City of Caesar, City of God

Millennium-Studien

zu Kultur und Geschichte
des ersten Jahrtausends n. Chr.

Millennium Studies

in the culture and history
of the first millennium C.E.

Herausgegeben von / Edited by
Wolfram Brandes, Alexander Demandt,
Peter von Möllendorff, Dennis Pausch,
Rene Pfeilschifter, Karla Pollmann

Volume 97

City of Caesar, City of God

Constantinople and Jerusalem in Late Antiquity

Edited by
Konstantin M. Klein and Johannes Wienand

DE GRUYTER

Diese Publikation wurde im Rahmen des Fördervorhabens 16TOA021 – Reihentransformation für die Altertumswissenschaften („Millennium-Studien") mit Mitteln des Bundesministeriums für Bildung und Forschung im Open Access bereitgestellt. Das Fördervorhaben wird in Kooperation mit dem DFG-geförderten Fachinformationsdienst Altertumswissenschaften – Propylaeum an der Bayerischen Staatsbibliothek durchgeführt.

ISBN 978-3-11-152144-2
e-ISBN (PDF) 978-3-11-071844-7
e-ISBN (EPUB) 978-3-11-071858-4
ISSN 1862-1139
DOI https://doi.org/10.1515/9783110718447

This work is licensed under the Creative Commons Attribution-NonCommercial-NoDerivatives 4.0 International License. For details go to http://creativecommons.org/licenses/by-nc-nd/4.0/.

Creative Commons license terms for re-use do not apply to any content (such as graphs, figures, photos, excerpts, etc.) that is not part of the Open Access publication. These may require obtaining further permission from the rights holder. The obligation to research and clear permission lies solely with the party re-using the material.

Library of Congress Control Number: 2022937689

Bibliographic information published by the Deutsche Nationalbibliothek
The Deutsche Nationalbibliothek lists this publication in the Deutsche Nationalbibliografie; detailed bibliographic data are available on the Internet at http://dnb.dnb.de.

© 2024 with the author(s), editing © 2022 Konstantin M. Klein and Johannes Wienand, published by Walter de Gruyter GmbH, Berlin/Boston.
This volume is text- and page-identical with the hardback published in 2022.
The book is published open access at www.degruyter.com.

www.degruyter.com

σὺ καὶ τὸ παρόν μοι θαῦμα διαζωγράφησον καὶ δὸς ἰδεῖν ὡς ἐν σκιᾷ καὶ τύπῳ τῆς πάλαι Ἱερουσαλήμ, ὅσα νῦν φιλανθρωπίᾳ Θεοῦ ἡ Θεοτόκος ἐνεδείξατο ὑπὲρ τῆς πόλεως ταύτης θαυμάσιά τε καὶ τέρατα.

It is for you to paint for me the current miracle, and to give the grace which I can see in the figure and the example of old Jerusalem, all these admirable miracles that the Mother of God accomplished for this city [i.e. Constantinople] because of the divine love for men.

Theodore Syncellus, *Homily on the Siege of Constantinople* §2 [626 AD]

Greek text after: Sternbach, L. (1900). *Analecta Avarica*, Cracow (p. 298).
Translation after: R. Pearse, Theodore Syncellus, Homily on the Siege of Constantinople in 626 AD (following Makk, F. [1975]. *Traduction et Commentaire de l'homélie écrite probablement par Théodore le Syncelle sur le siège de Constantinople en 626*, Szeged).

Preface and Acknowledgements

This book explores the entangled histories of Constantinople and Jerusalem, two pivotal urban centers of the late-antique world. Each city experienced an unparalleled rise to prominence between the fourth and seventh centuries AD, but the relationship between the two hubs as a result of their new status has gone unexplored. Continuous imperial building activity and ecclesiastical patronage transformed the two cities into symbols of Empire and Church, and Constantinople and Jerusalem were interconnected and interdependent in multiple ways. Here, a range of papers on art, ceremony, religion, ideology, imperial rule and Church institutions explores the literary and material evidence for the twinned histories of these two vibrant, inspiring, and fascinating centers.

Several research institutions have provided generous support as well as pleasant atmospheres for academic exchange. We want to thank the Seminar of Ancient History and Epigraphy (SAGE) at Universität Heidelberg; the Kenyon Institute of the Council for British Research in the Levant (CBRL); the Jerusalem Department of the German Protestant Institute of Archaeology in the Holy Land (DEIAHL); the Istanbul Department of the German Archaeological Institute (DAI); the International Academic Forum (IWH) at Universität Heidelberg; and the Leibniz-project 'Polyphony of Late Antique Christianity' at the Goethe-Universität Frankfurt am Main.

Kind friends and colleagues have contributed to making this book possible. Our special thanks go to Josephine Abu Sa'da, Wolfram Brandes, Hartmut Leppin, Felix Pirson, Maida Smeir, Kai Trampedach, Mandy Turner and Dieter Vieweger. We are grateful to John Noël Dillon, Robert Meyer, Johann Martin Thesz and Marlena Whiting for translation and language polishing. Laura Schöps drew the maps of Constantinople and Jerusalem (Maps 1 & 2). Neslihan Asutay-Effenberger and Shlomit Weksler-Bdolah generously shared their expertise on the topographies of Constantinople and Jerusalem. We are also grateful to Christian Michel and Anna Haake, who have helped us to prepare the manuscript for print. The book has benefited greatly from the helpful suggestions made by the anonymous reviewers.

Millennium Studies with its interdisciplinary approach to the cultural history of late antiquity is a fitting series for a book about Constantinople and Jerusalem, and we are grateful to the editorial board and De Gruyter for including our volume in their imprint. Heartfelt thanks go to Mirko Vonderstein, Benedikt Krüger, and Jessica Bartz for their excellent editorial work. Above all, we would like to thank the authors for their dedication, enthusiasm, and patience, which has made this volume possible in the first place.

Konstantin Klein & Johannes Wienand
October 2022

Contents

List of Figures —— XI

List of Abbreviations —— XIII

List of Contributors —— XVII

Konstantin Klein and Johannes Wienand
Constantinople & Jerusalem in Late Antiquity: Problems – Paradigms – Perspectives —— 1

Part One: The Centers of a New World Order

Kai Trampedach
The Making of the Holy Land in Late Antiquity —— 11

Rene Pfeilschifter
Always in Second Place: Constantinople as an Imperial and Religious Center in Late Antiquity —— 39

Part Two: Urban Topographies Connected

Neslihan Asutay-Effenberger and Shlomit Weksler-Bdolah
Delineating the Sacred and the Profane: The Late-Antique Walls of Jerusalem and Constantinople —— 71

Marlena Whiting
From the City of Caesar to the City of God: Routes, Networks, and Connectivity Between Constantinople and Jerusalem —— 111

Konstantin M. Klein
Neighbors of Christ: Saints and their *Martyria* in Constantinople and Jerusalem —— 139

Kai Trampedach
A New Temple of Solomon in Jerusalem? The Construction of the *Nea* Church (531–543) by Emperor Justinian —— 161

Part Three: The Power of Religion and Empire

Johannes Wienand
Eusebius in Jerusalem and Constantinople: Two Cities, Two Speeches —— 185

Nadine Viermann
Surpassing Solomon: Church-building and Political Discourse in Late Antique Constantinople —— 215

Jan-Markus Kötter
Palestine at the Periphery of Ecclesiastical Politics? The Bishops of Jerusalem after the Council of Chalcedon —— 241

Part Four: Jerusalem, Constantinople and the End of Antiquity

Paul Magdalino
The Church of St John the Apostle and the End of Antiquity in the New Jerusalem —— 263

James Howard-Johnston
Jerusalem in 630 —— 281

Lutz Greisiger
From 'King Heraclius, Faithful in Christ' to 'Allenby of Armageddon': Christian Reconquistadores Enter the Holy City —— 295

General Index —— 323

Names —— 329

Places —— 335

Literary Sources —— 339

List of Figures

Map 1:   City Map of Constantinople in Late Antiquity, © Laura Schöps
Map 2:   City Map of Jerusalem in Late Antiquity, © Laura Schöps
Fig 1:   Map of Istanbul, Theodosian Land Walls and the Gates, N. Asutay-Effenberger and G. Petras, adapted from Krischen 1938, p. 4, fig. 1 and Marcell Restle 1976
Fig 2:   Istanbul, Theodosian Land Walls, Main Wall, Outer Wall, Outer Ward and the Moat, Photo: N. Asutay-Effenberger
Fig 3:   Cross-Section Reconstruction of the Theodosian Land Walls, N. Asutay-Effenberger and G. Petras, adapted from Krischen 1938, fig. 4
Fig 4:   Istanbul, staircase behind the Sulukulekapı, Photo: N. Asutay-Effenberger
Fig 5:   Istanbul, casemates of the Outer Wall, Photo: N. Asutay-Effenberger
Fig 6:   Istanbul, Mevlevihanekapı, Outer Gate, Inscription, Van Millingen 1899, figure before p. 97
Fig 7:   Istanbul, bridge at the Belgradkapı, Photo: N. Asutay-Effenberger
Fig 8:   Istanbul, Theodosian Land Walls, Tower No. 18, Photo: N. Asutay-Effenberger
Fig 9:   Golden Gate and Küçük Altın Kapı [old postcard], private collection
Fig 10: Istanbul, Hypogeum at the Silivrikapı, Photo: N. Asutay-Effenberger
Fig 11: Istanbul, Gate of St Romanos, Photo: N. Asutay-Effenberger
Fig 12 a–b: Istanbul, Gate of St Romanos, Inscription, Photo: N. Asutay-Effenberger
Fig 13: Istanbul, Sulukulekapı [Field Side], Photo: N. Asutay-Effenberger
Fig 14: Map of Jerusalem in the mosaic floor at Madaba, after Vincent and Abel 1914, Pl. XXX, copied by P.M. Gisler O.S.B
Fig 15: Map of Jerusalem with the Early Byzantine city wall, after Tsafrir 2000. Drawing: Natalya Zak, courtesy of the Israel Antiquities Authority
Fig 16: Jerusalem, the Early Byzantine wall near Damascus Gate, after Hamilton 1944, Pl. 1.1
Fig 17: Jerusalem, late Roman wall cut by the corner of SE tower of Byzantine Wall, looking north, after Weksler-Bdolah/Lavi 2012
Fig 18: Jerusalem, corner of SE tower of Byzantine Wall, looking north, after Weksler-Bdolah/Lavi 2012
Fig 19: Jerusalem, the Early Byzantine wall in the Ophel excavations, looking north, after Mazar 2007, 191, Fig. 17.14: Courtesy of E. Mazar
Fig 20: Sketch map of routes in Anatolia and coastal highway to Alexandria, © M. Whiting
Fig 21: Sketch map of routes in Palaestina, © M. Whiting
Fig 22: Sketch map of Pilgrim's Road and pilgrimage sites in Anatolia, © M. Whiting
Fig 23: Frank G. Carpenter's World Travels, vol. 1, Garden City, NY, 1922, Frontispiece

List of Abbreviations

Abbreviations of journals and periodicals follow those used by *L'Année Philologique*. Abbreviations of authors and titles of works follow the 'Ancient Authors and Titles of Works' in *Brill's New Pauly*, the 'Abbreviations List' in *Oxford Classical Dictionary*, 4th Edition, and Lampe's *Patristic Greek Lexicon*. The following list assembles the most common bibliographical abbreviations used in this volume and abbreviations not listed in the works cited above.

AAAH	Acta ad archaeologiam et artium historiam pertinentia
AAWW	Anzeiger der Österreichischen Akademie der Wissenschaften in Wien, Philos.-Hist. Klasse
ACO	Acta Conciliorum Oecumenicorum
AB	Analecta Bollandiana
ADAJ	Annual of the Department of Antiquities of Jordan
AE	Année Épigraphique
AHC	Annuarium Historiae Conciliorum
AJAH	American Journal of Ancient History
AKG	Archiv für Kulturgeschichte
Altertum	Das Altertum, hrsg. vom Zentralinstitut für Alte Geschichte und Archäologie der Dt. Akademie der DDR
ANRW	Aufstieg und Niedergang der Römischen Welt
Anth. pal.	*Anthologia palatina*
AW	Antike Welt
BASO	Bulletin of the American Schools of Oriental Research
BCH	Bulletin de correspondance hellénique
BHG	Bibliotheca Hagiographica Graeca
BHL	Bibliotheca Hagiographica Latina
BJ	Bonner Jahrbücher des Rheinischen Landesmuseums in Bonn und des Vereins von Altertumsfreunden im Rheinlande
BMGS	Byzantine and Modern Greek Studies
Brev.	*Breviarium*
ByzF	Byzantinische Forschungen: internationale Zeitschrift für Byzantinistik
ByzZ	Byzantinische Zeitschrift
CCO	Collectanea Christiana Orientalia
CCSG	Corpus Christianorum, Series Graeca
CCSL	Corpus Christianorum, Series Latina
CFHB	Corpus Fontium Historiae Byzantinae
ChHist	Church History
Chron. min.	*Chronica minora*
Chron.	*Chronicon*
CIL	Corpus Inscriptionum Latinarum
CIIP	Corpus Inscriptionum Iudaeae/Palaestinae
CJ	The Classical Journal
COD	Conciliorum Oecumenicorum Decreta
Cod. Iust.	Codex Iustinianus
Cod. Theod.	Codex Theodosianus
CPh	Classical Philology
CSCO	Corpus Scriptorum Christianorum Orientalium
CSEL	Corpus Scriptorum Ecclesiasticorum Latinorum

CSSH	Comparative Studies in Society and History
DOP	Dumbarton Oaks Papers
EA	Epigraphica Anatolica: Zeitschrift für Epigraphik und historische Geographie Anatoliens
EHR	English Historical Review
Ep./Epp.	*Epistula/Epistulae*
ESI	Excavations and Surveys in Israel
Fr.	*Fragment*
GRBS	Greek, Roman and Byzantine Studies
HA-ESI	Hadashot Arkheologiyot. Excavations and Surveys in Israel
HE	*Historia ecclesiastica*
HebrUCA	Hebrew Union College Annual
HZ	Historische Zeitschrift
IEJ	Israel Exploration Journal
JbAC	Jahrbuch für Antike und Christentum
JECS	Journal of Early Christian Studies
JEH	Journal of Ecclesiastical History
JGS	Journal of Glass Studies
JHS	Journal of Hellenic Studies
JÖByz	Jahrbuch der Österreichischen Byzantinistik
JRA	Journal of Roman archaeology
JRS	Journal of Roman Studies
JSAI	Jerusalem Studies in Arabic and Islam
JSAH	Journal of the Society of Architectural Historians
LC	*Laus Constantini*
M&H	Medievalia et Humanistica: studies in medieval and Renaissance society
MAT	Memoire dell'Accademia delle Scienze di Torino
MDAI(I)	Mitteilungen des Deutschen Archäologischen Instituts (Abt. Istanbul)
MGH	Monumenta Germaniae Historica
MMJ	Metropolitan Museum Journal
NEAEHL	New Encyclopedia of archaeological excavations in the holy land
NSAJR	New Studies in the Archaeology of Jerusalem and its Region
OCP	Orientalia Christiana Periodica
PEFQSt	Palestine Exploration Fund Quarterly Statement
PEQ	Palestine Exploration Quarterly
PG	Patrologia Graeca
PL	Patrologia Latina
PLRE	Prosopography of the Later Roman Empire
PO	Patrologia Orientalis
P&P	Past and Present: a journal of historical Studies
QDAP	Quarterly of the Department of Antiquities of Palestine
RAC	Reallexikon für Antike und Christentum
RB	Revue Biblique
RE	Paulys Realencyclopädie der classischen Altertumswissenschaft
REArm	Revue des Études Arméniennes
REAug	Revue des Études Augustiniennes
REByz	Revue des Études Byzantines
REJ	Revue des Études Juives
RH	Revue historique
RSBN	Rivista di studi bizantini e neoellenici

RSR	Revue des Sciences Religieuses
SC	*De Sepulchro Christi*
SO	Symbolae Osloenses, auspiciis Societatis Graeco-Latine
StudMed	Studi Medievali
T&MByz	Travaux et mémoires du Centre de recherche d'histoire et civilisation byzantines
ThZ	Theologische Zeitschrift
TRE	Theologische Realencyclopädie
VC	*Vita Constantini*
VChr	Vigiliae Christianae: a review of early Christian life and language
Vit.	*Vita*
VS	*Vita Sabae*
ZAC	Zeitschrift für antikes Christentum
ZDPV	Zeitschrift des Deutschen Palästinavereins
ZPE	Zeitschrift für Papyrologie und Epigraphik

List of Contributors

Neslihan Asutay-Effenberger, Ruhr-Universität Bochum

Lutz Greisiger, Martin-Luther-Universität Halle-Wittenberg

James Howard-Johnston, University of Oxford

Konstantin Klein, University of Amsterdam

Jan-Markus Kötter, Heinrich-Heine-Universität Düsseldorf

Paul Magdalino, University of St Andrews

Rene Pfeilschifter, Julius-Maximilians-Universität Würzburg

Kai Trampedach, Ruprecht-Karls-Universität Heidelberg

Nadine Viermann, Durham University

Shlomit Weksler-Bdolah, Israel Antiquities Authority

Marlena Whiting, Johannes Gutenberg-Universität Mainz

Johannes Wienand, Technische Universität Braunschweig

City Map of Constantinople in Late Antiquity — XIX

1   Land wall (conjectured course) at the time of the Emperor Septimius Severus (193–211)
2   Land wall (conjectured course) at the time of the Emperor Constantine I (306–337)
3   Sea wall at the time of the Emperor Theodosius II (408–450)
4   Land wall at the time of the Emperor Theodosius II (408–450)
5   Augusteion
    a Hagia Sophia
    b Imperial palaces
    c Senate
    d Administrative basilica
    e Baths of Zeuxippus
6   Hippodrome
    α Egyptian obelisk of Theodosius I (390)
    β Serpent Column from Delphi
    γ Walled obelisk (10th c.)
7   Palace of Lausus (5th c.)
8   Forum Constantini with column of Constantine
9   Forum Tauri (Forum of Theodosius I)
10 Hagia Eirene (4th c.)
11 Church of the Theotokos Chalkoprateia (5th c.)
12 Church of St. Sergius and St. Bacchus (527–536)

Medrion (V)   Theodosian regio
Deuteron   district

▨ Acropolis of Byzantium
⛪ Church
🏛 Monastery
▨ Cistern
↘ Main Street

Map. 1: City Map of Constantinople in Late Antiquity, © Laura Schöps

XX —— City Map of Jerusalem in Late Antiquity

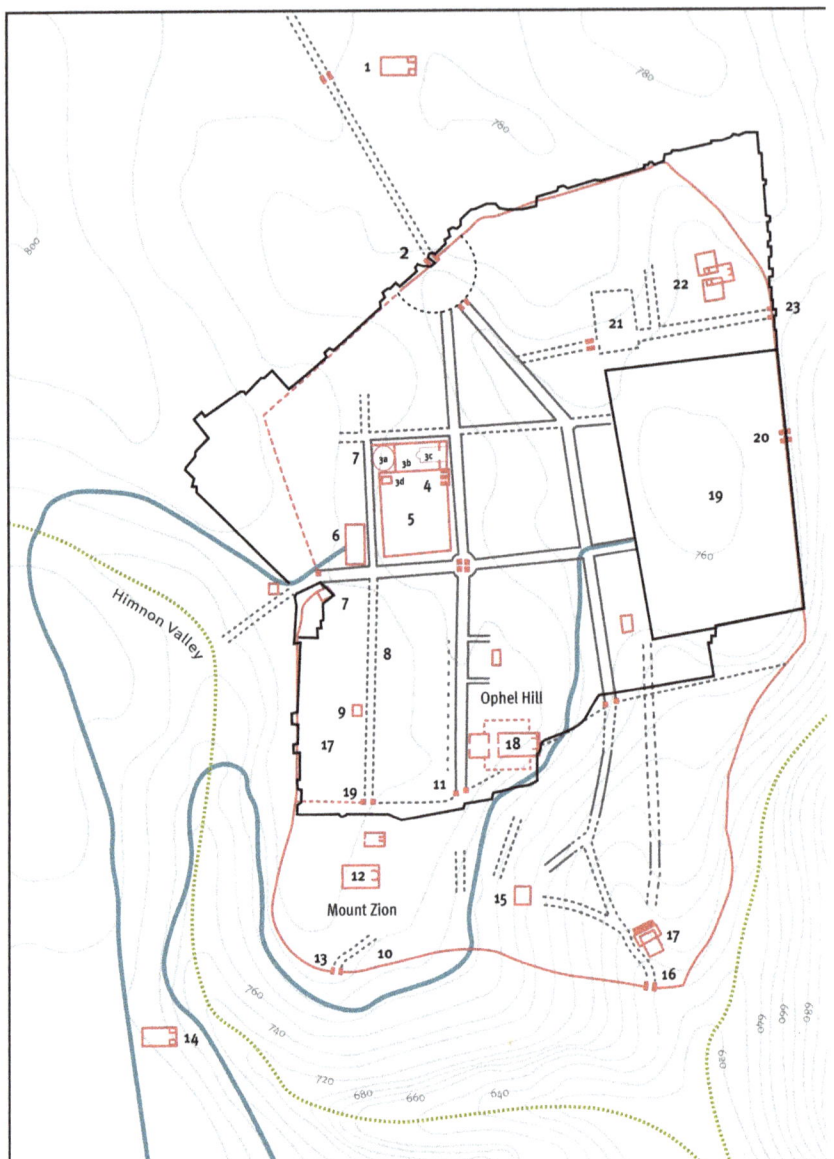

Map. 2: City Map of Jerusalem in Late Antiquity, © Laura Schöps

City Map of Jerusalem in Late Antiquity — XXI

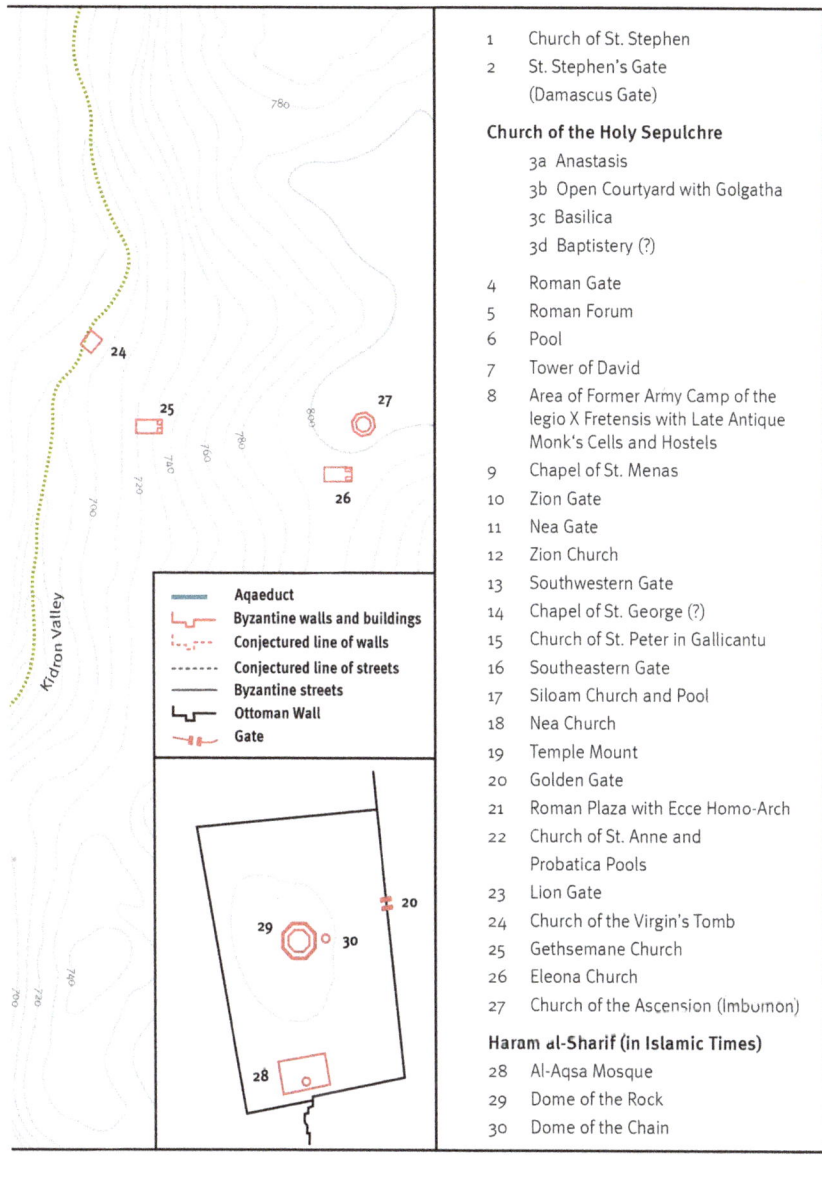

1 Church of St. Stephen
2 St. Stephen's Gate (Damascus Gate)

Church of the Holy Sepulchre
    3a Anastasis
    3b Open Courtyard with Golgatha
    3c Basilica
    3d Baptistery (?)

4 Roman Gate
5 Roman Forum
6 Pool
7 Tower of David
8 Area of Former Army Camp of the legio X Fretensis with Late Antique Monk's Cells and Hostels
9 Chapel of St. Menas
10 Zion Gate
11 Nea Gate
12 Zion Church
13 Southwestern Gate
14 Chapel of St. George (?)
15 Church of St. Peter in Gallicantu
16 Southeastern Gate
17 Siloam Church and Pool
18 Nea Church
19 Temple Mount
20 Golden Gate
21 Roman Plaza with Ecce Homo-Arch
22 Church of St. Anne and Probatica Pools
23 Lion Gate
24 Church of the Virgin's Tomb
25 Gethsemane Church
26 Eleona Church
27 Church of the Ascension (Imbomon)

Haram al-Sharif (in Islamic Times)
28 Al-Aqsa Mosque
29 Dome of the Rock
30 Dome of the Chain

Konstantin Klein and Johannes Wienand
Constantinople & Jerusalem in Late Antiquity: Problems – Paradigms – Perspectives

In the early fourth century AD, the city of Byzantium looked back on an urban history spanning almost a millennium: Greek colonists from Megara had founded the city in the first half of the seventh century BC. From the Archaic era to the Roman imperial period, however, the city had remained on the fringes of the larger power blocs, its geopolitical significance being largely defined by its location on the Bosporus, the maritime entrance to the Black Sea. The urban development of the city of Byzantium had always been limited, and it had never in any particular way been connected to the city of Aelia Capitolina in the province of Palestine, an even older city that was located about 1,200 Roman miles away in a different peripheral region of the vast Empire. In the early fourth century AD, the cities of Byzantium and Aelia Capitolina looked back on their own individual and separate millennium-old histories, and yet, at the same time, they faced the beginning of an entirely new era: no other two cities of the late-antique world experienced a more remarkable rise than the cities of Byzantium and Aelia Capitolina. Under their new and renewed names of Constantinople and Jerusalem, they rose to become the most important hubs of both the Christian Empire and the Church for centuries to come, and they were interconnected in an increasingly dense and complex net of reciprocal dependencies. The intensifying links between the two cities were reflected in the mid-620s by Theodore the Syncellus, an attentive observer who even saw in the capital of the Byzantine Empire 'the figure and the example of old Jerusalem'.

The impulse for this momentous and far-reaching development was given by the Emperor Constantine. In AD 326, he ordered the re-foundation of the city of Byzantium on the Bosporus, and only four years later, Constantinople was established as a new imperial residence. Initially, the city of Constantinople was an urban symbol, promulgating the lasting peace after the decisive military victory of Constantine over his remaining rival to the imperial throne. Over the years and decades that followed, the city transformed into the most important center of the Empire and for centuries served as the vibrant capital of the Byzantine Empire. Constantine also encouraged the construction of the first monumental churches in and around Aelia Capitolina / Jerusalem – a region that slowly but steadily transformed into the Christian Holy Land over the next centuries. The evolving Christian topography of the Biblical lands represented the power of Constantine's newly adopted Christian religion. Jerusalem, with the imperially founded Church of the Holy Sepulcher (consecrated in 335) at its heart eventually became a theological reference point of both the Christian Empire and the Church.

Throughout late antiquity, the two cities were constantly transforming (and transformable) spaces of religious-political interaction between the monarch, the

Church, and the population of the Empire. Imperial influence, initiatives by the Church, and projects by individuals transformed and reshaped both these significant urban centers into intertwined symbols of imperial and divine power and triumph. Constantinople and Jerusalem thus became important Christian realms of memory and identity as well as central places for Roman imperial representation and legitimation. The most vivid manifestation is to be found in the imperial building program and the development of sacred topographies in the two cities, but also in the translation of relics, in the imperial ceremonial, in the Church calendar, in the symbolic and pictorial idiom of the monarchy, and in pilgrimage. Each of the two cities, however, would run under their distinct frameworks with their own sets of rules for social interaction, communication, conflict resolution, ritual, and discourse. Presumably the most important factor reinforcing a fundamental asymmetry between the two cities was the emperor's almost continuous presence in Constantinople, but absence in Jerusalem: Heraclius in AD 630 was the first Christian emperor to visit the Holy Land – no less than three centuries after the implementation of the first imperial Church building projects in Jerusalem.

The chapters collected in this volume aim to shed light on the late-antique histories of these two cities, their roles for both the Roman monarchy and the Christian Church, their ideological impact, and their unique relationship of mutual influence and independent development. The individual chapters pursue a comparative approach, illuminating the reciprocal relations and interdependencies of Constantinople and Jerusalem in their late-antique contexts: To confine the role of Constantinople to the political and of Jerusalem to the religious sphere would not do justice to the complexity of both cities. Whereas the importance of religion in Constantinople is obvious, it is more difficult to answer the question as to how political (or politicized) late-antique Jerusalem actually was and how the character of the two cities changed over time.

The volume examines the roles and perceptions of Constantinople and Jerusalem from a range of different perspectives and various disciplines. An introductory section (*Part One: The Centers of a New World Order*), with two complementary chapters, locates both cities in their distinct, yet interconnected, late-antique contexts, while the chapters in the subsequent sections cover archaeology and urbanism (*Part Two: Urban Topographies Connected*), the role of religio-political ideologies (*Part Three: The Power of Religion and Empire*), and the rising importance of eschatology on the eve of the Arab conquests, including the historic reverberations of imperial entrances to the Holy City up until the 20th century (*Part Four: Jerusalem, Constantinople and the End of Antiquity*).

In order to understand how the individual parts of this book approach the late-antique cities of Jerusalem and Constantinople within this transformation of world-historical significance and how the individual chapters relate to one another, it will be useful to provide brief outlines of their aims and methods and to introduce their themes and arguments.

Part One: The Centers of a New World Order

The two chapters that form the opening section of this volume provide the basic historical framework. They investigate the long-term developments, and analyze the forces that shaped the late-antique metropolis of Constantinople on the one hand and the Holy Land with Jerusalem as its religious center on the other. The first of the two chapters presents a thorough study of the history of the Holy Land that re-evaluates the imperial influence exercised in the Holy City and its surroundings, while the second meticulously investigates the rise of Constantinople with particular attention paid to its relation to Jerusalem.

In the first chapter, *Kai Trampedach* draws a careful picture of the development and growth of Christian Jerusalem, firmly locating these processes within their Roman imperial context ('The Making of the Holy Land in Late Antiquity'). While for many Christians, and certainly for the emperor Constantine, it must have been clear that Jerusalem was and had always been a very special place, Trampedach shows that the parameters of the city's rise were confined within established traditions and models. This analysis provides an important reminder that while Jerusalem was conceived as the city of God, it became a city of the Caesars as well, who did lend their support to this religious center, but according to the same rules that applied for other cities in the late Roman Empire. At the same time, Trampedach's contribution on the city of Jerusalem firmly introduces important themes for the remaining volume, namely the rise of pilgrimage and desert monasticism, church constructions, as well as the capturing of the city by the Sasanians and the Arabs.

Rene Pfeilschifter investigates the political and religious impact of the new capital on the Bosporus and its complex relationship to Jerusalem ('Always in Second Place: Constantinople as an Imperial and Religious Center in Late Antiquity'). Constantinople became the center of the (East) Roman socio-political system which was characterized by an almost unbreakable bond between city and emperor. Pfeilschifter shows that, for Constantinople, being the city of Caesar went hand in hand with aspiring to become the city of God as well. As Constantinople lacked a distinctly pagan or Jewish character (as in Rome or Jerusalem respectively), an infusion of Christian elements faced fewer obstacles than elsewhere, and an important stimulus was the fact that the inhabitants of Constantinople persistently constituted themselves as a Christian community. In the process of becoming a city of God, Constantinople took more than it gave: It imported relics, eschatological meaning, and finally even the True Cross. Jerusalem received less in return, as Pfeilschifter shows. Above all, it did not become a political or administrative center. While Constantinople assumed functions that originally or primarily belonged to Jerusalem, the opposite did not occur. In fact, Constantinople did not become a model for any other city. In spite of all the importance and all the originality of its development, its political power was seen as having been transferred from Rome. Likewise, Constantinople's growing holiness and its importance for salvation only resulted in a Second, New Jerusalem.

Part Two: Urban Topographies Connected

Proceeding from the insights gained by Trampedach and Pfeilschifter in the opening chapters, the three case studies of the second section cast a close look at the urban, art historical, and archaeological developments in Constantinople and Jerusalem.

In their jointly written assessment of the late-antique city walls of Constantinople and Jerusalem, *Neslihan Asutay-Effenberger* and *Shlomit Weksler-Bdolah* start from close surveys of the construction methods, building techniques, and defensive qualities of the walls – both case studies are based on extensive archaeological fieldwork ('Delineating the Sacred and the Profane: The Late-Antique Walls of Jerusalem and Constantinople'). Both authors revise previous scholarly assumptions on the structure and chronology of the fortification systems. From there, the contribution tackles questions concerning the role of patronage for the walls and, in particular, what it meant for the population of Constantinople and Jerusalem that their cities became fortified. The contribution discusses the structural similarities and differences between the two fortification systems. It is striking that Jerusalem's walls deliberately incorporated largely unchanged and highly visible building blocks from dismantled Jewish structures, which were obviously meant to demonstrate the victory of Christianity over Judaism and to underline the founder's piety. The walls of Constantinople, on the other hand, were instead meant to express security and imperial power. Thus, the walls of the two cities delineate two different but complementary notions of the Christian monarchy.

In investigating the infrastructure that connected Constantinople with Jerusalem and vice versa, *Marlena Whiting* employs the concept of 'braided systems' ('From the City of Caesar to the City of God: Routes, Networks, and Connectivity Between Constantinople and Jerusalem'). As she demonstrates, a complex interplay of three key needs brought about and maintained the communication networks between the imperial and the holy city: the needs of the imperial administration and the military; the need to ensure the movement of goods and trade; and the need newly arising in the fourth century of ensuring the safety and comfort of pilgrims. The roads to Jerusalem served pilgrims so well because they connected theatres of military activity and trade nodes, because they were maintained for transport of important raw materials and money, and because they were also needed to feed the capital, including products such as the holy wine of Palestine.

In his contribution, *Konstantin Klein* casts a close look at the presence of saints as well as living holy men and women in the cities of Constantinople and Jerusalem ('Neighbours of Christ: Saints and their *Martyria* in Constantinople and Jerusalem'). Holy places commemorating the life and passion of Christ took a paramount role in Jerusalem from the beginning, but (in stark contrast to Constantinople) there were no churches and almost no private memorial sites for saints in Jerusalem before the mid-fifth century, and no attempts to incorporate living holy men and women within its walls. Then the situation changed rather suddenly: Klein shows that it was Constantinopolitan influence in Jerusalem, namely the sojourn of the empress Eudocia, which brought the cult of saints back to the Holy City that once had produced Christianity's first martyr, St Stephen. With the construction of the first church to him between 438 and 460, Jerusalem's ecclesiastical landscape opened up to *martyria* for saints, and Eudocia's endeavors were soon to be extensively imitated by other inhabitants of Jerusalem. At the same time, Eudocia also left her footprint on the urban topography of Constantinople. This set the stage for reciprocal influence of Christian topography between the Holy Land and the imperial capital on the Bosporus.

Kai Trampedach's contribution on the Justinianic Nea Church further explores this theme, focusing on one of the most ambitious imperial building programs in the history of Jerusalem ('A New Temple of Solomon in Jerusalem? The Construction of the Nea Church (531–543) by Emperor Justinian'). In this chapter, Trampedach examines the religious and political dimensions of the urban refurbishment in Justinianic times. Through a trenchant analysis of the archaeological remains and literary sources, Trampedach carves out the symbolic meaning of the edifice. Since the church did not highlight a locality of salvific history, our understanding of its position within the dense sacred topography of the Holy City depends on its spatial references and its embedment within the religious calendar of Jerusalem, among others. The analysis shows that the building was meant to compete not only with the Constantinian structures, but even with King Solomon's temple. As Trampedach is able to show, Justinian's building activities in the Holy Land also served specific political and religious aims in the center of imperial rule in Constantinople.

Part Three: The Power of Religion and Empire

The third part of the volume focuses on the ecclesiastical, political, and symbolic meaning of Constantinople and Jerusalem.

In his contribution, *Johannes Wienand* examines two of the earliest literary sources we have concerning the Constantinian re-foundations of Jerusalem and Constantinople: two orations by the bishop Eusebius of Caesarea, one given in 335 in the course of the inauguration ceremonies for the Constantinian basilica in Jerusalem, the other given in 336 in the imperial palace of Constantinople on the occasion of the festivities for the thirtieth jubilee of Constantine's reign ('Eusebius in Jerusalem and Constantinople: Two Cities, Two Speeches'). Both speeches deal with the ramifications of the Constantinian religious transformation for the Roman monarchy in a religiously heterogeneous empire. As the differences in character between the two speeches clearly show, the two cities of Jerusalem and Constantinople played diverging but complementary roles in the imperial concept of a Christian monarchy on the one hand and in the interpretations by a Christian bishop on the other. A close examination of the two speeches in their ceremonial contexts sheds light on the earliest phase of the formation of a Christian Roman Empire and the two single most important cities of the new era.

Nadine Viermann's contribution shows how references to Old Testament Jerusalem were exploited for the political discourse in sixth-century Constantinople ('Surpassing Solomon: Church-Building and Political Discourse in Late Antique Constantinople'). In particular, King Solomon (as the builder of the First Temple) was used as a role model and point of reference for the staging of a distinct imperial self-perception. Viermann employs the example of the church of St Polyeuctus, built by Juliana Anicia, to show how the building's various semantic levels demonstrate the imperial aspirations of its founder. The contribution does not only discuss the famous epigram inscription with its explicit references to King Solomon but also places St Polyeuctus in the context of Prophet Ezekiel's temple vision and of the contemporary eschatological expectations of the sixth century. This subversive and presumptuous concept of St Polyeuctus is contrasted with Emperor Justinian's reactions to Juliana's provocation that also took on the shape of explicit references to the Biblical king. The contribution shows that Solomon served as a multifaceted bearer of meaning in various communicative contexts. We can thus observe the creation of a *topos* predominated by the aspect of surpassing the Old Testament king and his Temple.

The chapter by *Jan-Markus Kötter* analyzes the impact the Council of Chalcedon (451) had on the status and standing of the Church of Jerusalem within the imperial church system ('Palestine at the Periphery of Ecclesiastical Politics? The Bishops of Jerusalem after the Council of Chalcedeon'). The outcome of the Council enabled Jerusalem to compete with the most important players within the empire-wide church hierarchy (Rome, Constantinople, Alexandria, Antioch). However, prestige and relevance were not precisely fixed but subject to a broad spectrum of negotiation processes. To understand the quest of the Jerusalem church for empire-wide recognition of privileged status, Kötter focuses in particular on the relations between Jerusalem and Constantinople, since the support of the imperial court had a crucial impact on the competition for authority and competences within the Church. Through an in-depth analysis of the relevant power brokers, their social networks, and their communication strategies, Kötter shows that the Church of Jerusalem enforced its claim to pre-eminence vis-à-vis the emperor on the one hand and the patriarchates on the other within a complex field between the two poles of autonomy and influence.

Part Four: Jerusalem, Constantinople and the End of Antiquity

The fourth part of the volume provides two case studies on the relationship between Constantinople and Jerusalem on the eve of the Arab expansion and an analysis of the historic reverberations of imperial entrances to the Holy City up until the 20th century.

Paul Magdalino's contribution analyzes the political and religious significance of the Church of St John the Apostle situated between the Hippodrome and the Hagia Sophia in Constantinople ('The Church of St John the Apostle and the End of Antiquity in the New Jerusalem'). The building process was begun under Phokas (602–610) and finished by Heraclius (602–641). It was the last recorded major religious foundation in Constantinople before the ninth century, and the last new construction of a major, free-standing public church. In more ways than one, therefore, it marks the end of late antiquity and early Christianity in Constantinople. Furthermore, the church was built in a distinctive form at a central and prestigious location. All this raises compelling questions about the motivation behind the remarkable edifice and the choice of its patron saint. Magdalino conclusively shows how all emperors of the early Byzantine era shared a strategy to accumulate relics and to increase the sacred status of Constantinople in order to transform it into a second Jerusalem and not, as a set of contemporary interpretations suggests, into a second Babylon.

James Howard-Johnston's contribution, on the other hand, analyzes the long-term political and religious repercussions caused by the capture of Jerusalem by Persian forces in spring 614 ('Jerusalem in 630'). On the Roman side, imperial propaganda focused on the True Cross, which had been seized and removed to the Persian capital. On March 21, 630, Heraclius staged a carefully orchestrated ceremony in Jerusalem to celebrate his victory in the long, hard-fought, ideologically charged war, by which the emperor finally restored Roman dominion over the eastern provinces and returned the True Cross to Jerusalem. The emperor tried to use his triumph to bring together the main sectarian factions of the Church, and to bring recalcitrant Jews into the Christian fold. His plans, however, were overtaken by the course of events: the existing world order was challenged by the Arab conquest and its underlying ideology of Holy War. Again the prime focus was Jerusalem, claimed by the Arabs as descendants of Ismael. The cities of Palestine capitulated by the spring of 635 at the latest. Three years later, another solemn ceremony was staged in Jerusalem to receive the second Caliph, Umar I, who was marking Islam's emergence as the new world power.

Lutz Greisiger takes in a diachronic array of entry ceremonies into the Holy City of Jerusalem, starting with Biblical paragons such as Melchizedek and King David, and Jesus Christ's entry to Jerusalem according to the Gospels ('From "King Heraclius, Faithful in Christ" to "Allenby of Armageddon": Christian Reconquistadores Enter the Holy City'). He defines both entries as epochal and – within their respective narratives – revolutionary acts. More than half a millennium later, Heraclius's visit to Jerusalem and his restoration of the True Cross can be interpreted as a similarly epochal change with striking eschatological undertones. Greisiger traces the impact of imperial entry ceremonies in Jerusalem throughout the Middle Ages when, e. g. Godfrey of Bouillon's entry into the city in 1099 following the Crusader conquest was clearly meant to emulate Heraclius's visit. The powerful imagery as well as the political importance the act engendered never became unfashionable, as Greisiger demonstrates in his discussion of the entries into Jerusalem by the Russian Grand Duke Konstantin Nikolayevich, the Austrian Emperor Franz Joseph, the German Emperor Wilhelm II – and in particular the highly symbolic and meticulously planned entry by General Allenby, who in 1917 took possession of the city of Jerusalem on behalf of the British Crown and was again likened to Godfrey of Bouillon. Strikingly, the manifold connections between Jerusalem and Constantinople salient in the late-antique *adventus* narratives became less important for the Christian 'conquerors' of the modern age.

Taken together, the chapters that make up this volume situate the entangled histories of late-antique Constantinople and Jerusalem in their wider cultural settings. As the City of Caesar and the City of God, Constantinople and Jerusalem are nodal points in a fascinating transition from the ancient Hellenistic and Roman worlds to the more regionalized but still deeply entangled medieval cultures between the Mediterranean and the Middle East.

Part One:
The Centers of a New World Order

Kai Trampedach
The Making of the Holy Land in Late Antiquity

The search for the places where Jesus Christ had taught or worked miracles – even places where he had merely been physically present – were of little interest to the early Christians. Their religion and faith were influenced by a spiritual and eschatological reading of God's revelation that differed greatly from the Jewish interpretation of the Bible. While earthly Jerusalem was necessarily doomed to destruction – according to Jesus' prophecy in the Gospel (Matthew 24:1–2) – it was the heavenly Jerusalem that became the object of Christian yearning. Accordingly, the current unholy state of Jerusalem and Judaea could be both explained and justified by opposition to Judaism. Seen in this light, the destruction of the city and the Temple during the reign of Emperor Vespasian and the official obliteration of its name with the founding of pagan Aelia Capitolina under Hadrian were simply manifestations of God's wrath toward the Jews for denying Christ. The Jews had all but lost the Holy Land, which therefore could now only exist spiritually.[1]

The Christian Understanding of Palestine before Constantine

As time passed, however, some Christians felt the need to preserve their collective religious memory. To the best of our knowledge, Melito of Sardis at the end of the second century was the first Christian to visit the sites where the story of Christian salvation took place. His motivation was to compile a reliable list of the books in the Biblical canon.[2] Scholarly interest was also the reason why Origen, in the first half of the third century, travelled to find some of the places mentioned in the Gos-

---

Note: This paper is based on reflections previously published in German in a somewhat peripheral volume: K. Trampedach, "Die Konstruktion des Heiligen Landes. Kaiser und Kirche in Palästina von Constantin bis Justinian", in *Die Levante. Beiträge zur Historisierung des Nahostkonfliktes*, ed. M. Sommer, (Freiburger Beiträge zur Entwicklung und Politik 27, Arnold-Bergstraesser-Institut), Freiburg i. Br. 2001, p. 83–110. In addition to the editors Konstantin Klein and Johannes Wienand I am grateful to John Noël Dillon and Marlena Whiting for assistance with the translation and for other suggestions.

1 See Wilken 1985, 688–689; Wilken 1992, 80 ff., esp. 96–97; Taylor 1993, 295: "There is no evidence at all that Jewish-Christians, or any other kind of Christians, venerated sites as sacred before the beginning of the fourth century."
2 Euseb. *HE* 4,26,14. On the motivation for Melito's journey to Jerusalem cf. the different views of Taylor 1993, 311, and Murphy-O'Connor 2010, 78–79.

pels.³ Alexander of Cappadocia may be considered the first to show an interest that went beyond learned curiosity: he came to Jerusalem in the mid-third century "to pray and visit the Holy Places."⁴ The exploration of Biblical topography, however, was not necessarily limited to its significance in the Gospels, as shown by the early writings of Eusebius: even when he was composing the *Onomasticon*, a list of Biblical sites with geographical and historical descriptions, he adhered to the spiritual interpretation of the Gospels.⁵

With Emperor Constantine's rise to power and his support of Christianity, it was not only Eusebius' parameters that fundamentally changed. Christianity suddenly acquired holy places located on earth, not in heaven, and growing streams of pilgrims set off for Palestine. Constantine, of course, was not solely responsible for this development; its roots lay deep in Christianity itself, particularly in the belief that Jesus of Nazareth was Christ or, to put it differently, that God had become flesh at a certain time and place. The divine revelation on which the new religion was based was part of a larger history. Hence, commemoration of the historical events of this revelation was at the heart of Christian tradition from the very beginning. Christians thus could not always remain indifferent to the places where the events of Gospels took place. As Robert Wilken puts it, "If there were no places that could be seen and touched, the claim that God entered human history could become a chimera. Sanctification of place was inevitable in a religion founded on history and on the belief that God 'became flesh' in a human being."⁶ Real, existing sites bore witness to the truth of the Bible and the Christian religion. These sites were bound to be transformed sooner or later into 'holy places,' for which the cult of martyrs served both as a model and as a structural parallel.⁷ The tombs of the martyrs attested to the truth of Christian faith and were also venerated by believers. To a certain extent,

---

3 Orig. *In Ioann.* 6,40–41.
4 Euseb. *HE* 6,11,2; cf. also Firmilian in Jer. *Vir. ill.* 54. Hunt, 1999, 25–40, suggests that there were indeed Christian pilgrims, but he also shows that, until Constantine constructed the central shrines commemorating Christian history, Christian visitors to Palestine found spiritual confirmation particularly in the 'negative evidence' it presented; cf. e.g. Hunt 1999, 31: "Pagan Aelia served as 'witness' for the worthlessness and insignificance of the 'Jerusalem below' which could no longer confine the glory of God."
5 While the *Onomasticon* was intended as a guide for those reading the Bible, it could also serve as a guidebook for pilgrims; see Wilken 1992, 99–100. For dating the *Onomasticon* before AD 300, Barnes 1981, 106 ff. D.E. Groh convincingly describes the purpose of the work as bringing "biblical, Roman, and Christian realities together in such a way that Christianity in [Eusebius'] own day can be seen to be the successor of the biblical realities in the Roman world", see Groh 1985, 23–31, esp. 29, and now Röwekamp 2017, 51–58.
6 See Wilken 1992, 91.
7 Hunt 1999, 28–29; Markus 1994, 257–271. Euseb. *VC* 3,28 revealingly calls the sepulcher of Christ "the revered and all-hallowed Testimony (*martyrion*) of the Saviour's resurrection" (translated here and in all other instances of this chapter by Av. Cameron and S.G. Hall 1999). For a thorough study of Christian theologians' reflections on Palestine and Jerusalem in pre-Constantinian times cf. Heyden 2014, 18–113.

the idea of the Holy Land was inherent in Christianity itself, but political and social circumstances ultimately determined whether and in what form this idea would take shape in the Roman province of Palestine.

Constantine's Constructions

Nevertheless, the swiftness, determination and certainty with which Constantine set the course of Palestine's future were remarkable. At the very beginning of the fourth century, a Roman official had not even heard of "Jerusalem."[8] At the Church Council of Nicaea (AD 325), the bishop of Aelia was nominally granted honorary precedence, but *de facto* he remained subordinate to the metropolitan of Caesarea, the provincial capital.[9] Immediately after the council, Constantine initiated a massive building program to lay the groundwork for the rise of Christian Jerusalem. Without the central holy places that Constantine ordered to be discovered and adorned, the subsequent pilgrim movement would not have been possible.[10] The emperor's approach shows remarkable theological and symbolic adroitness. The building program epitomized the fundamental doctrines of Christianity, just as they are mentioned in the Nicene Creed: the incarnation in Bethlehem, the passion and resurrection at Golgotha and the nearby sepulcher and, finally, the ascension on the Mount of Olives.

Constantine also did not neglect the sites of the Old Testament. At Mamre, where God first appeared to Abraham, the emperor built a church that demonstrated Christianity's claim to all Biblical history: according to the Christian interpretation, Abraham's theophany not only anticipated Christ's appearance typologically, but, for many Church Fathers, also confirmed the consubstantiality of God the Son and God the Father, as decreed at Nicaea against the Arians. It is unclear whether Constantine had this specifically in mind; however, it shows that the sites of the Holy Land were highly charged with theological messages that could be directed toward different audiences.[11]

---

8 Euseb. *De mart. Pal.* 11, 10–12.
9 Canon 7 of Nicaea (325) [COD, S. 8,25–31]: Ἐπειδὴ συνήθεια κεκράτηκε καὶ παράδοσις ἀρχαία, ὥστε τὸν ἐν Αἰλίᾳ ἐπίσκοπον τιμᾶσθαι, ἐχέτω τὴν ἀκολουθίαν τῆς τιμῆς, τῇ μητροπόλει σῳζομένου τοῦ οἰκείου ἀξιώματος. According to Heyden 2014, 119–122, the canon should be understood as an expression of the emperor's esteem for Jerusalem and as a "symbol of church unity". On the conflict of the sees of Caesarea and Jerusalem cf. Irshai 2011, esp. 27–34.
10 See Leeb 1992, 89: "Konstantin schafft bewußt ein neues christliches, religiöses Zentrum im Osten des Reiches. Er bzw. seine Berater werden so eigentlich zu den Erfindern und Schöpfern der Idee des ‚Heiligen Landes'. Erst jetzt hat Jerusalem die Voraussetzungen, zur ‚Heiligen Stadt' zu werden."
11 Euseb. *VC* 3,25 41. 51–53, *LC* 9,17; see Maraval 1985, 67–68; Leeb 1992, 90–91; Van Dam 2007, 301–302; Klein (forthcoming), ch. 2.5. The Constantinian buildings are mentioned in the earliest pilgrim account, which dates to AD 333; see *Itin. Burdig.* (ed. P. Geyer and O. Cuntz, CCSL 175, Turnhout 1965), 594 (Golgotha), 595 (Mount of Olives), 598 (Bethlehem) and 599 (Mamre).

The core element of Constantine's building projects in Palestine was the *Anastasis* complex or the Church of the Holy Sepulcher. It was meant to be the central Christian sanctuary of Palestine, and perhaps of the entire Roman Empire.[12] According to Eusebius, our main source for the period, Constantine "decided that he ought to make universally famous and revered the most blessed site in Jerusalem of the Savior's resurrection."[13] Constantine began by ordering the pagan temple at the site, most likely the main shrine (*capitolium*) of Aelia,[14] to be demolished and the rubble – tainted by idolatry – to be removed. Then, according to Eusebius, something totally unexpected happened: under the ruins of the temple, the tomb of the Savior came to light.[15] According to a letter preserved by Eusebius, the emperor ordered Makarios, the bishop of Jerusalem, to build the most magnificent basilica in the world. "It is right," the emperor added, after giving the bishop instructions as to how the basilica should be decorated, "that the world's most miraculous place should be worthily embellished."[16] In order to organize the building project, the bishop was directed to two high-ranking helpers: the emperor's "friend" and praetorian prefect *per Orientem*, Drakilianos, and the provincial governor. Makarios would coordinate with the emperor himself to select the columns and marble for the complex.[17]

But how did Constantine come upon the idea to transform Aelia into a/the "New Jerusalem"? According to Eusebius, the initiative derived solely from God's providence. Beyond this claim, there is only speculation. Perhaps Makarios, as scholars often assume, brought the matter to Constantine's attention at the Council of Nicaea,[18] or perhaps the initiative came from Christian circles at court (e.g. the imperial women, western bishops) or even from the emperor himself.[19] It is easier to understand *why* this idea was popular with the emperor. With his victory over Licinius, Constantine became the sole ruler of the Roman Empire. With the Council of Nicaea, he created, or so he thought, a homogeneous and united imperial church. From this moment on, he increasingly favored Christianity to the point of exclusion. Where else, if not in Jerusalem, could he pay homage to his new God in the most ostentatious manner? The presentational center of Rome was already occupied with pagan temples, and even an emperor like Constantine would not have dared to substantial-

---

12 Wilken 1992, 93–94; Drijvers 1992, 57.
13 Euseb. *VC* 3,25.
14 Bieberstein/Bloedhorn 1994, I, 144 ff. and II, 184; Belayche 1997; Murphy-O'Connor 1994 and 2010; Küchler 2014, 298; Klein (forthcoming), ch. 2. Against this view, cf. Gibson/Taylor 1994, 68 ff., who assume that only the temple of Venus, mentioned in Eusebius' account, was located at the place of the Church of the Holy Sepulcher, while they propose that the *capitolium* replaced the former fortress *Antonia* at the northeastern corner of the Temple Mount.
15 Euseb. *VC* 3,26–28.
16 Euseb. *VC* 3,31,3.
17 Euseb. *VC* 3,30–32; cf. Sozom., *HE* 2,26,3.
18 Krautheimer 1993, vol. 2, 514; see Stemberger 1987, 57; Hunt 1982, 7; Walker 1990, 188 and 194; Hunt 1997a, 405–424, esp. 411–412; Klein (forthcoming), ch. 2.1.
19 See Yarnold 1989, 105–109; Heyden 2014, 122–126.

ly transform this venerable heart of ancient Roman tradition. It is telling that all Constantinian churches in Rome were built at the edge of the city – even *extra muros* – and were not officially financed from the *fiscus* but rather from the imperial privy purse (the *res privata* or *patrimonium*).[20] The new city on the Bosporus was not, as is often inferred from later developments, designed as a new Christian capital, but rather was intended through and through to glorify its founder.[21] Palestine, however, was far from the political center of the empire and its conservative elites. There was no need to pay special attention to the sensibilities of its inhabitants: in Aelia, the emperor could clear away the main temple without attracting much attention.[22] And where could the triumphant mood of Christians be better – and more obviously – expressed than in the city that had rejected and executed the founding hero of the religion?[23] Eusebius' excitement is palpable when he describes the emperor's New Jerusalem: it stood "facing the famous Jerusalem of old, which after the bloody murder of the Lord had been overthrown in utter devastation, and paid the penalty of its wicked inhabitants."[24] At the same time, this remark shows how the very concept of an earthly, Christian Jerusalem posed a problem for Eusebius.[25] What, to him and other theologians, had been the most important feature distinguishing Christianity from Judaism was now on the brink of vanishing. The new Christian city, centered around the Holy Sepulcher, therefore had to be separated spatially from the old Jewish city centered around the Temple Mount. Dissociation from pagan Aelia, by contrast, was less politically charged; it sufficed to clear away its center, rearrange it, and invest it with new meaning. Apart from these adjustments, the new Jerusalem was also based on obvious continuities: it was to be expected that the tomb of Christ and Golgotha would be unearthed under the *capitolium* of Aelia. What other space would have been more fitting politically and theologically?[26]

---

20 Krautheimer 1993, 510 ff.; see also Krautheimer 1983, 29 – 30.
21 See Dagron 1974, 41– 42 and 542 ff.; Berger 2003, 63 – 72. It is noteworthy that a comparison of the Church of the Holy Sepulcher in Jerusalem and the Church of the Apostles in Constantinople shows that Constantine's self-glorification in 'his' city is closely modelled on Christ's glorification in Jerusalem; see Leeb 1992, 107 ff.
22 The Roman *legio X Fretensis*, which Vespasian installed on the ruins of old Jerusalem, had already been moved to Aila on the Red Sea under Diocletian; see Bieberstein/Bloedhorn 1994, I, 147–148; Kubitschek 1925.
23 Walker 1990, 15 – 16.
24 Euseb. *VC* 3,33,1.
25 Walker 1990, 311 ff.; Hunt 1997a, 417– 419.
26 Drijvers 2004, 10 – 16. Cf. Klein (forthcoming), ch. 2.4, on the originally anti-pagan direction of impact of the Encaenia; it was no coincidence that September 13th, the *dies natalis* of Jupiter Capitolinus, had been chosen as the date of the inauguration which was to be liturgically commemorated every year.

Helena's "Pilgrimage"

Constantine's building program was not the only imperial initiative that served to express the special status of Palestine and Jerusalem. In 326, shortly after Constantine commissioned the Church of the Holy Sepulcher, his mother Helena set out on her famous tour on the Eastern provinces.[27] Helena had received the rank of *Augusta* after the palace crisis culminating in the execution of Constantine's wife Fausta and his son Crispus. Evidence suggests that her journey in addition to other purposes had a penitential character and was an attempt to repair a tarnished relationship with the Church. The empress's active demonstration of imperial piety might have significantly improved the dynasty's Christian reputation and served broadly as shining example. Helena combined her "pilgrimage" with the traditional arrival ceremonial of an emperor in the provinces.[28] "As she visited the whole east in the magnificence of imperial authority, she showered countless gifts upon the citizen bodies of every city, and privately to each of those who approached her." According to Eusebius, she supported soldiers, the poor and downtrodden, and granted amnesty to prisoners and exiles.[29] This imperial generosity, of course, was not for its own sake. It was meant to influence public opinion and convey a new imperial image to the provincials. Combined with pilgrimage, however, the *iter principis* was fashioned anew in Christian form. The concept of the Roman Empire and the Roman monarchy, as represented symbolically by the journey of Helena Augusta, thus also changed. Upon reaching the destination of her pilgrimage, according to Eusebius, Helena applied "her outstanding intellect to enquiring about the wondrous land" and "accorded suitable adoration to the footsteps of the savior."[30] Helena's journey to the Eastern provinces had a major impact on the development of Christian pilgrimage in Palestine.[31] She and her son sponsored the construction of the Church of the Nativity in Bethlehem and the Church of the Ascension on the Mount of Olives. She probably also oversaw the rapid progress made on constructing the Church of the Holy Sepulcher.[32] Was Helena also involved in the discovery of the True Cross? The legend of her involvement first appeared in the latter half of the fourth century.[33]

If Eusebius' account is reliable, Constantine himself considered travelling to Palestine to celebrate his thirtieth jubilee, to take part in the consecration of the Church

---

27 Hunt 1982, 28 ff.
28 Halfmann 1986.
29 Euseb. VC 3,44. Drijvers 1992 is right to emphasize (65) that "she (sc. Helena) did not travel as a humble pilgrim but as an Augusta," although his reconstruction of the political and diplomatic circumstances of her journey is not convincing; see Grünewald 1995, 53–54.
30 Euseb. VC 3,42,2–3.
31 Holum 1990, 66–81, convincingly interprets Helena's journey against the background of the *itinera principum*.
32 Euseb. VC 3,41–43.
33 Cf. below, n. 66.

of the Holy Sepulcher in Jerusalem and to be baptized in the River Jordan.[34] Be that as it may, Constantine's journey never took place. The emperor nevertheless ensured that his new central church would have a magnificent dedication ceremony by ordering the Synod of Tyre to relocate to Jerusalem. The Anastasis compound thus was consecrated in the presence of imperial officials and numerous bishops from throughout the empire (although predominantly its eastern part). Eusebius reports that many speeches were held on this occasion, including his own, and emphasizes the connection with the emperor's *tricennalia*.[35] According to Eusebius, the joint celebration in Jerusalem sealed the alliance between the Roman emperor and the Christian God: while the emperor guaranteed the worthy veneration of Christ by magnificently adorning the Holy Places, God himself granted a long and successful reign to the emperor.

Eusebius' interpretation, of course, does not necessarily reflect the emperor's original intentions in every detail.[36] As a matter of fact, the Constantinian building program is revealing enough all by itself. It is accompanied by two imperial letters, considered genuine, quoted in Eusebius' text.[37] The first letter, to Bishop Makarios on the erection of the Church of the Holy Sepulcher, has been quoted and discussed above. The second letter was sent to Makarios and all the bishops of Palestine. In this document, Constantine complains that the recipients failed to inform him of the pagan pollution of certain holy places, so that it was left to his pious mother-in-law, Eutropia, to alert him to the fact.[38] Constantine connects this accusation of idolatry to a pagan altar near the oak of Mamre and dispatches the *comes* Acacius to purify the site and – following the instructions of the bishops – build a *basilica* there worthy of the Catholic and Apostolic Church. This letter again shows how earnestly the emperor personally cared for the development of the sacral topography in Palestine. At this point, we may therefore conclude that both Constantine and Helena showed remarkable commitment in initiating a development that would ultimately transform Palestine into the Holy Land of the Christian *oikumene*.

---

34 Euseb. *VC* 4,40,2. 4,62,2.
35 Euseb. *VC* 4,33. 43–47. Eusebius' speech on the consecration of the Church of the Holy Sepulcher is most probably transmitted together with the tricennial oration: Euseb. *LC* 11–18; see Drake 1976, 30–45; Barnes 1977, 341–345, and Wienand in this volume.
36 This interpretation is nevertheless important as an exemplary discourse. For Eusebius, the ideal Christian emperor had to take care of the Holy Places in Palestine. This argument was, as we shall see, taken up and modified as needed by several ecclesiastical dignitaries. On Eusebius' impact on other writers, Winkelmann 1964, 91–119, esp. 107–108: Eusebius' *VC* in particular was used by the church historians of the fifth century; see Leppin 1996, 40.
37 Euseb. *VC* 3,30–32. 3, 52–53; see Dörries 1954, 84 ff. and 321–322. In the early 1950s, the discovery of a papyrus proved that another often-questioned document (*VC* 2,24–42) was authentic; debate over the authenticity of the documents quoted in the *VC* subsequently came to an end; see Winkelmann 1962, 187–243, esp. 197–205; Tartaglia 1984, 17 ff.; Sansterre 1972, 159.
38 Hunt 1997a, 416.

The Bishop and the Emperor: Cyril of Jerusalem and Constantius II

Local church leaders embraced the opportunity that Constantine's foundations offered them. With the publication of his *Vita Constantini* shortly after the emperor's death, Eusebius, Bishop of Caesarea, might already have encouraged his successors to ensure the continuity of imperial policy toward Palestine. Bishop Cyril of Jerusalem openly expressed this expectation in a letter to Emperor Constantius regarding a cross of light that appeared in the sky over Jerusalem on May 7, 351. Cyril links the phenomenon to an apocalyptic prophecy of Christ: "And then shall appear the sign of the Son of man in heaven" (Matthew 24:30).[39] In doing so, he recalled the common expectations of the return of the Lord, which was traditionally linked with the Mount of Olives. The cross of light should revive the conviction that the Holy Land was not only the place of Christ's earthly presence, but also the future site of his return at the end of times.[40] At the same time, Cyril connects the auspicious sign with the reign of Constantius: "In the time of your blessed father Constantine of happy memory and most favored by God, the saving wood of the Cross was found in Jerusalem when God's grace rewarded the piety of his noble search with the discovery of the hidden holy places. But you, most pious Lord Emperor, have surpassed your father's piety with an even greater reverence for the divine, and in your time miracles have now appeared no longer from the ground but in the heavens."[41] According to Cyril's interpretation of the cross, Constantius, who at the time was suppressing Magnentius' usurpation in the West, had God on his side. The location of the phenomenon was far from immaterial: even more than Constantine's discovery of the Christian holy places, the heavenly sign illustrated God's favor toward the city where the events of the New Testament took place.[42] Cyril thus offered the em-

---

[39] Cyr. Jer. *Ep. ad Const.* 1. 6. The best edition of this letter is Bihan 1973, 264–296. On bishop Cyril of Jerusalem cf. Drijvers 2004, 153 ff. (chap. 6: "Promoting Jerusalem"); Van Nuffelen 2007; Kalleres 2015, 149–171.
[40] Hunt 1982, 156.
[41] Cyr. Jer. *Ep. ad Const.* 3 (trans. Yarnold 2000, 69).
[42] Cyril obviously succeeded in convincing the people to accept and disseminate his interpretation, as can be seen from the reactions attested by Sozom. *HE* 4,5 (trans. Chester D. Hartranft): "Men, women, and children left their houses, the market-place, or their respective employments, and ran to the church, where they sang hymns to Christ together, and voluntarily confessed their belief in God. The intelligence disturbed in no little measure our entire dominions, and this happened rapidly; for, as the custom was, there were travelers from every part of the world, so to speak, who were dwelling at Jerusalem for prayer, or to visit its places of interest, these were spectators of the sign, and divulged the facts to their friends at home. The emperor was made acquainted with the occurrence, partly by numerous reports concerning it which were then current, and partly by a letter from Cyrill the bishop. It was said that this prodigy was a fulfillment of an ancient prophecy contained in the Holy Scriptures. It was the means of the conversion of many pagans and Jews to Christianity."

peror the charisma of the holy places as a means of legitimating his rule. Cyril calls it the first fruits of his episcopate, which he offers the emperor through his letter.[43] It is not difficult to recognize Cyril's attempt to raise the dignity of his episcopal see; it is likely that he hoped for imperial support in his ecclesiastical quarrels with his metropolitan, Acacius of Caesarea.[44] Cyril's letter thus proposed an alliance that would not be confirmed until a hundred years later: Constantius' support for the Arians apparently precluded further steps down this path.

Julian's Attempt to Rebuild the Temple

Paradoxically, the next emperor to show interest in Jerusalem as a religious center was none other than Julian the Apostate. The sources credibly relate that in 363 Julian attempted to relocate the Jews to Judea and to rebuild the Jewish Temple in Jerusalem.[45] His motives are to be found in his religious policy.[46] Julian made a name for himself as *restaurator templorum* and attempted to promote and revive ritual sacrifice throughout the empire. By rebuilding the Temple in Jerusalem, he would have enabled the Jews to venerate their God with sacrifices once more. Julian potentially also attempted to win over the large Jewish communities of Babylonia on the eve of his war against the Persians. According to Ammianus, he also attempted "to extend the memory of his reign by great works."[47] The reference to the actions of Constantine in the Holy Land forty years earlier is obvious.[48] Julian, however, did not intend to undo Constantine's actions, but rather outdo them and thus deprive them of their significance. To do this, he devised a plan – from a Christian perspective, a diabolical one – that undoubtedly drew on the emperor's early religious upbringing. Julian intended to refute Christ's prophecy about the Temple[49] and, in doing so, strike at the heart of Christianity at the very site of its origin and recent glorification, since the destruction of the Jewish Temple was supposedly a sign sent by God signifying the transition from the old to the new covenant. The extent to which Julian's plans stirred up the Christian imagination can be surmised from the agitated reactions pre-

---

43 Cyr. Jer. *Ep. ad Const.* 7.
44 Sozom. *HE* 4,25; Theod. *HE* 2,27.
45 A careful reassessment of all available sources can be found in Blanchetière 1980, 61–81, and Levenson 2004.
46 For the following, see ibid., 72 ff.; Bowersock 1978, 88–90 and 120–122 (on the chronology of the events); Smith 1995, 216–217; Stemberger 1987, 163 ff.; Drijvers 2004, 130–137.
47 Amm. Marc. 23,1,2 (trans. J.C. Rolfe): *imperiique sui memoriam magnitudine operum gestiens propagare*.
48 This reference even extends to practical matters; cf. Amm. Marc. 23,1,2–3: just like Constantine, Julian assigned the task of swiftly carrying out his plans to the highest imperial officials (his 'friend' Alypius and the provincial governors).
49 Matthew 24:2: "[...] verily I say unto you, There shall not be left here one stone upon another, that shall not be thrown down"; similarly, Mark 13:2; Luke 19:44. 21:6; cf. also Daniel 9:26.

served in the sources, sometimes even decades later.⁵⁰ The project, however, failed, and the Christians naturally attributed this failure to God's intervention and used it as an argument in their apologetic writings. In the end, Julian's strategy accomplished the opposite of what he had intended: the importance of Jerusalem as an arena for religious competition became implanted in the Christian mentality. Only unrestrained possession of the Holy Land could secure the truth of the Gospels.

Julian's immediate successors, however, had other concerns than promoting the holy places of Palestine; their adherence to Arianism further inhibited their collaboration with the Church of Jerusalem. Only after Theodosius I had restored ecclesiastical unity could the province again become relevant to imperial policy. Although Theodosius did not act as a builder in Jerusalem,⁵¹ he granted legal privileges to the clergy responsible for maintaining the holy places.⁵² Various personal connections to aristocratic ascetics from the Theodosian court who permanently resided in Jerusalem filled the gap left by the lack of imperial activity.⁵³

The (Female) Pilgrim's Movement

I cannot discuss in detail every step of the theoretical elaboration and practical realization of the concept of the Holy Land. As early as the late 340s, Cyril included mention of Biblical places as visible and tangible testimonies to Christ in his baptismal catecheses. In doing so, he set the parameters for future theological reflection – especially, of course, in Jerusalem.⁵⁴ His sermons also suggest a lively culture of pilgrimage. The first pilgrim account, however, authored by a pious traveler from Bordeaux, dates even earlier: the so-called Pilgrim of Bordeaux travelled to the Holy Land in 333, i.e. before the completion of the Constantinian churches. The next pilgrim account to come down to us is that of Egeria, who travelled through the Holy Land between 381 and 384.⁵⁵ We also know of a large number of western noblemen and especially noblewomen in the late fourth and early fifth centuries who stayed in

---

50 See n. 44; Drijvers 2004, 131–132.
51 In the tradition of Constantine, he may have claimed theologically important places for Christianity, but *pace* Bieberstein/Bloedhorn 1994, I, 155–156; II, 118ff.; III, 243ff.; Röwekamp 1995, 66–67; Maraval 1985, 68–69; Stemberger 1987, 64; Küchler 2014, 427. 470, there is no evidence that he commissioned any buildings in Jerusalem, e.g. churches in the Garden of Gethsemane or on Mount Sion; Klein 2012, 95–107, here 98: "[...] for one hundred years after Constantine all new buildings in the city were commissioned, as far as we know, either by the clergy of Jerusalem using alms and donations from rich pilgrims or by these aristocratic pilgrims themselves, like Melania the Elder (monastery on the Mount of Olives) or the noblewomen Poemenia (the *Imbomon*)."
52 *Cod. Theod.* 16,2,26.
53 See Hunt 1982, 157ff.; Klein 2012, 98–99.
54 See Markus 1994, 259; Drijvers 2004, 154–156.
55 See Wilkinson 1999 [updated edition]; Röwekamp 1995. The joint efforts of pilgrims and monks to create a religious identity for Palestine are investigated in Sivan 1990, 54–65.

Jerusalem and Bethlehem for longer periods (and occasionally permanently) and became famous for founding pious establishments.[56] In some cases, their reason for moving to Palestine may have been the advance of barbarian tribes in the West.[57] Besides providing security, the Holy Land also functioned much more fundamentally and lastingly as a place of spiritual exile. Ascetic withdrawal from the world to Palestine did not entail a radical break with society;[58] it did, however, provide wealthy and important aristocrats an honorable means of escaping the burdens of their social status and professional duties. This new form of withdrawal was particularly attractive to Roman noblewomen.[59] By changing their lifestyle, they could gain power and influence in a different realm: honorable female aristocrats in Rome turned into revered ascetics and female benefactors in Jerusalem and Bethlehem.[60] Paulinus of Nola wrote about one such noblewoman, Melania the Elder: "Abandoning worldly life and her own country, she chose to bestow her spiritual gift at Jerusalem, and to dwell there in pilgrimage from her own body. She became an exile from her fellow citizens, but a citizen among the saints. With wisdom and sanctity she chose to be a servant in this world of thrall so as to be able to reign in the world of freedom."[61] Besides the promise of salvation, serving in Jerusalem could replace ruling in Rome. This form of serving, however, was merely another, more effective form of ruling, since it derived power from the true dominion in Heaven, for which it prepared one. To perform their new role successfully, noblewomen had to separate themselves from their usual environment spatially and socially. Not least in order to experience a distant echo of this heavenly freedom, Melania went to Jerusalem – as did her eponymous granddaughter and likewise Paula and Eustochium, the friends and sponsors of Jerome.[62] Especially the example of Melania the Younger shows that this new lifestyle did not deprive them of their hereditary contacts: in 436 she travelled to Constantinople to help arrange the marriage of the western emperor Valentinian III and Eudoxia, the daughter of Theodosius II, the emperor in the East. Her saint-like

---

56 Cf. Heyden 2014, 154–166. Overviews in Bieberstein/Bloedhorn 1994, I, 159–160, and in Stemberger 1987, 100. Translations of the respective source texts can be found in Wilkinson 1977, and in Donner 1979.
57 Clark 1989, 167.
58 The prolific writings of Jerome in Bethlehem show that besides the caring for pilgrims, he was still guaranteed active exchange with the outside world, see Rebenich 1992, 195 ff.
59 On the liberating call to asceticism cf. Feichtinger 1995, *passim*, esp. 238, 308 ff. and 319 ff. As Feichtinger shows, however, the greater possibilities ascetic women enjoyed met with corresponding strategies developed by male theologians and clerics to contain them. I would argue, however, that this 'containment' was more difficult to realize in the Holy Land than it was e. g. in the city of Rome or in Constantinople.
60 See Clark 1989, 173. For the elite self-perception (particularly that of newly converted Christians) of the Roman senatorial aristocracy, which maintained its prestige, connections and economic resources in the Holy Land, see Rebenich 1992, 181 ff. 193–194, and Hunt 1982, 76 ff.
61 Paul. Nol. *Ep.* 29,10 (trans. P.G. Walsh).
62 See Feichtinger 1995, 181 ff. (Paula), 188 ff. (Melania the Elder), 209 ff. (Eustochium), and 227 ff. (Melania the Younger); Heyden 2014, 243–248.

bearing endowed her with a great influence at the imperial court.[63] It is likely that she also convinced the mother of the bride, the empress Eudocia, to make a pilgrimage to the Holy Land.[64]

The Christian holy places were not, of course, attractive exclusively to women, even though the phenomenon emerges more prominently in connection with them. In addition to many pilgrims, important scholars such as Jerome and Rufinus, who resided in Palestine, also helped to promote the Holy Land and integrate it in the Christian mentality. Jerome called Jerusalem a "Christian Athens" and claimed that the most noble men and women of all nations gathered there to live according to Christian virtues.[65] On the whole, these pious expatriates in Palestine had broad spiritual and political influence.

The Discovery of the True Cross (and other Relics)

The fourth century witnessed what would become potentially the most important foundation myth of the Christian empire: the discovery of the True Cross by Empress Helena.[66] Neither Eusebius nor the pilgrim of Bordeaux, both contemporary sources, mention the *lignum crucis*. Soon afterward, however, Cyril of Jerusalem claims in his baptismal catecheses (348–350) that "the whole world has since [sc. since the crucifixion] been filled with the wood of the cross, piece by piece," and, in the letter to Emperor Constantius quoted above, he dates the discovery of the cross to the reign of Constantine.[67] In her account of her pilgrimage dating to 381–384, Egeria gives us a

---

63 Gerontios *Vit. Mel.* 50–56; see Hunt 1982, 221ff.; Holum 1982, 183–184.
64 It is also possible that Melania encouraged the Iberian prince Nabarnugios, who lived as a hostage at the imperial court, to escape to the Holy Land, where he became a monk and adopted the name Peter; cf. John Rufus *Vit. Pet. Iber.* 40–44 (Horn/Phenix).
65 Jer. *Ep.* 46,9; see Vogüé 1993, 51ff. Jerome, however, also made different proclamations. In *ep.* 58,2ff. he refers to the spiritual representation of Jerusalem in order to discourage his addressee (Paulinus of Nola) from a pilgrimage or permanent stay in the holy places (on the reasons behind this, cf. Hunt 1973, 480); similar reservations are expressed by Gregory of Nyssa, *ep.* 2 (PG 46, 1013C); cf. Markus 1994, 260.
66 Heid 2001; Heid 1989; Hunt 1982, 38ff.; Drijvers 1992, 81–93, and 2004, 167–175; Borgehammar 1991, 123ff. argues for the historicity of the legend. Heinen 1995, 83–117, esp. 113, writes that "[nichts] spricht […] dagegen und vieles dafür, daß Helena in der Tat Kreuz und Nagel gefunden hat." The arguments of Borgehammar and Heinen cannot be discussed here in detail, especially since the historicity of the legend is immaterial in the present context. It is noteworthy, however, that belief in the discovery of the cross did not become widespread until the late fourth century. Klein's argument (forthcoming) ch. 2.2–3, is the most plausible, namely, that, given Eusebius' silence on the matter, within one or at most two decades of the construction of the Anastasis compound a piece of wood was found that was believed to be the True Cross – and only later was connected with Empress Helena.
67 *Catech.* 4,10 (cf. 10,19. 13,4 – trans. E. Yarnold); *Ep. ad Constantium* 3 (cf. n. 41); see Drijvers 2004, 157–158.

vivid description of the liturgical importance of the relic at the time.⁶⁸ Neither Cyril nor Egeria, however, refer to Helena's role in connection with this. The legend first appears almost contemporaneously in the writings of Gelasius of Caesarea, which Rufinus used for his ecclesiastical history, and in an obituary composed in 395 by Ambrose, Bishop of Milan, for the late emperor Theodosius I.⁶⁹ Although the two accounts differ in details, they paint a similar picture of Helena's role. Ambrose's speech, which was part of a religious yet highly political ceremony,⁷⁰ is noteworthy in the present context for his explicit reference to the political and theological consequences of the discovery of the True Cross.⁷¹ Ambrose notably integrates the legend into his praise of this remarkable Christian emperor. According to Ambrose, Theodosius upon his death entered the kingdom of Christ, where he now dwells with Constantine – as almost his only worthy successor. Constantine, however, the archetypical Christian emperor, not only symbolically raised the cross by making Christianity the favored religion of the Roman Empire; he physically raised it by sending his pious mother to Jerusalem to uncover the Christian holy places. According to the logic of this political theology, Helena was the only person who could find the cross. Constantine was out of the question, since, as was well known, he did not visit Palestine in his lifetime. The Ambrosian Helena, however, who was compared to Mary the mother of Christ, supposedly was not content with merely finding the cross; she moreover endowed the empire with the genuine attributes of Christian faith. According to Ambrose, she had the nails of the cross made into a diadem and bridle that she sent to her son: "Constantine used both, and passed on the faith to subsequent rulers," Ambrose remarks, and after a few lines he continues: "a crown made from cross, so that the faith spreads its light; reins too from the cross so that power rules but here is just government, not unjust enactment."⁷² In Ambrose's account, the relics from Jerusalem with which Helena adorned the imperial insignia exemplify the connection between Christ and Roman imperial rule.⁷³

---

68 *Itin. Eg.* 37,1–3.
69 Rufin. *HE* 10,7–8; Ambr. *De obitu Theod.* 40–51, Heinen 1995, 88ff. To Drijvers 2004, 173 "it seems [...] not improbable that Cyril [sc. of Jerusalem] was responsible for the origin and composition of the story of Helena's *inventio crucis.*"
70 Heinen 1995, 91.
71 For the importance of the passage about Helena in the speech, see Steidle 1978, 94–112. The most important addressees of the speech were, of course, the sons of the deceased emperor, especially Honorius; see Steidle, 102ff.
72 Ambr. *De obitu Theod.* 47–48: *Utroque usus est Constantinus et fidem transmisit ad posteros reges. [...] corona de cruce, ut fides luceat, habena quoque de cruce, ut potestas regat sitque iusta mode ratio, non iniusta praeceptio.* English translation by J.H.W.G. Liebeschuetz, *Ambrose of Milan. Political Letters and Speeches*, Liverpool 2005, 200.
73 See Hunt 1997, 52ff. who discusses the importance of the Helena legend in Ambrose's funerary speech, esp. 57: "In his eternal realm in the heavenly Jerusalem Theodosius was brought closer to the faith of the holy places than he had ever been in real life."

They compelled the successors of Constantine and Theodosius to maintain a piety that also included care for the Christian holy places.

In the fourth century, the self-conception of Roman emperors and the normative imperial ideal proposed by theologians did not always coincide. It was only later emperors who began, especially in the city of Constantinople, to present themselves ever more in accordance with such Christian theological guidelines.[74] This development first peaked at the court of Arcadius and Theodosius II. The translation of several relics from Palestine to Constantinople attests to the process.[75] In order to procure the most precious relics, the emperor had to grant favors to the Palestinian Church. An episode transmitted in Theophanes' *Chronicle* will serve as an example: "In this year the pious Theodosius, in imitation of the blessed Pulcheria, sent much money to the archbishop of Jerusalem for distribution among those in need. He also sent a golden cross, set with precious stones to be fixed on the holy site of Calvary. The archbishop sent as a return gift the relics of the right hand of the first martyr Stephen, by means of Passarion, one of the holy men." Pulcheria and Theodosius received the relics in Chalcedon and brought them to the palace, where they erected a magnificent church for St Stephen.[76] The relics had been discovered in Palestine in 415,[77] and parts had been brought to Constantinople in 421.[78] It is likely that the timing of the translation was no coincidence: being engaged in an uncertain war with Persia at the time, the pious imperial court seems to have felt a special need for the divine support it expected to receive from the relics.[79] The bishop of Jerusalem, who had apparently profited from Pulcheria's generosity in the past, did not hesitate to underline Palestine's special relationship with the emperor by duly donating the relics.

Eudocia's Pilgrimage and Patronage

As we have seen, Theodosius II's patronage followed the precedent set by Constantine. Empress Eudocia's pilgrimage to the Holy Land in 438/439 was an even more

---

74 See Martin 1985; Diefenbach 1996, esp. 52ff.; Trampedach 2005b; Meier 2007.
75 Diefenbach 1996, 43ff.; idem 2002, 21–47, esp. 24.
76 Theoph. AM 5920 (p. 8687 de Boor / trans. Mango/Scott 1997, 135f). The reception of the relics may be depicted on the Trier Ivory; see Holum/Vikan 1979, 115–133 (with illustrations); Holum 1982, 102–109. For a different view cf. Klein in this volume.
77 *Epistula Luciani*, PL 41,807–818; see Clark 1982, 141ff.
78 Cf. Holum/Vikan 1979, esp. 127ff. Theophanes' credibility has been called into question by Wortley 1980, 381–394. Wortley notes that there is no mention of the translation prior to the ninth century chronicle. Reference to Passarion, who is known as an archimandrite and chorepiscopus from other sources, may, however, support its authenticity; cf. Cyril of Scythopolis, VE 16; VS 30; and Delmas 1900, 162–163.
79 See Holum 1977, 153–172, esp. 163ff.

prominent commemoration of Helena's (by then) legendary journey.[80] Like Helena, Eudocia travelled with a large entourage through the cities of the East, bestowing donations on them. Her entrance into Antioch seemed to have been the most impressive of all. Melania, whom the empress revered as a spiritual mother, came as far as Sidon to meet her on her way to Jerusalem. And in Jerusalem itself she was received not only by Bishop Juvenal, but also by Cyril, Patriarch of Alexandria. She took part in the consecration of two *martyria* that she generously supported and returned to Constantinople with several relics. Several years later, most likely in 444, Eudocia returned to the Holy Land, where she remained until her death in 460. The sources are too vague to determine what sort of court intrigue in Constantinople, if any, caused Eudocia's exile.[81] It was, however, an honorable exile, and there is no reason to assume that the empress did not enjoy her stay in Jerusalem. Even after finally breaking with the court a few years later, she resided in a palace in Bethlehem, received petitions, gave orders to soldiers and the local population and demanded strict obedience. The governor of Caesarea, as the local representative of imperial power, was allowed to interfere only at the empress's request.[82] Eudocia moreover must have commanded extensive financial resources, since she initiated the largest building activity in the Holy Land since Constantine. Not only did she build churches, monasteries, hospices, poor houses, and hospitals, she also erected or rebuilt or expanded Jerusalem's city walls, referring explicitly to a verse of Psalm 50: "Do good to Sion in your good pleasure (*eudokia*) and let the walls of Ierousalem be built."[83]

Eudocia also had influence in ecclesiastical matters. She appointed important priestly office-holders, e. g. in the Church of the Holy Sepulcher.[84] Even as an exile, Eudocia held sway over Jerusalem and its hinterland in a way that recalled every aspect of late imperial rule. The holy places gave her the ideal location to demonstrate her outstanding piety and to live a life that befitted an empress who was not bound to the regulations of court life. Eudocia's example would become very popular among imperial women: in 470 her eponymous granddaughter died in Jerusalem

---

80 Socr. *HE* 7,47; Gerontios *Vit. Mel.* 58–59; John Rufus *Vit. Petr. Iber.* 71 (Horn/Phenix); Marc. Com. 439,2; Evagr. *HE* 1,20; Hunt 1982, 229 ff., Holum 1982, 184–185; McNamara 1996, 51–80, esp. 57–58; Sivan 2008, 210–219; Klein 2011/2012, 85–95.
81 The story related in John Malalas 14,8 (276–277 Thurn) does not seem to have any historicity.
82 See Holum 1982, 218.
83 Ps. 50:20–21 of the LLX (ed. Rahlfs, trans. A. Pietersma): ἀγάθυνον, κύριε, ἐν τῇ εὐδοκίᾳ σου τὴν Σιων, καὶ οἰκοδομηθήτω τὰ τείχη Ιερουσαλημ; cf. Cyr. Scyth. *Vit. Euth.* 35; *Vit. Ioann.* 4; John Malalas 14,8 (277–278 Thurn); Evagr. *HE* 1,22; *Chron. Pasch.* p. 585 Dindorf; Armstrong 1969, 17–30, esp. 18–19; Hunt 1982, 237 ff.; Bieberstein/Bloehorn 1994, I, 160–161; Klein 2012, 158–160; idem 2011/2012, 89–95. According to Weksler-Bdolah (this volume), who studied the archaeological evidence, the construction of the late antique walls of Jerusalem date to the late fourth century or early fifth century at the latest; her assumption, however, that the literary sources confuse Eudocia with Eudoxia does not seem plausible to me, since there is no indication that the latter was involved in any way in the affairs of Jerusalem.
84 Cyr. Scyth., *VE* 30.

after escaping from her Vandal husband Huneric; similar cases of high-ranking female expatriates are known from the sixth century.[85]

The Ecclesiastical Elevation of Jerusalem

The concept of the Holy Land influenced ecclesiastical relations in Palestine from the very beginning. As mentioned above, as early as the Council of Nicaea, the Bishop of Jerusalem received an honorary position in the province of Palestine although he had to accept the metropolitan privileges of the See of Caesarea.[86] This compromise was not always uncontested. While Caesarea insisted on its traditional priority, Jerusalem could point to its continuously growing numbers of pilgrims. Jerusalem's claim to the Apostolic tradition was even more important; dogmatic controversies added to the rivalry. Caesarea, however, was able to maintain its priority until Juvenal became Bishop of Jerusalem. During his long episcopal rule (422–457), Jerusalem experienced a rapid, albeit not always straightforward, rise in the ecclesiastical hierarchy. Juvenal, being both ingenious and cunning, was not content merely to contest Caesarea's position as his predecessors had done; his ambitions went much further. The honorific rank he intended to win for Jerusalem was ultimately to be labelled a "patriarchate" and endowed with special privileges; he even demanded jurisdiction over the See of Antioch and the entire Diocese of Oriens. The devious paths Juvenal took in ecclesiastical politics to achieve this goal cannot be discussed in detail here.[87] Suffice it to say he did not hesitate to exploit the dogmatic controversies of the day for his own purposes. Even though he was one of the main protagonists of the so-called "Robber Council" (*latrocinium*) of Ephesus, he still managed to be on the winning side at the subsequent Council of Chalcedon. He thus secured patriarchal rank for his see, which was granted jurisdiction – if not over the entire Diocese of Oriens – over the three provinces of Palestine, which were removed from the ecclesiastical authority of Antioch. This success would not have been possible without the support of both the emperors Theodosius II and Marcian. In Juvenal they found a suitable individual to oversee the Holy Land and guarantee the enforcement of their ecclesiastical policies. This was a matter of considerable importance: given the large numbers of international pilgrims and the significance of the holy places themselves for imperial self-representation, the emperors had to vigorously fight heterodox movements in

---

85 Theoph. AM 5964 (p. 118 de Boor); Cyril of Scythopolis, *VS* 53–54. A roughly similar case from the late fourth century is mentioned by Zosimus 5,8,2: the widow and daughter of the eastern praetorian prefect Fl. Rufinus, who was murdered by troops outside Constantinople in 395, were granted safe conduct to sail to Jerusalem, where they lived for the rest of their lives.
86 See above, n. 19.
87 See the fundamental article by Honigmann 1950, 209–279; for the historical context, see also: Bacht 1953, 193–314, esp. 231–232; on the status of the episcopal see of Jerusalem after the Council of Chalcedon cf. Kötter, in this volume.

Jerusalem and its hinterland. For this, they needed a local supporter who enjoyed great ecclesiastical authority. The emperor Marcian accordingly repeatedly termed the See of Jerusalem "the See of the thrice-blessed Apostle Peter."[88]

Initially, however, the plan backfired. Juvenal's ambiguous role at the Council of Chalcedon had cost him the acceptance of his own community. Upon returning from the council he was ousted from his episcopal see. In his place, a certain Theodosius, a supporter of the deposed Alexandrian bishop Dioscurus, was elected patriarch by a large number of clerics and monks. Empress Eudocia also initially supported Theodosius. After many failed warnings and negotiations, and after Theodosius had consecrated numerous anti-Chalcedonian bishops, the emperor took drastic action. Theodosius himself was ousted and Juvenal re-instated with the support of soldiers in the summer of 453.[89] Several letters by Pope Leo the Great, who was a prominent defender of Chalcedon, show how important these matters were to church leaders. Even though he had little patience for Juvenal's intrigues and dogmatic inconstancy, Leo nevertheless expresses his hope that the Palestinian defectors would soon obey their legitimate bishop for "the sake of the testimony of the holy places" where they dwelled, and that they would soon return to the true faith.[90] In a letter dated February 4, 454, Leo congratulates Juvenal upon his return to the See of Jerusalem; Leo writes that the error and ignorance of a Jerusalemite Christian was far less excusable than that of anyone else. A Christian from Jerusalem gained knowledge of the Gospels not from books but from the testimony of the places themselves. Whereas Christians elsewhere had to believe, those in Jerusalem merely had to open their eyes and look around.[91] With this, Leo postulated an indivisible connection between the Holy Land and orthodoxy. According to this argument, the holy places themselves would refute potential heretics. For Leo, the Holy Land was destined to become the stronghold of orthodoxy. This line of thinking fell on fertile ground in Jerusalem and became a central aspect of the Jerusalemite self-conception.

Juvenal's return, however, was not a happy one. His position was precarious since most of the population opposed him. Two fortunate circumstances helped him to regain lost ground for himself and his Chalcedonian cause: first, Eudocia changed sides at the behest of Leo the Great and members of the eastern and western imperial courts. She set an example for many monks and laymen by re-entering com-

---

88 See Honigmann 1950, 256.
89 Bacht 1953, 244 ff.
90 Cf. *Ep.* 109 (Schwartz, ACO II 4,138.12ff. = 43,68 ff. Silva-Tarouca) from November 25, 452: *Qui ut eandem emendationem quam ille (sc. Iuvenalis) elegit, imitentur, optandum est, si vel ipsa sanctorum locorum circa quae habitant, testificatione resipiscant.* See Winkelmann 1988, 167–175, esp. 174–175.
91 Cf. *Ep.* 139 (Schwartz, ACO II 4, 92,7ff. = 53,21ff. Silva-Tarouca): *Quamvis enim nulli sacerdotum liceat nescire quot praedicat, inexcusabilior tamen est omnibus inperitis quilibet Hierosolymis habitans Christianus, qui ad cognoscendam virtutem evangelii non solum paginarum eloquiis, sed ipsorum locorum testimoniis eruditur. Et quod alibi non licet non credi, ibi non potest non videri. Quid laborat intellectus, ubi est magister aspectus?*

munion with Juvenal. Additionally, Euthymius, a highly revered monastic figure, had accepted the doctrine of Chalcedon from the very beginning and had rejected the offers made by the episcopal usurper Theodosius.[92] This had far-reaching consequences, and Euthymius' authority may also have influenced Eudocia's shift of allegiance.[93] Moreover, his disciples became the most important group in Palestinian monasticism and consequently occupied the most eminent episcopal sees of the Holy Land, including the patriarchate.[94] The spirit of compromise in ecclesiastical politics during the reign of Leo and Zeno bore fruit particularly in Palestine where the patriarchs staunchly implemented imperial policy. The *henotikon* edict of Emperor Zeno, issued in 482, which refrained from denouncing the Council of Chalcedon but certainly diminished its importance, resulted in the second Palestinian church union (the first was Eudocia's shift of allegiance). Consequently, most remaining anti-Chalcedonian monks returned to the Catholic Church.[95] This union also laid the basis for the political prominence of Palestinian monasticism in the sixth century.[96]

Holy Land Monasticism

In the late fifth century, the monks of the Judean desert in Palestine – and not the local patriarchs or bishops – became the most influential ambassadors of the Holy Land. This development went hand in hand with the contemporary tendency to attribute extraordinary power to holy men on account of their ascetic lifestyle. The monks of Palestine, however, were uniquely positioned to give this trend new impulses. In contrast to monks in Egypt,[97] Syria and Asia Minor, Palestinian monasticism was international. The monks came from all parts of the Roman world – partic-

---

92 Cyril of Scythopolis, *VE* 27. Even though the historicity of Euthymius's support for Chalcedon is undisputed, one can only speculate about his motives. The study by Binns 1994, esp. 186–187 is not particularly convincing on this matter. Euthymius may have realized that the Church of Jerusalem depended on imperial support.
93 Cyril of Scythopolis *VE* 30. Whenever Cyril recounts his heroes' victories in the battle for orthodoxy, however, his testimony is of dubious value for the historian. Eudocia's reconciliation with Juvenal and the Chalcedonian party did not stop her from continuing to support Monophysite monasteries, this time in compliance with the emperor Marcian; cf. Klein 2018a, 13–18; Binns 1994, 187.
94 Cf. Binns 1994, 161.
95 Cyril of Scythopolis *VE* 45, cf. Binns 1994, 188–189; Kötter 2013, 166–167; Kötter in this volume.
96 Cf. Trampedach 2005a.
97 Monasticism in Egypt also initially had a strong 'international' component (cf. e.g. Palladius, *Historia Lausiaca* or the *Historia Monachorum in Aegypto*). However, the devastating barbarian incursions in 404, 434 and 444 – and especially the doctrinal controversies following the Council of Chalcedon and Egypt's drift toward Monophysitism reduced this internationalism to some extent; cf. Griggs 1990, 209 ff. Cyril of Scythopolis (*VE* 32) mentions two archimandrites from Nitria who sought refuge from Monophysite attacks. One of them, Martyrius, originated from Cappadocia; the other, Elias, from Arabia. Both eventually became Patriarch of Jerusalem.

ularly, of course, from the East – and sometimes even from outside the borders of the empire.[98] This heterogeneity and its consequences were somewhat softened by a unique self-understanding: the hermits of the Judean desert regarded themselves as elite monks. Moreover, because of their predominantly foreign origins, the monks had no local roots and few contacts among the local population; their uninhabited desert abode and consequent problems of communication, of course, will have contributed to this isolation. In contrast to what Peter Brown has shown for the densely populated rural areas of Syria,[99] these reasons meant that the monks of Palestine neither could nor did act as intercessors or patrons for the population. Instead, they acted on account of an ecumenical responsibility and accountability that they derived from their geographical proximity to the Holy Sites. In their minds, they were truly "imperial monks."[100] Cyril of Scythopolis shows this in the first of his *Lives* by connecting the birth of Euthymius in Melitene in Armenia with the death of the Arian emperor Valens at the Battle of Adrianople.[101] Cyril regards the coincidence as a sign of God's providence, demonstrating the universal ecclesiastical and political importance of this monastic hero. Despite the catastrophic defeat of Roman troops, the coincidence is nonetheless a good omen: it stands for the beginning of the end of the Arian heresy. By means of this analogy, the hagiographer anticipates Euthymius' prominent role as the paradigmatic champion of the Orthodox Church from the very day of his birth. Cyril of Scythopolis, our main source for these events, wrote in the mid-sixth century. His depiction of both the character and importance of the Judean monks is static and therefore should not simply be applied to the actions of Euthymius, who lived a century earlier. Nevertheless, Euthymius' role marks the beginning of a development that extended to Cyril's own time, which we will briefly discuss below.

Sabas (439–532), one of Euthymius' disciples, perhaps accomplished best what Cyril of Scythopolis regarded as the divine mission of Judean desert monasticism. Sabas was not only a monastic hero; he also became famous as an organizer who literally colonized the desert with numerous monastic foundations.[102] In 493, together with a certain Theodosius, he was ordained an archimandrite by the patriarch.

---

98 For an overview of the places of origin of monks mentioned in the writings of Cyril of Scythopolis, cf. Schwartz 1939, 359 with n. 1; Trampedach 2005a, 292–294.
99 Brown 1982, 103–152. In referring to monks as patrons of the rural population, Brown (ibid., 145 ff.) also cites examples from Palestine; in contrast to Syria, however, these are exceptions, especially in the region of the Judean desert.
100 Cf. Hay 1996, 118–125, here p. 122: "In Palestine we observe an interesting progression. In the late fifth and sixth centuries, the leading monks repeatedly display an aggressive self-assurance that sees them present on the world stage, reflecting their re-integration, when deemed necessary, with the wider Christian community and their assumption of a leading role in theological and community affairs." On the following, see also my article on "Reichsmönchtum" (as n. 96).
101 Cyr. Scyth. *Vit. Euth.* 2; cf. Binns 1994, 1–2.
102 Chitty 1966, 105 ff.; Binns 1994, 161 ff.; Patrich 1995, 169 ff., esp. 203 ff. The archaeological evidence and the funding are studied by Hirschfeld 1992 and by Klein 2018b respectively.

Sabas was now responsible for the lauras in the vicinity of Jerusalem, and Theodosius for the coenobitic settlements.[103] With these appointments, the patriarch skillfully integrated the desert monks into the local church hierarchy. However, the arrangement also allowed monastic leaders to serve as representatives of the Church of Palestine.

The Roman emperors in the latter half of the fifth century pursued a conciliatory policy in their effort to resolve the divisions in the Church caused by the Council of Chalcedon. The policies of Emperor Anastasius (492–518) also, at least initially, took the same tack. However, when – in the second half of his reign – Anastasius himself became increasingly anti-Chalcedonian, conflict with the Church of Palestine became unavoidable.[104] In 511, the situation had become so precarious that Patriarch Elias of Jerusalem decided to send an illustrious delegation to the imperial court in Constantinople. Cyril of Scythopolis quotes the letter of credence signed by the patriarch: "The elite of the servants of God, good and faithful and leaders in the whole desert, including our Lord Sabas, the colonizer and guardian of our desert and luminary over all Palestine, I have sent to entreat your Majesty."[105] While the other monks quickly returned to Palestine, Sabas stayed in the capital for half a year to negotiate with the emperor. Yet, even though he found support among the female members of the imperial family, and even though Anastasius himself treated him with respect, Sabas obtained neither political guarantees nor tax remissions for the Church of Jerusalem. Anastasius, however, reassured the desert father that for the time being he would not take action against Patriarch Elias, who refused to follow the emperor's ecclesiastical policy. Moreover, he consigned a large amount of money to Sabas, which the latter distributed among the desert monasteries upon his arrival.[106]

The 'cease-fire,' however, was short-lived. Emperor Anastasius felt obliged to enforce his ecclesiastical policy in the Holy Land. Even when he had spoken with Sabas at the court in Constantinople, he had threatened to depose Elias "in order that the revered region that played host to God may not be sullied by the doctrines of Nestorius."[107] Two years later, he made good on his threat; in the meantime, Severus, the leading anti-Chalcedonian theologian at the time, was elected Patriarch of Antioch and enjoyed imperial support.[108] As Elias continued to refuse to condemn the Council of Chalcedon and to enter into communion with Severus, the emperor eventually attempted to depose him. Anastasius, however, did not expect the monastic resistance organized by Sabas and Theodosius. They managed to expel both the imperial officials and their military reinforcements from the city. In 515 Anastasius again at-

---

[103] Cyr. Scyth. *VS* 30; cf. Flusin 1983, 137 ff.; Binns 1994, 178–179; Patrich 1995, 287 ff.
[104] Cf. Honigmann 1951, 7 ff.; Jones 1964, 232 ff.; Frend 1972, 192 ff.
[105] Cyr. Scyth. *VS* 50 (trans. R.M. Price).
[106] Cyr. Scyth. *VS* 51–55; cf. Patrich 1995, 311 ff.
[107] Cyr. Scyth. *VS* 52.
[108] Cf. Charanis 1974, 72 ff.

tempted to depose Elias, this time by much more drastic means. He sent Olympus, the military commander (*dux*) of Palestine, to Jerusalem at the head of imperial troops. Olympus ousted Elias from his episcopal see and sent him to Aila (Aqaba) in exile. Elias was replaced by a certain John, who initially promised to re-enter into communion with Severus of Antioch and to condemn the Council of Chalcedon. However, John quickly broke his promise under the influence of Sabas and other leading desert fathers, since his ecclesiastical office depended on their regional support. The *dux* Anastasius, Olympus' successor, immediately went to Jerusalem and imprisoned John. When the latter again promised to meet the emperor's demands, he was released. Overnight, John summoned the desert monks to Jerusalem, where – according to Cyril of Scythopolis – more than ten thousand of them gathered. Only the basilica of St Stephen built by Eudocia was large enough to accommodate so great a number. In the presence of Hypatius, the emperor's nephew who happened to have made a pilgrimage to Jerusalem, the *dux* Anastasius, and the civil governor and consular Zacharias, the patriarch John – together with the monastic leaders Theodosius and Sabas – ascended the pulpit and condemned all enemies of the Council of Chalcedon; their speeches met with fervent acclamations from the monks. Hypatius was the first to give in or rather to deviate from his previous dogmatic beliefs: under oath he testified to his orthodoxy and gave the monks a generous donation of money. The *dux*, however, withdrew from Jerusalem to Caesarea out of fear of the monks.[109]

In this situation, with the emperor's reaction imminent, Theodosius and Sabas, acting as "combatants for piety, and generals and champions of orthodoxy" (in the words of Cyril of Scythopolis), issued a highly remarkable letter to Anastasius on behalf of the monks. Formally styled as a petition for peace for the Church of Jerusalem, this letter might more accurately be described as a declaration of war. In the petition, the monks claim that as inhabitants of the Holy Land, they have consistently observed the true and genuine faith through the agency of the holy places and the holy apostles. "Who are we, dwelling every day at the holy places, at which the mystery of incarnation of our great God and Savior was accomplished, where we touch the truth with our own hands, how then, more than five hundred years since the coming of Christ, are we of Jerusalem to learn the faith?" The monks announce to the emperor that they would never enter into communion with Severus or any other heretic. Moreover, they stress the complete agreement of all inhabitants of the Holy Land on this matter. Lastly, in the event of a violent intervention, they threaten the emperor with the following scenario: "the blood of all of us will willingly be shed and all the holy places be consumed with fire before such a thing come to pass in this holy city of God. For what benefit is there in the bare title of the holy

---

[109] Cyr. Scyth. *VS* 56.

places if they are so ravaged and dishonored?"[110] We do not know whether this forceful and bold demonstration by the monks impressed Anastasius. For the last two years of his reign, however, he refrained from risking the massacre predicted by the monks by not intervening at all. At the end of his life, he was forced to acknowledge that his church policy had failed, not least on account of the resistance of the Holy Land.

The Contributions of Justinian

The new dynasty that came to power in 518 made an about-face and favored the adherents of the Council of Chalcedon.[111] Now the monks of Jerusalem and the Judean desert could profit from their successful resistance to Anastasius' interventions. When Sabas – already over ninety years old – travelled to Constantinople for a second time to gain the emperor's support for the Palestinian provinces devastated in the Samaritan uprising, Emperor Justinian gave him a lavish reception. According to Cyril of Scythopolis, he sent the patriarch Epiphanius and the bishop Hypatius of Ephesus on imperial galleys to meet him. When the holy man was received at court, Justinian rose from his throne and prostrated himself, thus inverting the usual ceremonial and abasing himself and his office. Sabas purportedly even affronted the empress: the holy man ignored her request for a prayer for an heir, since he disapproved of her anti-Chalcedonian tendencies. Cyril of Scythopolis describes the negotiations between the emperor and the monk as an affair that gave both sides tangible benefits. Sabas received from the emperor the favors he had wanted: (1) tax relief for the Palestinian Church; (2) the rebuilding of church buildings destroyed during the Samaritan uprising; (3) the establishment of a hospital for the sick and for foreign persons in Jerusalem; (4) the construction and adornment of the *Theotokos* Church in Jerusalem, the foundation of which had already been laid by the patriarch Elias; (5) and the building of a desert fortress to protect the monasteries from Saracen incursions.

In return, the emperor would profit from the prayers of the desert monks, and Sabas prophesized their success: God would remunerate the emperor's beneficence toward the Holy Land with the acquisition of Africa, Rome, and the rest of the Western Roman Empire. At the same time, however, Sabas reminded the emperor of his duty to enforce orthodoxy everywhere. By regaining the West, Sabas says in Cyril's account, the emperor should liberate the holy Church from the stain of heresies (explicitly mentioning the Arian, Nestorian and Origenist heresies).[112]

---

110 Cyr. Scyth. *VS* 57; cf. Trampedach 2005a, 273–279. A markedly restrained answer in the form of a letter from the emperor is transmitted by Theodorus of Petra *Vit. Theodos.* 24, p. 60–61 (Usener); cf. Bacht 1953, 287.
111 Cf. Vasiliev 1950, 132ff.; Leppin 2011, 54–73.
112 Cyr. Scyth. *VS* 70–74; cf. Patrich 1995, 313ff.; Trampedach 2005a, 279–284.

This is undoubtedly a *vaticinium ex eventu*. Cyril wants to show that the welfare of the empire depended on the emperor's piety, which in turn manifests itself foremost in the fight for orthodoxy, reverence for holy men like Sabas, and care for the Holy Land. According to Cyril of Scythopolis, the prayers of the desert monks contribute significantly to the emperor's success.[113] As is well known, Justinian himself shared this view.[114]

Even after Sabas' death, the monks of Palestine enjoyed special status at the imperial court. Their delegates played a crucial role in the theological discussions with the anti-Chalcedonians in Constantinople in the 530s, culminating in the synod of 536, and also in the build-up to the fifth ecumenical council. However, they did not always speak with one voice. After the death of the great monastic leaders, controversy over the dogmatic reliability of Origen shook the solidarity of the Palestinian monks. Although the controversy was only a regional phenomenon, the emperor himself attended to the matter and condemned the Origenists in an edict in 544. The fact that even the fifth ecumenical council 553 addressed the issue and ruled in the emperor's favor shows how important the question of orthodoxy in the Holy Land had become to the emperor and the Church.[115]

Constantinople and Jerusalem now stood in a close relationship on several levels. Justinian made the idea of the Holy Land one of the primary aspects of his self-conception, as both his legislation and especially his building activity demonstrate.[116] It was under Justinian and his successors, up to Heraclius, that the ideas of the Holy Land and sacral monarchy were transformed into complementary elements of a unified political theology.[117] The alliance was not especially long-lived,

---

113 The relationship between holy man and emperor as described by Cyril is characterized by Flusin 1983, 207–208 as follows: "C'est lui [sc. Sabas] qui assure miraculeusement la sécurité et la prospérité de l'empire, la droiture et la réussite de la politique impériale. [...] L'empereur agit sur les conseils du moine; le moine prie, sans se mêler d'une tâche administrative; la collaboration des deux activités est nécessaire et efficace."

114 E.g., in the preface to his constitution *Deo auctore* from 530, Justinian states that all achievements, both military and legislative, were to be ascribed to God, under whose authority the emperor governed the empire, and whose providence inspired all projects and brought them to fruition; cf. Meier 2003, 104–136. God's support, however, on which Justinian purportedly based his rule above all else, was mediated not least by pious monks and especially by holy men like Sabas; cf. Hasse-Ungeheuer 2016, 120–129. 252–254.

115 Cf. Schwartz 1939, 387–408; Chitty 1966, 124ff.; Binns 1994, 201–217; Patrich 1995, 440–448; Capizzi 1994, 77ff.; Meier 2003, 279–289; Leppin 2011, 247–249; *The Acts of the Council of Constantinople of 553*, translated with an introduction and notes by R. Price, Liverpool 2012, vol. 2, 270–286; Hasse-Ungeheuer 2016, 211–223.

116 See the contributions of Trampedach and Viermann on the Justinianic church-building and political discourse in Jerusalem and Constantinople respectively, both in this volume, and cf. Sivan 2008, 219–225.

117 For a case from the reign of Maurice (582–602) that illustrates the post-Justinianic link between the concepts of the Holy Land and sacred monarchy, cf. Theoph. AM 6094 with Trampedach 2005a,

since Jerusalem was conquered by the Arabs in 638 and thus irrevocably lost to the Roman-Byzantine Empire. Even independently, however, both concepts proved to have a great future ahead of them.

Bibliography

Allen, P. & Jeffreys, E. (eds.) (1996). *The Sixth Century: End or Beginning?*, Brisbane.

Aretz, E. (ed.) (1995). *Der Heilige Rock zu Trier. Studien zur Geschichte und Verehrung der Tunika Christi*, Trier.

Armstrong, G.T. (1969). 'Fifth and sixth century church buildings in the Holy Land,' *Greek Orthodox Theological Review* 14, 17–30.

Bacht, H. (1953). 'Die Rolle des orientalischen Mönchtums in den kirchenpolitischen Auseinandersetzungen um Chalkedon (431–519),' in Grillmeier/Bacht 1953, 193–314.

Barnes, T. (1977). 'Two speeches by Eusebius,' *GRBS* 18, 341–345.

Barnes, T. (1981). *Constantine and Eusebius*, London.

Belayche, N. (1997). 'Du Mont du Temple au Golgotha. Le Capitole de la colonie d'Aelia Capitolina,' RHR 214, 387–413.

Berger, A. (2003). 'Konstantinopel, die erste christliche Metropole?,' in Brands/Severin 2003, 63–72.

Bieberstein, K. & Bloedhorn, H.-W. (1994). *Jerusalem: Grundzüge der Baugeschichte vom Chalkolithikum bis zur Frühzeit der osmanischen Herrschaft* (3 vols.). Wiesbaden.

Bihan, E. (1973). 'L'épître de Cyrille de Jérusalem à Constance sur la vision de la croix (BHG³ 413),' *Byzantion* 43, 264–296.

Binns, J. (1994). *Ascetics and ambassadors of Christ: the monasteries of Palestine*, Oxford.

Blanchetière, F. (1980). 'Julien Philhellène, Philosémite, Antichrétien: l'affaire du Temple de Jérusalem (363),' *Journal of Jewish Studies* 31, 61–81.

Bonamente, G. (ed.) (1993). *Costantino il Grande: dall' antichità all'umanismo*, Macerata.

Borgehammar, S. (1991). *How the Holy Cross was found: from event to medieval legend*, Stockholm.

Bowersock, G. (1978). *Julian the Apostate*, London.

Brands, G. & Severin, H.-G. (eds.) (2003). *Die spätantike Stadt und ihre Christianisierung*. Wiesbaden.

Brown, P. (1982). 'The Rise and the Function of the Holy Man in Late Antiquity,' in *Society and the Holy*, Berkeley, 103–152.

Capizzi, C. (1994). *Giustiniano I tra politica e religione*, Messina.

Charanis, P. (1974). *Church and State in the Later Roman Empire. The Religious Policy of Anastasius the First, 491–518*, Thessaloniki.

Chitty, D.J. (1966). *The Desert a City: An Introduction to the Study of Egyptian and Palestinian Monasticism under the Christian Empire*, Oxford.

Clark, E. (1982). 'Claims on the bones of Saint Stephen: the partisans of Melania and Eudocia,' *ChHist* 51, 141–156.

Clark, E. (1989). 'Piety, propaganda, and politics in the *Life of Melania the Younger*' in *Studia Patristica* 18, 167–183.

---

271 f.; the link was further developed by the emperor Heraclius (610–641); see Howard-Johnston, in this volume and esp. Viermann 2021, ch. 6.

Dagron, G. (1974). *Naissance d'une capitale: Constantinople et ses institutions de 330 à 451*, Paris.
Delmas, F. (1900). 'Saint Passarion,' *Échos d'Oient* 3, 162–163.
Diefenbach, S. (1996). 'Frömmigkeit und Kaiserakzeptanz im frühen Byzanz,' *Saeculum* 47, 35–66.
Diefenbach, S. (2002). 'Zwischen Liturgie und Civilitas. Konstantinopel im 5. Jahrhundert und die Etablierung eines städtischen Kaisertums,' in Warland 2002, 21–47.
Donner, H. (1979). *Pilgerfahrt ins Heilige Land. Die ältesten Berichte christlicher Palästinapilger (4.–7. Jahrhundert)*, Stuttgart.
Dörries, H. (1954). *Das Selbstzeugnis Kaiser Konstantins*, Göttingen.
Drake, H. (1976). *In praise of Constantine: A Historical Study and New Translation of Eusebius' Tricennial Orations*, Berkeley.
Drijvers, J.W. (1992). *Helena Augusta: The Mother of Constantine the Great and the Legend of her Finding of the True Cross*, Leiden.
Drijvers, J.W. (2004). *Cyril of Jerusalem: Bishop and City*, Leiden.
Feichtinger, B. (1995). *Apostolae Apostolorum. Frauenaskese als Zwang und Befreiung bei Hieronymus*, Frankfurt a. M.
Flusin, B. (1983). *Miracle et histoire dans l'œuvre de Cyrille de Scythopolis*, Paris.
Frend, W.H.C. (1972). *The Rise of the Monophysite Movement. Chapters in the History of the Church in the Fifth and Sixth Century*, Cambridge.
Gibson, Sh. & Taylor, J.E. (1994). *Beneath the Church of the Holy Sepulchre, Jerusalem: the archaeology and early history of traditional Golgotha*, London.
Griggs, C.W. (1990). *Early Egyptian Christianity: from its origins to 451 C.E.*, Leiden.
Grillmeier, A. & Bacht, H. (eds.) (1953). *Das Konzil von Chalkedon* (vol. II: *Entscheidung um Chalkedon*), Würzburg.
Groh, D.E. (1985). 'The Onomasticon of Eusebius and the rise of Christian Palestine,' *Studia Patristica* 18, 23–31.
Grünewald, Th. (1995). Review: 'Drijvers: Helena Augusta. The Mother of Constantine the Great and the Legend of Her Finding of the True Cross. Leiden: Brill (1992),' *Gnomon* 67, 51–56.
Halfmann, H. (1986). *Itinera principum: Geschichte und Typologie der Kaiserreisen im Römischen Reich*, Stuttgart.
Hasse-Ungeheuer, A. (2016). *Das Mönchtum in der Religionspolitik Kaiser Justinians I. Die Engel des Himmels und der Stellvertreter Gottes auf Erden*, Berlin.
Hay, K. (1996). 'Impact of St. Sabas: The Legacy of Palestinian Monasticism' in Allen/Jeffreys 1996, 118–125.
Heid, S. (1989). 'Der Ursprung der Helenalegende im Pilgerbetrieb Jerusalems,' *JbAC* 32, 41–71.
Heid, S. (2001). 'Die gute Absicht im Schweigen Eusebs über die Kreuzauffindung,' *Römische Quartalschrift für christliche Altertumskunde und Kirchengeschichte* 96, 37–56.
Heinen, H. (1995). 'Helena, Konstantin und die Überlieferung der Kreuzesauffindung im 4. Jahrhundert,' in Aretz 1995, 83–117.
Heyden, K. (2014). *Orientierung. Die westliche Christenheit und das Heilige Land in der Antike*, Münster.
Hirschfeld, Y. (1992). *The Judean Desert Monasteries in the Byzantine Period*, New Haven.
Holum, K. (1977). 'Pulcheria's crusade A.D. 421–422 and the ideology of imperial victory,' *GRBS* 18, 153–172.
Holum, K. (1982). *Theodosian Empresses: Women and Imperial Dominion in Late Antiquity*, Berkeley.
Holum, K. (1990). 'Hadrian and St. Helena: imperial travel and the origins of Christian Holy Land pilgrimage' in Ousterhout 1990, 66–81.
Holum, K. & Vikan, G. (1979). 'The Trier Ivory, Adventus ceremonial, and the relics of St. Stephen,' *DOP* 33, 113–133.

Honigmann, E. (1950). 'Juvenal of Jerusalem,' *DOP* 5, 209–279.
Honigmann, E. (1951). *Évêques et Évêques monophysites d'Asie Antérieure au VIe Siècle*, Louvain.
Hunt, E. (1973). 'Palladius of Helenopolis: A Party and Its Supporters in the Church of the Late Fourth Century", *JThS* 24, 456–480.
Hunt, E. (1982). *Holy Land Pilgrimage in the Later Roman Empire, A.D. 312–460*, Oxford.
Hunt, E. (1997a). 'Constantine and Jerusalem,' *JEH* 48, 405–424.
Hunt, E. (1997b). 'Theodosius I and the Holy Land,' *Studia Patristica* 29, 52–57.
Hunt, E. (1999). 'Were there Christian pilgrims before Constantine?' in Stopford 1999, 25–40.
Inowlocki, S. & Zamagni, C. (eds.) (2011). *Reconsidering Eusebius. Collected Papers on Literary, Historical, and Theological Issues*, Leiden.
Irmscher, J. (ed.) (1964). *Byzantinische Beiträge*, Berlin.
Irshai, O. (2011). 'Fourth Century Christian Palestinian Politics: A Glimpse at Eusebius of Caesarea's Local Political Career and its Nachleben in Christian Memory,' in Inowlocki/C. Zamagni 2011, 25–38.
Jones, A.H.M. (1964). *The Later Roman Empire 284–602. A Social, Economic and Administrative Survey*, Oxford.
Klein, K.M. (2011/2012). 'Do good in thy pleasure unto Zion. The Patronage of Aelia Eudokia in Jerusalem,' *Wiener Jahrbuch für Kunstgeschichte* 60/61, 85–95.
Klein, K.M. (2012). 'The Politics of Holy Space: Jerusalem in the Theodosian Era (379–357 CE),' in Weiss 2012, 95–107.
Klein, K.M. (2018a). 'Kaiser Marcian und die Monophysiten,' *Gymnasium* 125, 251–273.
Klein, K.M. (2018b). 'Von Hesychie zu Ökonomie. Zur Finanzierung der Wüstenklöster Palästinas (5.–6. Jh.),' *Millennium* 15, 37–67.
Klein, K.M. (forthcoming). *Jerusalem in der Spätantike. Von Constantin zu Iustinian*, Berlin.
Kötter, J.-M. (2013). *Zwischen Kaisern und Aposteln: Das akakianische Schisma (484–519) als kirchlicher Ordnungskonflikt der Spätantike*, Stuttgart.
Krautheimer, R. (1983). *Three Christian Capitals: Topography and Politics*, Berkeley.
Krautheimer, R. (1993). 'The ecclesiastical building policy of Constantine' in Bonamente 1993, II, 514.
Kubitschek, W. (1925). s.v. 'Legio X Fretensis,' *RE* 12.2, 1671–1677.
Küchler, M. (²2014). *Jerusalem. Ein Handbuch und Studienreiseführer zur Heiligen Stadt*, Göttingen.
Leeb, R. (1992). *Konstantin und Christus. Die Verchristlichung der imperialen Repräsentation unter Konstantin dem Großen als Spiegel seiner Kirchenpolitik und seines Selbstverständnisses als christlicher Kaiser*, Berlin.
Leppin, H. (1996). *Von Constantin dem Großen zu Theodosius II. Das christliche Kaisertum bei den Kirchenhistorikern Socrates, Sozomenus und Theodoret*, Göttingen.
Leppin, H. (2011). *Justinian. Das christliche Experiment*, Stuttgart.
Maraval, P. (1985). *Lieux saints et pèlerinages d'Orient: histoire et géographie: des origines à la conquête arabe*, Paris.
Markus, R. (1994). 'How on Earth Could Places Become Holy? Origins of the Christian Idea of Holy Places,' *JECS* 2, 257–271.
Martin, J. (1985). 'Zum Selbstverständnis, zur Repräsentation und Macht des Kaisers in der Spätantike,' *Saeculum*, 35, 115–131.
McNamara, J.A. (1996). 'Imitatio Helenae: Sainthood as an attribute of queenship,' in Sticca 1996, 51–80.
Meier, M. (2003). *Das andere Zeitalter Justinians. Kontingenzerfahrung und Kontingenzbewältigung im 6. Jahrhundert n. Chr.*, Göttingen.
Meier, M. (2007). 'Die Demut des Kaisers. Aspekte der religiösen Selbstinszenierung bei Theodosius II. (408–450 n.Chr.),' in *Die Bibel als politisches Argument. Voraussetzungen*

und Folgen biblizistischer Herrschaftslegitimation in der Vormoderne, ed. A. Pecar and K. Trampedach, Munich, 135–158.

Murphy-O'Connor, J. (1993). 'The Location of the Capitol in Aelia Capitolina,' *RB* 101, 407–415.

Murphy-O'Connor, J. (2010). 'The Argument for the Holy Sepulchre,' *RB* 117, 55–91.

Ousterhout, R. (ed.) (1990). *The Blessings of Pilgrimage*, Chicago.

Patrich, J. (1995). *Sabas, Leader of Palestinian Monasticism. A Comparative Study in Eastern Monasticism, Fourth to Seventh Centuries*, Washington D.C.

Rebenich, S. (1992). *Hieronymus und sein Kreis. Prosopographische und sozialgeschichtliche Untersuchungen*, Stuttgart.

Röwecamp, G. (ed.) (1995). *Egeria. Itinerarium. Lateinisch-deutscher Text mit Einleitung*, Freiburg.

Sansterre, J.-M. (1972). 'Eusèbe de Césarée et le "Césaropapisme",' *Byzantion* 42, 131–195, 532–594.

Schwartz, E. (1939). *Kyrillos von Skythopolis*, Leipzig.

Sivan, H. (1990). 'Pilgrimage, monasticism, and the emergence of Christian Palestine in the 4th century,' in Ousterhout 1990, 54–65.

Sivan, H. (2008). *Palestine in Late Antiquity*, Oxford.

Smith, R. (1995). *Julian's Gods: Religion and Philosophy in the Thought and Action of Julian the Apostate*, London.

Sommer, M. (ed.) (2001). *Die Levante. Beiträge zur Historisierung des Nahostkonfliktes*, Freiburg.

Steidle, W. (1978). 'Die Leichenrede des Ambrosius für Kaiser Theodosius und die Helena-Legende,' *VChr.* 32, 94–112.

Steinicke, M. & Weinfurter, S. (eds.) (2005). *Investitur- und Krönungsrituale. Herrschaftseinsetzungen im kulturellen Vergleich*, Köln.

Stemberger, G. (1987). *Juden und Christen im Heiligen Land. Palästina unter Konstantin und Theodosius*, Munich.

Sticca, S. (ed.) (1996). *Saints: studies in hagiography*, New York.

Stopford, J. (ed.) (1999). *Pilgrimage explored*, York.

Tartaglia, L. (1984). *Eusebio di Cesarea: sulla vita di Costantino*, Naples.

Taylor, J.A. (1993). *Christians and the Holy Places. The Myth of Jewish-Christian Origins*, Oxford.

Trampedach, K. (2001). 'Die Konstruktion des Heiligen Landes. Kaiser und Kirche in Palästina von Constantin bis Justinian,' in Sommer 2001, 83–110.

Trampedach, K. (2005a). 'Reichsmönchtum? Das politische Selbstverständnis der Mönche Palästinas im 6. Jahrhundert und die historische Methode des Kyrill von Skythopolis,' *Millennium* 2, 271–296.

Trampedach, K. (2005b). 'Kaiserwechsel und Krönungsritual im Konstantinopel des 5. bis 6. Jahrhunderts,' in Steinicke/Weinfurter 2005, 275–290.

Vasiliev, A.A. (1950). *Justin the First. An Introduction to the Epoch of Justinian the Great*, Cambridge Mass.

Viermann, N. (2021). *Herakleios, der schwitzende Kaiser. Die oströmische Monarchie in der ausgehenden Spätantike*, Berlin.

Vogüé, A de (1993). *Histoire littéraire du mouvement monastique dans l'antiquité. Première partie: La monachisme latin*, Paris.

Walker, P. (1990). *Holy City, Holy Places? Christian Attitudes to Jerusalem and the Holy Land in the fourth century*, Oxford.

Warland, R. (ed.) (2002). *Bildlichkeit und Bildorte von Liturgie. Schauplätze in Spätantike, Byzanz und Mittelalter*, Wiesbaden.

Weiss, J. (ed.) (2012). *Locating the Middle Ages: The Spaces and Places of Medieval Culture*, London.

Wilken, R.L. (1985). s.v. 'Heiliges Land,' *TRE* 14, 688–689.

Wilken, R.L. (1992). *The Land Called Holy*, New Haven.

Wilkinson, J. (1977). *Jerusalem Pilgrims Before the Crusades*, Warminster.
Wilkinson, J. (^{3}1999). *Egeria's Travels*, Warminster.
Winkelmann, F. (1962). 'Zur Geschichte des Authentizitätsproblems der *Vita Constantini*,' *Klio* 40, 187–243.
Winkelmann, F. (1964). 'Die Beurteilung des Eusebius von Caesarea und seiner *Vita Constantini* im griechischen Osten,' in *Byzantinische Beiträge*, ed. J. Irmscher, Berlin 1964, 91–119.
Winkelmann, F. (1988). 'Papst Leo I. und die sog. Apostasia Palästinas,' *Klio* 70, 167–175.
Wortley, J. (1980). 'The Trier Ivory reconsidered,' *GRBS* 21, 381–394.
Yarnold, E.J. (1989). 'Who Planned the Churches at the Christian Holy Places in the Holy Land?,' *Studia Patristica* 18, 105–109.
Yarnold, E.J. (2000). *Cyril of Jerusalem*, London.

Rene Pfeilschifter
Always in Second Place: Constantinople as an Imperial and Religious Center in Late Antiquity

Jerusalem and Istanbul are both metropolises of world standing. The former is of central importance for three world religions, and this is the principal reason why Jerusalem has played a key role in the Middle East conflict for many decades. Istanbul is less contested. The city in large part owes its fascination to the circumstance that not only is it one of the major urban centers of the Islamic world, but it also represents – now as in the past – a bridge to Europe. Neither of the two cities was originally intended to assume such a role. Even a millennium after their founding, and much longer in the case of Jerusalem, both cities were no more than regional centers. Despite its strategic location, Byzantion remained a polis of minor importance, while Jerusalem was the main urban center of a small nation that carried little weight in the conflicts of the Near Eastern world and paid the price for its intransigence towards the Romans with the eradication of this very center. It was late antiquity that made both cities great, more precisely Constantine the Great, who effectively became the (new) founder of both Constantinople and Jerusalem. Had he not expanded Byzantion and turned it into an imperial residence, Constantinople would never have become the seat of emperors and sultans. Jerusalem, on the other hand, presents a different case, as Constantine never set foot in it. Moreover, it was by no means inevitable, that a city which had played an important role in the formative years of Christianity should become relevant for Christians in the Late Roman present. It was primarily thanks to Constantine's intensive patronage that Jerusalem experienced such a rapid rise, and it was only because the city of Christ had become the object of pious longing that it was able to occupy an important place in the religious topography of Islam.

This article will focus on the city on the Bosporus. My approach will not be chronological, as the city's history would all too easily become imperial history – from the late fourth century onward, metropolis and Empire indeed appear to have formed an indissoluble whole. But why was this so? To put it differently: why did Constantinople not remain a mere residence, with the ultimately trivial function of providing the emperor and his entourage with housing and a functioning infrastructure? Why did Constantine's foundation step out of the shadow of Rome like no other imperial residence of the third and fourth centuries had done before? Why did Constantinople, of all places, become the Christian city of Caesar?

Note: I would like to thank Johann Martin Thesz, Marlena Whiting and Robert Meyer for the translation.

The first part of this article will try to answer these questions. In the following section, I shall attempt to sharpen the contours of Constantinople's sacred status, this being the precondition of its bond with Jerusalem. Finally, I will briefly address the question as to why Constantinople never attained paradigmatic status. Indeed, this capital never became a model, neither for Jerusalem nor for any other city.

Second Rome: The Making of the New Capital

Constantine had turned the city named after him into a Second Rome.[1] The old Byzantion was enlarged to four times its original size and the center laid out on a monumental scale. To populate the new capital, inhabitants were drawn from the surroundings and further afield, while an administration was installed, for the city at least.[2] When Constantine died in 337, all this seemed to have been in vain. Although his successors paid reverence to the new center on the Bosporus – Constantius II (337–361) and Valens (364–378) in particular made every effort to promote the city's development[3] – they seldom resided in Constantinople.[4] For the most part, the emperors only passed through the city, coming from the West or the Danube,

---

1 This section draws heavily on Pfeilschifter 2013.
2 Regarding Constantine and his new foundation, see Berger 2006, 441–450; Bassett 2004, 17–36; Dagron 1984, 19–47, 120–124; Mango 2004, 23–36; Millar 1992, 53–57; Bauer 1996, 257–261. Moser 2018, 57–72, now argues convincingly against the view that Constantine established even the nucleus of a second senate. For the further rise of Constantinople in the fourth century, see Dagron 1984, 48–72, 86–96, 124–137, 192–196, 519–522; Errington 2006, 142–168; Beck 1973b, 1–10; Mango 2004, 37–42.
3 For Constantius, see most recently Moser 2018, 131–168, 189–276. This emperor founded the Constantinopolitan senate in 350/51. For Valens, see Lenski 2002, 114, 278–280, 388, 399. Valens' commitment is all the more remarkable as he was not overly fond of the city that had supported the usurper Procopius (Socr. 4,38,5).
4 From 330 onward Constantine mostly resided in Constantinople. Constantius II came to the city following the death of his father; after 337, however, his presence in Constantinople is securely attested only for 342 (January), 346 (May to August), 349 (for an undetermined period of time), and 359/360 (late 359 to March 360). That he personally attended in 345 the ground-breaking of the baths named after him is, in my opinion, not at all implied by *Chron. Pasch.* p. 534 Dindorf. Julian was in Constantinople from December 361 to May 362. Valentinian I spent the first weeks of his reign there (March/April 364), elevating Valens to the co-emperorship at the Hebdomon in March. The latter resided in Constantinople from December 364 to July 365. In September of that year, Procopius was acclaimed emperor in Constantinople. After the suppression of the revolt in May 366, Valens probably spent the winter of 366/367 there (see Lenski 2002, 114 and n. 288), followed by a few days or weeks in December/January 370 (*Cod. Theod.* 5,1,2 with Mommsen's comment in the apparatus and Errington 2000, 902–904), several weeks in 370 (March/April), later six months (December to May 371), and less than two weeks in 378 (May/June). Omitting Procopius but calculating generously, this amounts to somewhere between three and a half to four years – from a total of 41 years. Here and in the following, all the details of imperial itineraries until 476 are based on Seeck 1919. See also Dagron 1984, 78–84; Destephen 2016, 41–62, 355–371.

on their way to the Persian border or vice versa. The emperor's whereabouts were dictated by military needs, and Constantinople lay far to the rear of the combat zone. When in the East, Constantius II favored Antioch, as did Valens. Constantinople was largely left to itself, and mostly gained notoriety on account of its fierce Christian sectarian disputes.

Things began to change with Theodosius I (379–395). This emperor preferred Constantinople to Antioch, which he never visited. The metropolis on the Bosporus became the customary residence of his family, and he himself resided in the city for more than half his reign.[5] Although personal preference was undoubtedly one of the reasons for this choice, the precarious political situation was certainly more important: the Danube border remained extremely vulnerable after Valens' catastrophe at Adrianople, and the political situation in the West was so unstable that Theodosius was in constant expectation of his presence being needed there (as did actually occur in two major military campaigns). Antioch, on the other hand, was too far on the periphery to allow for rapid interventions in the West, and relations with the Persian Empire were peaceful anyway.[6] Theodosius actively promoted the development of Constantinople, not only through building projects[7] but also in the field of church politics. He convened a council in Constantinople, brought relics into the city, confiscated the churches of the Homoeans, strengthened the small Nicaean congregation, and made their bishop one of the foremost of the Empire.[8]

Felix K. Maier, in a new study, convincingly demonstrates that during the fourth century non-military aspects of legitimation became ever more important in imperial (self-)representation. This was especially true for Theodosius I.[9] The development prepared the ground for the transition of 395. The unexpected death of Theodosius

---

5 November 380 to July 381; September 381 to May 384; September 384 to August 386; October 386 to August 387; July to September 391; November 391 to April 394. This adds up to more than nine years, from a reign of 16 years. See – in addition to Seeck 1919 – Dagron 1984, 84–85; Croke 2010, 242; Destephen 2016, 62–81, 371–382. In my opinion, Croke's postulated shift from military activity to a concentration on court and city, aimed at "protecting, improving, and promoting the lives of his imperial subjects" (244, 263–264, here 263), is not plausible for Theodosius I.
6 Van Dam 2010, 74, remarks: "The prominence of Constantinople had shifted the focus of the eastern emperors toward the northern frontiers". It was the other way around.
7 See Leppin 2003, 188–201; Ernesti 1998, 95–100, 143–154; Bauer 1996, 187–202; Isele 2010, 98–106; Matthews 1975, 118–121; Croke 2010, 257–262. Following Mango 2004, 43–45, Mayer 2002, 125–127, 136–137, places particular emphasis on the fact that Theodosius' building program – notably the Forum of Theodosius and the erection of an obelisk in the Hippodrome – was intended to create a visual similarity between Constantinople and Old Rome, and to establish it once and for all as the capital. That Theodosius wished to 'humiliate' (125) Rome, seems, however, rather exaggerated.
8 See Tiersch 2002, 111–124; Errington 1997, 33–43, 54–59, 61–62; Dagron 1984, 449–461; Liebeschuetz 1990, 157–165; Ritter 1965, 45–53, 92–96, 106–107, 112–115, 128–130, 233–235; Gómez-Villegas 2000, 119–131, 142–144, 153–165, 176–183; Ernesti 1998, 51–57, 60–63, 113; Leppin 2003, 58, 64–66, 73–79, 180.
9 Maier 2019, 339–450.

not only made Constantinople's status as new capital permanent, the year 395 actually represented a turning point for the political system. By this, I do not mean the division of the Empire into East and West, but the sudden withdrawal of Theodosius' sons and successors to their respective residences. This was at first only due to a coincidence: the two young emperors Arcadius and Honorius, while not incompetent, were by no means outstanding rulers. They both lacked the inclination and aptitude for military exploits and displayed a certain inertia. Honorius initially remained in Milan, before relocating to Ravenna in 402.[10] Very soon, however, the Western Empire proved unable to fend off its enemies. A turbulent political situation developed, leading to an increasingly desperate struggle for survival that did not allow for the long-term stabilization of stationary imperial rule.

In the East, Honorius' brother Arcadius and, to an even greater extent, the latter's son Theodosius II left their mark on an entire era. During the thirteen years of his reign, Arcadius only visited Asia Minor a few times on summertime retreats, in total probably spending no more than a year outside of Constantinople. Theodosius spent just one and a half years outside the city – in a reign of 42 years. Not a single week was spent on a military campaign. Yet, there would have been at least one urgent – and for earlier emperors, imperative – occasion for him to conduct a campaign. His uncle Honorius died childless in 423, leaving the whole Empire united under Theodosius' rule. At this point, his first priority should have been to travel to Italy and present himself to his new subjects. Instead, he remained in Constantinople and attempted to assert his authority over the West through a vice-regent of sorts: Honorius' last *magister militum*, Castinus. Barely four months later, however, a civil servant named John was acclaimed emperor in Rome. Even then, Theodosius showed no intention of leading his army to Italy. Instead, he simply relinquished his claim to sole rule and only sought to secure the West for his family. The emperor had a five-year-old cousin named Valentinian who was also Honorius' nephew and had even been born at the court in Ravenna, but had so far been ignored by Theodosius. Now he had Valentinian proclaimed emperor in Thessalonica (without going there himself), betrothed him to his daughter Eudoxia, and sent him with his mother Galla Placidia and a sizable army to Italy on a successful campaign against John.[11]

Was Theodosius too lethargic and a coward? It may be that he failed to recognize the needs of the people and the complexity of the practical requirements when he attempted to rule through a proxy. Since the third century, the Mediterranean world could barely be controlled from a single geographical point. Even sole rulers who hastened from one end of the Empire to the other had found it very difficult to do so, and with short-lived success. In any case, Theodosius would have had to revive

---

10 Only short visits to other, mostly nearby cities – never outside of northern Italy – interrupted Honorius' sojourn in Milan until 402. During the 21 years from 402 to his death in 423, Honorius probably spent only two and a half years away from Ravenna.

11 Olymp. *frg.* 43,1 Blockley; Philost. *HE* 12,13; Socr. *HE* 7,23,1–10; Hyd. s. a. 424. For the events, see Stein ²1959, 282–285; Bury 1923, 221–224; Oost 1968, 178–193; Stickler 2002, 27–35.

the tradition of the itinerant emperor that his grandfather had still adhered to. Yet, had he done so, the outcome would have been to once again strengthen the military as an 'acceptance group'.

In order to explain this, we must briefly look back at the Principate of the first two centuries AD. In those days, a socio-political order which Egon Flaig has described as an 'acceptance system' had established itself in the city of Rome. This concept refers to a rule that owes its existence to the 'losable' support of certain social groups, in contrast to a legitimacy that is thought to be 'un-losable' or conferred by a supreme authority. The stability of such a monarch's rule does not rest on lineage (dynastic principle) or on a transcendent legitimation (divine right) but on the support of the relevant socio-political groups. This support is not granted once and for all, but must be secured over and over again by the ruler. It can also be denied to him. Acceptance is a fleeting commodity. At any time, a challenger may rise and court the various socio-political groups: the ruler can be overthrown by a usurper.[12]

During the Principate, the key socio-political groups were the senatorial aristocracy, the *plebs urbana*, and the army. This bound the emperor to the city, especially since the primary military influence was long wielded by the Praetorians. Nevertheless, the emperor could allow himself to leave Rome for extended periods of time, even if the reason for the absence was not war – as in the case of Tiberius on Capri or of Hadrian's travels throughout the Empire. This did not pose a threat to the emperor's rule. During the course of the second century, the political situation on the Empire's borders started to become precarious. Marcus Aurelius spent seven years away from Rome. Finally, the bond between emperor and city dissolved during the crisis of the third century: the ruler marched with his army from one trouble spot to the next, with the result that the legions assumed control of elevating and deposing emperors. They had taken the place of the Praetorian Guard, and even more importantly, they had become the *only* relevant acceptance group. The Senate and the people stayed in Rome, the geographical distance depriving them of any appreciable influence on the exercise of power. Rome remained the venerable center of the Empire, but the emperors were merely visitors in their own city. This situation continued beyond the renewed stabilization of the Empire by Diocletian and Constantine, and into the reign of Theodosius I.[13]

It was the emperor's withdrawal to Constantinople that allowed him to shake off the domination of the soldiers and the demands of the generals. With the ruler now safely secluded in the city, his popularity among the army and the opinion of the troops were no longer crucial. The fact that the city on the Bosporus became the capital was, initially, perhaps only due to the personal preference of Theodosius I. However, unlike the provincial town of Ravenna, Constantinople was suited to accommo-

---

12 Flaig 2019.
13 Halfmann 1986 provides an itinerary until 284 and also analyses the choice of residences and the circumstances under which imperial journeys took place.

dating the emperor and his court on a permanent basis. There was a palace and a hippodrome, a senate and a municipal administration – and, above all, Constantinople was a metropolis. It was the most dynamic city in the world. The number of inhabitants had multiplied since its founding in 326, with an estimated 200,000 people living on the Bosporus around the middle of the fifth century. The entire city was filled with the sounds of building, trading, manufacturing, and living, while the government did what it could to regulate these activities in order to retain some measure of control over the development of the metropolis. Although since the death of Constantine no emperor had resided on the Bosporus for very long at a time, his city was better suited than any other in the eastern Mediterranean to assume the role of a capital, due to its infrastructure and its strategic location on the transport routes, but above all because of its population. There is nothing so effective at neutralizing military power as a large city with bustling life, countless people, and narrow streets.[14]

When Theodosius' grandson relinquished his claim to the Western Empire in 424, this was not a sign of lethargy but of political reason. Were he to spend too much time in Italy or Gaul to bring these provinces under his control, he would run the risk of losing the East in the meantime. The stability of his own, more modest realm was preferable to the high-risk gamble of attempting to exercise power over the entire Mediterranean by himself. Constantinople was the grandson's city of choice as well, probably again out of personal inclination but now also out of necessity.

That a system similar to the one in Rome soon developed in Constantinople had nothing to do with tradition or historical reminiscence. The continuity had been broken by more than 150 years of itinerant emperorship. However, since society had remained much the same, as had most aspects of imperial rule, and the conditions of the cities were nearly identical, in a similar context a comparable system evolved.

At first glance, such a continuity of similar conditions might appear unlikely given the already advanced Christianization of the Empire, the greater distance between the late-antique emperor and his subjects, and the dynastic principle. The Christian emperor's belief that he had been chosen by God was indeed somewhat at odds with the principles of the acceptance system. However, the resulting tension was offset by the fact that the emperor never succeeded in elevating his position into a transcendental realm. He had no monopoly on the interpretation of the divine will. God had conferred upon him the responsibility for the Empire. If the emperor failed to live up to this responsibility, every Christian subject was entitled to his own judgement – and the withdrawal of his support. The alleged seclusion of the late-antique emperor, which never allowed him to leave the palace and thus deprived him of any opportunity to meet his subjects, is a scholarly construct. Although the emperor was strongly elevated by representation and ceremony, he regularly moved about in Constantinople and interacted with the population. The dynastic idea also influenced

---

[14] An excellent outline of Constantinople's development is given by Beck 1973b, 7–12. For population figures, see Jacoby 1961, 102–109.

late-antique emperorship, as it does every monarchy. However, lineage or designation by the predecessor never shielded the emperor from usurpation: the manner in which power was wielded was more important than its source. The hereditary principle always remained restricted by the conditions of the acceptance system.

The relevant acceptance groups were, as in Rome, the soldiers, the elites, and the people. There was no army within the walls, and the guards and security forces were weak in numbers and strength. They could not control the city by force of arms. For the emperor, this was both an advantage and a disadvantage: the soldiers were not able to neutralize the other acceptance groups, but neither were they capable of striking down an insurgence. Furthermore, the bonds of loyalty that tied them to the emperor were particularly close. The acceptance of the military was thus relatively easy to obtain.

The elites, as an aristocracy of office, stood before the emperor as individuals. All decisions regarding their political and social advancement were made by him. For this reason, relations between aristocrats were determined by competition and not by solidarity. They never took a stand against the emperor. The most common form of acceptance withdrawal was not one of combined aristocratic opposition but of conspiracy. Furthermore, especially in the later fifth century, individual men of power attempted to dominate the emperor and to transfer the acceptance to a new position akin to that of a majordomo. These attempts failed sooner or later, as the loyalty of the socio-political groups remained oriented towards the emperorship.

Of greatest importance were the people. This acceptance group alone dared to voice open criticism of the emperor, articulating its concerns clearly and with astonishing unity. Since the individual disappeared in the crowd, he was protected by anonymity – the emperor could not hold large segments of the population accountable. The opposition to his rule expressed itself in words, but also in actions. Violence was the hallmark of popular expressions of will, especially in the absence of institutionalized mechanisms for the resolution of conflicts. Resistance not only emanated from the circus factions but from the people as a whole. It could be encountered in the Hippodrome or anywhere else in the city. The collective body of the people served as a permanent behavioral corrective, thus compelling the emperor to attend to the needs of the urban masses carefully.

The clergy naturally played an important role in a Christian empire. However, clerics did not constitute an acceptance group. The bishop of Constantinople was in some respects the most powerful churchman of the Empire – more on this below – but he never became the protector of his city as did so many bishops around the Mediterranean. The presence of emperor and court did not allow him to interfere in public administration, and in the face of many competing influences he was not even able to establish himself as the center of Christian social relations. The bishop was limited to his pastoral duties: spiritual succor, consolation, holding together his flock. Regarding monks, they were very often at odds with the bishop or with each other. Only rarely did they form a forceful lobby, and when they did, the government successfully denounced them as troublemakers. Their resistance was not acknowledged as such and thus only elicited repressive responses. This was not a problem for the so-called holy men. The authority of these exceptional ascetics rested upon their proximity to God. But this implied a distance to the petty affairs of the world which could be reduced only at the cost of sacrificing an enormous amount of social capital. Therefore, only rarely could holy men bring their reputation to bear, and they were unable to apply continuous pressure on the emperor. Their opposition was so sporadic that it was of little significance for the functioning of the acceptance system.

In spite of the acceptance groups' considerable potential for exerting influence, notably by the people, the emperor's position was by no means weak. If his behavior was more or less in accordance with Christian norms, if he embraced orthodoxy, and if he cared for the welfare of his subjects, he could hold on to power. The acceptance system in Constantinople provided a strong societal order inasmuch as it was fairly tolerant of an emperor's failings, up to a point. To endanger his throne, the ruler had to commit a number of serious errors regarding status recognition and interaction. For this reason, the emperor was rarely overthrown in the fifth and sixth centuries. Only a handful of usurpers appeared on the scene and even fewer succeeded.

Compared with the city of Rome, this socio-political order was considerably more robust and almost exclusively focused on Constantinople. This is clearly demonstrated by the emperor's much stronger connection to the city: the successors of Theodosius followed his example by confining themselves to Constantinople and rarely leaving the city. The emperor Marcian (450–457) conducted a short campaign in the Balkans at the beginning of his reign, something no emperor would do for the next 140 years.[15] It was not until 590 or 592 that Maurice broke with tradition and personally led a campaign in the Balkans. In Constantinople, however, the emperor's departure met with strong opposition, which was mirrored in an extremely unfavorable depiction of the campaign in the sources. Not only was the operation a failure – the enemy was not seen once – it was also marred by a solar eclipse, a sea storm, a raging boar, the birth of a freakish child with the tail of a fish, and a treacherous murder. Maurice' obstinate war was seen as a violation of the divine order. And there was another problem: the arrival of a Persian delegation forced the emperor to return briefly not long after his departure, and further diplomatic business compelled him to abort the campaign altogether. Thus, functional reasons also prevented the emperor from leaving Constantinople. An authorized representative who might

---

15 ACO II 1,1 p. 27–30; 1,2 p. 16, 29; 3,1 p. 21, 23; Theod. Lect. *Epit.* 360. Having received news of a Hunnic invasion, Marcian set out for the western Balkans in the late summer of 451. Soon thereafter, he was able to report the successful conclusion of the campaign. How far the emperor came and whether he actually caught sight of the enemy remains uncertain.

have received the negotiators did not exist. The emperor could not delegate such matters but had to settle them personally – in the capital.[16]

After this experience, Maurice stayed at home for the rest of his reign. It was not until 612 that an emperor joined the troops again. Having arrived in Caesarea in eastern Asia Minor, however, Heraclius was told by the commanding general and *magister militum* Priscus: "An emperor is not permitted to leave the palace and to be with the armies far afield." In the camp, Heraclius had no other choice but to endure the impertinence of his general – the soldiers apparently shared the opinion of their commander. The emperor did not meet the standard his subjects expected from his behavior. The full exercise of imperial power was dependent upon the degree of acceptance, and, being far from Constantinople, Heraclius could do very little – precisely because he was far from Constantinople. In Caesarea, he came to recognize that his authority did not count for much if the capital's acceptance groups were not there to support it. It is very telling that he was able to remove Priscus from office only later, in Constantinople.[17] A further campaign in the following year ended with the loss of Syria to the Persians. Heraclius had suffered a great loss of prestige, thus rendering it impossible for him to assume command again.[18]

In the following decade, the Romans witnessed the worst catastrophes in living memory: the Persians also occupied Egypt and parts of Asia Minor, the Avars gained the upper hand in the Balkans, Constantinople was afflicted by hunger and epidemics, and the Empire was on the brink of collapse. Yet, when Heraclius made plans for an African expedition, Patriarch Sergius was said to have made him swear in church that he would not leave the city.[19] By the year 622, however, the situation had become so desperate that hardly any opposition arose when he set out on a military campaign to Asia Minor. At least his goal was not Africa, and the emperor returned after the end of the campaigning season. But two years later, he left Constantinople for five years of continuous warfare, not even returning to the city during the great siege of 626.[20] Thus the bond between the emperor and Constantinople dissolved after all. But it was only a situation of extreme emergency that allowed an emperor

---

16 Theophyl. Sim. *Hist.* 5,16,1–6,3,8; Theoph. AM 6083 (p. 268–269 de Boor). For context, see Whitby 1983, 331–332; Whitby 1988, 156–157.
17 Niceph. *Brev.* 2: οὐκ ἐξὸν βασιλεῖ ἔφασκε καταλιμπάνειν βασίλεια καὶ ταῖς πόρρω ἐπιχωριάζειν δυνάμεσιν; *Vit. Theod. Syc.* 152–155; Seb. 33–34 (p. 112–113 Abgaryan); *Chron. Pasch.* p. 703 Dindorf. For historical context, see Kaegi 1973, 324–328; Viermann 2021, 153–156.
18 Seb. 34 (p. 114 f. Abgaryan); *Vit. Theod. Syc.* 166. See Kaegi 1973, 328–329; Stratos 1979, 67–73.
19 Niceph. *Brev.* 8.
20 For the year 622: Theoph. AM 6113 (p. 302–306 de Boor); Niceph. *Brev.* 12; Theod. Sync. *Obsid.* 12 (p. 302 Sternbach/Makk); 14 (p. 303); Seb. 38 (p. 124 Abgaryan) (with Howard-Johnston 1999, 213); Georg. Pis. *Exp. Pers.* 1,108–157; 2,8–3,340; *Bon.* 5–9; *Patr. Const.* 2,53. See Stratos 1968, 126–127; Kaegi 2003, 107–112; Oikonomidès 1975. Departure in 624: *Chron. Pasch.* p. 713–714 Dindorf; Theoph. AM 6114 (p. 306 de Boor); Seb. 38 (p. 123–124); Theod. Sync. *Obsid.* 11–12 (p. 302–303). See Gerland 1894, 331–337, 349–350; Stratos, 363–364; Whitby/Whitby 1989, 204–205; Howard-Johnston 1999, 213–214. For another interpretation of these years, see now Viermann 2021, 179–185.

to break with tradition, and thus also with the established system of rule. In the field, he indeed exposed himself once again to the determining influence of the army.

The emperor also rarely left the city on non-military business. Religious motives, for instance the fulfillment of a vow, were apparently deemed valid justification for absences, although the sources rarely speak of them.[21] Other than this, the emperor's presence is only attested in the city's immediate vicinity, in the suburban palaces in Europe or on the opposite shore of the Propontis. With very few exceptions, he was never more than a few hours away from the city. He could thus return at any moment and react to unexpected developments on the spot.[22] By this, I am referring not only to foreign envoys but also to conspiracies and uprisings, which nothing could quell as effectively as the emperor's personal intervention. When Tiberius II spent thirty days in a palace outside the city to attend the vintage, his opponents made plans for a coup. Tiberius had to hasten back with all speed to prevent the worst from happening.[23]

It was not just that Constantinople, like other capitals, benefited from its status as imperial residence and found its actual raison d'être therein. The emperor also was bound to the city. Constantinople was not simply the location of a palace. The exercise of imperial power, even the existence of emperorship itself, was only possible in the city. The fact that an acceptance system also emerged in Constantinople was certainly not a foregone conclusion, but it was not surprising in light of its similarity to Rome. What is surprising, however, is the concentration, the compression of this system within this one city, in a space of little more than fourteen square kilometers. The remainder of the vast Empire, the 'rest,' as one might say, did not belong to the political system.

The reason for this extreme separation of 'inside' and 'outside' was the city's geographical situation as well as its fortifications. The Bosporus lay at the junction of the sea routes from the Black Sea to the Aegean and the Mediterranean and of the land route connecting northwestern Europe to Asia. In spite of this, the city had to some extent been isolated since the days of its foundation: it was separated from the cities of Asia Minor by the sea, while the European hinterland had not been settled by the Greeks. Furthermore, the hinterland was inhabited by Thracian tribes who were separated from Byzantion by cultural differences and ethnic background, as well as a lesser degree of urbanization. This only began to change when Thrace became a Roman province in the first century AD, followed by a sharp increase in

---

21 In 515, after his victory over Vitalian, Anastasius travelled to the Sosthenion on the middle Bosporus, where the rebel had pitched his camp. Once there, he spent many days offering thanks in the Chapel of the Archangel Michael (Mal. 16,16; Ioann. Nic. 89,87). In 563, fulfilling a vow, Justinian visited a church in Germia in northern Galatia (Theoph. AM 6056 [p. 240 de Boor]). Cf. Destephen 2018.
22 The imperial residences were either located within a ten kilometer radius of the city or could easily be reached by a short boat ride. A list of Constantinople's suburban palaces is provided by Janin 1964, 138–153.
23 Greg. Tur. Franc. 5,30.

the importance of towns. However, Thrace never reached the levels of urbanization that characterized the core areas of the Mediterranean cultures, e.g., Greece, Italy, or even Africa. When Byzantion rose to become a metropolis in the reign of Constantine the Great and thereafter, a much sharper contrast developed between the capital and its surroundings compared to Rome and Latium.

In the nearly 900 years between its foundation by Constantine and the Fourth Crusade, not once the city was taken by force. This was not due to the idleness of its enemies – attempts were indeed made to conquer it – but to its strategic location and above all to the strength of its fortifications. The triangular area that roughly represents the layout of Constantinople was surrounded by the sea on two sides: by the Golden Horn to the north and by the Propontis to the south. The only thing that mattered here was to prevent the enemy from landing by boat. Particularly vulnerable sections of the coast were protected by fortifications, but as long as the Roman fleet controlled the sea and did not revolt, there was little to fear from this side. This was the situation throughout late antiquity for the most part, and remained so until the Islamic invaders deliberately attacked the long coastlines. The vulnerable side was the westward one, where the promontory on which the city lies suddenly widens to the north and west, to the hinterland and the European continent. This is where the fortification works were the strongest.

Between 405 and 413, massive walls roughly six and a half kilometers in length were erected between the Golden Horn and the Propontis.[24] In particularly vulnerable places, trenches up to 20 meters wide and 7 meters deep afforded additional protection. The walls themselves formed a continuous line of defense: behind the eight-meter-high outer wall with its 92 smaller towers stood, separated by a terrace, the main fortification, the inner wall. It was 11 meters high, nearly 5 meters wide, and fitted with 95 towers at intervals of 40 to 60 meters.[25]

After the completion of these Theodosian walls, the city could no longer be conquered if its inhabitants were united and at least halfway circumspect in defending themselves – a fact that has often been noted by scholars.[26] That being said, the key

---

24 Socr. *HE* 7,1,3; ILS 5339. After the publication of Speck's article 1973, 135–143, the broad consensus was that the wall was begun in 408 or soon thereafter and brought to completion in 413. This appeared to fit in well with the Hunnic incursion of Thrace in 408, which was a failure, but undoubtedly reminded Constantinopolitans that their city was not impregnable (*Cod. Theod.* 5,6,3; Sozom. *HE* 9,5; see Holum 1982, 88–89; Bayless 1977, 47–48). However, a subsequently discovered building inscription offers evidence for a construction period of nine years (Feissel 1995, 567). Since the year 413 is securely attested by *Cod. Theod.* 15,1,51, the only option is to push back the beginning of construction to 405. See Lebek 1995, 112–114, 117.
25 On this topic, see Asutay-Effenberger's contribution to this volume as well as her authoritative reconstruction 2007, 1–5, 13–35, 61–106, 148–169. See also Janin 1964, 265–283; Müller-Wiener 1977, 286–269, 297, 301. The building description by Meyer-Plath/Schneider 1943, 22–95 is indispensable. An excellent overall impression of the construction is conveyed by the drawings of Krischen 1938.
26 See e.g. Kaegi 1981, 19–20; Schreiner 2007, 31–37.

point has not yet been made. The impregnability of the city and, soon thereafter, the awareness of this circumstance shaped the socio-political system and the self-understanding of its inhabitants in a decisive manner. Due to the unconquerable walls, the acceptance system of late antiquity was much more focused on Constantinople than that of the Principate had been on Rome. As a consequence, in order to be emperor, one had to be present in the city and control it. At the same time, the ruler could not be overthrown or dislodged from the outside. This was the reason the field army and the other subjects of the Empire counted for little in comparison with the inhabitants of Constantinople. They alone could make or break the emperor. Constantinople was a political world unto itself. It only reacted to external disturbances to accommodate the wishes and needs of an acceptance group within the city.

Second Jerusalem? The New Navel of the Earth

If Constantinople was the seat of the emperor and the secular center of the Eastern Roman Empire, why was the city then referred to as – of all things – the "Second Jerusalem" as early as the sixth century? Throughout late antiquity, not a single emperor (with the exception of Heraclius, very late in the period) visited Jerusalem, let alone resided there. Moreover, this city was of little importance for the military and imperial administration. Conversely, Jerusalem was of course politically relevant due to its religious significance, but in this respect Constantinople not only ranked behind Jerusalem, but behind all metropolises of the Empire. Antioch, Alexandria, Rome, even Ephesus and Carthage had played important roles in the history of early Christianity – which partly explains why they were able to retain their prosperity and status in late antiquity. Byzantion, on the other hand, had been a non-entity during the first three centuries after Christ.

But could not the city of Caesar also be the city of God? In fact, both went hand in hand: the emperors were determined to develop Constantinople into a Christian center. Precisely because of its exalted political status, it was unthinkable that the city should remain second-rate in terms of religious importance. A Christian ruler was supposed to demonstrate his faith. He could do so by erecting buildings in the Holy Land. However, in his immediate surroundings he could find better ways and many more opportunities to display his piety. The ambiguous or, better yet, self-styled Christianity that had characterized Constantine's rule as well as his city had rapidly faded away with the progressing Christianization of the Empire.[27] Moreover, Constantinople lacked a distinctly pagan (as in Rome) or Jewish character (as in Jerusalem), making it easier to infuse with Christian elements.

---

[27] On Constantine's Constantinople, see most recently Wallraff 2013, 80–90, but also Johannes Wienand's contribution to this volume.

Because the city had been founded after the persecutions, relics of local saints and martyrs were in short supply. Obtaining them from elsewhere was difficult, as no one was willing to relinquish the religious and economic benefits that were associated with the possession of a reliquary shrine.[28] If anyone could break this resistance, it was the state. For this reason, the translation of relics constituted a perfect field of activity for the emperor, as it offered him an ideal opportunity to demonstrate his piety (in Constantinople, not in the provincial cities affected). This phenomenon began already with Constantius II: in the year 356, he had the mortal remains of the Pauline disciple Timothy transferred to the Church of the Holy Apostles, followed by those of Luke the Evangelist and of the Apostle Andrew in 357.[29] In February 360, the emperor personally attended the interment of the martyr Pamphilus and of two of his followers in the newly-consecrated Great Church.[30] Theodosius I used translations of relics to further his efforts to repress the Homoeans, but otherwise followed Constantius' lead. The relics of Saint Paul the Confessor, who had allegedly died as a Nicaean martyr, were brought into the city by order of Theodosius. He also single-handedly carried the Baptist's head, shrouded in the imperial purple cloak, to Constantinople – a particular demonstration of divine grace which God had denied his heretical predecessor Valens.[31] All later emperors followed this example, thus leading to the buildup of a collection of saints' relics that would remain without equal throughout the Middle Ages.[32] The acquisition of relics usually went hand in hand with the construction of a martyrium to house them. Theodosius I, for example, had the Prodromos Church at the Hebdomon built for the Baptist's head. This leads to a second area in which an emperor could demonstrate his Christianity to the city: the building of churches, not just for relics, but also for purposes far beyond that. Justinian's

---

28 For the martyrs of Byzantion and Constantinople in the fourth century, see Delehaye 1933, 232–237. On the nascent phenomenon of the translation of relics in the fourth century, see e.g. Brown 1981, 86–105, and Hunt 1981.
29 Philost. *HE* 3,2; 2a; *Chron. Pasch.* p. 542 Dindorf; *Consul. Constant.* s. a. 356–357. The chronology is disputed, Mango 1990a favors 336 for Luke and Andrew. For the dates adopted here, see Whitby/Whitby 1989, 33. For the *status quaestionis*, see KFHist E 7,2 p. 182–185, and G 1 p. 109–110.
30 Cedr. p. 523 Bekker; *Synax. eccl. Const.* p. 467 Delehaye (in the apparatus). On the itinerary of Constantius, see Seeck 1919, 207.
31 Socr. *HE* 5,9,1–2; Sozom. *HE* 7,10,4; 21,1–6.
32 Maraval 1985, 93–101, gives the evidence for the numerous translations of relics in chronological order. I only add a few overlooked references. The martyr Phocas under Arcadius: Ioann. Chr. *Phoc. mart.* 1 (PG 50,699–700); the monastic father Isaac under Theodosius II: *Vita Isaacii* 18 (for the date, see Cameron/Long 1993, 72–75); Forty Martyrs under Justinian: Proc. *Aed.* 1,7,3–5; Theodore of Sryceon under Heraclius: Niceph. Sceuoph. *Enc. Theod.* 44–48. The true number, however, is much higher, as is clear by the vast number of churches with relics that were brought to Constantinople at an unknown date. For the situation in the Middle Byzantine period, see Mergiali-Sahas 2001, 44–60; Klein 2006, 89–96.

Hagia Sophia is only the most famous example of a prolific religious building activity that all emperors regarded as their duty.[33]

Constantinople's Christian identity, much like that of Jerusalem, also benefited from the elevation of the local bishop's status. But what the bishop of Jerusalem had to procure on his own, his colleague in Constantinople secured with the active support of the emperor. The First Council of Constantinople, which convened in 381 under the auspices of Theodosius I, assigned him prime position immediately behind the bishop of Rome – simply because Constantinople was the Second Rome, that is, for purely political reasons. This was a blow to Alexandria, which had traditionally been the seat of the foremost bishop of the East. This primacy admittedly was only bestowed for honorary purposes. Constantinople remained, at least formally, under the jurisdiction of the metropolitan of Heraclea while the bishop was not given any prerogatives in other church provinces.[34] Nevertheless, the honorary primacy soon developed into a real one in Thrace and Asia Minor, less because of the ambitious aims of the bishops of Constantinople – although there was no lack of such[35] – but simply because of the gravitation of power: the government allotted resources and made important decisions, and no cleric stood closer to the court and the emperor than the bishop of the capital. This made him a suitable mediator and patron for other clerics,[36] but he was, of course, also a direct beneficiary.[37] When the Council of Chalcedon confirmed the bishop's primacy over Asia Minor and Thrace in 451, it adjusted canon law to the altered circumstances and made the position of the bishop

---

33 Maraval 1985, 401–410, gives a list of the martyria in the city, of which, however, a substantial number were financed by the elites outside the imperial family. See also Konstantin Klein's contribution to this volume. Additional money was spent on the maintenance of these churches and on endowments for poor people and strangers, which the emperor and the upper class regarded as a central norm of Christian charity. On this topic, see e.g. Diefenbach 1996, 53–55; Dagron 1989, 1074–1080.

34 Canon. conc. I Const. 3 (CCO p. 47–48 = COD⁴ p. 66); Socr. *HE* 5,8,13. See also Ritter 1965, 92–96; L'Huillier 1996, 119–125; Ubaldi 1903, 34–36; Errington 1997, 61–62; Dagron 1984, 455–461. A brief outline of the rise of Constantinople until the early seventh century is given by Dagron 2002, 24–32, and Elia 2002b, 97–105. The older literature can be found in Beck 1959, 30–32.

35 For example, John Chrysostom's resolute intervention in the affairs of the bishops of Asia Minor in 402 (Tiersch 2002, 309–326; Kelly 1995, 163–166, 172–180). For a general overview of the activities of the bishops of Constantinople outside their diocese, see Dagron 1984, 461–463, 465–473; Karlin-Hayter 1988, 179–210.

36 Providing access to court: *Vit. Porph.* 26–27; 37–40; 42–43; 45–46; 50–54; Cyr. Scyth. *Vit. Ioann.* 4; *Avell.* 116,25. In 546, Justinian even formalized the admission by decreeing that bishops had to be introduced by the patriarch (*Novell. Iust.* 123,9). Lobbying: Pall. *Dial.* 14 (p. 278 Malingrey). Opinion maker: Zach. *HE* 4,7–8.

37 This became most obvious in formal regulations, such as the subordination of the Illyrian church provinces to Constantinople in 421 or that of Cyzicus between 406 and 425 (*Cod. Theod.* 16,2,45; Socr. *HE* 7,28,2). See Gaudemet 1989, 392–393, 406–407; Tiersch 2002, 320–321; Norton 2007, 86–87.

of Constantinople (who would soon call himself patriarch) unassailable.[38] The importance of Antioch, Jerusalem, and even Alexandria declined in the following decades. Justinian, in the end, only acknowledged the primacy of Rome over Constantinople.[39] Towards the end of the sixth century, with the emperor's support, the bishop of Constantinople even assumed the title of an ecumenical patriarch – much to the dismay of Gregory the Great, who, not entirely without reason, viewed this as the beginning of a primacy of Constantinople over the other patriarchates of the East.[40]

The main stimulus for Constantinople to become the city of God, however, was the fact that its inhabitants persistently and repeatedly constituted themselves as a Christian community. This happened, for one, when they attended mass. The Great Church or, as it soon came to be called, the Hagia Sophia was the center of liturgical life in the city. But even a church of this size could only accommodate a fraction of all the worshippers: the population of Constantinople rose to 375,000 in the early years of Justinian's reign. Even if the plague that broke out in 541 killed more than 20 to 30% of the population – the most plausible estimate – this still left hundreds of thousands.[41] Regular church attendance thus promoted identification of the individual with the whole city only to a limited degree. The Christians were distributed over many churches. There was no parochial system, so believers were not bound to a particular church. It is nevertheless probable that the broader strata of society usually went to the church that was closest to them. There, the individual would occasionally get to see the emperor or the elites, who tended to choose their house of worship on the basis of the festival calendar or with respect to the saint whose inter-

---

38 Canon. conc. Chalc. 9; 17; 28 (ACO II 1,2 p. 160–161; 1,3 p. 88–89 = COD⁴ p. 142, 145, 150–151). See e.g. Frend 1972, 7–12; de Halleux 1989, 28–35; L'Huillier 1996, 231–236, 253 254, 267–296; Blaudeau 2006, 401–410; Herman 1973, 463–480 (clear analysis, albeit with a strong Catholic bias); Dagron 1984, 473–487.
39 Zeno's emphatic formulation of 477 is already quite remarkable: *sacrosanctam quoque huius religiosissimae civitatis ecclesiam matrem nostrae pietatis et Christianorum orthodoxae religionis omnium et eiusdem regiae urbis sanctissimam sedem* (*Cod. Iust.* 1,2,16,1). Justinian: *Novell. Iust.* 131,2 (545); *Cod. Iust.* 1,1,8,8–12 and 22 (533); see also *Novell. Iust.* 123,9 (546). See e.g. Chevailler/Chabanne 1984, 726–730, but also Dvornik 1966, 828–833.
40 Greg. M. *Ep.* 5,37; 39; 41; 44–45; 7,24; 28; 30–31; 8,29; 13,41. The term is analyzed by Tuilier 1966, 417–424, though he tends to ignore the implications for church politics by distinguishing between jurisdictional and dogmatic/ideological significance. The explicit assertion of communion with the whole of orthodox Christianity certainly implied a claim to supremacy, which Gregory clearly recognized. The relevant texts are collected by Vailhé 1908b and 1908a. For the conflict, see Dagens 1975, 466–473; Saitta 2002, 246–251; Eich 2016, 133–136.
41 The numbers are those of Jacoby 1961, who has dealt most thoroughly with the methodical difficulties confronting any reliable calculation. See also the remarks by Müller 1993, 17–20. On the number of victims claimed by the plague, see also Stathakopoulos 2004, 138–141 (20%); Leven 1987, 141, 146–148 (40%); Conrad 1996, 93 ("between one third and half of the entire population").

cession they hoped to obtain.⁴² This certainly strengthened the bond with the Empire and the existing social order, but it seems rather doubtful if such rare encounters did much to produce a specific identity of being part of a Christian Constantinople.

Processions were another matter. Open-air activities certainly could not accommodate an unlimited number of Christians, but they allowed a much larger crowd to participate. Moreover, the spatial limitations were less noticeable on the streets and squares, thus creating the subjective impression that many more people participated than was really the case. Processions were a common occurrence, for supplication and thanksgiving, celebration and mourning. While translations of relics were ultimately quite rare, there were many other occasions for processions, such as major church holidays, military victories, natural phenomena, catastrophes such as comets or fires – as well as the yearly remembrance of an induction of relics, particular earthquakes, an occurrence of ash rain, etc.⁴³ The annually recurring processions were thus supplemented by new ones that were themselves partly repeated in the following years. The frequency of processions was probably much higher than in Rome and Jerusalem, the two other cities of late antiquity whose liturgical landscapes are fairly well documented. A significant impulse in this direction was probably supplied by the tenacious struggle of the various Christian groups in the fourth century.⁴⁴ Public processions that ended in a church controlled by one's own denomination offered an almost ideal opportunity to both assert religious hegemony and invite the entire population to join in. The latter was the key to the popularity of the processions, even after the Nicaeans had gained the upper hand. Nowhere else could the feeling of be-

---

42 For the lack of a parochial system and the consequences thereof, see Dagron 1989, 1069–1074, 1083–1085; on the situation around 400, see Mayer 2000b, 79–80; Mayer 2000a, 56–62. For regular and public church attendance of the emperor, see McLynn 2004. Arcadius only occasionally frequented the services held by John Chrysostom, but this does not imply that he was not as consistent as his father in attending public services (thus McLynn 2004, 265–266); rather, he went to other churches in the city. There were of course also churches on the palace grounds: one, consecrated to the Archangel Michael, is attested for the sixth century. It was open to the wider public for worship (Theod. Lect. *Epit.* 483), and was thus not a palace chapel for the exclusive use of the court. The small Church of St Stephen, from the fifth century, only began to play a more important role in the religious life of the imperial family under Heraclius.
43 Evidence for the processions in Constantinople: Baldovin 1987, 182–189; Maraval 1985, 93–101; Croke 1981, 125 n. 19.
44 The best example is that of the night-time processions of the Homoeans around 400, which John Chrysostom countered with separate Nicaean ones. The result was stone-throwing and injuries, a sign how much was at stake when public space was occupied in this way (Socr. *HE* 6,8,1–9; see Tiersch 2002, 131–132). Baldovin 1987, 209–214, made the convincing case that the frequency of processions was not only higher than in Rome and Jerusalem, but also higher than in Constantinople of the tenth century. This may have to do with Baldovin's previous assumption that the Middle Byzantine emperors were less likely to take part in processions than those of late antiquity (202). This could be taken as an indication of how important the presence of the emperor was, but also as evidence for changes in public communication between the early seventh and the tenth century. However, there is no certainty in this matter.

longing to the city, to orthodoxy, and to the Empire be experienced in such a direct way.

The emperor frequently took part in the public processions and in the corresponding religious services. In pious community with his fellow Christians, the monarch could demonstrate his orthodoxy for all to see. Processions thus bridged the distance between the emperor and the urban population, and contributed significantly to the identification with the existing order and the integration into it. Sometimes the emperor even abstained from wearing his insignia and walked barefoot or clad like a common subject. In this way, the inhabitants of Constantinople found unity in the evocation of a joint Christianity.[45]

The form this might take is demonstrated by two anecdotes reported by the church historian Socrates. While Theodosius II was watching the chariot races, he was informed of his army's victory over the Western emperor John in 425. The emperor announced the news to the people and called on them to turn their attention from the entertainment and to thank God in unison. The audience quickly forgot about the games and formed a procession while still in the Hippodrome. Accompanied by song, it moved along with the emperor and arrived at a church where Theodosius and his subjects spent the rest of the day in prayer. The fact that the emperor spontaneously called for a joint procession and that the people complied without further ado indicates that such behavior was not uncommon, or rather, probably even the rule. On another occasion, the spectators who were gathered in the circus were surprised by a severe snowstorm. Theodosius again requested them to forget the games – which probably had been interrupted anyway – and to implore God for protection. The Constantinopolitans complied once again, while the emperor even intoned the pious hymns and marched, without his purple robe, among his people. The sky soon cleared, and the year was blessed with a good harvest. During processions, Socrates writes, "the whole city became a single church."[46]

Patriarch, churches, relics, processions – all this defined Constantinople as a Christian city, as one of the Empire's religious centers. This alone, however, was by no means sufficient to establish a spiritual connection with Jerusalem.[47] A few additional factors were required, and in the end even a crisis of global proportions.

Analogy with the Jerusalem of the past as it is described in the Old Testament held a certain importance, but in my opinion should not be overestimated. In the

---

[45] On the emperor's participation, see Diefenbach 1996, 43–52; Diefenbach 2002, 24–31; Martin 1997, 54–55; Meier 2003, 489–502. A list of the processions in which the emperor participated can be found in Pfeilschifter 2013, 339 n. 89.

[46] Socr. HE 7,22,15–18; 23,11–12. Socrates comments both events with nearly identical words: ὅλη μὲν ἡ πόλις μία ἐκκλησία ἐγένετο / ἐγίνετο (22,17; 23,12). There is a similar report about Maurice in 593: after news of a victory, the emperor spent the entire night praying in Hagia Sophia and led a supplicatory procession for further victories on the following day (Theophyl. Sim. Hist. 6,8,8; Theoph. AM 6080 [p. 262 de Boor]).

[47] Ousterhout 2006, 99–102, warns against such a premature conclusion, and rightly so.

sixth century, emperors such as Justinian and aristocrats such as Anicia Juliana erected churches that surpassed the Temple of Solomon and thus the old Jerusalem.[48] 'Surpassing' was in itself nothing unusual, and it is well known that Christians saw themselves as second to none – again and again and in many different fields. After all, it was they – and not the Jews – who were in possession of the revealed truth. At any rate, this demonstration of superiority over the kings of Jerusalem must have helped ensure that both cities could easily be associated with one another in the minds of the people of Constantinople. Of greater importance, however, were the relationships with the present, Christian Jerusalem as well as with the coming, prophesied Jerusalem.

Let us first turn to the present: several of the more precious relics that were brought to Constantinople came from Jerusalem. Initially poor in sacred objects, the imperial city was supplied from the best source and thus caught some of the glory that shone on the city of Christ.[49] The wife and the sister of Theodosius acquired relics of the protomartyr Stephen,[50] and later the garments and the girdle of the Virgin were deposited in Constantinople.[51] The most important relics, however, were the fragments of the True Cross, that is, of the cross on which Christ had been crucified. They reached the Bosporus in the fifth century, while the inhabitants of Constantinople began to believe that they had already been brought there in the time of Constantine.[52]

Now to the coming Jerusalem. From about AD 500 onward, there arose an eschatological apprehension that became one of the defining social currents in the sixth century, the more so since it was confirmed by political catastrophes, earthquakes, climate changes, floods, and especially by the above-mentioned plague.[53] But there was an upside to the Christian conception of the End of Days: the apocalypse would lead to the Last Judgement, the ultimate goal of Christian history, and at its end, according to Chapter 21 of the *Book of Revelation*, a new Jerusalem would descend from Heaven. In his contribution to this volume, Paul Magdalino plausibly argues that in this eschatological context the New, Second Jerusalem was identified with Constantinople. This way, the scenario of doom was supplemented by a more optimistic vision that did not contradict the first. The Roman Empire was intimately

---

48 On this topic, see Nadine Viermann's contribution to this volume.
49 For the Theotokos/Diomedes Monastery (or Church) at the Golden Gate, also called Jerusalem, see Janin 1969, 95–97 (an additional reference is Theod. Sync. *Dep.* 3).
50 Theoph. AM 5920 (p. 86–87 de Boor), with a depiction of the scene on the so-called Trier Ivory, see Holum/Vikan 1979, 120–127, 131–133 (a different interpretation in Wortley 1980); Marcell. *Chron.* 439,2. See also Konstantin Klein's contribution to this volume.
51 For the complexity of the sources, which nevertheless suggest a date still in the fifth century, see Shoemaker 2008.
52 See Klein 2004b, 33–41; Frolow 1961, 73–74, no. 13, 16, 36, 38.
53 Analysing eschatological beliefs has become a hot topic in the last decades. See e.g. Magdalino 1993, passim, esp. 3–19; Brandes 1997; Meier 2003, 64–94; Meier 2008, 46–50, 54–55; Magdalino 2008, 123–126.

linked to the history of salvation, even going so far as to imply that the latter was nearing completion.

Constantinople was first referred to as the Second Jerusalem around the year 500. The basis of comparison was the sacred topography. However, this identification remained extremely rare in the sixth century and does not appear outside of hagiographical sources.[54] For a breakthrough, an event was necessary that would threaten the very existence of Constantinople – one so great that it could only be addressed in apocalyptic terms. In 626, when the city against expectations withstood the siege by Avars and Persians while the emperor was fighting far away in the east, a priest at the Hagia Sophia, Theodore Syncellus, celebrated the saving of Constantinople in a sermon that couched the events in an imagery taken from the Old Testament: the emperor as the reborn David, the patriarch as the second Moses, and so forth. By the same token, the old Jerusalem and Constantinople are repeatedly equated and compared, of course to the latter's advantage.[55] The sermon culminates in an elaborate proof that in the siege of Constantinople the apocalyptic prophecy of *Ezekiel* 38 and 39 has been fulfilled. The onslaught of Gog and Magog, which also plays an important role in Chapter 20 of *Revelation*, has been repelled:

> What place can be called navel of the earth other than the city in which God established the emperorship of the Christians, and which He, due to its location in the very middle, set up as the intermediary between East and West? Leaders and nations and peoples banded together against it, but the Lord has quashed their power. To Sion he spoke: "Be of good courage, Sion, let not your hands be slack. See, your God is in you, he has the might to save you." There assembled before it the hosts of the nations from the utmost north, the horses and riders in their armor, and with them the Persians. And this had been revealed word for word by the prophet. The bows in their left hands shattered the power of our Lord, and the arrows in their right hands smashed the Virgin. And they tumbled in the mountains of Israel, becoming carrion for beasts and birds. These things were prophesied by the divine Ezekiel with the following words: "In that day, says the Lord, the Lord, I will give to Gog a place of renown, a tomb in Israel, the burial-place for the attackers in the sea, and there they shall bury the whole nation of Gog."[56]

---

54 *Vit. Dan.* 10: [...] ἄπελθε εἰς τὸ Βυζάντιον καὶ βλέπεις δευτέραν Ἱερουσαλήμ, τὴν Κωνσταντινούπολιν· ἀπολαύεις καὶ τῶν μαρτυρίων καὶ μεγάλων εὐκτηρίων [...]; Eustr. *Vit. Eutych.* 762; 2078–2079.
55 David: Theod. Sync. *Obsid.* 38 (p. 313 Sternbach/Makk); 52 (p. 320). Moses: 17–18 (p. 304–305). Jerusalem: 2–3 (p. 298–299); 8 (p. 301); 20 (p. 306); 27–31 (p. 309–310); 38 (p. 313); 50 (p. 319). See Viermann 2021, 221–225.
56 Theod. Sync. *Obsid.* 40–47 (p. 314–318 Sternbach/Makk): ὀμφαλὸν δὲ τῆς γῆς τίνα ἕτερον τόπον ὀνομάζεσθαι δίκαιον ἢ τὴν πόλιν, ἐν ᾗ τὰ Χριστιανῶν Θεὸς βασίλεια ἵδρυσε καὶ ἣν ὡς ἔκ τινος μεσαιτάτης περιωπῆς ἀνατολῇ τε καὶ δύει δι' ἑαυτῆς μεσιτεύειν ἐποίησε. κατὰ ταύτης ἄρχοντες καὶ λαοὶ καὶ ἔθνη συνήχθησαν, ὧν τὸ κράτος κατέβαλε κύριος ὁ εἰπὼν τὴν Σιών· 'θάρσει Σιών, μὴ παρείσθωσαν χεῖρές σου· ἰδοὺ ὁ θεός σου ἐν σοί, δυνατὸς τοῦ σώζειν σε'. ἐν ταύτῃ τῶν ἐθνῶν τὸ ἄθροισμα ἐκ τῶν ἐσχάτων τοῦ βορρᾶ παραγέγονεν, ἵπποι καὶ ἱππεῖς ἐνδεδυμένοι τοὺς θώρακας καὶ σὺν αὐτοῖς οἱ Πέρσαι· καὶ τοῦτο γὰρ ῥητῶς διὰ τοῦ προφήτου δεδήλωται· ὧν τὰ τόξα ἀπώλεσεν ἐκ τῆς ἀριστερᾶς χειρὸς ἡ ἰσχὺς τοῦ Θεοῦ ἡμῶν καὶ τὰ τοξεύματα ἐκ τῆς δεξιᾶς ἡ παρθένος συνέθλασεν· ἔπεσόν τε ἐπὶ

At that time, however, another decisive event had already occurred: the fall of the real Jerusalem. In the year 614, the Persians had taken the city, and later, after an uprising, massacred the Christian population. The Holy Lance and the Holy Sponge were brought to safety in Constantinople.⁵⁷ This was all the more important since the True Cross had been lost. When Heraclius began his reconquista a few years later, he did so under the banner of religion, even if the recovery of the Cross was not the main goal. But after he had succeeded, the emperor personally brought the True Cross back to Jerusalem in 630. According to the long accepted reconstruction, the True Cross, or at least what was believed to be the Cross, was taken directly to Jerusalem after its surrender by the Persians and subsequently remained there.⁵⁸ However, the sources contain strong evidence that the Cross was brought to Constantinople either before or immediately after it was returned to Jerusalem.⁵⁹ Should these indications turn out to be correct, they would testify to the enhanced sacred status of the capital during the hitherto greatest crisis of the Roman Empire. And even if they should prove incorrect, they would still constitute a no less remarkable testimony for the expectations of those who lived only a few decades later: it was perfectly believable that the reclaimed Cross had been presented to the capital as well.

Possible errors in this respect are at any rate easily understandable and excusable. Only a few years later, the Romans lost Jerusalem a second time, this time for good. Having learned from earlier mistakes, Heraclius evacuated the True Cross in time and brought it to the only conceivable place of exile: Constantinople.⁶⁰

τὰ ὄρη τοῦ Ἰσραὴλ θηρίοις καὶ πετεινοῖς δοθέντες κατάβρωμα. τὰ δὲ οὕτως ὑπὸ τοῦ Ἰεζεκιὴλ τοῦ θείου προφητευόμενα· 'ἐν τῇ ἡμέρᾳ ἐκείνῃ λέγει κύριος, κύριος, δώσω τῷ Γὼγ τόπον ὀνομαστὸν μνημεῖον ἐν Ἰσραήλ, τὸ πολυάνδριον τῶν ἐπελθόντων ἐν τῇ θαλάσσῃ, καὶ κατορύξουσιν ἐκεῖ πάντα τὸν λαὸν τοῦ Γὼγ' (46 [p. 317–318]; quotations: Zeph. 3:16–17 and Ezek. 39:10–11). For the "navel of the earth", see Alexander 1999.

57 *Chron. Pasch.* p. 705 Dindorf. See Flusin 1992, 180–181; Viermann 2021, 177–178. A small dating error in the *Chronicon Paschale* and the unclear circumstances of the surrender of the Holy Lance do not, in my opinion, provide sufficient grounds for shifting the arrival of the relics to the year 629 (as postulated by Klein 2004a, 34–40, Speck 2000b, 167–172, and Zuckerman 2013, 198–201). The passage clearly implies that the Holy Lance had fallen into Persian hands only shortly before and that it had now, for whatever reasons, been turned over to the Romans.

58 For this, see James Howard-Johnston's contribution to this volume and Flusin 1992, 293–312. For the spiritual meaning of the *restitutio crucis*, especially for the already dawning End of Days, see Flusin, 312–319; Drijvers 2002.

59 Before the return: Seb. *frg.* 2 (p. 433 Abgaryan) (translation in Mahé 1984, 231–231); Theoph. AM 6120 (p. 328 de Boor). This possibility is advocated by Klein 2004a, 41–43, and Booth 2014, 157–158 and n. 74. After the return: Niceph. *Brev.* 18. Zuckerman 2013, 201–218, harmonizes the sources by assuming that there were two returns in 629 and 630, interrupted by the presentation of the Cross in Constantinople. But see Mango 1990b, 185, on the difficulties in sources and chronology associated with its presence in Constantinople.

60 Seb. 41 (p. 131 Abgaryan); 42 (p. 136); Theoph. AM 6125 (p. 337 de Boor); Ps.-Šapuh p. 70–71 Darbinjan-Melikjan. Dating the conquest of Jerusalem is difficult. The city most probably fell between 635 and 637. See most recently Booth 2014, 242–243.

This did not mean that the sacred topography of Constantinople was henceforth configured in strict emulation of Jerusalem or even that the one city was considered a copy of the other.[61] The imperial traditions were too strong to permit this; furthermore, religious life, after three centuries, had acquired its own, distinct forms. But now, in the Middle Ages, at least the imperial capital was the place that came closest to the lost Jerusalem.[62]

Second Constantinople – and why this did not work

Constantinople took more than it gave. It imported relics, eschatological meaning, and finally even the True Cross. Jerusalem received little in return. Above all, it did not become a political center for the Empire and its administration. This was of course not the fault of Constantinople: the two cities did not interact with each other, and despite a hyperactive bishop of Jerusalem,[63] they were not even political players that might have competed for the first place within the Empire. However, it is still worth noting that Constantinople assumed functions that originally or primarily belonged to Jerusalem, whereas the opposite did not occur: Jerusalem did not become a Second Constantinople.

For this to happen, the city would have needed an emperor within its walls. Both geography and the development of international affairs prevented this from happening. Jerusalem lay on the eastern periphery of the Empire, too far away from the West and from the critical Danube border. The only thing that might have forced the emperor to reside here permanently would have been a protracted Persian war, as in the fourth and sixth centuries. Up to AD 400 the decision in favor of Constantinople was probably still reversible and/or an additional emperor in Asia still imaginable, following the example of Constantine's sons. But in the fifth century the relations with the Persian Empire were mostly peaceful. The factors that allowed Constantinople to become the imperial city were, conversely, detrimental to Jerusalem.

But even if an emperor had taken up residence in the Levant, he probably would have opted for Antioch, as his predecessors in the fourth century had done: the old Seleucid capital was not only the administrative center of the entire region, it was also situated at a strategically more convenient distance from the Persian Empire than the comparatively remote Jerusalem, which presented the additional disadvant-

---

[61] I follow the interpretation of Ousterhout 2006, 100–109: "more often than not, Jerusalem provided no more than a convenient metaphor for a sacred city, and not a typological model" (100).
[62] From then on, following the example of Theodore Syncellus, the comparison with Jerusalem started to become more popular. For the sources, see Fenster 1968, 109, 115, 121, 135, 139, 159–160, 177, 211, 214, 250, 280, 284.
[63] On this particular bishop, see Jan-Markus Kötter's contribution to this volume.

age of a landlocked location.[64] The latter city had never even been the seat of Roman governors: already in the early Empire, Iudaea or Palaestina had been ruled by a prefect residing in Caesarea Maritima, an arrangement that continued until the very end of antiquity.[65]

It is nevertheless tempting to envision for a moment what developments the permanent presence of an emperor might have triggered. What would such a Jerusalem have looked like? – Due to the settled presence of the court, the city is populated by several hundred thousand people. At least in the beginning, Latin plays a significant role. Over time its importance declines (as it did in Constantinople). Not only Greek, but also the Aramaic languages gain ground. The Romanness of the court and administration fades. The oriental Christianities exert great influence, while Western theology recedes into the background. The Jews soon come under pressure. They are exiled from Jerusalem and Iudaea, as the Christian emperor does not tolerate persons of the wrong faith in his city. In other respects, the emperor has far fewer possibilities to shape urban development. While Constantinople, as an almost untouched surface, was formed according to imperial needs, in Jerusalem the fact that its topography is intimately connected with the story of Christ sets narrow limits on any such endeavor.[66] The emperor is not only a Christian, he lives in one city with Christ. Therefore, the analogies between the heavenly and the earthly ruler are addressed more frequently and with greater intensity. The spiritual significance of emperorship is much more closely linked to Christianity than to its Roman, pagan roots. Whether this serves to strengthen it is a different question. It is of course conceivable that the emperor may be exalted to the point of becoming a Christ-like figure who cannot be overthrown under any circumstances. Conversely, the emperor's position may lose its worldly significance by no longer being autonomous from the religious sphere: the emperor becomes a mere symbol, while others make the decisions. Several shades of variation are possible, and even the extremes do not entirely exclude each other. However, one thing seems rather probable: in the shadow of Christ an acceptance system does not develop.[67]

These counterfactual reflections are meant to underline that the actual development of Late Roman emperorship represented only one of several historical possibilities. The option which was ultimately realized had much to do with the city of Caesar. The unique form which the emperorship assumed in the late-antique East would have been inconceivable anywhere but in Constantinople.

---

[64] See Marlena Whiting's contribution to this volume.
[65] See Haensch 1997, 227–237, and most recently Isaac 2011, 21–32.
[66] On the omnipresence of the traces of Christ in the sacred topography of Jerusalem, see Konstantin Klein's contribution to this volume and, in comparison with Constantinople, Ousterhout 2006, 109.
[67] That the exercise of power from such a religiously charged place was fraught with difficulties is also suggested by the fact that Jerusalem did not become the capital of any of the various Islamic empires. Leaving the Crusader states aside, this would only happen in modern Israel, but on a Zionistic, secular basis.

Jerusalem was not the only city on which Constantinople did not exert a powerful influence. In fact, it did not become a model for any other city. Not for Antioch or Alexandria, which cultivated their far older traditions. Not for the cities and towns of the Latin Middle Ages, which even early on were socially and culturally detached from Constantinople and, for precisely this reason, as alienated from it as they were dazzled by it.[68] Not even for Moscow, which was more eager to become the New Israel or the Third Rome than the Second Constantinople.[69] In this last case it is evident why the city on the Bosporus could not serve as a paradigm: Constantinople was always a 'second', never a 'first'. In spite of all the importance and all the originality of its development, its political power was seen as having been transferred from Rome. Likewise, Constantinople's growing holiness and its importance for salvation only resulted in a Second, New Jerusalem. The originals may have faded at times, but they were never forgotten. For centuries, the lost Jerusalem inspired the Catholic nations to undertake great wars to win it back. The fall of Constantinople in 1453, on the other hand, only triggered weak efforts. Even when the Ottoman Empire was put on the defensive from the 18th century onward, the liberation of Constantinople remained a vague aspiration, even for Russia. It was never fulfilled.

In fact, it was the Turks who enabled Constantinople to continue under conditions that were quite similar to the ancient and Byzantine ones. Though stripped of most of its religious claims, Constantinople nevertheless retained its original, worldly function as capital of an empire: from the city of Caesar to the city of Sultan. The Ottomans were thus the only ones for whom Constantinople was something like a 'first'. However, the founding of modern Turkey not only deprived the city of its empire but also of its status as a capital. Today Istanbul's appeal beyond the borders of Turkey is more of a touristic nature, even for the non-Turkish Islamic world. The sacral aura of Jerusalem has proved more enduring. That city not only attracts visitors from all over the world, its spiritual importance is also manifest in its considerable political weight. Whether this holds the promise for a better future of its inhabitants remains to be seen.

Bibliography

Actes (1989). *Actes du XIe Congrès International d'Archéologie Chrétienne. Lyon, Vienne, Grenoble, Genève et Aoste (21–28 septembre 1986)* (vol. 2), Rome.

Alexander, Ph.S. (1999). 'Jerusalem as the *Omphalos* of the World: On the History of a Geographical Concept,' in Levine 1999, 104–119.

---

[68] See only, on the example of palaces, Luchterhandt 2006.
[69] Raba 1995; Rowland 1996. In this respect as well, Moscow stands at the end of a chain of tradition that begins with Kyiv; see Philipp 1956.

Asutay-Effenberger, N. (2007). *Die Landmauer von Konstantinopel-İstanbul. Historisch-topographische und baugeschichtliche Untersuchungen*, Berlin.

Baldovin, J.F. (1987). *The Urban Character of Christian Worship. The Origins, Development, and Meaning of Stational Liturgy*, Rome.

Bassett, S. (2004). *The Urban Image of Late Antique Constantinople*, Cambridge.

Bauer, F.A. (1996). *Stadt, Platz und Denkmal in der Spätantike. Untersuchungen zur Ausstattung des öffentlichen Raums in den spätantiken Städten Rom, Konstantinopel und Ephesos*, Mainz.

Bauer, F.A. (ed.) (2006). *Visualisierungen von Herrschaft. Frühmittelalterliche Residenzen. Gestalt und Zeremoniell. Internationales Kolloquium 3./4. Juni 2004 in Istanbul*, Istanbul.

Bayless, W.N. (1977). 'The Preatorian [sic!] Prefect Anthemius: Position and Policies,' *Byzantine Studies* 4, 38–51.

Beaton, R. & Rouèche, Ch. (eds.) (1993). *The Making of Byzantine History. Studies Dedicated to Donald M. Nicol*, Aldershot.

Beck, H.-G. (1959). *Kirche und theologische Literatur im Byzantinischen Reich*, Munich.

Beck, H.-G. (ed.) (1973a). *Studien zur Frühgeschichte Konstantinopels*, Munich.

Beck, H.-G. (1973b). 'Großstadt-Probleme: Konstantinopel vom 4.–6. Jahrhundert,' in Beck 1973a, 1–26.

Berger, A. (2006). 'Konstantinopel (stadtgeschichtlich),' *RAC* 21, 435–483.

Blaudeau, Ph. (2006). *Alexandrie et Constantinople (451–491). De l'histoire à la géo-ecclésiologie*, Rome.

Booth, Ph. (2014). *Crisis of Empire. Doctrine and Dissent at the End of Late Antiquity*, Berkeley.

Brandes, W. (1997). 'Anastasios ὁ δίκορος: Endzeiterwartung und Kaiserkritik in Byzanz um 500 n.Chr.,' *ByzZ* 90, 24–63.

Brandes, W. & Schmieder, F. (eds.) (2008). *Endzeiten. Eschatologie in den monotheistischen Weltreligionen*, Berlin.

Brown, P. (1981). *The Cult of the Saints. Its Rise and Function in Latin Christianity*, Chicago.

Bury, J.B. (1923). *History of the Later Roman Empire from the Death of Theodosius I. to the Death of Justinian (A.D. 395 to A.D. 565)* (vol. 1), London.

Cameron, Al., Long, J. & Sherry, L. (1993). *Barbarians and Politics at the Court of Arcadius*, Berkeley.

Chevailler, L. & Chabanne, R. (1984). 'Justinien et la Pentarchie,' in *Sodalitas: scritti in onore di Antonio Guarino* 1984, Vol. 2, 721–730.

Conrad, L.I. (1996). 'Die Pest und ihr soziales Umfeld im Nahen Osten des frühen Mittelalters,' *Der Islam* 73, 81–112.

Croke, B. (1981). 'Two early Byzantine earthquakes and their liturgical commemoration,' *Byzantion* 51, 122–147.

Croke, B. (2010). 'Reinventing Constantinople: Theodosius I's imprint on the imperial city,' in McGill/Sogno/Watts 2010, 241–264.

Cross, F.L. (ed.) (1966). *Studia Patristica. Papers Presented to the Fourth International Conference on Patristic Studies Held at Christ Church, Oxford, 1963* (Pt. 1: Editiones, Critica, Philologica, Biblica), Berlin.

Dagens, Cl. (1975). 'L'Eglise universelle et le monde oriental chez saint Grégoire le Grand,' *Istina* 20, 457–475.

Dagron, G. (^{2}1984). *Naissance d'une capitale. Constantinople et ses institutions de 330 à 451*, Paris.

Dagron, G. (1989). 'Constantinople. Les sanctuaires et l'organisation de la vie religieuse,' in *Actes*, 1069–1085.

Dagron, G. (2002). 'Constantinople, la primauté après Rome,' in Elia 2002a, 23–38.

Delehaye, H. (^{2}1933). *Les origines du culte des martyrs*, Bruxelles.

Destephen, S. (2016). *Le voyage impérial dans l'Antiquité tardive. Des Balkans au Proche-Orient*, Paris.

Destephen, S. (2018). 'Le Prince chrétien en pèlerinage,' in Destephen/Dumézil/Inglebert 2018, 269–313.

Destephen, S., Dumézil, B. & Inglebert, H. (ed.) (2018). *Le prince chrétien de Constantin aux royautés barbares (IVe – VIIIe siècle)*, Paris.

Diefenbach, S. (1996). 'Frömmigkeit und Kaiserakzeptanz im frühen Byzanz,' *Saeculum* 47, 35–66.

Diefenbach, S. (2002). 'Zwischen Liturgie und *civilitas*. Konstantinopel im 5. Jahrhundert und die Etablierung eines städtischen Kaisertums,' in Warland 2002, 21–49.

Drijvers, J.W. (2002). 'Heraclius and the *Restitutio Crucis*. Notes on Symbolism and Ideology,' in Reinink/Stolte 2002, 175–190.

Durand, J. & Flusin, B. (ed.) (2004). *Byzance et les reliques du Christ*, Paris.

Dvornik, F. (1966). *Early Christian and Byzantine Political Philosophy. Origins and Background* (vol. 2), Washington, D.C.

Eich, P. (2016). *Gregor der Große. Bischof von Rom zwischen Antike und Mittelalter*, Paderborn.

Elia, F. (ed.) (2002a). *Politica retorica e simbolismo del primato: Roma e Costantinopoli (secoli IV– VII). Atti del convegno internazionale (Catania, 4–7 ottobre 2001). Omaggio a Rosario Soraci* (vol. 1), Catania.

Elia, F. (2002b). 'Sui *privilegia urbis Constantinopolitanae*,' in Elia 2002a, 79–105.

Ernesti, J. (1998). *Princeps christianus und Kaiser aller Römer. Theodosius der Große im Lichte zeitgenössischer Quellen*, Paderborn.

Errington, R.M. (1997). 'Church and state in the first years of Theodosius I,' *Chiron* 27, 21–72.

Errington, R.M. (2000). 'Themistius and his emperors,' *Chiron* 30, 861–904.

Errington, R.M. (2006). *Roman Imperial Policy from Julian to Theodosius*, Chapel Hill.

Feissel, D. (1995). 'BÉ Nr. 720,' *REG* 108, 566–568.

Fenster, E. (1968). *Laudes Constantinopolitanae*, Munich.

Flaig, E. (^{2}2019). *Den Kaiser herausfordern. Die Usurpation im Römischen Reich*, Frankfurt a.M.

Flusin, B. (1992). *Saint Anastase le Perse et l'histoire de la Palestine au début du VIIe siècle* (vol. 2: *Commentaire. Les moines de Jérusalem et l'invasion perse*), Paris.

Frend, W.H.C. (1972). *The Rise of the Monophysite Movement. Chapters in the History of the Church in the Fifth and Sixth Centuries*, Cambridge.

Frolow, A. (1961). *La relique de la Vraie Croix. Recherches sur le développement d'un culte*, Paris.

Gaudemet, J. (^{2}1989). *L'Église dans l'Empire romain (IV–V siècles)*, Paris.

Gerland, E. (1894). 'Die persischen Feldzüge des Kaisers Herakleios,' *ByzZ* 3, 330–373.

Gómez-Villegas, N. (2000). *Gregorio de Nazianzo en Constantinopla. Ortodoxia, heterodoxia y régimen teodosiano en una capital cristiana*, Madrid.

Grillmeier, A. & Bacht, H. (eds.) (^{4}1973). *Das Konzil von Chalkedon. Geschichte und Gegenwart* (vol. 2: *Entscheidung um Chalkedon*), Würzburg.

Hackel, S. (ed.) (1981). *The Byzantine Saint. University of Birmingham Fourteenth Spring Symposium of Byzantine Studies*, London.

Haensch, R. (1997). *Capita provinciarum. Statthaltersitze und Provinzialverwaltung in der römischen Kaiserzeit*, Mainz.

Halfmann, H. (1986). *Itinera principum. Geschichte und Typologie der Kaiserreisen im Römischen Reich*, Stuttgart.

de Halleux, A. (1989). 'Le vingt-huitième canon de Chalcédoine,' in Livingstone 1989, 28–36.

Herman, E. (1973). 'Chalkedon und die Ausgestaltung des konstantinopolitanischen Primats,' in Grillmeier/Bacht 1973, 459–490.

Holum, K.G. (1982). *Theodosian Empresses. Women and Imperial Dominion in Late Antiquity*, Berkeley.

Holum, K.G. & Vikan, G. (1979). 'The Trier Ivory, *Adventus* ceremonial, and the relics of St. Stephen,' *DOP* 33, 113–133.

Howard-Johnston, J. (1999). *Sebeos, The Armenian History Attributed to Sebeos. Translated, with notes, by R. W. Thomson. Historical Commentary by J. Howard-Johnston. Assistance from T. Greenwood* (vol. 2), Liverpool.

Hunt, E.D. (1981). 'The traffic in relics: Some late Roman evidence,' in Hackel 1981, 171–180.

Isaac, B. (2011). 'Introduction (Caesarea),' *CIIP* 2, 17–35.

Isele, B. (2010). *Kampf um Kirchen. Religiöse Gewalt, heiliger Raum und christliche Topographie in Alexandria und Konstantinopel (4. Jh.)*, Münster.

Jacoby, D. (1961). 'La population de Constantinople à l'époque byzantine: un problème de démographie urbaine,' *Byzantion* 31, 81–109.

Janin, R. (²1964). *Constantinople byzantine. Développement urbain et répertoire topographique*, Paris.

Janin, R. (1969). *La géographie ecclésiastique de l'Empire byzantine* (vol. 1.3: *Le siège de Constantinople et le patriarcat œcuménique. Les églises et les monastères*), Paris.

Kaegi Jr., W.E. (1973). 'New evidence on the early reign of Heraclius,' *ByzZ* 66, 308–330.

Kaegi Jr., W.E. (1981). *Byzantine Military Unrest 471–843. An Interpretation*, Amsterdam.

Kaegi Jr., W.E. (2003). *Heraclius. Emperor of Byzantium*, Cambridge.

Karlin-Hayter, P. (1988). 'Activity of the bishop of Constantinople outside his *Paroikia* between 381 and 451,' in ΚΑΘΗΓΗΤΡΙΑ 1988, 179–210.

ΚΑΘΗΓΗΤΡΙΑ. *Essays Presented to Joan Hussey for her 80th Birthday*, Camberley 1988.

Kelly, J.N.D. (1995). *Golden Mouth. The Story of John Chrysostom – Ascetic, Preacher, Bishop*, Ithaca N.Y.

Klein, H.A. (2004a). *Byzanz, der Westen und das ‚wahre' Kreuz. Die Geschichte einer Reliquie und ihrer künstlerischen Fassung in Byzanz und im Abendland (Spätantike – Frühes Christentum – Byzanz)*, Wiesbaden.

Klein, H.A. (2004b). 'Constantine, Helena, and the Cult of the True Cross in Constantinople,' in Durand/Flusin 2004, 31–59.

Klein, H.A. (2006). 'Sacred relics and imperial ceremonies at the Great Palace of Constantinople,' in Bauer 2006, 79–99.

Krischen, F. (1938). *Die Landmauer von Konstantinopel* (vol. 1: *Zeichnerische Wiederherstellung mit begleitendem Text. Lichtbilder von Th. von Lüpke*), Berlin.

Lebek, W.D. (1995). 'Die Landmauer von Konstantinopel und ein neues Bauepigramm (Θευδοσίου τόδε τεῖχος),' *EA* 25, 107–154.

Lenski, N. (2002). *Failure of Empire. Valens and the Roman State in the Fourth Century A.D.*, Berkeley.

Leppin, H. (2003). *Theodosius der Große*, Darmstadt.

Leven, K.-H. (1987). 'Die "Justinianische" Pest,' *Jahrbuch des Instituts für Geschichte der Medizin der Robert-Bosch-Stiftung* 6, 137–161.

Levine, L.I. (ed.) (1999). *Jerusalem. Its Sanctity and Centrality to Judaism, Christianity, and Islam*, New York.

L'Huillier, P. (1996). *The Church of the Ancient Councils. The Disciplinary Work of the First Four Ecumenical Councils*, Crestwood N.Y.

Lidov, A. (ed.) (2006). *Hierotopy. The Creation of Sacred Spaces in Byzantium and Medieval Russia*, Moscow.

Liebeschuetz, J.H.W.G. (1990). *Barbarians and Bishops. Army, Church, and State in the Age of Arcadius and Chrysostom*, Oxford.

Livingstone, E.A. (ed.) (1989). *Studia Patristica. Papers Presented to the Tenth International Conference on Patristic Studies Held in Oxford 1987* (Pt. 19: *Historica, Theologica, Gnostica, Liturgica, Biblica et Apocrypha*), Leuven.

Luchterhandt, M. (2006). 'Stolz und Vorurteil. Der Westen und die byzantinische Hofkultur im Frühmittelalter,' in Bauer 2006, 171–211.
Magdalino, P. (1993). 'The History of the Future and its Uses: Prophecy, Policy and Propaganda,' in Beaton/Roueché 1993, 3–34.
Magdalino, P. (2008). 'The End of Time in Byzantium,' in Brandes/Schmieder 2008, 119–133.
Mahé, J.-P. (1984). 'Critical remarks on the newly edited excerpts from Sebēos,' in Samuelian/Stone 1984, 218–239.
Maier, F.K. (2019). *Palastrevolution. Der Weg zum hauptstädtischen Kaisertum im Römischen Reich des vierten Jahrhunderts*, Leiden.
Mango, C. (1990a). 'Constantine's Mausoleum: Addendum,' *ByzZ* 83, 434.
Mango, C. (1990b). *Nikephoros Patriarch of Constantinople, Short History. Text, Translation, and Commentary*, Washington D.C.
Mango, C. (^{3}2004). *Le développement urbain de Constantinople (IVe–VIIe siècles)*, Paris.
Maraval, P. (1985). *Lieux saints et pèlerinages d'Orient. Histoire et géographie des origines à la conquête arabe*, Paris.
Martin, J. (1997). 'Das Kaisertum in der Spätantike,' in Paschoud/Szidat 1997, 47–62.
Matthews, J. (1975). *Western Aristocracies and Imperial Court A.D. 364–425*, Oxford.
Mayer, E. (2002). *Rom ist dort, wo der Kaiser ist. Untersuchungen zu den Staatsdenkmälern des dezentralisierten Reiches von Diocletian bis zu Theodosius II.*, Mainz.
Mayer, W. (2000a). 'Cathedral Church or Cathedral Churches? The Situation at Constantinople (c. 360–404 AD),' *OCP* 66, 49–68.
Mayer, W. (2000b). 'Who Came to Hear John Chrysostom Preach? Recovering a Late Fourth-Century Preacher's Audience,' *EThL* 76, 73–87.
McGill, S., Sogno, C. & Watts, E. (eds.) (2010). *From the Tetrarchs to the Theodosians. Later Roman History and Culture, 284–450 CE*, Cambridge.
McLynn, N.B. (2004). 'The transformation of imperial churchgoing in the fourth century,' in Swain/Edwards 2004, 235–270.
Meier, M. (2003). *Das andere Zeitalter Justinians. Kontingenzerfahrung und Kontingenzbewältigung im 6. Jahrhundert n. Chr.*, Göttingen.
Meier, M. (2008). 'Eschatologie und Kommunikation im 6. Jahrhundert n. Chr. – oder: Wie Osten und Westen beständig aneinander vorbei redeten,' in Brandes/Schmieder 2008, 41–73.
Mergiali-Sahas, S. (2001). 'Byzantine emperors and holy relics. Use, and misuse, of sanctity and authority,' *JÖByz* 51, 41–60.
Meyer-Plath, B. & Schneider, A.M. (1943). *Die Landmauer von Konstantinopel* (vol. 2: *Aufnahme, Beschreibung und Geschichte*), Berlin.
Millar, F. (^{2}1992). *The Emperor in the Roman World (31 BC–AD 337)*, London.
Moser, M. (2018). *Emperor and Senators in the Reign of Constantius II. Maintaining Imperial Rule Between Rome and Constantinople in the Fourth Century AD*, Cambridge.
Müller, A.E. (1993). 'Getreide für Konstantinopel. Überlegungen zu Justinians Edikt XIII als Grundlage für Aussagen zur Einwohnerzahl Konstantinopels im 6. Jahrhundert,' *JÖByz* 43, 1–20.
Müller-Wiener, W. (1977). *Bildlexikon zur Topographie Istanbuls. Byzantion – Konstantinupolis – Istanbul bis zum Beginn des 17. Jahrhunderts unter Mitarbeit von Renate und Wolf Schiele mit einem Beitrag von Nezih Fıratlı*, Tübingen.
Norton, P. (2007). *Episcopal Elections 250–600. Hierarchy and Popular Will in Late Antiquity*, Oxford.
Oikonomidès, N. (1975). 'A chronological note on the first Persian campaign of Heraclius (622),' *BMGS* 1, 1–9.
Oost, S.I. (1968). *Galla Placidia Augusta. A Biographical Essay*, Chicago.

Ousterhout, R. (2006). 'Sacred geographies and holy cities: Constantinople as Jerusalem,' in Lidov 2006, 98–116.
Paschoud, F. & Szidat, J. (eds.) (1997). *Usurpationen in der Spätantike. Akten des Kolloquiums "Staatsstreich und Staatlichkeit" 6.–10. März 1996 Solothurn/Bern*, Stuttgart.
Pfeilschifter, R. (2013). *Der Kaiser und Konstantinopel. Kommunikation und Konfliktaustrag in einer spätantiken Metropole*, Berlin.
Philipp, W. (1956). 'Die religiöse Begründung der altrussischen Hauptstadt,' in Woltner/Bräuer 1956, 375–387.
Raba, J. (1995). 'Moscow – The Third Rome or the New Jerusalem?,' *Forschungen zur osteuropäischen Geschichte* 50, 297–307.
Reinink, G.J. & Stolte, B.H. (eds.) (2002). *The Reign of Heraclius (610–641): Crisis and Confrontation*, Leuven.
Ritter, A.M. (1965). *Das Konzil von Konstantinopel und sein Symbol. Studien zur Geschichte und Theologie des II. Ökumenischen Konzils*, Göttingen.
Rowland, D.B. (1996). 'Moscow – The Third Rome or the New Israel?,' *Russian Review* 55, 591–614.
Saitta, B. (2002). 'Gregorio Magno e la primazia della sede romana,' in Elia 2002a, 239–261.
Samuelian, Th.J. & Stone, M.E. (eds.) (1984). *Medieval Armenian Culture*, Chico CA.
Schreiner, P. (2007). *Konstantinopel. Geschichte und Archäologie*. Munich.
Seeck, O. (1919). *Regesten der Kaiser und Päpste für die Jahre 311 bis 476 n. Chr. Vorarbeit zu einer Prosopographie der christlichen Kaiserzeit*, Stuttgart.
Shoemaker, S.J. (2008). 'The Cult of Fashion. The Earliest *Life of the Virgin* and Constantinople's Marian Relics,' *DOP* 62, 53–74.
Sodalitas. Scritti in onore di Antonio Guarino (vol. 2), Napoli 1984.
Speck, P. (1973). 'Der Mauerbau in 60 Tagen. Zum Datum der Errichtung der Landmauer von Konstantinopel mit einem Anhang über die Datierung der Notitia urbis Constantinopolitanae,' in Beck 1973, 135–178.
Speck, P. (ed.) (2000a). *Varia. 7*, Bonn.
Speck, P. (2000b). 'Zum Datum der Translation der Kreuzreliquien nach Konstantinopel,' in Speck 2000a, 167–179.
Stathakopoulos, D.Ch. (2004). *Famine and Pestilence in the Late Roman and Early Byzantine Empire. A Systematic Survey of Subsistence Crises and Epidemics*, Aldershot.
Stein, E. (^{2}1959). *Histoire du Bas-Empire* (vol. 1.1: *De l'État Romain à l'État Byzantin [284–476]*), Paris.
Stickler, T. (2002). *Aetius. Gestaltungsspielräume eines Heermeisters im ausgehenden Weströmischen Reich*, Munich.
Stratos, A.N. (1968). *Byzantium in the Seventh Century* (vol. 1: *602–634*), Amsterdam.
Stratos, A.N. (1979). 'La première campagne de l'Empereur Héraclius contre les Perses,' *JÖByz* 28, 63–74.
Swain, S. & Edwards, M. (eds.) (2004). *Approaching Late Antiquity. The Transformation from Early to Late Empire*, Oxford.
Tiersch, C. (2002). *Johannes Chrysostomus in Konstantinopel (398–404). Weltsicht und Wirken eines Bischofs in der Hauptstadt des Oströmischen Reiches*, Tübingen.
Tuilier, A. (1966). 'Le sens de l'adjectif οἰκουμενικός dans la tradition patristique et dans la tradition byzantine,' in Cross 1966, 413–424.
Ubaldi, P. (1903). 'La sinodo "ad quercum" dell'anno 403,' *MAT* 52, 33–97.
Vailhé, S. (1908a). 'Saint Grégoire le Grand et le titre de patriarche œcuménique,' *Echos d'Orient* 11, 161–171.
Vailhé, S. (1908b). 'Le titre de patriarche œcuménique avant saint Grégoire le Grand,' *Echos d'Orient* 11, 65–69.

Van Dam, R. (2010). *Rome and Constantinople. Rewriting Roman History during Late Antiquity*, Waco.
Viermann, N. (2021). *Herakleios, der schwitzende Kaiser. Die oströmische Monarchie in der ausgehenden Spätantike*, Berlin.
Wallraff, M. (2013). *Sonnenkönig der Spätantike. Die Religionspolitik Konstantins des Großen*, Freiburg.
Warland, R. (ed.) (2002). *Bildlichkeit und Bildorte von Liturgie. Schauplätze in Spätantike, Byzanz und Mittelalter*, Wiesbaden.
Whitby, L.M. (1983). 'Theophanes' Chronicle source for the reigns of Justin II, Tiberius and Maurice (A.D. 565–602),' *Byzantion* 53, 312–345.
Whitby, L.M. (1988). *The Emperor Maurice and his Historian: Theophylact Simocatta on Persian and Balkan Warfare*, Oxford.
Whitby, L.M. & Whitby, M. (1989). *Chronicon Paschale 284–628 AD. Translated with Notes and Introduction*, Liverpool.
Woltner, M. & Bräuer, H. (eds.) (1956). *Festschrift für Max Vasmer zum 70. Geburtstag am 28. Februar 1956*, Wiesbaden.
Wortley, J. (1980). 'The Trier Ivory reconsidered,' *GRBS* 21, 381–394.
Zuckerman, C. (2013). 'Heraclius and the return of the Holy Cross,' *T&MByz* 17, 197–218.

Part Two:
Urban Topographies Connected

Neslihan Asutay-Effenberger and Shlomit Weksler-Bdolah

Delineating the Sacred and the Profane: The Late-Antique Walls of Jerusalem and Constantinople

In the year 420, the emperors Theodosius II and Honorius sent a letter to the *praefectus praetorio* Monaxius. In most provinces of the Empire, the letter decreed, individuals were now permitted to defend their own estates and places with circuit walls. This law reacted to the changing security needs in the wake of robberies and hostile incursions, and it was issued in spite of the evident danger for the state posed by private fortifications.[1] On a small scale, the imperial letter reflected one of the main characteristics of urbanism in the reign of the Theodosian dynasty: the urban centers of the Empire, particularly in the East, were fortified. In most cases existing fortifications were repaired and enlarged, and sometimes new walls were built to adorn and protect a city. It is not always possible to identify the exact circle of commissioners, but in the case of the most massive re-fortification measures of the great late Roman cities, the building projects were favored, encouraged, and supported by the imperial court. Throughout the late Roman world, city walls most visibly symbolized imperial power and security in a period facing the onset of Barbarian incursions into the Empire.[2]

Both Constantinople and Jerusalem were encircled with impressive fortifications early in the fifth century: the walls of Constantinople were commissioned by Arcadius prior to his death, and built over the years 404/405–413 in the reign of Theodosius II. In Jerusalem, the exact period of construction, and the builder, are less clear. Apart from shared characteristics and a common historical context, the walls of Constantinople and Jerusalem exhibit individual traits, idiosyncratic features, and unique structural specifics. The aim of this contribution is to approach Constantinople and Jerusalem through the material culture, archaeology, and symbolism of their most extensive monuments: their late-antique walls. The first part, on the walls of Constantinople, was written by Neslihan Asutay-Effenberger,[3] the second part, deal-

---

[1] *Cod. Iust.* 8,10,10, on the law and its implications for the public sphere, cf. Connolly 2006–2007, 150–152.
[2] In Constantinople, the threat posed in 378 by Fritigern's army had deep and long-lasting repercussions: Socr. *HE* 5,1,3, Sozom. *HE* 7,1,2 and Amm. Marc. 31,16,4–7 on the defense of Adrianople, cf. Lenski 1997, 131–133. Regarding Jerusalem as a city on the imperial periphery, a massive re-building is characteristic of all capitals and important cities in the three Palaestinae (Caesarea Maritima, Scythopolis, and Aila).
[3] The walls of Constantinople have been studied in greater detail in the author's Habilitationsschrift, Asutay-Effenberger 2007.

ing with the walls of Jerusalem, by Shlomit Weksler-Bdolah.[4] The paper includes new archaeological evidence, and the comparison offers new perspectives on the City of Caesar and the City of God in late antiquity.

The City Walls of Constantinople

> For in reality there are two seas embracing it [i.e. the city of Byzantium], the Aegean on the one side and the sea called the Euxine on the other; these unite with each other to the east of the city, and rushing together as they mingle their waves, and pushing back the solid land by this invasion, they beautify the city as they surround it. [...] Thus the sea forms a garland about the city; the remainder of the city's boundary is formed by the land which lies between the two arms of the sea, and is of sufficient size to bind together there the crown of waters.[5]

With these words, Procopius described the geographical situation of the almost trapezoidal shape of the late-antique capital Constantinople, and its relation to the sea in the sixth century. At the same time, he implicitly indicated its congenial strategic position (Fig. 1).

The city in which Procopius lived was significantly larger than pre-Constantinian Byzantium or the city of Constantine I, which had been inaugurated on 11 May AD 330, when it covered roughly six square kilometers. In scholarly literature, it has often been assumed that the first fortification of Roman Byzantium was built adjacent to today's *Topkapı Sarayı* (Fig. 1). In a punitive action against Byzantium, Septimius Severus is said to have razed this old defense work in AD 196. According to more recent research, a wall reaching from the Golden Horn to the Sea of Marmara existed on the east side of what would later be the Forum of Constantine. Severus had this complex destroyed, and it was not reconstructed for some time.[6] The only remains of the Roman wall today are still in the vicinity of the Manganes, the former armory, at the seashore of *Marmara*.[7] The new land walls, erected on Constantine's behalf, stretched from the Rhabdos at the Sea of *Marmara* (nowadays in the borough

---

[4] For a detailed description of the wall segments of Jerusalem, cf. Weksler-Bdolah 2006–2007, Weksler-Bdolah 2020, 138–140, as well as the preliminary reports of recent finds: Sion/Puni 2011, Zelinger 2010 and Weksler-Bdolah/Lavi 2013. The views offered here below are an updated and revised version of Weksler-Bdolah 2006–2007.

[5] Proc. Aed. 5,3.10: πελάγη γὰρ δύο ἀμφ' αὐτὴν ὄντα, ὅ τε δὴ Αἰγαῖος καὶ ὁ Εὔξεινος καλούμενος Πόντος, ξυνιᾶσιν ἀλλήλοις ἔς τὰ πρὸς ἕω τῆς πόλεως καὶ ξυγκρουόμενα τῇ τοῦ ῥοθίου ἐπιμιξίᾳ, ταύτῃ τε τὴν ἤπειρον τῇ ἐσβολῇ βιαζόμενα, καλλωπίζουσι κύκλῳ τὴν πόλιν. [...] οὕτω μὲν οὖν στεφανοῖ τὴν πόλιν ἡ θάλασσα, ἐκδέχεται δὲ ἀνὰ τὸ λειπόμενον ἡ γῆ, μεταξὺ τοσαύτη οὖσα, ὅσον τὴν ἀπὸ τῆς θαλάττης στεφάνην ἐνταῦθα ξυνδεῖσθαι (trans. Dewing/Downey 1940, 57, 59).

[6] Cf. Müller-Wiener 1961, 165–175, Berger 1988, 203–206, Mango 2004, 13–21, and Schreiner 2007, 19, cf. Effenberger 2013, 215–274, esp. 234.

[7] Demangel/Mamboury 1939, 49–56 with plate 9.

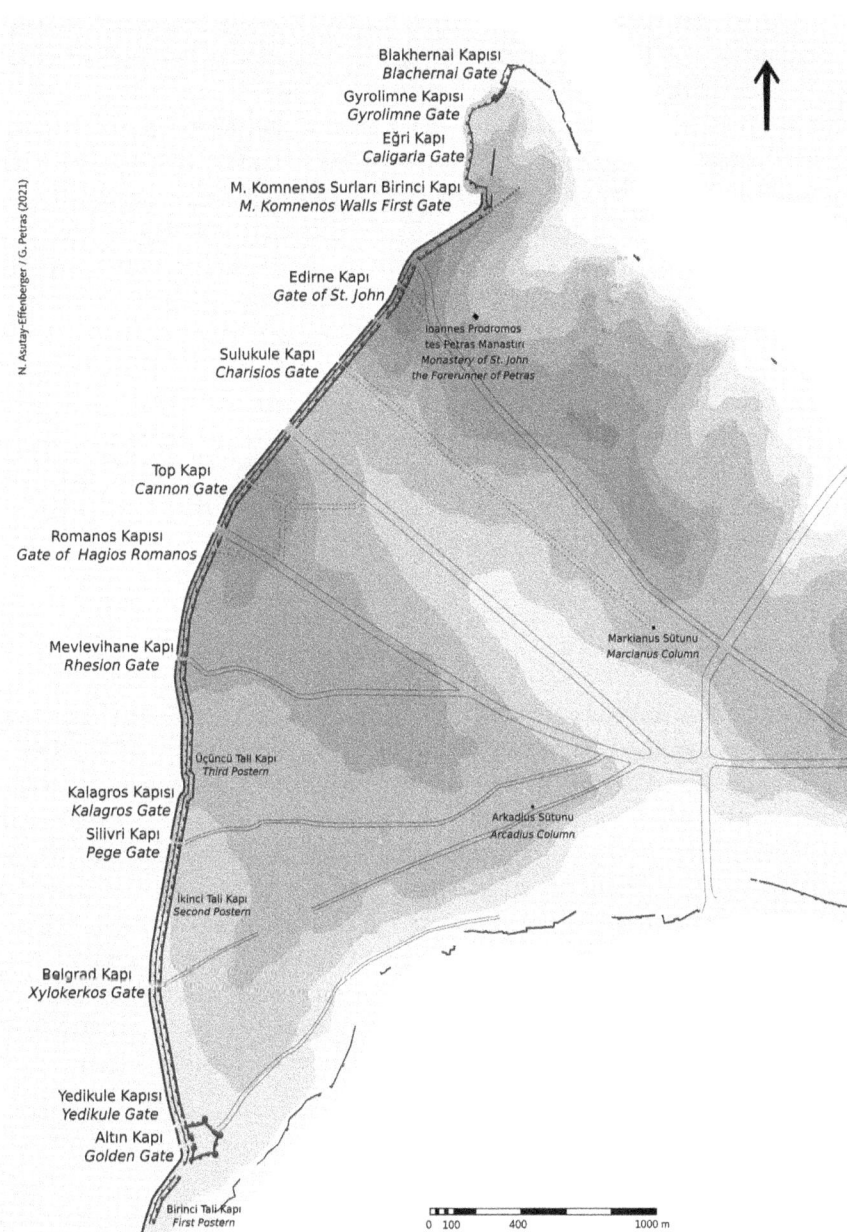

Fig. 1: Map of Istanbul, Theodosian Land Walls and the Gates, N. Asutay-Effenberger and G. Petras, adapted from Krischen 1938, p. 4, fig. 1 and Marcell Restle 1976.

of *Cerrahpaşa*) to the Church of St Anthony at the Golden Horn, near today's *Cibali*.[8] This complex has not left any traces in the modern cityscape of Istanbul, so we do not know its architectonic features. The only evidence derives from the vicinity of a Byzantine church in *Cerrahpaşa* (the *İsa Kapısı Mescidi*), where remains of the Constantinian Golden Gate still stood until AD 1509, when it was thrown down by a huge earthquake which Ottoman sources called *Kıyâmet-i Suğra* (Small Apocalypse).[9]

It is not clear whether at the time of Constantine the shoreline was protected by a defense system. According to the written sources, the walls were only erected in 439 during the reign of Theodosius II.[10] Moreover, the coastlines followed a different course in the fourth century and formed two large bays at modern *Yenikapı* and *Unkapanı*, so that the eastern part of the peninsula was only connected to the Thracian hinterland via a small isthmus (ca. 900 m wide). Both bays were later backfilled.[11] While the sea walls are only partly preserved, the Theodosian land walls continue to impress visitors to the west of the city up to the present day (Fig. 2): they were the largest and most complete urban defense work of late antiquity and the Byzantine Middle Ages.[12]

History and Architecture

The land walls were constructed in the reign of Theodosius II under the supervision of the *praefectus praetorio per Orientem*, Anthemius. According to an inscription which was discovered in the 1990s close to *Belgradkapı*, the building activities took nine years,[13] which means that the groundbreaking must have taken place in AD 404/405, still in the reign of Arcadius, who also might have had a share in the construction of the walls of Jerusalem. Theodosius was four years old when the work started, and thirteen when it was completed – Arcadius and Anthemius consequently played the crucial part. A law issued in AD 413 granted the prior owners of premises adjacent to the walls continuity of use, a fact which indirectly secures the date of completion. According to this text, the lower stories of the towers as well as the cemeteries and the vegetable gardens in the area were accessible to the previous owners of the grounds during times of peace.[14]

---

[8] On the Constantinian walls, cf. Asutay-Effenberger/Effenberger 2008, 13–44, and Asutay-Effenberger/Effenberger 2009, 1–29.
[9] Cf. Effenberger 2005, 35–36.
[10] For a discussion, cf. Mango 2001, 17–28. Future scholarly evaluations of the findings from the *Yenikapı* excavations will certainly help to answer this question, cf. Öztuncay/Karamani Pekin 2007, 164–242.
[11] Mango 2001, 24.
[12] For the most recent evaluation of the land walls, cf. Asutay-Effenberger 2007.
[13] Kalkan/Şahin 1993, 137–147. For a discussion, cf. Asutay-Effenberger 2007, 37–38.
[14] *Cod. Theod.* 15,1,51 (4 April 413). At some sections of the inner ward, graves are still visible.

Beyond their fortifying functions, the Theodosian walls also had a highly symbolic meaning. It was only with the Theodosian dynasty that Constantinople became a major Christian city, and its new walls were a visible indication of imperial power. Part of the stereotypical praise for cities (*laudes urbium*) mentioned the unscalability of the walls in with the same breath as churches, palaces, grand buildings, and the riches of the city "beloved by Christ."[15] During the siege by the Avars in 626, the Khan is said to have caught sight of a woman in magnificent dress striding over the wall – undoubtedly the Virgin Mary, as the inhabitants of Constantinople were certain.[16] Until late into the sixth century, two of the most significant Marian shrines were still located outside the Theodosian land walls: the Church of the Theotokos tes Peges[17] and the Blachernai,[18] "in order that both of them may serve as invincible defenses to the circuit-wall of the city," as Procopius explicitly stated.[19] This was long after Constantinople had become 'Theotokoupolis,' the city of the Theotokos,[20] and was also considered a 'New Jerusalem'. During its over thousand-year history, the imposing structure of the walls impressed besiegers and countless foreign visitors alike. The disappointment over the failure of the city walls was painfully felt after the conquest by the crusaders in 1204, which prompted Niketas Choniates' bitter outcry: "If those things for whose protection you were erected no longer exist, being utterly destroyed by fire and war, for what purpose do you still stand?"[21]

With the completing of the Theodosian land walls, the limit of the city was expanded ca. 1.5 km to the west and its territory increased to fourteen square kilometers. The preserved land walls cover a length of 5650 m. They start at the shore of the Sea of *Marmara* in the south and end at the so-called *Tekfur Sarayı*, a late Byzantine palace complex. Behind this palace, the twelfth century portion of the Blachernai wall starts, which was constructed in the reign of the emperor Manuel II Komnenos (AD 1143–1180).[22] According to previous scholarship, the Theodosian walls coincided with even older ones and ran across the borough of *Mumhane* in the direction of the Golden Horn. In the light of the most recent research, however, this position cannot be upheld: the Theodosian land walls presumably ran in a diagonal course from the area of *Tekfur Sarayı* to the Church of St Demetrius at the Golden Horn.[23] Of this section of the walls, however, no part is preserved.

---

15 Cf. the evidence presented in Fenster 1968.
16 *Chron. Pasch.* ad ann. 626 (trans. Whitby/Whitby 179–180).
17 On this church, cf. Janin 1969, 223–228.
18 On the church, cf. Mango 1998; Effenberger 2016.
19 Proc. *Aed.* 1,3,5–10 (trans. Dewing/Downey 1940, 41).
20 Mango 2000a, 17–25.
21 Niketas Choniates 591,16–18: "εἰ γὰρ ὧν ἕνεκα ἔκτισθε" εἶπον "ἐς τέλος ἤδη ἐξέλιπον, πυρὶ καὶ πολέμῳ ἠμαυρωμένα, τί ὑμῖν ἔτι καὶ τῷ ἑστάναι; καί τίνα περιστελεῖτε μετέπειτα ..." (trans. Magoulias 1984, 325).
22 Most recently Asutay-Effenberger 2013, 253–276; cf. also Asutay-Effenberger 2007, 118–146.
23 A long-standing theory accepted Blachernai as the XIV Region of the city and dated some wall remains (the so-called *Mumhane* Walls) to the Roman period. The written sources, the masonry,

While the sea walls of the city only exhibit a single defense line (curtain walls and towers),[24] the Theodosian land walls consist of three parallel rows (Figs. 2 and 3): the main wall (τὸ μέγας τεῖχος), the outer wall (προτείχισμα/ἔξω τεῖχος), and the moat (τάφρος/σοῦδα). In front of both the main and the outer walls lay wards (hereafter inner and outer ward). The curtain walls of the main wall are 12 m high and 4.80 m thick, with its thickness varying at several positions. At an interval of 50 to 70 m, rectangular and polygonal towers were installed. The polygonal towers are usually located at bends. According to the theory of Philon of Byzantium (ca. 200 BC), the 20 m high towers are only slightly connected to the curtain walls, so that in case of an earthquake the collapse of the whole area could be averted (Fig. 2).[25] Not all towers are preserved, and no contemporary source informs us about their exact number.[26] That said, the walls underwent several changes within the last millennium. Not only were existing towers repaired, but new towers were added. In their rhythm and shape, they differ from the Theodosian concept. Their architectural features and workmanship demonstrate dissimilar characteristics as well. This is clearly visible in the area of the so-called 'Sigma' and especially on the north side of the Lycos creek in the area of *Edirnekapı* (see below) (Fig. 1). In the first construction period, the land wall must have had a minimum of 94 and a maximum of 95 defense towers between the Sea of *Marmara* and *Tekfur Sarayı*. The question of how many towers there were on the lost line between *Tekfur Sarayı* and the Church of St Demetrius cannot be answered.

The u-shaped lower chambers of the towers, which do not have their own rear walls, are accessible from the curtain wall through a high arched niche (Fig. 4). They are covered by different types of vaults or wooden ceilings. In several rectangular towers, a lateral entrance is situated at the flank that opens to the inner ward. The upper stories, which rise above the level of the curtain walls and possess their own rear walls, can be reached via crenellated parapet-walks accessed by a double-flight staircase behind the gates (Fig. 4). Stairs were located at several other sections of the curtain wall walkway. One could reach the uppermost platform of the towers, where the war machines were mounted, through stairs, which were installed on the rear wall of the upper stories of the towers. Only the vaulted upper chambers were used for defensive purposes, and solely here can embrasures be found. The preserved

---

and several architectural peculiarities led to the assumption that the *Mumhane* wall was part of the wall of Heraclius from the seventh century. So far this line has always been connected with a wall segment at the Golden Horn between *Ayvansaray* and the church of St Demetrius. For a detailed discussion, cf. Asutay-Effenberger 2007, 13–27; see also Asutay-Effenberger 2013, 253–276.

24 On the sea walls, cf. Van Millingen 1899 and Janin 1962, 287–300. Cf. also Dirimtekin 1953 and Dirimtekin 1956.
25 Ph. Mech. 5,20–1,80 (ed. Schoene), Ph. Bel. 17–84 (ed. Diels/Schramm).
26 Cristoforo Buondelmonti, *Liber insularum archipelagi* 50 mentioned ninety-six towers: *turres in muro altiori* [sc. in the higher walls] *nonaginta sex*. Cf. Gerola 1931, 271. Many travelers speak of fantastical numbers such as 'a thousand'.

Fig. 2: Theodosian Land Walls, Main Wall, Outer Wall, Outer Ward and the Moat, Photo: N. Asutay-Effenberger.

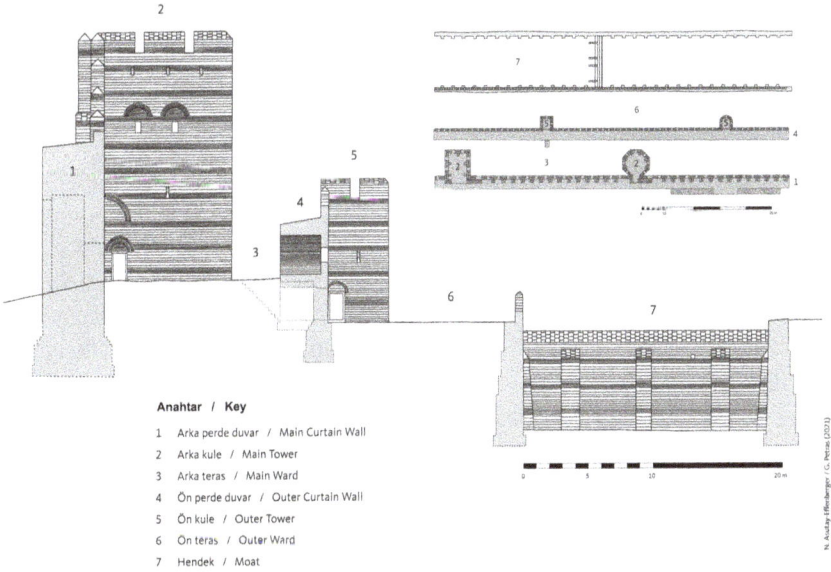

Fig. 3: Cross-Section Reconstruction of the Theodosian Land Walls, N. Asutay-Effenberger and G. Petras, adapted from Krischen 1938, fig. 4.

Fig. 4: Staircase behind the Sulukulekapı, Photo: N. Asutay-Effenberger.

original Theodosian towers usually had two loopholes at the front and three on each flank.[27] At certain intervals, the wall was pierced by the main gates between two gateway-towers (see below), which connect with the major streets or important arterial roads. Yet more small arched posterns are visible on some curtain walls, which correspond with the wards: the archways of the main gates were narrowed in the Middle Byzantine period, usually reusing pieces of the original furnishings.

The outer wall runs 15 m in front of the main wall (Figs. 2 and 3). The 8 m high curtain walls are 3.80 m thick. This line of the fortification includes rectangular or horseshoe shaped towers, which were always arranged between two main towers, through which the effectiveness of the entire wall as a fortification was strengthened. The outer towers could be accessed through an arched opening from the inner ward. Some of them had side gates and communicated with the outer ward. The curtain walls were reinforced through casemates (covered round paths) (Fig. 5). Above the casemates are crenellated parapet-walks. On the same alignment as the main gates, smaller gates were mounted at the outer wall. These were blocked by portcullises (see below).

The date of the construction of the outer wall has preoccupied researchers for a long time. Because of a Greek inscription on the lintel of the *Mevlevihanekapı* (Fig. 6), which mentions the year 447 and speaks of a building time of sixty days, it was occa-

---

27 The first stories, which were used as depots or as guard chambers possess only light/air slits.

Fig. 5: Casemates of the Outer Wall, Photo: N. Asutay-Effenberger.

sionally assumed that the outer line of the fortification was only erected in 447.[28] As Bruno Meyer-Plath and Alfons Maria Schneider have argued, the main wall is not strategically effective without the outer wall, thus both lines had to be planned at the same time.[29] Additionally, an examination of the written sources by the author revealed that the date 447 and the 60-day construction period correspond to a heavy earthquake that would have necessitated thorough repairs.[30] As mentioned above, the main wall was renovated several times throughout its history.

An 18 m wide moat runs along the outer wall, separated from it by 15 m (Fig. 2 and 3).[31] Its depth probably varies depending on the terrain. Its long sides were supported with buttresses. At nineteen points the moat is intersected by transverse walls, which divide it into smaller units. The eastern wall of the moat wall was enhanced with merlons; it gained the look and the function of a third defense line. It is assumed that some fosses were only in the area of the gates in the fifth century

---

28 For detailed discussion, cf. Asutay-Effenberger 2007, 35–53. For a Latin inscription with a comparable legend, which situated on northern console of the outer gateway, see Meyer-Plath/Schneider 1943,133, no 35.
29 Meyer-Plath/Schneider 1943, 17. For reconstruction drawings, cf. Krischen 1938.
30 Cf. note 28 above.
31 There are some deviations in measurements.

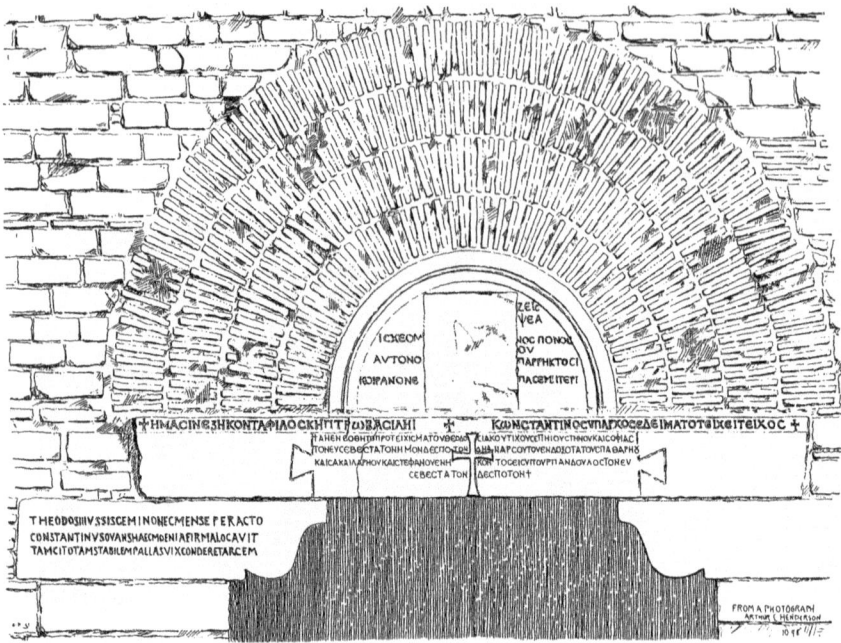

Fig. 6: Mevlevihanekapı, Outer Gate, Inscription, Van Millingen 1899, figure before p. 97.

and the final shape was only achieved around the year AD 1000.[32] Late Byzantine sources mention that the moat was filled with water. Furthermore, Meyer-Plath and Schneider discovered water pipes close to *Topkapı* in the area of the tower No. 63.[33] Originally, wooden bridges spanned the moat in front of the gates. They could be torn down in case of an attack. The stone bridges visible today are Ottoman constructions (Fig. 7). Below tower No. 75 (north of the modern *Adnan Menderes Bulvarı*), the Lycus creek entered the city and originally disembogued in the Sea of *Marmara* at the port of Theodosius (Fig. 1).[34] North of *Silivrikapı* (see below), between towers No. 40 and No. 42, the wall forms a trapezoidal recess, which is called "sigma" in the literature and did probably not belong to the Theodosian conception.

Arched posterns are located in the curtain walls between towers Nos 1–2, 11–12 (only the traces are visible today), 30–31, and 42–43.[35] The first main gate coming from the south is the Golden Gate (Porta Aurea/*Altın Kapı*) between two marble pylons (towers No. 9 and No. 10). Through this entrance, which was once decorated

---

[32] Meyer-Plath/Schneider 1943, 36. Cf. Müller-Wiener 1977, 286 (for the author raising doubts concerning this dating).
[33] Gerola 1931, 271 (Buondelmonti's "View with moat filled with water"). Manuel Chrysolaras 17,8 (German translation: Grabler, Europa 127). On the water pipes, cf. Meyer-Plath/Schneider 1943, 36–37.
[34] This is the modern location of the *Marmaray* main station *Yenikapı*.
[35] For a discussion of the lateral entrances, cf. Asutay-Effenberger 2007, 33–34, 71–72 and 78–83.

Fig. 7: Bridge at the Belgradkapı, Photo: N. Asutay-Effenberger.

Fig. 8: Theodosian Land Walls, Tower No. 18, Photo: N. Asutay-Effenberger.

with sculptures, the Via Egnatia (*strata nova*) led into the city (Figs. 1 and 9).³⁶ The gate owed its name to its gilded doors, and it served as a gate for imperial triumphs and processions throughout Byzantine history, at least into the thirteenth century. The Golden Gate, with its monumental size (66 m wide, 19.40 m high) and its gatehouse with three arched passageways, differs from all other entrances of the fortification. A higher central arch is flanked by two lateral archways. An inscription in golden letters was once mounted on the extrados of both the field and city side of the central entrance arch. The only traces left of the inscription today are some drill holes. Nevertheless, it was possible to decipher the text on this basis. The inscription on the city side read *haec loca Theudosius decorat post fata tyranni* ("Theodosius decorated this place after the demise of the tyrant") and on the field side *aurea saecla gerit qui portam construit auro* ("Golden Ages dawned when the gate was constructed").³⁷

Fig. 9: Golden Gate and Küçük Altın Kapı [old postcard], Private collection.

The inscription has sometimes been connected to the victory of Theodosius I (379–395 AD) over Magnus Maximus, which would suggest that the triumphal gate (or rather, triumphal arch) existed even before the construction of the walls. However,

---

36 Cf. Asutay-Effenberger 2007, 54–61.
37 Meyer-Plath/Schneider 1943, 125 no. 8.

the unfinished sculpture and the junction with the curtain walls on the south make it clear that the gate was only constructed after the completion of the walls, erected rapidly to replace an earlier gate.[38] A new interpretation of some underground remnants discovered in 1927 and in the 1930s confirms this assumption.[39] The emperor mentioned in the inscription therefore has to be identified with Theodosius II, the triumph over an unnamed tyrant refers to the defeat of the usurper John in AD 425.[40] The gate has been modified several times. The u-shaped outer wall with *Küçük Altın Kapı* (Small Golden Gate) in front of the terrace is a 9th century addition.[41]

The first gate in the curtain wall to the north, *Yedikulekapısı*, between towers No. 11 and 12, is an Ottoman construction.[42] Northwards, between the rectangular gateway-towers No. 22 and No. 23, is the so-called *Belgradkapı* gate complex (Figs. 1 and 7). It is usually identified as the Byzantine Xylokerkos gate.[43] It lies at the end of the route, altered by Constantine, of the Via Egnatia (*strata vetus*), the main street that led to the former Golden Gate of the Constantinian Walls. The third milestone of the city was also located here. All these factors lead to the assumption that *Belgradkapı* was the most important gateway of the wall until the construction of the Theodosian Golden Gate.[44] *Silivrikapı*, between two polygonal gateway-towers (Nos 35 and 36), and the Kalagros Gate between the unequal rectangular gateway-towers (Nos 39 and 40) are the next entrances to the north (Fig. 10). *Mevlevihanekapı*, which is protected by the rectangular gateway-towers No. 50 and No. 51, is the best-preserved entrance (Figs. 1 and 6).[45] Here the narrowing of the middle arch in the main gate as well as the holes of the portcullis on the outer gate are clearly visible, offering the best opportunity for studying a gate complex. The above-mentioned inscription on the lintel of the outer gate that refers to the year AD 447 was given the caption εἰς τὴν πόρταν (sic!) τοῦ Ῥησίου (Rhesion gate in the Anthologia Graeca, which establishes its original name during the Byzantine era.[46] However, according to the sources, the gate was also called Polyandrion/Myriandrion ('many men/a thousand men') in colloquial speech because of the cemeteries that were situated there.[47]

The Gate of St Romanos (Figs. 1 and 11) lies in a short distance further north, at the south side of the modern main artery (*Turgut Özal Bulvarı*), between the rectangular gateway towers No. 59 and No. 60.[48] This entrance does not have a Turkish

---

38 For detailed discussion and sources, cf. Asutay-Effenberger 2007, 54–61.
39 Macridy/Casson 1931, 63–84; for an interpretation, cf. Asutay-Effenberger 2007, 57–71.
40 Cf. Asutay-Effenberger 2007, 54–61.
41 Asutay-Effenberger 2007, 61–71.
42 Asutay-Effenberger 2007, 78–83.
43 Asutay-Effenberger 2007, 86 n. 349, cf. Meyer-Plath/Schneider 1943, 63.
44 For a discussion, cf. Asutay-Effenberger 2007, 60–61.
45 Meyer-Plath/Schneider 1943, 66–67.
46 Diehl. *Anth. Lyr. Graec.* 4,691.
47 Asutay-Effenberger 2007, 110.
48 Asutay-Effenberger 2007, 87–94.

Fig. 10: Hypogeum at the Silivrikapı, Photo: N. Asutay-Effenberger.

name. Until the discovery of an inscription on the preserved marble lintel of the main gateway in 2003, it was believed to be a 'military' gate.[49]

---

[49] Asutay-Effenberger 2003, 1–4, and Asutay-Effenberger 2004, 18–20. Philippides/Hanak 2011, 335 with note 167 argue that there were no gateway-towers, no inscriptions and no evidence for the street having been connected to the gate. Additionally, the term 'πόρτα' is only attested after the year 1204. They furthermore believe that this lintel might have been relocated to this gate by the workers during

Fig. 11: Gate of St Romanos, Photo: N. Asutay-Effenberger.

The inscription reads πόρτα μέση εἰσφέρουσα ἐπὶ τὸν ἅγιον Ῥωμανόν ("The middle gate, leading to Saint Romanos"), which does not leave any doubts that this is in fact the Gate of St Romanos (Fig. 12 a–b). It was one of the most important entrances into the city until the Ottoman conquest of Constantinople in 1453. Behind this gate ran the extension of the Mese, the 'middle street' of Constantinople. The gate was the center of the wall section called Mesoteichion.[50]

Fig. 12 a–b: Gate of St Romanos, Inscription, Photo: N. Asutay-Effenberger.

---

the construction of the former *Millet* Street (today's *Turgut Özal Bulvarı*) in the 1950s. The inscription on the lintel is without doubt from the Theodosian era, as Feissel 2006, 63 no. 196 has demonstrated, and the word πόρτα was used long before 1204 (cf. Asutay-Effenberger 2007, 87–98). The term could also be read in the inscription of the Golden Gate. Moreover, an eighteenth-century map of the city of Istanbul should be mentioned here, where remains of an old street outside St Romanos Gate are recorded (Kauffer/Lechevalier/Choiseul-Gouffier 1822, plate 68). But even more importantly, an organic relation between the lintel and all other architectural elements of the entrance could clearly be observed before its removal from its place in recent years (the broken lintel today lies upside-down on the ground in front of the gate). For further discussion, cf. the review of Philippides/Hanak 2011 by Michael Angold, www.history.ac.uk/reviews/review/1101 (last accessed August 8, 2022). See also Effenberger 2017, 191–225, esp. 200–210. The term "military gate" was never used in the Byzantine sources and is a 19th century invention!

50 For a discussion, cf. Asutay-Effenberger 2007, 106–110.

Topkapı is the last gate south of the Lycus creek. It stands between the rectangular gateway-towers No. 65 and No. 66 (Fig. 1). The entrance was mistakenly identified as the Gate of St Romanos, until the discovery of the above-mentioned inscription in 2003. There is a high probability that the *Topkapı* was the Byzantine Gate of Pempton.[51] The first main entrance north of the Lycus is *Sulukulekapı* (north of today's *Adnan Menderes Bulvarı*), which is flanked by rectangular towers No. 77 and No. 78 (Figs. 1, 4 and 13). The complex used to be incorrectly identified as the Gate of Pempton due to the erroneous equation of *Topkapı* with the Gate of St Romanos, but also based on mistaken interpretations of the sources and ignorance of the Ottoman literature. It is in fact the Byzantine Gate of Charisios.[52]

Fig. 13: Sulukulekapı [Field Side], Photo: N. Asutay-Effenberger.

The last main entrance north of the *Sulukulekapı* is *Edirnekapı* between the polygonal gateway towers No. 86 and No. 87 (Fig. 1).[53] Earlier research associated the complex with the Gate of Charisios.[54] Despite this, the Gate of St John mentioned in written and visual sources was never taken into consideration. The Gate of St John stood

---

51 For a discussion, cf. Asutay-Effenberger 2007, 94–96.
52 Meyer-Plath/Schneider 1943, 70, and Asutay-Effenberger 2007, 96–107; cf. also Asutay-Effenberger 2009, 29–31.
53 Meyer-Plath/Schneider 1943, 70–71, and Asutay-Effenberger 2007, 96–107.
54 Meyer-Plath/Schneider 1943, 70.

in this location and got its name from the nearby Church of St John. Only a few steps further along, the wall is today interrupted by *Fevzi Paşa* Street. The wall continues on the other side of the street with further towers until the *Tekfur Sarayı*. Behind the *Tekfur Sarayı*, the Blachernai Wall starts in the direction of the Golden Horn.⁵⁵ Although inscriptions are observable at many segments of the wall, apart from some gates (Golden Gate, *Belgradkapı* and *Mevlevihanekapı*), Theodosius was nowhere mentioned by name.⁵⁶

Masonry and Spolia

The Theodosian Land Wall is the earliest monumental structure featuring double-shell layered masonry with alternating ashlar and brick courses (Figs. 2 and 3).⁵⁷ The brick courses reinforced the construction and give the monument its polychromatic effect. The five-layered bricks are usually 37 × 37 × 4.5–5 cm. The layer of reddish mortar containing brick fragments is almost as thick as the bricks. The sharp-edged and accurately fitted limestone ashlars differ from tower to tower in their number of layers and only feature small joints. These characteristics of the Theodosian original construction are especially noticeable at towers Nos 14, 16, 17, 71 as well as occasionally at their neighboring curtain walls (Fig. 8).⁵⁸ The outer wall contains uneven ashlars and wider joints and was large parts of it were thoroughly renovated in Middle Byzantine times. The walls were damaged several times by natural disasters such as earthquakes, or by enemy attacks, and constantly repaired. Until the tenth/eleventh centuries, the repair works usually copied the Theodosian workmanship, however, re-used bricks and ashlars were often irregular, and the mortar layers were thicker. The masonry from the time of the emperor Michael II (AD 820–829) and his son Theophilos (AD 829–842) forms a contrast to this pattern, particularly in the segments of *Edirnekapı*, where big ashlars dominate the lower portions of the wall, with bricks used in the upper portion.⁵⁹ The wall sections of the eleventh and twelfth centuries demonstrate the recessed brick technique. In late Byzantine times, the masonry often featured one to three rows of bricks between the ashlars. There are also vertically mounted bricks between the ashlars. Epigraphically dated to the fifteenth century, these parts are usually listed without bricks. The polychrome arching at several sections, for example at the back of the gate at the Sigma, should be mentioned as another characteristic of the late Byzantine period.

Besides the *spolia* which once decorated the Golden Gate of the Theodosian walls, as mentioned in the written sources, there are hardly any other *spolia* to be

---

55 Asutay-Effenberger 2013, 253–276.
56 For the inscriptions in *Belgradkapı* and *Mevlevihanekapı*, see Asutay-Effenberger 2007, 35–38.
57 On the masonry, cf. Asutay-Effenberger 2007, 173–181.
58 Asutay-Effenberger 2007, 173–181.
59 Asutay-Effenberger 2019, 143–154.

found in the original late-antique parts of the walls. Obviously, the Constantinopolitan walls of Theodosius II were conceived as a prestigious new building project for which the re-use of older building materials was not considered appropriate. The most frequent use of *spolia* derive from the collapsed sections of the fortification such as ashlar and brick. Other architectural sculptures from some unknown monuments, fragments of the fallen inscriptions, tombstones were also used as building material, decorative, or apotropaic elements. All these instances of the use of *spolia* predominantly appear in parts of the walls which were renovated or added in the tenth century as well as in late Byzantine time, for example in the area between *Sulukulekapı* and *Edirnekapı* or near *Mevlevihanekapı*. The tenth century relief wall (among others with Herakles depictions) of the u-shaped construction in front of the Golden Gate can be mentioned here as the most imposing use of *spolia*.[60]

The Late-Antique Walls of Jerusalem

The Roman colony of Aelia Capitolina was founded in the second century over the remains of the Second Temple period Jewish city of Jerusalem.[61] The Roman city mostly ignored the remains of the Jewish city and made no use of the ruined fortifications, known as the First Wall, the Second Wall, and the Third Wall of the Second Temple Period.[62] The only exception was a segment of the western wall of the First Wall, where the Roman Tenth Legion was stationed.[63] It is widely accepted that the newly-founded colony of Aelia Capitolina was unwalled and its limits were marked by monumental, free-standing city gates.[64]

The accepted view associates the construction of Jerusalem's Late Roman fortifications with the departure of the *legio X Fretensis* during the reign of Diocletian, and suggests that around the year AD 300, a city wall following more or less the course of the present-day Ottoman city wall was built around the Roman colony.[65] The wall was expanded to incorporate Zion in the mid-fifth century, probably by the empress Eudocia who then resided in Jerusalem. Another opinion proposes that Aelia Capitolina remained unwalled throughout its existence and that only at a later date was Jerusalem surrounded with a wide circuit wall, which enclosed the present-day old city

---

60 Asutay-Effenberger 2007, 61–71.
61 For summaries on the archaeological remains of Aelia Capitolina and the city's layout, cf. Vincent/Abel 1914, 1–88, Geva 1993a, Tsafrir 1999a, Weksler-Bdolah 2020. Many scholars have suggested reconstructions for the city plan of Aelia Capitolina, e.g. Germer-Durand 1892, Bar 1993, Magness 2000, Eliav 2003, Avni 2005, Ehrlich/Bar 2004 *inter alia*.
62 Ios. *Bell. Iud.* 5,136 and 142–149.
63 Ios. *Bell. Iud.* 7,1–4.
64 Avi-Yonah 1976b, Geva 1993, Tsafrir 1999, 136, Bahat 1990 and Mazor 2004, 109–119.
65 Hamilton 1952, Avi-Yonah 1954, 147, Tsafrir 1975, 17–19, Tsafrir 1999a, 140–141, and Bahat 1990.

of Jerusalem, Mount Zion, the City of David, and the Ophel.[66] According to this proposal, the construction of the wall was probably related to the Christianization of the city and took place at some time during the fourth or fifth centuries (late-antique times).[67]

The earliest cartographic representation of Jerusalem appears on the Madaba Map, where it is depicted as an oval-shaped city surrounded with walls (Fig. 14).[68] These walls included the present-day Old City, Mount Zion, the City of David, and the Ophel hill. Seventeen square towers were integrated into the course of the walls, and another five or six towers may be reconstructed in the ruined part of the mosaic.[69]

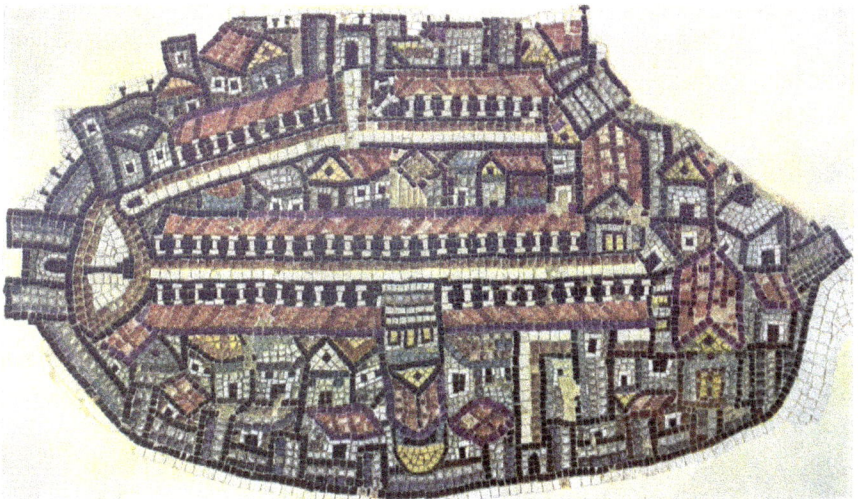

Fig. 14: Map of Jerusalem in the mosaic floor at Madaba, after Vincent and Abel 1914, Pl. XXX, copied by P.M. Gisler O.S.B.

Three main arched city gates were incorporated into the walls in the north, east, and west. The Madaba representation of the mid-sixth century sets a *terminus ante quem* for the construction of the walls. Many segments of the late-antique city wall are known around the circuit of the Old City of Jerusalem (Fig. 15). They were exposed

---

66 Geva 1993b, 761–762, Wilkinson 1990, 90, Wilkinson 2002, 51–53 and 314 with map 11, as well as Weksler-Bdolah 2006–2007, Weksler-Bdolah 2007, Weksler-Bdolah 2011, 418–420, and Weksler-Bdolah 2020, 138–140.
67 Geva 1993, 771–772. The chronology of the Roman and Byzantine periods used below reflects common scholarly modes of periodization. In Israeli research, especially on the history and archaeology of the Levant and the city of Jerusalem, a different periodization is common: 63 BC–70/135 AD (Early Roman), 70/135–324 AD (Roman/Late Roman), 324–636 AD (Byzantine).
68 Avi Yonah 1954.
69 Tsafrir 1999b, 345.

below the courses of the present-day Ottoman walls in the north and the west, around Mount Zion in the south and along the City of David and the Ophel hill in the east. Remains were exposed under the Ottoman walls on both sides of Damascus Gate (Fig. 16),[70] under the courses of the western Ottoman walls near David's Tower in the citadel,[71] further north, under the road which enters Jaffa Gate today,[72] and under the building of the Imperial Hotel, documented in the late nineteenth century.[73]

South of Jaffa Gate, the walls were documented in the Armenian Garden[74] as well as on the slopes of Mount Zion.[75] A southeastern corner of a gate-tower in the southeast corner of the walls, which was documented in the late nineteenth century by Frederick Bliss and Archibald Dickie[76] and re-excavated by Kathleen Kenyon,[77] was recently re-discovered in our excavations on behalf of the Israel Antiquities Authority (Figs. 17 and 18).[78] On the Ophel hill, segments of the walls have been investigated in the past (Fig. 19).[79]

The Mode of Construction and Perimeter of Jerusalem's Walls

The walls' mode of construction is similar around their entire circuit. The wall is built of ashlar, limestone blocks, arranged in levelled courses. Some of the blocks were originally prepared for the wall, as indicated by their smooth faces and medium size (height ca. 0.50–0.70 m, length ca. 0.7–1.40 m). Others were re-used Hasmonean blocks or re-cut Herodian blocks. The Hasmonean blocks were slightly smaller, and they were characterized by faces with margins along four sides and a central protruding boss. The re-cut Herodian blocks were the largest (height ca. 1 m and length ca. 1.7–2 m). Their faces had margins along two or three sides, and the central boss was flattened. Based upon their monumental size and shape, these blocks presumably originated from the ruins of King Herod's monumental buildings and were cut and reduced to fit their new setting, therefore having margins only along two or three instead of all four sides. In rare cases double-bossed blocks were used as well. The lower courses of the walls were laid in a stepped manner so that every course was

---

70 Hamilton 1944, fig. 3, Turler/De Groot/Solar 1979 and Avni/Baruch/Weksler-Bdolah 2001.
71 Johns 1950 and Geva 1983.
72 Sion/Puni 2011.
73 Merrill 1886, 20, Schick 1887 and Vincent/Steve 1954.
74 Tushingham 1985.
75 Bliss/Dickie 1894, Chen/Margalit/Pixner 1994 and the recent excavation of Zelinger 2010.
76 Bliss/Dickie 1898, 94–96 with plate XI.
77 Kenyon 1974, 269 with plate 6.
78 Weksler-Bdolah/Lavi 2013.
79 Warren/Conder 1884 Mazar 1995 and Mazar 2007, 181–200.

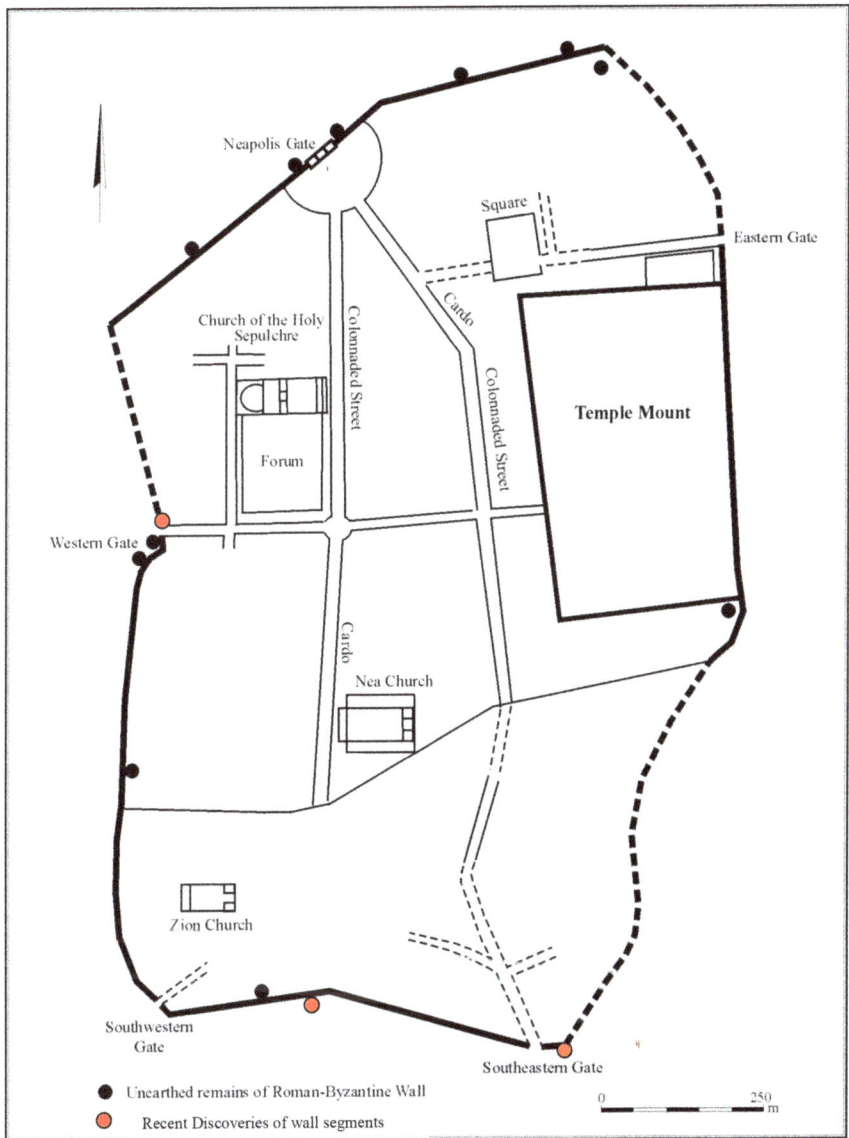

Fig. 15: The Early Byzantine city wall. Dots mark places where segments of the wall were exposed, red dots are the recent excavations finds, after Tsafrir 2000. Drawing: Natalya Zak, courtesy of the Israel Antiquities Authority.

set back in relation to the course which it overlaid, whereas the upper courses of the walls were laid vertically one above the other.

The similarity and the contemporary dating of all wall segments supports their interpretation as parts of a single wide circuit wall which was constructed some time before the mid-fifth century – a date supported by results of the recent excava-

Fig. 16: The Early Byzantine wall near Damascus Gate, after Hamilton 1944, Pl. 1.1.

Fig. 17: Late Roman wall cut by the corner of SE tower of Byzantine Wall. Looking north, after Weksler-Bdolah/Lavi 2012.

Fig. 18: Corner of SE tower of Byzantine Wall. Looking north, after Weksler-Bdolah/Lavi 2012.

tions. Inside Jaffa Gate, the excavators suggested a late-fourth century date for the construction of the wall.[80] On Mount Zion, the excavator dated a segment of a plaster floor that possibly abutted the inner face of the wall, but was damaged when the upper courses of the wall were robbed, as "not prior to 409 AD,"[81] and concluded the wall was built by the empress Eudocia in the mid-fifth century. However, an earlier possible date for the wall's construction in the late-fourth or early-fifth century should be considered, since the wall already existed once the floor was laid.[82] In another excavation,[83] the foundation trench of the wall's southeastern tower cut a late Roman wall (second to fourth centuries), clearly postdating it. The fact that no remains of the late-antique walls are known below the southern line of the Ottoman walls (which has been suggested in the past as the southern line of Aelia Capitolina's walls built in ca. AD 300), makes it less viable that Jerusalem's late-antique walls were built in two phases.

The perimeter of the walls enclosed the areas of the present-day Old City of Jerusalem, Mount Zion, the City of David, and the Ophel hill. The course was probably dictated by the size of the settled area of the city at this time, and by the natural top-

---

80 Sion/Puni 2011.
81 Zelinger 2010.
82 Weksler-Bdolah 2011.
83 Weksler-Bdolah/Lavi 2013.

Fig. 19: The Early Byzantine wall in the Ophel excavations. Looking north, after after Mazar 2007, 191, Fig. 17.14: Courtesy of E. Mazar.

ography. During their construction, remains of the Second Temple Period fortifications were integrated into the course of the walls, and also partly dictated its route. In the north, between Damascus Gate and Herod's Gate, the late-antique walls overlapped the route suggested as the line of the Second Wall.[84] In the west (north of David's Tower) the walls followed a segment of a wall documented at the end of the nineteenth century which has been suggested as the route of the Second or Third Wall.[85] South of David's Tower and around Mount Zion, the City of David, and the Ophel, the walls overlapped the route of the First Wall. Some of the old fortifications were incorporated into the late-antique walls, such as David's Tower and the eastern wall of the Temple Mount. The integration and usage of older fortifications within new lines of fortifications is a well-known fact. In Jerusalem, for example, the Hasmonean First Wall from the Second Temple period followed the course of Hezekiah's Wall of the First Temple period, integrating parts of older fortifications within its route.[86] Many sections along the Ottoman City walls of Jerusalem were built directly above or somewhat to the side of the remains of wall segments and towers from various periods, ranging in date from the Second Temple Period, to late-antique and medieval times.[87] A similar phenomenon has been documented in Italy, where fortifications in many towns were reconstructed in the third century incorporating gates and segments of previous walls.[88]

The walls' circuit was influenced by the size of the city at the time of its construction. The wide perimeter united the area of Aelia Capitolina with two hills which were part of the core of Biblical Jerusalem, but which were outside the city's boundaries in Roman times: the southeastern hill (the area of the Ophel and the City of David) and the south-western hill, which later became known as Christian Zion, which corresponds with areas of the modern Jewish and the Armenian Quarters within the Ottoman wall, as well as Mount Zion outside the wall. Since it appears that the southwestern hill was the campsite of the *legio X Fretensis*, it was not considered part of the city's boundaries in Roman times. Moreover, following the departure of the legion which was transferred to Aila in the late third century AD, the site of the camp remained uninhabited for some decades, perhaps due to its military ownership. It was finally released to civic use not before the second half of the fourth century.[89] In all likelihood, the construction of the city walls post-dated the expansion of the city into the empty areas of the southern hills, a process which now can be more accurately dated thanks to new archaeological material: the building of private residences on the southeastern hill started in the first half of the fourth century,[90] while the southwestern hill was released to civic use and predominantly became the home to several Christian monasteries, hermitages, and churches from the second half of the

---

84 Avi-Yonah 1968, 124 fig. 6.
85 Merill 1866, 23–24, Schick 1887, Vincent 1902, Vincent/Steve 1954, 96–98, Geva 1981, 64, and Seligman 2002.
86 Cf., for example, areas W and X-2, in Geva 2000, 134 and 206.
87 Weksler-Bdolah 2011.
88 Cf. Ward-Perkins 1984, 192.
89 Weksler-Bdolah 2014 and Weksler-Bdolah 2020, 134–137.
90 Gordon 2007 and Ben-Ami/Tchekhanovets 2013.

fourth century onwards. A recent excavation dated the external wall of the so-called King David's Tomb building to the late fourth century.[91] This building is traditionally identified as part of the late-antique Church of Zion. The construction of the city walls unified the area of the Roman city, the abandoned campsite of the *legio X Fretensis*, and the southeastern hill into one big entity: the holy city of Jerusalem as depicted in the Madaba mosaic.

The Use of Spolia

The Jerusalemite builders made extensive use of Hasmonean and Herodian ashlars in secondary use which were placed in the facing parts of the walls, so that a late-antique visitor to the city would necessarily see them. In addition to this, some re-used architectural fragments of distinctly classical carving were discovered in the core of the wall on Mount Zion.[92] The walls' construction was precisely executed all around its circuit with great care. The stone courses were leveled and arranged according to the size and texture of the stones, thus creating a unified homogenous appearance. It is obvious that the wall was built of carefully selected stones, medium-sized ashlars that were purposely hewn for this matter, Hasmonean stones, and Herodian blocks were used for the facing of the wall, whereas other carved masonry was used for the core. Just as in Constantinople, where all parts of the late-antique walls were newly built, the facing side of the Jerusalemite walls was designed in a manner that must have impressed the visitors to the city. The monumental appearance of the wall was created not only by its beauty, but also by the fact that the space immediately around the wall, both inside and out, was left vacant of buildings. Nowhere along the wall have remains of abutting structures been discovered, thus verifying the legal status of city walls and gates as *res sanctae* – holy things, which could not become the object of private ownership.[93]

The extensive use of *spolia* characterized the late-antique walls of Jerusalem, like buildings in many other cities of the Empire. The re-use of classical building materials as a symbol of the victory of Christianity over its predecessors while maintaining the connection to the classical heritage has been noted by many scholars.[94] In Jerusalem, Christianity rivaled the memory of Judaism more than it competed with paganism. The construction of the late-antique walls, which largely depended on the usage of stones from the ruined Temple Mount, or from other Second Temple Period Jewish buildings, can therefore be interpreted as a representation in stone of the vic-

---

[91] Reem 2013, 239.
[92] Chen/Margalit/Pixner 1994, 80.
[93] Johnson 1983, 62–63.
[94] Tsafrir 1998, Ward-Perkins 1984, 203–228, Wharton 1995, Saradi-Mendelovici 1990.

tory of Christianity over Judaism.⁹⁵ Moreover, the integration of monumental Herodian stones in the walls attest to the lesser importance of the Herodian monuments at the time of the walls' construction, and probably also to an explicit imperial permission to re-use them, as otherwise this would have been prohibited by law.⁹⁶ However, the walls were built about 300 years after the destruction of the Jewish city, and it might be argued that the builders of the wall used the abundant stones without recognizing them as Jewish. Yet, the selective choice of *spolia* only of Jewish origin does suggest that this was done on purpose, reflecting the builders' involvement and struggle with the Jewish history of Jerusalem.

However, the use of *spolia* in late-antique buildings and in particular in city walls can also be explained as a practical solution, making it possible to quickly remove ruined buildings, for example after an earthquake. This might be true for Jerusalem as well, which suffered a severe earthquake in AD 363, which was described in several historical documents, including a letter attributed to the city's bishop, Cyril of Jerusalem.⁹⁷ The damage caused by the earthquake is also attested in the archaeological evidence elsewhere in the city. Recently, a peristyle house of the fourth century whose destruction can be dated to the year AD 363, has been excavated south of the Temple Mount.⁹⁸ The lack of any archaeological evidence relating to the earthquake in any segment of the late-antique city walls does suggest that they were built later than AD 363. However, the meticulous construction of the late-antique walls as well as their overall shape shows that they were not built in haste or in war times, but were rather planned in advance and aimed at reflecting the prosperity, the high status, and wealth of the city at the time of construction. In addition to defending the holy city, they also demonstrated aesthetic beauty, which impressed the observers and mirrored the important status of Jerusalem.⁹⁹

Who Built the Walls of Jerusalem?

The walls' construction can be seen as part of a period abounding in building activity in Jerusalem in the fourth and fifth centuries, which was affiliated with the city's rise

---

95 Euseb. *d.e.* 3,140–141 describes Roman public buildings, which used the Jewish Temple's stones; cf. Tsafrir 1975, 95–96. It is possible that the builders of the late anitque walls would have been able to also find Herodian stones in the ruins of more recent, pagan buildings.
96 Cassiod. *Var.* 3,49 (ed. Fridh/Halpron – Lund 1973, CCSL 96) mentions an example from Catania, where the emperor's permission was requested in order to use the ruined amphitheatre's building materials for the reconstruction of the city walls. This indicated that the use of *spolia* was not spontaneous in late antiquity. Ruins had a legal status and a specific imperial decree was required in order to use them. Permission was granted or denied according to their state of preservation, their location, their symbolic significance or their aesthetic value; cf. Ward-Perkins 1984, 206–218.
97 Brock 1976, 103, and Brock 1977.
98 Ben-Ami/Tchekhanovets 2013.
99 Gregory 1982, 56–57.

in status and the advancement of Christianity. The reason for Jerusalem's importance in late antiquity was primarily religious and derived from its uniqueness as the physical center of Christianity and its status as a holy city. Even though no imperial building inscriptions from late-antique Jerusalem are (yet) known, the involvement of imperial and provincial authorities in the construction of the walls has often been suggested, prompted by the involvement of a late-antique empress alleged by the sources. This leads to the question of who funded the resources for the walls and what implications such a case of imperial involvement would have for Jerusalem. Around the year AD 400, city walls were constructed in several important cities of Palestine, such as the provincial capitals of Palaestina Prima and Palaestina Secunda – Caesarea Maritima and Scythopolis – as well as in the important city of Aila at the Red Sea in Palaestina Tertia.[100] Perhaps, Jerusalem, which began to flourish and underwent urban development due to the impact of Christianity, followed suit. This may be connected with the administrative reorganization of the area around this time, but perhaps also with security problems and the fear of barbarian invasions that shook the west of the Empire.

The evidence from the written sources confirms the dating of the walls' construction between the late fourth and the mid-fifth century.[101] In his account of the life of Peter the Iberian, the *Vita Petri Hiberi*,[102] John Rufus states that Jerusalem was unwalled at the time of Constantine: "When it was rebuilt by the Christian Emperor Constantine, the Holy City, Jerusalem, at first was still sparsely populated and had no [city] wall, since the first [city] wall had been destroyed by the Romans. There were few houses and [few] inhabitants."[103] Many pilgrims, for example the Pilgrim of Bordeaux, Egeria, as well as Paula and Jerome, visited Jerusalem during the course

---

[100] On Caesarea Maritima, cf. Lehmann 1994, on Scythopolis, cf. Tsafrir/Foerster 1997, 102, and Mazor 2004, 28, and on Aila, cf. Parker 2003, 332.

[101] Sh. Weksler-Bdolah would like express her gratitude to Dr Leah di Segni for her help in translating and discussing the various sources mentioned below.

[102] The account was written in the late fifth century probably by John Rufus and is preserved in a Syriac and a Georgian translation. The Syriac version was edited and translated into German by Raabe 1895 and translated into English by Horn/Phenix 2008. The Georgian version was translated into English by Lang 1976, 57–80. Some passages of the text exist in Hebrew translations by A. Horvitz, cf. Tsafrir 1975, 37–38, Tsafrir 1999, 303, and Bitton-Ashkelony 1989, 108.

[103] Ioh. Ruf. *Vit. Petr. Hib.* 64 (ed. Horn/Phenix = Raabe 1895, 44), cf. Tsafrir 1975, 37–38 as well as Tsafrir 1999b, 274–275 and 303. Yoram Tsafrir doubted the credibility of John Rufus' testimony, however, given that the information provided in this passage is in accordance with other fourth- and fifth-century accounts, it seems that one should accept it. Moreover, the emphasis on the fact that the city was unwalled in the times of Constantine, whereas Peter the Iberian, who arrived in 437/438 entered through 'holy walls' (see below), adds to the historicity of the description. The Georgian version gives the following passage: "At this time, the holy city of Jerusalem was still lacking in inhabitants, as well as being deprived of walls, since the former walls had been destroyed by the Romans," cf. Lang 1976, 65–66, which implies that Jerusalem was deprived of walls when Peter the Iberian visited the city.

of the fourth century.[104] Their reports reflect the emergence of Jerusalem's sacred topography, the construction of churches in holy places, and the development of a specific local liturgy.[105] The pilgrims' acquaintance with the limits of the city is obvious. The pilgrim of Bordeaux left Jerusalem to climb Zion,[106] Paula "entered Jerusalem", and "passing on, she climbed Zion."[107] According to Egeria, Jerusalem was entered and exited through a city gate.[108] It appears that the city domain was well defined and marked by city gates, or some other boundary markers. A circuit wall was not mentioned in any of these accounts, most likely, it seems, because no such wall existed at that time. Indeed, it is possible to argue that the circuit wall was not important, and therefore not described by the pilgrims, but such a claim ignores the considerable significance of city walls in late antiquity. Furthermore, the reference of the writers to segments of older walls and ruined gates encountered in Zion and near the pool of Siloam[109] indicates that they in fact paid attention to fortifications, considered them important, and wrote about them even when they lay in ruins. It is reasonable to assume that if a circuit wall had existed when they visited Jerusalem in the fourth century, they would not have failed to mention it. Moreover, the description and reference to the city walls in the fifth-century accounts (once the walls were already built), supports the assumption that the late-antique city walls were not ignored.

The walls of Jerusalem are first mentioned by Eucherius, in his letter to Faustinus, written in the first half of the fifth century: "The site of the city is almost forced into a circular shape, and is enclosed by a lengthy wall, which now embraces Mount Zion, though this was once just outside."[110] The description fits with Jerusalem as

---

104 On the *Itinerarium Burdigalense*, cf. the commentaries by Tsafrir 1975, 32–34 and 91–94, Wilkinson 1981, 123–147, and Limor 1998, 30–34. On the *Itinerarium Egeriae*, cf. Wilkinson 1981, 122–147, and Limor 1998, 88–114, and on Paula and Jerome, cf. Hier. *ep.* 108 with the commentaries and discussions in Tsafrir 1975, 113, Limor 1998, 142–143, and Wilkinson 2002, 79–92.
105 For detailed studies, cf. Wilkinson 1981, Wilkinson 2002, Limor 1998, Limor 1999, Hunt 1982, Tsafrir 1975, Tsafrir 1999 as well as the references given below.
106 *Itin. Burdig.* 592: *Item exeuntibus Hierusalem, ut ascendas Sion* ("Moreover, as you leave Jerusalem to climb Zion").
107 Hier. *Ep.* 108,9: *ingressa est Hierosolymam*. Paula passed on her left the tomb of Queen Helena of Adiabene and then entered Jerusalem.
108 *Itin. Eg.* 36,3 and 43,7.
109 For the wall near the pool of Siloam, cf. *Itin. Burdig.* 592,1: *in ualle iuxta murum est piscine* ("in the valley beside the wall is the pool"), for the wall of Zion, cf. *Itin. Burdig.* 592,5: *intus autem intra murum Sion* ("inside the wall of Sion"). Ruined gates are mentioned in Hier. ep. 108,9: *non eas portas, quas hodie cernimus in fauillam et cinerem dissolutas* ("not meaning the gates we see now, which have been reduced to dust and ashes").
110 Eucherius 6,25,3 (Freypont 1965, 237–243). The account was translated and interpreted by Tsafrir 1975, 132–134 (Hebrew); Limor 1999, 159–160 (Hebrew) and Wilkinson 2002, 94–98 (English). It is widely accepted to relate the account to bishop Eucherius of Lyons, who died between 449–455 AD. However, the formula *ut fertur* in the title of Freypont's edition, implies that at least in the editor's eyes, the account may not be authentic.

portrayed in the Madaba Map and provides a *terminus ante quem* for the construction of the circuit wall before Eucherius' death. Yet, the arrival of Peter the Iberian in Jerusalem, ca. AD 437–438, may set an earlier *terminus ante quem* for the construction of the circuit wall, relying on the narrative provided by John Rufus:

> When they had reached the outskirts of the holy city of Jerusalem which they loved, they saw from a high place five stades away the lofty roof of the holy church of the Resurrection, shining like the morning sun, and cried aloud, 'See, that is Sion the city of our deliverance!' They fell down upon their faces, and from there onwards they crept upon their knees, frequently kissing the soil with their lips and eyes, until they were within the holy walls (Syriac:'shure qaddishe') and had embraced the site of the sacred cross on Golgotha.[111]

As the sense of ܫܘܪܐ ('shura') in Syriac is usually 'city walls,' the description seems to attest to the existence of fortifications in Jerusalem when Peter entered the city in AD 437–438,[112] while it cannot be ruled out that reference is being made to ruined fortifications such as the 'Zion wall' which was mentioned by the Pilgrim of Bordeaux in the west, or the Temple Mount's wall in the east.[113]

A number of accounts from the sixth century (Malalas, Cassiodorus, the Piacenza Pilgrim, and the Chronicon Paschale)[114] attest to the involvement of the empress Eudocia in rebuilding of the walls in Jerusalem, influenced by Psalm 51:18: 'Let it be thy pleasure (εὐδοκία) to do good to Sion, to build anew the walls of Jerusalem'.[115] The accounts vary, stating that Eudocia enlarged the city and surrounded its circumference with better walls, improved their condition, or renewed the whole circuit of the Jerusalem walls. Modern scholars suggest interpreting these statements as reflect-

---

[111] John Rufus *Vita Petri Hiberi* 38 (= Raabe 26–27), trans. Lang 1976, 54. The Georgian version is slightly shorter, but very close to the Syriac version, cf. Bitton-Ashkeloni 1999, 107–108. Coming from Constantinople by foot, Peter and his companions could have reached Jerusalem from the west, north or east, depending on the route they used. Their first sight of Jerusalem, while standing on a high place, may allow to specify on this this: The view of the Church of the Holy Sepulcher, opposite of it the Church of Ascension on the top of the Mount of Olives, as provided in the Syriac version of the *Vita*. This description suggests that their viewpoint was a high place northwest of the present day Old City of Jerusalem (maybe near the so-called Russian Compound), and their entrance took place, accordingly, through one of the western or northern gates.
[112] Cf. Payne Smith, s.v. "ܫܘܪܐ" p. 568, given 'city walls' and 'bulwark' as the most common translation. However, we cannot exclude the possibility that John Rufus, by using this expression, meant the precinct walls of the Church of the Holy Sepulcher or the Second Temple Period walls of the Temple Mount visible to travelers who were coming to Jerusalem from the Jericho road – or even the remains of the Second Temple Period 'Zion wall' mentioned by the Pilgrim of Bordeaux (see above). Shlomit Weksler-Bdolah would like to express her gratitude to Sebastian Brock and Brouria Bitton-Ashkeloni for discussion on the Syriac terminology.
[113] Shlomit Weksler-Bdolah would like to thank Leah Di Segni for her helpful remarks relating this account.
[114] Ioh. Mal. *Chron.* (357–358, Dind.), Cassiod. *Exp. in Ps.* 50 (CC 97, 468), *Itin. Plac.* 1c (confusing her name), and *Chron. Pasch.* ad ann. 585.
[115] Cf. also Hunt 1982, 221–248.

ing Eudocia's renewal of the ancient wall around Zion (the Second Temple Period's 'First Wall'), therefore naming it 'Eudocia's wall',[116] whereas the ancient accounts clearly attribute the enclosing of the whole city and the renewal of the whole circuit of walls to Eudocia. Attributing the whole line of fortifications to Eudocia suggests its probable dating between AD 437/438, the time of her first pilgrimage to Jerusalem,[117] or to between AD 444, when she returned to Jerusalem for good, and Eucherius's death sometime between AD 449–455.[118] This, however, contradicts John Rufus's testimony, if with his references to 'holy walls' he is describing the city walls of Jerusalem. The archaeological record, too, seems to favor an earlier date for the construction of the walls in the late fourth century or early fifth century at the latest.[119]

If we accept such a dating (i.e. late fourth/early fifth centuries AD), the attribution of the wall to Eudocia in the historical sources may be explained either in the sense that she restored an existing wall, or simply by a confusion in the tradition. As the first account which associated Eudocia with the wall's reconstruction was written about a century after her death, there may have been some uncertainty and confusion with regard to her life and deeds.[120] The existence of three successive Byzantine empresses with almost similar names in the course of the fifth century – Eudoxia, Arcadius's wife, Eudocia, Theodosius II wife, and Eudoxia, Theodosius II's daughter – undoubtedly caused confusion, as seen in coins[121] and legends.[122] Oddly, Cassiodorus and the Piacenza Pilgrim, in telling the story, give the name of the em-

---

116 Conrad Schick was the first who identified the Zion wall, which were unearthed by Frederick Bliss and Archibald Dickie, with the wall built ca. 440 by the empress Eudocia (Bliss 1894, 254). His suggestion was commonly accepted, cf. Dalton 1895, 28, Avi-Yonah 1976b, 621–622, Tsafrir 1975, 21 and 132–135, as well as Tsafrir 1999, 287–295. Bliss suggested two phases in the development of the late-antique walls on Mount Zion: First, around the beginning of the fifth century (a wall which was built to protect the Church of Zion and which did not include the Pool of Siloam within its precinct). Then, around 450, Eudocia rebuilt the wall (named by Bliss 'upper wall') around Zion and the pool, cf. Bliss/Dickie 1898, 307–309 and 321–323.
117 The suggestion of attributing Eudocia's initiative to her first pilgrimage (around 438), was made by Leah Di Segni, who suggested comparing it with the enlargement of Antioch's walls due to Eudocia's endeavors (Ioh. Mal. 14 (346–357, Dind.), Evagr. HE 1,20, cf. also Holum 1982, 117–118).
118 Dalton 1895, 28 dated the rebuilding of the walls by Eudocia to between 438–454.
119 The pottery assemblage characterizing the surface of the wall builders, consisted mostly of local ware, dated from the late third to the fifth century, thus enabling to relate the wall with Eudocia. Yet, the lack of imported ware, that is usually more abundant in assemblages from the fifth century AD, suggested the wall was build prior to the fifth century, when imported ware had become more abundant. Shlomit Weksler-Bdolah would like to thank Jodi Magness for this comment.
120 John Malalas, for example, not always distinguished between authentic history and popular memories (such as folk tales) of events, cf. Holum 1982, 114.
121 Boyce 1954.
122 Drake 1980, 148–155.

press as Eudoxia, although they identify her as Theodosius II's wife. Might the wall have been initiated by Eudoxia, and falsely attributed to Eudocia?[123]

Conclusion

The walls of Constantinople and Jerusalem were not constructed simultaneously, but close together in time. The frequent references in the ancient sources to imperial involvement in the holy city supports the assumption that not only in Constantinople did the city walls constitute a highly visible imperial monument, but that the imperial family was involved in building the walls of Jerusalem as well: Aelia Eudoxia, wife of Arcadius and mother of Theodosius II, or Eudocia, wife of Theodosius II, may have played a decisive role. But even if both the walls of Constantinople and the walls of Jerusalem were in one sense or another imperial building projects, they significantly differed in their design, function, and symbolism.

The Theodosian walls of Constantinople, constructed between 404/405 and 413 AD, were the largest urban defense work of late antiquity. They were completed in the reign of Theodosius II, who, however, was only four years old when construction works started and thirteen when the walls were finished. The original planning and initiative should thus be attributed to his father, Arcadius, and to the *praefectus praetorio per Orientem* Anthemius. In Jerusalem, the overall similarity of the excavated wall segments suggests that the whole circuit of the walls was built in one single phase within a rather short period of time. Jerusalem's late-antique wall unified within its course the Roman *colonia* Aelia Capitolina, the Christian hill of Zion (in the area of the abandoned campsite of the *lexio X Fretensis*) as well as the southeastern hill (with the area of the Ophel and the city of David). The archaeological evidence suggests a time frame for the construction between the late fourth and the mid-fifth century.

The walls of Constantinople were the first monumental structure built in layered masonry. The parts which were later changed and added differ from the Theodosian workmanship; the parts which were constructed in late Byzantine times are noticeably different. Hardly any *spolia* were used in the initial construction: the Constantinopolitan walls were a prestigious and completely new building project for which the re-use of older building materials was not considered appropriate. As in Constantinople with its ostentatiously new walls, the Jerusalem walls were likewise built in a manner that must have impressed visitors to the city. However, the con-

---

[123] Aelia Eudoxia married Arcadius at 395 AD, she was proclaimed Augusta at 400 AD and died in 404 AD. Eudoxia was involved in the Holy Land, and was portrayed as a devoted supporter of Christianity in the Imperial Court (Holum 1982). An inscription incised on the pedestal of a statue which was unearthed in the city of Scythopolis reads: 'Artemidorus set up a golden (statue of) Eudoxia, the queen of all earth, visible from every place in the country' (Tsafrir 1998, 217), indicating her appreciation in the capital of Palaestina Secunda.

scious selection and integration of *spolia* of Jewish origin suggests a distinct symbolic message, reflecting the builders' involvement and struggle with the Jewish history of Jerusalem.

In both cities, the walls considerably expanded the cities' limits, reflecting a period of expansion and growth in the early fifth century. While in Constantinople the wall enlarged the walled territory towards the west, in Jerusalem the perimeter of the walls united the area of the Roman city, the abandoned campsite of the Roman legion, and the hill which once formed the core of the Biblical city into one entity: the holy city of Jerusalem. The Theodosian walls of Constantinople were a highly visible display of imperial power, and they were obviously also meant to fortify the capital of the Roman Empire: the construction of the walls answered the need for monarchic representation and security for the inhabitants of the City of Caesar. The walls of Jerusalem, the City of God, on the other hand, were built as a vigorous symbol of Christian victory over Judaism. They reflect the desire of the builders to preserve the urban heritage, and more precisely – to preserve Jewish "symbols" of the Second Temple period – such as the Herodian stones, which were traditionally associated with the Herodian Temple Mount, and at the same time change their meaning.

Bibliography

Asali, K. (ed.) (1990). *Jerusalem in History*, London.
Asutay-Effenberger, N. (2003). 'Die Entdeckung des Romanos-Tores an den Landmauern von Konstantinopel,' *ByzZ* 96, 1–4.
Asutay-Effenberger, N. (2004). 'Romanos-Kapısı ve Mesoteikhon: Sultan II. Mehmet, İmparator XI. Konstantin Palaiologos ve Urban'ın Dev Topunun Kuşatma Esnasındaki Mevziileri,' *Türk Eskiçağ Bilimleri Enstitüsü Haberler* 18, 18–20.
Asutay-Effenberger, N. (2007). *Die Landmauer von Konstantinopel-İstanbul. Historisch-topographische und baugeschichtliche Untersuchungen*, Berlin.
Asutay-Effenberger, N. (2008). 'Das Kloster des Ioannes Prodromos τῆς Πέτρας in Konstantinopel und sein Bezug zur Odalar und Kasım Ağa Camii,' *Millennium* 6, 299–327.
Asutay-Effenberger, N. (2009). 'Nochmals zum Charisiostor an der Theodosianischen Landmauer,' *JÖByz* 59, 29–31.
Asutay-Effenberger, N. (2010). 'Kitâb-ı Bahriye Berlin ve Londra Yazmalarındaki İstanbul Haritalarının Kaynağı ve Bazı Bizans Anıtları Üzerine,' in Emecen 2010, 213–226.
Asutay-Effenberger, N. (2013). 'The Blachernai Palace and its defence,' in Redford/Ergin 2013, 253–276.
Asutay-Effenberger, N. (2019). "Die Theophilos-Türme in den Blachernen, in Neslihan Asutay-Effenberger/Falko Saim, *Sasanidische Spuren in der byzantinischen, kaukasischen und islamischen Kunst und Kultur*, Mainz, 143–154.
Asutay-Effenberger, N. & Effenberger, A. (2008). 'Eski İmaret Camii, Bonoszisterne und Konstantinsmauer,' *JÖByz* 58, 13–44.
Asutay-Effenberger, N. & Effenberger, A. (2009). 'Zum Verlauf der Konstantinsmauer zwischen Marmarameer und Bonoszisterne und zu den Toren und Straßen,' *JÖByz* 59, 1–29.
Avi-Yonah, M. (1939). 'Greek and Latin inscriptions from Jerusalem and Beisan,' *QDAP* 8, 54–61.
Avi-Yonah, M. (1953). 'The Madeba Mosaic map,' *Eretz-Israel* 2, 129–156 [in Hebrew].

Avi-Yonah, M. (1954). *The Madaba Mosaic map*, Jerusalem.
Avi-Yonah, M. (1968). 'The Third and Second Walls of Jerusalem in the New Testament Age,' *IEJ* 18, 98–125.
Avi-Yonah, M. (ed.) (1976a). *The Encyclopedia of Archaeological Excavations in the Holy Land* (vol. 2), Ann Arbor.
Avi-Yonah, M. (1976b). 'Jerusalem, Aelia Capitolina, and the Byzantine period,' in Avi-Yonah 1976a, 610–626.
Avni, G. (2005). 'The urban limits of Roman and Byzantine Jerusalem: A view from the necropolis,' *JRA* 18, 373–397.
Avni, G., Baruch, Y. & Weksler-Bdolah, S. (2001). 'Jerusalem, the Old City – Herod's Gate (A-2877),' *Hadashot Arkheologiyot, Excavations and Surveys in Israel* 113, 76–79.
Bahat, D. (1990). *The Illustrated Atlas of Jerusalem*, New York.
Bahat, D. & Ben-Ari, M. (1972). 'Excavations in Zahal Square,' *Qadmoniot* 19–20, 118–119 [in Hebrew].
Baldovin, J. (1987). *The Urban Character of Christian Worship: The Origins, Development and Meaning of Stational Liturgy*, Rome.
Bar, D. (1993). 'The southern boundary of Aelia Capitolina and the location of the Tenth Roman Legion's Camp,' *Cathedra* 69, 37–56 [in Hebrew].
Ben-Ami, D. & Tchekhanovets, Y. (2013). 'A Roman mansion found in the City of David,' *IEJ* 63, 164–173.
Ben-Dov, M. (1994). 'Excavations and architectural survey of the archaeological remains along the southern wall of the Jerusalem Old City,' in Geva 1994a, 311–320.
Berger, A. (1988). *Untersuchungen zu den Patria Konstantinupoleos*, Bonn.
Bitton-Ashkelony, B. (1999). 'The Pilgrimage of Peter the Iberian,' *Cathedra* 91, 97–112 [in Hebrew; English summary 180].
Bliss, F. (1894). 'Second report on the excavations of Jerusalem,' *PEFQSt* 27, 243–257.
Bliss, F. & Dickie, A. (1898). *Excavations in Jerusalem 1894–1897*, London.
Boyce, A. (1954). 'Eudoxia, Eudocia, Eudoxia: dated solidi of the fifth century,' *American Numismatic Society Museum Notes* 6, 131–142.
Brock, S. (1976). 'The rebuilding of the Temple under Julian: A new resource,' *PEQ* 108, 103–107.
Brock, S. (1977). 'A letter attributed to Cyril of Jerusalem on the rebuilding of the Temple,' *Bulletin of the School of Oriental and African Studies* 40, 267–286.
Broshi, M. & Gibson, S. (1994). 'Excavations along the western and southern walls of the Old City of Jerusalem,' in Geva 1994a, 147–155.
Broshi, M. & Tsafrir, Y. (1977). 'Excavations at the Zion Gate, Jerusalem,' *IEJ* 27, 28–37.
Bührig, C. (2001). 'Some aspects of the monumental gate *extra muros* of Gadara from the late Roman period seen in its context of urban development,' *SHAJ* 7, 547–552.
Cambi, N. & Marin, N. (ed.) (1998). *Acta XIII Congressus Internationalis Archaeologiae Christianae, Split-Porec 25.9.–1.10.1994* (vol. 2), Vatican City.
Chen, D., Margalit, S. & Pixner, B. (1994). 'Mount Zion: discovery of Iron Age fortifications below the Gate of the Essenes,' in Geva 1994a, 76–81.
Christie, N. & Loseby, S. (ed.) (1996). *Towns in Transition: Urban Evolution in Late Antiquity and the Early Middle Ages*, Berkeley.
Connolly, S. (2006–2007). 'Fortifying the City of God: Dardanus' inscription revisited,' *CJ* 102, 145–154.
Crowfoot, J. (1929). 'Excavations in the Ophel, 1928, preliminiary report to December 8,' *PEFQSt* 61, 9–16.
Crowfoot, J. & Fitzgerald, G. (1929). *Excavations in the Tyropoeon Valley, Jerusalem*, London.
Dalton, J. (1895). 'Note on the First Wall of ancient Jerusalem and the present excavations,' *PEFQSt* 28, 26–29.

Demangel, R. & Mamboury, E. (1939). *Le quartier des Manganes et la première région de Constantinople*, Paris.
Dever, W.G. (ed.) (1994). *Preliminary excavation reports: Sardis, Bir Umm Fawakhir, Tell el- Umeiri, The Combined Caesarea Expeditions, and Tell Dothan*, Ann Arbor.
Dirimtekin, F. (1953). *Fetihten önce Marmara surları*, Istanbul.
Dirimtekin, F. (1956), *Fetihten önce Haliç surları*, Istanbul.
Di Segni, L. (1995). 'The involvement of local, municipal and provincial authorities in urban building in late antique Palestine and Arabia,' in Humphrey 1995, 312–332.
Di Segni, L. (1999), 'Epigraphic documentation on building in the provinces of Palaestina and Arabia, 4th–7th c.,' in Humphrey 1999, 149–178.
Drake, H. (1980). 'The legend of Constantine and Eudoxia: sources, date, significance,' in Orlandi 1980, 132–158.
Effenberger, A. (2005). 'Die Illustrationen. Topographische Untersuchungen Konstantinopel/İstanbul und ägaische Örtlichkeiten,' in Siebert/Plassmann 2005, 13–89.
Effenberger, A (2013). 'Zur Wiederverwendung der venezianischen Tetrarchengruppen in Konstantinopel,' *Millennium* 10, 215–274.
Effenberger, A. (2016) 'Marienbilder im Blachernenheiligtum' *Millennium* 13, 275–325.
Effenberger, A (2017) 'Die Kirche des hl. Romanos in Konstantinopel und ihr Umfeld,' *Millennium* 14, 191–225.
Ehrlich, M. & Bar, D. (2004). 'Jerusalem according to the description of the Bordeaux Pilgrim: geographic and theological aspects,' *Cathedra* 113, 35–52 [in Hebrew].
Eliav, Y.Z. (2003). 'The urban layout of Aelia Capitolina: a new view from the perspective of the Temple Mount,' in Schäfer 2003, 241–278.
Emecen, F. (ed.) (2010). *İmparatorluklar Başkentinden Kültür Başkentine İstanbul*, Istanbul.
Erim, K. (1986). *Aphrodisias: City of Venus Aphrodite*, London.
Feissel, D. (2006). *Chroniques d'épigraphie byzantine 1987–2004*, Paris.
Fenster, E. (1968). *Laudes Constantinopolitanae*, Munich.
Freypont, I. (ed.) (1965). Eucherius, *De situ Hierosolymae, epistola ad Faustinum Presbyterum* (CCSL 175), Turnhout.
Germer-Durand, J. (1892). 'Aelia-Capitolina,' *RB* 1, 369–387.
Gerola, G. (1931), 'Le Vedute di Costantinopoli di Cristoforo Buondelmonti,' *Studi Bizantini e Neoellenici* 3, 249–279.
Geva, H. (1981). 'The Tower of David – Phasael or Hippicus?,' *IEJ* 31, 57–65.
Geva, H. (1983). 'Excavations in the Citadel of Jerusalem, 1979–1980 (preliminary report),' *IEJ* 33, 55–71.
Geva, H. (1993a). 'Jerusalem, the Roman Period,' in Stern/Lewinson-Gilboa/Aviram 1993, II, 758–766.
Geva, H. (1993b). 'Jerusalem, the Byzantine Period, the city wall,' in Stern/Lewinson-Gilboa/Aviram 1993, II, 770–772.
Geva, H. (ed.) (1994a). *Ancient Jerusalem Revealed*, Jerusalem.
Geva, H. (1994b). 'Excavations in the Citadel of Jerusalem, 1976–1980,' in Geva 1994a, 156–167.
Geva, H. (ed.) (2000). *Jewish Quarter Excavations in the Old City of Jerusalem, Conducted by Nahman Avigad, 1969–1982* (vol. 1: *Architecture and Stratigraphy: Areas A, W and X-2, Final Report*), Jerusalem.
Goldfuss, H. (1984). 'Jerusalem, Jaffa Gate,' *ESI* 3, 53–55.
Gordon, B. (2007). 'The Byzantine quarter south of the Temple Mount enclosure,' in Mazar 2007, 201–215.
Gregory, E. (1982). 'Fortifications and urban design in early Byzantine Greece,' in Hohlfelder 1982, 43–64.

Ariel, D.T., Shiloh, Y. & De Groot, A. (eds.) (1992). *Excavations at the City of David 1978–1985, Directed by Yigal Shiloh* (vol. 3: Stratigraphical, Environmental, and Other Reports), Jerusalem.
Hadidi, A. (ed.) (1992). *Studies in the History and Archaeology of Jordan* (vol. 4), Amman.
Hamilton, R. (1944). 'Excavations against the North Wall of Jerusalem, 1937–8,' *QDAP* 10, 1–54.
Hamilton, R. (1952), 'Jerusalem in the fourth century,' *PEQ* 84, 83–90.
Hennessy, J. (1970). 'Preliminary report on excavations at the Damascus Gate, Jerusalem, 1964–1966,' *Levant* 2, 22–27.
Hirschfeld, Y. & Foerster, G. (1993). 'Tiberias,' in Stern/Lewinson-Gilboa/Aviram 1993, IV, 1470–1473.
Hohlfelder, R. (ed.) (1982). *City, Town and Countryside in the Early Byzantine Era*, New York.
Holum, K. (1982). *Theodosian Empresses: Women and Imperial Dominion in Late Antiquity*, Berkeley.
Horn, C.B. & Phenix, R.R. (eds. and transl.) (2008). *John Rufus: The Lives of Peter the Iberian, Theodosius of Jerusalem, and the Monk Romanus* (Writings from the Graeco-Roman World 24), Atlanta.
Humphrey, J. (ed.) (1995). *The Roman and Byzantine Near East. Some Recent Archaeological Research* (vol. 1), Ann Arbor.
Humphrey, J. (ed.) (1999). *The Roman and Byzantine Near East. Some Recent Archaeological Research* (vol. 2), Ann Arbor.
Hunt, E. (1982). *Holy Land Pilgrimage in the Later Roman Empire, AD 312–460*, Oxford.
Janin, R. (^{2}1962). *Constantinople Byzantine: développement urbain et répertoire topographique*, Paris.
Janin, R. (^{2}1969). *La géographie ecclésiastique de l'Empire Byzantin, Première Partie. La Siège de Constantinople et le Patriarchat oecuménique* (vol. 3: Les Églises et le Monastères), Paris.
Johns, C. (1950). 'The Citadel, Jerusalem: a summary of work since 1934,' *QDAP* 14, 121–190.
Johnson, S. (1983). *Late Roman Fortifications*, London.
Kalkan, H. & Şahin, S. (1993). 'Ein neues Bauepigramm der Theodosianischen Landmauer von Konstantinupolis aus dem Jahr 447,' *EA* 22, 137–147.
Kauffer, F., Lechevalier, J. & de Choiseul-Gouffie, M. (1822). *Voyage pittoresque de la Grèce* (vol. 2.2), Paris.
Kehrberg, I. & Manley, J. (2001). 'New archaeological finds for the dating of the Gerasa Roman city wall,' *ADAJ* 45, 437–446.
Kehrberg, I. & Manley, J. (2002). 'The 2001 Season of the Jarash City Walls Project: preliminary report,' *ADAJ* 46, 197–204.
Kehrberg, I. & Manley, J. (2003). 'The Jerash City Walls Project (JCWP) 2001–2003: report of preliminary findings of the second season 21st September – 14th October 2002,' *ADAJ* 47, 83–86.
Kenyon, K. (1968). 'Excavations in Jerusalem, 1967,' *PEQ* 100, 97–109.
Kenyon, K. (1974). *Digging up Jerusalem*, London.
Kloner, A. (1986). 'The "Third Wall" in Jerusalem and the "Cave of the Kings" (Josephus War V 147),' *Levant* 18, 121–126.
Krischen, F. (1938). *Die Landmauer von Konstantinopel I: Zeichnerische Wiederherstellung*, Berlin.
Kühnel, B. (1987). *From the Earthly to the Heavenly Jerusalem: Representations of the Holy City in Christian Art of the first Millennium*, Freiburg.
Lander, J. (1984). *Roman Stone Fortifications: Variation and Change From First Century A.D. to the Fourth*, Oxford.
Lang, D.M. (ed. and trans.) (^{2}1976). 'A Militant Ascetic: Peter the Iberian, Bishop of Mayuma by Gaza,' in *Lives and Legends of the Georgian Saints, Selected and translated from the original texts*, Oxford, 57–80.

Lapin, H. (ed.) (1998). *Religious and Ethnic Communities in Later Roman Palestine*, Bethesda.
Lavan, L. (ed.) (2001). *Recent Research in Late Antique Urbanism*, Ann Arbor.
Lehmann, C. (1994). 'The excavation of Caesarea's Byzantine city wall, 1989,' in Dever 1994, 121–131.
Lenski, N. (1997). '*Initium mali Romano imperio*: contemporary reactions to the Battle of Adrianople,' *Transactions of the American Philological Association* 127, 129–168.
Levine, L.I. (ed.) (1999). *Jerusalem: Its Sanctity and Centrality to Judaism, Christianity and Islam*, New York.
Lewin, A. (2001). 'Urban public building from Constantine to Julian: the epigraphic evidence,' in Lavan 2001, 27–37.
Liebeschuetz, W. (1972). *Antioch: City and Imperial Administration in the Later Roman Empire*, Oxford.
Limor, O. (1998). *Holy Land Travels and Christian Pilgrims in Late Antiquity*, Jerusalem [in Hebrew].
Limor, O. (1999), 'Christian pilgrims in the Byzantine period,' in Tsafrir/Safrai 1999, 391–416 [in Hebrew].
Macridy, T. & Casson, S. (1931). 'Excavations at the Golden Gate, Constantinople,' *Archaeologia* 81, 63–84.
Magness, J. (1993). *Jerusalem Ceramic Chronology circa 200–800 CE*, Sheffield.
Magness, J. (2000). 'The north wall of Aelia Capitolina,' in Stager/Greene/Coogane 2000, 328–339.
Mango, C. (1998). 'The origins of the Blachernae shrine at Constantinople,' in Cambi/Marin 1998, II, 61–76.
Mango, C. (2000a). 'Constantinople as Theotokoupolis,' in Vassilaki 2000, 17–25.
Mango, C. (2000b). 'The Triumphal Way of Constantinople and the Golden Gate,' *DOP* 54, 173–186.
Mango, C. (2001). 'The shoreline of Constantinople in the fourth century,' in Necipoğlu 2001, 17–28.
Mango, C. (^{2}2004). *Le développement urbain de Constantinople (IVe–VIIe siècles)*, Paris.
Mazar, B. (1969). 'The excavations in the Old City of Jerusalem,' *Eretz-Israel* 9, 161–174 [in Hebrew].
Mazar, E. (1995). 'The Ophel Wall in Jerusalem in the Byzantine period,' in Safrai/Faust 1995, 48–63 [in Hebrew].
Mazar, E. (ed.) (2007). *The Temple Mount Excavations in Jerusalem 1968–1978, Directed by Benjamin Mazar: Final Reports* (vol. 3: *The Byzantine Period, Qedem 46*), Jerusalem.
Mazar, E. & Mazar, B. (1989). *Excavations in the South of the Temple Mount*, Jerusalem.
Mazor, G. (2004). *Free standing city gates in the eastern provinces during the Roman Imperial period*, Bar Ilan University, Ramat-Gan (PhD Diss.) [in Hebrew].
Meynersen, F. (2001). 'The Tiberias Gate of Gadara (Umm Qays): reflections concerning the date and its reconstruction,' *ADAJ* 45, 427–432.
Merrill, S. (1886). 'Recent discoveries at Jerusalem,' *PEFQSt* 18, 21–24.
Meyer-Plath, B. & Schneider, A.M. (1943). *Die Landmauer von Konstantinopel II: Aufnahme, Beschreibung und Geschichte*, Berlin.
Müller-Wiener, W. (1961). 'Zur Frage der Stadtbefestigung von Byzantion,' *BJ* 161, 165–175.
Müller-Wiener, W. (1977). *Bildlexikon zur Topographie Istanbuls. Byzantion – Konstantinupolis – Istanbul bis zum Beginn des 17. Jahrhunderts*, Tübingen.
Necipoğlu, N. (ed.) (2001). *Byzantine Constantinople: Monuments and Everyday Life*, Leiden.
Nicholas, D. (1997). *The Growth of the Medieval City From Late Antiquity to the Early Fourteenth Century*, London.
Orlandi, T. (ed.) (1980). *Eudoxia and the Holy Sepulchre: A Constantinian Legend in Coptic*, Milan.

Öztuncay, B. & Karamani Pekin, A. (2007). *Marmaray: Gün Işığında. İstanbul'un 8000 yılı. Marmaray ve Sultanahmet kazıları*, Istanbul.
Parker, S. (2003). 'The Roman Aqaba Project: the 2002 campaign,' *ADAJ* 47, 321–333.
Parrish, D. (ed.) (2001). *Urbanism in Western Asia Minor: New Studies on Aphrodisias, Ephesos, Hierapolis, Pergamon, Perge and Xanthos*, Ann Arbor.
Philippides, M. & Hanak, W. (2011). *The Siege and Fall of Constantinople in 1453: Historiography, Topography, and Military Studies*, Farnham.
Piccirillo, M. (ed.) (1999). *The Madaba Map Centenary 1897–1997: Travelling Through the Byzantine-Umayyad Period*, Jerusalem.
Pixner, B. & Margalit, S. (1989). 'Mount Zion: the Gate of the Essenes re-excavated,' *ZDPV* 105, 85–95.
Plaum, H.-G. (1952). 'La fortification de la ville d'Adraha d'Arabie, 259/260–274/275, d'après des inscriptions récemment découvertes,' *Syria. Archéologie, art et histoire* 29, 307–330.
Raabe, R. (ed.) (1895). *Petrus der Iberer, Vita Petri Iberi a Joanne Rufo*. Leipzig.
Ratte, C. (2001). 'The urban development of Aphrodisias in Late Antiquity,' in Parrish 2001, 116–147.
Redford, S. & Ergin, N. (eds.) (2013). *Cities and Citadels in Turkey From the Iron Age to the Seljuks*, Leuven.
Reem, A. (2013). 'King David's Tomb on Mount Zion: theories vs. the archaeological evidence,' in Stiebel et al. 2013, 221–242.
Reich, R. & Shukron, E. (1994). 'Jerusalem – Mamilla,' *ESI* 14, 92–96.
Restle, M. (1976). *Istanbul – Bursa – Edirne – Iznik. Baudenkmäler und Museen*, Stuttgart.
Roueché, C. (1989). *Aphrodisias in Late Antiquity*, London.
Rubin, Z. (1999). 'Jerusalem in the Byzantine period – a historical survey,' in Tsafrir/Safrai 1999, 199–238 [in Hebrew].
Safrai, Z. & Faust, A. (eds.) (1995). *The First Conference on Recent Innovations in the Study of Jerusalem*, Tel Aviv [in Hebrew].
Saradi-Mendelovici, H. (1990). 'Christian attitudes toward pagan monuments in Late Antiquity and their legacy in later Byzantine centuries,' *DOP* 44, 47–61.
Sartre, M. (1985). *Bostra des origins à l'Islam*, Paris.
Schäfer, P. (ed.) (2003). *The Bar Kokhba War Reconsidered: New Perspectives on the Second Jewish Revolt Against Rome*, Tübingen.
Schreiner, P. (2007). *Konstantinopel. Geschichte und Archäologie*, Munich.
Schick, C. (1887). 'Notes from Jerusalem,' *PEQ* 18, 213–221.
Segal, A. (1981). 'Tadmor/Palmyra,' *Qadmoniot* 14, 2–14 [in Hebrew].
Seigne, J. (1992). 'Jérash romaine et byzantine: développement urbaine d'une ville provinciale orientale,' in Hadidi 1992, 331–341.
Seligman, J. (2001). 'Yet another medieval tower and section of Jerusalem's ancient walls (Armenian Patriarchate Road),' *Atiqot* 42, 262–276.
Seligman, J. (2002). 'Jerusalem's ancient walls strike again: the Knights Palace Hotel,' *Atiqot* 43, 73–85.
Siebert, I. & Plassmann, M. (eds.) (2005). *Cristoforo Buondelmonti. Liber Insularum Archipelagi. Universität- und Landesbibliothek Düsseldorf Ms. G 13. Faksimile*, Wiesbaden.
Sion, O. & Puni, S. (2011). 'Jerusalem, Jaffa Gate,' *HA-ESI* 123, http://www.hadashot-esi.org.il/report_detail_eng.aspx?id=1779&mag_id=118 (last accessed August 8, 2022).
Sivan, R. & Solar, G. (1994). 'Excavations in the Jerusalem Citadel, 1980–1988,' in Geva 1994, 168–176.
Stager, L.E., Greene, J.A., & Coogane, M.D. (eds.) (2000). *The Archaeology of Jordan and Beyond: Essays in Honor of James A. Sauer*, Winona Lake.

Stern, E., Lewinson-Gilboa, A. & Aviram, J. (eds.) (1992/1993). *The New Encyclopedia of Archaeological Excavations in the Holy Land* (4 vols.), New York.

Stiebel, D.G. et al. (eds.) (2013). *New Studies in the Archaeology of Jerusalem and its Region*, Jerusalem.

Tsafrir, Y. (1975). *Zion: The South Western Hill of Jerusalem and its Place in the Urban Development of the City in the Byzantine Period*, The Hebrew University of Jerusalem, Jerusalem (PhD Diss.) [in Hebrew].

Tsafrir, Y. (1978). 'The gates of Jerusalem in the account of Muqadassi: new identifications on the basis of Byzantine sources,' *Cathedra* 8, 147–155 [in Hebrew].

Tsafrir, Y. (1998). 'The fate of pagan cult places in Palestine: the archaeological evidence with emphasis on Beth Shean,' in Lapin 1998, 197–218.

Tsafrir, Y. (1999a). 'The topography and archaeology of Aelia Capitolina,' in Tsafrir/Safrai 1999, 115–166 [in Hebrew].

Tsafrir, Y. (1999b). 'The topography and archaeology of Jerusalem in the Byzantine period,' in Tsafrir/Safrai 1999, 281–352 [in Hebrew].

Tsafrir, Y. (1999c). 'Byzantine Jerusalem: the configuration of a Byzantine city,' in Levine 1999, 133–150.

Tsafrir, Y. (1999d). 'The holy city of Jerusalem in the Madaba Map,' in Piccirillo 1999, 155–164.

Tsafrir, Y. (2000). 'Procopius and the Nea Church in Jerusalem,' *Antiquité Tardive* 8, 149–164.

Tsafrir, Y. & Foerster, G. (1989). 'On the date of the "Sabbatical Year Earthquake",' *Tarbiz* 58, 357–362.

Tsafrir, Y. & Foerster, G. (1997). 'Urbanism in Scythopolis-Beth Shean in the fourth to seventh centuries,' *DOP* 51, 85–146.

Tsafrir, Y. & Safrai, S. (eds.) (1999). *The History of Jerusalem: The Roman and Byzantine periods (70–638)*, Jerusalem.

Turler, D., De Groot, A. & Solar, G. (1979). Jerusalem, Excavations between Damascus Gate and the New Gate. *Hadashot Arkheologiyot* 69/71, 56–57 [in Hebrew].

Tushingham, A.D. (1985). *Excavations in Jerusalem 1961–1967 I. Excavations in the Armenian Garden on the Western Hill*. Toronto, 60–107.

Van Millingen, A. (1899). *Byzantine Constantinople: The Walls of the City and Adjoining Historical Sites*, London.

Vassilaki, M. (ed.) (2000). *Representations of the Virgin in Byzantine Art*, Milan.

Vincent, L.-H. (1902). 'La deuxième enceinte de Jerusalem,' *RB* 11, 31–57.

Vincent, L.-H. & Abel, F.-M. (1914). *Jérusalem, récherches de topographie, d'archéologie et d'histoire* (vol. 2: *Jérusalem nouvelle* [1926]), Paris.

Vincent, L.-H. & Steve, M.-J. (1954). *Jérusalem de l'Ancien Testament. Récherches d'archéologie et d'histoire*, Paris.

Walmsley, A. (1996). 'Byzantine Palestine and Arabia: urban prosperity in Late Antiquity,' in Christie/Loseby 1996, 126–158.

Ward-Perkins, B. (1984). *From Classical Antiquity to the Middle Ages: Urban Public Building in Northern and Central Italy AD 300–850*, New York.

Warren, C. & Conder, C.R. (1884). *The Survey of Western Palestine* III: *Jerusalem*, London.

Weksler-Bdolah, S. (2001). 'Jerusalem, the Old City walls,' *HA–ESI* 113, 79–80.

Weksler-Bdolah, S. (2003). *The fortifications of Jerusalem during late Roman, Byzantine and early Islamic periods (3rd/4th to 8th cent.)*, The Hebrew University of Jerusalem, Jerusalem (M.A. thesis) [in Hebrew].

Weksler-Bdolah, S. (2006–2007). 'The fortifications of Jerusalem in the Byzantine period,' *ARAM* 18–19, 85–112.

Weksler-Bdolah, S. (2007). 'Reconsidering the Byzantine period city wall of Jerusalem,' *Eretz-Israel* 28, 88–101 [in Hebrew; English summary on p. 12*].

Weksler-Bdolah, S. (2011). 'On the date of construction of the southern wall of Mt. Zion during the Byzantine period,' *Qadmoniot* 141, 57 [in Hebrew].

Weksler-Bdolah, S. (2014). 'The Tenth Legion's Camp: nonetheless on the southwestern hill,' *New studies on Jerusalem* 20, 219–238 [in Hebrew; English summary on pp. 48*–50*].

Weksler-Bdolah, S. (2020). *Aelia Capitolina: Jerusalem in the Roman Period in Light of Archaeological Research* (Mnemosyne supplements 432), Leiden.

Weksler-Bdolah, S. & Lavi, R. (2013). 'Jerusalem, Siloam,' *HA-ESI* 125, http://www.hadashot-esi.org.il/report_detail.aspx?id=4343&mag_id=120 (last accessed August 8, 2022).

Wharton, A. (1995). *Refiguring the post-classical city: Dura Europus, Jerash, Jerusalem and Ravenna*, Cambridge.

Wightman, G. (1989). *The Damascus Gate, Jerusalem*, Oxford.

Wightman, G. (1993). *The Walls of Jerusalem from the Canaanites to the Mamluks*, Sydney.

Wilkinson, J. (^{2}1981). *Egeria's Travels to the Holy Land*, Warminster.

Wilkinson, J. (1990). 'Jerusalem under Rome and Byzantium,' in Asali 1990, 75–104.

Wilkinson, J. (2002). *Jerusalem Pilgrims Before the Crusaders*, Warminster.

Zelinger, Y. (2010). 'Jerusalem, the slopes of Mount Zion,' *HA-ESI* 122, http://hadashot-esi.org.il/Report_Detail_Eng.aspx?id=1530&mag_id=117 (last accessed August 8, 2022).

Marlena Whiting
From the City of Caesar to the City of God: Routes, Networks, and Connectivity Between Constantinople and Jerusalem

In many ways it is appropriate to think of Constantinople and Jerusalem as poles of the late antique world, and as each other's antipodes. To regard the former as being the seat of imperial and earthly power and the other the locus of heavenly power, and the travel between them dictated solely by these concerns, with pilgrims drawn to the sacred pole and bureaucrats drawn to the secular one. But to do so would not do justice to the nature of these two cities as urban centers, and the wide range of motivations for travel that the two could command. It also under-emphasizes the importance of the places in between these two nodes through which travelers of all kinds would have to pass, on a journey that took many weeks.

The fourth century saw the emergence of new roles for the ancient cities of Constantinople and Jerusalem, the former as an administrative capital, and the latter as a spiritual one. Although these roles would continue to coalesce throughout the fourth through seventh centuries, the need for communications infrastructure to connect the two cities resulted in investment throughout the period. Three main concerns would ensure that communication routes were kept open: the needs of the imperial administration and the military, the need to ensure the movement of goods and trade, and the new need that arose after the fourth century, the need to ensure the safety and comfort of pilgrims to the holy sites of Christianity. In this article I argue that it is by considering these three strands in tandem as part of an integrated system that we can appreciate the developments that went into maintaining the communications networks between the imperial city of Constantinople and the holy city of Jerusalem in the fourth through seventh centuries.

In this article I will outline more precisely what I mean by an integrated system using my chosen term, *braided network*. I will then demonstrate the applicability of the concept to the communications routes between Constantinople and Jerusalem, with specific reference to the fourth through seventh centuries. I will examine what drew diverse types of traveler to each city, and then place the cities in a wider regional framework by looking at the roads that connected them. Specifically, I will challenge the modern convention of referring to the trans-Anatolian route as

---

Note: My thanks to Konstantin Klein for the invitation to contribute to this volume. Part of the research for this article was carried out at the Research Center for Anatolian Civilizations (ANAMED) in Istanbul as a Visiting Fellow in 2016.

∂ OpenAccess. © 2022 Marlena Whiting, published by De Gruyter. This work is licensed under the Creative Commons Attribution-NonCommercial-NoDerivatives 4.0 International License.
https://doi.org/10.1515/9783110718447-005

the 'pilgrims' road', which is misleading in light of the complex nature of the braided network.[1]

Braided Network System

In trying to understand the interplay of politics, economics, and religious motivations on the road networks of Late Antiquity, I have found it helpful to think in terms of *braided systems*.[2] A braided system, like a plait of hair or fibers, is made up of several strands that are bound together, but also intersect and diverge. Like a braided river system, to extend the analogy, in which it is the force of the water through the system that determines which channels merge together, and whether new channels open up, different networks within the system have greater force at different times, influencing how the braided system as a whole develops. This is a useful way of thinking about the road system in Late Antiquity: built by the imperial administration and the military for communication and supply needs, but equally used for other purposes, like trade and pilgrimage. The latter categories have an impact on the former, as the imperial administration set up customs stations and protected roads used by merchants, investing in infrastructure, or providing protection and charitable institutions along routes used by pilgrims. The distinct motivations of each group might tug the system in new directions: a remote shrine (a hermit's cell or healing spring) could become a popular pilgrimage site, or the source of an exotic trade item could attract merchants. But the other strands will react and follow to support or benefit from the new node. To gain a holistic picture of the networks linking Constantinople and Jerusalem in the fourth through seventh centuries, I will proceed to examine the three main identifiable strands in the braided system: 1) administrative (and military) traffic, 2) trade, and 3) pilgrimage. First, it is necessary to consider the importance of our cities for each type of travel.

Capita Viae: Constantinople and Jerusalem

Constantinople and Jerusalem had very different functions from one another in Late Antiquity, as seen elsewhere in this volume, and thus different attractions as destinations for travel. Both were unique among the cities of the late antique world, and Jerusalem's status as a holy city for Christianity definitely colored much of its other

---

[1] The term "Pilgrim's Road" first appears in the works of William Ramsay (1890, 197; 1899, 166), and refers – in the singular – to the route of the Bordeaux Itinerary, and is adopted by French (1981). The route has no known ancient name, and I will use the singular form for the sake of convenience. However, the tendency to romanticize the name is problematic, as I will discuss below.
[2] Whiting 2020, 63–65.

interactions. Nevertheless, they did both have relevance for officials and merchants, as well as for pilgrims, in multifaceted networks as we shall see below.

For Constantinople, it is easy to understand the convergence of administrative, mercantile, and religious interests on the capital of the empire. The administrative role of the city as the imperial capital is particularly salient. The imperial court as well as its attendant offices and law courts would be the primary motivator to ensure the movement of information. The movement of information of course equated to a movement of people who were the only physical means by which messages could be conveyed. In 330, Constantinople replaced Nicomedia within a Tetrarchic system which included capitals at Trier, Milan, Sirmium (and Ravenna from 402). Antioch also hosted the imperial court at one time or another; Valens spent the winter of 385–386 in Ankara. Rome continued to be the seat of the Senate, although a senate was also established at Constantinople.[3] Until the early fifth century, the court was often itinerant, following the person of the emperor – or emperors – between capitals and on military campaigns. There was also a strong tendency towards centralization of the government, and most administrative, legal, and financial matters were addressed directly by the emperor.[4] For example, the monk Sabas of the Judean Desert traveled to Constantinople twice, once in 511 to petition the Emperor Anastasius on doctrinal matters, and for the second time in 530 to the court of Justinian to request remission of taxes for the provinces of Palaestina Prima and Secunda following the Samaritan revolts, and funds to rebuild churches and improve security.[5] Religious and political-administrative matters centralized around the emperor.

This centralization necessitated an investment in infrastructure. In fact, Lukas Lemcke has recently argued that the official imperial communications service, known in Late Antiquity as the *cursus publicus*, was restructured and experienced a "golden age" in the fourth century in part due to mobility of the emperor. This generated the need to maintain communications on diverse subjects, not just channeling information from the provinces to Constantinople when the emperor was in residence there, but needing to locate the emperor in whatever province he might be, should he be absent.[6] As the emperor increasingly became based at Constantinople, so too did all the branches of central government, and the city's natural advantages as a communications hub were amplified. Of course, the vast majority of information traffic issuing from the capital was not destined specifically for Jerusalem. The focus of military operations, for example, in the east was mainly on the Mesopotamian frontier, and there were communications routes to northern Mesopotamia that did not require crossing the Taurus Mountains (the main natural barrier to north-south communications between Anatolia and Syria / the Levant).[7]

---

3 Jones 1964, 133.
4 Jones 1964, 403–406.
5 Cyr. Scyth. *VS* 50–55, 71–74.
6 Cf. Lemcke 2016, esp. 27–29.
7 Comfort 2009, Comfort/Abadie-Reynal/Ergeç 2000.

The emperor also served as arbiter in religious disputes, as seen above in the case of Sabas' first journey to Constantinople. In the fourth and early fifth centuries Constantinople lacked official ecclesiastical authority; instead it derived symbolic authority from its status as the imperial capital. It was not until the council of Chalcedon in 451 that Constantinople was elevated to a patriarchate. Nevertheless, it was a frequent location for church councils. The seven ecumenical church councils between 325 and 787 were all convened in Asia Minor – and three of them in Constantinople – partly because it served as a sort of cross-roads location between east and west, and partly to be near the emperor who had to convene the council and ratify its decisions. Bishops traveling for church councils counted as imperial officials and were granted the right to use the *cursus publicus*, although this was not necessarily a frequent occurrence.[8] Furthermore, Constantinople's status as a religious center was enhanced through acquisition of important relics and famous churches that made it a pilgrimage destination in its own right.[9]

In the fourth and fifth centuries, Constantinople had an estimated population of around 500,000.[10] The sheer scale of the urban population means that the city has been seen as a black hole into which the produce of the empire disappeared. 80,000 inhabitants were entitled to the free ration of grain and oil, the *annona civitatis*, which was mainly imported from Egypt. Although the state played a role in some of this circulation, particularly of the grain originating in Egypt, recent studies show that diverse products reached the capital via diverse exchange mechanisms.[11] Three quarters of the city's population was not entitled to the grain ration, and had to source their staples and extras through other means. Constantinople was the biggest center of consumption in the Late Antique world. Marlia Mundell Mango's work on the commercial map of Constantinople has shown there were extensive and numerous facilities, both state-owned and private, dedicated to food storage, production and distribution/sale (like warehouses, bakeries, and markets).[12] But it was not the case that products only flowed to the capital to be consumed there; Constantinople was an important production site, especially of luxury and state-controlled goods, like precious metalware. Some valuable items of Constantinopolitan workmanship doubtless found their way into the churches of the Holy Land. For example, the chronicler Theophanes records for the year 427/428 that Theodosius II sent to Jerusalem, in addition to money, "a golden cross, set with precious stones to be fixed on

---

8 Lemcke 2016, 85–87.
9 The relics of Prophet Samuel were brought from the Holy Land to Constantinople overland in 407; Jerome comments on the crowds "from Palaestina to Chalcedon" (*unde Palaestina usque Chalcedonem*) who turned out to watch the progress. Jer. *Adversus Vigilantium* 5.
10 Mango 1985, 51 estimates the population of that period at 300,000–400,000. Durliat 1990, 259–261, 269, offers a higher estimate of 600,000–650,000.
11 Kingsley/Decker 2001.
12 Mundell Mango 2000.

the holy site of Calvary".[13] Although it is not specified it seems fair to speculate that this cross was the product of a Constantinopolitan workshop. Constantinople was more than just a center of consumption, drawing products and people in. It was also an unavoidable nodal point in the overland communications network between Europe and the East Mediterranean.

At the Jerusalem end, the story is rather different. As Benjamin Isaac drily puts it: "Roads lead to Jerusalem because people want to go there, not because it is a natural halting place or caravan city."[14] In Late Antiquity, the city's place at the center of the emerging concept of a Christian 'Holy Land,' as a destination in its own right, had a palpable effect on the city's status. Certainly the city's importance in the eyes of the imperial administration and the military (in whose interests the road networks were maintained) must have diminished after the legion stationed there, the *Legio X Fretensis*, was relocated to Aila c. 284. Although the city may have retained cultural importance in the region, it is difficult to see it as a locus of administrative importance on the empire-wide level. The provincial capital was at Caesarea Maritima. Even within the Christian church's administrative hierarchy, the bishop of Jerusalem was initially subordinate to the metropolitan bishop at Caesarea Maritima, until the elevation of Jerusalem to status of patriarchate in 451.[15] However, the structuring of Jerusalem and its hinterland as a *terra sancta*, especially the large numbers of monastics who came to reside in the city and its environs created a significant power base in religio-political issues, enabling it to rival Constantinople, Antioch, and Alexandria in the east and exercise considerable influence.

What then of military or strategic matters? As seen from the case of Sabas, monks could petition the emperor on issues that could be considered matters of strategy. Sabas requested funds for a fort to protect his Judean desert monasteries "on account of the inroads of the Saracens", much as the monks in Sinai had requested Justinian fortify their monastery.[16] This again testifies to the influence that one strand might have on another in a braided network: the increased presence of pilgrims and monasteries and their steadily accruing wealth made them vulnerable to raiding, and thus in need of imperial resources to protect them. After the end of the third century, the Levant was not particularly heavily garrisoned. There were forts in the desert areas, along the Strata Diocletiana from the Negev to the Middle Euphrates, but not much in the way of forts in the urbanized areas. Antiochus Strategos mentions a garrison at Jericho during the Persian invasion of 614.[17] Ironically, it was the communications routes that proved vulnerable: when the Persians invaded

---

[13] Theoph. AM 5920 (AD 427/8).
[14] Isaac 1990, 105.
[15] Cf. contribution by Kötter in this volume.
[16] Cyr. Scyth. *VS* 72, though Sabas' fortification was never built. Isaac 1990, 93. On Sinai, see Proc. Aed. 5,8,9.
[17] Conybeare 1910, 505.

they did so not from the east, but from the west, where the coastal highway had provided them with access to Caesarea Maritima from Antioch.

Our understanding of Jerusalem as an economic operator is heavily influenced by its holy status. 'The Economics of Byzantine Palestine' published in 1958 by Michael Avi-Yonah mainly focuses on church finances, and despite advances in the field, not much has changed in terms of scholarly focus on the economic life of Jerusalem itself.[18] The church was a major consumer of luxury products like metalware and textiles, probably mainly acquired as gifts. However, for example the large amount of incense used in the liturgy could make Jerusalem a logical market for products from the Red Sea and Arabian trading circuits in a pattern of direct exchange.[19]

Pilgrimage is often emphasized as an economic force, and that pilgrims' desire for tokens and memorabilia drove manufacture. Pilgrim tokens are assumed to have been produced in Jerusalem based on the iconography matching *loca sancta* there.[20] Hexagonal glass pilgrim flasks with both Christian and Jewish motifs are also presumed to have been produced in or just outside Jerusalem in the sixth and seventh centuries.[21] Pottery typology indicates that Jerusalem might have been a center for regional types of pottery, but previous research has focused particularly on types that are associated with religious contexts (candlestick/slipper lamps).[22] This can be considered the direct impact of one strand in the braided network (pilgrimage) on another (trade and manufacture). However, so far the assumption that Jerusalem is the production center for these goods is based on typology rather than petrographic analysis to determine the source of the clay, and to my knowledge no production sites have been found in Jerusalem or its immediate environs,[23] but the variety of pottery found in the city from regions adjacent to Jerusalem does suggest that Jerusalem was part of local regional circulation of products not exclusively associated with pilgrimage.[24]

Jerusalem's activity in the regional agrarian economy has been investigated in relation to the extensive capacity for wine production at monasteries near Jerusalem,

---

18 Cf. Kingsley 2004, 74–78 for a critique of the focus on ecclesiastical "artificial economy", and suggestions for reframing the question.
19 Eivind Seland (2012) has studied the fourth-century *Liber Pontificalis* for evidence of exotic products acquired through trading networks in the Red Sea for use in the liturgy in the city of Rome; it seems logical that Jerusalem would have been reliant on similar trading networks.
20 Rahmani 1993.
21 Barag 1970.
22 Magness 1993, 176 notes their limited distribution outside Palestine and suggests Jerusalem as their site of production. Cf. also Magness 1996, 39. Cf. Magness 1993, 178–181, on pottery production in Jerusalem.
23 One type of lamp is known to have been produced at Beit Nattif, 20 km SW of Jerusalem, in the fourth to fifth centuries. Gardner 2014, 286.
24 Magness 1993, 182.

for the production of so-called Gaza wine.²⁵ Gaza wine gets its name from the amphorae which transported it around the Mediterranean and the Red Sea, which were produced mainly at Gaza and Ascalon, but also at other sites in Palestine (both monastic and secular) and even at Aila on the Red Sea.²⁶ An agricultural boom in the Byzantine period led to expansion in many previously marginal areas, particularly in the Negev Desert southwest of Jerusalem, and installations related to wine production are prevalent throughout Palestine.²⁷ This wine was drunk in Constantinople at the coronation of Justin II and was praised by Gregory of Tours.²⁸ Of course, part of its desirability and 'brand' derived from its origin in the Holy Land, and it is possible that the monks in and around the Holy City were actively involved in this economic activity.

The previous sections have demonstrated the wide range of activities taking place in each of the *capita viae* of our imaginary journey, and the different kinds of motivations for travelers to make that journey. The analogy of braided networks that simultaneously cater to the needs of various kinds of travelers can be extended: journeys making use of these networks and infrastructure need not have exclusively one motivation. Particularly for late antiquity, the way that Christianity permeates many aspects of daily life (and the way it colors our sources, many of which are hagiographies), means that many journeys involved prayer or a visit to a shrine and could take on attributes of pilgrimage. This can often make it difficult to decode what is a pilgrimage and what is not, and is further reason why thinking in terms of braided networks can be useful.

For example, the journeys famously made by empresses such as Helena (in 327) and Eudocia (in 438) to Jerusalem are often referred to in scholarship as pilgrimages because of their acts of piety and patronage there. Socrates tells us that Eudocia's first journey to Jerusalem in 438 was made in answer to a vow, and Sozomen tells us that Helena traveled to Jerusalem for the purpose of prayer.²⁹ However, even among ancient sources the pilgrimage motivation is disputed, and a wider look at the sources shows us that these visits to Jerusalem took place as part of larger journeys that themselves are modeled on the imperial grand tour (*iter principis*).³⁰ Eusebius of Caesarea describes Helena as journeying through the eastern provinces in imperial magnificence and notes that she bestowed countless benefits on cities,

---

25 Kingsley/Decker 2001, 10–11. See also Decker 2013.
26 This type is most commonly known as Late Roman (LR) 4. Cf. Pieri 2005 for a summary, also Riley 1975, 30–31, Dixneuf 2005, 54–55, Mayerson 1992. Imitations at Aila: Melkawi/'Amr/Whitcomb 1994.
27 Kingsley 2002.
28 Coripp. *In Laud. Iust.* 4,6. Greg. Tur. *Hist. Franc.* 7,29. The fourth-century text *Expositio totius mundi et gentium* also praises the wine of Palestine (29). For more on ancient discussions of Palestinian wine, cf. Mayerson 1993.
29 Socr. *HE* 7,47; Sozom. *HE* 2,1.
30 Holum 1990.

individuals, and soldiers, dispensing both money, charity, and justice.[31] Evagrius Scholasticus, describing Eudocia's first 'pilgrimage' notes of her visit to Antioch that she used it to proclaim her affinity with Antioch's philosophical (pagan) tradition, and to perform acts of civic patronage by rebuilding the city's walls.[32] To Eudocia is also attributed a poem discovered at the baths at Hammat Gader near the shores of Lake Tiberias. The poem is classicizing in style, yet in the sixth century at least the same baths were regarded as a place of miraculous healing.[33] Is Eudocia's presence there an act of civic or religious patronage? Sometimes the strands in the braided network are not at all distinct.

Another example of a journey where the strands are indistinct is the journey from Jerusalem to Constantinople made by the aristocrat-turned-ascetic Melania the Younger in 436. She traveled from Jerusalem to Constantinople to be involved in the marriage negotiations of the daughter of Theodosius II to Valentinian III, and to convert her uncle who was a pagan senator.[34] Thus the purpose of her visit was partly official, partly personal and partly religious. Her uncle managed to supply her with some sort of permit to use the facilities of the *cursus publicus*. Although she was nominally traveling in the guise of an imperial official, the journey offered her many opportunities to demonstrate her holiness. She often resided in churches instead of inns, like a pilgrim. The power of her sanctity was able to surmount bureaucratic hurdles. The fact that it took the station master at Tripoli some time to realize that this senator's niece wielding a dubious official permit and trying to requisition more animals than she was entitled to was in fact a holy woman on a mission from God, shows that in Late Antiquity the lines could be very blurred indeed.

The Journey: Routes and Processes

And what then of the process of getting from Constantinople to Jerusalem or vice versa? Not everyone could be a Sophia and be miraculously transported from one to the other.[35] For most this meant a long journey of over a month, passing through localities each with their own characteristics and roles to play in regional and interregional networks.

Furthermore, it is important to note that the routes that 'directly' connected Constantinople and Jerusalem are far from direct, instead passing through a series of nodes, and relying on a combination of land and sea travel. They rely on routes and nodes that were originally conceived of for different purposes. The trans-Anato-

---

31 Euseb. *VC* 3,44.
32 Evagr. *HE* 1,20–21. He is the one who expresses skepticism of "other historians" who claim Eudocia's motives were solely religious.
33 On Eudocia's inscription, cf. Green/Tsafrir 1982. Baths for healing: *Itin. Plac.* 7.
34 Gerontius *Vit. Mel. Jun.* 50–56.
35 Cf. Klein this volume.

lian highway to Antioch (known in modern scholarship as the Pilgrim's Road) was a military-administrative highway, as was the 'coastal corridor' connecting Antioch and Alexandria via the Mediterranean coast. These were adapted and maintained in Late Antiquity for the purpose of integrating Jerusalem into the communications network.

In the following section I will trace the main overland routes as divided into three stages (Constantinople-Ancyra-Antioch, the coastal highway between Antioch and the coast of Palaestina, and the overland journey between the coast and Jerusalem). I will consider the route both as geographically determined by the physical landscape but also consider the cultural landscape of cities and their function as nodes in braided networks in their own right. I will also consider the very specific impact of pilgrimage on the routes.

Before focusing on the overland routes, a brief consideration of the maritime routes would be pertinent. Late Antique Constantinople was a port city, separated from the Asian landmass by the Bosporus (c. 3 km from the mouth of the Golden Horn to Chalcedon); Jerusalem is located 50 km inland and not connected to any navigable waterways. Any journey from one to the other would necessitate a combination of water and land travel.

To access the Levantine coast from Constantinople requires sailing through the Sea of Marmara and out the Dardanelles into the Aegean, essentially island-hopping from one island to another, or tramping along the coast, which provided opportunities to sleep on land (avoiding night sailing) and refreshing the supplies of fresh water on board. A ship could also keep within sight of the coastline, avoiding the open sea. Rhodes and Cyprus are important island stops for accessing the Levantine coast. The frequency of small islands and the shape of the coastline of Asia Minor are both helpful and harmful as they could serve as both a refuge and a hazard. The sheer number of shipwrecks found along coast of Asia Minor from the Bronze Age onward gives an idea of the statistics of running afoul of the local geology.

The coast of the Levant is rather different, a straight coastline with sandy beaches but exposed to the open sea and wind.[36] Anchorages are frequent with a port on average every 6 km.[37] The large number of available ports would give many alternatives to a traveler, particularly in the case of pilgrims making their way to Jerusalem. Even ports that did not possess a direct inland access towards Jerusalem or other cities would be easily linked by the coastal highway to another city that joined with the road network of the interior. For example, Dor (Tantura) was apparently not directly connected by an official highway with the interior, and traffic from Dor likely made its way either south to Caesarea Maritima (a distance of about 13 km) or north to Ptolemais (c. 35 km) before linking up with inland routes.

---

36 Kingsley 2004, 28–33, on historical versus present-day conditions.
37 De Graauw/Maione-Downing/McCormick 2013.

The main advantage of sea travel compared to land travel was speed. For example, between 401 and 402, Porphyry of Gaza sailed from Gaza to Constantinople, via Rhodes. The journey there took 20 days – 10 to Rhodes and a further 10 the Constantinople, and the return journey, aided by the prevailing northerly winds, took only 10 days.[38] The journey by land between Gaza and Constantinople could be reckoned at anywhere between 20 and 54 days.[39] The disadvantages of sea travel were the dangers, unpredictability, and dependence on the seasons and weather. There was also the cost of chartering passage to consider. For travelers with permission to use the services of the *cursus publicus*, the permit issued by the state was only valid for travel by land.

The *cursus publicus*, in addition to only servicing travel overland, also only operated on roads classed as public highways, *viae publicae*. Nevertheless, it is estimated that the Roman Empire was covered by a network of some 80,000 kilometers of public highways.[40] These public highways had two main functions, first to connect destinations of importance (the *capita viae*), and second, to achieve that connection in the most efficient way possible. The most efficient – and historical sources suggest, the most used – overland route between Constantinople and Jerusalem relying on the *viae publicae* consists of three stages. The first is the traversing of the Anatolian interior and crossing the Taurus mountains to Antioch (the so-called Pilgrim's Road). The second stage is the coastal corridor following the Mediterranean shore south from Antioch to one of any number of cities of coastal Palestine from which to commence the third stage: journeying across the interior towards Jerusalem.

The roads and routes that were used to connect Constantinople and Jerusalem were of course not an innovation of the fourth century. The famous imperial roads followed ancient routes that were for a large part constrained by natural features of the landscape. For example, any route connecting Asia Minor with the Levant must cross the Taurus Mountains: the most natural place to do this is through the so-called Cilician Gates (Gülek Boğazı). This is true even today, and the Tarsus-Ankara highway squeezes through the pass at an elevation of 1050 m above sea level.

In addition to mountain passes, other naturally or physically predetermined factors, such as river crossings, the availability of drinking water, or the need for overnight accommodation will affect all travelers in our braided system equally. If they are traveling by foot, most persons, regardless of motivation, will travel at more or

---

38 Marcus Diaconus *Vit. Porph.* 26–27, 34, 37 and 56–57.
39 The estimates derive from a combination of documents. For Gaza-Antioch, the papyrus account of Theophanes (ca. AD 320) gives a duration of 14 days. Matthews 2006, 61. For Antioch-Constantinople the *magister officiorum* Caesarius (AD 387) took 6 days in a mule-drawn chariot. Lib. *Or.* 21,15. The Bordeaux Traveler (AD 333) records 40 (overnight) stops for the same journey. *Itin. Burd.* 570–581.
40 To this can be added approximately 320,000 km of secondary roads. Sidebotham 2011, 125. The confirmation of a road as a *via publica* depends on milestones and itineraries. Roads that are archaeologically attested but where no official evidence survives may well have been *viae publicae*, but are more safely categorized as highways or 'major thoroughfares'.

less the same rate (5 km/h on level terrain, or 25–30 km per day) and require lodging at identical intervals. Passages through more difficult terrain will require infrastructure as well. Egeria mentions stopping overnight at the inn at Mansucrene after a day's travel, before climbing to the Cilician Gates the following morning (an effort which doubtless necessitated plenty of rest, and plenty of daylight).[41] Routes will also tend to follow the path of least resistance. As these are often determined by natural features they tend to be resistant to change, and so Roman engineered roads of the 1st–3rd centuries are found laid over routes of much greater antiquity, and modern highways follow their course today.

Stage 1: Constantinople–Antioch

Let us begin with the stage from Constantinople to Antioch (Fig. 20). In tracing the route of this first stage, the very first natural barrier is the Bosporus. Constantinople's location controlling the waterways of the Black Sea and the Sea of Marmara was in many ways considered ideal, but presented problems for overland connectivity, considering that Constantinople was also the pinnacle of the Balkans and Thrace, the terminus for the Via Egnatia. A bridge was constructed under Justinian across the Golden Horn upstream of the modern Atatürk Bridge, but did not solve the problem of connecting the European side of the Bosporus with the Asian side.[42] This was resolved by relying on ships and ferries to take passengers across, and was clearly not regarded as much of an obstacle, as casual notes in the itineraries of the Bordeaux Traveler and Egeria indicate.[43]

The route known as the Pilgrim's Road then follows the coast to Nicaea before turning eastwards towards Ancyra (Ankara) in central Anatolia. From there the route turns south, following the foothills of the Cappadocian mountains, keeping to the eastern edge of the featureless central Anatolian plateau and the Tuz Gölü Salt Lake, passing through Tyana and then through the Taurus Mountains at the Cilician Gates. On the other side of the mountains it passes through the metropoleis of Cilicia – Tarsus, Adana, and Mopsuestia (Yakapinar/Misis) – before crossing the Amanus Mountain range, via the 'Amanid Gates' (Kara Kapı) squeezing between the mountains and the coast at Porta/Portella ('Jonah's Pillars') another mountain crossing known as the Syrian Gates at Belen south of Alexandria ad Issum (Iskenderun), which placed the traveler within a day's journey of Antioch. This route is just over 1000 km long. It served in the Roman period when it was constructed, and in

---

41 *Itin. Eg.* 10,7.
42 *Chron. Pasch.* 618,14–19; the *Notitia Urbis Constantinopolitanae* (mid-fifth c.) also mentions a wooden bridge across the Golden Horn. Seeck 1876, 240.
43 *Itin. Burd.* 571, *Itin. Eg.* 23,8. However, the emperor Julian forbade captains from ferrying some troublesome petitioners to Constantinople, and they found themselves stranded at Chalcedon. Amm. Marc. 22,6,4.

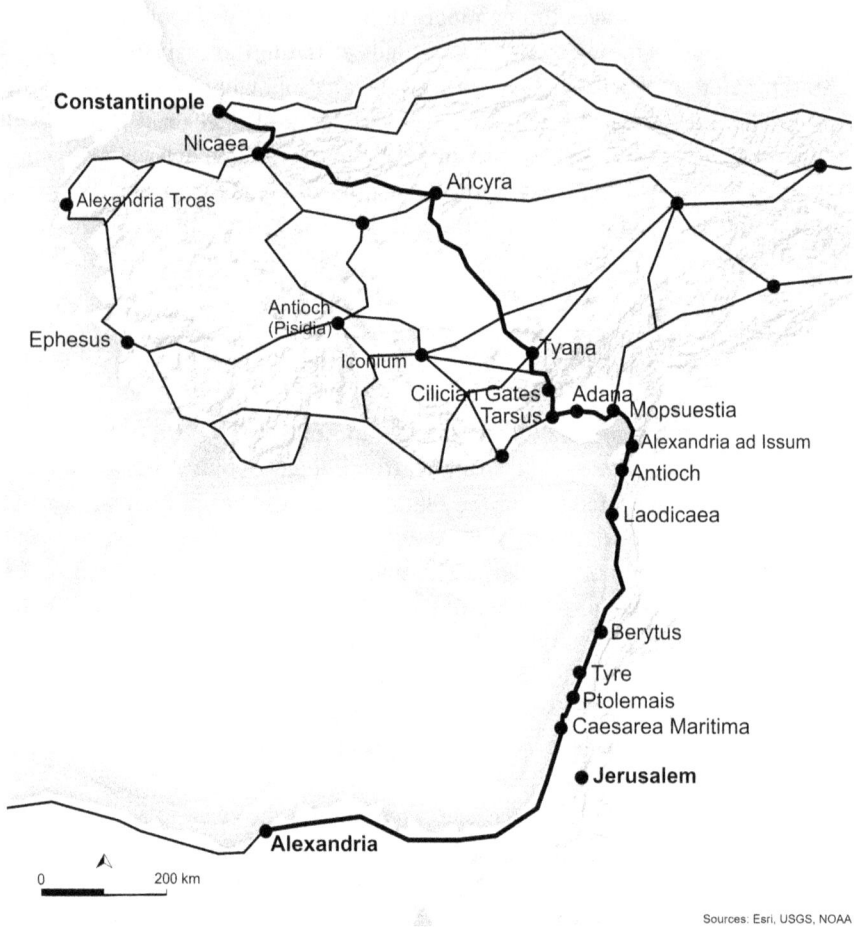

Fig. 20: Sketch map of routes in Anatolia and coastal highway to Alexandria, © M. Whiting.

Late Antiquity as well, as an interregional highway. Its main purpose was to provide overland connection between Europe on the one hand and Syria, the Levant, and beyond, on the other, and the pass through the Taurus was – and is – the only direct way to achieve that.

Although we know from historical sources that this was the preferred overland route of many travelers including the Bordeaux Traveler, Egeria, Melania the Younger, and Caesarius the *magister militum*, it was by no means the only route across Anatolia. Compare, for example, the itineraries of the Apostle Paul in the first century AD, to cities like Iconium and Pisidian Antioch, Ephesus and Alexandria Troas on the Aegean, none of which are on the Pilgrim's Road. Paul's route turns westward north of the Cilician Gates, following the first-century AD road known as the Via Sebaste, connecting the Taurus pass with Ephesus via Iconium.[44]

On the Peutinger Map (of first- to fourth-century date[45]), the Pilgrim's Road route is not even accurately represented. From this document one would gain the impression that there was no direct link from the Cilician Gates to Tyana, but that traffic had to pass by way of Iconium (Konya – Yconio on the Peutinger Map). The earliest milestone evidence along the corresponding section of the Pilgrim's Road dates to the reign of Caracalla (AD 216); the inscription specifically refers to repairs on the roads and bridges, thus the initial paving predates this inscription.[46]

Paul's objective was to proselytize and engage with communities – and the central Anatolian plateau was comparatively devoid of cities. The advantage of the Pilgrim's Road is its speed, the relative levelness of its terrain compared to the western, coastal areas. The coast of Asia Minor is fairly mountainous, with deep river valleys running perpendicular to the coastline, making coastal overland communications difficult and slow. The river deltas are prone to siltation and the ground is marshy and at risk of seasonal flooding. The Pilgrim's Road, skirting the eastern edge of the central Anatolian plateau/Konya plain is altogether quicker, even if it does miss some of the cultural highlights.

The focus on Jerusalem as a destination for pilgrims in Late Antiquity overshadows what was perhaps the most important nodal point in the communications network of the East Mediterranean: the city of Antioch. Antioch was, at its height in the fourth and fifth centuries, a city of some 200,000 people, embellished with temples, churches, colonnades, shops, public baths and other public amenities. It was an important center for philosophical learning, and thus also became an important locus of theological learning as well, which would see Antioch be prominent in the theological disputes of the age. Antioch also had a religious landscape with many churches and relics, including the relics of Simeon the Elder Stylite.

In the late third century, Antioch was made the capital of the administrative diocese of Oriens, which extended from southeast Anatolia east to the Tigris, and south to the Red Sea. As such, it was the residence of the *comes Orientis*, the *magister militum per orientem*, and the governor of the province of Syria. It was also the seat of the Patriarchate of the East. For administrative purposes, thus, Antioch was the most important city of the Near East, its status similar to that of Alexandria in Egypt. Antioch served as the imperial capital under Constantius II and Valens, because of its proximity to the Mesopotamian frontier. It is sometimes characterized as a 'frontier

---

44 On Paul's itineraries through Asia Minor, see French 1994; for an illustrated guide, see Cimok 2004, esp. pages 109–116 for the Taurus crossing.

45 The version preserved today is a thirteenth-century copy of a map probably drawn up in the early to mid-fourth century, itself possibly based on a first- or second-century original. For a recent discussion on the dating, see Talbert 2010. See also French 1981, Table 9a–11a, 118–122.

46 *RRMAM* 3.3, No. 166: *Viam Tauri vetustate [conl]apsam conplanatis monti[bus e]t caesis rupibus ac dilata[tis i]tineribus cum pontibus institutis restituit.*

capital' despite being hundreds of miles from the actual frontier, since it served as the base of operations and winter camp for a number of Persian campaigns, notably during the reigns of Julian, Justinian, Phocas (led by future emperor Maurice), and possibly Heraclius in the 630's.[47] This role fell to Antioch in part for geographic reasons. The northern reaches of the Orontes river valley provided transverse access to the interior of Syria and thence the Euphrates and Tigris frontiers. Antioch also had access to the sea via its port at Seleucia Pieria, and north-south communications, as we have seen, via the coastal highway.[48] The agricultural hinterland of Antioch, which included the much-studied Limestone Massif, was greatly expanded in the late antique period and was capable of supporting the large population of the city and a wintering army (with a few notable exceptions, e. g. under Julian). Antioch was also an important terminus for long-distance trade, as the same routes that in war time led to the Mesopotamian frontier also connected with known trading posts e. g. at Batnae (Suruç)[49] Antioch was geographically best placed to gather together the roads from the interior, and disperse them north and south. In the sixth century Antioch experienced repeated earthquakes, fire, plague and two sacks by the Persians. However, there was no real possibility for Antioch, however beset, to fade into obscurity – its function as a hub was too important. In many ways the same goes for the other cities of the Levantine coast: the Piacenza Pilgrim (c. 570) described that many of the cities were partly ruined, but it was unavoidable that he should nonetheless pass through them in order to reach Jerusalem.[50]

Stage 2: The Coastal Highway

From Antioch the road headed south, re-joining the coast at Laodicea (Latakia). Especially through Lebanon (*provincia Phoenicia*) the coast road is constrained to a narrow corridor by the steep Anti-Lebanon mountains rising to the east. Recent studies have highlighted some of the communications challenges on the routes inland to Baalbek and the Bikaa Valley.[51] The Mount Carmel range marks the southernmost point of these inaccessible coastal mountains, and after Ptolemais (Akko) the interior of the Levant becomes more accessible. The distance from Antioch to Ptolemais is 445 km. The coastal highway continues down the length of the Mediterranean coast, all the way to the Nile Delta and Alexandria, and was thus yet another crucial

---

47 Kaegi 2003, 230.
48 I have elsewhere expressed skepticism about the Orontes itself as the channel for transport of goods, there are many rapids that make navigation uncertain, and furthermore, Seleucia Pieria is not located at the mouth of the Orontes. Instead, the river valley provides a convenient route for land transport. Whiting 2017.
49 Amm. Marc. 16,3,3. records that an international trading fair took place there every September.
50 *Itin. Plac.* 1–2.
51 Abou Diwan/Doumit 2017.

interregional highway. The coastal road is quite ancient, its antiquity is epigraphically attested for example at the Nahr al-Kalb gorge 15 km north of Berytus (Beirut) where numerous inscriptions from the 13th century BC to the 21st century attest to its importance as a thoroughfare.[52] Another indication that this road was an interregional highway rather than a regional one, is that the Roman road does not pass directly through all of these cities. Some of them, having a stronger relationship with the sea than the land, are located on promontories that would require the road to detour. Thus the Roman road probably passed directly through Berytus and Laodicaea (Latakia) but by-passed Byblos and Tyre, with milestones marking the junctions for transverse roads to these cities.[53]

The coastal highway continues south from Ptolemais toward Caeasarea Maritima, where physical remains of the road are attested between Caesarea and 'Atlit, south of Haifa (Fig. 21). The milestones found along the road indicate roadworks were carried out between the second and third centuries; no milestone records the earliest phase of the engineered road.[54] The extension of the road south to Joppa (Jaffa) was repaired in the Byzantine period, evidence of the route's continued importance as part of a continuous artery connecting the entire eastern Mediterranean, and the ongoing investment in its infrastructure.[55]

Stage 3: Inland Towards Jerusalem

South of the Mount Carmel mountain range it was possible to depart from the coastal highway at any of the larger settlements (e. g., Caesarea Maritima, Joppa, Ascalon, Gaza) that served as junctions for the public highways, and turn inland towards Jerusalem. The Piacenza Pilgrim departed for the interior from Ptolemais, touring the northern sites of the Galilee first, then traveling to the Jordan River and then westwards towards Jerusalem.[56] The seventh-century pilgrim itinerary of Epiphanius, which recommends Tyre (40 km north of Ptolemais) as a port for the Holy Land, may have a similar itinerary in mind.[57]

From the coastal plain the elevation of the terrain increases at steady increments. To look at it on the map, there are north-south bands of increasing elevation, with transverse routes of access at various points. To look at it from the ground, the landscape is hilly, and the routes skirt the peaks of the hills. Each city serves as a junction for several other routes to other cities. Caesarea Maritima has at least

---

52 Paine/Hitchcock 1873, 111–112; the most recent inscription dates from 2000, see Lindering 2012 (2018).
53 Goodchild 1949, 106.
54 Roll 1996, 553.
55 Roll 1996, 558.
56 *Itin. Plac.* 4–17.
57 Epiphanius Hagiopolita *Itin.* 1.

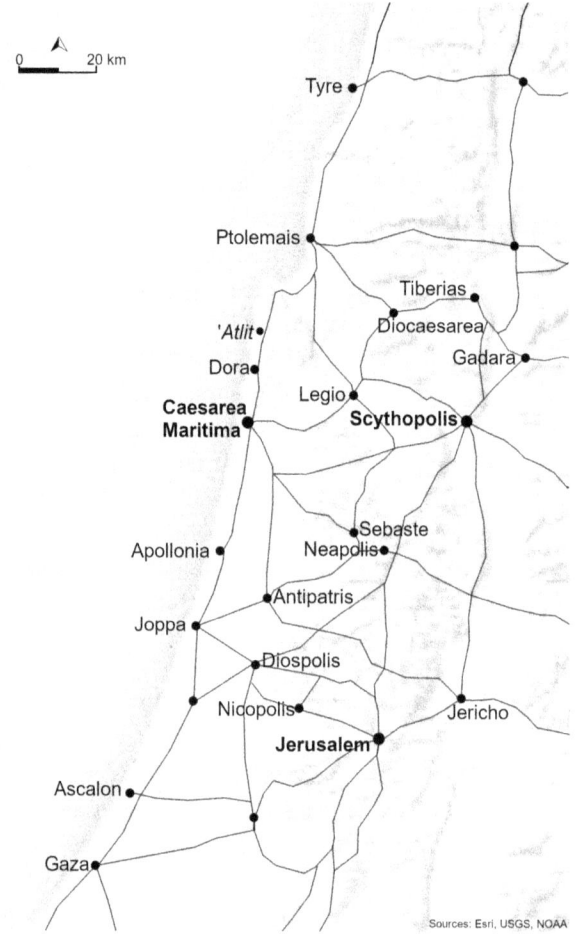

Fig. 21: Sketch map of routes in Palaestina, © M. Whiting.

four inland routes departing from it; Jerusalem likewise has five roads entering it from various directions. Each city is well-connected, but given the sheer number of roads and junctions, the possible permutations are numerous, and it is clear that various routes might have been preferred for different reasons. For those interested in holy sites, from Caesarea Maritima it was possible to arrive at Jerusalem passing through Antipatris, Lydda-Diospolis and Emmaus/Nicopolis, the route taken for example by Paula and Jerome, and completed in reverse by the Bordeaux Traveler.[58] It was equally possible to take the coastal road from Caesarea further

---

58 Hier. *Ep.* 108,8.

south to Joppa, and then to towards Jerusalem via Lydda-Diospolis etc., with little apparent difference in distance covered or time required.[59]

As I have been demonstrating throughout, the main purpose of the roads that linked Constantinople to Jerusalem was not to provide a direct connection between the two cities, instead the route took advantage of existing connections (to Antioch or Alexandria) to make it possible to complete the journey in what I have separated into three stages. Furthermore, even in Late Antiquity this route was not maintained exclusively for Christian (i.e. pilgrimage) purposes, but the imperial administration and military, as well as trade, had a significant share in the traffic along these routes.

Nevertheless, the Christianization of the Roman Empire with Jerusalem as its spiritual center did create new pressures on the road network. In the following section I will explore how the existing road network responded to the needs of Christian users, and how the interplay of the different groups in the braided system remained active.

Infrastructure Maintenance, Patronage, and Civic Responsibility

To resume our metaphor of the braided network, in the case of infrastructure that serves a wide variety of users, who is responsible for maintaining it? The government? The Church? The emperor? Typically of Late Antiquity, the answer is all three. Emperors or high government officials like the governors or prefects financed large infrastructure projects, while local officials were responsible for day-to-day maintenance. Changes throughout the period in responsibility for communications infrastructure are a by-product of many of the social changes taking place in the fourth and fifth centuries and beyond. These changes include the so-called "flight of the *curiales*" and decline of classical civic administration, and the concomitant rise of Christianity.[60]

Up to the mid-fourth century, road repairs were often recorded on milestones, usually bearing the name of the ruling emperor and other times the names of lesser officials (including those responsible for commissioning the work). Road work carried out as part of a military campaign might have the name of the legion who provided the labor. Including the name of the emperor was a propaganda statement of imperial hegemony. Many of the milestones recorded along the Pilgrim's Road, along the coastal highway, and in Palaestina, have some primary but mainly secondary inscriptions of Constantine and his sons from the period 333–337, and it might be tempting to read them as endorsements of the new Christian Holy Land. However,

---

59 This route is described in reverse in Theodosius' *De situ terrae sanctae*, 4. It would probably take three to four days.
60 Whittow 1990.

this should not be seen as an overtly Christian message or a promotion of the road for Christian pilgrimage. Instead the message is one of political and dynastic unity and stability following the civil wars of Constantine's early reign and the execution of his eldest son, Crispus.[61] Two milestones of Julian (361–363) were discovered along the so-called 'Pilgrim's Road,' one in Pontus/Bithynia and one near Ancyra[62]; it is clear that the Hellenophile Julian was *not* promoting Christian travel to the Holy Land. Instead it is likely related to his campaigns against Persia and sojourn in Antioch.

The lack of the overtly Christian associations even by the late fourth century is further made clear by a road inscription at Nahr al-Kalb commemorating the widening of a road cut in the rock during the governorship of Proc[u]lus in 382–383. This inscription invokes a pagan god (the Phoenician god, Malek, associated with Zeus), and is written in Homeric Greek intended to appeal to the intellectual elite of the curial classes of the Hellenized cities (who were still in charge of road maintenance).[63] The strongly pagan intellectual character of the cities of Phoenicia – and corresponding lack of sites Christian holy sites – is likely why Jerome glosses over them when describing Paula's journey to the Holy Land after arriving at Antioch in 384.[64]

In many ways, the Nahr al-Kalb inscription is emblematic of the state of affairs in the fourth century. In this period, ordinary maintenance of roads, bridges, etc. was primarily the responsibility of local city governments (the *boulē* or *curia*) and their elite members, the *curiales*. They were also responsible for the operation of the *cursus publicus* within their city's territory. Responsibility for the *cursus publicus* was a *munus* – a civic obligation – bestowed on the member of the *curia* elected to the position of *manceps* for a period of five years. Fodder for the animals was provided for by the *annona*, i.e. tax revenue, but the *manceps* had to make up any shortfall from his own resources. This and other civic *munera* were thus increasingly unappealing and unviable to local *curiales*. Legislation throughout the fourth and fifth centuries attempted to enforce this obligation, stressing that no class be exempt from contributing to road maintenance – these laws expanded to include imperial domains and the Church among those responsible for maintaining roads and bridges.[65]

Bishops, based largely in cities, gradually assumed much of the administrative authority that had previously resided with the *curiales*, who were abandoning their

---

61 See Goodchild 1949, 117–127, Fischer/Isaac/Roll 1996, 295, Isaac/Roll 1982, 95, Thomsen 1917, 93. On milestones in the fourth century and beyond, see Whiting 2015. In fact, of the 128 milestones dating from the reign of Constantine found in Asia Minor, only eight are on the 'Pilgrim's Road'.
62 *RRMAM* 3.3, No. 87(A), 139, *RRMAM* 3.2, No. 115(4), 184–185.
63 Hall 2004, 144–145, Hajjar 1990, 2505.
64 Hier. *Ep.* 108,8: *Omitto Coeles Syriae, et Phoenicis iter (neque enim hodoeporicon ejus disposui scribere): ea tantum loca nominabo, quae sacris Voluminibus continentur.* The Piacenza Pilgrim c. 570 describes the inhabitants of Sidon as very bad people (*homines in ea pessimi*), possibly a comment on their lack of piety? *Itin. Plac.* 2.
65 *Cod. Theod.* 15,3,1–6. A law of Arcadius and Honorius dated to 399 specifically mentions the 'immense ruin of the highways'. *Cod. Theod.* 15,3,4.

stations for less onerous positions (e.g. posts in the imperial administration – or joining the Church). Thus the Church was responsible not only for ecclesiastical matters but also the organizing of charity and hospitality (which included pilgrims), but also road infrastructure and bridges. A bridge located ca. 50 km southwest from Ankara has an inscription saying it was completed by the Bishop Paul.⁶⁶ Theodoret, Bishop of Cyrrhus in northwest Syria, noted that he paid for two bridges to be built near the city "from the revenues of [his] see".⁶⁷ This was still local government, but in a different guise.

In more complicated cases, however, it was necessary for the higher echelons of government to get involved. For example, a series of three bridges built leading to Seleucia Pieria in 524 was overseen by the *comes Orientis*.⁶⁸ In *De Aedeficiis* (thus occurring pre-550), Procopius records a series of complex bridge repairs in Cilicia, at Tarsus, Adana, and Mopsuestia, attributed by the author to Justinian himself (and thus presumably paid for from state revenue).⁶⁹ Procopius states that the condition of the bridges had made the road (which in this case is the Pilgrim's Road) impassable, and that their condition was due to "the neglect of the authorities" (τῇ τῶν προεστηκότων ὀλιγωρίᾳ).⁷⁰ Whether we are to infer corruption or simply a lack of funds, clearly the by now foundering local government system had broken down, and imperial intervention was necessary to restore the bridges: their role in sustaining this key interregional communications route was of too much importance to let them crumble.⁷¹

As society changed, the Christianization of infrastructure and amenities became more pervasive. A useful example is the village of Sykeon in Galatia (ca. 300 km SW of Constantinople). Justinian built a bridge there, and a church next to the bridge "to be a refuge for travelers in winter".⁷² However, we know from the *vita* of the holy man/bishop Theodore of Sykeon that within a short time a secular lodging house catering to imperial officials and merchants also appeared at this important halting point.⁷³ However, once Theodore gained fame as a holy man, the place became a

---

66 Ramsay 1883, 22, No. 11; possibly the same Bishop Paul of Ankara (ca. 580) mentioned in the *Vit. Theod. Syceon.*, 58 and 79. Cf. Foss 1977, 59.
67 Theodor. *Ep.* 81, dated c. 449.
68 *IGLS* III.2 no. 1142. Similarly, at Philadelphia in Isauria, the *comes Orientis* Auxitius is credited with having spent 3,000 solidi towards restoring a bridge sometime in the fifth or sixth century. Bean and Mitford 1970, 219–220, no. 251; *PLRE* II, 206 = Auxitius.
69 Proc. *Aed.* 5,5,4–20.
70 Proc. *Aed.* 5,5,6.
71 Procopius also mentions a new road cut through the mountains north of Antioch on this route. Proc. *Aed.* 5,5,1–3. According to David French, an Austrian team has observed traces of a rock-cut road in that area. French 1993, 454. Road works in Cilicia and Cappadocia under Justinian are not exclusively confined to this highway, however.
72 Proc. *Aed.* 5,4,4.
73 *Vit. Theod. Syceon.* 3, 6. Theodore was born in the reign of Justinian, and died in 613.

place of regional pilgrimage, and, thanks to its location, one of interregional pilgrimage as well.

The 'Pilgrim's Road'

The Christianization of travel infrastructure to pilgrimage is most evident in Palaestina, in the region around Jerusalem which abounded with sites to which could be assigned Biblical associations, and could thus be incorporated into a Christian travel network, providing the appropriate kinds of hospitality to pilgrims.[74] This is particularly evident on the route from Jerusalem to Jericho and the Jordan River, where roadside churches and hostels at regular intervals (in part thanks to imperial patronage) appropriated and mimicked the facilities of secular road networks. This formed a kind of *cursus sanctus*, one might say, mirroring the structure of the *cursus publicus*. We also see this on the Joppa-Jerusalem route with the construction of roadside monasteries, but also with state involvement in security installations, like watchtowers and guardhouses.[75] Even sites with no overt scriptural provenance could integrate themselves into the *cursus sanctus*, by appropriating a Biblical locus, by acquiring relics, and by building churches and religious buildings. Emmaus/Nikopolis came to be associated with the resurrected Christ's meeting with his two disciples, although the Emmaus of the New Testament story is a different location. The church at the port city of Dor was likely sanctified through the acquisition of relics; a reliquary was found in a side chapel during excavations.[76] The empress Eudoxia endowed a pilgrim hostel at a monastery near Gaza.[77]

What then of the other regions through which pilgrims, particularly those traveling over land, had to pass, namely Phoenicia and the provinces of central Anatolia? Both of these regions were holdouts of paganism throughout the fourth century and beyond and lacked a ready-made Christian topography, which had to be developed through the promotion of martyr cults and holy persons. Very few pilgrim accounts mention Phoenicia in any detail. Jerome skips it for lacking sites of interest. Along the densely urbanized Levantine coast, hospitality through church authorities could have been readily available, as we saw with the journey of Melania the Younger to Constantinople. The Piacenza Pilgrim in the 570's notes that many of these cities were in a ruinous state, but that Ptolemais had a great number of monasteries.[78]

---

[74] Hunt 1982, 54 refers to an "alternative system of Christian hospitality".
[75] Fischer et al. 1996, watchtower at Khirbet al Atrash, 124–125, guardhouse at Khirbet ad Dureihima, 149.
[76] Dauphin 1993.
[77] Marcus Diaconus, *Vit. Porph.* 53..
[78] *Itin. Plac.* 1–2. The cities had been damaged by an earthquake in the reign of Justinian: *tempore Iustiniani imperatoris subuersa est a terrae motu*.

Attempting to answer the question of pilgrim-specific amenities on the route through central Anatolia is a bit more complex. The area that the route passes through is vast and consists of numerous micro-regions. The archaeological investigations are sporadic, and synthesizing studies are few. In his 1981 study of the Pilgrim's Road, French described most of the roadside settlements as 'mounds'.[79] More recent archaeological investigations have been carried out at some sites, but it is still difficult – and beyond the scope of this article – to piece together a coherent story for the demographic and cultural landscape for the regions through which the Pilgrim's Road passed, and harder still to assess how this might have directly served pilgrims between Constantinople and Jerusalem. The indicators present in other regions, such as saints' shrines and monasteries specifically related to the highway, prove elusive, particularly in the archaeological record. Four points seem relevant with regard to reconstructing a Christian pilgrimage route through Anatolia: 1) the settlement pattern and its characteristics, 2) the process of Christianization of the area, 3) the Christian legends associated with localities, and 4) the evidence from pilgrim authors regarding the sacred topography of Anatolia and Asia Minor.

Firstly, the settlement pattern. In contrast to the Levantine coast, for example, the Pilgrim's Road passes through a landscape that is not heavily urbanized. While there are cities in central Anatolia, in most cases the road does not pass through the city itself, but through its rural hinterland, populated mainly with villages and the occasional imperial estate. Even settlements that have the official status of 'city,' like Faustinopolis, may have been little more than villages.[80] Furthermore, the road stations whose names are known to us from literary sources might not have been situated in the settlement from which they derive their name. For example, French identified the road station for Andabilis as a site located about 4 km from the village of Andabilis (Yeniköy), the 'parent site' for the road stop. The reasons for selecting a location for a road stop are different for those for selecting a permanent settlement (e.g., accessibility vs. defensibility). Sites like these do not automatically benefit from urban amenities, especially those that could be provided by a city-based ecclesiastical administration. Gregory of Nazianzus evoked life in one such a roadside station (at Sasima, in Cappadocia): "dust everywhere, noise, carriages, lamentations, groans, tax-collectors, tortures and fetters; a population of total strangers and vagabonds."[81].

Second, the process of the Christianization of the area has bearing on the visibility of Christian shrines and hospitality. The cities of Anatolia are sometimes regarded as holdouts of paganism, but this probably only applies to the urban elites. Bishops of Ancyra and Tarsus were present at the council of Nicaea in 325, and Ancyra was originally considered as a venue for that council. So both Christians and pagans were

---

[79] "Mound" in this case denotes a settlement mound, *hüyuk* or *tell*, which is an indicator of the presence of a multi-period settlement.
[80] Turchetto 2015, 186. Cf. Trombley 2001.
[81] Greg. Naz. *Carm.* 2,1.

active in these cities throughout the fourth century. Furthermore, cities were more likely to be the site of martyr cults, as the original trial, execution, and burial of the martyr was more likely to have taken place in a city. This was the case with the cult of the martyr Plato of Ancyra, whose veneration was carried by Ancyra natives to Constantinople and the Holy Land.[82] The process of conversion of the countryside is typically slower than that of the cities.[83] It is therefore possible that Christianity was slower to transform some of the rural locales through which the Pilgrim's Road passed. However, the unlikely elevation of Sasima to episcopal see in 372 shows that the transformation of rural areas was being implemented. The process was probably complete in the fifth century, and by the sixth century tales of local holy men were popular among rural communities.

This brings us to the third point, namely the role of narrative, landscape, and memory in the construction of sites of pilgrimage. It is noteworthy that many of the legends associated with holy sites in Anatolia date from the medieval period, and do not seem to trace back to late antiquity. This is the case with an early church building at Andabilis, which in the medieval period acquires the legend of having been built by Helena during her journey to the Holy Land. Medieval frescoes show that the church was dedicated to Constantine and Helena, but it is unclear – and unlikely – that the legend goes back all the way to the fourth century. Another case in point is the legend of the martyr Orestes of Tyana.[84] According to early martyrology, he was martyred 24 km from the city, having been dragged there by a wild horse and his body cast into a river. It is not until a twelfth-century version that this event is associated with a specific locale – a thermal spring at Batos – and that healings are said to occur there. There are many thermal springs in the Tyana area, some of which were consecrated to Zeus and considered holy sites in pagan times, but do not appear to have been recorded as famous sites of Christian pilgrimage and healing. Nevertheless, Gregory of Nazianzus, writing in 382, twice mentions a bath at Xanxaris (thought by Berges and Nollé to be identifiable with Aqua Calidae, a road station mentioned on the Peutinger Map and by the Bordeaux Traveler), and his second letter mentions that he is staying at a monastery there.[85] Could this be a glimpse of possible "alternative Christian hospitality", to which Gregory as a man of the church would have been entitled, possibly more so than a lay pilgrim?

Finally, we must consider the evidence from pilgrim itineraries. Egeria (ca. 380) mentions the shrine of Euphemia at Chalcedon, but nothing of religious interest between Tarsus and Chalcedon. It is a journey that would have taken several weeks, yet she finds nothing worth recording. The sites that are of interest to her lie off the route of the Pilgrim's Road: she makes a detour of several days from Tarsus to visit Seleucia and the shrine of Thecla, and she expresses hope to visit Ephesus on a separate

---

82 On the cult of Plato in Late Antiquity, see Foss 1977.
83 E.g. Caseau 2004.
84 For primary texts relating to Tyana and its hinterland, cf. Berges/Nollé 2000.
85 Greg. Naz. *Ep.* 125, 126. Berges/Nollé 2000, 406.

journey, after her return to Constantinople.[86] The pilgrim itinerary of Theodosius, dating to ca. 530, mentions a number of holy shrines in Asia Minor relating to apostles and martyrs, at Caesarea, Gangra, Euchaita, and Sebastia, however Ancyra and the shrine of Plato is the only one mentioned that actually lies along the Pilgrims' Road (Fig. 22).[87] We also know of several other major pilgrimage and healing shrines, for example, of Michael the Archangel at Germia in Galatia.[88] However, it seems from the accounts of Egeria and Theodosius, written a century and a half apart, that there was not much to interest a Holy Land pilgrim directly on the Pilgrim's Road. Instead the Pilgrim's Road is revealed as dependent on the state network, but braided by many users. Ancyra emerges as an important node in this braided network, with a garrison, but also famous for trade, especially textile production.[89]

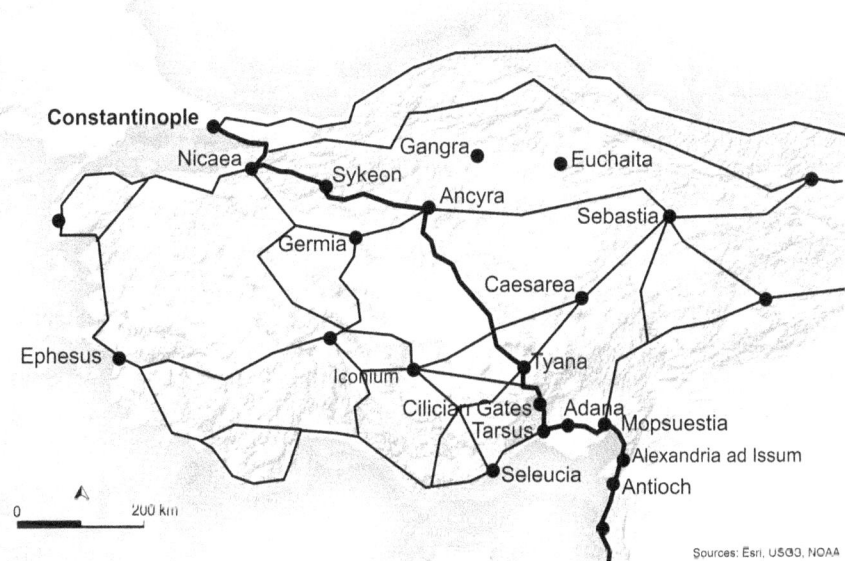

Fig. 22: Sketch map of Pilgrim's Road and pilgrimage sites in Anatolia, © M. Whiting.

In reality, the term 'Pilgrim's Road' is something of a misnomer. When considering the motivations for travel between Constantinople and Jerusalem it is easy to see the lure of the Holy City and its shrines and thus over-ascribe a pilgrim's motivation to the majority of journeys. The fault for this lies, in part, in modern nomenclature. The name Pilgrim's Road was originally ascribed to the Constantinople-Ancyra-Tar-

---

86 *Itin. Eg.* 22,1–23,6, Ephesus: 23,10.
87 Theodosius *De situ terrae sanctae* 15.
88 Niewöhner 2017, 342–348.
89 Foss 1977, 31. Cf. also Foss 1977, 56 for the suggestion that it was merchants from Ancyra who spread the cult of Plato the Martyr, especially to Constantinople.

sus road by William Ramsay, and the name chosen because it is the route described in the Bordeaux Itinerary, whose anonymous author has traditionally been known as the 'Pilgrim of Bordeaux'. Hence, the *Pilgrim's* Road. This is the term adopted by David French, as the complete route has no known ancient name (although the section through the Taurus mountains was apparently known as the Via Tauri).[90] However, over time there has been some slippage of the apostrophe – instead of referring to a pilgrim in the singular, it has come to be referred to as the *Pilgrims'* Road (plural), assumed to be on account of it being the route for countless pilgrims *en route* to Jerusalem.[91] As I have shown, this is problematic for a number of reasons. Firstly, it is far from the only route that travelers, pilgrims or otherwise, could have used for traveling through Anatolia and Asia Minor. And secondly, it implies that the bulk of travelers were pilgrims, or even that the road's *raison d'être* was pilgrimage, which obscures the vast amount of travel for other reasons that took place along this route. It conveys the idea that the primary *caput viae* was Jerusalem, and ignores other more probable destinations for the bulk of traffic in Late Antiquity, principally the capital of the eastern diocese, Antioch. Finally, it promotes the idea that Asia Minor was devoid of sites of interest to pilgrims, when, in reality, many sites of great renown were simply not located on this artery.

Conclusion

There is no single 'Pilgrims' Road' between Constantinople and Jerusalem. There is no way to get from Constantinople to Jerusalem that does not involve a mixture of sea and land travel. There is no fixed overland route (though it is constrained by natural geographic features at some points). There were different options for crossing Asia Minor or for accessing Jerusalem from the coast, although some seem to have been more popular than others.

It also wasn't just pilgrims on the road. Although Jerusalem is difficult to uncouple from its sacred attributes, other factors also placed the city within regional and interregional networks, of which the wine trade is but one aspect. Constantinople is a hub for a complex system of networks in which Jerusalem is but one node. The roads which reached Jerusalem were in part maintained and served pilgrims so well because they connected other locations like Antioch or Alexandria or any of the dozens of cities in between. They connected with theaters of military activity, with important raw materials and the empire's agricultural tax base, which was partly used to feed the capital, but produce also entered Constantinople (and other cities) via mechanisms of trade, including the holy wine of Palestine.

---

90 *RRMAM* 3.3, No. 166.
91 Cf. Hunt 1997, 256.

While it is tempting to see Constantinople and Jerusalem as opposites: one the secular capital of the Byzantine world and the other its spiritual capital, with pilgrims constantly flowing from one to another, this is a misleading perception of the roles played by both cities and the networks that existed connecting them. It is important to situate these cities in their landscape and recognize the spaces in between not as empty places on a map but integral nodes in complex and interweaving networks.

Bibliography

Abou Diwan, G. & Doumit, J. (2017). 'The Berytus-Heliopolis Baalbak road in the Roman period: a least cost path analysis,' *Mediterranean Archaeology and Archaeometry* 17, 225–241.

Agius, D.A., Cooper, J.P., et al. (eds.) (2011). *Navigated Spaces, Connected Places Proceedings of Red Sea Project V held at the University of Exeter September 2010*, Oxford.

Avi-Yonah, M. (1958). 'The Economics of Byzantine Palestine,' *IEJ* 8, 39–51.

Barag, D. (1970). 'Glass Pilgrim Vessels from Jerusalem—Part I,' *JGS* 12, 35–63.

Bean, G.E. & Mitford, T.B. (1970). *Journeys in Rough Cilicia, 1964–1968*, Vienna.

Berges, D. & Nollé, J. (2000). *Tyana: Archäologisch-historische Untersuchungen zum südwestlichen Kappadokien*, Bonn.

Beyer, D., Henry, O., et al. (eds.) (2015). *La Cappadoce méridionale, de la préhistoire à la période byzantine*, Istanbul.

Bieliński, P., Gawlikowski, M., et al. (eds.) (2014). *Proceedings of the 8th International Congress on the Archaeology of the Ancient Near East 30 April – 4 May 2012, University of Warsaw, Volume 2 Excavation and Progress Reports, Posters*, Wiesbaden.

Bonifay, M. & Tréglia, J. (eds.) (2007). *LRCW 2, Late Roman Coarse Wares, cooking wares and amphorae in the Mediterranean: archaeology and archaeometry*, Oxford.

Bowden, W., Lavan, L., et al. (eds.) (2004). *Recent research on the late antique countryside*, Leiden.

Cameron, Av. & Garnsey, P. (eds.) (1997). *The Cambridge ancient history, vol. XIII: The Late Empire, A.D. 337–425*, Cambridge.

Caseau, B. (2004). 'The fate of rural temples in Late Antiquity and the Christianisation of the countryside,' in Bowden/Lavan/et al. 2004, 105–144.

Cimok, F. (2004). *Journeys of Paul: from Tarsus to the ends of the earth*, Istanbul.

Collar, A. and Kristensen, T.M. (eds.) (2020). *Pilgrimage and Economy in the Ancient Mediterranean*, Leiden.

Comfort, A. (2009). 'Roads on the Frontier between Rome and Persia: Euphratesia, Osrhoene and Mesopotamia from AD 363 to 602,' PhD Dissertation, University of Exeter.

Comfort, A. & Abadie-Reynal, C., et al. (2000). 'Crossing the Euphrates in Antiquity: Zeugma Seen from Space,' *Anatolian Studies* 50, 99–126.

Conybeare, F.C. (1910). Antiochus Strategos' Account of the Sack of Jerusalem in A.D. 614 *EHR* 25, 502–517.

Dauphin, C. (1993). 'Dora-Dor: A Station for Pilgrims in the Byzantine Period on Their Way to Jerusalem,' in Tsafrir 1993, 90–97.

Decker, M. (2013). 'The end of the Holy Land wine trade,' *Strata: Bulletin of the Anglo-Israel Archaeological Society* 31, 103–116.

de Graauw, A., Maione-Downing, B., et al., (2014). *Geodatabase of Ancient Ports and Harbours*, hdl:1902.1/22612, Harvard Dataverse, V4.

Dixneuf, D. (2005). 'Production et circulation des biens à Gaza durant l'Antiquité tardive: le témoignage des amphores,' in Saliou 2005, 51–74.
Durliat, J. (1990). *De la ville antique à la ville byzantine. Le problème des subsistances*, Rome.
Fischer, M. & Isaac, B.H., et al. (1996). *Roman Roads in Judaea II: the Jaffa–Jerusalem Roads*, Oxford.
Foss, C. (1977). 'Late Antique and Byzantine Ankara,' *DOP* 31, 27–87.
Franconi, T.V. (ed.) (2017). *Fluvial Landscapes of the Roman World*, Portsmouth, R.I.
French, D.H. (1994). 'Acts and the Roman Roads of Asia Minor,' in Gill/Gempf 1994, 49–58.
French, D.H. (1993). 'A Road Problem: Roman or Byzantine?,' *MDAI(I)* 43, 445–454.
French, D.H. (1981–8). *Roman Roads and Milestones of Asia Minor (RRMAM)*, Oxford.
Gardner, G.E. (2014). 'City Of Lights: The Lamps of Roman and Byzantine Jerusalem,' *Near Eastern Archaeology* 77, 284–290.
Gill, D. & Gempf, C. (eds.) (1994). *The Book of Acts in its First Century Setting, Volume 2: Graeco-Roman Setting*, Grand Rapids, MI.
Goodchild, R.G. (1949). 'The Coast Road of Phoenicia and its Roman Milestones,' *Berytus* 9, 91–127.
Green, J. & Tsafrir, Y. (1982). 'Greek Inscriptions from Ḥammat Gader: a poem by the Empress Eudocia and two building inscriptions,' *IEJ* 32, 77–96.
Hajjar, Y. (1990). 'Baalbek: grand centre religieux sous l'Empire,' in *ANRW II.18.4*, 2458–2508.
Hall, L.J. (2004). *Roman Berytus: Beirut in Late Antiquity*, London.
Holum, K.G. (1990). 'Hadrian and St. Helena: imperial travel and the origins of Christian Holy Land pilgrimage,' in Ousterhout 1990, 66–81.
Hunt, E.D. (1982). *Holy Land pilgrimage in the later Roman Empire, AD 312–460*, Oxford.
Hunt, E.D. (1997). 'The church as a public institution,' in Cameron/Garnsey 1997, 238–276.
Isaac, B.H. (1990 [1992]). *The Limits of Empire: the Roman Army in the East*, Oxford.
Isaac, B.H. & Roll, I. (1976). 'A Milestone of A.D. 69 from Judaea: The Elder Trajan and Vespasian,' *JRS* 66, 15–19.
Jones, A.H.M. (1964). *The Later Roman Empire, 284–602: A Social, Economic and Administrative Survey*, Oxford.
Kaegi, W.E. (2003). *Heraclius, Emperor of Byzantium*, Cambridge.
Kingsley, S. & Decker, M. (2001). 'New Rome, new theories on inter-regional exchange. An introduction to the east Mediterranean economy in Late Antiquity,' in Kingsley/Decker 2001, 1–27.
Kingsley, S. & Decker, M. (eds.) (2001). *Economy and Exchange in the East Mediterranean during Late Antiquity: Proceedings of a Conference at Somerville College, Oxford, 29th May, 1999*, Oxford.
Kingsley, S.A. (2002). *A Sixth-Century AD Shipwreck off the Camel Coast, Israel: Dor D and Holy Land Wine Trade*, Oxford.
Kingsley, S.A. (2004). *Shipwreck Archaeology of the Holy Land: Processes and Parameters*, London.
Lavan, L. (ed.) (2001). *Recent Research in Late-Antique Urbanism*, Portsmouth, R.I.
Lemcke, L. (2016). *Imperial Transportation and Communication from the Third to the Late Fourth Century: The Golden Age of the Cursus Publicus*, Leuven.
Lindering, J. (2012 [2018]). 'Lykos (Nahr al-Kalb),' *Livius.org: Articles on ancient history*, http://www.livius.org/articles/place/lykos-nahr-al-kalb (last accessed August 8, 2022).
Magness, J. (1993). *Jerusalem Ceramic Chronology: Circa 200–800 CE*, Sheffield.
Magness, J. (1996). 'Blessings from Jerusalem: Evidence for Early Christian Pilgrimage,' *Eretz-Israel: Archaeological, Historical and Geographical Studies* Joseph Aviram Volume, 37–45.
Mango, C. (1985). *Le développement urbain de Constantinople (IVe–VIIe siècles)*, Paris.

Matthews, J. (2006). *The Journey of Theophanes: Travel, Business, and Daily Life in the Roman East*, New Haven.

Mayerson, P. (1992). 'The Gaza "Wine" Jar (Gazition) and the "Lost" Ashkelon Jar (Askalônion),' *IEJ* 42, 76–80.

Mayerson, P. (1993). 'The Use of Ascalon Wine in the Medical Writers of the Fourth to the Seventh Centuries,' *IEJ* 43, 169–173.

Melkawi, A. & 'Amr, K., et al. (1994). 'The excavation of two seventh-century pottery kilns at Aqaba,' *Annual of the Department of Antiquities of Jordan* 38, 447–468.

Mundell Mango, M. (2000). 'The Commercial Map of Constantinople,' *Dumbarton Oaks Papers* 54, 189–207.

Niewöhner, P. (ed.) (2017). *The Archaeology of Byzantine Anatolia: From the End of Late Antiquity Until the Coming of the Turks*, Oxford.

Ousterhout, R. (ed.) (1990). *The Blessings of Pilgrimage*, Urbana.

Paine, J.A. & Hitchcock, R.D. (1873). 'The Greek Inscription at Dog River,' *Palestine Exploration Fund Quarterly* 17, 111–112.

Pieri, D. (2007). 'Les centres de production d'amphores en Méditerranée orientale durant l'Antiquité tardive: quelques remarques,' in Bonifay/Tréglia 2007, 611–625.

Rahmani, L. (1993). 'Eulogia Tokens from Byzantine Bet She'an,' *'Atiqot* 22, 109–119.

Ramsay, W.M. (1883). 'Inscriptions de la Galatie et du Pont,' *BCH* 7, 15–28.

Ramsay, W.M. (1890). *The Historical Geography of Asia Minor*, London.

Ramsay, W.M. (1899). *A Historical Commentary on St. Paul's Epistle to the Galatians*, London.

Riley, J.A. (1975). 'The Pottery from the First Session of Excavation in the Caesarea Hippodrome,' *BASO* 218, 25–63.

Robinson, D. & Wilson, A. (eds.) (2011). *Maritime Archaeology and Ancient Trade in the Mediterranean*, Oxford.

Saliou, C. (ed.) (2005). *Gaza dans l'Antiquité Tardive: archéologie, rhétorique et histoire: actes du colloque international de Poitiers, 6–7 mai 2004*, Salerno.

Seeck, O. (1876). *Notitia Dignitatum: accedunt notitia urbis Constantinopolitanae et Laterculi provinciarum*, Berolini.

Seland, E. (2011). 'The *Liber Pontificalis* and the Red Sea trade of the early-mid fourth century AD,' in Agius/Cooper/et al. 2011, 117–126.

Sidebotham, S.E. (2011). *Berenike and the ancient maritime spice route*, Berkeley, CA.

Talbert, R.J.A. (2010). *Rome's World: The Peutinger Map Reconsidered*, Cambridge.

Thomsen, P. (1917). 'Die römischen Meilensteine der Provinzen Syria, Arabia und Palaestina,' *Zeitschrift des Deutschen Palästinavereins* 40, 1–103.

Trombley, F.R. (2001). 'Town and *territorium* in Late Roman Anatolia (late 5th–early 7th c.),' in Lavan 2001, 217–232.

Tsafrir, Y. (ed.) (1993). *Ancient churches revealed*, Jerusalem.

Turchetto, J. (2015). 'Beyond the myth of the Cilician Gates. The ancient road network of central and southern Cappadocia,' in Beyer/Henry/et al. 2015.

Whiting, M. (2020). 'Braided Networks: Pilgrimage and the Economics of Travel Infrastructure in the Late Antique Holy Land,' in Collar/Kristensen 2020, 62–90.

Whiting, M. (2017). 'Gift of the Orontes: fluvial landscapes of northwest Syria in late antiquity,' in Franconi 2017, 127–137.

Whiting, M. (2015). 'Milestones in Late Antique Palaestinae and Arabia,' *The Ancient Near East Today: Current News about the Ancient Past*, 3 August 2015, http://asorblog.org/2015/08/06/milestones-in-late-antique-palaestinae-and-arabia (last accessed August 8, 2022).

Whittow, M. (1990). 'Ruling the Late Roman and Early Byzantine City: A Continuous History,' *P&P* 129, 3–29.

Konstantin M. Klein

Neighbors of Christ: Saints and their *Martyria* in Constantinople and Jerusalem

Introduction

In the late fifth century, Matrona, a noblewoman from Perge in Pamphylia, was facing a crisis. Married to a husband she did not like, she left for Constantinople in order to conduct a saintly life of praying and fasting, day and night. Her husband Domitianus was deeply angered, and even more so when Matrona decided to disguise herself as a eunuch and enter the monastery of Bassianus.[1] But she was soon discovered and asked to leave. Matrona left once more (and once more in drag) this time for Jerusalem[2] – her husband as ever in hot pursuit. Sending him on the wrong track south to Mount Sinai, she settled in a pagan temple near Beirut, preferring the presence of ghastly demons over that of her lawfully wedded husband. Once she succeeded in driving out all the evil spirits, however, Matrona longed for nothing more than to return to Constantinople to find Bassianus, her spiritual advisor, even though she knew that her husband Domitianus would probably be in the city as well. Pondering over suitable alternative locations to go, Matrona fell asleep. In a dream, three armed men appeared to her, competing with each other as to who would be chosen to take her for a wife. Matrona refused, for God was by now her only bridegroom, and, according to her sixth-century *Vita*, the whole matter appeared to her to be very improper. Nevertheless, she asked the three knights for their names. It turned out the oldest was called Alexander, another Antiochus, and the youngest Constantine. At the end, the men put an end to their dispute by casting lots. It fell to the youngest, Constantine.[3] When Matrona woke up, she perceived what the revelation of the vision meant; she gave up going to Alexandria or Antioch, and left for Constantinople, where she established a monastery.[4] Years later Matrona died in the odor of sanctity *and* as a legal citizen of Constantinople,[5] a city which had gladly ac-

---

[1] Cf. *Vit. Matr.* 4, cf. Patlagean 1976, 612–615.
[2] Cf. *Vit. Matr.* 13–14. The *Vita* mentions, among other churches, Justinian's *Nea* which provides a *terminus post quem* of 543.
[3] Cf. *Vit. Matr.* 25.
[4] *Vit. Matr.* 36. The monastery was located within the Theodosian land walls in a place called Severiana and was completed in 413. The name may derive from Severus, a patron of Bassianus, cf. Berger 1988, 526.
[5] *Vit. Matr.* 36: νόμιμος Κωνσταντινουπόλεως οἰκήτωρ γενομένη. The *Vita* suggests that the possession of land in Constantinople made Matrona a lawful resident of the city.

cepted her in the pantheon of living holy men and women, and venerated her as a saint soon after her demise.

The *Jacobite Synaxarion* (Codex Parisinus 4869) records an originally Coptic legend transmitted in Arabic about a woman called Sophia living in Constantinople at the time of the Emperor Arcadius and John Chrysostom, who was her alleged spiritual advisor. Even though the manuscript witness is late, Michel van Esbroeck proposed that the legend itself dates to the late fifth century. Sophia bore three sons, but, after the death of her parents and husband, sought counsel from Chrysostom as she did not want to remarry and was at the same time afraid to join a monastery fearing the disapproval of her children. Distraught, Sophia lay prostrate before a large cross, and, like Matrona, eventually fell asleep. In her dream it was the Virgin Mary who appeared to her and said that if Sophia wanted to please God, he would not call her in this city. She, the Virgin, would have Sophia speak to her son. When Sophia woke up, she discovered that she had been transferred to Jerusalem.[6]

Both female figures, legendary as they may be, are remarkable. Matrona stands out because she is caught in a bigamous love affair – one that still does not leave enough room for her husband. She is obviously enamored with the heavenly bridegroom, but at the same time she is deeply in love with the city of Constantinople. This city, however, is not fit to house her alleged contemporary, Sophia, who is transferred in a cloud to Jerusalem. The Holy City is, according to the story's subtext, a place much more suitable to house Sophia, the Holy Wisdom, within its walls. It is remarkable that in the Matrona legend Jerusalem does not qualify as a destination for her. In Sophia's case, however, Jerusalem is the *only* option during her lifetime. However, after her death, Sophia, Wisdom, returns to Constantinople, which, as I will show, plays an important part in the logic of the narrative.

How can these two legends about holy women help us to understand the role that saints – living as well as deceased – played in the two cities? The following pages aim to demonstrate how during the assumed lifetime of Matrona and Sophia, i.e., in the second half of the fifth century, a fundamental change occurred in Jerusalem concerning the relationship between saints and city – and how this change was directly influenced by contemporary developments in Constantinople.

Holy Women between Constantinople and Jerusalem

At the end of the fourth century, the pilgrim Egeria, a woman much more 'real' than Matrona and Sophia, but nevertheless quite elusive considering the numerous questions her pilgrim account leaves us with, was travelling to the Holy Land. Returning from an excursion into the Judaean desert, she passed through a remote desert valley where she discovered a hermit's cell. This is how she presents her quest for more in-

---

6 Cf. van Esbroeck 2001, 132–133.

formation: "You know how inquisitive I am, and I asked what there was about this valley to make this holy monk build his cell there. I knew there must be some special reason."[7] The pilgrim learned that this was the valley of Kerith where the prophet Elijah was once fed by the ravens.[8] She had good reasons to ask, for she was assuming that there could not be a place, which was so clearly marked and honored by a hermitage, without carrying any deeper religious meaning. Following Egeria's footsteps, it becomes clear that every holy place, even the fairly minor ones, were kept in the collective memory of the monks and pilgrims and commemorated by a landmark. Her mind-set was typical of the antique attitude towards the *lieux de mémoire* of the Graeco-Roman world; what Lucan had remarked in a different context and at a different time, *nullum est sine nomine saxum*[9] (there is no stone which does not carry a name, i.e., its specific history), was also true for the late antique Holy Land. Egeria's account also makes it clear that 'stones' which were *not* connected to Biblical history (and they were not numerous to begin with) did not incite much interest in late antique pilgrims. By paying reverence to the holy places the Biblical narrative could be illustrated and verified. The past merged into the believers' individual presence when they directly experienced the physical places that had once been in contact with Old Testament prophets or with the Messiah.[10] Jews and Christians alike interpreted Psalm 137 as an admonition to keep up the importance of the Holy Land's *omphalos*, not only as a metaphor but as a physical place: "If I forget thee, O Jerusalem …".[11]

The city was surrounded by a multitude of holy places and it emerged as the epicenter of Christian yearning not least because collective memory kept alive their precise and genuine location.[12] Whether this historic exactness was (as in some, or perhaps even many cases) a recent invention, was not questioned by late antique pilgrims and was unimportant for them, just as it shall not concern us here in this study. The sources speak of almost archaeological endeavors, not only the zealous

---

7 *Itin. Eg.* 16,3: *Tunc ego, ut sum satis curiosa, requirere cepi, quae esset haec uallis ubi sanctus, monachus nunc, monasterium sibi fecisset; non enim putabam hoc sine causa esse* (trans. Wilkinson 1999, 128).
8 Egeria rendered the name of the brook to 'Corra' in Latin; cf. 1 Kings 17:3–6.
9 Lucan *Phars.* 9,973 – referring to the plains of the Scamander and the fallen city of Troy.
10 Cf. Halbwachs 2008, 1.
11 Cf. Assmann 2009, 21, see especially Ps 137:5–6: "If I forget you, O Jerusalem, let my right hand wither! Let my tongue cling to the roof of my mouth, if I do not remember you, if I do not set Jerusalem above my highest joy."
12 Cf. Stroumsa 1989, 17. The image of Jerusalem as the navel of the world, however, can be traced back to no earlier than the Hasmonean revolt of the second century BC. The reading of the reference in Ezekiel (9:37), *tabbur ha-'aretz*, generally translated as 'navel of the world,' is doubtful as the verbal root *t–b–r* is not attested in early Semitic, and its translation as 'navel' postdates the Septuagint, cf. Alexander 1999, 104–110. Rabbinic sources from Late Antiquity often mention Jerusalem as an *omphalos*. The sixth-century Madaba mosaic map presents – in opposition to the real topography – the Church of the Holy Sepulcher at the very center of the city – clearly as the *omphalos* of Christianity.

late antique 'archaeologists' Macarius and Helena in Jerusalem[13] – one can also find the same mind-set when Egeria tried to link a deserted Bedouin campsite to a resting place of the Israelites, or when Jerome's companion Paula identified the ruins of Biblical Dor,[14] or, back in the capital, where the princess Pulcheria stood at the edge of a Constantinopolitan excavation trench unearthing the relics of the Forty Martyrs of Sebaste.[15]

In Palestine, the discovery of more and more holy places[16] is directly connected with the desire of more and more pilgrims who wanted to visit them and the attitudes of the Church of Jerusalem which gradually understood the symbolic capital of its sacred space, promoted it, and sometimes had to create it.[17] Despite the constant power struggle between the metropolis in Caesarea and the Bishopric of Jerusalem, no major competition between the different episcopal sees regarding rights of ownership of the various holy sites is recorded. In a lengthy letter to the provincials of the East,[18] Constantine had stated that the holy places belonged to the churches.[19] During the reign of Theodosius I, the administration of such sites became a more important economic factor as they enjoyed tax exemptions after a law dated to 381,[20] and with its elevation to a Patriarchate at the Council of Chalcedon, Jerusalem eventually presided over the three Palestinian provinces which contained most of the holy places.[21]

---

13 On the discovery of the Tomb of Christ, cf. Hunt 1997.
14 Cf. Hier. *Ep.* 108,8,2.
15 Sozom. *HE* 9,2, cf. also Bowes 2008, 1.
16 This can be illustrated by comparing the geographical focus of different pilgrim accounts: whereas the pilgrim of Bordeaux did not visit the holy places around Mt Sinai, Egeria's account gives an evocative description. Egypt became a goal of Christian pilgrimage only in the late fourth century, Egeria, Melania the Elder, Jerome and Paula being among its first visitors. The Galilee region became integrated in the typical pilgrimage routes even later, the pilgrim of Piacenza (c. 570) being one of the first authors who wrote about important places such as Nazareth (*Itin. Plac.* 4–7, esp. 5).
17 Cf. Hunt 1997 (for the growing understanding of holy places discovered by Macarius of Jerusalem), Drijvers 2004 (for Cyril of Jerusalem and the promotion of holy space), and Wilkinson 2002, 61 (for the house of Pilate, St Sophia, and the *lithostroton* as an example for a deliberate change of location of a holy site).
18 Cf. Euseb. *VC* 2,24–42. For a commentary to the *Letter to the East*, its authenticity, composition, and distribution, cf. Cameron/Hall 1999, 239–242.
19 Euseb. *VC* 2,40: Καὶ μὴν καὶ τοὺς τόπους αὐτούς […] τίς ἂν ἀμφιβάλοι μὴ οὐχὶ ταῖς ἐκκλησίαις προσήκειν, ἢ οὐχὶ καὶ προστάξειεν ἄν.
20 *Cod. Theod.* 16,2,26: *Universos, quos constiterit custodes ecclesiarum esse vel sanctorum locorum ac religiosis obsequiis deservire, nullius adtemptationis molestiam sustinere decernimus* […].
21 Cf. Price/Gaddis 2005b, 15, and Wilkinson 2002, 59; Phoenicia and Arabia were administered from Antioch.

A City of Saints

Before casting a closer look at the holy sites in Jerusalem it is necessary to return to Constantinople and to briefly summarize the evidence on the ground. Even though the physical remains of many Constantinopolitan churches have vanished beneath the layout of the modern city, and even though the sources are often much later and interwoven with legends, enough exists to reconstruct the ecclesiastical landscape in Constantine's new capital.[22] For the reign of Theodosius II the *Notitia Urbis Constantinopolitanae*[23] mentions fourteen churches,[24] of which twelve are listed in the description of the city's *regiones*. For some of these churches, the *Notitia* does not give specific names.[25] Then there was the church named St Sophia[26], and two churches dedicated to St Irene.[27] Both Sophia and Irene, of course, did *not* commemorate respective female saints. The dedication to the Holy Wisdom, the incarnated *logos*, may partly be due to the lack of local saints in fourth-century Constantinople, but in general patron saints were rather unusual except for places which actually contained relics or *martyria*. For the fourth-century inhabitants of Constantinople, however, it was clear that Sophia and Irene were not persons.[28]

Turning back to the *Notitia* (and leaving the church of Anastasia[29] aside for a moment), four churches commemorated specific saints: Menas,[30] Paul,[31] Acacius (a martyr from Nicomedia)[32] and the originally Constantinian Church of the Holy Apostles,[33]

---

[22] Cf. Bowes 2008, 103.
[23] The *Notitia* dates to approximately AD 447–450, cf. Bury 1916, 442–443, and Havaux 2017, 6–9, arguing for an earlier dating to AD 425–427.
[24] NUC 242.
[25] In the *Caenopolis* (NUC 237), in the *Homonea* (237), in the thirteenth *regio* (Sycena) (240), and in the fourteenth *regio* (241).
[26] NUC 231.
[27] NUC 231 and, in *regio* 7, 235.
[28] Cf. Proverbs 8:22–25. Cf. Grégoire/Kugener 1930, 16 with n. 1, for a similar case of the church of St Irene in Gaza: "Les premières églises chrétiennes portèrent, comme les temples, les édifices et autres locaux publics de l'époque hellénistique, des inscriptions ou enseignes. Le sens de celles-ci devait être à la fois symbolique et profane. Les noms de Σοφία, Εἰρήνη, et même Μαρία se prêtaient parfaitement à cet usage. Plus tard on crut que les églises portant ces 'vocables' étaient consacrées à 'sainte Sophie' ou à 'sainte Irène'."
[29] NUC 235.
[30] NUC 233.
[31] NUC 235. The church of St Paul commemorated Bishop Paul of Constantinople (AD 342–350), whose remains were buried there c. 381, cf. Woods 2001, 207. Sozomen (*HE* 7,10) and Socrates Scholasticus (*HE* 5,9) reveal, however, that by the mid fifth century the population of Constantinople was convinced that the church in fact contained the relics of Paul the Apostle.
[32] NUC 237. The church may date to the time of Constantine, cf. Mango 1986, 34. Even though the existence of a church at the time of Constantine's death has been called into question, there seem to be no doubt of the existence of a church (and a cult) of St Acacius at the place of the church by the time of John Chrysostom's episcopate (AD 398–404) who held two sermons in the church,

containing the relics of Luke and Andrew (transferred there in 357 or in 360[34]) as well as Timothy.[35] Constantine also perhaps commissioned the reconstruction of the earlier church of Irene, the enlargement of the shrine to Acacius, and the new foundation to Mocius outside the city walls, who was a Constantinopolitan martyr from the time of the Diocletianic persecutions.[36] However, the evidence for this is all mid-fifth century or later, "well after", as Kim Bowes remarks, "the Constantinian myth-machine was set into motion."[37] Constantinopolitan bishops were rather reluctant builders: the church dedicated to Bishop Paul, mentioned in the *Notitia*, is said to have been founded by Macedonius, while Sozomen mentions Chrysostom dedicating a church to two of Bishop Paul's secretaries.[38] Gregory Nazianzen's short-lived episcopate saw the foundation of his 'alternative see,' the house-church Anastasia, named in reference to the hoped-for resurrection of a true, pro-Nicean faith.[39] When St Marcianus (d. 471) came to Constantinople, he re-built the Anastasia – this time not identifying the *patrocinium* with an ideological concept, but with a saint, Anastasia, whose relics were brought into the church in a public procession.[40]

The fifth century witnessed an enormous rise in the number of religious buildings, many of them commissioned by members of the court: Arcadia, the sister of Theodosius II, ordered the construction of a church (and monastery) dedicated to Andrew, called 'by-the-judgment' (ἐν τῇ Κρίσει).[41] Her sister Pulcheria added a church to Lawrence in the 420s;[42] a church to Euphemia was located at the former palace of the eunuch Antiochus in the area between the hippodrome, the *Mese*, and the Binbirdirek Cistern, another one for the same saint was begun by Licinia Eudoxia, the daughter of Theodosius.[43] The veneration of Stephen in Constantinople

---

cf. Woods 2001, 203–204. He proposes that the Church of St Acacius was in fact a church built by Acacius, a member of the Constantinian entourage who demolished the pagan sanctuary at Mamre and supervised the building of the new Constantinian church there, cf. Euseb. *VC* 3,52.
33 *NUC* 238. On Constantine's church building activities, cf. Marinis 2022, 181.
34 Cf. Woods 1991, 286–292.
35 Cf. Woods 1991, 290.
36 Cf. Woods 2001, 204, and Johnson 2022, 214.
37 Cf. Bowes 2008, 107.
38 Cf. Bowes 2008, 107. The church of Paul is somewhat confusing as Paul was Macedonius' great enemy and the church was eventually dedicated to the former by Theodosius as a means of proclaiming a final pro-Nicean victory. Furthermore, although Paul is said to have built it, he was also proclaimed bishop there and thus the construction may date to before his first elevation in 338. On the church of the *Notarii*: Sozom. *HE* 4,3 with Janin 1953, 391–392.
39 Cf. Snee 1998, 158–160, and Bowes 2008, p. 117 with n. 373.
40 Cf. Saradi 1995, 97 with n. 45.
41 Cf. Janin 1953, 34.
42 Marcellinus Comes *Chron.* a.c. 439, a.c. 453, cf. also Janin 1953, 312–315. The basilica of St Lawrence built by the empress Pulcheria and completed in 453 stood close to the Golden Horn, near modern Ayakapı (according to Janin 1953, 303–4) or farther to the northwest, at modern Balat (according to Berger 1988, 530). It must have been fairly close to Matrona's nunnery, cf. *Vit. Matr.* 38.
43 Cf. Neumann/Belting 1966, 107.

has a complex and sometimes contradictory literary tradition. It appears that the first church was built by the praetorian prefect Aurelianus. However, he could not procure Stephen's relics, so he had to make do with the body of a contemporary living holy man, the monk Isaac. It appears, as suggested by Paul Magdalino, that the empress Eudocia had intended to place the relics of Stephen which she brought from Palestine in her new palace-church in the tenth region, but these relics seem to have wound up in Pulcheria's church to Lawrence.[44] The court advisor Paulinus is attested as the founder of the monastery of SS Cosmas and Damianus in AD 439 which was later renovated by Justinian.[45] In 462, the consul Studios, a Roman patrician who had settled in Constantinople, built a church consecrated to John the Baptist. Literary sources from the same century mention churches to Thomas[46] and Theodore.[47] A certain Baras who came from Egypt to Constantinople during the reign of Zeno (474–491 AD) is said to have founded another monastery of John the Baptist. The aristocrat Eusebia had constructed a *martyrion* outside the city where she placed her own coffin as well as the relics of the Forty Martyrs which were later re-discovered by Pulcheria. A family friend of Eusebia's, the praetorian prefect Caesarius, added a church to Thyrsus, another Asia Minor martyr. In AD 394 his predecessor as prefect, Rufinus, had completed a similar project on his estate in Chalcedon with a *martyrion* for Peter and Paul whose relics he had obtained during a trip to Rome.[48] A poem of 76 hexameter lines which is preserved in the *Palatine Anthology* and on the capitals of the later church mentions that it was the empress Eudocia who founded a church to Polyeuctus,[49] a military saint martyred at Melitene in the mid-third century. It was enlarged and splendidly rebuilt by Anicia Juliana, perhaps in order to stress her family links with Eudocia.[50] This sixth-century 'Temple of Byzantium' followed the Old Testament descriptions of the measurements of the Temple.[51] To this evidence we can add the shrines for deceased Constantinopolitan holy men: starting with a Theodosian monastery to Dios, a monk from Syria, moreover the rivalry between Saturninus and Victor for housing the monk Isaac, who died in 406,[52] and also the saint-like veneration

---

44 Cf. here below as well as Bowes 2008, 112, and Magdalino 2001, 58–59 and 61–64.
45 Proc. *Aed.* 1,6.
46 *Vit. Matr.* 29.
47 *Vit. Matr.* 33. The church was situated on the Mese in the vicinity of the church of St Sophia and was rebuilt by Sphoracius following a fire, perhaps after 465, cf. Mango 1993b, 25–28.
48 Cf. Bowes 2008, 111–112.
49 For the archaeological remains of the church near the Şehzade Camii in Istanbul's Saraçhane quarter, cf. Mango/Ševčenko 1961, 243–247.
50 Cf. Harrison 1989, 33. The poem states that Eudocia did not built the church as large not because of any restraint or lack of resources, but because she had a divine premonition that her family and descendants would have the knowledge and resources to provide grander embellishment.
51 Cf. 1 Kings 6–7, 2 Chron 3–4, as well as Ezekiel's heavenly temple (40–43), cf. Harrison 1989, 137–139. Cf. also Nadine Viermann's contribution in this volume.
52 Saradi 1995, 88–90, Janin 1953, 84, and Krausmüller 2022, 200.

of Isaac's successor Dalmatius,[53] and – similarly – the veneration for Alexander Acoemetus[54] and his successor Marcellus. In summary, until the end of the fifth century, one can trace churches and *martyria* for at least 27 saints in Constantinople (plus the Forty Martyrs), with two places for Andrew, John the Baptist, and Euphemia, and two, perhaps three, for Stephen. Additionally, one could mention the by-then personified patrons Anastasia, Irene, and Sophia.[55] Finally, for the sixth century, further churches to Diomedes, Peter and Paul, and Sergius and Bacchus would have supplemented the ecclesiastical landscape of Constantinople. What is remarkable is the city's attempt to add local saints to the urban pantheon. The martyrs Acacius, Mocius, and, although of a different time, Bishop Paul were among them – but also living holy men and women like Matrona who were accepted with open arms and after their deaths venerated in the city's collective memory: "[T]he new capital, so conscious of acquiring the mark of nobility, achieves a nobility worthy of its universal prestige."[56]

A City of Christ

At the end of the fourth century, Egeria eagerly reported on *lieux de mémoire* in the Holy Land. A list derived from her account offers a slightly different picture to that we have just encountered in Constantinople, as it features numerous Old Testament figures who had lived or died there. All in all, she mentions a number of *loca sancta* that located precisely the assumed dwelling-places of almost thirty saintly figures.[57] When it comes to Jerusalem, however, Egeria's focus narrowed. Every single place she mentioned, was related to Christ alone.

The first account which informs us about the Christian topography of Jerusalem, the pilgrim of Bordeaux, did still record two categories of sights: firstly, a large corpus of buildings and landmarks encountered on or in close vicinity to the Temple Mount, and secondly those which are related to Christian salvation history. From his itinerary it becomes clear that the new Christian Jerusalem was contrasted to the Jerusalem of old – with King Solomon functioning as some sort of intermediary. However, the Bordeaux Pilgrim is our sole witness to buildings or objects on the Tem-

---

53 On the so-called monastery of Dalmatius, cf. Saradi 1995, 90–91.
54 Cf. *Vit. Alex. Acoi.* 43 with Caner 2002, 274.
55 To put it in Michel van Esbroeck's words: "[w]hile Constantine had simply built the church of Peace, the name became Saint Irene." Cf. van Esbroeck 2001, 139, see also Socr. *HE* 1,16.
56 Van Esbroeck 2001, 135.
57 The account mentions sites connected with Moses (*Itin. Eg.* 2,1), Elijah (4,2), Aaron (4,4), Joshua (5,4), Joseph (7,7.9), Reuben, Gad and Manasseh (10,4), Balak the son of Beor (12,10; it should be "son of Zippor", cf. Wilkinson 1999, 124 with n. 2), Balaam the Seer (12,2), Job (13,1), Melchizedek (13,4), Abraham (14,2), John the Baptist (15,1), Thomas (17,1), King Abgar and his servant Ananias (17,1), Rebecca and Eleazar (20,4), Helpidius (20,5), Terah, Sarah and Lot (20,9), Nahor and Bethuel (20,10), Rachel (20,11), Jacob (21,1), and Laban (21,4).

ple Mount, a space that becomes suspiciously empty within a very short time, certainly by Egeria's visit in AD 381–384. If we combine the fourth century accounts, i.e. the pilgrim of Bordeaux, Egeria's description of the Jerusalemite liturgy, and the Armenian lectionary, we get a picture of the city's religious topography.

The Bordeaux pilgrim mentioned various sets of pools, e.g. at Bethesda and at Siloah, which will be examined below – even though they did not carry any deeper meaning in his account. Going south he entered the Mt Sion area where Egeria in her day would see the Church of Holy Sion. The Bordeaux Pilgrim only mentioned the house of Caiaphas with the column of flagellation in it – there was no church yet at this spot. He passed by the house of Pilate, i.e. the city's *praetorium*, also only a 'place' in communal memory, not yet a church. His next sight was the new *basilica* built by Constantine and the rock of Golgotha. On the ascent of the Mount of Olives, Egeria noted a church.[58] Both of our pilgrims noted the Constantinian church on top of the mountain, the so-called Eleona commemorating the Ascension; a localization, however, which had yet to be defined as Egeria mentions both the church and additionally the actual place where the Lord ascended to Heaven, the so-called *Imbomon* – which very shortly after Egeria's visit would be transformed into a church through the patronage of the Roman matron Poemenia. Finally, both pilgrims mentioned Bethany with the vault in which Lazarus was laid – also no church building yet in their times, but soon to come, commemorating the meeting between Christ and the sisters Martha and Mary.[59]

If one contrasts the evidence of the fourth century with that of the early and midsixth century (namely the pilgrim accounts of Theodosius and the so-called Piacenza Pilgrim, dating to before 518 and *c.* 570 respectively), several changes can be noticed. The house of Caiaphas was now called the Church of St Peter[60] and the house of Pilate was by now a Church of St Sophia, the Holy Wisdom which inspired Christ's response to Pilate.[61] The column of flagellation, once in the house of Caiaphas, had moved into the Church of Holy Sion,[62] a place which seems to have functioned to a certain extent as a storeroom for sacred objects: the 'cup of the Apostles' was kept there as were the stones with which Stephen was martyred.[63] The pool of Siloah in the 570s had next to it a church commemorating the miracle of Jesus healing the blind man.[64] The twin pools of Bethesda were covered by a Church of Mary.[65] Accord-

---

58 *Itin. Eg.* 36,1–2.
59 Cf. *Itin. Eg.* 25,11; 29,3–6, Bieberstein/Bloedhorn 1994, I, 156.
60 Theodosius 7b.
61 Theodosius 7b and *Itin. Plac.* 23.
62 Theodosius 7b and *Itin. Plac.* 22. Egeria saw the column of the flagellation of Christ in the Church of the Holy Sepulcher and the Piacenza Pilgrim would even encounter a second column outside the city, cf. *Itin. Plac.* 25.
63 *Itin. Plac.* 22.
64 *Itin. Plac.* 24, cf. John 9.
65 Theodosius 8b as well as *Itin. Plac.* 27.

ing to the Gospel of John, this was the place of Christ's healing of the paralytic, and the place was commemorated as such during the fifth century. The association with the spot as the birthplace of the Virgin (hence today's name of the church, St Anne's, the mother of Mary) must have been fairly recent at the time when Theodosius was writing.

In addition to the few actual churches of the fourth century, many of the previous holy places (the houses of Caiaphas and Pilate, the two pools) were now transformed into churches. Despite this building activity, one thing remained largely unchanged: all these churches were still closely connected to the Gospel story:[66] the importance of St Peter and St Sophia, for example, did not spring from their respective names, but from the fact that they commemorated the places of Christ's trial, just as the churches erected over the two pools testified to the exact place were the Lord had worked miracles. Unlike the evidence in other parts of the late Roman Empire, particularly Constantinople, Jerusalem did not contain any significant number of sanctuaries dedicated to Christian saints.

Introducing the Cult of Saints to the Holy City

None of this would be particularly remarkable if there had not also been a fifth-century church of St Stephen, even though it is the only 'non-Jesus-related' church that is recorded in the sources.[67] This building was connected to Eudocia, the wife of Theodosius II, who had left the court for Jerusalem once on a pilgrimage in 438–439, and then, for good, in 442/443. The church was located outside the northern city walls, and its foundation was clearly connected with Eudocia's first stay in the city and her successful *translatio* of some of the saint's relics to Constantinople.[68] The consecration of the large basilica was a major event in Jerusalem[69] and Eudocia had invited Cyril of Alexandria to conduct the service.[70] We can be certain that the empress knew about the considerable popularity of the Protomartyr throughout the whole

---

[66] A letter attributed to Cyril of Jerusalem on the rebuilding of the Jewish Temple in AD 363, discovered, edited and translated by Sebastian Brock, mentions a 'Church of the Confessors' (chap. 6) unique to this letter. Even if the letter is genuine (Brock assumes that it was written at the beginning of the fifth century by an author who had certain knowledge of both the historical episode and the topography of Jerusalem), the best explanation of the mention of this church seems to follow Brock in interpreting it as a mistranslation, so that underlying the Syriac was the Greek μαρτύριον, i.e. the term by which the Constantinian basilica of the Holy Sepulcher was generally known in these times, cf. Brock 1977, 277.
[67] Cf. also Klein 2019, 106–114.
[68] Cf. below; on the consecration, cf. John Rufus *Vit. Petr. Hib.* 49 with Clark 1982, 141–156, and Leyerle 2002, 350.
[69] For the construction of the church, cf. Socr. *HE* 7,47,3 and Evagr. *HE* 1,22.
[70] Cf. Clark 1982, 151, Horn 2006, 75, and Bitton-Ashkelony/Kofsky 2006, 49–50.

Empire,[71] and it is likely that she recognized that a space dedicated exclusively to the saint was still missing within the sacred topography of Jerusalem. After all, the martyr's bones had been discovered already in 415[72] and were still being temporarily stored in the Holy Sion, a church actually commemorating the events of Pentecost.[73]

It seems that in Jerusalem the veneration of Christ was – for understandable reasons – so important and dominant that the commemoration of saints and martyrs was less distinctive than in other cities of the early Byzantine Empire. And indeed, the sacred topography for such places of remembrance remained extraordinarily vague. Besides Eudocia's foundation, we can only find a very small number of sacred places which were not connected directly to the life and passion of Christ: Palladius of Helenopolis and Rufinus of Aquileia mention that a shrine on the eastern Mount of Olives was dedicated to John the Baptist, although the information we possess is far too limited to be able to locate it.[74] Unlike in other cities, most of the early monasteries in Jerusalem did not carry the name of a specific saint. Eudocia built a hospice with a chapel dedicated to St George; this again formed an exception.[75] It is interesting to note that a fifth-century Coptic encomium on St George is attributed to a certain Theodosius, Bishop of Jerusalem. The text is generally thought to be authentic,[76]

---

71 Stephen's death was interpreted as an echo of the Crucifixion. Therefore, the church of Stephen donated by Eudocia can be interpreted as resembling the revelation of the True Cross by Helena and the erection of the Church of the Holy Sepulcher by Constantine. Cf. Clark 1982, 142, as well as Hunt 1982, 212 and 220. Several other church foundations in honor of St Stephen allegedly made by Eudocia belong to the realm of myth. This is particularly true for those church foundations associated with depositions of St Stephen's foot (on this cf. the erroneous remarks in Holum 1982, 195, and Hunt 1982, 233), for example, in Safranbolu in Paphlagonia. A dedicatory inscription confirming the empress' involvement was first mentioned by Doublet 1889, 293–299, and has since been assumed to be genuine by Elizabeth Clark, Kenneth Holum and especially Enrico Livrea, who dedicated an entire article to it, trying to justify its linguistic oddities (cf. Livrea 1996). Only Mango 2004, 24 with nn. 14–16, and *passim*, observed that the inscription is a nineteenth century forgery.

72 For the case of Stephen, it is noteworthy that the discovery of the relics of James, the first Bishop of Jerusalem, in 351 on the Mount of Olives, apparently had no impact on the localization of the Pentecost events at Mount Sion (assumed to be James' house). The saint's relics were collected and briefly placed in the Church of Holy Sion. Apparently, the obsession with finding the exact position of holy places only concerned Christ and not saints and martyrs, as we also shall see in the case of Stephen; cf. esp. Rubin 1999, 154–155, and Abel 1919, 480–499.

73 Among the relics and holy objects presented to the Piacenza pilgrim in the Church of Holy Sion, there was also a reliquary of the head of the martyr Theodota, cf. *Itin. Plac.* 22. For the discovery of St Stephen's relics, see Hunt 2001, 171.

74 Cf. Bieberstein/Bloedhorn 1994, III, 416.

75 Cf. Cyr. Scyth. *Vit. Ioann.* 204,9 and Bieberstein/Bloedhorn 1994, II, 51–52. Blake Leyerle suggested that Eudocia's foundation of St Stephen also included an important hospital; cf. Leyerle 2002, 360 and 369–372.

76 The first account of George's martyrdom is said to have been written in Greek by Pasicrates, allegedly the servant of the saint, a source which existed in a Syriac translation in the seventh century which shows close resemblances to an early-fifth century Coptic version preserved in the Bodleian and edited and translated by E.A. Wallis Budge in 1888; cf. Budge 1888, xxxi. This collection of

and its author has thus to be identified with the anti-Chalcedonian monk-made-patriarch of 452–453, i.e. during the time Eudocia resided in the city. If the text is indeed genuine, one may suggest a certain mutual influence between the literary preoccupation with George and the attribution of Eudocia's hospice, as the empress maintained close contact with the anti-Chalcedonian party while living in Jerusalem.[77]

The remaining evidence for the veneration of saints in Jerusalem is meager. A chapel dedicated to the military saint Menas was founded by a Roman noblewoman, Bassa.[78] From Cyril of Scythopolis' description it becomes clear that this chapel was built in imitation of Eudocia's church of St Stephen – perhaps directly influenced by the empress's foundation. The monk Theognius, who came to Jerusalem in AD 454/455, stayed at a monastery on the Mount of Olives which had been founded shortly before his arrival by the noblewoman Flavia, who also build a church to the martyr Julian.[79] Again, this church post-dates the church of St Stephen by more than a decade.[80] The distribution of these chapels shows a concentration of *martyria* on the Mount of Olives. This is confirmed by the sixth-century pilgrims[81] who mention certain tombs there,[82] however, all of these were small, mostly private shrines. We know of a monk, Gabrielius, who stemmed from Euthymius' monastery in the desert and became a protégé of Eudocia's in Jerusalem after she was back on the Chalcedonian path. This Gabrielius used to withdraw for certain periods of the year to a recluse's

---

the Coptic tradition on St George also contains an encomium written by a certain Theodosius, Bishop of Jerusalem, for which neither Budge nor Georg Röwekamp in the respective *LACL* entry found reasons to assume that it might not be genuine (cf. Budge 1888, xxvii): as this bishop is referred to in the encomium on St George by Theodotus of Ancyra (*fl.* 431–432) and as there is no reason to suppose an interpolation of the name (cf. Budge 1888, 236 with n. 1), it is likely that the alleged author of the text is indeed referring to the monk Theodosius who was raised to the Patriarchal see in 452. From John Rufus' *De obitu Theodosii* we know that the anti-Chalcedonian patriarch fled to Egypt after 453 – which would explain the transmitting of the text in Coptic – until the imprisonment of Abba Romanus in Antioch made Theodosius leave his hiding place and travel to the city on the Orontes (John Rufus, *De obit. Theod.* 2–3). For the Coptic scribes of the manuscripts a false attribution to Theodosius would also make no sense, as due to the secrecy and brevity of his presence in Egypt he remained a fairly elusive character to the Egyptian anti-Chalcedonians.

77 I have argued elsewhere that Eudocia's support for the anti-Chalcedonians of Palestine was backed and approved by the court of Marcian and Pulcheria, cf. Klein 2018.
78 A letter dating to late AD 453 from Pulcheria to Bassa is preserved among the post-conciliar documents in the Greek acts of Chalcedon, cf. *ACO* 2,1,3:494–495.
79 Cyr. Scyth. *Vit. Theog.* 241,20.
80 Finally, Cyril again mentions a shrine of the military saint Theodore with a *terminus ante quem* of 532; however, such a chapel is not attested archaeologically. Cf. Cyr. Scyth. *VS* 185,4 with Bieberstein/Bloedhorn 1994, II, 98. It is important to note that the fact that although no more places of remembrance are recorded in the sources, this does not necessarily mean that they did not exist. The small number of mentions may result from the nature of the sources; the few examples are mostly recorded by Cyril of Scythopolis who was an insider to the area.
81 Theodosius 6.
82 For James, Zacharias, Simeon, cf. Theodosius 9; for Zebedee and Cleophas, cf. *Itin. Plac.* 16; for Pelagia, cf. *Itin. Plac.* 16; and for Hesychius, cf. *Itin. Plac.* 27.

cell on the Mount of Olives, where he had set up a martyr's shrine.[83] Places like this are clearly not comparable to Eudocia's basilica which was, according to Cyril of Scythopolis, so enormous as to host a very large congregation. It is obvious that there was a difference between this building and the small private shrines on the Mount of Olives, none of which is attested *before* the beginning of the construction of St Stephen's church.[84] Most of the places commemorating saints were erected by Roman noblewomen (such as Melania, Flavia, and Bassa), i.e. not by the clergy of Jerusalem but from outsiders to the city like Eudocia herself. She was the first founder in the city who acknowledged the growth in importance of the public veneration of relics and saints which had begun at the end of the fourth century. Coming from the center of power in Constantinople with its numerous churches, this cult of saints was well-known to her.[85] A second novelty of Eudocia's foundation is that Stephen's stoning was located in a *different* place to that in which the basilica was placed. Every single church built in Jerusalem before the 440s was meticulously located at what was thought to be the exact place hallowed by divine presence. As a result of this, the late antique religious buildings in Jerusalem are characterized by a near-obsession with the search for the 'correct place.' The church of St Stephen, in contrast, was placed at the main arterial road leading to Neapolis and Damascus, thus resembling a pattern of building large churches outside the city centers as in Rome or Milan[86] rather than following the local traditions in Jerusalem. With this choice of location, the new church was both influenced by the city's street layout and proved influential itself: everyone who entered the city had to pass by it, and many wrote about it.[87]

Nevertheless, the construction of Eudocia's church in Jerusalem still shows how dominant the connection between *places of events* and *places of remembrance* was in

---

83 Gabrielius built himself a small hermitage where he used to withdraw at Epiphany and where he died as a miracle worker and was also buried there. Cyril of Scythopolis mentions his knowledge of Latin, Greek, and Syriac (*Vit. Euth.* 56,6–18).
84 The exception here are Melania's endeavors to promote her own *martyrion* for the same relics.
85 Cf. Brown 1981, 92–95. Even after Eudocia's time, the veneration of saints and martyrs remained somewhat tentative. The legend of the discovery of the relics of Jacob in the Kidron Valley was clearly modelled on the discovery of St Stephen, even though the account claims that it already happened during the reign of Valens. However, no chapel for Jacob is attested before the eighth century. Finally, a church for John the Baptist is not attested before the Sassanid devastation of the city (AD 614) and John Moschus mentions a church of SS Cosmas and Damianus for the year 615, once again maybe in the Kidron Valley. Moreover, Biblical figures were remembered in Jerusalem as well, from the sixth to the tenth century: a grotto was shown to be the prison of Jeremiah and a memorial place of Isaiah existed in the Kidron Valley, both not included on the normal pilgrim routes, cf. Bieberstein/Bloedhorn 1994, I, 158–159 as well as III, 234 and 408. For the implications of the growing cult of saints for Jerusalem, cf. Kretschmar 1977, 111. For Eudocia's political activities in the Holy Land, see the monographs by Binns 1994, Bitton-Ashkelony/Kofsky 2006 and Horn 2006 as well as Kofsky 1997, 209–222.
86 Cf. Krautheimer 1983, *passim*.
87 Similarly, Eudocia's church of St Polyeuctus in Constantinople was carefully positioned on a processional route on the Mese from the Forum of Theodosius to the Church of the Holy Apostles, cf. Harrison 1989, 34.

people's minds: from the sixth century onwards, a tradition appears identifying the place of the Church of St Stephen as the exact location of the martyr's stoning.[88] A little later, the local priests were even able to show pilgrims the stones of Stephen's martyrdom in the church – perhaps those the Piacenza Pilgrim had seen at Sion, although there has never been a lack of stones in Jerusalem. As a consequence, the northern city gate, today's Damascus Gate, changed its name to St Stephen's Gate in Eudocia's times. We may draw comparisons to similar phenomena in Constantinople where the church commemorating Bishop Paul was a hundred and fifty years later thought to be a church to St Paul the Apostle; whereas the church to Acacius, as already demonstrated by David Woods,[89] was in fact a church originally built by a member of Constantine's entourage, the *comes* Acacius, and relatively soon was thought to be commemorating the martyrdom of St Acacius.[90] And, of course, the *Vita Sophiae* mentioned in the beginning, provided an alternative, perhaps more easily comprehensible, tradition for the Church of St Sophia. It is not surprising that in the same period, a second Sophia tradition was also evolving which described the death of Sophia during the reign of Emperor Hadrian: a saint who had three martyr daughters, aptly named Pistis, Elpis, and Agape.[91]

The construction of Eudocia's church to St Stephen also constituted a new form of congregational space by its sheer size which surpassed all of Jerusalem's churches except for the Constantinian basilica. It goes beyond enhancing places of remembrance with religious buildings in the manner of Jerusalemite building tradition before her. Whether this was a deliberate action or not, is impossible to tell. The evidence shows that in the years after Eudocia's death, the strict observation of correct locations had become more blurred. For Jerusalem this was completely new – and somewhat visionary. When after a long break of imperial activity Justinian decided to launch a vast building program in the city,[92] his main church, the *Nea*, was in fact a church dedicated to the Virgin and inaugurated on the feast day of Mary's presentation in the Temple, but it did not commemorate a particular spot in which the event had taken place and/or was preserved in local tradition. In the position for his church, Justinian thus had a free choice, and the *Nea*'s location should rather be seen as an imperial response to the growing population in the city[93] as it extended the colonnaded *cardo* to the south, that is to an area that had not been densely populated before.

---

88 Bieberstein/Bloedhorn 1994, II, 231–232.
89 Cf. above note 32.
90 Cf. Bowes 2008, 113 for similar thoughts on the places of remembrance of St Philip and St Celerina in Constantinople.
91 Cf. van Esbroeck 2001, 129–134.
92 Trampedach 2001, 108–110.
93 Binns 1994, 92, and Stathakopoulos 2008, 310.

New Saints for Constantinople

While Eudocia's decision to build a church dedicated to St Stephen in Jerusalem may have been surprising for this city (though very much in line with the empire-wide cult of saints), her Church of St Polyeuctus in Constantinople seems a more surprising choice. When she reached the capital in the fall of AD 439, she carried with her a precious gift for the city:

> Eudocia, the wife of the emperor Theodosius, returned from Jerusalem to the imperial city, bringing with her the relics of the most blessed Stephen, the first martyr, which were placed in the basilica of St Lawrence where they are venerated.[94]

The entry in the *Chronicon* of Marcellinus Comes gives no explanation for why relics as important as those of Stephen brought to the capital by someone as important as Eudocia were deposited in a church commemorating a different saint, St Lawrence, and built by a different founder, Pulcheria. Kenneth Holum has argued that Theodosius' sister had founded this church upon Eudocia's arrival to receive the newly translated relics, and that "in this way Pulcheria turned Eudocia's downfall to her own profit."[95] The latter claim can be easily dismissed, as the deposition in AD 439 could hardly be connected with Eudocia's alleged downfall of 443. Nevertheless, it is odd that – if Pulcheria was indeed Eudocia's rival – the latter permitted for no obvious reason that her sister-in-law earned the merits for the successful translation, especially as Eudocia had her own church of St Polyeuctus constructed roughly at the same time. Although the rivalry scenario is tempting, no contemporary source reports any enmity between the two *Augustae* "who appear[ed] to be one," as Cyril of Alexandria put it. There is no reason to interpret the latter line as a sarcastic statement, as Holum did.[96] If one steps aside from the notion of competition between the two *Augustae*, and accepts that they even may have cooperated (appearing to be one), the sources arguably make more sense. Sozomen, who was very keen on portraying Pulcheria in panegyric terms, did not mention a church dedicated to St Lawrence. It is true that his *Historia ecclesiastica* terminates in the year AD 439, however, there must have been a church foundation structurally complete enough to house the relics by that time. The historian's silence can be explained with a later entry in Marcellinus Comes' *Chronicon:* only in 453, fourteen years after the deposition of the relics of St Stephen in Constantinople, did Pulcheria's church receive the relics of St Lawrence sent from Pope Leo I from Rome in the wake of the negotiations at the

---

[94] Marcellinus Comes, *Chron.* a. 439(2): *Eudoxia uxor Theodosii principis ab Hierosolymis urbem regiam remeavit, beatissimi Stephani primi martyris reliquias, quae in basilica sancti Laurentii positae venerantur, secum deferens.* The confusion between Eudoxia and Eudocia is a common mistake in the sources, from the dating and the context it is clear that 'Eudocia' must be meant in this instance.
[95] Holum 1982, 137; cf. 196 for an alleged foundation in AD 439.
[96] Cf. *ACO* I,1,3,77,79–80.

Council of Chalcedon.⁹⁷ Therefore, Sozomen could not have reported on a Church of Lawrence, since it did not exist as such at the time of his writing. On the other hand, the statement concerning the year 439 made by Marcellinus Comes is likewise not wrong, as in his times the church was, of course, dedicated to and known as St Lawrence. From the available evidence it seems that both Pulcheria and Eudocia built churches in Constantinople without exactly knowing which relics would eventually wind up in them. This does, of course, not mean that these buildings were mere blank canvasses, but rather that both *Augustae* had certain hopes and aspirations concerning the relics that they desired for their religious foundations. One could compare these pious hopes to the grand plan of the Church of the Holy Apostles a century earlier, which ideally would have housed relics of twelve important saints, an enterprise that proved unrealistic as time went on.⁹⁸ Moreover, it appears possible to determine the envisaged patron saints of these two churches, which must have been under construction in the 430s:⁹⁹ I would suggest that for Pulcheria's church it was St Lawrence from the very beginning. In comparison with this saint, however, St Polyeuctus, who eventually became commemorated in Eudocia's church, appears as a rather minor figure. The fitting match for the deacon Lawrence was, of course, none other than the deacon Stephen. Scholars have speculated on the connection between the empress and the saint: Polyeuctus was martyred in the hometown of the desert monk Euthymius, a figure of authority for Eudocia in Palestine. However, there is nothing to suggest that the empress met the desert monk during her pilgrimage of AD 438/439, let alone came under his influence.¹⁰⁰ It is possible to assume that she had never even heard the name of St Polyeuctus until her second stay in the Holy Land. Upon her return to the capital in 439, the relics of Stephen were deposited in Pulcheria's church. If we accept that the empresses collaborated, this act is not surprising: the conjunction of the two saints made sense, both were deacon-martyrs, whose relics were housed together in Rome.¹⁰¹ Perhaps Eudocia and Pulcheria had hoped to accelerate the translation of Lawrence's relics to Constantinople by offering the bones a place near to Stephen – or, Pulcheria's church simply was closer to completion, assuming that Eudocia's foundation may have fallen behind due to her absence of approximately a year and a half. It is likely that the cooperation between the two empresses continued after Eudocia left Constantinople for good: she still had funds at her disposal,¹⁰² which clearly exceeded those of ordinary pilgrims, and

---

97 Cf. Marcellinus Comes, *Chron.* a. 453(5).
98 Cf. Mango 2009, 53 and 55–57.
99 Cf. Magdalino 2001, 61–65, suggesting that the Church of St Polyeuctus may have been planned to be dedicated to some other saint.
100 Eudocia's first stay in Jerusalem was relatively short; I will discuss the chronology of this pilgrimage elsewhere.
101 According to the *translatio* of the bones of St Stephen from Constantinople to Rome (dating, most likely, to the late eighth century); cf. Costambeys/Leyser 2007, 279–281.
102 Cf. John Rufus *Vit. Petr. Hib.* 166.

she owned property in the Holy Land, and perhaps resided in a suitable palace in Bethlehem.[103] Moreover, there is reason to assume that at least two church buildings in Jerusalem and Constantinople respectively show interaction between the Holy Land and the capital dating to after the time of Eudocia's second departure: Eudocia's Constantinopolitan church received relics of St Polyeuctus only after the empress had met Euthymius in the Judean Desert in the late 440s, and the Jerusalemite Church of St Stephen was decorated with costly capitals (either directly imported from Constantinople or executed in Constantinopolitan style).[104]

New Saints for Jerusalem

The stimulus for the veneration of saints in Jerusalem came from outside. What may be a mere coincidence is that most of these important outsiders who built churches in honor of saints in the city (Eudocia, Melania, and Bassa), all had at times switched their allegiance to the anti-Chalcedonians. Even though the difference between the cult of saints among Chalcedonians and anti-Chalcedonians has not been explored, the latter's interest in making the saints at home in Jerusalem appears remarkable, especially when we combine this with the possibility that the anti-Patriarch Theodosius really authored an encomium on St George, and that, of course, Peter the Iberian – the anti-Chalcedonian *par excellence* – carried a large box of relics of Persian martyrs with him when he escaped from Constantinople to Jerusalem.[105]

In this context, Michel van Esbroeck's dating[106] of the Sophia legend to the fifth century, relating to the riots of 451–453, makes perfect sense. The Virgin Mary had transferred the widow Sophia from Constantinople to Jerusalem, the only place where Sophia could be reunited with God. It was also predicted that Sophia would return to the capital, after her death.[107] For the anti-Chalcedonians, wisdom was widowed from all that kept her in Constantinople: only in Jerusalem did the faith remain intact. "[O]rthodoxy originate[d] in Jerusalem; and Sophia of Constantinople [was] no longer justified by her roots [...] but through the [J]erusalemite preservation in the fertile soil of the true doctrine of the Holy City."[108] It is not surprising that the church in the *praetorium*, the place of Christ's trial, was built in the 450s and named St Sophia, nor is the proposed date of the writing-down of the legend, the reign of the Miaphysite emperor Anastasius, when – in the eyes of the Miaphysites – Sophia could at last return home.

---

103 *Vit. Bars.* 93,4.
104 Cf. Verstegen 2018, 71.
105 Cf. John Rufus *Vit. Petr. Hib.* 26–28 and 31–35.
106 Van Esbroek 2001, 138.
107 Cf. van Esbroeck 2001, 133.
108 Van Esbroeck 2001, 137.

If there was an actual connection between the cult of saints, religious affiliation, and building politics, we might ask what the Chalcedonian response to this might have looked like. And indeed, we can trace a reaction of the spearhead of pro-Chalcedonians in the Jerusalem area, the desert monastery of Euthymius, located in close proximity to the Holy City. In the wake of the turmoil of AD 451–453, all of these outsider/anti-Chalcedonian foundations of churches and *martyria* of saints were seized by monks from the desert: Euthymius had his disciple Gabrielius join Eudocia at St Stephen's,[109] Bassa's church of St Menas received the Euthymian monk Andrew as a supervisor,[110] and Flavia's monastery was run by the Chalcedonian Theognius.[111] Moreover, a little later, in AD 473, i.e. twenty-two years after Chalcedon, thirteen years after Eudocia's death, the time was ripe for the generation of an entirely new saint for Jerusalem: Euthymius himself.[112]

Things unfolded quickly after his death: at the recommendation of Chrysippus, guardian of the Cross and a former disciple of Euthymius, the Patriarch Anastasius, a former monk of the desert monasteries, invited Martyrius and Elias, two disciples of Euthymius, to attend his dead body, leaving Fidus, a disciple of Euthymius and now a deacon of the latter's monastery, with the "responsibility for building a burial vault for the translation of the precious remains to a becoming place."[113] He employed craftsmen and workers from Jerusalem who demolished the hermit's original cave and built a large vaulted chamber with Euthymius' tomb in the middle. The Patriarch had already sent the tombstone in advance along with a silver crucible and surrounding railings. On 7 May, he came down to the monastery and translated the relics to the prepared place, carrying them in his own hands.[114]

It had taken Euthymius' disciples three and a half months to present Jerusalem and its surroundings with its newest saint: Euthymius, the Chalcedonian hero, father of the monks, colonizer of the desert. The step from 'living holy man' to 'venerated saint' was just a small one. For understanding both the foundation of Eudocia's church to St Stephen, but also the veneration of contemporary living saints in Jerusalem, it is the religious landscape of Constantinople that may give us further answers.

---

109 Cf. Cyr. Scyth. *Vit. Euth.* 53,5–54,11. Gabrielius also became the executor of Eudocia's will.
110 Cf. also Cyr. Scyth. *Vit. Euth.* 53,5–54,11. Bassa was apparently quicker to join the Chalcedonian cause, as Pulcheria addressed her in a letter asking her to convince Eudocia to defect from Miaphysitism.
111 Cf. Cyr. Scyth. *Vit. Theog.* as well as Paul of Elusa, *Vit. Theog.* 5.
112 Cf. Cyr. Scyth. *Vit. Euth.* 59,16–61,4.
113 Cyr. Scyth. *Vit. Euth.* 60,27–61,3.
114 Cyr. Scyth. *Vit. Euth.* 61,18–62,1.

Bibliography

Abel, F.-M. (1919). 'La sépulture de Saint Jacques le Mineur,' *RB* 16, 480–499.
Alexander, P. (1999). 'Jerusalem as the *Omphalos* of the World: On the History of a Geographical Concept,' in Levine 1919, 104–119.
Assmann, A. (2009). *Erinnerungsräume. Formen und Wandlungen des kulturellen Gedächtnisses*, Munich.
Bassett, S. (ed.) (2022). *The Cambridge Companion to Constantinople*, Cambridge.
Berger, A. (1988). *Untersuchungen zu den Patria Konstantinupoleos*, Bonn.
Bieberstein, K. & Bloedhorn, H. (1994). *Jerusalem: Grundzüge der Baugeschichte vom Chalkolithikum bis zur Frühzeit der osmanischen Herrschaft* (3 vols.), Wiesbaden.
Binns, J. (1994). *Ascetics and Ambassadors of Christ: The Monasteries of Palestine 314–631*, Oxford.
Bitton-Ashkelony, B. & Kofsky, A. (2006). *The Monastic School of Gaza*, Leiden.
Bowes, K. (2008). *Private Worship, Public Values, and Religious Change in Late Antiquity*, Cambridge.
Brock, S. (1977). 'A Letter Attributed to Cyril of Jerusalem on the Rebuilding of the Temple,' *Bulletin of the School of Oriental and African Studies* 40, 267–286.
Brown, P. (1981). *The Cult of Saints: Its Rise and Function in Latin Christianity*, London.
Budge, E.A. (1888). *The Martyrdom and Miracles of Saint George of Cappadocia: The Coptic Texts Edited with an English Translation*, London.
Bury, J. (1916). 'The Date of the *Notitia* of Constantinople,' *EHR* 31, 442–443.
Cameron, Av. & Hall, S. (1999). *Eusebius, Life of Constantine: Translated with Introduction and Commentary*, Oxford.
Caner, D. (2002). *Wandering, Begging Monks: Spiritual Authority and the Promotion of Monasticism in Late Antiquity*, Berkeley.
Clark, E. (1982). 'Claims on the Bones of St Stephen: The Partisans of Melania and Eudocia,' *ChHist* 51, 141–156.
Cooper, K. & Hillner, J. (eds.) (2007). *Religion, Dynasty, and Patronage in Early Christian Rome, 300–900*, Cambridge.
Costambeys, M. & Leyser, C. (2007). 'To Be the Neighbour of St Stephen: Patronage, Martyr Cult, and Roman Monasteries, c. 600–900,' in Cooper/Hillner 2007, 262–287.
Dagron, G. (1974). *Naissance d'une capitale: Constantinople et ses institutions de 330 à 451*, Paris.
Doublet, G. (1889). 'Inscriptions de Paphlagonie,' *BCH* 13, 293–319.
Drijvers, J. (2004). *Cyril of Jerusalem: Bishop and City*, Leiden.
Grégoire, H. & Kugener, M.-A. (1930). *Marc le Diacre: Vie de Porphyre Évêque de Gaza*, Paris.
Hackel, S. (ed.) (2001). *The Byzantine Saint*, Crestwood.
Halbwachs, M. (2008). *La Topographie Légendaire des Évangiles en Terre Sainte: Étude de Mémoire Collective*, Paris.
Harrison, R. (1989). *A Temple for Byzantium: The Discovery and Excavation of Anicia Juliana's Palace Church in Istanbul*, Austin.
Havaux, M. (2017). 'Théodose II, Constantinople et l'Empire: Une nouvelle lecture de la *Notitia Urbis Constantinopolitanae*,' *RH* 681, 3–54.
Holum, K. (1982). *Theodosian Empresses: Women and Imperial Dominion in Late Antiquity*, Berkeley.
Horn, C. (2006). *Ascetics and Christological Controversy in Fifth Century Palestine: The Career of Peter the Iberian*, Oxford.
Hunt, E. (1982). *Holy Land Pilgrimage in the Later Roman Empire: AD 312–460*, Oxford.

Hunt, E. (1997). 'Constantine and Jerusalem,' *JEH* 48, 405–424.
Hunt, E. (2001). 'The Traffic in Relics: Some Late Roman Evidence,' in Hackel 2001, 171–180.
Johnson, M. (2022). 'Sacred Dimensions: Death and Burial,' in Bassett 2022, 213–227.
Klein, K. (2018). 'Marcian und die Monophysiten,' *Gymnasium* 125, 251–273.
Klein, K. (2019). 'Zur spätantiken Kaiserin als Stifterin,' *Plekos* 21, 87–115.
Kofsky, A. (1997). 'Peter the Iberian: Pilgrimage, Monasticism and Ecclesiastical Politics in Byzantine Palestine,' *Liber Annuus* 47, 209–222.
Krausmüller, D. (2022). 'Sacred Dimensions: Constantinopolitan Monasticism,' in Bassett 2022, 200–213.
Krautheimer, R. (1983). *Three Christian Capitals: Topography and Politics*, Berkeley.
Kretschmar, G. (1977). 'Die Theologie der Heiligen in der frühen Kirche,' in von Lilienfeld 1977, 77–125.
Janin, R. (1953). *La Géographie Ecclésiastique de l'Empire Byzantin. 1er Part: Le Siège de Constantinople et la Patriarcat Œcuménique* (vol. 3: *Les Église et les Monastères*), Paris.
Jeffreys, E. (ed.) (2008). *The Oxford Handbook of Byzantine Studies*, Oxford.
Levine, L. (ed.) (1999). *Jerusalem: Its Sanctity and Centrality to Judaism, Christianity and Islam*, New York.
Leyerle, B. (2002). 'Children and Disease in a Sixth Century Monastery, What Athens Has to Do with Jerusalem,' in Rutgers 2002, 349–372.
Lilienfeld, F. von (ed.) (1977). *Aspekte frühchristlicher Heiligenverehrung*, Erlangen.
Livrea, E. (1996). 'L'Imperatrice Eudocia Santa?,' *Zeitschrift für Papyrologie und Epigraphik* 119, 50–54.
Magdalino, P. (2001). 'Aristocratic *Oikoi* in the Tenth and Eleventh Regions of Constantinople' in Necipoğlu 2001, 53–69.
Mango, C. (1986). *Byzanz*, Stuttgart.
Mango, C. (ed.) (1993a). *Studies on Constantinople*, Aldershot.
Mango, C. (1993b). 'Epigrammes Honorifiques, Statues et Portraits à Byzance,' in Mango 1993a, 25–28.
Mango, C. (2004). 'A Fake Inscription of the Empress Eudocia and Pulcheria's Relic of Saint Stephen,' *Nea Rhome* 1, 23–35.
Mango, C. (2009). 'Constantine's Mausoleum and the Translation of Relics,' *ByzZ* 83, 51–62.
Mango, C. & Ševčenko, I. (1961). 'Remains of the Church of St. Polyeuktos at Constantinople,' *DOP* 15, 243–247.
Marinis, V. (2022). 'Sacred Dimensions: Church Building and Ecclesiastical Practice,' in Bassett 2022, 180–199.
Mourad, S., Koltum-Fromm, N. & Der Matossian, B. (eds.) (2018). *Routledge Handbook on Jerusalem*, London/New York.
Necipoğlu, N. (ed.) (2001). *Byzantine Constantinople: Monuments, Topography and Everyday Life*, Leiden.
Neumann, R. & Belting, H. (1966). *Die Euphemia-Kirche am Hippodrom zu Istanbul und ihre Fresken*, Berlin.
Patlagean, E. (1976). 'L'Histoire de la Femme Déguisée en Moine et l'Évolution de la Sainteté Féminine à Byzance,' *StudMed* (ser. 3) 17, 612–615.
Price, R. & Gaddis, M. (eds.) (2005a). *The Acts of the Council of Chalcedon*, Liverpool.
Price, R. & Gaddis, M. (2005b). 'General Introduction,' in Price/Gaddis 2005a, 1–85.
Rubin, Z. (1999). 'The Cult of the Holy Places and Christian Politics in Byzantine Jerusalem,' in Levine 1999, 151–162.
Rutgers, L. (ed.) (2002). *Essays on Classical, Jewish, and Early Christian Art and Archaeology*, Leuven.

Saradi, H. (1995). 'Constantinople and its Saints (IVth–VIth. c.): The Image of the City and Social Considerations,' *StudMed* 36, 87–110.

Snee, R (1998). 'Gregory Nazianzen's Anastasia Church: Arianism, the Goths, and Hagiography,' *DOP* 52, 157–186.

Sommer, M. (ed.) (2001). *Die Levante: Beiträge zur Historisierung des Nahostkonflikts*, Freiburg.

Stathakopoulos, D. (2008). 'Population, Demography, and Disease,' in Jeffreys 2008, 309–316.

Stroumsa, G. (1989). 'Religious Contacts in Byzantine Palestine,' *Numen* 36, 16–41.

Talbot, A.-M. (1996). *Holy Women in Byzantium: Ten Saints' Lives in English Translation*, Dumbarton Oaks.

Trampedach, K. (2001). 'Die Konstruktion des Heiligen Landes: Kaiser und Kirche in Jerusalem von Constantin bis Justinian,' in Sommer 2001, 83–110.

Van Esbroeck, M. (2001). 'The Saint as a Symbol,' in Hackel 2001, 128–140.

Verstegen, U. (2018). 'Byzantine Jerusalem,' in Mourad/Koltun-Fromm/Der Matossian 2018, 64–76.

Wilkinson, J. (1999). *Egeria's Travels*, Warminster.

Wilkinson, J. (2002). *Jerusalem Pilgrims Before the Crusades*, Warminster.

Woods, D. (1991). 'The Date of the Translation of the Relics of SS. Luke and Andrew to Constantinople,' *VChr* 45, 286–292.

Wilkinson, J. (2001). 'The Church of "St." Acacius at Constantinople,' *VChr* 55, 201–207.

Kai Trampedach
A New Temple of Solomon in Jerusalem? The Construction of the *Nea* Church (531–543) by Emperor Justinian

The buildings constructed by Emperor Justinian (r. 527–565) not only fundamentally changed Constantinople, but also Jerusalem. Justinian reshaped the urban structure of Jerusalem especially by expanding the *cardo maximus* and constructing a new Church of Mary, the so-called Nea. Two contemporary, completely independent authors and witnesses with very different intellectual backgrounds give us information about these building projects, which continued for a period of twelve years, from 531 to 543: the historian Procopius of Caesarea and the hagiographer Cyril of Scythopolis. These literary sources are complemented by archaeological findings. The part of Jerusalem where these Justinianic buildings stood was thoroughly investigated from 1969 to 1982 by Israeli archaeologists led by Nahman Avigad. The part of their research relevant to my topic was published by Oren Gutfeld in 2012 as volume 5 of *Jewish Quarter Excavations in the Old City of Jerusalem*. In this article, I will discuss Procopius and Cyril's statements about the Nea and compare them to the findings of the archaeological investigation (Section II). On this basis, I will ask what symbolic and theological messages Emperor Justinian associated with the building of the Nea in Jerusalem (Section III). In doing so, I will discuss the theory that Justinian wanted his church to be understood as a typological successor to the Jewish Temple: accordingly, Justinian intended the Nea to be not only a new church of Mary in Jerusalem, but also a new Temple of Solomon.[1] First, however, I will sketch a brief overview of Justinian's building activity in the Holy Land, which provides the context for the emperor's building measures in Jerusalem (Section I).

Note: A German version of this paper appeared in *Millenium* 12, 2015, 155–177. I am grateful to Hartmut Leppin and Wolfram Brandes (both Frankfurt a. M.) for suggestions, and especially to John Noël Dillon (Berkeley) for comments and translation, including the citations from the Greek sources. Special thanks go to Michael Chronz (Bonn) who called my attention to the topic many years ago and who gave useful hints.

[1] This theory is not new, but was supported or considered by Amitzur 1996; Shahid 2006; Taylor 2008; Gutfeld 2012, 491–494, in part with various arguments that will be examined more closely in this article.

OpenAccess. © 2022 Kai Trampedach, published by De Gruyter. This work is licensed under the Creative Commons Attribution-NonCommercial-NoDerivatives 4.0 International License.
https://doi.org/10.1515/9783110718447-007

I

The reign of Emperor Justinian (527–565) may be considered the apogee of late-antique sacred building activity in Palestine, and especially in Jerusalem. As Procopius lists in his *Buildings* in detail, the emperor himself furnished the money for monasteries, churches, poorhouses, hostels, cisterns and fountains, and even fortresses to protect the monks and pilgrims from desert nomads. He additionally invested in four major projects, three of which Procopius describes at length: 1) the construction of the *cardo maximus* and Nea Church in Jerusalem; 2) the construction of a massive defensive wall around the Theotokos Church built by Zeno on Mount Garizim in Samaria, to protect it from Samaritan attacks; 3) the construction of a church on Mount Sinai and a fortress at the foot of the mountain; and 4) (missing in Procopius, perhaps because the project was not completed until after *Buildings* was composed) the restoration and expansion of the Church of the Nativity in Bethlehem.[2] This list immediately raises the question of why the emperor carried out so may large and expensive projects in Palestine. What interest did Justinian have in Jerusalem and the Holy Land?

Two answers spring to mind: first, Palestine was vitally important for the emperor's religious policy. In contrast to Egypt and Syria, after initial resistance the Chalcedonian definition of faith had largely prevailed in Palestine. The patriarchs of Jerusalem and especially the monks of the Judean desert had vigorously maintained their allegiance to Chalcedon in the face of the intervention of the anti-Chalcedonian emperor Anastasius. After the accession of Emperor Justin in 518, who again made Chalcedon the official orthodoxy, the Holy Land thus automatically became a bastion of the emperor's religious policy in the East. The Church of Jerusalem played a key part in Justinian's efforts to restore the unity of the Church and to find a compromise formula that all parties could accept. Bishops and especially monks from Palestine took a leading role in the negotiations. The emperor, in turn, vigorously intervened in person both with theological treatises and official resources when the unity of the Palestinian Church was threatened in the late 530s and early 540s by the so-called Origenists.[3]

Second, on account of the great number of pilgrims who traveled to the holy sites from every corner of the Empire, it was important to the emperor to remain on good terms with the local authorities. In this way, the emperor could take advantage of a particularly powerful stage for representation. Emperor Justinian used this stage and

---

[2] Proc. *Aed.* 5,6–9; Armstrong 1969, 23–28; on the Church of the Nativity in Bethlehem, cf. M. Avi-Yonah, in: *The New Encyclopedia of Archaeological Excavations in the Holy Land*, Jerusalem 1994, vol. 1, 205–208; cf. Cameron 1985, 94–98, esp. 95 with n. 88.
[3] Cf. Trampedach 2005, 273–279, 284.

made the idea of the Holy Land a key element of his self-conception.⁴ In a novel from 536, Justinian praises Palestine as a province of distinguished cities, of good and learned citizens, of renowned men of God, and "what is the greatest of all," the site where Jesus Christ appeared on Earth.⁵ Another decree from the same year awarded the Church of Jerusalem important financial privileges. The emperor offers the following justification, among others:

> When God, the lord of all and also creator of all things, deigned to give so great a privilege to it [Jerusalem] over other cities, namely that there he would rise from the dead after the flesh, it is clear why We too, who follow the Lord God and his great miracles, have given it a privilege over other churches: thus may it enjoy the benefit of Our law, which we offer to it as a gift, granting it advantages and honoring it in every way.⁶

Benefactions for Jerusalem are part of the emperor's ideological self-conception: as Justinian himself stresses, they are an expression of the *imitatio dei* or *mimesis theou* to which the emperor feels particularly bound. Like Constantine in the fourth century and – to a lesser extent – Empress Eudocia in the fifth,⁷ Justinian also honored the Holy Land with intense building activity – to an extent that is unparalleled outside Constantinople, even for this building-mad emperor, with the exception of the fortifications on the eastern frontier of the Empire.⁸

Among Justinian's building projects in the Holy Land, those in Jerusalem were undoubtedly the most significant, and not only on account of the site; the expenses the emperor had to meet to expand the *cardo maximus* and construct the Nea Church were several times greater than those for other buildings in the Holy Land. The mosaic map of Madaba, created in the second half of the sixth century, provides us with an especially vivid impression of contemporary Jerusalem. The map gives an astonishingly accurate picture of Jerusalem, provided one disregards two characteristic theological-ideological distortions: a) the Anastasis complex appears precisely on the major diameter of the elliptically shaped city and thus is placed by the creators of the mosaic in the center of the image, just as the Holy City itself stands at the center of the world; and b) the existence of the Temple Mount is hidden from observers of the mosaic. The topographical location of the *cardo maximus* and the Nea Church,

---

4 For the context, see above my chapter on 'The Making of the Holy Land in Late Antiquity,' pp. 32–34.
5 Nov. 103, praef. (ed. Schoell/Kroll, p. 497, 3–13).
6 Nov. 40, Cap. I. (ed. Schoell/Kroll, p. 261, 1–10).
7 Cf. Klein 2011/12, 85–95.
8 Since all four building projects mentioned occupied symbolic sites, they were particularly well-suited to promote the process of de-Judaizing Palestine under the banner of Christianity – a goal clearly connected to Justinian's anti-Jewish legislation. Cf. Shahid 2005, 374: "It is only natural for an emperor of such anti-Jewish cast of mind to direct his attention to Palestine in order to convert it from a Jewish Promised Land to a Christian Holy Land." To that effect Shahid ibid., 382–384, convincingly interprets the prooemium of Nov. 103 (cited above), in which the emperor showers lavish praise not only on Jesus Christ, but also on the emperors Vespasian and Titus.

which extends eastward at its southern end, is indicated correctly on the Madaba Map, emphasizing the size and significance of these Justinianic building projects.[9]

II

In his *Life of St Sabas*, composed around 555, Cyril of Scythopolis relates how the aged desert father obtained several significant privileges for the Church of Palestine during his visit to Constantinople in 531.[10] The Nea allegedly played an important part in the negotiations. According to Cyril, Sabas asked the emperor to build and decorate the Theotokos Church in the Holy City; its foundation had been laid not long before under the archbishop of Jerusalem, Elias (494–515).[11] As Cyril continues to relate, the emperor eagerly fulfilled the monastic leader's wish, provided money, and sent the architect Theodorus to Jerusalem to build the church. Without encroaching on the overarching authority of Archbishop Peter, he commissioned Barachos, the bishop of Bakatha, to oversee the construction, which lasted twelve years until the dedication of the building. "It is superfluous," Cyril remarks in conclusion, "to describe the size, the incredible brilliance, and the rich ornamentation of this venerable building; it stands before our very eyes, surpassing all previous marvels and tales at which men have wondered and that the Hellenes have recorded in their histories."[12]

Cyril's account stresses three things to put Justinian's achievement in the right light: 1) By building the new Theotokos Church in Jerusalem, the emperor continues and completes a project initiated years before by Patriarch Elias. 2) The initiative to have Justinian build the church, as Cyril expressly emphasizes, was taken by the Church of Palestine and its envoy, the monastic leader Sabas.[13] 3) The emperor carried out the task requested of him very eagerly by providing for its financing, a competent engineer (μηχανικός), and a suitable overseer. The division of labor Cyril describes precisely matches his ideal: the emperor proves and distinguishes himself as

---

[9] Cf. Tsafrir 1999, esp. 155–158; Mucznik-Ovadiah-Turnheim 2004, esp. 23. On the purpose and significance of the map, cf. the illuminating reflections of Shahid 1999.

[10] Cyr. Scyth. VS 70–73 (171,26–178,18 Schwartz); cf. Trampedach 2005, 279–284. Diekamp 1899, 11–15, has shown that a year must be added to Cyril's dating after 529 so that Sabas' journey to Justinian in Constantinople takes place in the year 531 (instead of 530). Stein 1944, 171–180, defended this conclusion against the objections of Schwartz 1939, 343–346, furnishing additional evidence in support; cf. also di Segni 2012, 261 with n. 4.

[11] Cyr. Scyth. VS 72 (175,11–15).

[12] Cyr. Scyth. VS 73 (177,14–178,4). It emerges from another passage in his work (*Vit. Euth.* 49 [71,16–20]) that as a young monk Cyril had personally participated in the dedication of the Nea in November 543.

[13] Cyril's account closes with the declaration: καὶ οὗτος μὲν τῆς τοῦ θείου Σάβα τετάρτης αἰτήσεως ὁ καρπός.

helper of the Church of Jerusalem, which is represented by its patriarchs and especially by holy desert fathers like Sabas.[14]

With the verdict quoted above, Cyril agrees with Procopius, writing at roughly the same time, who likewise praises the church as a marvel. In contrast to Cyril, Procopius fortunately did not consider a detailed description superfluous: he particularly emphasizes the enormous difficulties that had to be overcome to construct the church.[15] The different focus of the two works derives from their different genres and intended audiences. While Cyril writes to glorify the Church of Palestine and its monks,[16] Procopius' work is an original, classicizing imperial panegyric, which uses the imperial building projects in Constantinople and the provinces to illustrate the emperor's devotion to God as vividly as possible.[17] The panegyrical nature of *Buildings* could explain why Procopius's description of the Nea mentions neither the laying of the foundation by the patriarch of Jerusalem, nor the initiative taken by the desert father Sabas, nor the officials charged to carry out the construction, but rather heaps all praise for the undertaking on Justinian. According to Procopius, the emperor ordered the church to be built on the highest hill in Jerusalem specifying its width and length and other details.[18] This contradicts Cyril's report that Patriarch Elias had laid the foundation.[19] Yet, even if Cyril did not invent this account, he certainly may have exaggerated it, and the claim that Sabas initiated the project could also be hagiographical exaggeration. Cyril similarly attributes Justinian's later military successes in Africa and Italy to Sabas' prophesies and prayers. In the case of the Nea, Cyril had a vested interest in crediting the Church of Palestine and its monastic leader with the initiative for the magnificent new building in Jerusalem. I will come back to this problem.

Procopius' account of the building and the shape of the church accords well with the archaeological research directed by the Israeli archaeologist Nahman Avigad in

---

14 Thus, according to Cyr. Scyth. VS 72 (175,15), after asking the emperor to finish the Theotokos Church in Jerusalem, Sabas adds the patronizing remark: τοῦτο γὰρ μάλιστα πρέπει καὶ τῆι ὑμετέραι εὐσεβείαι. Justinian's efforts to provide financing, materials, and responsible personnel recall Constantine's orders for constructing the Anastasis Basilica: cf. Euseb. VC 3,31–32. The *mechanikós* Theodorus, sent by the emperor to Jerusalem from Constantinople, is probably the same man praised by Procopius (Bell. 2,13,26) as an outstanding engineer in connection with the successful defense of Dara against the Persians in 540 (ἐπὶ σοφίᾳ τῇ καλουμένῃ μηχανικῇ λογίῳ ἀνδρός): cf. Martindale, PLRE III B, 1249 (s.v. Theodorus 13).
15 Proc. Aed. 5,6.
16 Cf. Trampedach 2005.
17 Cf. Cameron 1985, 84–112; with respect to the date, I accept the arguments for placing its date of composition ca. 544: Cameron 1985, 9–12, 85–86; Greatrex 1994; Howard-Johnston 2000, 20–22.
18 Proc. Aed. 5,6,4: ἐπέστελλε γὰρ αὐτὸ Ἰουστινιανὸς βασιλεὺς ἐν τῷ προὔχοντι γενέσθαι τῶν λόφων, δηλώσας ὁποῖον τά τε ἄλλα δεήσει καὶ τὸ εὖρος αὐτῷ καὶ μῆκος εἶναι.
19 This contradiction between Cyril and Procopius has curiously gone virtually unnoticed by scholars: cf. Bieberstein/Bleedhorn 1994, II 292; Shoemaker 2002, 101–102; Küchler 2007, 527; di Segni 2012, 259; Gutfeld 2012, 488–489. The authors' different emphases, however, have been noted by Tsafrir 2000, 151. 154; Shahid 2005, 377 n. 15.

the 1970s, which led to the discovery of substructures and remains of the foundation of the church.[20] This is also true of the most spectacular find, which the excavators discovered in a cistern immediately abutting the church's southern retaining wall, accessible from the north by a gallery furnished with stairs: on the south side, facing the entrance, they found a building inscription framed by a *tabula ansata*:

> Κ(αὶ) τοῦτο τὸ ἔργον ἐφιλοτιμήσατο ὁ εὐσεβ(έστατος) ἥμων βασιλεὺς Φλ(άουιος) Ἰουστινιανὸς προνοία κ(αὶ) σπουδὶ Κωνσταντίνου ὁσιωτά(του) πρεσβ(υτέρου) κ(αὶ) ἡγουμέ(νου) ἰνδ(ικτιῶνος) ιγ' +
>
> This work, too, our most pious emperor, Flavius Justinian, generously carried out, with the care and initiative of the most holy presbyter and hegumen, Constantine, in the thirteenth year of the indiction.[21]

The work mentioned here is naturally the cistern in which the inscription was placed. The inscription remained hidden from the public and could at most have been seen at the dedication of the building complex. In Justinian's long reign, a thirteenth indiction year occurred three times: 534/5, 549/50, and 564/65. Since the substructures to which the cistern belongs undoubtedly must have been constructed before the church itself was built, several scholars have favored the first date.[22] Mention of the presbyter and hegumen Constantine, however, whom John Moschus also calls "hegumen of holy Maria, Theotokos, the Nea," argues against this date. It is highly unlikely that the monastery founded to supervise the sanctuary had already existed several years. Moreover, the introductory "too" (καί) in the inscription apparently refers to the already completed Nea. Thus, as argued by Leah di Segni, it seems most plausible to assume that the massive vaults on the southeastern side of the Nea complex were expanded with a subterranean cistern under Abbot Constantine in 549/50 and that the inscription documents this project.[23]

The four main difficulties connected with the construction according to Procopius can easily be visualized in the archaeological findings: 1) the foundation and substructures; 2) the transport of building materials; 3) the construction of the

---

[20] Cf. Avigad 1979; Avigad 1983, 229–246; Avigad 1993; Tsafrir 2000; Gutfeld 2012, esp. 226–245.
[21] CIIP 1,800; cf. now di Segni 2012.
[22] E.g., Cameron 1985, 95; Amitzur 1996, 174; Muznik-Ovadiah-Turnheim 2004, 28; Küchler 2007, 527.
[23] Di Segni 2012, 261–262, also considers the date 564/565 possible. Shortly after the Nea was dedicated, Patriarch Peter appointed the Origenist monk John the Eunuch, former abbot of the monastery of Martyrius, as the hegumen of the monastery attached to the Church (Cyr. Scyth. VS 86 [193, 17–18]). In light of the Origenist controversy, it is possible that John was replaced before 549/50 by the Constantine named in the inscription. Among the *hegoumenoi* of the Nea monastery mentioned in the stories of John Moschus, Constantine (6), Eudoxius (187), and Abramius (68. 187), the first-named is presumably identical with the local builder of the cistern. Also in this probable case, an early date would be incompatible with the internal chronology of John Moschus. Cf. also Avigad 1993, 134–135; Feissel 2000, 99–100.

roof; and 4) the columns. I will discuss these difficulties and the solutions found for them in order.

1. Procopius describes the hilly topography of Jerusalem, with its abrupt transitions between mountain and valley, as a particular challenge for the builders and architects. The top of the hill was actually too narrow for a church of the Nea's size; accordingly, massive substructures were built on the south-eastern side. The excavations confirm Procopius' account. Above all else, they revealed precisely this extensive foundation work, which still impresses modern observers (*Aed.* 5,6,2–7). Procopius' panegyrical exaggeration thus is not completely unfounded: "Thus the building rests partly on solid rock and partly floats in the air, after the emperor's might added mass to the hill" (*Aed.* 5,6,8).

2. Procopius emphasizes the size of the stones used in the construction and the difficulty of transporting them (*Aed.* 5,6,9–13). These statements were also confirmed by the archaeological investigation. The blocks excavated in the area of the apses and the southeastern corner are indeed of a remarkable size – particularly for a late-antique building.[24] Quarries are conjectured to the north of the late-antique city and make it clear why it was necessary to widen the streets to build the Nea, as reported by Procopius, for logistical reasons alone. The archaeological excavations and restorations in the southern part of the Cardo give a particularly good impression of these measures: rock up to 6 m in height was removed to level the stairway, which presumably already existed on the hilly terrain, and it was widened so that ox-carts could deliver the blocks of stone needed to construct the church. The ground thus was also prepared for the representative colonnaded street that impressively linked the Nea and the Anastasis Basilica.[25]

3. Procopius elaborates on the problem of constructing the roof, understandably in the case of the Nea: its naves measured 74.6 m and an inner width of 52.3 m had to be spanned. Procopius describes the long search for sufficiently large trees; at last, he writes, an extensive cedar forest was located, from which the church roof could be fabricated at a height appropriate to its length and width (*Aed.* 5,6,14–15). Naturally, there are no archaeological remains that could illustrate how this challenge was met.

4. According to Procopius, the columns presented the builders with a similar problem to the roof construction (*Aed.* 5,6,17–18). Initially, no columns tall and strong enough to support the roof were available. The city's location in the mountainous inland, Procopius writes, hindered the importation of columns, which had to be monolithic according to late-antique custom. "But when the emperor," Procopius writes, "was frustrated over the difficulty of constructing the work, God revealed a kind of stone suited to this purpose in the mountains nearby, whether it had lain

---

24 According to Tsafrir 2000, 154–155, the blocks will have weighed four tons on average; some individual blocks weigh even twice as much. Ben-Dov 1985, 238, who excavated the southeastern corner immediately beyond the Ottoman city walls, mentions (probably inexactly) blocks weighing 5–15 tons.
25 Cf. Tsafrir 2000, 155–162; Gutfeld 2012, 97–100, 484–487.

there hidden before or was first created then. There is good reason in both cases to attribute the cause to God. We who measure all things with our humanly power consider many things sheerly impossible, but nothing on earth is impossible or undoable to God. Thus a great number of massive columns from that place, which resemble the color of burning fire, support the church on all sides, some above and some below, and others in the stoas that surround the entire church except the side facing east. Two such columns standing before the door of the church are exceptionally massive and probably second to none in the entire world" (*Aed.* 5,6,19–22). Procopius then gives a brief description of the narthex, atrium, propylaea, and two hospices connected to the building complex for strangers and the destitute sick. This description ends with the remark that the emperor provided the church of the mother of God with considerable incomes (*Aed.* 5,6,23–26).[26] The lack of archaeological evidence has prevented us from forming a clear picture of these latter parts of the building.[27] Matters are different, however, in the case of the fire-red columns, the process of whose discovery leads Procopius to add theological reflections in his idiosyncratic manner. According to Yoram Tsafrir, the raw material for the columns may have been provided by the red-colored stone known today as *mizzi ahmar*, which may be found at sites to the north, northwest, and northeast of the present-day Old City of Jerusalem. Tsafrir interprets Procopius' account of Justinian's "miraculous discovery" of this stone as suggesting that Justinian's stone masons used this stone for the first time on a large scale for a monumental structure. There is in fact no archaeological evidence that *mizzi ahmar* was used in any earlier period of Jerusalem's building history. It was used, however, soon after: the almost fifty columns of the Church of the Nativity in Bethlehem, probably renovated by Justinian, apparently come from the same source of stone. If this theory is correct, then the costly expansion of the Cardo southwards will have had an immediate, practical purpose in addition to representation and symbolism: as a smooth ramp that made it significantly easier to bring the very long column shafts from the quarries in the north to the construction site.[28]

---

26 The hospices for strangers and the sick (as well as the monastery) attached to the Nea are mentioned by the pilgrim from Piacenza (23), who wrote about his journey to the Holy Land around 570. In his account of the conquest of Jerusalem by the Persians in 614, the monk Antiochus Strategos includes among the thirty-five places where the victims of the Persian massacre were laid out after their departure: the Nea (no. 5 on the list), the library of the Nea (no. 8), and the imperial home for the elderly (no. 25); cf. Milik 1960/61, esp. 133, 145–151.
27 Gutfeld 2012, 226–245, attempts to create a reconstruction with several illustrations that combines the archaeological findings and Procopius' description.
28 Tsafrir 2000, 162–164 (who incidentally also conjectures [cf. ibid. n. 35 and fig. 13] that the approximately 12 m long monolithic column of *mizzi ahmar*, which on account of a crack was left unfinished in the quarry near the Russian cathedral northwest of the Old City where it may be viewed today in a pit, was also intended for the Nea); cf. Gutfeld 2012, 490–491. The assumption of Ben-Dov 1985, 239–240 (accepted by Shahid 2005, 381) that Procopius' language is an attempt to conceal the fact that the ruins of the Jewish Temple were plundered to erect the Nea, and that the columns in

On the basis of the conclusions reached thus far, I would now like to discuss the motives that led to the construction of the Nea. But first I must return to the question of authorship. In light of what has been stated above, I believe it is clear that Cyril's account, despite his apparently accurate information, gives at least one false impression. The patriarch Elias can not have laid the foundation for a building of this size on this site. He would have severely lacked both the resources and the logistical capacity. At most, it is conceivable that he began to build a much smaller church for Mary, although it must remain uncertain whether he did so on the site of the future Nea or elsewhere in Jerusalem. Procopius explicitly states, as mentioned above, that the emperor personally chose the site, the form, and the dimensions of the church. This statement is naturally an exaggeration, but it is not a topos: Procopius makes no other such claim anywhere else in his *Buildings*.[29] Even in the case of the Hagia Sophia in Constantinople, he is much more reserved and indicates the importance of the experts, especially the architects and engineers Anthemius of Tralles and Isidorus of Miletus, who supported the emperor's ambitions. He continues,

> Indeed, this too was a sign of God's honor for the emperor, namely that He provided him with the most suitable men to carry out the work to be done. And one might also marvel at the sagacity of the emperor for this reason: because he of all men was able to select the most suitable men for the most earnest of undertakings.[30]

Despite its general formulation, Procopius ignores this thought in his description of the Nea and merely mentions "builders" (ἐπιδημιουργοὶ τοῦ ἔργου) who carry out Justinian's plans. As with the Hagia Sophia, the sagacity of the emperor and God's grace combine in the construction of the Nea so that the work is a success, but in the case of the Nea it comes without the intervention of eminent collaborators. "Emperor Justinian wrought these things with human strength and skill, but his pious faith rewarded him with honor and assisted him in this undertaking."[31] The panegyrical emphasis of this is in my opinion not empty words, but rather suggests that Justinian really was involved in the construction of the Nea with an intensity comparable only to that lavished on the Hagia Sophia. It is very probable that he made use of the collaborators mentioned by Cyril, especially the architect and engineer Theodorus, whom he sent from Constantinople to Jerusalem.[32] The account of the laying of

---

particular came from it, is unconvincing. The columns of the Herodian Temple were 'only' 27 feet = 8.64 m high (i.e., smaller than those of the Nea) and were normally constructed of drums: Jos. *Ant.* 15,413; cf. Avigad 1983, 150–165.

29 Cf. Amitzur 1996, 162–163.
30 Proc. *Aed.* 1,1,25–26.
31 Proc. *Aed.* 5,6,16. After this comes the account (quoted in part above) of the miraculous discovery of the quarry that provided the perfect raw material for the columns of the nave and atrium.
32 Above the substructures on the southeast side, where the large cistern with the dedicatory inscription was built presumably later (see above), the excavators uncovered the walls and stone floor of a building that may be identified as the monastery attached to the Nea or the hospices mentioned by

the foundation by Patriarch Elias (494–515), by contrast, is less convincing, particularly since it leaves unanswered the question as to why Elias' successors John (515–524) and Peter (524–552) did not resume building after 518, when construction interrupted by the confusion caused by Anastasius' interference with the Church of Palestine could have been continued. Be that as it may, since the hypothetical foundation of Elias will have lain idle for more than fifteen years, and since the concept realized by the emperor far surpassed the financial and logistical capabilities of the Church of Jerusalem, I think it is justified to conclude that Justinian built an entirely new Nea that had nothing to do with any such original plans (if they existed). We thus may now ask what symbolic and theological messages Emperor Justinian wanted to transmit by building the Nea in Jerusalem.

III

After the Hagia Sophia in Constantinople, the Nea was the second largest and second most expensive church that Justinian had built. Its dimensions and lavish architecture surpassed even the rebuilt Church of the Apostles in Constantinople and the Basilica of St John in Ephesus.[33] This surely indicates the enormous significance Justinian attached to Jerusalem. But what scope was there for an ambitious ecclesiastical building project in Jerusalem? The key sites of the Gospels were already occupied. The Christian topography of Jerusalem in 531 already contained churches in remembrance of Easter and Pentecost and the miracles of Jesus, and churches built over the graves and relics of martyrs. The Nea, however, had no such associations; at the date of its construction, it was the only prominent church in Jerusalem that was not built, at, over, or on a Biblical *lieu de mémoire*.[34] It goes without saying that it is unlikely such a theologically ambitious emperor as Justinian would have built a monumental church in Jerusalem that made no reference to the biblical importance of the site.

A glimpse at the physical topography of Jerusalem reveals how this historical deficit was supposed to be overcome. Separated by valleys, the Nea sits at approximately the same height as the Temple Mount and the Anastasis complex. If one connects these three points, an equilateral triangle is made. "Emperor Justinian ordered that the church be built on the highest of the hills," writes Procopius,[35] and we have seen that he had to make great efforts to achieve this goal. The elevated site thus must have been very important to him, and naturally it was also well-suited to in-

---

Procopius. These walls are built of alternating layers of stone and brick. The excavator Nahman Avigad (1979, 33; 1984, 236; cf. Gutfeld 2012, 146) plausibly conjectures that this technique, which was widespread in Constantinople but previously unknown in Jerusalem, was introduced there by the imperial architect Theodorus.
33 For comparisons with other churches built under Justinian, see also Gutfeld 2012, 487–488.
34 Cf. the sketch in Bieberstein/Bloedhorn 1994, I 153–164.
35 Proc. *Aed.* 5,6,4.

crease the monumentality of the construction. Beyond this, the emperor apparently intended to use the special position of the church to connect it to the other two prominent points in Jerusalem: the Anastasis complex and the Jewish Temple Mount.

Not only its position on the opposite hill, but also its size and ornamentation made the Nea a rival to the central Constantinian church of the city. Yet the expansion of the Cardo created a direct, representational connection between the two monumental church complexes. The correlation between the two could be described as follows: with his basilica for Mary, Emperor Justinian placed a similarly ambitious Christian sanctuary alongside Constantine's church for Jesus Christ as a worthy counterpart.[36] No amount of glory in the world, after all, could have made it surpass the site of the passion and resurrection of Christ.

After some 250 years of insignificance, Constantine had reestablished Jerusalem as a major Christian site. In his *Vita Constantini*, the theologian Eusebius of Caesarea describes the emperor's *new* Jerusalem "opposite that famed Jerusalem of old, which after the bloody murder of the Lord paid for the godlessness of its inhabitants with its overthrow in utter devastation."[37] This sentence discloses the problem Eusebius saw in the existence of an earthly Jerusalem of Christians. What he and other theologians had considered one of the most important marks of difference from Judaism now threatened to vanish. Therefore, the new Christian city centered around the Holy Sepulcher was emphatically removed from the God-forsaken Jewish city focused on the Temple Mount in spatial terms and yet remained connected to it by supplanting the Temple Mount, interpreted as triumphing over it. The topography suggests a similar dialectic at work in the case of Justinian's church, particularly since it rose above the ruins of the Temple Mount, by then used as a trash heap, more visibly than the Anastasis complex.[38]

In Christian Jerusalem, the question of the relationship to the Jewish Temple arises all by itself, but it was also a delicate subject even in Constantinople at this time. Anicia Juliana, a wealthy aristocrat with imperial ancestors, commissioned the construction of what was at the time the largest and most magnificent church in Constantinople; dedicated to the martyr Polyeuctus, the church was completed in the 520s. From the dedicatory inscription, which praises the achievement and noble ancestry of the commissioner in poetical language, it emerges that Anicia Juli-

---

[36] According to Küchler 2007, 529–530, the Nea on the Madaba mosaic serves "wie ein Gegenstück zur Grabeskirche": "Darin wird die ehrgeizige Absicht Justinians ersichtlich, am prachtvoll verlängerten *Cardo maximus* Konstantins die größte Marienkirche Palästinas zu errichten.".
[37] Euseb. *VC* 3,33,1.
[38] On the topography, see Gutfeld 2012, 4–6 (with fig. 2), 141, and the conclusion 491: "By emphasizing the construction of the church on the highest hill in the city, was Procopius referring to Justinian's intent to have it overlook the ruins of the Temple Mount – and thus underscore Christianity's superiority and victory over Judaism?" Cf. also Amitzur 1996, 171; Jacobs 2004, 151; Shahid 2005, 377–378.

ana intended the Church of Polyeuctus to surpass the Temple of Solomon.[39] Justinian apparently interpreted the church and this claim as a challenge, to which he responded with the rebuilding of the Hagia Sophia. Accordingly, in the contemporary tradition the Hagia Sophia in Constantinople is repeatedly compared to the Temple of Solomon: in a famous hymn, Romanus the Melodist compared the reconstructed Hagia Sophia of Justinian in Constantinople to two models in Jerusalem, namely, the Temple of Solomon and the Anastasis and Church of Zion of Constantine and Helena.[40] If this comparison suggested itself for theological reasons for the most important and largest church of the capital, that must have been even more true for a monumental church constructed in Jerusalem itself. And Justinian famously is supposed to have proclaimed at the dedication of the Hagia Sophia: "I have outdone thee, Solomon!"[41] In the year 531, however, when the plans to build the Nea were being drawn up, Justinian could not have known that he would soon have the opportunity (in consequence to the devastation caused by the Nika Revolt in January 532) to rebuild the Hagia Sophia. Accordingly, the visit to Constantinople by the desert father Sabas may have presented Justinian with a welcome occasion to realize his goal of surpassing the Temple of Solomon (and the Church of Polyeuctus of Anicia Juliana) in Jerusalem, the biblical city, itself.[42] It thus is also plausible from the perspective of Constantinople that the emperor conceived of the Nea in order to surpass the Jewish Temple.

The Nea is dedicated to Mary, Mother of God. As Mischa Meier has shown, Emperor Justinian embraced the growing reverence of Mary among the general population and promoted the cult of Mary throughout the Empire, presumably in response to the various crises of the time.[43] Procopius emphasizes one aspect of the policy, namely, the building of churches: "Emperor Justinian built many churches dedicated to the Mother of God throughout the Empire of such magnificence and size and constructed at such extravagant expense that if one were to observe just one of them by itself, he would suppose that Justinian had built this one work alone and had la-

---

39 *Anth. Pal.* 1,10,48–50; cf. Harrison 1990, 137–139; Bardill 2006. Debates about Jerusalem and the Temple in the second half of the sixth century, in which even the re-erection of the Jewish Temple seemed imaginable, are attested by the *Erotapokriseis* of Pseudo-Kaisarios (ed. R. Riedinger, Berlin 1989) IV 218: cf. Papadoyannakis 2008. On the 'better-than-Solomon' competition in contemporary Constantinople, see the contribution to this volume by Nadine Viermann.
40 Rom. Mel. 54,21–22; cf. *Anonymi in Hagiam Sophiam Hymnus* in: Trypanis 1968, no. 12, strophes 3 and 13 (p. 142 and 145); Coripp. *In laud. Iust.* 4,283 with commentary by Cameron 1976, 204–205.
41 Script. Orig. Const. p. I 105,4–5 Preger. Although this statement is attested in a late and unreliable source, in light of the contemporary parallel evidence it should not be dismissed too easily as unhistorical, as Meier 2003, 189, stresses.
42 Cf. Amitzur 1996, 174, and esp. Shahid 2005 (who stresses Justinian's imperial self-representation as a 'better-than-Solomon' emperor [374, 376, 380, 385]).
43 Meier 2003, 502–528.

bored over it intensively for his entire reign."⁴⁴ The Nea naturally belongs in this context.

The "old" churches dedicated to Mary in Jerusalem at the Pool of Bethesda and Gethsemane recalled Mary's birth, celebrated on September 8, and her childhood home, over which the church was allegedly built, as well as her death and grave.⁴⁵ The Nea, by contrast, as mentioned, is not directly connected to any biblical site. A connection to the events of the Gospels could be created only by integrating the church liturgically into the calendar of feast days in Jerusalem. But how was that managed? How was the Nea integrated into the liturgical calendar of Jerusalem?

The chronological proximity of the date of the dedication of the church, November 20 (543) and the 'The Presentation of Mary' (ἡ ἐν τῷ ναῷ εἴσοδος τῆς Ὑπεραγίας Θεοτόκου) on November 21 is surely no coincidence.⁴⁶ When exactly this feast was incorporated in the liturgical calendar of Jerusalem is unknown; the liturgical tradition puts the beginning of the feast in the mid-sixth century.⁴⁷ Probably, therefore, the Presentation of Mary linked up with the dedication of the church and in that way entered into the liturgical calendar of Jerusalem (from where it spread first in the Eastern, then also in the Western Church). The feast of the Presentation of Mary celebrates the entry of the three-year-old Mary into the Temple and her nine-year-long stay there, as depicted in the apocryphal Protoevangelium of James.⁴⁸ The hymns that are still sung today on this occasion in the Orthodox Church celebrate Mary as "living temple" (ναὸς ἔμψυχος) or as "God-bearing temple" (ναὸς θεοχώρητος) or as the "most pure temple of the savior" (καθαρώτατος ναὸς τοῦ Σωτῆρος).⁴⁹ This language, which apparently derives from Athanasius of Alexandria, was powerfully deployed by John Chrysostom and Cyril of Alexandria and became downright conventional from the time of the Council of Ephesus on.⁵⁰ In the age

---

44 Proc. Aed. 1,3,2; cf. Meier 2003, 514 with n. 448.
45 Cf. Bieberstein/Bloedhorn 1994, III 167–169 (on St Mary at the Pool of Bethesda), III 251–256 (on the Church of the Sepulcher of St Mary); Küchler 2007, 245–246, 470–471. No contemporary source explains the name 'Nea'. In the unlikely view of Bieberstein 1989, the Nea took its name not in distinction to an earlier church of St Mary but in reference to the city district of Neapolis.
46 Tarchnischvili 1959–60, n. 1373; Garitte 1958, 389. 391. Mimouni 1995, 512–514, rejects a connection between the two feasts.
47 Cf. Baldovin 1987, 54. 239; Mimouni 1995, 376–377; Schoemaker 2003, 116; for the history of the Jerusalem liturgy in general, see H. Brakmann, RAC 17 (1996), 706–712.
48 Protoev. Jac. 7–8.
49 ΜΕΓΑΣ ΙΕΡΟΣ ΣΥΝΕΚΔΕΜΟΣ, for November 21, 707–714.
50 G.W.H. Lampe, A Patristic Greek Lexicon, Oxford 1961, s.v. ναός H. 2. Approximately at the same time as Athanasius (cf. esp. de incarnatione 8,3: Αὐτὸς [sc. τοῦ Θεοῦ Λόγος] γὰρ δυνατὸς ὢν καὶ δημιουργὸς τῶν ὅλων, ἐν τῇ παρθένῳ κατασκευάζει ἑαυτῷ ναὸν τὸ σῶμα, καὶ ἰδιοποιεῖται τοῦτο ὥσπερ ὄργανον, ἐν αὐτῷ γνωριζόμενος καὶ ἐνοικῶν) Eusebius of Caesarea used the temple as a metaphor with respect to Christ's human nature, but without making any connection to the Virgin Mary and characteristically on the occasion of the dedication of the Church of the Holy Sepulcher in Jerusalem (LC 14,3: θείου λόγου οἰκητήριον νεώς τε ἅγιος ἁγίου θεοῦ). On Cyril's Mariology, cf. Limberis 1994, 107–116, esp. 109–110.

of Justinian, the Mother of God was celebrated in countless hymns as ναὸς ἔμψυχος and with similar expressions.[51] The Nea was the centerpiece of the stational liturgy of Jerusalem not only on the feast of Mary's entry into the Temple, but also on other days, in connection with major feasts such as Epiphany, the Assumption, and Encaenia (*enkainia*), and also in commemoration of its founders Theodora and Justinian, as emerges from the Georgian lectionary.[52] In the passages that were read or sung on these days in the Nea, at least those for the dedication of the church on November 20 and for the fourth day of the *enkainia* refer to the Temple.[53] We thus may confirm that the Nea towered over the Temple of Solomon not only physically: as its liturgical integration into the church calendar makes clear, since it was dedicated to the Mother of God (*theotokos*) as the true, genuine Temple of God, it surpassed the Jewish Temple theologically as well. The Nea was thus not only the new Church of Mary in Jerusalem, but rather in a sense a new and better Temple.

For this assumption, however, we cannot cite the author Procopius, as Oren Gutfeld does, for instance, who discusses the relationship between the Nea Church and the Temple of Solomon in the concluding chapter of the excavation publication (chap. 23: "Discussion and Summary").[54] Since Gutfeld does not distinguish between the author of the text and the author of the building described in the text, he credits Procopius with astonishing theological knowledge: It seems that Procopius was also hinting at the prophet Isaiah's vision of the End of Days: 'In the last days the mountain of the Lord's temple will be established as the highest of the mountains; it will be exalted above the hills, and all nations will stream to it.' (Isaiah 2:2)."[55] This claim, however, stands in clear contradiction to the intellectual profile of a classicizing panegyrist interested more in the technology, logistics, and engineering artistry of the buildings he describes than in theological subtleties.[56] Moreover, there is no

---

51 Rom. Mel. 35, stanzas 2 and 5 (Maas/Trypanis p. 277–278); Trypanis 1968, no. 1 (Akathistos Hymn), stanza 23 (p. 39); no. 11 (On the Assumption of the Holy Virgin Mary), stanza 19 (p. 137); no. 12 (On the Dedication of the Hagia Sophia), stanza 3 (p. 142).
52 On the fourth day of the Octave of Epiphany: Tarchnischvili 1959–60, n. 124. March 16: Tarchnischvili 1959–60, n. 258; cf. Garitte 1958, 178. June 26: Tarchnischvili 1959–60, n. 1063; cf. Garitte 1958, 260. August 3: Tarchnischvili 1959–60, n. 1123; cf. Garitte 1958, 293. August 17: Garitte 1958, 305. September 12: Tarchnischvili 1959–60, n. 1232; cf. Garitte 1958, 328. On the fourth day of the Octave of the Enkainia: Tarchnischvili 1959–60, n. 1251; cf. Garitte 1958, 331. On the Georgian lectionary, cf. Baldovin 1987, 72–80; the development of the liturgy of Mary in Jerusalem is discussed by Schoemaker 2002, 132–141.
53 On November 20: Ps. 131 (David vows to build the Temple); Hebr. 3,1–6 (Christ is higher than Moses); on the fourth day after the Enkainia, cf. Leeb 1970, 77, 96.
54 Gutfeld 2012, 491–493, here 491: "it is hard to discern the great similarities between Procopius' description of the Nea Church and biblical descriptions of Solomon's Temple."
55 Gutfeld 2012, 491; cf. Taylor 2008, 52, who vaguely states that its location on the highest hill in Jerusalem "recalls Isaiah 2:2."
56 Howard-Johnston 2000, esp. 29, credits Procopius with such a marked interest in building materials and techniques that he proclaims him first and foremost an architect/engineer: "the expertise which he brought to Belisarius' staff was technical rather than literary or legal or organisational."

evidence that Procopius possessed any theological learning that would have enabled him to make subtle allusions to Old Testament prophets. When Procopius cites scripture, which is seldom, he does so openly, usually in abbreviated form, and sometimes incorrectly.[57]

Gutfeld also associates the discovery of the cedar forest in Procopius with the story of the "cedars of Lebanon" in the Book of Kings, which King Hiram of Tyre had felled and sent to Solomon for the Temple.[58] Besides the unremarkable fact that cedar was used as a building material in both cases, there are no similarities to be found between the texts; Procopius does not even mention Lebanon. Again, there is not the slightest indication that Procopius knew the Old Testament text or was thinking of it; on the contrary, his account shows with perfect clarity why the discovery of the cedar forest was so important for the unusually broad roof and thus for completing the construction of the church.

It is another remark of Procopius' that suggests a Solomonic motif, but of which he himself was unaware. Procopius mentions two especially tall and uniquely massive columns before the entrance to the basilica, without explaining their function or significance. Several scholars have filled this gap with reference to an analogy in the Old Testament:[59] according to 3 Kings 7:1–9 (LXX), King Solomon had two magnificent columns, called Jachum and Baaz (or Jachin and Boaz in the MT), erected in the vestibule of the main temple chamber. Unfortunately, we cannot tell from Procopius' description where exactly in the Nea complex the two potentially analogous Justinianic columns stood. How should the location πρὸ τῆς τοῦ νεὼ θύρας be interpreted? The columns could not have been erected in the narthex, which Procopius mentions next. As Gutfeld remarks, "the narthex was particularly narrow and such massive columns could not have been properly viewed, and certainly not properly appreciated by visitors. In addition, they would not have allowed for the presence

---

57 Cf. Rubin, RE 23 (1957), 341–343 (s.v. Prokopios von Kaisareia). The Old Testament material that appears in *Buildings* is scanty and unspecific: Procopius mentions the Babylonian captivity of the Jews in order to explain the name of the northern Syrian town Cyrus (2,11,2). He reports that Moses is said to have received the Ten Commandments from God on Mount Sinai and then shared them with men (5,8,8), without discussing further Old Testament stories associated with the site (e.g., the legend of the burning bush). Procopius even mentions a Solomonic temple, not in connection with Jerusalem, but rather with the Libyan city of Boreium; there, he says, "the Jews had an ancient temple that they especially revered and honored since, they say, Solomon built it when he was ruling over the Jewish people" (6,2,22). Procopius does not quote or paraphrase passages from the Septuagint. In building the Nea, did Justinian perhaps have Isaiah 2:2 or even – as Amitzur 1996, 166–167 speculates – Ezekiel 40 in mind? There is no definite indication that he did. It is as a metaphor for the spiritual Church that the verse is understood in the commentaries to Isaiah of Eusebius of Caesarea (PG 24, 101–105), John Chrysostom (PG 56, 28–29) and Cyril of Alexandria (PG 70, 67–72).
58 Gutfeld 2012, 492; cf. Shahid 2005, 377.
59 Amitzur 1996, 166; Shahid 2005, 377; Taylor 2008, 52; Gutfeld 2012, 243–244 (with fig. 5.23), 492–493.

of a gallery above the narthex, as required by Procopius' account." For lack of a better one, the excavators adopted a solution that in my opinion is still unsatisfactory:

> With all the difficulties it entails, we propose that the two columns stood on either side of the central apse, and that Procopius' description began in the east while facing west, his back towards the apse. First he surveyed the basilica, then turned back towards the apse and described the two massive columns, after which he proceeded westward to the narthex and atrium.[60]

This reconstruction not only contradicts Procopius' wording; it reduces the analogy of the Nea columns to Jachin and Boaz, since they would not be standing before the church, as the latter did before the Temple of Solomon. The excavators did not consider the possibility that the columns may have stood in the atrium adjoining the narthex. Without any comparable cases, however, this idea seems likewise rather improbable. Hence the question can only be answered conditionally: if Justinian attempted to imitate the columns before the Temple of Solomon with the two giant columns before or in the Nea, he would have revived a tradition that could put his church in a particularly close relationship to God and compensate for its lack of a basis in the New Testament.

Another famous remark of Procopius is as mysterious as the exact location of the two giant columns. In his history of the Vandalic War, the historian reports that at Belisarius' Vandalic triumph in 534, the Jewish treasure that Titus had brought with other booty to Rome in 70 after the capture of Jerusalem, and which the Vandals had seized and brought to Carthage in 455, was carried through the streets of Constantinople and into the Hippodrome. Procopius adds that out of fear, on the advice of a Jew, the emperor then quickly had the treasure transferred to the Christian churches of Jerusalem (ἔδεισέ τε καὶ ξύμπαντα κατὰ τάχος ἐς τῶν Χριστιανῶν τὰ ἐν Ἱεροσολύμοις ἱερὰ ἔπεμψεν).[61] Unfortunately, this imprecise remark in Procopius is the last information transmitted about the Jewish temple treasure.

This action already seems strange because late-antique emperors usually had no second thoughts about the repatriation of sacred objects, but rather on the contrary made great efforts to obtain relics from all parts of the Empire, and naturally from the Holy Land in particular, for the capital Constantinople and their palaces. If we follow Procopius, we might plausibly conjecture that Justinian had destined these objects to be kept and displayed in the Nea, his new temple in Jerusalem.[62] Yet several pieces of evidence argue against the credibility of Procopius' report:[63] in his account of the looting of Rome by Gaiseric, Procopius does not mention the Jewish

---

60 Gutfeld 2012, 243. The excavators believe they have found a foundation stone for a monumental column in the eastern wall on the north side of the apse; they reconstruct a column diameter of 2.40 m and a height of 17.75 m (including base and capital).
61 Proc. Bell. 4,9,5–9.
62 Taylor 2008.
63 Cf. Boustan 2008, 356–362.

treasure. Instead, he mentions elsewhere that, during the sack of Rome in 410, Alaric looted "the treasures of Solomon, the king of the Hebrews, a most spectacular sight: for most of them were decorated with emerald; the Romans had seized them long ago from Jerusalem," and brought the treasure to Carcassonne in southern Gaul (*Bell.* 5,12,41–42).[64] Procopius does not comment on the contradiction. Other, earlier and independent sources, such as Jordanes and Victor Vitensis, who describe the looting of Rome by Gaiseric, apparently knew nothing about the κειμήλια of Solomon. The way in which Procopius justifies moving the temple treasures to Jerusalem is also utterly untrustworthy. It is a Jew who is supposed to have caused the emperor (through the intercession of someone in the emperor's circle) to restore the valuables from the Temple to Jerusalem ("the place where Solomon the king of the Jews had once placed them"). According to Procopius, the Jew succeeded in convincing Justinian that his own palace in Constantinople might suffer the same fate as the palaces in Rome and Carthage because of the presence of the Jewish temple treasure. Yet how could these objects have presented a threat under the banner of orthodox Christianity? Has Procopius here ascribed his own superstition to the emperor?[65] According to Shahid, who attempts to bolster Procopius' account with two further arguments, "the existence of the Vessels in Constantinople would have been grist to the mill of the late Anicia Juliana, especially if they had been deposited in the Church of Polyeuctus, thus endowing it with an unusual sanctity." But why would Justinian have placed the vessels in the Church of Polyeuctus? He could have had them temporarily kept in the palace church and then donated them to the Hagia Sophia in 537. Shahid's second argument is no more plausible:

> The superstitious emperor may have remembered from reading the book of Daniel in the Old Testament that the misuse to which the vessels had been put by the Neo-Babylonian king Belshazzar finally led to the destruction of his kingdom. After he used the Vessels at his banquet,

---

64 Proc. *Bell.* 5,12,41–42: ἐν τοῖς ἦν καὶ τὰ Σολόμωνος τοῦ Ἑβραίων βασιλέως κειμήλια, ἀξιοθέατα ἐς ἄγαν ὄντα. πρασία γὰρ λίθος αὐτῶν τὰ πολλὰ ἐκαλλώπιζεν, ἅπερ ἐξ Ἱεροσολύμων Ῥωμαῖοι τὸ παλαιὸν εἷλον. In connection with "Belisarius' triumph," Procopius similarly states (*Bell.* 4,9,5): τὰ Ἰουδαίων κειμήλια (...), ἅπερ ὁ Οὐεσπασιανοῦ Τίτος μετὰ τὴν Ἱεροσολύμων ἅλωσιν ἐς Ῥώμην ξὺν ἑτέροις τισὶν ἤνεγκε.

65 But why should Procopius have invented this strange story? Boustan 2008, 360, gives the following answer: "It offers Procopius an effective rhetorical strategy for linking the triumph to the glorious victories of the Flavians over an earlier 'internal enemy' – in their case, the Jews rather than the Vandals – but without actually having to contend with the inconvenient traces that the vessels might have left behind in the capital." This explanation gains in plausibility if one presumes Procopius has largely exaggerated (rather than invented) the account. Perhaps that is why Procopius avoids naming specific objects. At any rate, it is difficult to imagine that Procopius, who considers emeralds worth mentioning in the case of Carcassonne (see above) would pass over in silence spectacular objects like the seven-armed menorah or the golden showbread table, if they had been carried through Constantinople with Belisarius in triumph.

the moving finger appeared on the wall and prophesied his downfall, in the four mysterious words that Daniel interpreted for him.[66]

But why would the orthodox emperor Justinian identify with the heathen king Belshazzar (Dan. 5:1–5 LXX)? Aside from his blasphemous treatment of the temple vessels, such an interpretation relies on the absurd assumption that Justinian as head of orthodox Christianity would not have considered himself the rightful owner of the temple vessels. According to all that we know about Justinian's religious self-understanding, the opposite must have been the case.

If Belisarius did indeed bring any objects from the temple treasure from Carthage to Constantinople, and the entire story has not been fabricated by Procopius, but merely exaggerated, and if Justinian sent these objects to Jerusalem, then he did so not out of religious fear, but rather to lend visible support to the contention of the triumph of Christianity over Judaism at the place of the appearance, suffering, and resurrection of Christ. Such a calculation, however, would presume that the objects from the Solomonic (actually, Herodian) Temple would be presented to a broad Christian public. The Nea, which was already under construction in 534, would have been an ideal stage for this purpose. Yet the sources tell us no such thing. For lack of evidence, it must remain doubtful whether the Jewish treasure ever reached this church or any other place in Jerusalem.[67]

We unfortunately soon lose track of the completed building in the obscurity of history. The pilgrim from Piacenza, who traveled to the Holy Land in 570, and John Moschus in the early seventh century, mention the Nea.[68] The Nea is also mentioned in a mosaic inscription that adorns the grave of one Kyriakos, who died on December 11, 566, in Jericho.[69] The church was apparently damaged but not destroyed during the capture of Jerusalem by the Persians in 614. There is scattered evidence of cult continuity until the early ninth century, probably in a small part of the gigantic building complex.[70] The *Commemoratorium de casis dei*, dating to the year 808, lists the Nea as damaged by an earthquake and prescribes it a clergy of twelve persons.[71] Eutychius of Alexandria in 935, however, reports that the Nea was destroyed in 614 and not rebuilt.[72] Although this statement is not credible on account of mentions of the Nea in the sources until the early ninth century and the lack of archaeological evi-

---

[66] Shahid 2005, 375–376.
[67] Taylor 2008, 54, believes, on the contrary, that the treasure reached Jerusalem, but was hidden: "The absence of any reference to the Temple treasure in the few accounts we do have may be due to the fact that it was not on show but stored below in the vaults, guarded by the monks and by the apotropaic care of the Mother of God."
[68] *Itin. Plac.* 23,1; Joh. Mosch. 6, 61, 68 and 187; cf. Küchler 2007, 530–532.
[69] SEG 8,315; Milik 1960/61, 147; Gutfeld 2012, 250.
[70] Schick 1995, 332–333; cf. Avni 2010.
[71] Cf. McCormick 2011, 103–111.
[72] Breydy 1985, I 98–99, II 118–119.

dence, it at least shows that already in the tenth century the Nea had largely vanished from the scene. The destruction of the Nea is remarkable – a unique occurrence that demands an explanation: since the Nea was not tied to a *lieu de mémoire* in a narrow sense, but rather derived its significance from an artificial theological concept, despite its former monumentality and liturgical centrality, it could vanish from the sacred topography of Jerusalem after the ninth century unmourned and unsung. Besides, the theological concept lost its point (it was, so to say, "historically overcome") as soon as the Temple Mount ceased to be in ruins– serving as a trash heap and thus referring to the destroyed Jewish Temple in a negative way – but was developed into the religious center of Islamic Jerusalem through the construction of the Dome of the Rock and the Al-Aqsa Mosque at the turn of the seventh and the eighth centuries.

Bibliography

Amitzur, H. (1996). 'Justinian's Solomon's Temple in Jerusalem,' in Poorthuis/Safrai 1996, 160–175.

Armstrong, G.T. (1969). Fifth and Sixth Century Church Buildings in the Holy Land, *Greek Orthodox Theological Review* 14, 17–30.

Avigad, N. (1979). 'Die Entdeckung der "Nea" genannten Marienkirche in Jerusalem,' *AW* 10.3, 31–35.

Avigad, N. (1983). *Discovering Jerusalem*, Nashville.

Avigad, N. (1993). 'The Nea: Justinian's Church of St. Mary, Mother of God, Discovered in the Old City of Jerusalem,' in Tsafrir 1993, 128–135.

Avni, G. (2010). 'The Persian Conquest of Jerusalem (614 C.E.) – An Archaeological Assessment,' *BASO* 357, 35–48.

Baldovin, J.F. (1987). *The Urban Character of Christian Worship. The Origins, Development, and Meaning of Stational Liturgy*, Rome.

Bardill, J. (2006). 'A New Temple for Byzantium: Anicia Juliana, King Solomon, and the Gilded Ceiling of the Church of St. Polyeuktos in Constantinople,' in Bowden/Gutteridge/Machado 2006, 339–370.

Ben-Dov, M. (1985). *In the Shadow of the Temple*, Jerusalem.

Bieberstein, K. (1989). 'Die Porta Neapolitana, die Nea Maria und die Nea Sophia in der Neapolis von Jerusalem. Beobachtungen zur Stadtentwicklung in byzantinischer und frühbarabischer Zeit,' *ZDPV* 105, 110–122.

Bieberstein, K. & Bloedhorn, H. (1994). *Jerusalem. Grundzüge der Baugeschichte vom Chalkolithikum bis zur Frühzeit der osmanischen Herrschaft* (3 vols.), Wiesbaden.

Boustan, R.S. (2008). 'The Spoils of the Jerusalem Temple at Rome and Constantinople: Jewish Counter-Geography in a Christianizing Empire,' in Gardner/Osterloh 2008, 327–372.

Bowden, W., Gutteridge, A. & Machado, C. (eds.) (2006). *Social and Political Life in Late Antiquity*, Leiden.

Breydy, M. (1985). *Das Annalenwerk des Eutychios von Alexandrien. Ausgewählte Geschichten und Legenden kompiliert von Sa'id ibn Batriq um 935 A.D.* (2 vols.), Leuven.

Cameron, Av. (ed./trans.) (1976). *Flavius Cresconius Corippus: In laudem Iustini Augusti minoris libri IV*, London.

Cameron, Av. (1985). *Procopius and the Sixth Century*, Berkeley.

Di Segni, L. (2012). 'Greek Dedicatory Inscription from the Vaulted Structure of the Nea Church,' in Gutfeld 2012, 259–267.
Evangelatou-Notara, E. (ed.) (2005). *Kletorion eis mnemen Nikou Oikonomide*, Athens.
Feissel, D. (2000). 'Les édifices de Justinien au témoignage de Procope et de l'épigraphie,' *Antiquité Tardive* 8, 81–104.
Gardner, G. & Osterloh, K.L. (eds.) (2008). *Antiquity in Antiquity. Jewish and Christian Pasts in the Graeco-Roman World*, Tübingen.
Garitte, G. (1958). *Le Calendrier Palestino-Géorgien du Sinaiticus 34 (Xe siècle)*, Bruxelles.
Geva, H. (ed.) (1994). *Ancient Jerusalem Revealed*, Jerusalem.
Greatrex, G. (1994). 'The Dates of Procopius Work,' *Byzantine and Modern Greek Studies* 18, 101–114.
Gutfeld, O. (2012). *Jewish Quarter Excavations in the Old City of Jerusalem conducted by Nahman Avigad, 1969–1982* (vol. 5: *The Cardo [Area X] and the Nea Church [Areas D and T]. Final Report*), Jerusalem.
Harrison, M. (1990). *Ein Tempel für Byzanz. Die Entdeckung und Ausgrabung von Anicia Julianas Palastkirche in Istanbul*, Stuttgart.
Howard-Johnston, J. (2000). 'The Education and Expertise of Procopius,' *Antiquité Tardive* 8, 19–30.
Jacobs, A.S. (2004). *Remains of the Jews. The Holy Land and Christian Empire in Late Antiquity*, Stanford.
Klein, K.M. (2011/2012). 'Do good in thy pleasure unto Zion. The Patronage of Aelia Eudokia in Jerusalem,' *Wiener Jahrbuch für Kunstgeschichte* 60/61, 85–95.
Küchler, M. (2007). *Jerusalem. Ein Handbuch und Studienreiseführer zur Heiligen Stadt*, Göttingen.
Leeb, H. (1970). *Die Gesänge im Gemeindegottesdienst von Jerusalem (vom 5. bis 8. Jahrhundert)*, Vienna.
McCormick, M. (2011). *Charlemagne's Survey of the Holy Land: Wealth, Personnel, and Buildings of a Mediterranean Church between Antiquity and the Middle Ages*, Washington D.C.
Milik, J.T. (1960–1961). 'La Topographie de Jérusalem vers la fin de l'epoque byzantine,' *Mélanges de l'Université Saint Joseph de Beyrouth* 37, 127–189.
Mimouni, S.C. (1995). *Dormition et l'Assomption de Marie. Histoire des Traditions Anciennes*, Paris.
Mucznik, S., Ovadiah, A. & Turnheim, Y. (2004). *Art in Eretz Israel in Late Antiquity*. Tel Aviv.
Papadoyannakis, Y. (2008). 'A Debate about the Rebuilding of the Temple in Sixth-Century Byzantium,' in Gardner/Osterloh 2008, 373–382.
Piccirillo, M. & Alliata, E. (eds.) (1999). *The Madaba Map Centenary (1897–1997). Travelling Through the Byzantine Umayyad Period*, Jerusalem.
Poorthuis, M. & Safrai, Ch. (eds.) (1996). *The Centrality of Jerusalem. Historical Perspectives*, Kampen.
Reich, R. (1994). 'The ancient burial ground in the Mamilla neighbourhood, Jerusalem,' in Geva 1994, 111–118.
Schick, R. (1995). *The Christian Communities of Palestine from Byzantine to Islamic Rule. A Historical and Archaeological Study*, Princeton.
Shahid, I. (1999). 'The Madaba Mosaic Map Revisited: Some New Observations,' in Piccirillo/Alliata 1999, 147–154.
Shahid, I. (2005). 'Justinian and the Christianization of Palestine,' in Evangelatou-Notara 2005, 373–385.
Shoemaker, S. (2002). *Ancient Traditions of the Virgin Mary's Dormition and Assumption*, Oxford.
Stein, E. (1944). 'Cyrille de Scythopolis. À propos de la nouvelle édition de ses œuvres,' *AB* 62, 169–186.

Tarchnischvili, M. (1959–1960). *Le Grand Lectionnaire de l'église de Jérusalem (Ve–VIIIe siècle)* (vols. I & II), Louvain.
Taylor, J. (2008). 'The Nea Church,' *Biblical Archaeology Review* 34.1, 51–59.
Trampedach, K. (2005). 'Reichsmönchtum? Das politische Selbstverständnis der Mönche Palästinas im 6. Jahrhundert und die historische Methode des Kyrill von Skythopolis,' *Millenium* 2, 271–296.
Trypanis, C.A. (1968). *Fourteen Early Byzantine Cantica*, Vienna.
Tsafrir, Y. (ed.) (1993). *Ancient Churches Revealed*, Jerusalem.
Tsafrir, Y. (1999). 'The Holy City of Jerusalem in the Madaba Map,' in Piccirillo/Alliata 1999, 155–163.
Tsafrir, Y. (2000). 'Procopius and the *Nea* Church in Jerusalem,' *Antiquité Tardive* 8, 149–164.

Part Three:
The Power of Religion and Empire

Johannes Wienand
Eusebius in Jerusalem and Constantinople: Two Cities, Two Speeches

Two of the earliest literary sources we have for the Constantinian refoundations of Jerusalem and Constantinople are from one and the same author: the bishop, theologian, and church historian Eusebius of Caesarea. In AD 335 and 336, he delivered two speeches in Jerusalem and Constantinople respectively.[1] Both orations deal, in a way, with the role of the first Christian emperor and the significance of his pious deeds. Although the speeches were given by the same orator within a short period of time, both on important ceremonial occasions, they differ significantly in content and purpose. As I will show in this paper, these differences tell us much about the different roles and settings of Jerusalem and Constantinople within the early Christian empire, about the impact of imperial absence in Jerusalem and imperial presence in Constantinople, and about the relation between church and state in the incipient Christian monarchy.

For Eusebius himself, the two speeches were so closely related that he decided to publish them as two interlinked appendices to his *Vita Constantini*.[2] After centuries of manuscript tradition, the orations appeared to be one coherent text, subdivided into 18 paragraphs, titled with the heading Εἰς Κωνσταντῖνον τὸν βασιλέα τριακονταετηρικός – 'In Praise of Constantine for the thirtieth jubilee of his reign'. In some manuscripts, however, a gap survived in the middle of the text, between the tenth and eleventh paragraph, and sometimes the two halves are headed by different titles – paragraphs 1 to 10 are called τριετηρικός ('tricennial oration'), para-

---

[1] The standard edition of the two speeches is Heikel 1902, 193–259; Harold Drake is currently preparing a new analysis of the orations of Constantine and Eusebius for the series *Die Griechischen Christlichen Schriftsteller* (Berlin, Akademie-Verlag) – I am grateful for the opportunity to read the manuscript. An anonymous English translation has been published by Samuel Bagster & Sons in London (Anonymous 1845, 293–380). A revised version by E. C. Richardson can be found in *Nicene and Post-Nicene Fathers* (Schaff/Wace 1890, vol. 2.1, 581–610). The English translation usually used today was published by Drake 1976, 83–102 ('In Praise of Constantine') and 103–127 ('On Christ's Sepulcher'), a German translation was published by Schneider 2020, 84–175 ('De laude Constantini') and 178–275 ('De verbo Dei'). I am grateful for the opportunity to consult the manuscript of Schneider's commentary and translation before publication. In the present chapter, the translations are taken from Drake 1976 (for SC and LC) and Cameron/Hall 1999 (for VC).
[2] The *Vita Constantini* was published only after Eusebius' death, most likely by his successor Acacius; see Cameron/Hall 1999, 9–12, with further references. The four books of the *Vita* have been published together with three appendices: the two orations discussed here and Constantine's *Oration to the Assembly of Saints*. Drake (forthcoming), ch. II.A makes the plausible suggestion that Eusebius was responsible for connecting the two speech manuscripts so closely that they could appear as one coherent text. Eusebius himself refers in VC 4,46 to the joint publication of his two orations.

graphs 11 to 18 bear the title βασιλικός ('imperial oration').[3] On the basis of these and other discrepancies, modern philology has reconstructed the original appearances of the two orations.[4] And since Eusebius alludes to the speeches in his *Vita Constantini*, providing additional information, it is possible to reconstruct in broad strokes their different historical settings.[5]

In the first ten paragraphs, an imperial encomium has survived in its entirety. This speech is today usually called *Laus Constantini, Triakontaeterikos*, or 'Tricennial Oration'. Eusebius gave this speech on the occasion of the festivities for the thirtieth jubilee of Constantine's reign, which were held on 25 July 336.[6] In an audience chamber of the imperial palace in Constantinople, the bishop delivered his praise before the emperor himself and possibly further members of the Constantinian dynasty, flanked by the emperor's ministers and the imperial bodyguard.[7] There seems to have been a small, select audience consisting of high-ranking notables and a number of bishops.[8] The speech is the earliest surviving Christian panegyric in honor of a Roman monarch.[9] Although the manuscript of this oration has survived as the *first* part of the appendix to the *Vita Constantini*, in terms of chronology it is the *later* of the two speeches.

The earlier speech, preserved in paragraphs 11 to 18, has an intricate history with at least two phases of revision.[10] The core of the surviving text seems to have been part of a manuscript for a sermon-like lecture on questions of cosmology, Christolo-

---

[3] Heikel 1902, CIV–CVI; Schwartz 1907, 1428.
[4] Drake (forthcoming), ch. II.A provides an in-depth assessment of the internal structures of the speeches, their formation, their relation to one another and their historical settings, which I largely follow here. See also Drake 1970, 89 (for a different view: Schneider 2007, 466 n. 322).
[5] Euseb. *VC* 4,33, 4,43–47.
[6] For the date and context of the tricennial oration, see Drake 1970, 1–2 n. 1; Drake 1975; Drake 1976, 51–52 with n. 35. Eusebius himself provides additional information regarding the setting of his speech in *LC* Prol., 1,1, 2,5, 3,1–2, 6,1, 6,10, 6,18, 9,11, 9,18, 10,7. Further information can be derived from Euseb. *VC* 4,46.
[7] *LC* 9,11.
[8] Eusebius mentions the presence of other bishops in *VC* 4,46. "Ministers and servants" and "his faithful lifeguards" are referred to in *LC* 9,11. In 3,4 the bishop alludes to the presence of Constantius Caesar.
[9] It was not the first panegyric held by a Christian on the Christian emperor, but none of the earlier encomia have survived. Eusebius of Nicomedia gave a laudatory speech on the emperor during the council of Nicaea in 325: Euseb. *VC* 3,11 and Theod. *HE* 1,7,10 (see Barnes 1978, 56–57; Brennecke 1994, 432; Cameron/Hall 1999, 265; Schneider 2007, 322 n. 184); Eusebius of Caesarea delivered ὕμνοι on Constantine on the twentieth jubilee of his reign (most likely in the emperor's absence): Euseb. *VC* 1,1,1 (for diverging interpretations, see Brennecke 1994, 436; Cameron/Hall 1999, 183–184); several orations in honor of the absent emperor were delivered during the inauguration ceremonies of the Constantinian church complex in Jerusalem in 335: Euseb. *VC* 4,45 (see below). In contrast to the tricennial oration, these earlier speeches were presented mainly in a primarily ecclesiastical context before a largely Christian audience, mostly in the emperor's absence.
[10] See the lucid analyses in Drake 1976, 42–43; Barnes 1977, 344; Maraval 1997, 244; Drake (forthcoming), ch. II.A.

gy, and soteriology – a lecture Eusebius gave in the course of the *encaenia* festivities held in Jerusalem from 13 to 20 September 335, i.e. the inauguration ceremonies for the Constantinian church complex that was built over the places of Christ's crucifixion, burial and resurrection – and that is best known by its generic name 'Church of the Holy Sepulcher'.[11] The speech is today usually called *Oratio de Sepulchro Christi* ('On Christ's Sepulcher').[12] Some weeks after the event, Eusebius had the opportunity to present the oration again, this time before the emperor in the imperial palace at Constantinople, presumably when the bishop traveled to the new capital on the Bosporus in early November 335 as part of a delegation of bishops trying to settle the dispute with Athanasius at the imperial court.[13] When he was granted the opportunity to deliver a speech before the emperor, Eusebius seems to have reused a substantial section of his Jerusalem lecture (11,8–17,15), to which he added a newly composed introduction (11,1–7) and ending (18,1–3) specifically designed to fit the occasion in Constantinople.[14] The bishop apparently made one final modification, but only a very slight one, when he prepared the text for publication as an appendix to the *Vita Constantini:* he added the first sentence to paragraph 11 in order to connect the text to the preceding tricennial oration.[15]

Strictly speaking, therefore, Eusebius gave *three* speeches, although the first two were closely related, apparently consisted in large parts of the same material, and survive in the form of one text only:

(1) A lecture presented at some point between 13 and 20 September 335 in the course of the inauguration ceremonies of the Constantinian church complex in Jerusalem. A section of this speech has survived in paragraphs 11,8–17,15 of the text known today as *Oratio de Sepulchro Christi*.

(2) A speech presented before the emperor in the imperial palace at Constantinople in early November 335. Apart from the first sentence in paragraph 11, which has been added only for publication of the text, the speech manuscript Eusebius used on this occasion seems to be identical (or almost identical) with the text today known under the title *Oratio de Sepulchro Christi:* it consists of a large section of the Jerusalem lecture with a new introduction and ending.

(3) A panegyrical oration presented before the emperor in the imperial palace at Constantinople on 25 July 336. The speech manuscript Eusebius used on this occasion seems to be identical (or almost identical) with the text today known under the title *Laus Constantini*.

---

[11] The historical context will be considered below.
[12] In view of the main focus on questions of theology, Schneider prefers the title *De verbo Dei* ('On the Logos of God'); see Schneider 2020, 13.
[13] The Festal Index for 335/336 dates the banishment of Athanasius to November 7, 335 (p. xvii trans. Burgess/Williams 1854).
[14] Drake (forthcoming), ch. II.A. convincingly shows which portions of the *SC* originally belonged to the Jerusalem lecture and which passages were newly composed.
[15] Maraval 1997, 240; Drake (forthcoming), ch. II.A.

In the two surviving speech manuscripts, Eusebius deals with the Christian monarchy and its implications for salvific history. Interestingly, however, the speeches take different stances on the issue. The discrepancy is instructive. It sheds light on the different circumstances under which the Roman state and the Christian church interacted in the two cities of Jerusalem and Constantinople. Closer scrutiny of the speeches within their historical settings will offer valuable insights into the role Constantine's two most important city refoundations played in the earliest phase of the Christian empire.

Eusebius in Jerusalem

The inauguration festivities of the Constantinian church complex in Jerusalem seem to have been the ceremonial climax of all the smaller and larger occasions for celebrating Constantine's commitment to the Holy Land.[16] Constantine ordered the erection of a basilica over a rock that had been identified as Golgotha, and on a spot where shortly before, in the process of clearing the site, an artifact assumed to be the Cross of Christ had been found. Right next to the basilica, where later the Anastasis rotunda was to be built, the Savior's Tomb had been unearthed, the very spot of Christ's resurrection, over which an aedicula was built in Constantinian times.[17] The basilica and the aedicula were connected via an open courtyard. The *martyrion* – as Eusebius calls the Constantinian church complex comprising these structures – thus marked and highlighted localities of utmost significance for Christian salvation history. At the same time, the edifice was an imperial building project in honor of the emperor's *summus deus*. Accordingly, its inauguration was an event of importance also on the level of imperial self-display.[18] Not surprisingly, then, court representa-

---

[16] On Constantine's role in the construction of a Holy Land, see Kai Trampedach's chapter to this volume.

[17] In discussing the *assumed* Cross of Christ, Borgehammar 1991 found a way to avoid the fruitless question of authenticity. On the *inventio crucis*, see below. The Anastasis rotunda over the supposed burial place of Christ was probably finished and consecrated only after Constantine's death: Wilkinson 1981, 40, 313 dates the inauguration of the Anastasis rotunda to the period between 337 and 348; according to Borgehammar 1991, 98, 101, the building was completed even later, but before Egeria's pilgrimage to the Holy Land. The term *martyrion* was later used to denote the basilica only, but for Eusebius the *martyrion* is the whole Constantinian building complex (see Hunt 1982, 13; Rubin 1982, 84; Walker 1990, 268). On the Constantinian church building complex in Jerusalem, Klein (forthcoming), ch. 2 – I am grateful for the opportunity to read the manuscript – and Kelley 2019; Yasin 2012, 941–942; Avni/Seligman 2003. Older literature includes Coüasnon 1974, 15; Corbo 1981; Hunt 1982, 11; Rubin 1982, 81; Kühnel 1987, 81; Ousterhout 1990; Walker 1990, 251; Patrich 1993, 103–112; Gibson/Taylor 1994, 77; Biddle 1999, 65–72, 109–119 (see also Biddle 2000, esp. 23–62). On the wider context of Constantine's church building program, see Armstrong 1974; Leeb 1992, 71–120; Krautheimer 1993; de Blaauw 2007; Lenski 2016, 179–196.

[18] According to Eusebius (*VC* 4,40,2), Constantine "reckoned his own thirtieth anniversary an auspicious occasion for thanksgiving to the universal King of All, and decided that it would be fitting to

tives and clerics likewise partook in the ceremonies. Constantine dispatched a range of members of the imperial administration, first and foremost the *notarius* Marianus. Marianus was not a very high-ranking official, but he had a good reputation among Christians, making him Constantine's first choice as his prime representative on the occasion.[19] According to Eusebius, Marianus was distinguished for his faith and his acquaintance with the Scriptures, and he was a confessor already during the Diocletianic persecution. Now, as the highest-ranking imperial representative in Jerusalem, he was in charge of the inauguration ceremonies. He gave a welcome address and held feasts and symposia. He also dispensed largesse to the citizens and made donations and votive offerings to the church.[20]

Apart from the court representatives, a whole range of clerics joined the ceremonies. Constantine had asked the bishops attending the synod of Tyre, which was still ongoing in early September, to make free use of the imperial post service and travel to Jerusalem in order to participate in the festivities.[21] Eminent bishops of all provinces, so Eusebius writes in his *Vita Constantini*, followed the emperor's call.[22] In particular, Eusebius points out numerous bishops from the Eastern provinces, even a bishop from the Persian Empire, and a whole mass of attendants. Some of the clerics were actively involved in the *encaenia* ceremonies, as Eusebius relates: the servants of God (οἱ τοῦ θεοῦ λειτουργοί) adorned the festivities with εὐχαί and διαλέξεις – with prayers and lectures.[23] In view of these sermons, Eusebius emphasizes three different rhetorical genera: (1) eulogies for the Christian emperor (with particular emphasis on the emperor's commitment to Jerusalem), (2) lectures on systematic theology, and (3) exegetical readings of Scripture.[24] Eusebius himself gave several public talks on the occasion, among them – so he claims – *ekphraseis* of the imperial wisdom-doctrines and interpretations of biblical prophecies.[25]

---

carry out the consecration of the *martyrion* which had been constructed with all artistic endeavours in Jerusalem". Drake (forthcoming), ch. II.C argues that this implies that "Constantine initially intended to coordinate the dedication with the start of his Jubilee Year on July 25". The extension of the Council of Tyre seems to have impeded this plan.

19 PLRE 1 Marianus 2; Euseb. *VC* 4,44. Eusebius does not mention Marianus by name in the passage itself, but he is mentioned in the corresponding *kephalaion* and in Sozom. *HE* 1,26. Eusebius counts Marianus among the close intimates of the emperor, but since he was just a *notarius*, this is unlikely to be true.

20 Euseb. *VC* 4,44.
21 See Drake 1987, 198–199 on the chronology of the Council of Tyre and the *encaenia* celebration.
22 Euseb. *VC* 4,43.
23 Euseb. *VC* 4,45,1.
24 Euseb. *VC* 4,45: "(1) ... Some praised the Godbeloved Emperor's devotion to the Savior of all, and recounted in detail the magnificent work connected with the *martyrion*; some with festive sermons based on divine doctrines provided a variety of intellectual delights for all to hear. (2) Others gave expositions of the divine readings, disclosing hidden meanings ...".
25 Euseb. *VC* 4,45,3: "This was the occasion when we also, being honored with favors beyond us, graced the feast with various addresses to those assembled, at one time interpreting in a written

The text that has survived in paragraphs 11,8 to 17,15 seems to be a substantial portion of the original manuscript of one of these sermon-like lectures. The text is devoted to cosmological, Christological, and soteriological discussions. The arguments are partly composed as a diatribe: Eusebius defends the core aspects of the Christian doctrines of God and salvation against a fictitious pagan opponent. At least in the surviving section of his lecture, Eusebius decided not to praise the material properties of the acclaimed church building, nor to pay tribute to the classical virtues of its pious builder, *pietas* and *munificentia*. Rather, Eusebius focused on the religious significance of the acts of divine salvation that occurred at the Christian loca sancta which the Constantinian basilica and the aedicula over the Tomb of Christ were meant to highlight, but Eusebius did not talk about the localities itself or about the imperial edifice. The exclusive focus on Christian theology and the absence of any allusions to the role of the first Christian monarch as a church builder are not self-explanatory – even less so since the inauguration ceremony at which Eusebius delivered his speech was obviously meant to bring together the two fields of church and state.

In the fourth book of his *Vita Constantini*, Eusebius describes the inauguration ceremonies in detail. Eusebius explicitly calls the festivities in Jerusalem a 'synod', which he parallelizes with the council of Nicaea that took place ten years earlier:

> (1) This second synod, the greatest of those we know, the Emperor assembled in Jerusalem, following that first synod, which he had brilliantly celebrated in the capital of Bithynia. That one however was a celebration of victory, which offered prayers of thanksgiving in the twentieth year of his reign for the defeat of enemies and foes at the very Palace of Victory (Nicaea); this one beautified the third decade, as the Emperor consecrated the *martyrion* to God, the Giver of all good things, as a peace-time dedication around the Savior's tomb.[26]

The two synods, so Eusebius says, were the most considerable gatherings of Christian bishops convoked by Constantine. The council of Nicaea, which was held in connection with the emperor's *vicennalia*, is characterized as ἐπινίκιον, i.e. as a victory celebration after the end of the civil war against Licinius in 324. The synod for the dedication of the Constantinian church complex in Jerusalem, in contrast, was held in connection with the tricennial celebrations under the heading of 'peace'. In this sense, Eusebius understands the Constantinian edifice as εἰρήνης ἀνάθημα – as an imperial votive offering given by the Christian emperor to God as a reward for the enduring peace within the Roman Empire. By this is meant the inner stability that characterized Constantine's regime since he has attained sole rule more than ten years earlier. In the same way as the closing ceremonies of the council of Nicaea were substantially subjected to court etiquette and to the logic of monarchic repre-

---

work the elaborate descriptions of the Emperor's philosophical ideas, at another making figurative thoughts from the prophets apply to the symbolic rites presently in hand."

26 Euseb. *VC* 4,47.

sentation, so also the synod of Jerusalem seems to have been closely bound to imperial protocol.[27]

Eusebius describes the ceremonies against the backdrop of this idiosyncratic mélange between Christian religion and Roman state. Interestingly, he does not recount Christian services conducted by clerics, but refers to certain persons who took an active role although, so he claims, they were unable to make their own contribution to understanding Christian philosophy. Instead, they appealed to God by means of bloodless and mystical sacrifices, praying for lasting peace throughout the Roman Empire and for divine protection of the church, the emperor, and his sons.[28] Eusebius implies that the *encaenia* festivities have been organized along a series of religious performances conducted primarily by court representatives. In this peculiar Constantinian blend between the imperial cult and Christian observances, religious performances with Christian overtones filled the gap caused by the incipient dissolution of pagan emperor worship, while Christian clergy members were still far from having a monopoly of defining and conducting the official religious observances for the emerging Christian monarchy.[29]

Thus, a variety of actors from different backgrounds joined the inauguration ceremonies of the Constantinian church complex in Jerusalem to celebrate the completion of an imperial building project. The festivities thereby served as a platform for various representatives of state and church to mediate and negotiate the image of the Roman ruler whose religious role was more ambiguous than ever before. The most contested aspect was the position of the Roman ruler in the cosmological fabric of Christian philosophy and in salvific history. While some seized the opportunity to praise God for His authorship of salvation, others praised the emperor's closeness to his protective deity and lauded his victories, his dynasty, and his construction works. Consequently, the ceremonial character of the festivities oscillated between the celebration of imperial power and success on the one hand and salvific history and theology on the other.

This ambivalence is manifest also on the level of time. The chronology of the *encaenia* festivities is characterized by a remarkable amalgam of Christian memorial culture and court culture, i.e., by peculiar overlaps between religious and imperial calendars. According to the Armenian Lectionary, the *encaenia* celebrations began on 13 September; Egeria tells us that the festivities were celebrated for eight days, which means they ended on 20 September.[30] Within this week of celebrations, two

---

[27] Eusebius, who partook in the events, describes in great detail the closing ceremony of the council of Nicaea in *VC* 3,10–15. For the council in general, see Kim 2020; older literature includes Luibhéid 1982 and Brennecke 1994; for the wider context: Hanson 1988.
[28] Euseb. *VC* 4,45,2. On the wider context of the end of pagan sacrifice in late antiquity, see Stroumsa 2009.
[29] On the role of bishops in the incipient Christian monarchy, see Drake 2000; Rapp 2005; Fear 2013.
[30] See Renoux 1969; Borgehammar 1991, 99–103; van Tongeren 2000, 27–37; Findikyan 2010; *Itin. Eg.* 48–49.

days seem to have been the most important ones: 14 and 18 September. Both dates have a deep meaning for Constantine's standing as a sole ruler over a reunited and peaceful empire, for the Constantinian dynasty, and for the emperor's relation to his protective deity.

From the Armenian Lectionary we know that on 14 September the commemoration of the Cross was liturgically celebrated in the Church of the Holy Sepulcher;[31] Egeria also reports that the *encaenia* festivities took place "on the very date when the Cross of the Lord was discovered".[32] This means that the consecration proper of the church building was linked to the anniversary day of the finding of the True Cross. The *inventio crucis* seems to have been the most important liturgical celebration within the course of the *encaenia* celebrations.[33] The available sources imply that the 'discovery' of the Holy Cross was a major symbolic event in the course of the urban restructuring of Jerusalem under Constantine.[34] The relic contributed to a significant transformation of the city's sacred topography which now centered around a new focal point: Golgotha and the nearby tomb of Christ. Both sites were revealed when Constantine had earlier structures removed, first and foremost the Hadrianic temple of Jupiter.[35]

Now, in Constantinian times, the newly recovered sites of Golgotha and Christ's Tomb were located *within* the city. This was considered by some to be out of line with what the Gospels say about their locations – but there seems to have been a tradition connecting the spots in question to New Testament salvation history, and "with his spirit moved by the Savior himself" Constantine knew where "against all expectations" he could expect the Rock of Calvary and the Tomb of Christ to appear.[36] Po-

---

[31] *Arm. Lect.* II, 225 ed. Renoux (English translations in Conybeare 1905 and Aivazian 2021).
[32] *Itin. Eg.* 48,1.
[33] See Borgehammar 1991, 99–103, and Tongeren 2000, 27–37, with further references.
[34] All later authors ascribe the discovery to Helena, but Eusebius says nothing about the discovery of the cross or a potential role of Helena; for a possible explanation, see Heid 2001. For a critical assessment of the sources, see Klein (forthcoming), ch. 2. On the tradition of Helena and her finding of the relic of the cross, see Drijvers 1992. It is not easy to assess the role of the cross for the Constantinian monarchy more generally. On the coins, other Christian symbols (above all the Chi-Rho) are clearly more important. All in all, there is only limited evidence as to how Constantine exactly used the sign of the cross as a symbol of divine power and success for his own monarchic representation; see Dinkler 1965.
[35] Euseb. *VC* 3,25–28 claims it was a temple for Aphrodite/Venus, but Jer. *Ep.* 58,3 and other evidence suggests that it was the Hadrianic temple of Jupiter; see Klein (forthcoming), ch. 2; for the archaeological situation, see Rubin 1982; Gibson/Taylor 1994.
[36] Euseb. *VC* 3,25 and 28. The sites were almost certainly located outside the second wall, and the area where the Church of the Holy Sepulcher was later erected was used as a quarry in the early first century AD. The German Protestant Institute of Archaeology (in cooperation with the Technische Universität Ilmenau) has conducted several geomagnetic surveys that suggest a possible trajectory of the second wall east of the Church of the Holy Sepulcher (see Vieweger et al. forthcoming; I am grateful for the opportunity to read a draft of the article). On the archeology and early history of traditional Golgotha, see also Gibson/Taylor 1994.

tentially on purpose, the sites (and in consequence also the Constantinian church complex) occupied the formerly pagan religious center of the city (just as the Hadrianic structures might have superimposed a spatial reference point of earlier Jewish/Christian memorial culture). Furthermore, Golgotha and the tomb of Christ were also located opposite the Temple Mount, a fact Eusebius thought worth emphasizing in his *Vita Constantini*.[37] In the same breath, Eusebius called the Constantinian church ἡ νέα Ἰερουσαλήμ – "the New Jerusalem" – in direct opposition to the "Jerusalem of old".[38] This strongly suggests that the Constantinian church complex was conceived as a Christian counterpart to the Jewish Temple. Constantine thus appears as a new Salomon, erecting the Temple of the New Covenant – a reading supported by the fact that the date of 14 September was also considered to be the anniversary of the inauguration of the Solomonic Temple.[39] The inauguration of the edifice thus symbolizes the dawn of a new salvific era.

Further religious overtones in the anniversary of the *inventio crucis* and the day of the dedication of the church might be seen in the fact that in the year 335, the date of 14 September fell on the *dies Solis*, the day of the Sun. Among the regular days of the week, it was certainly the most important day for Constantine, devoted to his former protective deity Sol invictus, which he had chosen as a personal companion in 310. When the pagan sun god became more and more problematic in the course of the intensifying Christianization of the Roman monarchy, Constantine increasingly abandoned explicit references to his divine companion in the early 320s, but at the same time he reinforced the image of a ruler endowed with solar power.[40] In the context of this development, the *dies Solis* was promoted by means of certain judicial regulations to serve as the prime day of the imperial cult.[41] Against this background, the day of 14 September 335 was certainly a day of particularly intense religious and imperial connotations.

The second most important day in the course of the *encaenia* festivities of 335 was the date of 18 September. On this very day, Constantine raised Dalmatius, the eldest son of his half-brother Flavius Dalmatius, to the rank of Caesar.[42] Dalmatius was the only member of the lateral line of his family whom Constantine invited to

---

37 Euseb. *VC* 3,33,1 (ἀντιπρόσωπος).
38 Euseb. *VC* 3,33; see Wilkinson 1979, 351–352; Ousterhout 1990.
39 Euseb. *VC* 3,33,1; see Drake (forthcoming), ch. II.C; see also Schwartz 1987.
40 On this development, see Wallraff 2001; Berrens 2004; Wienand 2011 and 2012, 296–335; on solar power in particular, see Drake 2009.
41 The Constantinian regulations regarding the *dies* Solis are preserved in *Cod. Iust.* 3,12,2 (3 March 321) and *Cod. Theod.* 2,8,1 (3 July 321); see Dörries 1954, 181-182, 226, 322, 345-346; Bacchiocchi 1977; Cameron/Hall 1999, 317; Wallraff 2001, 96-109, with further references on p. 96 n. 31; Girardet 2007, 285-287.
42 *Chron. Min.* 1,235; see RE Delmatius 3; PLRE 1 Dalmatius 7; Barnes 1982, 43; Klein 1979, 106–109; Barnes 2011, 162; Wienand 2013, 40.

join the imperial college.⁴³ Dalmatius descended from Theodora, the second wife of Constantine's father Constantius.⁴⁴ The emperor apparently chose the day for elevating Dalmatius primarily because it was the anniversary of the battle of Chrysopolis. His victory in this decisive confrontation of the civil war against Licinius had made Constantine sole ruler in 324. Quite obviously, both events (the anniversary and the elevation) have purposefully been connected, and it was certainly not by chance that Constantine chose the year of his *tricennalia* (which ran from 25 July 335 to 25 July 336) for this significant reconfiguration of the imperial college:⁴⁵ even Eusebius clearly points out the connection between the three ten-year-cycles of Constantine's rule on the one hand and the elevation of his Caesars on the other.⁴⁶ Even more, the bishop closely connected the dedication of the *martyrion* church with the celebration of the Constantinian dynasty, suggesting that the elevation of Dalmatius (which most likely was carried out in Constantinople) was reflected in one way or another also in the *encaenia* ceremonies. Again, the leading concept seems to have been the notion of 'peace,' which stood at the center of a triadic concept composed around the emperor's victoriousness (battle of Chrysopolis), the universal concord within the im-

---

43 Within the imperial college, Dalmatius held the lowest rank. He was granted his own images on the imperial coinage; on the epigraphic record, which is more ambivalent, see Grünewald 1990, 152–153. According to Aurelius Victor (*Caes.* 41,15), the promotion of Dalmatius was conducted *obsistentibus valide militaribus* – a view that is obviously influenced by hindsight. In 336, Dalmatius probably married Helena, Constantine's youngest daughter. Nevertheless, the decision to include Dalmatius in the ruler college led to a grim rivalry between the two family lines, foremost the bloody purges after the emperor's death in 337, in which almost all members of the lateral line including Dalmatius were killed on the orders of Constantine's sons (on the events of 337, see Burgess 2008). These events had serious repercussions down until the reign of Julian (360–363), see Baker-Brian/Tougher 2020.
44 PLRE 1 Theodora 1; Wienand 2013, 24–26, 39, 40–41.
45 It was not the first time Constantine chose meaningful dates for rearranging the imperial college: when he raised Crispus and Constantinus to Caesars, he chose 1 March 317 – the 25ᵗʰ *dies imperii* of his own father Constantius I (according to inclusive reckoning). Constans was elevated to the rank of Caesar on 25 December 333, i.e. on the *natalis invicti* or *natalis Christi*.
46 Euseb. *VC* 4,40,1–2. The bishop is notoriously imprecise regarding the accession dates and even abstained from mentioning Dalmatius, who suffered a *damnatio memoriae* after he was murdered in the political purges of 337. Eusebius also ignored Crispus, Constantine's oldest son, who was put to death on the emperor's command in the course of the so called 'palace crisis' of 326 and who was also subjected to a *damnatio memoriae*. Thus, Eusebius only mentions three Caesars: Constantine Iunior, elevated "at the time of his father's tenth anniversary", Constantius "about the time of the twenty-year celebration", and Constans, "promoted about the end of the third decade". Eusebius is quite imprecise regarding the dates of the Caesars' appointments. Crispus and Constantinus Iunior were promoted on 1 March 317, i.e. on the 25ᵗʰ *dies imperii* of Constantius I; Constantius Iunior was elevated on 8 November 324; and Constans was appointed on 25 December 333 (i.e. the *natalis invicti* or Christi). Thus, Dalmatius was the only Caesar who was actually elevated in the course of one of Constantine's major ruler anniversaries. However, the fact that Eusebius takes for granted the connection between Constantine's *tricennalia* and the expansion of the imperial college suggests that this was an aspect of Constantinian representation familiar to his contemporaries.

perial dynasty (elevation of Dalmatius), and the divine support of the Constantinian monarchy (dedication of the *martyrion* church).

Now, in the lecture-sermon Eusebius delivered on the occasion of the *encaenia* ceremonies, the bishop significantly departed from the Constantinian interpretation of the building and its religious context. First of all, the bishop completely ignored all the intricate layers of meaning just carved out – although the fact that he refers to these aspects in his *Vita Constantini* clearly shows that he was well aware of them. He also abstained from praising Constantine's Christian-friendly religious policy in his speech, and he did not even highlight the emperor's pious church-founding activity. Instead, Eusebius at first retraced the conceptual foundations of Christian cosmology, then – in a Christological middle part – he discussed the incarnation, death, and resurrection of Christ, and finally he dealt with the soteriological ramifications of divine revelation up to his own time. Instead of praising the Christian emperor and his church building activity, Eusebius chose to focus on the corresponding doctrines of Christian belief: the Christological middle part of the lecture specifically refers to the salvific events that were supposed to have happened on the very spot where now Eusebius was giving his talk in the newly built Constantinian church.

As it seems, Eusebius made no efforts to link his discourse to the official reading of the *encaenia* ceremonies. Quite the contrary: the way in which Eusebius, in his speech, depicted the Christian God, differed in various respects from the way the *summa divinitas* usually appeared in Constantinian representation. In the cosmological part of his speech, Eusebius introduced the proposition that God alone was the cause of all historic development. From this premise the bishop then deduced – in the soteriological part of the oration – the provocative conclusion that God alone fought the enemies of Christianity and eliminated the error of polytheism, that he alone gave new hope to the Christians, and that he alone rebuilt their churches – accomplishments Constantine undoubtedly claimed for himself:

> (5) Now let anyone who so wishes come forth and explain who it was who, after such destruction and ruin, restored the sacred buildings from top to bottom; who, after the loss of all hope, decided on a second rebuilding, even greater than the former? And, surely the greatest marvel of the account, He [= God] did rebuild, not after the demise of those persecutors, but while these vey exterminators were yet alive, so that through their own mouths and their own writing they should themselves sing the recantation of what they had done.[47]

Eusebius then even drew an unflattering comparison between the power of an earthly ruler on the one hand and the power of God and Christ on the other:[48] "What sovereign ever wielded power for so many ages? Who else continues to command after death, to raise trophies over his enemies, and to subordinate every land and country and city, both Greek and barbarian, subduing his adversaries with an invisible and

---

47 Euseb. *SC* 17,5.
48 Euseb. *SC* 17,11.

hidden hand?" Eusebius knew very well that Constantine put himself on a par with Christ – just about a year later, in his tricennial oration, the bishop himself reinforced the idea of a close companionship between a semi-divine emperor and Christ. His Jerusalem lecture, however, Eusebius delivered in an environment more strongly influenced by the ecclesiastical sphere, at a certain distance from the imperial court. Here he pointed out and emphasized not the parallels but rather the fundamental differences between the ruler of All and Christ on the one hand and the ruler of the Roman state on the other.

In the cosmological passages of the lecture, Eusebius argued that the true source of divine power did not lie in the sun, but in the one God of All.[49] The bishop here implicitly addressed the persistent impact of the sun-cult on the religious image of the Christian monarch: a topic that was of great importance to the bishop precisely because solar symbolism had a late heyday in the last decade of Constantine's rule.[50] In the early 320s, solar and Christian facets of imperial representation had begun to merge – a process that formed a new image of the Roman monarch who now himself appeared as highly charged with solar power. On the imperial coins and medallions, where this process can be traced most accurately, Constantine was now regularly portrayed with a nimbus – a solar aura – and with the traditional gesture of Sol invictus: raising the right hand and holding a globe in the left.[51]

The formation of a new *imago* of the Roman emperor went hand in hand with the formation of a new state and ruler cult, which can best be seen in the military sector, but which has also transformed religious observances at court and in the provinces: new military rites to be held on the *dies Solis*, the day of the Sun, went without pagan sacrifices and were thus open to Christian interpretations, but they also incorporated traditional aspects of sun worship. The soldiers were supposed to assemble on a sacred site outside the *castra*, raise their hands towards the sun and recite a prayer to the *summus deus* on behalf of the emperor and his dynasty.[52] At that time, explicitly pagan imagery had largely disappeared from imperial representation, while Christian symbols adorned the military standards and the emperor's dress uniform.[53] In this distinctively Constantinian mélange, traditional and innovative tendencies intermingled and formed a new image of the Roman emperor – an image that clearly appealed to Christian religion, while still depicting the monarch as a semi-divine entity with privileged access to the divine, as a figure transcending earthly limitations, and as an object of human veneration. Devotion to the sun was probably the most persistent aspect of pagan tradition within Constantine's monarchic representation. In re-

---

[49] Euseb. *SC* 11,8.
[50] On the cult of the sun in Eusebius' writings, see Amerise 2007. On the role of solar power for the late antique Roman monarchy more broadly, see Wallraff 2001 and 2011 and Drake 2009.
[51] See Wienand 2012, 296–335.
[52] Euseb. *VC* 4,18–20 and *LC* 9,9–10; see Wienand 2012, 319–328.
[53] Euseb. *VC* 4,18,3–20,2 and *LC* 9,9–10; see Wienand 2012, 319–328. The prayer has overtones of a religious confession.

defining the cosmological significance of the sun, Eusebius obviously intended to advance and disseminate a reading of the Christian emperor more plainly pertaining to cosmological conceptions of the Christian tradition.

Finally, Eusebius also provided a keen reinterpretation of the concept of 'peace' in his Jerusalem lecture – the official motto of Constantine's tricennalia and his church building program in the Holy Land. According to Eusebius, the δύναμις of the cosmic ruler alone brought about universal peace on earth, and God alone can ensure persistent peace. For Eusebius, this insight was the *kephalaion* of his lecture, the focal point of his whole argument.[54] In the bishop's account of peace, there was not much room for the praise of the emperor's accomplishments.

Given that a Christian bishop was speaking and not an imperial official, the obvious discrepancies between the official conception of the *encaenia* ceremonies and Eusebius' account are not peculiar *per se*, but they are striking in so far as Eusebius was here speaking in a ceremonial environment largely governed by court etiquette, and that he intended to be heard also by those close to the emperor. Several passages show that Eusebius did not exclusively address the devoted Christians among his audience or the members of the local parish.[55] Eusebius obviously seized the favorable moment when more public attention than ever was being paid to Jerusalem and when relevant parts of the imperial administration, up to the emperor himself, directly or indirectly partook in the events. The speech is remarkable in that it provides a Christian reasoning about the relation between divine providence and salvific history to be heard at least by some of the many ears of the Roman emperor – a reasoning that in various respects departed intentionally from what Eusebius could expect the emperor to want to hear.

However, Eusebius did not intend to draw a dividing line between the emperor's conception of state religion on the one hand and 'true' Christianity on the other. Rather, the bishop seems to have tried to make his audience believe that his reasoning represented the religious knowledge and understanding of Constantine himself: in this sense, the speech apparently belongs to the speech genre that Eusebius has called "*ekphraseis* of the imperial wisdom-doctrines".[56] Eusebius attributed the theological insights carved out in the lecture to the pious church builder himself. At least this is what Eusebius did when – two months later – he presented parts of his lecture again, this time before the emperor in Constantinople: in the newly added preface (SC 11,1–7) Eusebius claims to be an interpreter and enunciator of the true religious beliefs of the emperor. Eusebius may have pursued this rhetorical strategy already in his Jerusalem lecture, potentially in the original introductory or concluding passages (that were omitted when Eusebius revised the manuscript and added the new intro-

---

54 Euseb. *SC* 17,12.
55 The fact that the text is composed as a diatribe suggests that the bishop addresses an audience that consists not only of Christians. The political impact of his argument implies that he intended to reach the imperial representatives.
56 Euseb. *VC* 4,45,3.

duction and conclusion for his speech to be delivered before Constantine in the imperial palace at Constantinople). The self-portrayal as interpreter of Constantine's religious understanding allowed Eusebius to portray his own interpretation not as an external ascription by an outsider, but rather as the proper intention of the benefactor himself, which Eusebius merely had to explicate. An orator who portrays himself as an interpreter of the emperor's religious beliefs is obviously pursuing a rhetorical strategy to render credible his own interpretation, and – which is even more important – this allowed Eusebius to manipulate the conception of a Christian ruler from within.

Why did Eusebius think such a modification was necessary? At court, the traditional ruler qualities of *virtus, humanitas, providentia* and *pietas* still served as the cornerstones of imperial self-display, while Christian layers of meaning were only employed selectively, and they were cautiously embedded into the traditional modes of interaction.[57] But this consensus-oriented adjustment of Constantine's religious approach was not unproblematic for the most ambitious Christians, even if they appreciated the official recognition of Christianity overall. To be sure, most Christians attending Eusebius' lecture will have embraced the end of persecution and the emperor's endorsement of Christianity, but some of them were likely irritated by the emperor's idiosyncratic approach of merging monarchic representation with Christian religion. Such an ambivalent assessment of Constantine's religious policy can also be seen in Eusebian thought: in his writings, a basic inclination to support the recent developments interferes with more or less explicit criticism of certain aspects of Constantine's self-depiction as Christian monarch.[58]

This ambivalent assessment can clearly be seen also in the Jerusalem lecture, where Eusebius undermined basic axioms of Constantine's religious self-conception as a Christian ruler. Although the bishop received with great enthusiasm Constan-

---

[57] A nice example of the resulting mélange in courtly representation is provided by the figure poems of Publilius Optatianus Porphyrius, a Roman senator who put his remarkable poetic ability into the service of Constantine; on Optatianus and his poems, see Polara 1973; Polara 1976; Bruhat 1999; Wienand 2012, 355–420; Squire/Wienand 2017; Körfer 2020. In his highly artistic *carmina figurata*, Optatianus combined Greco-Roman mythology with set-pieces of Christian thought and symbolism to create a novel form of imperial eulogy. *Carmen* 19 is a particularly elaborate figure poem. In the ground text of the poem, Optatianus celebrates the emperor's virtues in a quite traditional manner. The colored intext verses that are woven into the ground text depict the Christian monogram Chi-Rho, Constantine's victorious sign, within an image that stands for the emperor's military prowess: a war ship can be seen with oars and a helm and a ram. The sails are drawn in the form of the Chi-Rho, and a letter combination stands for the *vota vicennalia*, the public vows for the twentieth jubilee of the emperor's reign. In Optatianus' poems, Christian elements are not in conflict with references to the pagan tradition. For Optatianus, the religious transformation of the Roman monarchy was fairly unproblematic These poems clearly show that at the imperial court, where the *carmina* have been presented and received, the religious transformation proceeded harmoniously.

[58] Eusebius' stance towards Constantine was long viewed as purely affirmative, but over the past decades, scholarship has developed more subtle approaches; see, for instance, Corke-Webster 2019; Inowlocki 2011.

tine's renunciation of polytheism, he had certain reservations regarding the concrete design of Constantine's Christian monarchy. However, it was not the bishop's intention to organize resistance against the Roman ruler, or simply to criticize him for his views. Eusebius seems to have aimed at contributing to the development of a Christian monarchy that could keep up with the demands of even its most ambitious and challenging Christian subjects. Eusebius had obviously understood that the image of a Christian emperor could only be formed and transformed from within. This is probably the most important reason why the aged bishop ventured to join the inauguration ceremonies in Jerusalem: this spectacular encounter between state and church offered Eusebius an excellent opportunity to communicate his views about the religious development of the Roman Empire vis-à-vis an audience composed of state representatives as well as Christian clerics and parishioners.

But Eusebius seems to have been aware of the fact that he would not be able to decisively influence the self-conception of the distant ruler with his Jerusalem lecture alone. The monarch and his closest advisors took part in the events only indirectly, and there was no guarantee that the leading circles took note of the documentation about the speeches given on the occasion. The chances to influence the emperor via the state representatives attending the ceremonies were limited: the highest official was a *notarius*, or probably a governor. No *comes* or other high-ranking official was in Jerusalem in 335, and no member of the imperial family attended the festivities; indeed, after Helena's death in the early 330s there was not much expectation of another imperial visit to the Holy Land, although occasionally Constantine seems to have entertained the thought of being baptized in the waters of the Jordan river.[59]

Eusebius knew that in the peripheral city of Jerusalem, even in such an advantageous situation, he could at best reach a handful of middle-ranking officials, apart from his fellow Christians. To be sure, even this was of great importance for him, since – according to his understanding – the endorsement of Christianity by the Roman state was of great concern to everybody. Eusebius' aim was to sensitize all social strata to the merits and detriments of the recent developments in order to influence the Roman monarchy in a way that would properly serve the interests of the church. His function as metropolitan bishop of Caesarea lent Eusebius an aura of authority, so that his auditorium certainly attached great importance to his views. But Eusebius knew that in the end the image of a Christian ruler was not framed in Jerusalem, that he instead had to advance to the very center and the ceremonial core of the Roman monarchy. He had to ascribe to the emperor his ideas of a truly Christian monarchy in the imperial palace at Constantinople – in the "adyton of the holy palace, the inner, most inaccessible of all places", as Eusebius himself called it.[60]

---

[59] Euseb. *VC* 4,62.
[60] Euseb. *LC* Prol. 4.

Eusebius in Constantinople, Take One

Only two months after the festivities in Jerusalem, Eusebius took part in a delegation of bishops who traveled to Constantine's court in Constantinople in order to inform the emperor about the outcome of the synod of Tyre and to settle the dispute with Athanasius. It was the first time the aged bishop had traveled to Constantinople. In his *Vita Constantini*, Eusebius provides a vivid account of how the metropolis on the Bosporus developed into the urban center of the evolving Christian monarchy.[61] Eusebius mentioned no biblical sites, as there were none. But in his account Constantinople was nonetheless the ideal hub of a Christian empire: Eusebius talks of "very many places of worship" and "very large martyr-shrines" and claims the city was "consecrated to the martyrs' God".[62] In Eusebius' account, Constantinople was not only a city with a Christian tinge, but a capital with an outright antipagan character:

> Being full of the breath of God's wisdom, which he reckoned a city bearing his own name should display, he saw fit to purge it of all idol-worship, so that nowhere in it appeared those images of the supposed gods which are worshipped in temples, nor altars foul with bloody slaughter, nor sacrifice offered as holocaust in fire, nor feasts of demons, nor any of the other customs of the superstitious.[63]

In his passages about the religious character of Constantinople, Eusebius is conspicuously vague about details. The only Christian building he names explicitly is a shrine (νεών) newly erected by Constantine in honor of the Holy Apostles, where Constantine was later to be buried.[64] There were other Christian buildings not mentioned by Eusebius, the construction of which might have begun under Constantine: the Church of S. Irene, a basilica outside the city walls dedicated to the martyr Mocius, and a Church of Acacius inside the walls.[65] But these buildings provided little

---

[61] Euseb. *VC* 3,3, 48–49, 54,2–3; on Eusebius' image of Constantinople, see Drake 1988; for imperial Constantinople in late antiquity, see Rene Pfeilschifter's chapter in this volume, see also Magdalino 2022; Bauer 2001; Brubaker 2001; Dagron 1984; Janin 1964. On Constantinian Constantinople in particular, see Dagron 1974, 13–115; Olbrich 2006 and 2015; Bassett 2004, 50–78, Moser 2018, esp. 45–82.
[62] Euseb. *VC* 3,48,1.
[63] Euseb. *VC* 3,48,2.
[64] Euseb. *VC* 4,58–60. According to Eusebius, Constantine has dedicated this building "to perpetuate for all mankind the memory of our Savior's apostles" and "prepared the place there for the time when it would be needed on his decease, intending with supreme eagerness of faith that his own remains should after death partake in the invocation of the Apostles". It is not entirely clear if Eusebius is speaking about two buildings – a Church of the Holy Apostles and a mausoleum – or about one; see Downey 1951, 53–80; Krautheimer 1975, 72–73; Bonamente 1988, 118; Mango 1990, 51–61; Leeb 1992, 93–120; Winkelmann 1962, 238–239. Johnson 2020, esp. 80–81 argues that at Eusebius' time "there was a single church building, not a church and a separate mausoleum" (p. 81).
[65] Socr. *HE* 1,16; Sozom. *HE* 8,17,5; Socr. *HE* 6,23. See Dagron 1974, 388–389; Mango 1985, 35–36.

more than Christian overtones to a city which was clearly laid out primarily as a major residential city serving the needs of the court. The central focal points of the urban design were the palace/hippodrome complex, the newly erected circular Forum of Constantine around a monumental statue of the emperor on a huge porphyry column, the impressively colonnaded *Mese* (the main axis of the city), and the Constantinian city walls.[66] Constantine had filled the public spaces of his newly designed prestige city with artwork brought together from the entire empire, particularly from the East. Many religiously connoted objects originally displayed in pagan temples or sanctuaries were among the items used for embellishing the city. According to what we know about the statues and sculptures transferred to Constantinople, the items represented the whole depth of Greco-Roman history, mythology, and religion.[67] As it seems, they were meant to make visible the greatness and splendor of the Constantinian empire and the glory of Roman dominion over the *orbis terrarum*. In religious terms, the spectrum of artwork brought to Constantinople obviously conveyed the idea of a plurality of religious references, ranging from the pagan past to Christianity. For Eusebius' reading of Constantinople, this harmonious collocation of pagan and Christian references posed a certain problem. At least he thought it necessary in his *Vita Constantini* to reinterpret the pagan implications in purely Christian terms:

> ... the sacred bronze figures, of which the error of the ancients had for a long time been proud, he displayed as a contemptible spectacle to the viewers, in another the Sminthian, in the Hippodrome itself the tripods from Delphi, and the Muses of Helicon at the palace. (3) The city named after the Emperor was filled throughout with objects of skilled artwork in bronze dedicated in various provinces. To these under the name of gods those sick with error had for long ages vainly offered innumerable hecatombs and whole burnt sacrifices, but now they at last learnt sense, as the Emperor used these very toys for the laughter and amusement of the spectators.[68]

This passage shows that Eusebius saw an emerging center of an evolving *imperium Romanum* when he came to Constantinople, but that he wanted to see an emerging center of the *orbis Christianus*. Constantine indeed stripped the statues brought to his new residential hub of their original cultic contexts, but the traditional pagan overtones were largely retained. The fact that Constantine also founded a new cult for Tyche in Constantinople – "which was anything but strictly Christian" – quite clearly shows that in the very center of his empire the first Christian monarch provided suitable room also for traditional religion.[69] Eusebius must have sensed that the emper-

---

66 On the hippodrome, see Akyürek 2021 and Dagron 2011; on the porphyry column, see Fowden 1991; on the walls, see the chapter by Neslihan Asutay-Effenberger and Shlomit Weksler-Bdolah in this volume.
67 On the Constantinian artwork in Constantinople, see Bassett 2004, 50–78; Berger 2021.
68 Euseb. *VC* 3,54,2–3.
69 For the quotation, see Lenski 2015, 351.

or's approach to Constantinople was significantly different from his approach to Jerusalem.

When Eusebius arrived in this emerging center of the Constantinian empire, he was summoned, together with the other bishops of his delegation, to the imperial palace in order to meet the emperor in person.[70] The prime purpose of the encounter was to resolve the conflict around Athanasius, who had left the synod of Tyre to appeal to the emperor directly. Beyond this case, Eusebius had other points on his agenda as well. Somehow he managed to be granted extra time to appear before the emperor.[71] According to his own request, as he relates in the *Vita Constantini*, he was allowed to present to the emperor a theological discourse relating to the Church of the Holy Sepulcher. Eusebius himself described this remarkable encounter in his *Vita Constantini*:

> **33** (1) One other thing seems to me to be unforgettable, a deed which the marvellous man did in our own presence. On one occasion, emboldened by his devotion to divine things, we asked permission to deliver an address about the Savior's tomb for him to hear. He listened with rapt attention, and where a large audience was standing around right inside the palace he stood up and listened with the others. When we begged him to rest on the imperial throne which was nearby, he would not do so, but made a shrewdly considered critique of the speech, and affirmed the truth of its doctrinal theology. (2) Since it took a long time and the speech still continued, we suggested breaking off; he however would not allow it, but urged us to go on to the end. When we asked him to sit he kept refusing, saying at one time that when the doctrine of God was being discussed, it was wrong for him to relax while he listened, and at another that it was good and beneficial for him to stand: it was a holy thing to listen to divinity standing up. When this too came to an end, we returned home and took up our regular business.[72]

What Eusebius recited in front of the emperor was apparently a large section of his Jerusalem lecture, to which he added a newly composed introduction and conclusion designed particularly for presentation before the emperor. It is not exactly clear why Eusebius chose not to write a completely new oration. Maybe it was only on short notice that he was granted the opportunity to appear before the emperor, so that he might not have had enough time to compose a new oration. This, at least, is implied by the fact that the newly added sections do not seem to fit very well with the main part of the speech. The passage quoted above also indicates that the bishop misapprehended how exactly his speech was expected to be delivered and received, which also points to a largely improvised situation. But the fact that he took over in

---

70 On the archaeology of the late antique imperial palace at Constantinople, see Westbrook 2019.
71 The encounter seems to have been of limited ceremonial character. The bishops' main task was to inform the emperor of the results of the synod of Tyre. It seems plausible to assume that they were also asked to report about the events in Jerusalem. Since Eusebius' speech does not provide details about the inauguration ceremonies or the Constantinian church building, but focuses on the salvific aspects of the biblical sites in Jerusalem, the presentation of the speech seems not to have been a regular part of the bishops' report about the *encaenia* ceremonies.
72 Euseb. *VC* 4,33.

an unmodified form the bulk of his Jerusalem sermon also shows that Eusebius ultimately underestimated what difference it made whether he spoke in the emperor's absence in Jerusalem or in his presence in Constantinople.

It is quite clear that the bishop did not succeed in controlling the message. According to how Eusebius himself recounts the encounter in his *Vita Constantini*, Constantine omitted the usual formalities of court ceremonial when he listened to the bishop's speech. Although Eusebius repeatedly asked Constantine to take a seat on his throne, the emperor persistently – and in an increasingly disgruntled manner – refused. He rather remained standing among his friends and advisors, and he even intervened in Eusebius' speech as if it were a statement of a council member during a session of the *consilium*. This procedure inevitably led to a considerable protraction, so that Eusebius at one point even wanted to break off his talk in order to comply with the time limits set for his presentation. The emperor, however, asked him to proceed.

When Eusebius described these events, he tried to explain the emperor's unexpected behavior in terms of humility: according to Eusebius' reasoning, the situation showed the emperor's reverence for God and proved Constantine's expertise in theological matters. However, the orator and the monarch obviously had divergent ideas of how the speech should be presented and how speaker and monarch should interact. Eusebius wanted to present his speech within the framework of court ceremonial, as if he were a regular panegyrist submitting an encomium before the enthroned emperor. But Constantine had obviously been informed about the contents and nature of Eusebius' speech beforehand. The emperor dismissed Eusebius' plea to take his place on the throne with the argument that it would be inappropriate to follow a theological discourse in a relaxed position. And indeed, Eusebius' speech dealt with cosmological, Christological, and soteriological issues, but it was not an encomium. In the main part of his speech, Eusebius did not even allude to Constantine's church building program in the Holy Land. Only the newly added introduction and conclusion contained laudatory aspects referring to the emperor's pious deeds.

But it was not only content that mattered: Constantine was probably also concerned about Eusebius' conception of religious competence and authority, in particular about the bishop's self-confident appearance as interpreter of divine knowledge. In his newly added introduction, Eusebius emphasized that the subsequent considerations were not meant to instruct Constantine, who had been initiated into the secrets of the Christian faith by repeated personal revelations of God. Rather, the bishop wanted to be some kind of ὑφερμηνευτής ('interpreter') who interprets the emperor's religious insights for those not yet initiated into the divine rites. In this sense, Eusebius calls himself an ἄγγελος, a messenger of Constantine's pious soul:

> (1) To this imperial composition about the Universal Sovereign, Constantine, Great Victor, let us attach for you revelations about solemn mysteries. These, of course, are not intended to initiate you, who have been instructed by God, nor to lay bare secrets for you, to whom well before our account God Himself, 'not by men nor through men' but by means of the Common Savior Him-

self and frequent enlightening visions of His Divinity revealed and uncovered the secrets of the holy rites. Rather it is to lead untaught men into light and to suggest to the unknowing the causes and foundations of your religious deeds of piety ... (17) I pray I may be a kind of interpreter of your intentions and become the reporter of your devout soul, in order to teach all that it is necessary and proper that everyone be taught in whom a desire exists to learn the principles of the power of our Savior God, for which He who long ago pre-existed and had charge of the universe at length came down to us from heaven, assumed a human nature, and underwent death.[73]

With these introductory remarks Eusebius made plain his intention to attribute to the emperor's pious understanding the insights carved out in the main part of his oration. There, however, Eusebius retained the critical assessment of the emperor's position in a Christian cosmos which he had presented a couple of weeks earlier before a significantly different audience in Jerusalem. But now the bishop stood in front of the emperor himself when he explained that God alone fought the enemies of Christianity and eliminated the error of polytheism, that God alone gave new hope to the Christians, and that God alone had rebuilt their churches;[74] and now it was the emperor who listened when Eusebius drew an unflattering comparison between the power of an earthly ruler on the one hand and the power of God and Christ on the other.

Those who carefully listened to the bishop's words must have realized that these assertions were seriously out of line with Constantine's idea of his role as a Roman Christian emperor. And Eusebius must have known this too. But the bishop seems to have entertained the hope that in the course of this personal encounter he might be able to influence the image of a Christian emperor maintained by Constantine and his closest companions, and that his ideas about the relation of Christian cosmology and Roman dominion might ultimately find their way into the ceremonial heart of the Roman monarchy. This seems to be the reason why the bishop so eagerly wanted his speech to be delivered within the regular framework of court ceremonial: a eulogistic oration before the enthroned emperor is usually performed as a ritual of consensus. The speaker takes care that his account is closely aligned with the emperor's self-image; in return, the orator's attributions are almost automatically confirmed and endorsed merely by the fact that the emperor provides the proper ceremonial environment and dignifies the occasion with his presence.

In the case of a conventional imperial panegyric this did not pose a problem, since the emperor could rely on the strictly affirmative stance of his eulogists. However, the Christianization of the Roman monarchy substantially modified the framework conditions of imperial representation. The two Eusebian speeches – the earliest surviving Christian speeches delivered before the emperor – show that the communicative function of a Christian oration before the Roman monarch does not necessarily correspond to a conventional panegyric. The Eusebian speeches are not

---

73 Euseb. *SC* 11,7.
74 Euseb. *SC* 17,5.

meant as a dazzling display of the orator's virtuosic skill in praising the emperor, his dynasty, and his deeds, and they do not aim at increasing the emperor's willingness to accept a petition, as many traditional panegyric orations do.[75] The bishop had other intentions. His prime interest was to contribute to the formation of a Christian image of the Roman ruler. As a Christian orator at court, Eusebius employed his skill to communicate a *normative* model of a Christian Roman monarchy. While a typical panegyrist employed unconditional affirmation as a means to win the emperor's inclination for supporting a certain request, Eusebius primarily tried to establish specific ideological standards a Christian emperor should meet – an approach with a subversive potential.

The misunderstandings regarding the role of Eusebius' speech point to the fact that at this time it was not yet routine for a bishop to give an oration before the emperor at court. From the very beginning, in his dealings with Christian clerics, Constantine preferred ecclesiastical synods as the most functional environment for exchange between state and church.[76] Among other reasons for choosing this policy, a synod offered the bishops much better conditions than the palace for getting in contact with the center of imperial power. Successfully maneuvering within court culture was not easy, it presupposed control of extended personal networks within the Roman aristocracy, which again required a substantial financial background and the proper *paideia*, i.e., the necessary habitus including the ability to interpret the topical language and the corresponding gestures usually employed at court – abilities Eusebius (and with him other clerics) quite obviously lacked (at least this is what the curious encounter between bishop and emperor in November 335 suggests).[77]

Thus, adequate communicative channels fitting the needs of clerics could not be easily implemented within the well-established and self-contained social structures of the central administration. The fact that Constantine largely confined his interaction with Christian clerics to synods was accordingly to the advantage of bishops, but at the same time this policy partly sealed off the imperial court culture from the influence of Christian agents. Very early on, Eusebius seems to have recognized that this development limited the influence of the church on the formation of a Christian ruler image. With his appearance before the emperor in the palace at Constantinople, the bishop obviously tried to pave a way for the church into the ceremonial heart of the Roman monarchy in order to occupy this crucial discursive field as well. The bishop's conspicuous efforts to enter the innermost spheres of the secluded palace thus show that he intended to transform the figure of the Roman ruler harmoniously from within, not through a conflictual process.

---

[75] On the late antique imperial panegyrics, see MacCormack 1976; Nixon/Rodgers 1994; Whitby 1998; Lassandro 2000; Rees 2002; Wienand 2012, 26–43; Omissi 2018; Omissi/Ross 2020.
[76] Girardet 1975 and 1989; Young 2021; Pigott 2019; MacMullen 2006.
[77] According to Gibbon 1909–1914, II, 136, Eusebius was "practiced in the arts of courts". At best, this is only partly true.

Now, Constantine decided to grant the request of the honorable bishop and to let him deliver his speech in the imperial palace. But the emperor had also taken the appropriate measures to ensure that he himself would retain interpretive sovereignty regarding his self-conception as a Christian monarch. By omitting the usual court ceremonial, Constantine avoided an *a priori* endorsement of Eusebius' reasoning. According to the account in the *Vita Constantini*, it was Constantine who "analyzed the content of the speech with the fullest concentration of his thoughts and who confirmed the truth of the theological doctrines".[78] Thus, through his interventions in the delivery of the speech, Constantine managed to reserve for himself the final judgment about the bishop's statements. While Eusebius tried to explore the emperor's readiness to accept a role subordinate to him as a bishop as far as divine knowledge was concerned, Constantine at once turned the tables on Eusebius. The bishop seems not to have expected such a powerful neutralization strategy. The unforeseen development of the encounter obviously irritated him: he concluded his account of these events with the puzzled remark "when this too came to an end, we returned home and took up our regular business". There is no mention of positive feedback from the emperor, as Eusebius would receive one year later, when he got a second chance to appear before the emperor as an orator at court.

Eusebius in Constantinople, Take Two

On the second try, Eusebius was more successful. On 25 July 336 he once more entered the imperial palace in Constantinople – and this time officially as an imperial panegyrist. For the closing ceremonies of the thirtieth jubilee of Constantine's reign, the bishop stepped before the emperor to celebrate his *tricennalia* with a specifically composed eulogy.[79] In addition to the emperor himself and an exclusive audience, Constantine's son was also present, and possibly also the other Caesars.

Eusebius' tricennial oration seems to have been the first Christian panegyric to be given on such an outstanding imperial occasion in a palatial audience chamber at court – in front of the enthroned emperor clad in his imperial garb, flanked by his sons and his closest friends and advisors. Whether Eusebius was given the opportunity for his second appearance at court due to another request of his own or whether he was specifically invited as encomiast, we cannot say. In any case, he had a second chance, and this time he had obviously obtained all necessary information about the exact procedure and about the status of his oration in advance, so he could present a fitting speech that was embedded into court ceremonial like a regular panegyric.

The imperial experiment of letting the aged bishop perform an imperial encomium on such an outstanding occasion succeeded to the emperor's satisfaction. In his

---

78 Euseb. *VC* 4,33,1.
79 On the date of Eusebius' oration, see Drake 1975.

Vita Constantini, Eusebius remarks that the emperor was full of joy after the speech, and that he expressed his sympathy towards Eusebius and other attending bishops during a subsequent banquet: "The friend of God (i.e. Constantine), while he listened to it, was like a man overjoyed; he said so himself after the hearing, when he dined with the bishops present and received them with every kind of honor".[80]

Eusebius was aware of the world-historic significance of these exceptional events. Accordingly, he did not want to leave the question of dissemination to chance. He included the account of the incident quoted above in the *Vita Constantini*, and he prepared the manuscript of his oration for publication as an appendix to his *Vita Constantini* – together with the manuscript of his first speech before the emperor and together with the text of Constantine's *Oration to the Assembly of Saints*.[81]

Regarding its basic layout and its contents, Eusebius' tricennial oration fundamentally differs from both the original Jerusalem lecture and its modified version. God is again the principal cosmic power, to which the sun is explicitly subordinate. But now the position of the earthly ruler has completely changed. In his Jerusalem lecture and thus also in his first speech before the emperor in Constantinople, Eusebius avoided ascribing salvific significance to his figure of a Christian emperor. In his tricennial oration, in contrast, Constantine appears as θεῷ φίλος, as 'friend of God,' who is situated on a par with Christ and who is depicted as highly charged with solar power.[82] In this picture, the emperor is situated in the sphere of the divine, and he possesses an unrivalled proximity to God and Christ. Constantine obtains his victories with heavenly assistance, and his victory sign is a beacon of hope for all Christians.

In his tricennial oration, Eusebius obviously seeks to fulfil all formal requirements of an imperial eulogy, and to cover all traditional thematic fields of Roman panegyric – even such fields as military representation, including references to victories over barbarians.[83] Nevertheless, Eusebius has an idiosyncratic approach to epideictic rhetoric. Within his densely woven net of references to central aspects of Constantinian self-display, Eusebius carefully preserves the necessary room to subtly adjust the parameters of the ruler image to a Christian framework.[84] Throughout the whole speech, Eusebius thus manages to relativize the salvific significance of

---

80 VC 4,46.
81 On the *Oration to the Assembly of Saints*, see Cristofoli 2005 and the introduction in Girardet 2013; see also Bleckmann 1997.
82 For more detailed accounts of how Eusebius construed the Christian monarch in his tricennial oration, see Drake 1976, 3–79; Wienand 2012, 421–482; Schneider 2020, 29–41 and 47–51; Drake (forthcoming), ch. II.B.3. On the wider context of the Christian emperors of late antiquity and their position toward God, see Meier 2003.
83 Euseb. LC 6–7, see Wienand 2012, 444–448.
84 On the wider context of Christian redefinition of the imperial role in the fourth century, see Drake 2015.

the earthly ruler, which – at first glance – he seems to have emphasized unconditionally.

Regardless of whether Eusebius talks about the emperor's role as a victor, about Constantine's solar power, or about the salutary sign, basically, the bishop is always concerned with one and the same aspect: the emperor's piety and his stance toward truth. As champion of the Christian God, the Eusebian Constantine does not fight for the glory and felicity of the *imperium Romanum* like the emperor of a traditional panegyric, and his victories do not stand for his unrivaled providence and virtue. Rather, Eusebius depicts Constantine even with respect to his military endeavors as "a paradigm of piety and truth for all on earth":

> (3) For how could one bear the likeness of monarchical authority who has formed in his soul the myriad falsely depicted images of demons? How can he be ruler and lord of all who has bound himself to countless malignant masters, who is a slave of shameful pleasures, a slave of unbridled lust, a slave of ill-gotten gain, a slave of ill-temper and wreath, a slave of fear and frights, a slave of bloodthirsty demons, a slave of soul-destroying spirits? (4) Wherefore let the friend of the All-Ruling God be proclaimed our sole sovereign with truth as witness, the only one who is truly free, or rather truly a lord. Above care for money, stronger than the passion for women, victor of physical pleasures and demands, the conqueror, not the captive, of ill-temper and wrath, this man truly is the Autokrator, bearing the title that conforms to his moral conduct. Really a Victor is he who has triumphed over the passions which have overcome mankind, who has modelled himself after the archetypal form of the Supreme Sovereign, whose thoughts mirror its virtuous rays, by which he has been made perfectly wise, good, just, courageous, pious, and God-loving.[85]

When Eusebius talks about Constantine's victories, he is primarily interested in the emperor's fight against the error of the polytheist religion and against Christian heresies. The conceptual reference point of this battle is the emperor's εὐσέβεια, his piety towards the Christian God. This allows Eusebius to formulate his concept of a Christian ruler on the basis of what might be called probationary affirmation. To be sure, Eusebius was highly interested in developing argumentative means for immunizing the Christian monarchy against the threat of subversion, as he saw the Christian monarchy as a necessary prerogative for an enduring prosperity of Christianity within the Roman state. But he also traced out the predetermined breaking points of monarchic legitimation within a Christian *orbis Romanus*: Christian piety became the most important factor, while military success *per se* loses its justificatory power. The Eusebian model of Christian panegyric, developed to provide the philosophical foundation for a novel image of a legitimate ruler, was also a benchmark for judging the Christian monarch.

---

85 Euseb. *LC* 5,3–4.

Conclusion

Eusebius' endeavor of implanting his normative concept of legitimate Christian rule in the heart of the Constantinian monarchy was not in vain. His contribution to framing the Christian ruler image was probably among the bishop's most effective and lasting achievements, although he represented only one of many groups competing for influence on the emperor's self-conception. To achieve success, however, Eusebius had to make far-reaching concessions to the demands of imperial representation. His journey from the Holy Land to the center of earthly rule is indicative of the long way Christian philosophy had to go to arrive at the idea of an emperor beloved by God – even if the emperor in question was willing to cover part of the distance himself.

Constantine subjected the Roman monarchy to a profound religious transformation, but it seems he tried to keep a certain distance between church and state in order not to lose interpretive sovereignty to an institution largely unacquainted with the art of imperial politics. Eusebius, on the other hand, intended to merge the two fields, although he obviously realized that the structural differences between the two spheres could not be overcome at once. But regardless of the persistent disparity between the *orbis Christianus* and the *orbis Romanus*, the bishop's commitment and the emperor's endorsement brought closer together Jerusalem and Constantinople, the very poles of an emerging new world order.

Bibliography

Aivazian, A. (ed.) (2021). *The Lectionary of the Armenian Apostolic Orthodox Church*, New York.

Akyürek, E. (2021). *The Hippodrome of Constantinople*, Cambridge.

Amerise, M. (2007). 'Monotheism and the Monarchy: The Christian Emperor and the Cult of the Sun in Eusebius of Caesarea,' *JbAC* 50, 72–84.

Anonymous (ed.) (1845). *The Life of the Blessed Emperor Constantine, in Four Books, From 306 to 337 A.D., by Eusebius Pamphilus*, London.

Armstrong, G. (1974). 'Constantine's Churches: Symbol and Structure,' *JSAH* 33, 5–16.

Avni, G. & Seligman, J. (2003). 'New Excavations at the Church of the Holy Sepulchre Compound,' in Bottini et al. 2003, 153–162.

Bacchiocchi, S. (1977). *From Sabbath to Sunday: A Historical Investigation of the Rise of Sunday Observance in Early Christianity*, Rome.

Baker-Brian, N. & Tougher, Sh. (eds.) (2020). *The Sons of Constantine, AD 337–361: In the Shadows of Constantine and Julian*, Cham.

Barnes, T.D. (1977). 'Two speeches by Eusebius,' *GRBS* 18, 341–345.

Barnes, T.D. (1978). 'Emperor and Bishops, A.D. 324–344. Some Problems,' *AJAH* 3, 53–75.

Barnes, T.D. (2011). *Constantine, Dynasty, Religion, and Power in the Later Roman Empire*, Chichester.

Bassett, S. (2004). *The Urban Image of Late Antique Constantinople*, Cambridge.

Bassett, S. (ed.) (2022). *The Cambridge Companion to Constantinople*, Cambridge.

Bauer, F.A. (2001). 'Urban Space and Ritual: Constantinople in Late Antiquity,' *AAAH* 15, 27–61.

Berger, A. (2021). *The Statues of Constantinople*, Cambridge.
Berrens, S. (2004). *Sonnenkult und Kaisertum von den Severern bis zu Constantin I. (193–337 n. Chr.)*, Stuttgart.
Biddle, M. (1999). *The Tomb of Christ*, Stroud.
Biddle, M. (2000). *The Church of the Holy Sepulchre*, New York.
Bleckmann, B. (1997). 'Ein Kaiser als Prediger: zur Datierung der Konstantinischen Rede an die Versammlung der Heiligen,' *Hermes* 125, 183–202.
Bonamente, G. (1988). 'Apoteosi e imperatori cristiani,' in: Bonamente/Nestori 1988, 107–142.
Bonamente, G. & Nestori, A. (eds.) (1988). *I cristiani e l'impero nel IV secolo. Colloquio sul cristianesimo nel mondo antico*, Macerata.
Bonamente, G. & Fusco, F. (eds.) (1993). *Costantino Il Grande: Dall'Antichità all'Umanesimo*, Macerata.
Borgehammar, S. (1991). *How the Holy Cross Was Found. From Event to Medieval Legend*, Stockholm.
Bottini, G.C., Di Segni L. & Chrupcala L.D. (eds.) (2003). *One Land Many Cultures: Archaeological Studies in Honour of S. Loffreda*, Jerusalem.
Brennecke, H.C. (1994). 'Nicäa I.,' *Theologische Realenzyklopädie* 24, 429–441.
Brubaker, L. (2001). 'Topography and Public Space in Constantinople,' in de Jong/Theuws 2001, 31–44.
Bruhat, M.-O. (1999). *Les Carmina figurata de Publilius Optatianus Porfyrius: La métamorphose d'un genre et l'invention d'une poésie liturgique impériale sous Constantin*, Paris (PhD Diss.).
Bruun, P. (1962). 'The Christian Signs on the Coins of Constantine,' *Arctos. Acta Philologica Fennica N.S.* 3, 15–35.
Burgess, H. & Williams, H.G. (trans.) (1854). *The Festal Epistles of S. Athanasius, Bishop of Alexandria*, Oxford.
Burgess, R. (2008). 'The Summer of Blood: The "Great Massacre" of 337 and the Promotion of the Sons of Constantine,' *DOP* 62, 5–51.
Cain, A. & Lenski, N. (eds.) (2009). *The Power of Religion in Late Antiquity. Selected Papers From the Seventh Biennial Shifting Frontiers in Late Antiquity Conference*, Farnham.
Cameron, Av., & Hall, S.G. (1999). *Eusebius: Life of Constantine*, Oxford.
Conybeare, F. C. (ed.) (1905). *Rituale Armenorum: Being the Administration of the Sacraments and the Breviary Rites of the Armenian Church Together with the Greek Rites of Baptism and Epiphany* (transl. A. J. Maclean), Oxford.
Corbo, V.C. (1981). *Il Santo Sepolchro di Gerusalemme. Aspetti archeologici dalle origine al periodo crociato* (3 vols.), Jerusalem.
Corke-Webster, J. (2019). *Eusebius and Empire: Constructing Church and Rome in the Ecclesiastical History*, Cambridge.
Coüasnon, C. (1974). *The Church of the Holy Sepulchre*, Oxford.
Cristofoli, R. (2005). *Costantino e l'Oratio ad sanctorum coetum*, Naples.
Dagron, G. (1974). *Naissance d'une capitale. Constantinople et ses institutions de 330 à 451*, Paris.
Dagron, G. (1984). *Constantinople imaginaire. Études sur le recueil des Patria*, Paris.
Dagron, G. (2011). *L'hippodrome de Constantinople. Jeux, peuple et politique*, Paris.
de Blaauw, S. (2007). 'Konstantin als Kirchenstifter,' in Demandt/Engemann 2007, 163–171.
de Jong, M. & Theuws, F. (eds.) (2001). *Topographies of Power in the Early Middle Ages*, Leiden.
Demandt, A. & Engemann, J. (eds.) (2007). *Konstantin der Große: Geschichte, Archäologie, Rezeption*, Trier.
Dinkler, E. (1965). 'Das Kreuz als Siegeszeichen,' *Zeitschrift für Theologie und Kirche* 62, 1–20.
Dörries, H. (1954). *Das Selbstzeugnis Kaiser Konstantins*, Göttingen.

Downey, G. (1951). 'The builder of the original Church of the Apostles at Constantinople. A contribution to the criticism of the Vita Constantini attributed to Eusebius,' *DOP* 6, 53–80.

Drake, H.A. (1970). *Semper Victor Eris: Evidence for the Policy and Belief of Constantine I Contained in Eusebius' Tricennial Oration*, Ann Arbor (PhD Diss.).

Drake, H.A. (1975). 'When was the "de Laudibus Constantini" delivered?,' *Historia* 24, 345–356.

Drake, H.A. (ed.) (1976). *Eusebius: In Praise of Constantine. A Historical Study and New Translation of Eusebius' Tricennial Orations*, Berkeley.

Drake, H.A. (1988). 'What Eusebius Knew: The Genesis of the Vita Constantini,' *CPh* 83, 20–38.

Drake, H.A. (2000). *Constantine and the Bishops: The Politics of Intolerance*, Baltimore.

Drake, H.A. (2009). 'Solar Power in Late Antiquity,' in Cain/Lenski 2009, 215–226.

Drake, H.A. (2015). 'Speaking of Power: Christian Redefinition of the Imperial Role in the Fourth Century,' in Wienand 2015, 291–308.

Drake, H.A. (forthcoming). *The Orations of Constantine and Eusebius*, Berlin.

Drijvers, J.W. (1992). *Helena Augusta. The Mother of Constantine the Great and the Legend of her Finding of the True Cross*, Leiden.

Ehling, K. & Weber, G. (eds.) (2011). *Konstantin der Große. Zwischen Sol und Christus*, Mainz.

Fear, A. et al. (eds.) (2013). *Role of Bishop in Late Antiquity: Conflict and Compromise*, London.

Findikyan, M. D. (2010). 'Armenian Hymns of the Holy Cross and the Jerusalem Encaenia,' *REArm* 32, 25–58.

Fowden, G. (1991). 'Constantine's Porphyry Column: The Earliest Literary Allusion,' *JRS* 81, 119–131.

Gibbon, E. (1909–1914). *The History of the Decline and Fall of the Roman Empire* (7 vols.), London.

Gibson, S., & Taylor, J. (1994). *Beneath the Church of the Holy Sepulchre in Jerusalem: The Archaeology and Early History of Traditional Golgotha*, London.

Girardet, K.M. (1975). *Kaisergericht und Bischofsgericht. Studien zu den Anfängen des Donatistenstreites (313–315) und zum Prozeß des Athanasius von Alexandrien (328–346)*, Bonn.

Girardet, K.M. (1989). 'Konstantin d. Gr. und das Reichskonzil von Arles (314). Historisches Problem und methodologische Aspekte,' in Papandreou et al. 1989, 151–174.

Girardet, K.M. (2007). 'Vom Sonnen-Tag zum Sonntag. Der dies solis in Gesetzgebung und Politik Konstantins d. Gr.,' *ZAC* 11, 279–310.

Girardet, K.M. (trans.) (2013). *Konstantin: Rede an die Versammlung der Heiligen*, Freiburg.

Grünewald, T. (1990). *Constantinus Maximus Augustus. Herrschaftspropaganda in der zeitgenössischen Überlieferung*, Stuttgart.

Hanson, R.P.C. (1988). *The Search for the Christian Doctrine of God: The Arian Controversy 318–381*, Edinburgh.

Heikel, I.A. (ed.). (1902). *Eusebius Werke* (vol. 1: *Über das Leben Constantins, Constantins Rede an die Heilige Versammlung, Tricennatsrede an Constantin*), Leipzig.

Hunt, E.D. (1982). *Holy Land Pilgrimage in the Later Roman Empire AD 312–460*, Oxford.

Inowlocki, S. (ed.) (2011). *Reconsidering Eusebius: Collected Papers on Literary, Historical, and Theological Issues*, Leiden.

Janin, R. (²1964). *Constantinople byzantine. Développement urbain et répertoire topographique*, Paris.

Johnson, M.J. (2020). 'Constantine's Apostoleion: A Reappraisal,' in Mullett/Ousterhout 2020, 79–98.

Johnson, S.F. (2012). *The Oxford Handbook of Late Antiquity*, Oxford.

Kelley, J.L. (2019). *The Church of the Holy Sepulchre in Text and Archaeology: A Survey and Analysis of Past Excavations and Recent Archaeological Research with a Collection of Principal Historical Sources*, Oxford.

Kim, Y.R. (ed.) (2020). *The Cambridge companion to the Council of Nicaea*, Cambridge.
Klein, K. (forthcoming). *Jerusalem in der Spätantike. Von Constantin zu Iustinian*, Berlin.
Klein, R. (1979). 'Die Kämpfe um die Nachfolge nach dem Tode Constantins des Großen,' *ByzF* 6, 101–150.
Körfer, A.-L. (2020). *Kaiser Konstantin als Leser. Panegyrik, performance und Poetologie in den carmina Optatians*, Berlin.
Krautheimer, R. (²1975). *Early Christian and Byzantine Architecture*, Hammondsworth.
Krautheimer, R. (1993). 'The Ecclesiastical Building Policy of Constantine,' in Bonamente/Fusco, vol. 2, 509–552.
Kühnel, B. (1987). *From the Earthly to the Heavenly Jerusalem. Representations of the Holy City in Christian Art of the First Millennium*, Freiburg.
Lassandro, D. (2000). *Sacratissimus Imperator. L'immagine del princes nell' oratoria tardoantica*, Bari.
Leeb, R. (1992). *Konstantin und Christus. Die Verchristlichung der imperialen Repräsentation unter Konstantin dem Großen als Spiegel seiner Kirchenpolitik und seines Selbstverständnisses als christlicher Kaiser*, Berlin.
Lenski, N. (2015). 'Constantine and the Tyche of Constantinople,' in Wienand 2015, 330–352.
Lenski, N. (2016). *Constantine and the Cities: Imperial Authority and Civic Politics*, Philadelphia.
Luibhéid, C. (1982). *The Council of Nicaea*, Galway.
MacCormack, S.G. (1976). 'Latin Prose Panegyrics: Tradition and Discontinuity in the Later Roman Empire,' *REAug* 22, 29–77.
MacMullen, R. (2006). *Voting About God in Early Church Councils*, New Haven.
Magdalino, P. (2022). 'Imperial Constantinople,' in Bassett 2022, 135–149.
Mango, C. (1985). *Le Développement urbain de Constantinople (IVe–VIIe siècles)*, Paris.
Mango, C. (1990). 'Constantine's Mausoleum and the Translation of Relics,' *ByzZ* 83, 51–61.
Maraval, P. (1997). *Le christianisme de Constantin à la conquête arabe*, Paris.
Meier, M. (2003). 'Göttlicher Kaiser und christlicher Herrscher? Die christlichen Kaiser der Spätantike und ihre Stellung zu Gott,' *Altertum* 48, 129–160.
Moser, M. (2018). *Emperor and Senators in the Reign of Constantius II: Maintaining Imperial Rule Between Rome and Constantinople in the Fourth Century AD*, Cambridge.
Mullett, M. & Ousterhout, R. (eds.) (2020). *The Holy Apostles: A Lost Monument, a Forgotten Project, and the Presentness of the Past*, Washington D.C.
Nixon, C.E.V. & Rodgers, B.S. (1994). *In Praise of Later Roman Emperors. The "Panegyrici Latini"; Introduction, Translation, and Historical Commentary with the Latin Text of R. A. B. Mynors*, Berkeley.
Olbrich, K. (2006). 'Constantiniana Daphne. Die Gründungsmythen eines anderen Rom?,' *Klio* 88, 483–509.
Olbrich, K. (2015). 'Die Gründung Konstantinopels zwischen Sagenkreisen und Zeitzyklen: Versuch einer Rekonstruktion constantinisch-augusteischer Kultprogramme,' *Klio* 97, 176–228.
Omissi, A. (2018). *Emperors and Usurpers in the Later Roman Empire: Civil War, Panegyric, and the Construction of Legitimacy*, Oxford.
Omissi, A. & Ross, A.J. (eds.) (2020). *Imperial Panegyric from Diocletian to Honorius*, Liverpool.
Ousterhout, R. (1990). 'The Temple, the Sepulchre and the Martyrion of the Saviour,' *Gesta* 29.1, 44–53.
Papandreou, D., Bienert, W.A. & Schäferdiek, K. (eds.) (1989). *Oecumenica et Patristica*, Chambésy.
Patrich, J. (1993). 'The Early Church of the Holy Sepulchre in the Light of Excavations and Restoration,' in Tsafrir 1993, 101–117.
Pigott, J.M. (2019). *New Rome Wasn't Built in a Day: Rethinking Councils and Controversy at Early Constantinople 381–451*, Turnhout.

Polara, G. (1973). *Publilius Optatianus Porfyrius: Carmina*, Torino.
Polara, G. (ed.) (1976). *Publilius Optatianus Porfyrius: Carmi*, Naples.
Rapp, C. (2005). *Holy Bishops in Late Antiquity: The Nature of Christian Leadership in a Time of Transition*, Berkeley.
Rees, R. (2002). *Layers of Loyalty in Latin Panegyric: AD 289–307*, Oxford.
Renoux, C.V.P. (1989). *Le lectionnaire de Jérusalem en Arménie: Le Čašocʻ*, Turnhout.
Rubin, Z. (1982). 'The Church of the Holy Sepulchre and the conflict between the sees of Caesarea and Jerusalem,' *Jerusalem Cathedra* 2, 79–105.
Schaff, P. & Wace, H. (eds.) (1890). *Eusebius Pamphilius: Church History, Life of Constantine the Great, Oration in Praise of Constantine*, Oxford.
Schneider, H. (ed.) (2007). *Eusebius von Caesarea: De vita Constantini / Über das Leben Konstantins*, Turnhout.
Schneider, H. (trans.) (2020). *Eusebius von Caesarea: De laude Constantini / De verbo Dei = Lobrede auf Konstantin / Über den Logos Gottes*, Freiburg.
Schwartz, E. (1907). 'Eusebios von Caesarea,' *Real-Encyclopädie der classischen Altertumswissenschaft* 6/1, 1370–1439.
Schwartz, J. (1987). 'The "Encaenia" of the Church of the Holy Sepulchre, the Temple of Solomon and the Jews,' *ThZ* 43, 265–281.
Squire, M. & Wienand, J. (eds.) (2017). *Morphogrammata / The Lettered Art of Optatian: Figuring Cultural Transformations in the Age of Constantine*, Paderborn.
Stroumsa, G. (2009). *The End of Sacrifice: Religious Transformations in Late Antiquity*, Chicago.
Tongeren, L. v. (2000). *Exaltation of the Cross. Towards the Origins of the Feast of the Cross and the Meaning of the Cross in Early Medieval Liturgy*, Leuven.
Tsafrir, Y. (ed.) (1993). *Ancient Churches Revealed*, Jerusalem.
Vieweger, D. et al. (forthcoming). 'Geophysikalische Erkundung der Lage und des Verlaufs der herodianischen Stadtmauer unter dem heutigen christlichen Viertel der Altstadt von Jerusalem,' *ZDPV*.
Walker, P.W. (1990). *Holy City, Holy Places? Christian Attitudes to Jerusalem and the Holy Land in the Fourth Century*, Oxford.
Wallraff, M. (2001). *Christus verus Sol. Sonnenverehrung und Christentum in der Spätantike*, Münster.
Wallraff, M. (2011). 'Konstantins 'Sonne' und ihre christlichen Kontexte,' in Ehling/Weber 2011, 42–52.
Westbrook, N. (2019). *The Great Palace in Constantinople: An Architectural Interpretation*, Turnhout.
Whitby, M. (1998). *The Propaganda of Power. The Role of Panegyric in Late Antiquity*, Leiden.
Wienand, J. (2011). 'Ein Abschied in Gold. Konstantin und Sol invictus,' in Ehling/Weber 2011, 53–61.
Wienand, J. (2012). *Der Kaiser als Sieger. Metamorphosen triumphaler Herrschaft unter Constantin I.*, Berlin.
Wienand, J. (2013). 'La famiglia e la politica dinastica di Costantino,' in *Costantino I. Enciclopedia Costantiniana sulla figura e l'immagine dell'imperatore del cosiddetto Editto di Milano 313–2013*, Rome, vol. 1, 23–52.
Wienand, J. (ed.) (2015). *Contested Monarchy: Integrating the Roman Empire in the 4th Century AD*, Oxford
Wilkinson, J. (²1981). *Egeria's Travels to the Holy Land*, Jerusalem.
Winkelmann, F. (1962). 'Zur Geschichte des Authentizitätsproblems der Vita Constantini,' *Klio* 40, 187–243.
Yasin, A.M. (2012). 'Sacred Space and Visual Art,' in Johnson 2012, 935–969.
Young, R.K. (ed.) (2021). *The Cambridge Companion to the Council of Nicaea*, Cambridge.

Nadine Viermann
Surpassing Solomon: Church-building and Political Discourse in Late Antique Constantinople

Introduction

When Emperor Justinian first set foot in the newly constructed Hagia Sophia, he supposedly uttered the words: "Praise be to God, who found me worthy to carry out such a work: I have outdone you, Solomon."[1] This famous declaration has resonated with both ancient historians and archaeologists, who usually understand it as a reflection of a Roman emperor's grandiose ambition to follow in the footsteps of the Jewish King Solomon. It derives from the Διήγησις περὶ τῆς ἁγίας Σοφίας (*Diēgēsis peri tēs Hagias Sophias*), a legendary account of the construction of the Hagia Sophia, usually dated to the ninth century and transmitted as part of the *Patria Konstantinoupoleos* compiled in the tenth century.[2] Beyond the passage quoted above, there is further evidence for the connection between Solomon, the Hagia Sophia, and Justinian in the *Patria Konstantinoupoleos*. The chapter περὶ στηλῶν, for instance, reports that Justinian had a statue of Solomon erected in the Basilica Cistern facing the Hagia Sophia; supposedly since the new church surpassed the Temple of Jerusalem both in size and beauty.[3] Gilbert Dagron has moreover stressed that the *Diegesis* interweaves allusions to the Old Testament throughout the narrative of the construction of the Hagia Sophia.[4] Thus, before entering the church for the first time and uttering

---

Note: I thank the editors of this volume for the opportunity to return to the topic of my Magister thesis (Heidelberg 2012) in this chapter and for providing valuable feedback. I also thank Kai Trampedach for having supervised both my Magister and PhD thesis and for his academic guidance over the past decade.

1 Δόξα τῷ θεῷ τῷ καταξιώσαντί με τοιοῦτον ἔργον ἀποτελέσαι· ἐνίκησά σε, Σολομῶν; from: *Diegesis* 27, ed. Preger 1901, 105; on this episode, see Dagron 2003, 109–110.
2 Edition of the *Patria* in Preger 1901/1907; edition of the *Diegesis*, Preger 1901, 74–108; cf. Preger, 1901a. On the date of the *Diegesis*, see Preger 1901a, 458–460; Dagron 1984, 265–269; on its legendary character, see Dagron 1984, 269–275. On the *Patria Konstantinoupoleos* in general, see Dagron 1984, Kazhdan 1991, and the most recent translation by Berger 2013; for the image of Justinian as propagated in this legendary account, see Prinzing 1986, 86–89.
3 Ἡ δὲ καθεζομένη ἐπὶ δίφρου ἐκεῖσε μεγάλη στήλη ἐστὶν || τοῦ Σαλομῶντος, ἣν ἀνέστησεν ὁ μέγας Ἰουστινιανὸς κρατοῦντα τὴν σιαγόνα αὐτοῦ καὶ ὁρῶντα τὴν ἁγίαν Σοφίαν ὅτι ἐνικήθη εἰς μῆκος καὶ κάλλος ὑπὲρ τὸν παρ' αὐτοῦ κτισθέντα ναὸν ἐν Ἱερουσαλήμ (Preger 1907, 171). See Dagron 1984, 268. On the statue of Solomon, see also the chronicle of Michael Glycas (twelfth cent.), *Annalium* 4,268–269; cf. Magdalino 1987, 58 n. 42.
4 See Dagron 1984, 293–298.

those legendary words, Justinian had a thousand oxen and countless other animals sacrificed in the forum, a practice that recalls Jewish sacrificial ritual rather than Christian liturgy.[5]

Both the content and symbolism of the *Diegesis* reflect, to a large extent, conditions in the ninth century;[6] however, the frequency and prominence of the connections between Solomon and Justinian in the *Patria Konstantinopoleos* are striking and cannot be explained entirely by the historical context of the text. In order to trace how the link between the Byzantine emperor and the Jewish king rose to such prominence, it must be taken into account that Solomon had already played a vital role in Constantinople long before the *Diegesis*. The dedicatory inscription of the Church of St Polyeuctus, sponsored by the noblewoman Anicia Juliana in the early sixth century, may be regarded as the earliest evidence that explicitly links Solomon to the imperial capital. Slightly later in the sixth century we have two hymns on Justinian and his building activities. Later yet, Solomon appears in Gorippus' verse panegyric on Justin II.[7] In this chapter, I revisit the evidence for the reception of King Solomon and the Jewish Temple in sixth-century Constantinople to demonstrate the role that a specific idea of Jerusalem played in the political discourse of the imperial capital. The analysis traces how the reference to Solomon was established as a powerful and persistent topos in the context of imperial church-building – a topos that still figured prominently centuries later in the *Patria Konstantinoupoleos*.

Juliana

Over the course of the 520s, Constantinople witnessed the completion of the Church of St Polyeuctus, which can be described as magnificent and innovative both in terms of its architecture and its decoration. Remains of this church, including fragments of

---

5 *Diegesis* 27, ed. Preger 1901, 104–105.
6 See Dagron 1984, 265–314, esp. 269, 309. The connection between the Hagia Sophia and the Temple of Solomon also appears in a Jewish chronicle composed in eleventh-century Italy, which mentions a certain Rabbi Shefatiya who was summoned to Constantinople for a discussion with the emperor Basil I (867–886). The discussion reported in the chronicle ultimately revolves around the question of whether greater expense was made for the Temple of Solomon or for Justinian's Hagia Sophia. The chronicle is edited in Neubauer 1985, 111–132; for a translation of the Basil passage, see Salzmann 1924, 70–74; on the relationship between the chronicle and the *Diegesis*, see Dagron 1984, 307–309; cf. also Scheja 1962 (1963), 48.
7 On the high number of references to Solomon in the sixth century, cf. Cameron 1976, 204–205; Dagron 1984, 303–306; Prinzing 1986, 89–91; Koder 1994, 135–138, and Ousterhout 2010, esp. 247. The earliest evidence for the explicit connection between the Jewish Temple and Christian churches is the speech of Eusebius of Caesarea for the dedication of the church of Tyre: *HE* 10,4, esp. 10,4,3; on the reception of the Jewish Temple in the context of Christian building activity, see Ousterhout 2010 and Deliyannis 2015.

the dedicatory inscription, were recovered in excavations in the Saraçhane neighborhood of Istanbul.[8] The surviving foundations and fragments of the architectural decoration furnish ample material for debate over how the original building should be reconstructed.[9] The *patricia* Anicia Juliana who sponsored the church was an illustrious figure: on her mother's side, she was the great-granddaughter of Theodosius II and Eudocia; on her father's side, she was a descendant of the famous family of the Anicii.[10] Her father, Flavius Anicius Olybrius, briefly ruled over the western half of the Roman Empire in 472. In 480, Juliana married Flavius Areobindus Dagalaifus, who was offered the crown in 512 during the Trisagion Riot against Emperor Anastasius.[11] Their son, Flavius Anicius Olybrius had to go into exile after the Nika Riot against Justinian.[12] Anicia Juliana herself was a staunch defender of the Council of Chalcedon; her correspondence with the Pope, preserved in the *Collectio Avellana*, reveals her to be one of the driving forces behind resolving the Acacian Schism.[13] Juliana's wealth was legendary: she founded several churches and figures prominently in the dedicatory miniature of the famous Vienna Dioscurides.[14] Besides the Church of St Euphemia and the Theotokos Church in the Honoratae Quarter,[15] her most important project was undoubtedly the Church of St Polyeuctus. Originally, the

---

[8] On the basis of the remains of the dedicatory inscription, which survives independently as *Anth. pal.* 1,10, the excavated structures could securely be identified as the Church of St Polyeuctus; see Mango/Ševčenko 1961.

[9] The fundamental publication on the Church of St Polyeuctus is the excavation report by Harrison 1986; see also Harrison 1984 and Harrison 1990. Bardill 2006 questions Harrison's reconstruction of the roof of the church as a dome, arguing instead for a gabled roof. New light on the architectural reconstruction has been shed by Venla-Eeva Kakko (MA thesis, Albert-Ludwigs-Universität Freiburg, *non vidi*). For a recent assessment of the reconstruction, see Effenberger 2019; Fabian Stroth (Albert-Ludwigs-Universität Freiburg) is currently preparing a new reconstruction of the church.

[10] PLRE II 468; a genealogy of Juliana's maternal family is provided by Harrison 1986, 419, fig. C. For Juliana's family and their presence in Constantinople, see Begass 2018, 351–380; cf. Caprizzi 1996, 13–35, and ead. 1968.

[11] PLRE II 143–144; on the Trisagion Riot, see Marcellinus Comes, a. 512, and Malalas (ed. Dindorf), 407; cf. Meier 2007; on Areobindus, see Begass 2018, 362–378.

[12] PLRE II 795; Malalas (ed. Dindorf), 478 reports that Justinian recalled him from exile in 533 and restored his property.

[13] *Coll. Avell.* 164, 179, 198; on their correspondence, see Caprizzi 1996, 78–91, and Pizzone 2003, 125–127.

[14] On the Vienna Dioscurides (ed. O. Mazal 1998/1999) and its relationship to Anicia Juliana, see especially Brubaker 2002 and Kiilerich 2001.

[15] On the Church of St Euphemia, see Konstantin Klein's chapter in this volume; Caprizzi 1996, 102–104; Effenberger 2019, 172–173. The choice of Euphemia as patron saint may also be interpreted as a statement on church politics: a native of Chalcedon, in whose martyrium the Council had been held in 451, Euphemia had become the figurehead of the Dyophysite position; see Caprizzi 1996, 118–119. The dedicatory inscriptions in the Church of St Euphemia have also been preserved in the Palatine Anthology (1,12–17); see Connor 1999, 502–504. On the church at Honoratae, see Effenberger 2019, 171–172. For Juliana's sponsorship of churches, see also Dirschlmeyer 2015, 164–181.

church had been dedicated by Juliana's great-grandmother Eudocia,[16] rising on a prominent site between the forum of Theodosius and the Church of the Holy Apostles near the northern branch of the Mese.[17] Juliana's reconstruction was completed before her death in 527/528.[18]

The impact of the St Polyeuctus Church becomes specifically evident in the monumental dedicatory inscription,[19] which uses King Solomon as a reference to bolster Juliana's position in Constantinople's political landscape. To fully grasp Juliana's message, however, it is necessary to analyze the inscription as an integral part of the church architecture. Judging from scholia in the Palatine Anthology and the design of surviving architectural elements, the following arrangement can be reconstructed:[20] via a propylon to the south, visitors could enter the atrium of the church, where lines 42–76 of the inscription were exhibited on five plaques (πίνακες).[21] The church itself stood to the east of the atrium and could be approached by a flight of stairs. After crossing a narthex, visitors reached the quadratic interior of the church, its sides stretching just over 50 m with an apse projecting to the east. The transition between the side aisles and an expanded central nave was subdivided into semicir-

---

[16] On potential reasons for Eudocia dedicating her church to the rather obscure martyr Polyeuctus, see Konstantin Klein's chapter in this volume; cf. Pizzone 2003; Klein 2019, 111–114; Effenberger 2019, 169–171.
[17] On the topography, see Mango/Ševčenko 1961, 244; cf. Harrison 1986, 9–10, 405–406 and Harrison 1990, 34. On the neighborhood, which was in the hands of several aristocratic families, see Magdalino 2001.
[18] For the date of Juliana's Church of St Polyeuctus, see Mango/Ševčenko 1961, 245; Harrison 1984; Bardill 2004, 62–64, 111–116 on dating of the brick stamps and Bardill 2006, 340. On the basis of the brick stamps, Begass 2018, 368–370, 378–379 proposes that the reconstruction of the church was begun after Areobindus had been awarded the consulate in 506; after the Trisagion Riot in 512, which had led to further estrangement between the emperor Anastasius und Juliana's family, the construction was paused for several years and only resumed after Anstasius' death and the accession of Justin I.
[19] *Anth. pal.* 1,10, ed. H. Stadtmüller, *Anthologia Graeca* 1, Leipzig 1894, 4–7; see the Greek text and translation of the inscription in Harrison 1986, 5–7.
[20] A scholion, connected by an asterisk to verse 41, appears next to verses 30–32: "This is written in a circle in the *naos* [of the church]" (Ταῦτα μὲν ἐν τῷ ναῷ ἔνδοθεν κύκλῳ περιγράφονται). A scholion at the end of verse 41 locates the second part of the poem "in the entrance of the same church" (ἐν τῇ εἰσόδῳ τοῦ αὐτοῦ ναοῦ), "outside the narthex" (ἔξωθεν τοῦ νάρθηκος). Another comment appears next to verses 59–61, giving more detail about where the second half of the inscription was placed: "There are four plaques on which this is written, with five or six verses on each" (τέσσαρες εἰσὶ πίνακες ἐν ᾧ [sic] ταῦτα περιγράφονται ἀνὰ στίχους πέντε ἢ καὶ ἕξ). A final scholion accompanies lines 63–66: "This is the last plaque, to the right of the entrance, on which this is written" (ἔσχατός ἐστι πίναξ ὁ πρὸς τοῖς δεξιοῖς μέρεσι τῆς εἰσόδου ἐν ᾧ ἐπιγέγραπται ταῦτα). The scholia are reproduced in Harrison 1986, 7, and Mango/Ševčenko 1961, 245–246.
[21] No remains of the plaques were found during excavations. In research, it is debated how the verses were distributed over the plaques and how the latter were set up in the atrium; cf. Mango/Ševčenko 1961, 246; Connor 1999, 495; Whitby 2006, 161; Speck 1991; for a recent reconstruction of the plaques and the western façade in general, see Effenberger 2019, 161–166.

cular exedrae, which – in all probability – supported a gallery.²² Lines 1–41 of the inscription ran around the central nave on the architrave of the aforementioned exedrae at a height of about 6 m, as is undoubtedly shown by the surviving remains.²³ The individual letters, which are worked in marble in high relief, are surrounded by simple moldings and were originally set against a blue background. An elaborate decorative scheme of grape vines and leaves adorned the surfaces above the inscription.²⁴

In my analysis I follow the path taken by a visitor to the church and – in contrast to the way the text is arranged in the Palatine Anthology – start by discussing the verses set on the *pinakes* in the atrium (42–76) before I proceed into the actual space of the church itself (1–41). Verses 42–76 can be divided into two sections: an encomium in honor of the founder (42–50) and an ekphrasis of the church (51–76).²⁵ After the rhetorical question that introduces the text, ("What choir is sufficient to sing the work of Juliana?"), we are given a truly illustrious gallery of predecessors: "Juliana, who, after Constantine, embellisher of his Rome, after the holy golden light of Theodosius, and after the royal descent from so many forebears, accomplished in a few years a work worthy of her family, and more than worthy?"²⁶ Immediately, in the first verses, Juliana is represented as the culmination of a lineage stretching back to Constantine, the founder of the Christian Empire. While "royal descent" refers to imperial genealogy, the climax Constantine-Theodosius-Juliana does not so much represent a real lineage as it creates an overarching relationship that supersedes kinship. Constantine's building activity and Theodosius' religious integrity are re-created in Juliana's work – the Church of St Polyeuctus – and simultaneously elevated to a new level. The following verses venture beyond the gallery of exemplary Christian emperors and bring a further person into play, which brings us back to the origin of this chapter: "She [Juliana] alone has conquered time and surpassed the wisdom of celebrated Solomon, raising a temple to receive God, the

---

22 For the partitioning of the interior space of the church, I find the reconstruction in Bardill 2006 more plausible. On Harrison's reconstruction, see Harrison 1990, 127–134 with several (hypothetical) illustrations of the ground plan and profile of the church; see also Harrison 1986, 406–411.
23 The precise findspot of the remains (Harrison 1986, 407) allows us to infer that the text of the inscription began in the southeast corner of the nave and continued clockwise until it reached the northeast corner.
24 On the execution of the inscription, see Harrison 1986, 414, and Harrison 1990, 81. Peacocks are a main decorative feature of the church, five of which adorn each exedra; their bodies, necks, and heads projected into the room in high relief; see Harrison 1986, 416, and Harrison 1990, 84. On the architectural decoration, which might merge classical stylistic elements with Persian/Sassanid motifs, see Russo 2004, Canepa 2006 and Effenberger 2019.
25 For detailed interpretations of the content and language of the epigram, see Connor 1999, Whitby 2003, and Whitby 2006.
26 Ποῖος Ἰουλιανῆς χορὸς ἄρκιός ἐστιν ἀέθλοις, / ἣ μετὰ Κωνσταντῖνον, ἑῆς κοσμήτορα Ῥώμης, / καὶ μετὰ Θευδοσίου παγχρύσεον ἱερὸν ὄμμα / καὶ μετὰ τοσσατίων προγόνων βασιληίδα ῥίζαν, / ἄξιον ἧς γενεῆς καὶ ὑπέρτερον ἤνυσεν ἔργον / εἰν ὀλίγοις ἐτέεσσι; (*Anth. pal.* 1,10,42–47). The English translation here and subsequently is taken from Harrison 1986, 5–7.

richly wrought and graceful splendor of which the ages cannot celebrate."[27] As the sponsor of the church, Juliana is not only rooted in the Christian imperial tradition, but is also connected to King Solomon by the attribute of wisdom. However, the quality of the connection to Solomon contrasts with those in the preceding verses. Juliana presents herself and her achievements in line with historical exempla like Constantine and Theodosius. While she carries on their legacy, in the case of Solomon the aspect of surpassing is clearly paramount. In a rhetorical syncrisis, Juliana emerges as superior to the Old Testament king.[28]

The "richly wrought and graceful splendor" of the Church of St Polyeuctus in verse 50 marks a transition to the second section, the ekphrasis. The spacious structure of the church, the layout of its interior, and its decorative elements are evoked in epic vocabulary. The climax of the ekphrasis describes a depiction of the baptism of Constantine "over the arch of the court" (ὑπὲρ ἄντυγος αὐλῆς). Judging from this, Constantine, whom the epigram stylizes as Juliana's model and predecessor, also figured prominently in the iconographical program of the church.[29] The concluding verses 74–76 recapitulate Juliana's achievements on behalf of her ancestors, herself, her children, and her descendants.

Transitioning from the *pinakes* to the interior of the church, the poem's encomiastic nature reaches its full potential. In the style of a *basilikos logos*,[30] Juliana's illustrious dynastic ancestry is emphasized: after Eudocia, who had already built a church for the martyr Polyeuctus on the same site, it was Juliana, the "bright light of blessed parents, sharing their royal blood in the fourth generation" (ζαθέων ἀμάρυγμα τοκήων, τέτρατον ἐκ κείνων βασιλήϊον αἷμα λαχοῦσα), who gave the church its ultimate glory worthy of the martyr, "increasing the glory of her many-sceptred ancestors" (κῦδος ἀεξήσασα πολυσκήπτρων γενετήρων). The poet highlights Juliana's orthodoxy (ὀρθὴν πίστιν) as the basis for her accomplishments. After lavishly praising her achievements as a builder, her εὐσέβεια and her ἀρετή, the saints are called upon to protect her and her family and to carry her fame "as long as the Sun drives his fiery chariot" (εἰσόκεν ἥλιος πυριλαμπέα δίφρον ἐλαύνει).

The recurrent theme of the dedicatory epigram, indicated by ubiquitous imperial terminology, is undoubtedly Juliana's royal ancestry and her ability to worthily represent her forebears with her present accomplishments. In formal terms, Homeric vo-

---

[27] Χρόνον δ' ἐβιήσατο μούνη, / καὶ σοφίην παρέλασσεν ἀειδομένου Σολομῶνος, / νηὸν ἀναστήσασα θεηδόχον, οὗ μέγας αἰὼν / οὐ δύναται μέλψαι χαρίτων πολυδαίδαλον αἴγλην (*Anth. pal.* 1,10,47–50).
[28] On the various rhetorical means with which a connection to the past can be created, see Rapp 2010, 176–180.
[29] The depiction of Constantine was most probably applied on the outer wall of the church facing the atrium, see Effenberger 2019, 163–166. Scholars have plausibly argued that the depiction of Constantine in the St Polyeuctus Church was the earliest pictorial evidence to represent Constantine's legendary baptism by the Roman Pope Silvester; see Fowden 1994 and Milner 1994, 79; already suggested by Mango/Ševčenko 1961, 245 with n. 14
[30] Cf. Whitby 2006, 166.

cabulary is combined with a rhetorically ambitious language inspired by classical and Hellenistic poetry, highlighting terms with Christian connotation.[31] Still, when compared to the poem's classical or classicizing legacy, the Christian terminology remains on the sideline; in the ekphrasis, for example, which clearly follows the longstanding tradition of describing secular monuments, Christian symbolism is completely omitted.[32]

In order to fully grasp the dedicatory inscription, we must ask who its intended audience was. Whereas only a small minority of churchgoers might have actually walked through the nave deciphering the splendid letters of the first forty-one lines affixed well above eye level, the epigram's message was simultaneously communicated in the finery of the architectural decorations.[33] Moreover, the inscription might have become part of a ceremonial performance: recitation of the verses as part of the liturgy is just one of many ways in which the text could have been made accessible to a broader mass of churchgoers.[34] With its archaizing and unusual vocabulary, however, the text seems to primarily speak to a clearly defined and exclusive audience – whether through reading or other channels of communication.[35] Only those who had an outstanding classical education would have been able to appreciate the entire semantic range.[36] This form of communication corresponds to Juliana's self-awareness as member of a social elite, a dynastically legitimated aristocracy in full possession of the highest degree of classical education. The inscription should thus be understood as an elitist statement and mark of distinction, both for the woman who commissioned it and for those who were able understand it.

In the poem, Solomon serves a clear function: by referring to the Jewish king, Juliana can extend the gallery of her illustrious predecessors past the Christian em-

---

31 Or as Connor 1999, 489 summarizes: "A richly textured interplay of classicising and pagan imagery is assimilated to Christian meaning." On the language of the epigram, see also Whitby 2006, 175– 180.
32 With the exception of the isolated word θεηδόχον (verse 49) as an attribute to νηόν, no indication is given of the liturgical function or spiritual relevance of the building. Such Christian symbolism can be detected in earlier sources and becomes standard of the course of the sixth century. Cf. Eusebius' ekphrasis of the church of Tyre (see Smith 1989, Wilkinson 1982), Paul the Silentiary's ekphrasis of the Hagia Sophia (see especially Macrides/Magdalino 1988), and also hymns, such as the anonymous kontakion on the re-consecration of the Hagia Sophia in the year 562 (discussed below) or the inauguration hymn for the Hagia Sophia in Edessa (see Palmer 1988).
33 On the decorations, see above n. 24; cf. James 2007a on ways in which texts could be perceived other than through reading, also with respect to the epigram in the Church of St Polyeuctus (James 2007a, 188–192).
34 Focusing on other churches, Papalexandrou 2001 has studied the performative aspect of inscriptions (in buildings) that could be read or recited during ceremonies as a commemorative act.
35 The fact that the inscription survived in the Palatine Anthology proves that the text was either read from stone or circulated in other form to eventually find its way into the Anthology.
36 Connor 1999, 499–500. on the audience and potential reception of the inscription. See also James 2007b, 191: "The high style of Anicia Juliana's epigram suggests that its intended reading audience was the classically educated, highly literate upper class."

perors back to the Old Testament; yet, by surpassing Solomon's wisdom, she unmistakably distinguishes herself from him. In addition to wisdom, Solomon and Juliana share yet another feature: their building activity. The νηὸς θεηδόχος (verse 49) built by Juliana unmistakably evokes the νηός of Solomon, the Temple of Jerusalem. Martin Harrison, the excavator of the church, argued that Juliana's church had been constructed in imitation of the Temple of Solomon. According to him, the specific decorations of the Church of St Polyeuctus echoed the biblical description of Solomon's Temple (1 Kings 7:13–51; 2 Chron. 3–4).[37] Harrison also referred to the measurements of the church to support this idea, arguing that the quadratic ground plan covered exactly 100 × 100 royal cubits – the dimensions attested for the Jewish Temple in the Old Testament.[38] Harrison's argument, however, obscures the fact that, in the Old Testament, 100 × 100 royal cubits do not refer to the temple built by Solomon, but rather to the visionary temple of Ezekiel (Ez. 40:5–42:20).[39] Ezekiel's vision, which he received during the Babylonian Exile after the destruction of Jerusalem, reflects not only on God's wrath, as manifested in the destruction of the temple, but also conceives of a new, pure temple, the dimensions of which are dictated by God himself to be realized in the future by upright rulers.[40]

With the eschatologically charged temple of Ezekiel,[41] Juliana might have intended to evoke a heavenly Jerusalem in Constantinople and stylize herself as the upright ruler of the vision.[42] As tempting as this possibility sounds, doubts emerge upon closer inspection: besides the questionable hypothesis that the footprint of the building had actually been intended to measure 100 x 100 royal cubits,[43] several features of the church militate against this theory. Juliana's representation, as revealed in the Church of St Polyeuctus as a whole and the epigram in particular, does not seem to

---

37 Palms/palmettes, cherubim, blossoms, pomegranates, and arrangements of trellises and lilies also figure in Juliana's church, see Harrison 1984; Harrison 1986, 410–411 and Harrison 1990, 137–144. Building on Harrison's theory, Shahid 2004 believes that references to the Jewish Temple can be identified already in the Church of St Polyeuctus built by Eudocia.
38 Harrison 1986, 410, and Harrison 1990, 137: none of the standard units of Byzantine measurement could reasonably be applied to the building. The square foundation that determines the plan of the church measures 51.45 m by 51.90 m, which, accepting Harrison's assumption that a normal cubit measured approximately 0.445 m and a royal cubit 0.518 m, would give dimensions precisely of 100 x 100 royal cubits (allowing for minor measuring discrepancies); cf. Ousterhout 2010, 243–246.
39 1 Kings 6:2 and 2 Chron. 3:3 give the dimension of the Temple of Solomon as 60 x 20 ordinary cubits. For the royal cubit, see Ez. 40:5 and Ez. 41:13–15 for the precise measurements; see Milner 1994, 74–75; Bardill 2006, 342–343.
40 On the vision of Ezekiel, see Pohlmann 1996/2001.
41 On the eschatological associations, see Bardill 2006, 342.
42 See Milner 1994.
43 It cannot be proven with certainty that the royal cubit is the unit of measurement on which the dimensions of the church are based. The precise metrological value of a royal cubit is difficult to determine: the relationship between meters and a Byzantine cubit varies from publication to publication. While Harrison 1986, 410, and Harrison 1990, 137 presumes 0.445 meters for a normal cubit, Schilbach 1970, 20 accepts 0.468 meters.

incorporate sophisticated theological elements let alone eschatological allusions. On the contrary, what emerges from the text is Juliana's ambition to create a monument that endures through the ages and proves worthy of herself and her ancestors for all time.[44] Christian references appear primarily in the emphasis on Juliana's orthodoxy; beyond that, the noblewoman articulates her self-representation by referring to aristocratic tradition and using classical or classicizing forms of expression. Rather than insisting on an eschatological interpretation, I understand the reference to Solomon and his Temple in Juliana's epigram as a cipher for a magnificent, royal, dynastically legitimated building program – the distinctive features of which are adapted to contemporary circumstances in the Church of St Polyeuctus.

In the context of the 520s, the Church of St Polyeuctus can be read as a clear political statement, as a commentary on monarchic succession and the condition of the political elite in the imperial capital.[45] With her dynastic genealogy, her traditional aristocratic lineage, and her classical education, Juliana enjoyed an abundance of distinctions that the men on the imperial throne lacked.[46] Justin I, who came to power in 518, had risen from humble, non-aristocratic origins on the Balkans; his nephew Justinian, who succeeded him in 527, shared the same background.[47] In the Church of St Polyeuctus, Juliana went beyond competition within the aristocracy and dared to challenge the reigning emperor, suggesting that her family might be better suited for the throne. In line with Christian emperors of the past, Solomon provides Juliana with a truly royal aura.

---

[44] Connor 1999, 499 proposes that the Church of St Polyeuctus was conceived as the final resting place for Juliana, so as to immortalize her memory and simultaneously anticipate her eternal life with God. The decorative elements that Connor interprets as funerary motifs (in particular, the peacocks and vines branches) are understood by Bardill 2006, 345 as allusions to the Paradise that awaited Juliana; Effenberger 2019, 180–181 proposes that an annex building west of the main church, usually labelled as baptistery, was in fact Juliana's funerary chapel.

[45] Begass 2018 (see n. 18 above) plausibly argues that Juliana's reconstruction of the St Polyeuctus Church had already begun in the first decade of the sixth century during the reign of the Emperor Anastasius. This, of course, would affect the political message that the building was meant to convey. However, it is highly likely that the epigram, on which I primarily base my argument, was composed and put up not under Anastasius but in a later stage of the construction work, that is, after Justin's accession in 518.

[46] Canepa 2006, 7 interprets the Church of St Polyeuctus as a "polemical statement" against the current rulers; for further attempts to place Juliana's church in the contemporary political context, see Harrison 1984; Harrison 1986, 418–420; Harrison 1990, 137–144; Fowden 1994; Milner 1994; Shahid 2004; Bardill 2006 and Begass 2018, 368–380.

[47] On the accession of Justin, see e.g. Leppin 2011, 43–73. On Justinian's path to power, see Croke 2007.

Justinian

If we read the Church of St Polyeuctus as a polemical commentary on the political conditions in the imperial capital, as Juliana's attempt to publicly highlight her family's dynastic claims, it remains to be asked how Justin or Justinian might have reacted to such an act of provocation. While the sources give us no direct information about potential confrontations between Justin I and Juliana, matters seem different with Justinian, who was elevated to the rank of Augustus on April 1, 527, a few months before his uncle's death. Gregory of Tours relates that Justinian sought Juliana out to ask her for a donation to the public treasury. In order to avoid supporting the emperor, Juliana cunningly liquidated all her property to pay to gild the roof of the Church of St Polyeuctus. Humiliated at the sight of the work, Justinian was forced to retreat empty-handed, since he did not dare to rob a church of its property.[48] Despite the predominantly legendary nature of this anecdote, written in faraway Gaul six decades after the Church of St Polyeuctus had been built, it reflects the tense relations between Juliana and Justinian.

The assumption that several families competed for visibility and monarchic prestige in Constantinople by means of church building is corroborated by the evidence of the Church of SS Sergius and Bacchus: Having been dedicated by Justinian at the edge of the Palace of Hormisdas shortly after his coronation in 527, it featured a dedicatory inscription circling the interior on the architrave – just like in the Church of St Polyeuctus.[49] The content of Justinian's inscription differs considerably from the Polyeuctus epigram, but the particular, unusual way in which it was presented, encircling the church space, certainly reflects the church dedicated by Juliana.[50]

Justinian had proved himself a prolific church builder from early on in his reign: besides the Church of SS Peter and Paul[51] and the aforementioned Church of SS Sergius and Bacchus, he began constructing the highly symbolic Nea Church in Jerusalem.[52] In 532, another unique 'opportunity' presented itself: As the people of Con-

---

48 Greg. Tur. *De glor. mart.* (PL 71) 793–795; the passage in Gregory of Tours has also been used as evidence for the reconstruction of the Church of St Polyeuctus; cf. Bardill 2006, 348–349; Harrison 1986, 8–9 with Latin text and translation; Mango/Ševčenko 1961, 245.
49 On the Church of SS Sergius and Bacchus and its date, see Mango 1972, Krautheimer 1974, Mango 1975, Bardill 2000, Shahid 2003, Croke 2006, and Bardill 2017.
50 For a comparison of the two inscriptions in formal terms and in terms of content, as well as the churches as a whole, see Connor 1999, 511–512, Bardill 2000, 4, Shahid 2003, 476–480, and Croke 2006, 50–51; cf. Ousterhout 2010, 243–247. The Church of SS Sergius and Bacchus does not bear any direct reference to Solomon or Jerusalem.
51 No archaeological remains of the Church of SS Peter and Paul have survived, but the dedicatory inscription has been transmitted in *Anth. pal.* 1,8. Justinian asked the pope to send relics to Constantinople to adorn the church (*Coll. Avell.* 187); see Croke 2006, 27–28 with n. 12; see also Proc. *aed.* 1,4,1–8.
52 On Justinian's Nea in Jerusalem, its theological implications and its relationship to the Jewish Temple, see Kai Trampedach's chapter in this volume.

stantinople rose against Justinian in the Nika Riot, the city descended into chaos for several days in a row; many buildings, including the Theodosian Hagia Sophia were burnt down, leaving a massive open space in the very center of the city. After he had succeeded in putting down the revolt by force, Justinian rebuilt the Hagia Sophia in only a few years, erecting a monument of such costliness and magnificence that it eclipsed all other churches in the capital, including the Church of St Polyeuctus.[53]

The reference to Solomon, after having been introduced into the monarchic discourse of Constantinople through the Polyeuctus epigram, was picked up in connection to Justinian's Hagia Sophia. Several sources indicate that the Old Testament king and his Temple played a crucial role in how the newly built Hagia Sophia was perceived by contemporaries. The first evidence can be found in Romanos the Melodist's hymn "On Earthquakes and Fires" remembering the chaos of the Nika Revolt and Justinian's reconstruction of the great church.[54] Although it is impossible to reconstruct beyond doubt when the hymn was originally performed, it must have been closely connected to the completion of the Hagia Sophia and might even have served as an inauguration hymn.[55] As opposed to the dedicatory epigram of the Church of St Polyeuctus cut in stone, the hymn – at least in its original context – must be understood as a primarily oral medium: it was sung during service in front of the whole congregation.[56] Whereas the Polyeuctus epigram can be interpreted as an elitist statement intended primarily for an exclusive audience, the hymn addressed the broad mass of churchgoers. Johannes Koder characterizes such hymns as the "most modern mass-medium of the sixth century"; in vocabulary and meter, they reflect the spoken Greek of the early Byzantine period and accordingly were accessible to a wide audience.[57]

The hymn "On Earthquakes and Fires", which consists of a proem and twenty-five stanzas (*oikoi*), can be divided essentially into two halves. The first half – taking a generalizing, catechetical tone – explores the subject of human sinfulness and the

---
53 On the Nika Riot, see Cameron 1976, esp. 278–281; Greatrex 1997; Meier 2003b; Leppin 2011, 142–148, and Pfeilschifter 2013, 178–210.
54 The hymn is preserved under the title κοντάκιον κατανυκτικὸν ψαλλόμενον εἰς ἕκαστον σεισμὸν καὶ ἐμπρησμόν; edition and translation in Grosdidier de Matons 1981, 470–499 no. 54 with commentary ibid. 455–469; German translation by Koder 2005, 274–284 no. 23. On Romanos Melodos himself, see Koder 2005, 25–33, and Grosdidier de Matons 1974, 353–424. For detailed analysis of the form and content of the hymn, see Catafygiotu-Topping 1978; Grosdidier de Matons 1981, 455–469; Barkhuizen 1995; Silvano 2004, and Nickau 2002.
55 On the original performance, see Maas 1906, 2–7; Grosdidier de Matons 1981, 457–459; Mitsakis 1971, vol. 1, 389–390; Catafygiotu-Topping 1978, 23; Barkhuizen 1995, 1; Silvano 2004, 53–54, 60; Koder 2008(2010), 278; Leppin 2011, 194. Attempts to determine the original context range from the laying of the cornerstone of the new church shortly after the suppression of the revolt to the inauguration ceremony of the finished church at Christmas 537.
56 On the genre and its presentation, see Koder 2005, 17–24.
57 Quotation from Koder 2005, 22 ("das modernste Massenmedium des sechsten Jahrhunderts"); on Romanos' audience and on the language of the hymns, see Hunger 1984; Follieri 1991, 9; Koder 1999; Silvano 2004, 61; and Koder 2008(2010).

misfortunes that a philanthropic God inflicts on his people in order to lead them to repentance. In the second half (*oikoi* 13–25), those ideas are transferred to the reality of the Christian community in Constantinople culminating in several encomiastic stanzas (*oikoi* 21–24) that dwell on Justinian's achievements for the city and its people.[58]

The hymn's penitential nature is already revealed in the proem: God, who is given the epithets κύριος and σωτήρ, is begged for εὐσπλαγχνία (mercy) which he should grant those who turn to him full of θλῖψις (dismay/fear) and μετάνοια (regret/repentance) in order to receive eternal life.[59] The following stanzas conjure an image of God as a δεσπότης ἀγαθός who is benevolent toward mankind in principle, but turns to harsh methods on account of man's foolishness. The notion of theodicy is then applied to episodes from the Old and New Testament. Moses and the Israelites exemplify the dichotomy of God's love of mankind (φιλανθρωπία) and the wrath (ὀργή) that their sinfulness provokes; divine mercy (εὐσπλαγχνία) eventually comes to the fore at Moses' behest. The Canaanite woman from the Gospel of Matthew (15:21–28) also faces God's wrath before penitently asking for eternal life. Building on this, *oikos* 6 emphasizes the importance of prayer and establishes the image of God as a father (ὥσπερ γὰρ πατήρ) who urges his negligent community to cultivate virtue (σωφροσύνη). *Oikoi* 8 and 9 introduce the metaphor of mankind as a plant that "received the source of all sin against God from the root of the first-created [= Adam];"[60] stanza 10 recalls further episodes from the New Testament in order to illustrate how those who trust in Christ (τοῖς πεποιθόσιν ἐπ' αὐτῷ) are granted salvation (σωτηρία). Finally, stanzas 11 and 12 serve to recapitulate the themes explored up to that point and transfer them to the reality of the audience.[61]

In *oikos* 13, Romanos starts explicitly addressing the metropolitan public: events from Constantinople's recent past are depicted as divine acts to heal the community (ἐν ἔργοις τὴν θεραπείαν τὴν ἡμῶν). On account of human sins (ἐκ τῶν ἁμαρτιῶν ἡμῶν), God first sent earthquakes and then – since this warning proved ineffective – let drought follow as a second plague. Yet, even the drought only exacerbated the moral state of mankind, and so the third divine blow took aim at "the very table of grace" (αὐτὴν τὴν τράπεζαν τῆς χάριτος). "He [God] made up His mind to burn down the holy things of the church, just as formerly He surrendered the sacred

---

[58] On the structure of the hymn, see Catafygiotu-Topping 1978, 24–25; Grosdidier de Matons 1981, 460; Barkhuizen 1995, 2–3; Nickau 2002, 605–608.
[59] Ζωὴν τὴν αἰώνιον thereafter recurs as a refrain.
[60] Ναρκοῦν λαμβάνει τὴν ἀρχὴν τὸ γένος τῶν ἀνθρώπων ἐκ τῆς τοῦ πρωτοπλάστου / ῥίζης τοῦ ἁμαρτάνειν ἐξ ἐναντίας τῷ Θεῷ· (Grosdidier de Matons 1981, 54.9). The English translation here and subsequently is taken from Carpenter 1973, 239–248 (slightly modified).
[61] This is made explicit in the first verse of *oikos* 12: "Let us see easily and clearly ..." (ῥᾳδίως ἴδωμεν σαφῶς); the hymn also subsequently addresses the community collectively in the first-person plural.

ark to those of another race."⁶² The next two *oikoi* (15 and 16) give a dramatic depiction of the devastating fire that destroyed large parts of the capital, and eventually refer to the collective trauma that dominated the capital even years after the event: "All men know what happened at the time; probably the memory of events took our minds and thoughts as prisoners of war and made our tongues rather hesitant to tell about them."⁶³ While it remains debated as to which historical events the first and second plague (earthquake and draught) are connected,⁶⁴ there is no doubt about the third plague: Romanos is referring to the Nika Riot of 532 and the destruction of the Hagia Sophia and the Hagia Eirene. In *oikos* 17, the hopelessness that prevailed in Constantinople after the disaster is contrasted with God's mercy (παρέχει τὸν οἰκτιρμὸν πᾶσιν ὁ δεσπότης). Only on those who failed to become virtuous "did He unleash His wrath at the point of sword" (ἐπάγει ὀργὴν ἐν στόματι μαχαίρας). In the "point of sword" we find a clear reference to the massacre in the Hippodrome with which Justinian quelled the riotous masses.⁶⁵

In *oikos* 18, the theme of prayer is reintroduced: facing the terrifying events, the pious turn to God begging him for mercy (ἐλεημοσύνη). Romanos places the emperor together with his consort, the empress Theodora, among those beseeching God and quotes his prayer as follows: "Grant to me, Savior, as to Thy David to conquer Goliath, for my hope is in Thee. As Merciful, save Thy faithful people, and grand to them eternal life."⁶⁶ This prayer is striking for various reasons: formally, it represents a parallel to the prayer of Moses, who in *oikos* 4 likewise begs God for the salvation of his people. Romanos, however, goes further, explicitly having Justinian refer to King David of the Old Testament as an example of pious victory.⁶⁷ By directly quoting his prayer, Romanos lifts Justinian above the masses and places him in the tradition of Old Testament leaders as spokesman for his people and intermediary before God. Just as Moses prayed for the Israelites, just as David saved his people with his victory over Goliath, Justinian saves the people of Constantinople. His prayer indeed made an impact: hearing voices of "those who cried out and those who ruled" (τῶν κραζόντων καὶ τῶν βασιλευόντων) – Romanos says in *oikos* 19 – God granted the mourning and devastated city of Constantinople his "humane pity" (τοὺς φιλανθρώπους

---

62 Καυθῆναι συγχωρήσας τὰ ἅγια τὰ τῆς ἐκκλησίας, / ὡς καὶ πρώην ἀλλοφύλοις ἐκδέδωκε κιβωτὸν τὴν θείαν· (Grosdidier de Matons 1981, 54.14). On the Ark of the Covenant, see 1 Sam. 4:1–5:12; it is noteworthy that the Hagia Sophia is paralleled with the Old Testament Ark of the Covenant.
63 Ἅπαντες ἴσασιν εἰκὸς τὰ τότε γεγονότα, ὧν εἰκότως ἡ μνήμη / τὸν νοῦν αἰχμαλωτίζει καὶ τὴν διάνοιαν ὑμῶν / καὶ ὀκνηροτέραν καὶ τὴν γλῶτταν τὴν ἡμῶν / ποιεῖ πρὸς τὴν διήγησιν (Grosdidier de Matons 1981, 54.15).
64 See Grosdidier de Matons 1981, 462–464.
65 See Barkhuizen 1995, 14.
66 Δός μοι, βοῶν, σωτήρ, ὡς καὶ τῷ Δαυίδ σου / τοῦ νικῆσαι Γολιάθ· σοὶ γὰρ ἐλπίζω· / σῶσον τὸν πιστὸν λαόν σου ὡς ἐλεήμων, / οἷσπερ καὶ δώσῃς ζωὴν τὴν αἰώνιον (Grosdidier de Matons 1981, 54.18). On the David and Goliath episode, see 1 Sam 17.
67 On the chain Moses – David – Justinian, cf. Catafygiotu-Topping 1978, 30–31; Barkhuizen 1995, 13–14; Silvano 2002, 57 with n. 109, and Nickau 2002, 611.

οἰκτιρμούς). *Oikos* 19 moreover serves to recall the city's suffering, climaxing in the destruction of the θρόνος τῆς ἐκκλησίας, the throne of the Church, to which *oikos* 20 is dedicated. In antitheses, the state of destruction is contrasted with erstwhile magnificence: Σοφία and Εἰρήνη, personifying the destroyed churches, have been thrown to the ground; brilliance and beauty have given way to decay and fear.

The recollection of disaster sets the scene for the encomium[68] on Justinian starting in *oikos* 21, which again begins by looking back to the Old Testament. The opening lines evoke the image of the Temple of Jerusalem (τὸν ναὸν τὸν μέγιστον), "that the all-wise Solomon over a very long time raised up, adorned, and embellished with infinite wealth."[69] This positive depiction, however, is short-lived and abruptly reversed in the second half of the stanza: the sanctuary was not only destroyed, but remained in ruins and rises no more (μένει ἐκπεσὼν καὶ οὐκ ἀνέστη). In keeping with the story of the Gospels, Romanos then contrasts the fallen temple with the achievements of the New Covenant: "The people of Israel were deprived of his temple; but we, instead of that, now have the holy Resurrection and Zion, which Constantine and the faithful Helena gave the world two hundred and fifty years after the fall [of the temple]."[70] Here, the familiar image of the Church of the Holy Sepulcher as antithesis to the destroyed Temple of Jerusalem[71] is merely another step toward Romanos' main argument. In the following verses, he shifts from Jerusalem to Constantinople: while 250 years passed between the destruction of the Jewish Temple and the construction of Constantine's churches in Jerusalem, "just one day after the disaster, work was begun on having the church restored. It was brilliantly decorated and brought to completion."[72] At the end of stanza 22, Romanos does not fail to mention those responsible for these building projects: "The rulers prided themselves on the expenditure; the Master dispenses eternal life."[73]

---

68 On the encomium of Justinian, cf. Barkhuizen 1995, 16–18.
69 ὃν Σολομῶν ἐκεῖνος ὁ πάνσοφος χρόνῳ μακροτάτῳ / ἀνεγείρας καὶ κοσμήσας ἐποίκιλε πλούτῳ ἀπεράντῳ (Grosdidier de Matons 1981, 54.21).
70 Λαὸς μὲν ὁ τοῦ Ἰσραὴλ ναοῦ ἀποστερεῖται· ἡμεῖς δὲ ἀντ' ἐκείνου / Ἀνάστασιν ἁγίαν καὶ τὴν Σιὼν ἔχομεν νῦν, / ἥνπερ Κωνσταντῖνος καὶ Ἑλένη ἡ πιστὴ / τῷ κόσμῳ ἐδωρήσαντο / μετὰ διακοσίους πεντήκοντα χρόνους τοῦ πτωθῆναι (Grosdidier de Matons, 1981, 54.22). It is noteworthy that this passage mentions only Constantine's building projects in Jerusalem. Not a word is said about the founding of Constantinople and the churches built in the capital. In this way, the passage is less about Constantine as emperor than it is about the significance of the church he built in Jerusalem as antithesis of the Jewish Temple.
71 Cf. Euseb. *Vit. Const.* 3,33,1–2; on this passage, see Ousterhout 1990 and Ousterhout 2010, 233–239.
72 Ἀλλ' ἐνταῦθα μετὰ μίαν τῆς πτώσεως ἤρξαντο ἡμέραν / τὸ τῆς ἐκκλησιᾶς ἐγείρεσθαι ἔργον· / καὶ φαιδρύνεται λαμπρῶς καὶ τελειοῦται· (Grosdidier de Matons 1981, 54.22). With respect to the date of the hymn's presentation, the verb τελειοῦται in the present tense could be interpreted indicating that the church is about to be completed or already is completed.
73 Οἱ μὲν βασιλεῖς δαπάνην φιλοτιμοῦνται, ὁ δὲ δεσπότης ζωὴν τὴν αἰώνιον (Grosdidier de Matons 1981, 54.22).

Just as the hardships that befell the people of Constantinople are explained with reference to basic human sin, Justinian's activity is placed into an explicitly Christian framework: Romanos depicts him as the pious leader of his people and their intermediary before God in imitation of Moses and David; the reconstruction of the Hagia Sophia relates to the famous Solomon and his Temple. However, similar to the mechanism employed in Juliana's case, the aspect of surpassing the past prevails: Romanos compares both the long time (χρόνῳ μακροτάτῳ) that Solomon needed to build the Temple, as well as the 250 years that lay between the destruction of the Temple and the building of Constantine's churches, with the rapidity of Justinian's endeavor. In contrast to the Polyeuctus epigram, however, the aspect of surpassing Solomon is anchored in Christian logic that understands the relations of the Old Testament as antecedents to Christ's incarnation and events yet to come. Thus, both the Temple of Solomon and the churches of Constantine figure as antecedents to the Hagia Sophia.[74] Romanos makes no attempt to construct a real imperial genealogy for Justinian like the one Juliana displayed in the Polyeuctus epigram. Instead, Justinian emerges as the peak of a spiritual line originating in the Old Testament. Moreover, the hymn defines the emperor's relationship to God: the verse "The rulers prided themselves on the expenditure; the Master dispenses eternal life," distinguishes the physical, earthly level of Justinian from the spiritual, heavenly realms of God. Nevertheless, there is a clear parallel between the earthly *basileus* and heavenly *despotes*, reflecting official imperial ideology.[75]

Eventually, stanzas 23 and 24 give another detailed account of the emperor's accomplishments for the capital and its population. "Now they [Justinian and Theodora] have revealed things that are great, brilliant, and worthy of wonder, indeed surpassing all the men of old, they who at this time reverently manage affairs of the Romans. In a short time, they rebuilt the entire city so that the hardships of all who had suffered were forgotten. The very structure of the church is erected with such excellence that it imitates Heaven, the divine throne, which indeed offers eternal life."[76] The verb ἀνέστησαν takes up the contrast with the Jewish Temple, which had never been rebuilt, and aligns Justinian's work of restoration with Christian resurrection; for Constantinople, the emperor's building projects correspond to God's gift of eternal life. Romanos concludes by representing the newly built church as

---

[74] On the antithesis Solomon – Justinian, see Catafygiotu-Topping 1978, 32–33; Koder 1994; and Nickau 2002, 614.

[75] This parallel, supported by the μὲν-δέ construction, is also highlighted by Catafygiotu-Topping 1978, 34; similarly Silvano 2002, 58. Nickau 2002, 615–616, in contrast, interprets this verse as downplaying Justinian's achievements – unconvincingly, in my view.

[76] Μεγάλα ὄντως καὶ φαιδρὰ καὶ ἄξια θαυμάτων καὶ ὑπερβεβηκότα / ἅπαντας τοὺς ἀρχαίους βασιλεῖς ἔδειξαν νυνὶ / οἱ ἐν τῷ παρόντι τῶν Ῥωμαίων εὐσεβῶς / τὰ πράγματα διέποντες· / ἐν χρόνῳ γὰρ ὀλίγῳ ἀνέστησαν ἅπασαν τὴν πόλιν, / ὡς καὶ λήθην ἐγγενέσθαι τοῖς πάσχουσι πάντων τῶν δυσκόλων· / ὁ οἶκος δὲ αὐτὸς ὁ τῆς ἐκκλησίας / ἐν τοσαύτῃ ἀρετῇ οἰκοδομεῖται / ὡς τὸν οὐρανὸν μιμεῖσθαι, τὸν θεῖον θρόνον, / ὃς καὶ παρέχει ζωὴν τὴν αἰώνιον (Grosdidier de Matons 1981, 54.23).

mimesis of Heaven and reflection of God's throne. While Juliana's dedicatory inscription is mostly lacking in Christian symbolism, Romanos' hymn expresses such symbolism to perfection. The relation between the earthly church (θρόνος τῆς ἐκκλησίας) and the heavenly/divine throne (τὸν θεῖον θρόνον) corresponds to the parallel between the earthly *basileus* and the heavenly *despotes*. The concluding prayer that makes up stanzas 24 and 25 continues this tone and beseeches God "to strengthen the undertaking and grounding of his church" (τὸ τῆς ἐκκλησίας στερεῶσαι τῆς αὐτοῦ ἐγχείρημα καὶ ἕδρασμα) so as to bring joy to the rulers (βασιλεῖς), the citizens (πολῖται), and the priests (ἱερεῖς). Recalling the terror and confusion to which the capital had been exposed, Romanos concludes by praying to Christ to save the entire city, churches, and emperors: Σῶτερ, (...) πᾶσαν σῶσον τὴν πόλιν, σῶσον τὰς ἐκκλησίας, σῶσον δὲ καὶ τοὺς βασιλεῖς.

As indicated at the beginning of this section, the Nika Riot radically challenged Justinian's authority and could only be brought under control through military force causing a high number of casualties. In this context, the hymn paints a picture of a severely traumatized city struggling to overcome the rift between the emperor and his people. Romanos' perspective can be understood as a coping strategy: he presents a means for the congregation to deal with the horrific events of the immediate past by developing a specific, religiously oriented interpretation.[77] Its gist is to present the Nika Riot in line with natural disasters as divine punishment; instead of making specific actors responsible for burning down the churches or the massacre in the Hippodrome, Romanos places human sin and divine wrath in a universal context. This interpretation not only serves to exculpate Justinian from slaughtering his people,[78] but also shows him in a pointedly positive light during this critical phase of reintegration. By virtue of his exceptional piety, the emperor, as the spokesman for his subjects who have succumbed to sin, shares in God's salvific master plan. Against the background of disaster, his Christian integrity and his accomplishments for the good of the city – both as the intermediary between his people and God and as the rebuilder of the destroyed church – come to the fore; his reconstruction of the Hagia Sophia is emblematic of God's pity. The hymn makes no explicit reference to Justinian being almost overthrown by collective dissent; on the contrary, it – almost cynically – propagates harmony between the urban population and the emperor, as he and his wife are depicted among those praying to pacify God's wrath. In Romanos' interpretation, Solomon, together with Moses and David, not only serves as an illustrious archetype from the Old Testament that reinforces the emperor's position in the imperial capital; by referring to Solomon's Temple, the reconstruction of

---

[77] For nuanced interpretations of the hymn in its historical context, see especially Nickau 2002 and Silvano 2004.
[78] His harsh actions against the rebels met with criticism elsewhere; for example, Malalas (ed. Dindorf), 476; cf. Proc. *hist. arc.* 7 on Justinian's relationship with the circus factions.

the Hagia Sophia, which grew out of the Nika Riot, is represented as fulfilling Old Testament models – thus sanctioning both building and builder.[79]

The question whether Justinian himself commissioned "On Earthquakes and Fires" has to remain open.[80] Nonetheless, it is highly likely that the emperor appreciated Romanos' interpretation of the recent past and his own role in it. As discussed above, hymns seem to have been the most sensible medium for reaching a broad audience and communicating a certain message. By establishing a religiously charged interpretation of the Nika Riot, the hymn served as a means of reinforcing Justinian's authority; it contributed to restoring the *consensus omnium* in Constantinople and to reuniting the estranged parties – βασιλεῖς, πολῖται and ἱερεῖς.

Next to "On Earthquakes and Fires", another contemporary source, an anonymous hymn, connects Solomon with Justinian and his Hagia Sophia. Although this second hymn does not offer such clear references to the lived experience of the community as the one analyzed above, we can clearly reconstruct the context in which it was originally performed. The acrostic gives the title ΤΩΝ ΕΓΚΑΙΝΙΩΝ Ο ΥΜΝΟΣ, and *oikos* 2 explicitly refers to the inauguration of the Hagia Sophia.[81] Since the invocation of the emperor in the concluding prayer in stanza 18 appears in the singular, the hymn must have been composed after Theodora's death in 548. That only leaves the rededication of the Hagia Sophia on Christmas 562, after its dome had collapsed following an earthquake.[82] In his edition, Constantine A. Trypanis argues that the hymn should be understood as a popular counterpart to the ekphrasis of Paul the Silentiary, which was recited on the same occasion several days later in the imperial palace and the patriarch's residence.[83]

The overarching theme of the hymn is the question of whether or how God could find a dwelling place on earth. Solomon's statement in 2 Chron 6:18 – Εἰ θεὸς μετ' ἀνθρώπων οἰκήσει – is interpreted as prophesying the incarnation, which in turn lays the ground for earthly churches: "Having once resided in flesh the Word consents, by the operation of the Spirit, to reside in temples built by hand, assuring his presence by mystical rites."[84] However, it soon becomes apparent that the hymn does not refer to churches in general, but to the Hagia Sophia in particular: "This is why we have now consecrated the sanctuary of Wisdom as a manifestly di-

---

[79] On the connection between the Hagia Sophia and the Temple of Solomon, see Ousterhout 2010, 239–243 and Scheja 1962 (1963), who argues that the dimensions of the Hagia Sophia should be understood as an imitation of the Temple.
[80] On the relationship between Justinian and Romanos, see Koder 2008 (2010); Koder 1994, 141.
[81] "This is why we have now consecrated the sanctuary of Wisdom..." Διὰ τοῦτο προφθάσωμεν τῆς Σοφίας τὸ ἁγίασμα; cf. also *oikos* 7. The hymn is edited in Trypanis 1968, 139–147; the English translation here and subsequently is taken from Palmer 1988, 140–144; on the question of authorship, see Trypanis 1968, 139, and Palmer 1988, 138.
[82] On the date, see Trypanis 1968, 139, and Palmer 1988, 137–138.
[83] Trypanis 1968, 139, following Friedländer 1912, 110; cf. Palmer 1988, 138.
[84] Ἐν σαρκὶ ἐνοικήσας ὁ Λόγος κατοικεῖν ἐν ναοῖς χειροτεύκτοις εὐδοκεῖ ἐνεργείᾳ τοῦ πνεύματος / μυστικαῖς τελεταῖς τὴν αὐτοῦ παρουσίαν πιστούμενος (Trypanis 12.4).

vine place for the honor and worship of the mystery."⁸⁵ This church alone is deemed worthy to serve as the "most sacred residence of God" (τὸ θαυμάσιον τέμενος τοῦτο τοῦ θεοῦ), as a "kind of heaven on earth" (οὐρανός τις ἐπίγειος), "since it surpasses the whole of mankind's knowledge of architectural technology" (τεχνικὴν ἅπασαν ὑπερανέχον ἐπιστήμην ἀνθρώπιον ἐν τοῖς δώμασιν).

After *oikoi* 6–9 draw an epic comparison between the church and the firmament (στερέωμα), *oikos* 10 again turns to the Old Testament: Moses had seen the image of the Tabernacle (σκηνὴν μαρτυρίου), but he could not describe it in words; thus Bezalel, "endowed with the wisdom of God" (ὑπουργὸν ... σοφίαν [ἐκ] θεοῦ), was entrusted with building it. In stanza 12, the hymn transitions from the Old Testament to sixth-century Constantinople, linking the two spheres by the following analogy: "We have the Savior as our lawgiver, as all-holy Tabernacle this divinely constructed temple, we propose our believing Basileus for Bezalel's office."⁸⁶ With the Tabernacle established as the model for the Hagia Sophia, Justinian turns into another Bezalel, enlightened by God's wisdom. From Moses and Bezalel, the poet moves on to Solomon and his Temple in Jerusalem, which is described in stanzas 13 and 14: "That temple was commonly known as the place of God, to which appeal was made by all; and the whole of Israel flooded to it under compulsion, driven together by the whip of the Law, for in it they used to make their offerings."⁸⁷ Following the description of the Jewish Temple, the familiar topic of surpassing Old Testament models is taken up again: "But they [the Jews] would certainly have to give us the credit for surpassing them, for the very evidence of the senses demonstrates that this divine *chef d'oeuvre* transcends everything; and its buttress is Christ."⁸⁸ While the Temple of Jerusalem gathered only one nation, and did so under the compulsion of the law, all people freely acknowledge their admiration for the Hagia Sophia, "so that even the unbelievers admit unequivocally that the one who lives in it is God."⁸⁹ The differences between the Jewish Temple and the Hagia Sophia are detailed further in *oikos* 16, contrasting the bloody sacrifices of the Jews with the Christian spiritual sacrifice. In the concluding prayer, the poet addresses God:

> O Savior, born of a virgin, preserve this house until the consummation of the world! (...) Heed the cries of the servants of thine house and grant peace to thy people by banishing heresies and

---

[85] Διὰ τοῦτο προφθάσωμεν τῆς Σοφίας τὸ ἁγίασμα / ὡς βασίλεια ἐμφανῶς θεϊκὰ πρὸς ἀνευφήμησιν καὶ λατρείαν τοῦ μυστηρίου (Trypanis 12.2).
[86] Νομοθέτην ἡμεῖς τὸν σωτῆρα κεκτημένοι, σκηνὴν παναγίαν τὸν θεάρμοστον ἔχομεν τοῦτον / ναόν, ἐν Βεσελεὴλ βασιλέα πιστὸν προβαλλόμενοι (Trypanis 12.12).
[87] Ὑπὸ πάντων ἐπίκλητος τόπος τοῦ θεοῦ τῷ ὀνόματι εἶναι ὁ ναὸς ἐθρυλεῖτο ἐκεῖνος, / καὶ εἰς τοῦτον ὁ πᾶς Ἰσραὴλ ἐπειγόμενος [συν]έρρεε / νομικῇ μάστιγι σθνλασμένος, / ἐν αὐτῷ γὰρ προσέφερον τὰ καρπώματα (Trypanis 12.14).
[88] ἐν ἡμῖν δὲ τὰ κρείττονα καὶ βεβαίως [γὰρ] ἀνευφήμουν <ἂν>· / ἀνεδείχθη γὰρ ἀληθῶς αἰσθητῶς [ἅμα καὶ νοητῶς] τὸ μεγαλούργημα ὑπεραῖρον τοῦτο τὸ θεῖον / ὑπὲρ <ἅ>παντα, ὃ στηρίζει Χριστός (Trypanis 12.14).
[89] ὅθεν καὶ ἄπιστοι μετὰ θάρσους ὁμολογοῦσιν, / ὡς ἐστὶν αὐτοῦ ὁ οἰκήτωρ θεός (Trypanis 12.15).

crushing the strength of the barbarians! Keep the faithful priest(s) and the Basileus safe and adorned with all piety.[90]

Whereas "On Earthquakes and Fires" explicitly addresses past calamities and offers a strategy to reintegrate the community after traumatizing events, the anonymous inauguration hymn strikes a purely celebratory tone: reference to the collapse of the dome is lacking.[91] The gist of the second hymn is to underscore the significance of the Hagia Sophia as *the only* worthy dwelling place for God on earth, as the center of the Christian *kosmos*. Setting the Hagia Sophia above other churches is initially legitimated by the technological superiority of the building; in a second step, the Church is distinguished as housing the divine by typologically linking it to the Jewish Tabernacle. Jewish cult sites, which were regarded as the dwelling places of God in Old Testament times, are presented as ephemeral steps toward divine incarnation and Christian churches in which God's presence manifests itself through the Eucharist.[92] Beyond that, Solomon's Temple serves to contrast Jewish compulsion with the voluntary initiative of Christians; the hymn indeed mentions its magnificent decoration, albeit noting that the Hagia Sophia obviously eclipses it. By virtue of analogy to Bezalel, the emperor is presented as a builder endowed with divine wisdom, but he takes second place to the magnificence of the church.[93] No direct comparison between Justinian and Solomon is made.

The last evidence for the topos of surpassing Solomon and his temple stems from Corippus' verse panegyric in honor of Emperor Justin II, written shortly after his coronation in 565.[94] After interpreting Justinian's construction of the church of the Holy Wisdom as prophesying the reign of Justin II and his wife Sophia and briefly describing the church and its symbolism, the poet concludes: "Let the description of Solomon's temple now be stilled" (4,283: *Salomoniaci sileat descriptio templi*). In this case, Solomon's Temple is not referred to as an Old Testament archetype foretelling Christian churches; it rather serves as one of the *cunctorum miracula nota locorum* (4,284) that have been overshadowed by the Hagia Sophia.

---

90 Σύ, σωτήρ, ὁ τεχθεὶς ἐκ παρθένου, διαφύλαξον τοῦτον τὸν οἶκον ἕως τῆς συντελείας τοῦ κόσμου,/ (...) / [καὶ] τὰς φωνὰς πρόσδεξαι τῶν οἰκετῶν σου / καὶ εἰρήνην τῷ λαῷ σου χαριζόμενος [καταπέμψον] / τὰς αἱρέσεις ἐκδίωξον καὶ βαρβάρων ἰσχὺν σύντριψον, / ἱερεῖς δὲ καὶ βασιλέα πιστοὺς πάσῃ συντήρησον εὐσεβείᾳ κεκοσμημένους (Trypanis 12.18).
91 We may suspect implicit references in certain verses, such as in *oikos* 14, which brings forward the idea that Christ will support the building (ὁ στηρίζει Χριστός).
92 See Palmer 1988, 148.
93 It is also interesting that the priests are mentioned before the emperor in the concluding prayer.
94 Edition and translation by Cameron with commentary on the Solomon comparison in Cameron 1976, 204–205. On the date of the work, see Cameron 1976, 4–7.

Conclusion

With respect to the overarching theme of this volume, this chapter traces an ideological connection between Constantinople and Jerusalem,[95] highlighting the presence and impact of an Old Testament king in the political discourse of the Byzantine imperial capital.[96] The sources discussed here show how the idea of Solomon was evoked to convey specific political messages. Both Solomon and his temple could be endowed with multiple layers of meaning. Neither the Polyeuctus epigram nor the hymns on the Hagia Sophia claim that either church imitates or revives the Jewish Temple in the imperial capital.[97] Instead, we witness the creation of a powerful topos governed by the claim of *surpassing* the Old Testament king and his temple. The differences in how the Polyeuctus epigram, on the one hand, and the hymns on the Hagia Sophia, on the other hand, refer to Solomon attest to distinct strategies of communication. In light of the declining relevance of the Anicii in the imperial capital, Juliana created an imperial aura that draws on every category of former greatness: it stretches from her imperial ancestors over the Christian emperors par excellence, Theodosius and Constantine, to the Jewish King Solomon and his temple in Jerusalem. Romanos' hymn, by contrast, refers to Solomon and his Temple in order to bestow Justinian's building project, which grew out of the Nika Riot, with a distinctively positive Christian meaning. It interprets both destruction and rebuilding of the Hagia Sophia as part of God's salvific master plan, rehabilitates Justinian as a pious leader of his people, and thus strengthens the emperor's position within the political structure of the capital. The anonymous hymn uses the Temple of Solo-

---

95 The topos of surpassing Solomon was part of a wider process that bestowed the capital with attributes of Jerusalem; Constantinople was established as New Jerusalem in addition to its status as New Rome; cf. the chapter by Paul Magdalino in this volume. The perception of Constantinople as New Jerusalem is documented as early as the sixth century: cf. *Vita Danielis Stylitae* 10: "Go to Byzantium and you will see the Second Jerusalem, Constantinople" (ἀπελθε εἰς τὸ Βυζάντιον καὶ βλέπεις δευτέραν Ἰερουσαλήμ, τήν Κωνσταντινούπολιν). On Constantinople as New Jerusalem, cf. e.g. Meier 2003a, 65 n. 94; Külzer 2000, esp. 58–59 and Magdalino 1993, 11–12. Besides the discursive presence of Jerusalem in Constantinople, relics frequently made their way from Jerusalem to Constantinople; see especially Ousterhout 2012; Ousterhout 2006, and (with respect to the Hagia Sophia) Scheja 1962 (1963). In my postdoctoral project, I investigate the translation of relics to Constantinople from the forth to the seventh century as a means to construct a Christian sacred topography in the imperial capital.
96 The references to Solomon discussed here are by no means the only ones made between an Old Testament figure and a late Roman / Byzantine emperor; numerous examples have been collected in Rapp 2010. The Old Testament in late antiquity served as a "guiding principle" alongside others, such as Roman imperial tradition, for discussing and negotiating Byzantine monarchy; see the pointed remarks of Dagron 2003, 50.
97 Such a claim would in fact bear negative connotations in a Christian sense; cf. Dagron 1984, 304; Milner 1994, 75; Ousterhout 2010, 225.

mon as a foil to present the Hagia Sophia as God's rightful dwelling place, while simultaneously celebrating the achievements of its builder, Justinian.

In conclusion, it seems plausible that Solomon's presence in the hymns correlated with the efforts Justinian made in order to respond to Juliana's provocation. The hymns on the Hagia Sophia pick out the vision of Solomon from Juliana's representation, adapt it to Justinian's own strategy, and transform it into an argument in his favor. Glancing at the *Patria Konstantinopouleos*, we may conclude that, in the long run, Justinian's reference to Solomon had a bigger impact than Juliana's. The evidence analyzed above indicates that the connection between Justinian's building activity and the Jewish Temple reached a broad public: the hymns spread the idea much further than Juliana's epigram, an essentially elitist statement. On that basis, the connection between the Byzantine emperor and the Old Testament king became deeply ingrained in the political discourse of the capital; it remained rooted in the collective memory to such an extent that it could re-emerge prominently in the *Diegesis*, although in a slightly distorted way.

Justinian, however, was not the last Byzantine emperor to appropriate the topos of surpassing Solomon. After a substantial gap in new imperial church building projects, Basil I dedicated the Nea Ekklesia in or adjoining the imperial palace in the late ninth century. Relating the inauguration ceremony, various chronicles report what at first glance appears to be a strange legend: the emperor supposedly sacrificed a statue of Solomon from the Basilica Cistern in the substructures of his church.[98] Apparently, the topos of surpassing Solomon and his Temple, as it was established in the sixth century, not only found its way into the *Diegesis* but also impacted the ideology of imperial church building up to the ninth century and beyond.[99]

Bibliography

Abramea, A., Lalou, A.E. & Chrysos, E.K. (eds.) (2003). *Byzantium. State and Society*, Athens.

Accorinti, D. & Vian, F. (eds.) (2003). *Des Géants à Dionysos. Mélanges de mythologie et de poésie grecques offerts à Francis Vian*, Alexandria.

Asutay-Effenberger, N. & Daim, F. (eds.) (2019). *Sasanischische Spuren in der byzantinischen, kaukasischen und islamischen Kunst und Kultur*, Mainz.

Bardill, J. (2000). 'The Church of Sts. Sergius and Bacchus in Constantinople and the Monophysite Refugees,' *DOP* 54, 1–11.

Bardill, J. (2004). *Brickstamps of Constantinople* (2 vols.), Oxford.

---

[98] Leo Gramm. 257; Ps. Sym. 692; Geo. Mon. Cont. 844; see Dagron 1984, 269, 309; Magdalino 1987, 58 with references to the sources and ibid. passim on the Nea Ekklesia. On the statue of Solomon, see n. 3 above. On imperial church building after Justinian, cf. Paul Magdalino's chapter in this volume.
[99] For the transmission of the legendary account of Justinian, the Hagia Sophia, and its connection to Solomon (also beyond the *Diegesis*), see Prinzing 1986, 89–92. In the eleventh century, Psellos compared the Peribleptos Church, sponsored by Romanos III Argyros (1028–1034), to both the Temple of Solomon and Justinian's Hagia Sophia, although in a critical way; see ibid. 91.

Bardill, J. (2006). 'A New Temple for Byzantium. Anicia Juliana, King Solomon, and the Gilded Ceiling of the Church of St. Polyeuktos in Constantinople,' in Bowden et al. 2006, 339–370.

Bardill, J. (2017). 'The Date, Dedication, and Design of Sts. Sergius and Bacchus in Constantinople,' *Journal of Late Antiquity* 10, 62–130.

Barkhuizen, H.J. (1995). 'On Earthquakes and Fires,' *JÖByz* 45, 1–18.

Beaton, R. & Roueché, C. (eds.) (1993). *The Making of Byzantine History. Studies Dedicated to Donald M. Nicol on his Seventieth Birthday*, Aldershot.

Begass, Ch. (2018). *Die Senatsaristokratie des oströmischen Reiches, ca. 457–518*, Munich.

Berger, A. (trans.) (2013). *Accounts of Medieval Constantinople: The Patria*, Cambridge, MA.

Boschung, D., Danner, M. & Radtki, C. (eds.) (2015). *Politische Fragmentierung und kulturelle Kohärenz in der Spätantike*, Paderborn.

Bowden, W., Gutteridge, A. & Machado, C. (eds.) (2006). *Social and Political Life in Late Antiquity*, Leiden.

Brubaker, L. (2002). 'The Vienna Dioskorides and Anicia Juliana,' in Littlewood 2002, 189–214.

Canepa, M.P. (2006). 'The Late Antique *Kosmos* of Power: International Ornament and Royal Identity in the Sixth and Seventh Centuries,' *21st Annual Byzantine Studies Congress*, London, http://www.wra1th.plus.com/byzcong/paper/I/I.3_Canepa.pdf (last accessed August 8, 2022).

Cameron, Al. (1976). *Circus Factions: Blues and Greens at Rome and Byzantium*, Oxford.

Cameron, Av. (ed./trans.) (1976). *Flavius Cresconius Corippus: In laudem Iustini Augusti minoris libri IV*, London.

Caprizzi, C. (1968). 'Anicia Giuliana (462 ca. – 530 ca.). Ricerche sulla sua Famiglia e la sua Vita,' *RSBN* 5, 191–226.

Caprizzi, C. (1996). *Anicia Giuliana. La Comittente (c. 463 – c. 528)*, Milan.

Carile, A. (ed.) (2004). *La Persia e Bisanzio. Convegno internationale (Roma 14–18 ottobre 2002)*, Rome.

Carpenter, M. (trans.) (1973). *Kontakia of Romanos, Byzantine Melodist; vol. 2: On Christian Life*, Columbia.

Catafygiotou-Topping, E. (1978). 'On Earthquakes and Fires: Romanos' Encomium to Justinian,' *ByzZ* 71, 22–35.

Cattin, G. (ed.) (1991). *Da Bisanzio a San Marco: Musica e liturgia*, Bologna.

Connor, C. L. (1999). 'The Epigram in the Church of Hagios Polyeuktos in Constantinople and its Byzantine Response,' *Byzantion* 69, 479–527.

Croke, B. (2006). 'Justinian, Theodora, and the Church of Saints Sergius and Bachus,' *DOP* 60, 25–63.

Croke, B. (2007). 'Justinian under Justin. Reconfiguring a Reign,' *ByzZ* 100,1, 13–56.

Dagron, G. (1984). *Constantinople imaginaire. Études sur le recueil des Patria*, Paris.

Dagron, G. (2003). *Emperor and Priest*, Cambridge.

Deliyannis, D.M. (2015). 'Church-Building in Rhetoric and Reality in the 5th–7th Centuries,' in Boschung et al. 2015, 159–182.

Dirschlmayer, M. (2015). *Kirchenstiftungen römischer Kaiserinnen vom 4. bis zum 6. Jahrhundert – die Erschließung neuer Handlungsspielräume*, Münster.

Effenberger, A. (2019). '"Sasanidischer" Baudekor in Byzanz? – Der Fall der Polyeuktoskirche in Konstantinopel,' in Asutay-Effenberger/Daim 2019, 155–193.

Follieri, E. (1991). 'L'innografia bizantina dal contacio al canone,' in Cattin 1991, 1–32.

Fowden, G. (1994). 'Constantine, Silvester and the Church of S. Polyeuctus in Constantinople,' *JRA* 7, 274–284.

Friedländer, P. (1912). *Johannes v. Gaza und Paulus Silentiarius*, Leipzig.

Greatrex, G.B. (1997). 'The Nika Riot: A Reappraisal,' *JHS* 117, 60–86.

Grosdidier de Matons, J. (1964–1981). *Romanos le Melode, Hymnes* (5 vols.), Paris.

Grosdidier de Matons, J. (1974). *Romanos le Melode et les origins de la poésie réligieuse à Byzanze*, Paris.
Harrison, M. (1984). 'The Church of St. Polyeuktos in Istanbul and the Temple of Solomon,' in Mango 1984, 276–279.
Harrison, M. (ed.) (1986). *Excavations at Saraçhane in Istanbul; vol. 1: The Excavations, Structures, Architectural Decoration, Small Finds, Coins, Bones, and Molluscs*, Princeton.
Harrison, M. (1990). *Ein Tempel für Byzanz. Die Entdeckung und Ausgrabung von Anicia Julianas Palastkirche in Istanbul*, Stuttgart.
Hunger, H. (1984). 'Romanos Melodos, Dichter, Prediger, Rhetor – und sein Publikum,' *JÖByz* 34, 15–42.
James, L. (2007a). '"And Shall these Mute Stones Speak?". Text as Art,' in James 2007b, 188–206.
James, L. (ed.) (2007b). *Art and Text in Byzantine Culture*, Cambridge.
Johnson, S.F. (ed.) (2006). *Greek Literature in Late Antiquity: Dynamism – Didacticism – Classicism*, Aldershot.
Kazhdan, A. (1991). s.v. 'Patria of Constantinople,' in *Oxford Dictionary of Byzantium* 3, 1598.
Kiilerich, B. (2001). 'The Image of Anicia Juliana in the Vienna Dioscurides: Flattery or Appropriation of Imperial Imagery?,' *SO* 76, 169–190.
Klein, K. (2019). 'Zur spätantiken Kaiserin als Stifterin,' *Plekos* 21, 87–115.
Koder, J. (1994). 'Justinians Sieg über Salomon,' in Mpratziōtē 1994, 135–142.
Koder, J. (1999). 'Romanos Melodos und sein Publikum. Zur Einbeziehung und Beeinflussung der Zuhörer durch das Kontakion,' *AAWW* 134, 63–94.
Koder, J. (trans.) (2005). *Romanos Melodos. Die Hymnen* (2 vols.), Stuttgart.
Koder, J. (2008[2010]). 'Imperial Propaganda in the Kontakia of Romanos the Melode,' *DOP* 62, 275–291.
Krautheimer, R. (1974). 'Again Saints Sergius and Bacchus at Constantinople,' *JÖByz* 23, 251–253.
Külzer, A. (2000). 'Konstantinopel in der apokalyptischen Literatur der Byzantiner,' *JÖByz* 50, 51–76.
Leppin, H. (2011). *Justinian. Das christliche Experiment*, Stuttgart.
Lidov, A.M. (ed.) (2006). *Ierotopija: The Creation of Sacred Spaces in Byzantium and Medieval Russia*, Moscow.
Littlewood, A.R. (ed.) (2002). *Byzantine Garden Culture*, Washington.
Maas, P. (1906). 'Die Chronologie der Hymnen des Romanos,' *ByzZ* 15, 1–44.
Macrides, R. & Magdalino, P. (1988). 'The Architecture of Ekphrasis: Construction and Context of Paul the Silentiary's Poem on Hagia Sophia,' *Byzantine and Modern Greek Studies* 12, 47–82.
Magdalino, P. (1987). 'Observations on the Nea Ekklesia of Basil I,' *JÖByz* 37, 51–64.
Magdalino, P. (1993). 'The History of the Future and its Uses: Prophecy, Policy and Propaganda,' in Beaton/Roueché 1993, 3–34.
Magdalino, P. (ed.) (1994). *New Constantines*, Aldershot.
Magdalino, P. (2011). 'Aristocratic Oikoi in the Tenth and Eleventh Regions of Constantinople,' in Necipoğlu 2011, 53–69.
Magdalino P. & Nelson, R. (eds.) (2010). *The Old Testament in Byzantium*, Washington.
Mango, C. (1972). 'The Church of Saints Sergius and Bacchus at Constantinople and the Alleged Traditions of Octagonal Palatine Churches,' *JÖByz* 21, 189–193.
Mango, C. (1975). 'The Church of Sts. Sergius and Bacchus Once Again,' *ByzZ* 68, 385–392.
Mango, C. (ed.) (1984). *Okeanos: Essays Presented to Ihor Ševčenko on his 60th Birthday by his Colleagues and Students*, Cambridge, MA.
Mango, C. & Ševčenko, I. (1961). 'Remains of the Church of St. Polyeuktos at Constantinople,' *DOP* 15, 243–247.
Mazal, O. (ed.) (1998/1999). *Der Wiener Dioskurides* (2 vols.), Graz.

Meier, M. (2003a). *Das andere Zeitalter Justinians. Kontingenzerfahrung und Kontingenzbewältigung im 6. Jh. n. Chr.*, Göttingen.
Meier, M. (2003b). 'Die Inszenierung einer Katastrophe: Justinian und der Nika-Aufstand,' *ZPE* 142, 273–300.
Meier, M. (2007). 'Σταυροθεὶς δι' ἡμᾶς – Der Aufstand gegen Anastasios im Jahr 512,' *Millennium* 4, 157–237.
Milner, C. (1994). 'The Image of the Rightful Ruler: Anicia Juliana's Constantine Mosaic in the Church of Hagios Polyeuktos,' in Magdalino 1994, 73–81.
Mitsakis, K. (1971). *Byzantine Hymnographia*, Thessaloniki.
Mpratziōtē, L. (ed.) (1994). *Thymiama stē mnēmē tēs Laskarinas Mpura 1*, Athens.
Necipoğlu, N. (ed.) (2011). *Byzantine Constantinople. Monuments, Topography and Everyday Life*, Leiden.
Neubauer, A. (1895). *Medieval Jewish Chronicles* (vol. 2), Oxford.
Nickau, K. (2002). 'Justinian und der Nika-Aufstand bei Romanos dem Meloden. Zum Kontakion 54 M.-Tr. (=54 Gr.),' *ByzZ* 95, 603–620.
Ousterhout, R. (1990). 'The Temple, the Sepulchre, and the Martyrdom of the Savior,' *Gesta* 29, 44–53.
Shahid, I. (2006). 'Sacred Geographies and Holy Cities: Constantinople as Jerusalem,' in Lidov 2006, 98–116.
Shahid, I. (2010). 'New Tempels and New Solomons: The Rhetoric of Byzantine Architecture,' in Magdalino/Nelson 2010, 223–253.
Shahid, I. (2012). 'The Sanctity of Place and the Sanctity of Buildings: Jerusalem versus Constantinople,' in Wescoat 2012, 281–306.
Palmer, A. (1988). 'The Inauguration Anthem of Hagia Sophia in Edessa,' *BMGS* 12, 117–167.
Papalexandrou, A. (2001). 'Text in Context: Eloquent Monuments and the Byzantine Beholder,' *Word and Image* 17, 259–283.
Pfeilschifter, R. (2013). *Der Kaiser und Konstantinopel. Kommunikation und Konfliktaustrag in einer spätantiken Metropole*, Berlin.
Pizzone, A.M.V. (2003). 'Da Melitene a Costantinopoli: S. Polieucto nella politica dinastica di Giuliana Anicia. Alcune osservazioni in margine ad A. P. I 10,' *Maia* 55, 107–132.
Pohlmann, K.-F. (1996/2001). *Der Prophet Hesekiel/Ezechiel* (2 vols.), Göttingen.
Preger, T. (ed.) (1901/1907). *Scriptores originum Constantinopolitanarum* (2 vols.), Leipzig.
Preger, T. (1901a). 'Die Erzählung vom Bau der Hagis Sophia,' *ByzZ* 10, 455–476.
Prinzing, G. (1986). 'Das Bild Justinians I. in der späteren Überlieferung der Byzantiner vom 7. bis 15. Jahrhundert,' in Simon 1986, 1–99.
Rapp, C. (2010). 'Old Testament Models for Emperors in Early Byzantium,' in Magdalino/Nelson 2010, 175–197.
Russo, E. (2004). 'La scultura di S. Polieucto e la presenza della Persia nella cultura artistica di Costantinopoli nel VI secolo,' in Carile 2004, 737–862.
Salzmann, M. (1924). *The Chronicle of Ahimaaz*, New York.
Scheja, G. (1963). 'Hagia Sophia und Templum Salomonis,' *Istanbuler Mitteilungen* 12, 44–58.
Schilbach, E. (1970). *Byzantinische Metrologie*, Munich.
Shahid, I. (2003). 'The Church of Sts. Sergios and Bakhos in Constantinople: Some New Perspectives,' in Abramea et al. 2003, 467–480.
Shahid, I. (2004). 'The Church of Hagios Polyeuktos in Constantinople: Some New Observations,' *Graeco-Arabica* 9–10, 343–355.
Silvano, L. (2004). 'Echi di propaganda giustinianea in un contacio di Romano il Melodo (no 54 Maas-Trypanis),' *Porphyra* 3, 107–120.
Simon, D. (ed.) (1986). *Fontes Minores 7*, Frankfurt.
Smith, C. (1989). 'Christian Rhetoric in Eusebius' Panegyric at Tyre,' *VChr* 43, 226–247.

Speck, P. (1991). 'Juliana Anicia, Konstantin der Große und die Polyeuktoskirche in Konstantinopel,' *Varia* 3, 133–147.
Trypanis, C.A. (1968). *Fourteen Early Byzantine Cantica*, Vienna.
Wescoat, B.D. (ed.) (2012). *Architecture of the Sacred*, Cambridge.
Whitby, M. (2003). 'The Vocabulary of Praise in Verse-Celebrations of 6th-Century Building Achievements: AP 2.398–406, AP 9.656, AP 1.10, and Paul the Silentiary's Description of St Sophia,' in Accorinti/Vian 2003, 593–606.
Whitby, M. (2006). 'The St. Polyeuktos Epigram (AP 1.10): A literary Perspective,' in Johnson 2006, 159–188.
Wilkinson, J. (1982). 'Paulinus' Temple at Tyre,' *JÖByz* 32, 553–561.

Jan-Markus Kötter
Palestine at the Periphery of Ecclesiastical Politics? The Bishops of Jerusalem after the Council of Chalcedon

Chalcedon 451: Ambition and Challenge

The Council of Chalcedon in 451 awarded ecclesiastical jurisdiction over the three provinces of Palestine to the church of Jerusalem. Insofar as Jerusalem hereby was invested with supra-metropolitan prerogatives, it became what later (and perhaps also already at the time, although this question does not interest us here) would be called a 'patriarchate'.[1] The patriarchal rights may have had primarily internal significance – namely, superior jurisdiction in Palestine –, but Jerusalem's elevation was at least implicitly tied to an ambition directed outwards as well, namely to the ambition of taking a leading role within the network of churches in the late-antique Roman Empire. Such a role, however, was by no means ensured by the simple conferral of higher ecclesiastical rank *per se*. It depended rather on how other players received it; hence, on whether they recognized Jerusalem's claims as legitimate or not. The council of 451 thus did not guarantee the greater significance of Jerusalem in the empire-wide Church, but at most provided a basis for it. The new status of the church of Jerusalem first had to prove its effectiveness in contemporary conditions.[2]

Recognition of Jerusalem's central ecclesiastical role was under threat from the beginning because the great churches of the empire had by no means worked out among themselves what factors legitimated such a role. Neither of the two fundamental positions in this respect – the analogy of governmental and ecclesiastical structures advocated by Constantinople and the Roman concept of a canonically sanctioned apostolic succession – necessarily saw Jerusalem as one of the central churches of the Roman Empire. It was no coincidence that the church of the Holy

---

[1] The origins of the title 'patriarch' are obscure. It was used more frequently after Chalcedon but became standard only in the sixth century. It shall nonetheless be used in this chapter, since all of the five major (and thus: 'patriarchal') churches had received supra-metropolitan prerogatives by 451 at the latest. On the concept: Chabanne/Chevailler 1984, 723–724; Gahbauer 1993, 51–58; Hall 2000, 731–732; Norton 2007, 141–144. On Jerusalem's elevation in 451: Evagr. *HE* 2,18 [p. 92,10–14].

[2] Ranks were not established by conciliar decree *per se*, but rather by agreement among ecclesiastical protagonists regarding the reception, acceptance, or rejection of hierarchical claims. Thus, the Council of Chalcedon was not the end of the process of the hierarchical development of the Church, but only the beginning. On the social theory of a transactional development of structures, which emphasizes reciprocity in the relationship of structures and actors: Coleman 1994, 1–23.

Land did not break into the ranks of the patriarchates until 451: since Jerusalem was not a provincial capital, the local church could not benefit from drawing analogies between the secular and ecclesiastical administration, but rather had long been at odds with the church of its own provincial capital Caesarea. When the Council of Nicaea first affirmed the superior ecclesiastical rights of Rome, Alexandria, and Antioch in 325 (with Rome in particular subsequently citing this tradition with ever more emphasis), there had been no room for Jerusalem. The somewhat unspecified honorary precedence that Jerusalem should have had according to the Council of Nicaea could not be converted into specific rights. However, it did show that the city could not be ignored completely in the development of ecclesiastical hierarchies.[3]

Despite this, by 451 developments had not yet reached a point where Jerusalem's new status could be welcomed warmly across the empire. Bishop Leo of Rome had reservations about the hierarchical measures of Chalcedon, since these also benefited Rome's main rival, Constantinople. Likewise, many in Alexandria refused to recognize the council at all. Since the good will of Constantinople and the emperor had been bought at Chalcedon with dogmatic concessions by Juvenal, the bishop of Jerusalem, a continued good will of the capital could not be counted on. And since Jerusalem's elevation ultimately came at the expense of a weakened Antioch, we should also presume reservations from this quarter as well.[4] Jerusalem was thus initially faced with the challenge of living up to its new role. With respect to the internal implementation of higher jurisdiction of the bishop of Jerusalem, this was unproblematic. Indeed, as early as 451, Bishop Juvenal faced a Palestinian rebellion, but it grew from the ranks of the monks. The ecclesiastical hierarchy of Palestine aligned itself with Jerusalem at an early date: indeed, the rebellion actually contributed towards this alignment when its leader, Theodosius, put himself in Juvenal's place and by intervening in episcopal investiture used his office to reshape the ecclesiastical hierarchy of the region.[5]

---

3 Canon 7 of Nicaea (325) [COD, p. 8,25–31]: Ἐπειδὴ συνήθεια κεκράτηκε καὶ παράδοσις ἀρχαία, ὥστε τὸν ἐν Αἰλίᾳ ἐπίσκοπον τιμᾶσθαι, ἐχέτω τὴν ἀκολουθίαν τῆς τιμῆς, τῇ μητροπόλει σῳζομένου τοῦ οἰκείου ἀξιώματος. On the development to the Chalcedonian period, Kötter 2013, 85–86, 90.

4 On the reception of the Council of Chalcedon: Brennecke 1998, 24–53; Grillmeier 1991. Despite its age, the collection of essays edited by Heinrich Bacht and Alois Grillmeier on the Council of 451 remains noteworthy: Bacht/Grillmeier 1953.

5 The rebellion was genuinely motivated by matters of doctrine, as a letter of Marcian to the monks of Sinai shows: ACO II.1,3, 131–132. For overviews of the revolt: ACO II.1,3, 131–132; Evagr. *HE* 2,5; Zach. *HE* 3,3; Theoph. AM 5945 [452/3, p. 107,6–27]. Cf. Grillmeier 1991, 113–120; Heyer 1984, 70–73; Honigmann 1950, 247–254; Klein 2018a, 172–4; Klein 2018b, 254–260; Leuenberger-Wenger 2019, 398–400; Perrone 1980, 88–103; Solzbacher 1989, 184–197. The monks, who were not part of the ecclesiastical hierarchy, played an especially important role for the patriarchs of Jerusalem. Cf. Chitty 1966, 110; Grillmeier 2004, 45–47; Heyer 1984, 57; Leuenberger-Wenger 2019, 523–525; Perrone 1998b *passim*.

Jerusalem's jurisdiction in Palestine itself was thereby recognized by all parties across the doctrinal spectrum.[6]

It remained to be seen whether the new patriarchate could also assert itself externally in the world of ecclesiastical 'superpowers'. How great a contribution would Jerusalem be permitted to make to contemporary controversies? How important were the positions taken by the Holy City to other players? And how pronounced was its bishops' interest in getting involved beyond their own jurisdiction? More specifically: could Jerusalem maintain its internal autonomy against external encroachments, and could it in turn influence events outside its own territory? Since individual late-antique churches structurally lacked means of enforcement to secure their interests in the face of resistance without relying on the imperial court, the players in the imperial capital at Constantinople intrinsically had an important part in these questions of autonomy and influence.[7]

This connection is particularly clear in the case of the other great churches: internal divisions in Antioch after Chalcedon again and again gave the capital the opportunity to intervene in the internal ecclesiastical affairs of Syria and to strengthen friendly bishops against their opponents. In Alexandria, by contrast, similar intervention was possible only with great effort. At the latest under Emperor Anastasius, a factual freedom of the church of Egypt from imperial encroachment was no longer fundamentally questioned, whereby the church of Alexandria in turn sacrificed some of its influence on events outside of Egypt. And while the popes of Rome repeatedly attempted to exert influence in the East, it became increasingly clear to them that their real power outside Italy depended on either the *a priori* acceptance of their claims by their addressees or on enforcement by the eastern Roman emperors. Simultaneously, the political disintegration of the empire ensured that Constantinople could no longer directly influence the Roman church, the independence of which was thus comparatively secure.[8]

Jerusalem's elevation thus awaited confirmation by subsequent events. These events will be examined below up to the year 518, that is, the point in time where the death of Emperor Anastasius led to an important reversal of the doctrinal position of imperial-ecclesiastical policy. The period under consideration here – especially the later reign of Anastasius – is well-documented compared to the otherwise quite scanty historical record of the ecclesiastical engagement of the bishops of Jeru-

---

[6] The situation in Palestine was fundamentally different from that in, e.g., Rome, where Chalcedonian doctrine was undisputed but the hierarchical measures of the council – particularly the so-called 'canon 28' – were not recognized.
[7] This interplay of ecclesiastical players and the monarchy as enforcer is the functional core of the late-antique 'Reichskirche'. Cf. Kötter 2014b, 3–8.
[8] On the early reception of the Council of Chalcedon and on the situation of the five patriarchates at this early stage: Kötter 2013, 47–55, 69–90.

salem.⁹ Building on a chronological survey of the events, this chapter will focus on the categories of internal autonomy from encroachment and of influence on external developments. By this, some light should be shed on the consolidation phase of the patriarchate of Jerusalem.

Jerusalem and the Reception of Chalcedon: A History of Events

Juvenal of Jerusalem paid a high price for his success at Chalcedon. Although at the so-called 'Robber Council' of Ephesus in 449 he had stood with Bishop Dioscorus of Alexandria in support of the radical Miaphysite theology of the Constantinopolitan archimandrite Eutyches, he changed sides two years later and accepted the formula proposed in Chalcedon that Christ was one person ἐν δύο φύσεσιν. As a reward, he was given jurisdiction over the three Palestines.[10]

Immediately after the council, it emerged that many of his former adherents were not at all prepared to treat their own dogmatic positions with similar flexibility. Monks in particular, under the leadership of Theodosius, were outraged by the adoption of what was in their eyes a Nestorian creed and by their own bishop's approval of it. Upon returning from Chalcedon, Juvenal was immediately called upon to recant, which he refused to do, intimating that he had merely carried out the emperor's will. While Juvenal fled and took refuge in Constantinople, the rebels elevated their leader Theodosius to be the bishop of Jerusalem and immediately set about reshaping the hierarchy of Palestine in accordance with their positions.[11] Not until Emperor Marcian systematically intervened on behalf of *his* council in 454 was the rebellion

---

[9] The following documents survive: a *synodikon* of Bishop Martyrius of Jerusalem to Bishop Peter Mongus of Alexandria [Zach. HE 5,12]; the text of the so-called *Palestinian Union* [Zach. HE 5,6]; a letter of Palestinian monks to Bishop Alcison of Nicopolis [Evagr. HE 3,31;33]; a letter of the archimandrites Sabas and Theodosius to Emperor Anastasius [Cyr. Scyth. VS 57]. Narrative sources are limited primarily to the monks' lives of Cyril of Scythopolis. On these, see Trampedach 2005, 285–292.
[10] Zach. HE 3,3 clearly makes this connection. Juvenal's support of the Chalcedonian *ekthesis* [ACO II.1,2, 128–130] was not insignificant: the bishop of Jerusalem was important already simply because of his seniority – he had been bishop since 422: Honigmann 1950, 237. For the promotion of Jerusalem in Chalcedon cf. Leuenberger-Wenger 2019, 66; 312–314.
[11] Juvenal retorted to the rebels that opposition to himself, who supported the resolutions of the imperial council, was opposition to Emperor Marcian: Zach. HE 3,5 [p. 109,17–22]. On the implication for the freshly acquired status of the patriarchate: Klein 2018b, 257. The monks obviously preferred a monastic form of Christological mysticism that had more in common with a Miaphysite theology than the Chalcedonian theology of separate natures: Solzbacher 1989, 185. Incidentally, it was precisely because of the disruptions resulting from the impossibility of regulating among different groups of monks that Chalcedon had canonically placed the ecclesiastic hierarchy over the monastic hierarchy, cf. Wipszycka 2018 *passim*. On the sources and scholarship on the rebellion: n. 5.

put down: Juvenal returned, and Theodosius fled.[12] Thanks to imperial support, Juvenal's position within his church was now relatively secure, but a comprehensive reconciliation apparently did not occur. It seems that hold-outs among the monks maintained anti-Chalcedonian positions for a long time. However, in Palestine, in contrast to Egypt and Syria, this did not result in inextricable tensions that might have destabilized the region over the long term. The peculiar composition of Palestinian monastic groups, which were recruited primarily from outside the region and thus were less capable of mobilizing and influencing the faithful of Palestine, as well as shared concern for the sacred sites, which transcended doctrinal controversy, made the conflict in the Holy Land take a less radical course than in neighboring regions.[13]

Nevertheless, a critical attitude toward Chalcedon within Palestine was not at all exclusively restricted to the monks. This emerged clearly in 475: the usurper Basiliscus had driven Emperor Zeno from Constantinople and in his search for supporters of his policy he relied on those who had consistently opposed the council of 451. Basiliscus therefore not only recalled the Egyptian leader of the Miaphysites, Timotheus Aelurus, from exile, but also scrapped the Council of Chalcedon in an *enkyklion*.[14] Anastasius of Jerusalem, the successor of the deceased Juvenal, approved this document and was by no means the only one. Yet when uprisings in Constantinople forced Basiliscus to annul the *enkyklion* in an *antenkyklion*, nothing is known of the approval of this second document by Anastasius. When Zeno again steered a Chalcedonian course after Basiliscus' fall in 476 and hordes of bishops hastened to excuse their prior acceptance of the *enkyklion* before Patriarch Acacius of Constantinople, it was Anastasius who refused to do so, as Zacharias Rhetor stresses.[15]

Anastasius, under whom internal tensions in Palestine had apparently continued to fester, died early in 478. His successor Martyrius successfully reconciled the hostile parties in the same year. The so-called *Palestinian Union* simply avoided taking a

---

12 Marcian's crucial part in the suppression of the rebellion is indicated in a synodal letter of Juvenal [ACO II.5, 9,1–29] and a letter of thanks written by Pope Leo [Leo M. *Ep.* 126 (ACO II.4, 81,31–82,13)].
13 Cf. Kennedy 2000, 601; Leuenberger-Wenger 2019, 401–402; Moss 2016; 68–69; Perrone 1998a, 15–16, 20–21; Roldanus 1998, 128; Solzbacher 1989, 196–197; Winkelmann 1980, 98–99. Furthermore, the Council of Chalcedon was less discredited in Palestine than in Egypt, where it was associated with a hierarchical defeat on account of the deposition of their regional leader, Dioscorus of Alexandria.
14 Cf. Cod. Vat. gr. 1431,73 [p. 49,1–51,30]; Evagr. *HE* 3,4; Zach. *HE* 5,2. On the origins, content, and transmission of the *enkyklion*: Blaudeau 2003, 156–163. The sources usually indicate that Basiliscus was influenced by Timotheus Aelurus.
15 Zach. *HE* 5,5. Cf. also: Simplic. *Ep. ad Acac.*, 121,25–30. The *antenkyklion*: Cod. Vat. gr. 1431,74 [p. 52,1–20]; Evagr. *HE* 3,7. Anastasius would have benefited from the new doctrinal development in the event that a new ecumenical council, being pushed by Aelurus, was about to be convened in Jerusalem. Patrich 1995, 301 explains that only the bishop's advanced age protected him from persecution after Zeno's imperial and Chalcedonian restoration. According to Fedalto 1988, 1001, Anastasius died in January 478. In contrast to other players, the bishop had not even been condemned by a synod, while simple metropolitan bishops, like Paul of Ephesus, were indeed punished.

clear position regarding the controversial Council of Chalcedon: while the councils of Nicaea, Constantinople, and Ephesus I are explicitly accepted, the same is not true of the synod of 451, although it is not explicitly condemned.[16] Keeping quiet about the crucial, controversial point proved to be a viable way for leaders in Palestine to acknowledge shared ecclesiastical convictions while putting an end to the disputes over Chalcedon. Therefore, the *Union* became the direct model for a famous edict of Emperor Zeno: with the *Henotikon* of 482, Zeno hoped to achieve church unity between the moderate Chalcedonian Acacius of Constantinople and the moderate anti-Chalcedonian Peter Mongus of Alexandria. Just like the *Union*, the *Henotikon* explicitly only recognized the councils of 325, 381, and 431, but avoided at the same time explicit condemnation of Chalcedon. Instead, it mentioned an anathema of Nestorius and Eutyches, which was already accepted by all sides.[17] Since this document actually succeeded in producing a settlement between Constantinople and Alexandria, Zeno soon extended the validity of the edict: on this basis, broad ecclesiastical unity was quickly achieved in the eastern empire.[18]

While the *Henotikon* soon encountered resistance in the conflict-ridden areas of Egypt and Syria – the disputes over Chalcedon had played out here much more rigidly than in Palestine, which destroyed an overall willingness of many of those involved to compromise – Martyrius of Jerusalem had no difficulty approving the edict. Since it traced its origin directly back to the *Palestinian Union*, it did not lead to tensions in Palestine. On the contrary, the ecclesiastical unity of the *Henoti-*

---

16 The *Union* is transmitted only in Zach. *HE* 5,6 [Vol. 1, 153,14–154,8]: *Quisquis ergo huic fidei definitioni cccxviii patrum nostrorum sanctorum episcoporum qui Nicaeae congregati sunt contraria sentit, quam secuti sunt et confirmaverunt cuique adsensi sunt et cl episcopi qui in urbe regia convenerunt fideles et veri, et synodus quae Ephesi habita est, aut sensit aut docuit, anathema sit, si aliam doctrinam vel disciplinam habet quae in variis locis facta est, sive Arimini sive Sardicae sive Chalcedone* […] [vol. 1, 153,25–31]. That the *Union* became the model for the *Henotikon* [cf. n. 17] is undisputed. Cf. Frend 1972, 174–175; Grillmeier 1991, 284; Perrone 1998b, 88; Winkelmann 1980, 98–99.
17 Cod. Vat. gr. 1431,75 [p. 52,21–54,21]; Evagr. *HE* 3,14. Liberat. 17, 113–117 gives a Latin translation, Zach. *HE* 5,8 a slightly abridged Syrian version. The controversial concluding sentence, which does not condemn Chalcedon but relativizes it, derives almost verbatim from the *Palestinian Union* (cf. n. 16): πάντα δὲ τὸν ἕτερόν τι φρονήσαντα ἢ φρονοῦντα ἢ νῦν ἢ πώποτε ἢ ἐν Χαλκηδόνι ἢ ἐν οἱαιδήποτε συνόδωι ἀναθεματίζομεν […]. On the *Henotikon* and its significance for imperial ecclesiastical politics: Blaudeau 2006, 206–231; Blaudeau 2007, 77; Brennecke 1998, 43–47; Frend 1972, 174–183; Gray 1979, 28–34; Grillmeier 1991, 285–290; Kinzig 2016, 629–630; Kötter 2013, 61–68; Maraval 2001, 133–135; Meier 2009, 46–51; Ritter 1982, 273–274. The anathematization of both Eutyches and Nestorius illustrates how the document, much like Chalcedon itself, was intended to serve as a *via media* between the two poles of the doctrinal controversy. This was hardly perceived, however, in the subsequent elaboration of the theological developments and the general tendency towards theological prejudice. Cf. Kötter 2011, 53; Kötter 2014a, 167.
18 Martyrius of Jerusalem [letter of Martyrius to Peter Mongus: Zach. *HE* 5,12] and Peter Knapheus of Antioch soon approved the *Henotikon*; Zach. *HE* 6,1 explicitly refers to this church unity. Although the popes in Rome did not join the compromise, ecclesiastical unity in the very part of the empire over which the emperor actually had control was achieved.

kon stabilized conditions in Palestine, which were laid on a quite similar foundation of reconciliation. Accordingly, Martyrius' successor Sallustius even actively defended the compromise against Bishop Euphemius of Constantinople, whose contacts to the church of Rome threatened the ecclesiastical unity achieved by the *Henotikon*, which cannot have been in Jerusalem's interest. Together with the bishop of Alexandria, Sallustius passed on to the new emperor, Anastasius, a letter from Euphemius to Rome and thus brought him under suspicion of political-doctrinal disloyalty.[19]

It nonetheless soon appeared that neither the Palestinian settlement nor the empire-wide compromise of the *Henotikon* were particularly stable. Emperor Anastasius held Zeno's course and even systematically expanded his conciliatory policy: the *Henotikon* ought no longer to serve only as a stopgap to open controversy, but as a common basis on which the disputing parties could positively agree despite their differences over Chalcedon.[20] But hardliners in both doctrinal camps increasingly expressed criticism of the document, which according to their respective positions did not go far enough in rejecting Chalcedon or in embracing it.[21] Anastasius' own frequent interventions in ecclesiastical politics bear some responsibility for the hardening of these fronts until his death in 518. And the church of Palestine appears as a dynamic factor in this process, too, as it developed more and more into the real defender of Chalcedon in the East. In 492, under the supporter of the *Henotikon*, Sallustius, the distinctly Chalcedonian Theodosius and Sabas were appointed archimandrites of the monks of Palestine. Just two years later the two monks found an ally in the like-minded Elias, who was appointed bishop of Jerusalem after the death of Sallustius.[22] Elias was a moderate Chalcedonian who approved the *Henotikon*, but he did not keep silent about Chalcedon: he wished to recognize the council explicitly for its condemnation of Nestorius and especially for the condemnation of Eutyches. The bishops Macedonius of Constantinople and Flavian of Antioch took a

---

19 Zach. *HE* 7,1. Nothing more is known about Sallustius.
20 Evagr. *HE* 3,30 [p. 125,32–126,8] reports that in the emperor's effort to restore peace in the Church, he neither publicly proclaimed nor condemned Chalcedon, but for the most part gave individual bishops free rein within the limits of the *Henotikon*.
21 The theological fronts actually grew further apart in the wake of the *Henotikon*: under Zeno, doctrinal differences were still relatively small, and the churches fairly evenly divided between Chalcedonians and anti-Chalcedonians. From 482, and particularly under Anastasius, the disintegrative effects of the document became ever more obvious. In addition to existing tensions, the interpretation of the *Henotikon* with respect to Chalcedon became a matter of dispute. Haacke 1953, 126–130 already observed this further differentiation of positions in the first part of Anastasius' reign. For the structural problems of the *Henotikon* cf. Kötter 2014a *passim*.
22 All three were students of Euthymius, who had supported the council during the rebellion of the Palestinian monks. Cf. Chitty 1966, 89–90. The archimandrites served as the link between the monks and the clergy. They were appointed by the bishop of Jerusalem; in the case of Sabas and Theodosius, this occurred under pressure from the monks [Cyr. Scyth. *VS* 30 (p. 114,23–26)]. On the role of the archimandrites: Bacht 1953, 296–299; Patrich 1995, 287–290; Rousseau 1997, 43–44. In particular on Sabas: Patrich 1995, 37–48, 287–299. It is impossible to say now whether these appointments led to the doctrinal reorientation in Palestine or are indicative of existing trends.

similar line.[23] When Emperor Anastasius took a new, more clearly anti-Chalcedonian stance in his religious policy after 507, the three bishops were ultimately deposed. Ironically, it was Elias who had been at least indirectly responsible for this, by breaking the compromise of the *Union* in 507 and permitting the Chalcedonian monk Nephalius to expel anti-Chalcedonian groups of monks from their monasteries in Palestine. A certain Severus set out for Constantinople in order to lead protests against this and soon became the emperor's most important theological advisor.[24]

While Severus now worked against the bishop of the imperial capital, Macedonius, Flavian in Syria came into conflict with Severus' partisan Philoxenus of Hierapolis, a conflict in which Elias also became embroiled. As the disputes within the different regions worsened and expanded, Macedonius finally fell in 511, and Flavian shared his fate just one year later.[25] Elias, however, was able to defend himself against his enemies' machinations. He relied on the support of Sabas and Theodosius: the former even campaigned for his bishop directly in the capital.[26] It was none other than Severus who succeeded Flavian as bishop of Antioch in 512. It comes as no surprise that Elias, who enjoyed the support of the Palestinian monks, refused to accept him into ecclesiastical communion and thus ultimately stood in the way of the emperor's goal of achieving renewed, comprehensive church unity in the East. Anastasius accordingly had great interest in forcing the bishop of Jerusalem to recognize Severus, which by no means prevented Elias from refusing the bishop of Antioch repeatedly.[27] Therefore, in 516 – or rather: finally, in 516 – Emperor

---

[23] On the collaboration of Macedonius, Flavian, and Elias: Cyr. Scyth. *VS* 50 [p. 140,18–24]. Cf. also Liberat. 18,128.

[24] Zach. *VS*, 102–103. According to the interpretation of the doctrinal reversal by Perrone 1980, 151–173, the banishment was its initial event. It remains an open question whether the presence of Severus in the capital gave impetus to the Miaphysite reorientation of Anastasius' religious policy or whether the stage had already been set for it, as argued particularly by Meier 2009, 241–247. Cf. further Dijkstra/Greatrex 2009, 233–234 and Moss 2016 *passim*, who points to the fact that there was occasional disagreement between Anastasius and Severus as well; after becoming bishop of Antioch, Severus had *nolens volens* to adapt a more conciliatory position vis-à-vis the dogmatic disputes of his time. Nevertheless, his positions were still not acceptable to his determined Chalcedonian opponents.

[25] A detailed account of the events surrounding the deposition of Macedonius is given by Zach. *HE* 7,8. Cf. Dijkstra/Greatrex 2009, 235–239. Elias and Flavian refused to recognize Macedonius' deposition but did not deny communion to his successor Timotheus: Evagr. *HE* 3, 33 [p. 132,19–22]. Cf. also Cyr. Scyth. *VS* 50 [p. 140,24–141,3]. Theoph. AM 6005 [512/3, 157, 25–30] criticizes this conduct. On the role of Severus in Macedonius' deposition: Frend 1979, 190–193. Flavian's deposition is described by Evagr. *HE* 3,32 and Zach. *HE* 7,10. Cf. also: Joh. Nik. 89,69–70; Theoph. AM 6004 [511/2, 156,9–19].

[26] Cyr. Scyth. *VS* 50–54 gives a detailed account of Sabas' diplomatic trip to Constantinople, where he personally interceded with the emperor on behalf of Elias and Chalcedon. Cf. Hay 1996, 120–121; Patrich 1995, 303–305, 311–313; Trampedach 2005, 279–284.

[27] Anastasius had, for instance, provided the deliverers of a *synodikon* from Severus to Palestine with a military escort. The envoys were nonetheless driven away by Sabas' and Theodosius' monks. Severus then turned to Anastasius and informed him of the incident. Cf. Evagr. *HE* 3,33; Cyr. Scyth. *VS* 56 [p. 148,22–149,6].

Anastasius had Elias deposed. In consideration of the bishop's conduct since 512, this must have required massive state intervention, which the emperor could afford only after putting down a fairly serious revolt in the Balkans.[28] Elias moreover appears to have lost the unconditional support of his monks, without whom he could not hold out against the growing imperial pressure.[29]

Elias' successor John would discover just how important Sabas and Theodosius were for the position and stance of the bishop of Jerusalem: John owed his office entirely to the fact that he had promised the emperor and his representatives in Palestine that he would enter into communion with Severus. Sabas and Theodosius, however, urged him to break his promise. But they were not yet prepared to defend the bishop against the political reaction to this step: John was imprisoned by the *dux Palaestinae* in order to compel him to recognize Severus after all. The two archimandrites, however, convinced the bishop in turn to feign acquiescence to this demand, whereupon John was released from custody. The planned ceremony at which he would express ecclesiastical unity with Severus was thwarted: Sabas and Theodosius gathered their followers together, appeared jointly with the bishop before the congregation of Jerusalem, placed Severus under anathema, and explicitly recognized Chalcedon. The surprised *dux Palaestinae* preferred to beat a hasty retreat to Caesarea.[30] Emperor Anastasius indignantly summoned Sabas and Theodosius (but not John!) to Constantinople. The two monks disobeyed this order, and instead sent the emperor a manifesto in which they threatened to spill their own blood rather than allow themselves to be forced into unity with heretics.[31] Anastasius had no choice but to take

---

28 The *comes foederatorum* Vitalian had, *inter alia* for doctrinal reasons, repeatedly marched on Constantinople. On Vitalian's rebellion: Malal. 16,16; Marc. Com. *a*.514–515; Zach. *HE* 7,13; Theoph. AM 6006 [513/4]. Cf. also: Meier 2007, 203–207; Meier 2009, 296–301.
29 At least Flavian of Antioch had repeatedly made concessions to his opponents, which can be traced in the sources. Corresponding information for Elias is lacking; that he had finally officially rejected the Council of Chalcedon, as Theoph. AM 6003 [510/1, 153,24–25] claims, is unlikely in light of subsequent developments: he still refused to enter into communion with Severus. But the confusion over an allegedly forged anathema of Elias against Chalcedon [Evagr. *HE* 3,31] at least suggests the bishop's engagement in support of the council was not always certain. Elias had perhaps made concessions that went too far in the eyes of his monks, which is why they distanced themselves from him. A passage of Zach. *HE* 7,10 might be interpreted to that effect: Elias supposedly responded to a letter of Severus'. Cf. Trampedach 2005, 273–276.
30 Cyr. Scyth. *VS* 56 [p. 150,8–152,12]. Cf. Bacht 1953, 285–286; Frend 1972, 151–153; Patrich 1995, 306–309. A nephew of Anastasius who was also present was able to escape the unpleasant situation by making a large donation of money. Bishop John may be regarded as one of the more or less 'lukewarm' supporters of the imperial dogmatic course, who Severus in Syria had tried to avoid (with good reason) promoting to higher ecclesiastical ranks: Van Nuffelen & Hilkens 2013, 565–569.
31 Cyr. Scyth. *VS* 57 [p. 155,11–13]: ζωῆς γὰρ καὶ θανάτου κειμένων ἐν τῶι περὶ πίστεως λόγωι ὁ θάνατος ἡμῖν ἐστιν προτιμότερος. The monks linked their orthodoxy with the immediate holiness of the tradition of the church of Palestine: [...] τὴν ἀληθῆ καὶ ἀφαντασίαστον ὁμολογίαν καὶ πίστιν ἄνωθεν καὶ ἐξ ἀρχῆς διὰ τῶν μακαρίων καὶ ἁγίων ἀποστόλων παραλαβόντες ἅπαντες οἱ τῆς ἁγίας γῆς ταύτης οἰκήτορες [...] ibid., 153,9–12]. On the text of the archimandrites: Trampedach 2005, 276–279.

their threat seriously. Since, on the one hand, its sacred sites gave Palestine great ideological significance for the entire empire and, on the other, it was unanimous in its rejection of Severus and therefore at least largely peaceful, the emperor acquiesced to events and left the region alone.[32] The Chalcedonians had prevailed in Palestine. Accordingly, it was a synod in Jerusalem in 518 that was among the first to confirm the new direction taken in the imperial ecclesiastical policy of Emperor Justin after Anastasius' death.[33]

The Autonomy of the Patriarchate of Jerusalem

A large part of the conflict-ridden dynamics of the development of the late-antique Church derived from the attempts of individual churches to intervene in the development of others and/or in the development of the doctrine and hierarchy of the imperial Church.[34] Since the rights of individual churches in their dealings with others throughout the empire were not fixed, but rather were based on experience and the degree to which they could be enforced, individual bishops tended to broaden their own scope for action by meddling in the internal affairs of other communities. Such testing of ecclesiastical power relations was likely to succeed only if it could count on secular enforcement to sanction it. To that extent, Jerusalem had to defend its autonomy in the hierarchical-doctrinal controversies of the post-Chalcedonian period not only against other churches, but especially against the imperial monarchy, whose authority made ecclesiastical intervention in the affairs of other churches possible in the first place.[35] Structurally, a patriarchate's ability to assert itself depended primarily on its relationship with the imperial capital. Already in 451, it was primarily Emperor Marcian's desire for unity that had rewarded Juvenal for changing sides at

---

32 Cf. Cyr. Scyth. *VS* 57 [p. 158,3–7], who, however, incorrectly explains the emperor's retreat as resulting from pressure imposed by Vitalian. Vitalian had actually been defeated by that point, the precondition for Anastasius being able to depose Elias at all. It had probably been intimated to the emperor that there would be a high number of casualties if he proceeded further on his path. Cf. Grillmeier 2004, 72–75.
33 The players in Jerusalem did not even wait for the emperor's command before taking such a step: Sabbait. 28; 30; Cyr. Scyth. *VS* 60 [p. 162,13–18]. Cf. Grillmeier 2002, 8–9; Heyer 1984, 82.
34 Kötter 2014b, 8–20.
35 On the principles behind imperial intervention: Bringmann 1998, 64–65; Ullmann 1976, esp. 1–9. The legal basis was the emperor's responsibility for *ius publicum*. Christian authorities did not have a consistent theory of their own with which to oppose him, and the New Testament's statements about the imperium [cf. Jn 18 36; Rom 13 1–7; Rev 18] are inconsistent. Cf. Meyendorff 1989, 29. It nonetheless seems that the segmented structure of the Church could not be transformed smoothly into an empire-wide organization, particularly since only a player outside the Church could grant this organization an empire-wide sanction. The voluntary subordination of individual bishops to others, on the other hand, could not be taken for granted and was difficult to enforce by purely ecclesiastical means. Enforcement from outside with imperial resources, however, frequently led to resistance. Cf. Kötter 2014b, 8–13.

the Council of Chalcedon with jurisdiction over the ecclesiastical provinces of Palestine. Juvenal himself knew very well to whom he owed his rank; he indicated it clearly to the rebellious monks in Palestine.[36] He likewise owed his reinstatement in 454 to Emperor Marcian. By fleeing to Constantinople, Juvenal himself had brought about the emperor's intervention in the internal affairs of Palestine, to his own advantage.

Marcian thereby demonstrated that individual emperors could theoretically reorder affairs in Palestine according to their own will at any time. The precondition for that was the will to do so: Marcian, for example, cannot have had any interest immediately after Chalcedon in directly calling his ecclesiastical efforts into question. He therefore directed all his energy towards reinstating Juvenal and expelling his rival bishop Theodosius.[37] That decisive imperial intervention in Palestine continued to be effective was demonstrated half a century later by Emperor Anastasius, who, in 516, succeeded in deposing Bishop Elias. But it is also clear in both Marcian's and Anastasius' case that it was by no means sufficient for the emperor merely to make his will known in order to countermand the will of the local players in Palestine. The events following the deposing of Elias, and the fact that this issue was addressed only after Anastasius had put down a rebellion in the Balkans, suggest that the emperor had to rely on considerable coercive force in 516 to remove Elias from office.[38]

Intervention in Palestine was costly, and therefore, authorities in Constantinople did not rush to resort to it. A glance at the situations in which emperors and their ecclesiastical allies avoided intervention makes this clear: above all, the fact that Bishop Anastasius of Jerusalem did not renounce the *Enkyklion* of Basiliscus of 475 is noteworthy in this context. But it is all the more remarkable that Emperor Zeno left him alone in this respect, despite his own decidedly Chalcedonian course after his restoration to office.[39] It is moreover striking that Elias' deposition in 516 took place a considerable time after that of his allies Macedonius in 511 and Flavian in 512. Lastly, we can confirm that after the final condemnation of Severus by Sabas, Theodosius, and John in 517, Emperor Anastasius was willing to punish the rebels, but in light of their explicitly expressed readiness for martyrdom he abandoned

---

[36] Cf. n. 11. It is hardly a coincidence that Juvenal fled to Constantinople.
[37] Emperor Marcian had already emphatically confirmed 'his' council in four decrees: ACO II.1,3, 119–124. He also interceded with Leo of Rome for the approval of the conciliar decrees, since the pope had refused to recognize the entire council on account of his rejection of 'canon 28'. Marcian informed Leo that the opponents of Chalcedon would exploit Leo's ambivalence to make a united front against the council: cf. ACO II.1,2, 61,7–16. As Chalcedon encountered increasing resistance in the East, Rome's explicit approval of its dogmatic content became ever more important.
[38] This also explains the late date of Elias' deposition (516) in comparison to those of his allies Macedonius (511) and Flavian (512). These coercive measures, however, proved to be ineffective against John of Jerusalem – or at least were not more effective than the intimidation by his monks.
[39] Paul of Ephesos and Peter Knapheus of Antioch were deposed, while the bishops of the diocese of Asia begged Acacius of Constantinople for forgiveness for their defection: Evagr. *HE* 3,8–9. Nothing like this is known for Anastasius of Jerusalem.

this plan relatively quickly. Although Palestine's resistance was one reason for the ultimate failure of Anastasius' religious policy, as will be shown below, the emperor was not prepared at this point to intervene decisively in the internal affairs of the church of Jerusalem and Palestine.[40]

There were various reasons for this repeated reluctance on the part of the emperors to involve themselves in Jerusalem. First of all, a comparison with other large episcopal sees in the empire shows that the effectiveness of imperial intervention in specific ecclesiastical regions was determined by geographical factors: the greater the distance between a region and the imperial centre Constantinople, the less likely (or at least the more costly) successful intervention became. For Constantinople, it was far easier to intervene in Antioch than in Alexandria or Jerusalem. The patriarchs of the Syrian metropolis in particular were especially dependent on imperial favor in the post-Chalcedonian period.[41] Furthermore, during the reign of Anastasius, the Syrian church exhibited a second characteristic that made intervention there easier, and easier to justify: doctrinal positions in the jurisdiction of Antioch were far more fragmented than in Jerusalem or Alexandria.[42] The emperors, in general, tended not to take action in ecclesiastical-political issues on their own initiative. Evagrius emphasizes a certain reluctance on the part of Anastasius, and this may have been intensified by the negative reception of Zeno's *Henotikon* in Rome, as the popes complained that the document lacked a sufficient ecclesiastical-institutional basis. It is thus no surprise that the measures of Anastasius' religious policy responded to initiatives and petitions from within the Church, making his ecclesiastical actions dependent on ecclesiastical impetus. That opened up more opportunities for intervention in the deeply divided region of Syria than in the doctrinally far more homogeneous (or at least quieter) Palestine. While Flavian of Antioch was undermined by his internal enemies in Syria, Elias of Jerusalem did not face such a threat to the same extent.

But it was not only that excuses for intervention in Palestine were lacking: the relative cohesion of Palestine also made intervention riskier and effective intervention more difficult. Thus, after 482, the emperors no longer attempted to take an active role in directing ecclesiastical relations in Alexandria, which was largely dominated by the Miaphysites. Likewise, in Palestine, success against the unified

---

40 This despite the fact that Sabas and Theodosius did not hold back harsh criticism in their letter to Anastasius [Cyr. Scyth. *VS* 57]. Anastasius' intervention may have seemed too costly precisely because of the monks' declared readiness for martyrdom and their reference to the holy sites.
41 Anastasius had been involved in all episcopal appointments in Constantinople and Antioch since his accession. The emperor had even actively approved Flavian's elevation, despite his later deposition: Theoph. AM 5991 [498/9, 142,9–12]. Imperial influence in the investiture of Severus is well known.
42 Both positions, Chalcedonian and anti-Chalcedonian, were widely held in Syria, both among monks and in the church hierarchy. Thus the bishops of Antioch were permanently dependent on imperial support. Cf. Kötter 2013, 87, 231–232, 243–245.

Chalcedonians after 507 at the latest could not be guaranteed even by the deployment of military coercion, all the more since such action would have endangered the holy sites. Anastasius briefly succeeded in reorganizing affairs in Palestine in 516; however, it is characteristic of the situation that the local monks around Sabas and Theodosius could put more pressure on the new bishop, John, than the imperial deputy, the *dux Palaestinae*, could. Thus, Jerusalem was able to demonstrate its independence of development under Anastasius: all by itself, this relatively small region successfully denied Severus ecclesiastical communion for the entire duration of his time in office.[43] For Emperor Anastasius and Severus structural reasons made it difficult and ultimately too risky to pursue their objectives in the Holy Land by force.

In all this, Jerusalem admittedly was hardly the highest priority in the emperors' ecclesiastical-political measures. Zeno had already demonstrated in 476 that the disobedience of the bishop of the Holy City might have to be accepted, when he failed to force Bishop Anastasius to approve his measures against Basiliscus. Also, with respect to Emperor Anastasius, there is no doubt that he *could* have brought about a change in Palestine by force. Sabas and Theodosius presumed as much when they declared themselves ready to die as martyrs before the prospect of such imperial intervention.[44] But Anastasius was not prepared to shed blood to force Jerusalem to support his policy. The ecclesiastical unity of the *really* key sees had ultimately been attained under Severus: Constantinople, Alexandria, and Antioch were in communion. The mere fact that Elias became the focus of imperial interest only long after Macedonius of Constantinople and Flavian of Antioch had been ousted supports this picture of the secondary importance of Palestine, as does the lack of clarity regarding the jurisdictions of Antioch and Jerusalem, still observable in the post-Chalcedonian period. Especially in the struggle of Severus' ally Philoxenus against Flavian of Antioch, the synods convened against Flavian were also directed against Elias; they thus were synods of the entire political *dioecesis Oriens*. It appears that the intent was to decide the cases of the two patriarchs together. The extent to which that challenged Jerusalem's autonomy, which had obtained its rank in 451 against the will of Antioch,[45] is illustrated by the fact that, as new bishop of Antioch, Severus attempted to force Elias of Jerusalem to enter into communion. The violent Chalcedonian reaction of Palestine to Severus' appointment as bishop of Antioch at least in part derived from a need to dissociate itself from its Syrian ecclesiastical rival.

---

43 The same is naturally also true of the bishops of Rome. Their case, however, is structurally different: since Rome was not directly under Anastasius' rule, he could not have forced it to accept Severus even if he wanted to.

44 Cf. n. 31.

45 Cf. Evagr. *HE* 2,4, who attempts to represent Antioch's loss of Palestine as a mutually agreed compromise. Juvenal had in fact claimed far greater territories for Jerusalem as early as 449: Honigmann 1950, 221–215, 224–227. Nonetheless, the measure can only be seen as a defeat for Antioch. Evagrius' assessment merely reflects his Antiochene perspective.

The Influence of the Patriarchate of Jerusalem

It is difficult to assess Jerusalem's influence on imperial-ecclesiastical developments because the bishops of Jerusalem, in contrast to their peers in Rome, Constantinople, or Alexandria, never claimed the power to make declarations binding to the entire Church.[46] Their demands instead always emerged from specific local and regional contexts, as in the case of the struggle against Anastasius, Severus, and Philoxenus.[47] Nonetheless, Jerusalem played its part in the development of the imperial Church after Chalcedon: the church of Jerusalem was decisively involved in the fundamental divisions with respect to the reception of Chalcedon. Juvenal's expulsion in 451, for example, was one of the factors that led to imperial-ecclesiastical approval of the Council of Chalcedon in the first place: Leo of Rome, in particular, had at first been reluctant to recognize the council on account of its hierarchical measures, which favored Constantinople. Not until Emperor Marcian impressed on him the necessity of at least professing the creed of Chalcedon in light of the anti-Chalcedonian uprisings in Egypt and Palestine was Leo ready to oblige; his support thus ensured the reception of the council despite initial resistance from many quarters.[48] Since endorsing Chalcedon meant the pope also lent his support to Juvenal, it was the very resistance that the new patriarch encountered in Palestine that ultimately led to the recognition of his new ecclesiastical role.

The next stage in the reception of Chalcedon was influenced by Jerusalem far more directly: Zeno's *Henotikon* had followed the example of the *Palestinian Union* of Martyrius of Jerusalem, which made the Palestinian church the direct inspiration for imperial-ecclesiastical policy. Hence, as long as the *Henotikon* was able to produce doctrinal compromise across the empire, it also stabilized the position of Jerusalem within the imperial Church.[49] Therefore, Bishop Sallustius was prepared to discredit Euphemius, his peer in Constantinople, when he distanced himself to an

---

46 Rome formulated claims of primacy that included the preeminence of the declarations of the popes. Therefore, the bishops of Rome had a far more immediate interest in the unity of the Church than the bishops of other major churches, who – even against outside intervention – relied much more heavily on ecclesiastical sectionalism.

47 In 511, Sabas petitioned the emperor on Elias' behalf not to give up the tenets of Chalcedon, but that hardly entailed a claim to general leadership in religious policy by Jerusalem. The request derived instead from Sabas' intercession on Elias' behalf in the specific situation: the monk had traveled to the court primarily to petition the emperor for leniency for Elias on account of his contact with Flavian of Antioch. For a detailed account of the delegation and Sabas' conversations with the emperor, see Cyr. Scyth. *VS* 50–54. Cf. Patrich 1995, 303–305, 311–313; Trampedach 2005, 279–284. Cf. n. 26.

48 For the letter of Emperor Marcian to Pope Leo: ACO II.1,2, 61,7–16. For Leo's acceptance (solely) of the doctrinal rulings of Chalcedon: Leo M. *Ep.* 114 [ACO II.4, 70,19–71,22]. The pope reveals categorically that it was only the threat from the opponents of the council that moved him to approve it.

49 The *Henotikon* would show, however, that Palestine, marked as it was by specific traditions, could not serve as a model for the entire empire. Cf. Kötter 2014a, 166–167.

alarming degree from the conciliatory document. The church of Jerusalem attempted, insofar as its means permitted, to ensure imperial support. This obviously was possible only as long as there was at least a rough common doctrinal basis between the Holy Land and the emperor in Constantinople.

Finally, the Chalcedonian volte-face of imperial religious policy under Justin in 518 was provoked by the failure of Anastasius' anti-Chalcedonian policy,[50] in which Jerusalem played an important role. Anastasius' failure was due to ecclesiastical-political dynamics that had, *inter alia*, originated in Palestine. Thus, Severus' flight from Palestine to the capital in 507 had helped radicalize the ecclesiastical parties and thereby discredited the *Henotikon* as a conciliatory document.[51] It was above all the triumph of Sabas, Theodosius, and John, who successfully evaded the emperor's and Severus' grasp, that will have given impetus to the Chalcedonian cause throughout the empire. Severus, for example, encountered resistance in his own jurisdiction on account of his radical doctrinal position; developments in neighbouring Palestine will have scarcely mitigated it.[52] To put it bluntly: the failure of Anastasius' religious policy does not date to the Chalcedonian restoration under Justin, but rather began with the successful resistance of the seemingly secondary patriarchate of Jerusalem. The question of how Justin might have responded in ecclesiastical political terms had *all* the patriarchates of the East been unified with regard to the *Theologumena* of Severus must at least be considered.[53]

---

50 Justin's motives are not entirely clear. Possibly, he was put under pressure by the Chalcedonian *comes foederatorum*, Vitalian, like Anastasius before him: Gray 1979, 46; Haacke 1953, 141. Justin's Illyrian origins are often cited as a potential source of sympathy for Roman positions. Cf. Capizzi 1969, 37; Jones 1964, 268; Meyendorff 1989, 208. Menze 2008, 18–22 at any rate considers it difficult to view the emperor as a staunch Chalcedonian *a priori*. Prior to 518, he was probably indifferent. Other reasons than his personal disposition must have influenced his decision to break with the course taken by Anastasius. Besides pressure from Vitalian, the "gestörtes Verhältnis zwischen Kaiser und hauptstädtischer Bevölkerung" (Meier 2007, 229) under Anastasius might be cited.
51 Severus himself only unwillingly recognized the *Henotikon*. He made clear what he thought of the emperor's constant efforts towards compromise in a letter to a friendly monk: "What has thrown the churches into confusion down to the present day is this, the fact that those who are in power halt between the two sides, and wish always to please both sides" [Sev. Ant. Ep. CL 37 (p. 292–293)].
52 Some centers of resistance formed in *Syria Secunda*. Cf. the affair concerning Kosmas of Epiphania and Severianus of Arethusa: Evagr. HE 3,34; Sev. Ant. Ep. SL 1,21. Epiphanius of Tyre (Flavian's brother), Dionysius of Tarsus, Julian of Bostra, Peter of Damascus, and Marinus of Berytus refused to follow Severus. Cf. Sev. Ant. Ep. SL 1,21; Sev. Ant. Ep. CL 51 [p. 325–326]; Zach. VS, 114. On resistance to Severus: Allen/Hayward 2004, 12–13; Bacht 1953, 287–289; Honigmann 1947, 157; Honigmann 1951, 38–39, 45–46; Leuenberger-Wenger 2019, 432–434.
53 Zach. HE 7,12 sees broad church unity under Severus' influence as actually achieved. According to Zach. HE 8,1 [vol. 2, 16–18], the imperial official Amantius attempted to use this as an argument in 518 to convince Justin to change his pro-Chalcedonian policy: *Chirographum trium patriarcharum et episcoporum complurium dicionis vestrae nondum aruit, qui scripserunt et synodum anathematizaverunt.*

On the significance of Chalcedonian Palestine for the course of empire-wide ecclesiastical affairs, we may conclude by citing an instructive example: around 512, Palestinian Chalcedonian monks wrote a letter to the Illyrian bishop, Alcison of Nicopolis,[54] who had played a central role in the defection of Illyrian bishops from communion with the church of Constantinople. These bishops placed themselves under the wing of Rome, which led Pope Hormisdas to assert stricter Chalcedonian positions vis-à-vis the eastern churches and the imperial efforts of reconciliation, and to rule out any concessions on the part of Rome in increasingly blunt terms.[55] The position of Rome, which was influenced and emboldened by the Chalcedonian revival in the East, would prove decisive in 518/19 for resolving the so-called 'Acacian Schism' between Rome and Constantinople.[56] Rome's experience of the Chalcedonian revival in the East primarily came from the Balkans; this region, however, was apparently in touch with developments in Palestine. Palestine's resistance thus made ripples far beyond the territory of the patriarchate of Jerusalem and its goal of merely preserving its internal autonomy.

Conclusion

Did Jerusalem succeed in transforming its ecclesiastical elevation in 451 into enhanced significance? The reign of Anastasius demonstrates that the church of Jerusalem, even in the event of conflict with players supported by the emperor, was capable of preserving its independence of development. Various attempts at encroachment could ultimately be thwarted by Palestine's relatively uniform doctrinal position. It also emerges, however, that, in the eyes of others, Jerusalem did not play a particularly central role: Emperor Anastasius could quite easily refrain from decisively enforcing his policy in the Holy Land, probably not least because he wished to avoid shedding blood at the holy sites. The patriarchate had thus asserted itself as an independent player, but, admittedly, it stood to benefit from Palestine's secondary importance regarding the strategy of the emperor and of the other patriarchates.

Accordingly, the bishops of Jerusalem refrained from formulating any similarly far-reaching demands with respect to their own influence on the development of the church as a whole, in contrast, for example, to the bishops of the 'two Romes'. Palestine was well aware of its prominent position as the church of the Holy Land, of course – Sabas and Theodosius stressed precisely that when they at-

---

54 This letter is in Evagr. *HE* 3,31;33.
55 Hormisdas wrote to his Gallic colleague Avitus of Vienne in 517 about what further actions he believed the growing ecclesiastical resistance in the East required: in light of the situation, a delegation was necessary either to persuade those in power in Constantinople to change course or to discredit them in the eyes of the opposition in the East: Avell. 137,12.
56 On the Acacian Schism, cf. Kötter 2013 *passim*.

tempted to prove the correctness of their doctrinal positions to the emperor in 517[57] – but we do not see Palestinian players making fundamental demands for any sort of supra-regional leadership of the Church on that basis. On the other hand, the developments in Palestine were hardly bereft of all significance for other churches or for the emperors: it was definitely noted what happened in Palestine, and, above all, it was noted how Constantinople reacted. In the period under consideration, the church of Jerusalem repeatedly gave impetus to or promoted developments that had ramifications beyond the narrow confines of Palestine. The region was thus far from being on the absolute periphery of ecclesiastical politics. However, a brief comparison with the other great episcopal sees of the empire[58] further qualifies this conclusion: while Jerusalem may not have been on the periphery, in its significance for the development of the imperial Church, it was definitely the most peripheral of the many centers vying for power and influence.

Bibliography

Allen, P. (2000). 'The Definition and Enforcement of Orthodoxy,' in Cameron 2000, 811–834.
Allen, P. & Jeffreys, E. (eds.) (1996). *The Sixth Century. End or Beginning?*, Brisbane.
Andresen, C. (ed.) (1982). *Die Lehrentwicklung im Rahmen der Katholizität*, Göttingen.
Bacht, H. (1953). 'Die Rolle des orientalischen Mönchtums in den kirchenpolitischen Auseinandersetzungen um Chalkedon (431–519),' in Bacht/Grillmeier 1953, 193–314.
Bacht, H. & Grillmeier, A. (eds.) (1953). *Das Konzil von Chalkedon. Geschichte und Gegenwart* (vol. 2: *Entscheidung um Chalkedon*), Würzburg.
Blaudeau, Ph. (2003). 'Antagonismes et convergences: regard sur les interprétations confessantes du gouvernement d'un usurpateur: Basilisque (475–476),' *Mediterraneo antico* 6, 155–193.
Blaudeau, Ph. (2006). *Alexandrie et Constantinople (451–491). De l'histoire à la géo-ecclésiologie*, Rome.
Blaudeau, Ph. (2007). 'Motifs et structures de divisions ecclésiales. Le schisme Acacien (484–519),' *AHC* 39, 65–98.
Brennecke, H.C. (1998). 'Chalkedonense und Henotikon. Bemerkungen zum Prozeß der östlichen Rezeption der christologischen Formel von Chalkedon,' in Roldanus/van Oort 1998, 24–53.
Bringmann, K. (1998). '*Imperium* und *Sacerdotium*. Bemerkungen zu ihrem ungeklärten Verhältnis in der Spätantike,' in Kneissl/Losemann 1998, 61–72.
Cameron, Av. (ed.) (2000). *Late Antiquity: Empire and Successors, A.D. 425–600*, Cambridge.
Capizzi, C. (1969). *L'imperatore Anastasio I (491–518). Studio sulla sua vita, la sua opera e la sua personalità*, Rome.
Chabanne, R. & Chevailler, L. (1984). 'Justinien et la pentarchie,' in Giuffrè 1984, 721–730.
Chitty, D.J. (1966). *The Desert a City. An Introduction to the Study of Egyptian and Palestinian Monasticism under the Christian Empire*, Oxford.
Coleman, J.S. (1994). *Foundations of Social Theory*, Cambridge Mass.

---

57 Cf. n. 32.
58 For a detailed comparative analysis of the five major episcopal sees of the time, see Kötter 2013, 224–254.

Dijkstra, J. & Greatrex, G. (2009). 'Patriarchs and Politics in Constantinople in the Reign of Anastasius (with a Reedition of *O.Mon.Epiph.* 59),' *Millennium* 6, 223–264.

Fedalto, G. (1988). *Hierarchia ecclesiastica Orientalis. Series episcoporum ecclesiarum christianarum Orientalium* (vol. 2: *Patriarchatus Alexandrinus, Antiochenus, Hierosolymitanus*), Padua 1988.

Frend, W.H.C. (1972). *The Rise of the Monophysite Movement. Chapters in the History of the Church in the Fifth and Sixth Centuries.* New edition, Cambridge.

Frend, W.H.C. (1979). 'The fall of Macedonius in 511 – a suggestion,' in Ritter 1979, 183–195.

Gahbauer, F.R. (1993). *Die Pentarchie-Theorie. Ein Modell der Kirchenleitung von den Anfängen bis zur Gegenwart*, Frankfurt a.M.

Giuffrè, V. (ed.) (1984). *Sodalitas. Scritti in onore di Antonio Guarino* (vol. 2), Naples.

Gray, P.T.R. (1979). *The Defense of Chalcedon in the East (451–553)*, Leiden.

Grillmeier, A. (^{2}1991). *Jesus der Christus im Glauben der Kirche* (vol. 2.1: *Das Konzil von Chalcedon [451]. Rezeption und Widerspruch [451–518]*), Freiburg.

Grillmeier, A. (2002). *Jesus der Christus im Glauben der Kirche* (vol. 2.3: *Die Kirche von Jerusalem und Antiochien nach 451 bis 600*), Freiburg.

Grillmeier, A. (^{2}2004). *Jesus der Christus im Glauben der Kirche* (vol. 2.4: *Die Kirche von Alexandrien mit Nubien und Äthiopien nach 451*), Freiburg.

Haacke, Rh. (1953). 'Die kaiserliche Politik in den Auseinandersetzungen um Chalkedon (451–553),' in Bacht/Grillmeier 1953, 95–177.

Hall, S.G. (2000). 'The Organization of the Church,' in Cameron 2000, 731–744.

Hay, K. (1996). 'Impact of St. Sabas: The Legacy of Palestinian Monasticism,' in Allen/Jeffreys 1996, 118–125.

Heyer, F. (1984). *Kirchengeschichte des Heiligen Landes*, Berlin.

Honigmann, E. (1947). 'The Patriarchate of Antioch. A Revision of Le Quien and the Notitia Antiochena,' *Traditio* 5, 135–161.

Honigmann, E. (1950). 'Juvenal of Jerusalem,' *DOP* 5, 209–279.

Honigmann, E. (1951). *Évêques et évêchés monophysites d'Asie antérieure au VIe siècle*, Leuven.

Jones, A.H.M. (1964). *The Later Roman Empire 284–602. A Social Economic and Administrative Survey* (3 vols.), Oxford.

Kennedy, H. (2000). 'Syria, Palestine and Mesopotamia,' in Cameron 2000, 588–611.

Kinzig, W. (2016). 'Herrschaft und Bekenntnis. Überlegungen zur imperialen Normierung des christlichen Glaubens in der Spätantike,' *HZ* 303, 621–642.

Klein, K. (2018a). 'Acceptation et résistance après le concile de Chalcédoine. Conversion de lieux et de personnes dans la Palestine de l'Antiquité tardive,' *Archives de sciences sociales des religions* 182, 169–189.

Klein, K. (2018b). 'Kaiser Marcian und die Monophysiten,' *Gymnasium* 125, 251–273.

Kneissl, P. & Losemann, V. (eds.) (1998). *Imperium Romanum. Studien zu Geschichte und Rezeption. Festschrift für Karl Christ zum 75. Geburtstag*, Stuttgart.

Kofsky, A. & Stroumsa, G. (eds.) (1998). *Sharing the Sacred. Religious Contacts and Conflicts in the Holy Land. First–Fifteenth Centuries CE*, Jerusalem.

Kötter, J.-M. (2011). 'Stability and Threat to the Order of the Church. Some Thoughts on the Personalization of the Church in Late Antiquity,' *InterDisciplines* 2, 37–64.

Kötter, J.-M. (2013). *Zwischen Kaisern und Aposteln. Das Akakianische Schisma (484–519) als kirchlicher Ordnungskonflikt in der Spätantike*, Stuttgart.

Kötter, J.-M. (2014a). 'Das Henotikon Zenons (482). Zum Scheitern eines kaiserlichen Einheitsbekenntnisses,' in Linder et al. 2014, 161–174.

Kötter, J.-M. (2014b). 'Die Suche nach der kirchlichen Ordnung. Gedanken zu grundlegenden Funktionsweisen der spätantiken Reichskirche,' *HZ* 298, 1–28.

Linder, M. et al. (eds.) (2014). *Religion und Herrschaft in der Antike (Keryx 3)*, Graz.

Leuenberger-Wenger, S. (2019). *Das Konzil von Chalcedon und die Kirche. Konflikte und Normierungsprozesse im 5. und 6. Jahrhundert*, Leiden.

Maraval, P. (2001). 'Die Rezeption des Chalcedonense im Osten des Reiches,' in Pietri 2001, 120–157.

Meier, M. (2007). 'Σταυρωθεὶς δἰ' ἡμᾶς – Der Aufstand gegen Anastasios im Jahr 512,' *Millennium* 4, 157–237.

Meier, M. (2009). *Anastasios I. Die Entstehung des Byzantinischen Reiches*, Stuttgart.

Menze, V.L. (2008). *Justinian and the Making of the Syrian Orthodox Church*, New York.

Meyendorff, J. (1989). *Imperial Unity and Christian Divisions. The Church 450–680 A.D.*, New York.

Moss, Y. (2016). *Incorruptible Bodies. Christology, Society, and Authority in Late Antiquity*, Oakland.

Norton, P. (2007). *Episcopal Elections 250–600. Hierarchy and Popular Will in Late Antiquity*, Oxford.

Patrich, J. (1995). *Sabas, Leader of Palestinian Monasticism. A Comparative Study in Eastern Monasticism, Fourth to Seventh Centuries*, Washington D.C.

Perrone, L. (1980). *La chiesa di Palestina e le controversie cristologiche. Dal concilio di Efeso (431) al secondo concilio di Costantinopoli (553)*, Brescia.

Perrone, L. (1998a). 'Christian Holy Places and Pilgrimage in an Age of Dogmatic Conflicts. Popular Religion and Confessional Affiliation in Byzantine Palestine (Fifth to Seventh Centuries),' *Proche-Orient chrétien* 48, 5–37.

Perrone, L. (1998b). 'Monasticism as a Factor of Religious Interaction in the Holy Land during the Byzantine Period,' in Kofsky/Stroumsa 1998, 67–95.

Pietri, L. (ed.) (2001). *Der lateinische Westen und der byzantinische Osten (431–642)*, Basel.

Ritter, A.M. (1982). 'Dogma und Lehre in der Alten Kirche,' in Andresen 1982, 99–283.

Ritter, A.M. (ed.) (1979). *Kerygma und Logos. Beiträge zu den geistesgeschichtlichen Beziehungen zwischen Antike und Christentum. Festschrift für Carl Andresen zum 70. Geburtstag*, Göttingen.

Roldanus, J. (1998). 'Stützen und Störenfriede. Mönchische Einmischung in die doktrinäre und kirchenpolitische Rezeption von Chalkedon,' in Roldanus/van Oort 1998, 123–146

Roldanus, J. & van Oort, J. (eds.) (1998). *Chalkedon: Geschichte und Aktualität. Studien zur Rezeption der christologischen Formel von Chalkedon*, Leuven.

Rousseau, Ph. (1997). 'Eccentrics and Coenobites in the Late Roman East,' *ByzF* 24, 35–50.

Solzbacher, R. (1989). *Mönche, Pilger und Sarazenen. Studien zum Frühchristentum auf der südlichen Sinaihalbinsel – Von den Anfängen bis zum Beginn islamischer Herrschaft*, Altenberge.

Trampedach, K. (2005). 'Reichsmönchtum? Das politische Selbstverständnis der Mönche Palästinas im 6. Jahrhundert und die historische Methode des Kyrill von Skythopolis,' *Millennium* 2, 271–296.

Ullmann, W. (1976). 'The Constitutional Significance of Constantine the Great's Settlement,' *JEH* 27, 1–16.

Van Nuffelen, P. & Hilkens, A. (2013). 'Recruitment and Conflict in Sixth-Century Antioch: A Micro-Study of *Select Letters* 6,1,5 of Severus of Antioch,' *ZAC* 17, 560–575.

Winkelmann, F. (1980). *Die östlichen Kirchen in der Epoche der christologischen Auseinandersetzungen (5. bis 7. Jahrhundert)*, Berlin.

Wipszycka, E. (2018). 'The Canons of the Council of Chalcedon Concerning Monks,' *Augustinianum* 58, 155–180.

Part Four:
Jerusalem, Constantinople and the End of Antiquity

Paul Magdalino
The Church of St John the Apostle and the End of Antiquity in the New Jerusalem

The overwhelming presence of Justinian's Hagia Sophia in the literature and landscape of Constantinople has tended to overshadow the significance of the church buildings that came before it, and, more especially, of those that came after it, during the long sixth century. While certain predecessors of the rebuilt Great Church, notably Juliana Anicia's St Polyeuktos and Justinian's own SS Sergios and Bacchos, have received much scholarly discussion, largely because of their surviving remains, the numerous church foundations that are recorded from the century after 537 have been virtually ignored by modern scholarship outside the topographical studies based largely on textual evidence. Yet it is abundantly clear from this evidence that the new Hagia Sophia, though no doubt meant to be the church to end all churches, actually gave new impetus to the trend of which it marked the culmination. Justinian himself did not feel deterred from making new foundations, just as, in the legislative sphere, he added his Novels to his supposedly conclusive Corpus of Roman law. Neither were his successors inhibited by his achievement: every one, from Justin II to Heraclius, made at least one major ecclesiastical construction or renovation, and this is not to mention the often substantial contributions of imperial relatives, imperial officials, and the occasional patriarch.[1] None of these constructions was on the outsize scale of Hagia Sophia, but some were evidently big by normal standards,[2] and all were public buildings in prominent urban locations. Seen in the context of this building program, Hagia Sophia appears as just one part, albeit the most spectacular, of a sustained official effort to sanctify the urban landscape. That the program and the major investments it required added up to a conscious policy rather than an accidental series of haphazard initiatives is suggested by the reference, in Tiberius II's Novel of c. 580 dealing with the *domus divinae* of the crown domain, to "the department in charge of the new churches".[3] This can only have been a financial unit set up by Justinian or Justin II in order to manage estates and revenues that were dedicated to financing the construction and the maintenance of recent and, perhaps, projected imperial church foundations.

What was the rationale behind this massive, collective investment in church building, which was a huge strain on the budget of a state whose military expendi-

---

[1] See below; for Justin II, see Cameron 1980, 62–84.
[2] See for example Anna Komnene and Nikephoros Gregoras on Justin II's church of St Paul at the Orphanage: *Annae Comnenae Alexias* 15,7,4, ed. D.R. Reinsch and A. Kambylis, CFHB 40/1 (Berlin – New York 2001), 482 (ναὸν ... μεγέθει μέγιστον); *Nicephori Gregorae Byzantina Historia*, I, ed. L. Schopen, I (Bonn 1829), (μέγιστος νεὼς τοῦ μεγάλου Παύλου).
[3] Zepos/Zepos 1931, I, 20; cf. Kaplan 1976, 12ff.

ture was steadily rising, even as its resources stagnated or declined? I would like to approach this question by looking at the foundation that seems, from the available evidence, to have been the last in the series, and therefore the last major new church to be built in Constantinople before the late ninth century. This was the church of St John the Apostle, situated between the Hippodrome and Hagia Sophia, close to the starting gates of the races, and across the road from the Milion.[4] It is referred to as being "at the Diippion",[5] "at the Million",[6] and "near Hagia Sophia/the Great Church".[7] According to the *Patria*, it was started by the emperor Phokas, (602–610), who dedicated it to his patron saint; it was then finished by Heraclius (602–610), Phokas' successor, who put a roof on the building and rededicated it to the Apostle John.[8] Although the *Patria* is not the most reliable of sources, its account gains some credibility in this instance from the Acts of the Sixth Ecumenical Council (681), which mention a scribe's workshop near the church of "Ioannophokas".[9] Further confirmation is provided by the festal calendar of tenth-century Constantinople, from which it is clear that the church of St John the Apostle "near the Great Church" was not only the principal urban venue for the *synaxis* of the apostle on 26 September, but also contained oratories where eight martyr saints, including St Phokas, were celebrated.[10] One manuscript of the *Patria* says that the building was roofed by Romanos I Lekapenos (920–944), which probably means that he restored it. In 1181 the church was the scene of fighting between the regency government of Alexios II and the faction loyal to Alexios' half-sister Maria: from their position on the roof, the government's soldiers were able to shoot down on their opponents who occupied the top of the Milion.[11] The church was visited by Anthony of Novgorod in 1200,[12] and in 1403 by Clavijo, who describes it as dedicated to St John Prodromos;[13] it is described as functioning, though in need of upkeep, in a patriarchal document of 1402.[14] After

---

4 Janin 1969, 264–267; Mango 1950, 152–161
5 *Patria* of Constantinople, ed. Th. Preger, *Scriptores originum Constantinopolitanarum* (Leipzig 1901, 1907), 168–170; see also Niketas Choniates, n. 11 below
6 *Patria* ed. Preger, *Scriptores*, loc.cit.
7 *Synaxarium Ecclesiae Constantinopolitanae*, ed. H. Delehaye, AASS ad Propylaeum Novembris (Brussels 1902), cols. 82, 150–151.
8 *Patria*, ed. Preger, *Scriptores*, 168–170.
9 ACO II/2/2, 652.
10 *Synaxarium*, ed. Delehaye, *Acta Sanctorum*, cols 69–70 (St Phokas), 79–82 (St John), 150–151 (St Tryphon), 305–306 (SS. Eustratios, Auxentios, Eugenios, Mardarios, Orestes), 437 (St Tryphon), 596–598 (St Antipas), 810 (St Orestes), 835–836 (St Phokas), 855–856 (St John Stratiotes), 866 (encaenia of the church).
11 Niketas Choniates *Hist.*, ed. J.-L. van Dieten, CFHB 11 (Berlin-New York 1975), I, 236.
12 Ed. and trans. G. Majeska in Spingou 2022, 512–513.
13 de Clavijo (ed. López Estrada 1943, 40–41). I follow the identification suggested by Grélois 2007, challenging the earlier assumption that Clavijo was referring to St John Stoudios, which affected the English translation by G. Le Strange, *Clavijo, Embassy to Tamerlane, 1403–1406* (London, 1928), 68.
14 F. Miklosich and J. Mueller, *Acta et diplomata graeca medii aevi sacra et profana*, II (Vienna 1862), 495–496.

1453, it was transformed into a menagerie, and as such features in the accounts of many travellers to the Ottoman capital in the sixteenth and early seventeenth centuries. According to a Greek notice in an Athonite manuscript, the building was destroyed by an earthquake in 1510, but even in its ruined state it continued for another century to serve as the sultan's 'lion house' and to make an impression on visitors through its distinctive architecture.[15] It has recently been shown, from the unpublished travelogue of Julien Bordier, who accompanied the French ambassador to Constantinople from 1605 to 1610, that the church was finally demolished at this time and its building materials used in the construction of the Sultan Ahmed mosque.[16]

Thanks to the accounts, and the sketches, of the European travellers, we are unusually well informed about the appearance of this building.[17] According to Clavijo, it was very tall, with a completely round nave, seven altars, twenty-four *vert-gris* marble columns, and fine mosaic decoration that completely covered the walls. Its round, domed form is emphasised by later writers, as well as in the drawings of Cristoforo Buondelmonti,[18] Hartmann Schedel,[19] Melchior Lorich,[20] and Pieter Coeck van Aelst. The Englishman John Sanderson, in 1594, even mistook its remains for those of a theatre.[21] The Hapsburg envoy Reinhold Lubenau, who saw it in 1587, refers it as a "large, old Christian church, right by the Atmeidan square," and gives a detailed description of the menagerie that it housed, which yields valuable information about its architecture. Eight lions were kept there, each of them tethered to a pillar, and a variety of other wild beasts were penned up in a series of chapels – between four and ten, depending on how one reads the description.[22] When Julien Bordier visited the site some twenty years later, the building had been pulled down, and "the entire square" of the Hippodrome was "filled with a wondrous quantity of dressed stone originating from the ... demolition" of the church. This

> had a circular plan ... I can reckon what it had been in its entirety on the basis of its ruins. For it is true that this temple was wondrous, its interior entirely covered, from top to bottom, on the vaults as well as on the walls and other areas, with very fine and rich mosaics, on which were represented all the figures of the Apocalypse ... One would scarcely believe how much fine worked stone was pulled from this church; those that composed round pillars had a diameter of eight or ten feet and a height of three or four. Those from the portals or other areas measured a *toise* [1.95 m.] or a *toise* and a half in length, and a thickness of half a toise.[23]

---

15 Mango 1950, 158–159.
16 Grélois 2007, 369–372; Grélois 2010, I, 216–218.
17 See, in addition to the studies by Mango 1950; Grélois 2007 and 2010; Asutay-Effenberger/Effenberger 2004, 51–93.
18 Paris, Bibliothèque Nationale, MS Lat. 2383, fol. 34 v., reproduced in *Hippodrome*, ed. Pitarakis, I, 215, and Kafesçioğlu 2009, 154.
19 Kafesçioğlu 2009, 165.
20 E. Fischer et al, *Melchior Lorck*, vol. 4: *The Constantinople Prospect* (Copenhagen 2009).
21 Cited by Mango 1950, 158, who suggests an identification with the Carceres of the Hippodrome.
22 Ed. W. Sahm, *Beschreibung der Reisen des Reinhold Lubenau*, I (Königsberg 1912), 152–154.
23 Cited by Grélois 2010, 217–218.

We may wonder about these measurements, and about the subject matter of the mosaics, but we need not doubt the overall reliability of Bordier's account, which was evidently based on his own observations and conversations with people who had seen the church before its recent demolition.

Putting this information together, we can envisage the church of St John Diippion as a large, tall structure with a centralised plan, consisting of a circular nave off which there opened a concentric ring of adjoining rooms. On the main liturgical axis there would have been the main apse of the sanctuary to the east, and the narthex, which according to the *Synaxarion* housed the tomb of a recent, tenth-century saint.[24] On the north and south sides were a series of apsidal side-chapels, the *Capellen* of Lubenau's description, which in his day were reserved to different species of wild beasts, and in Byzantine times had surely been dedicated to the various saints whose cults were celebrated in the church. From the tenth-century *Synaxarion*, it is clear that six saints and one group of martyrs were commemorated in the church, making a total of seven "cults".[25] This matches Clavijo's reference to seven altars, which together with Lubenau's mention of eight pillars, suggest an octagonal plan, with the entrance door and the main apse on the east-west axis, and six apses on the remaining sides of the octagon, three to the north and three to the south. The church apparently had two types of columnar support: the *vert-gris* marble columns seen by Clavijo, and the composite cylindrical stone piers whose dismantled sections Bordier saw in the Hippodrome. Clavijo and Bordier both mention the mosaic decoration, and another sixteenth-century visitor, Stefan Gerlach, confirms Bordier's information that the church was built of dressed stone.[26] The images of the church in the fifteenth and sixteenth-century panoramas further suggest that the building had a gallery and was surrounded by a circular colonnade. Finally, a reference to the church's 'stoas' in the patriarchal document of 1402 would seem to indicate the existence of a peristyle atrium.

The church of St John at the Diippion must have been one of the more imposing landmarks of medieval Constantinople, by virtue of its distinctive design, its expensive stone and mosaic fabric, and its central location in a monumental ensemble that comprised the Milion, Hagia Sophia, the Baths of Zeuxippos, not to mention the Hippodrome, the main entrance to which it dominated. It is of special interest for the modern historian because, if it was indeed the work of the emperors Phokas and Heraclius, it is the last recorded major religious construction in Constantinople before the ninth century, and the last ever new foundation of a major, free-standing public church: that is, a church that was not part of a palatine, monastic, or previously existing ecclesiastical complex. In more ways than one, therefore, it marks the end of late antiquity and early Christianity in Constantinople. As such, it raises many ques-

---

24 Delehaye, *Synaxarium*, 11 March.
25 See above, n. 10.
26 *Tagebuch* (Frankfurt 1674), 79.

tions. In the context of Constantinople and Jerusalem in late antiquity, what interests us is the question of motivation. Why did Phokas choose to build this church? Why did he build it round? Why did Heraclius complete the building and dedicate it to St John the Apostle, Evangelist and Theologian?

According to the *Patria*, Phokas built the church to commemorate an incident involving the horse relay station that had existed there before he became emperor. The army had sent him to demand payment of their wages, and he had escaped the wrath of the emperor Maurice by taking some horses from the stable and hobbling the rest to prevent pursuit. Whether or not there was more to this story than a rather fanciful etymology of the word Diippion, it does not preclude the more prosaic explanation that Phokas built a church because it was expected of him as emperor, that this was an important part of what emperors and their associates were supposed to do in the post-Justinianic age. If we look at the record of Phokas' immediate predecessors, we can see that he was conforming to a pattern. The sources attribute no less than eight church constructions or renovations to Justin II and Sophia, including the great church of St Paul at the Orphanage and the church of St James at the Chalkoprateia.[27] Justin's *praipositos* Narses is reliably attested as the builder of the church of St Panteleemon attached to the hospital that bore his name.[28] The reigns of Justin's successors Tiberius II and Maurice were not so productive, but Tiberius is credited with starting and Maurice with finishing the church of the Forty Martyrs at a prominent central location.[29] Maurice is further said to have restored the church of St Theodore at *ta Sphorakiou*, near Hagia Sophia, and to have added a church of St George to the same complex. Among the churches attributed to Maurice's close associates, we may mention those of the Theotokos τῶν Ἀρεοβίνδου built by his brother Peter and the Theotokos τῆς Διακονίσσης on the city's central avenue, founded by the patriarch Kyriakos;[30] the importance of the latter is reflected in the fact that it later served as the 'home' church of the Green faction.[31] It is clear that Phokas could not ignore these precedents, especially since he had come to power in a violent coup d'état concluding with the systematic murder of Maurice and his whole family. This put Phokas under pressure to prove that he was at least as worthy to rule as the regime he had overthrown. His church foundation indeed suggests a determination to go one better than his predecessors, to make his contribution to the city's landscape stand out from theirs. He erected the church of St Phokas at an even more central and prestigious location, as part of the city's most imposing monumental ensemble. He also

---

[27] Theoph. *Chron.*, ed. C. de Boor (Leipzig 1883, repr. Hildesheim 1980), I, 244; trans. Mango/Scott 1997, 361; *Patria*, ed. Preger, *Scriptores*, 263; Janin, *Églises et monasteries*, 253–5; Cameron 1980.
[28] Anon. *Synopsis chronike*, ed. K. Sathas, Μεσαιωνικὴ Βιβλιοθήκη, VII, 107; *Patria*, ed. Preger, 249; cf. Berger 1988, 591–596.
[29] Theoph. *Chron.*, ed. C. de Boor, I, 268; trans. Mango/Scott 1997, 390.
[30] Theoph. *Chron.*, ed. de Boor, I, 277 (trans. Mango/Scott 1997, 401); *Patria*, ed. Preger, *Scriptores*, 250.
[31] See Dagron 2000, 84–85, 157–158.

gave it a distinctive form that did not, to my knowledge, correspond to any of the other major churches within the city, but did closely resemble two prominent Justinianic structures in the European suburbs. One was the church of the Archangel Michael at Anaplous on the Bosphoros, which Procopius describes in the *Buildings*.[32] The other was the church of St John the Baptist at the Hebdomon, which Procopius says was identical to the church at Anaplous in every way, and whose basic resemblance to the church built by Phokas is confirmed by the *Patria*, which describes it as "the round-roofed church with the apses".[33] We do not know whether Phokas visited the church of the Archangel Michael at Anaplous, but we know that he both knew and liked the church of St John Prodromos at the Hebdomon. For this was the church in which Phokas was crowned emperor by the patriarch Kyriakos on 25 November 602, and from which he made his ceremonial progress through the city to the Palace, riding in a chariot drawn by a quadriga of white horses.[34] The church he built near the Milion thus commemorated, both geographically and symbolically, the end of the process by which he had taken possession of the city from Maurice. In this connection, we should also note that it commanded the space, the Diippion, through which the chariots and horses were led to the starting gates of the Hippodrome racetrack by the teams of the Blue and Green factions who had been so conspicuous in the transfer of authority.[35] By marking the spot with a replica of his own coronation church, dedicated to his own patron saint, Phokas was erecting a very explicit monument to his personal imperial power. Only a triumphal column would have been more explicit. Yet here too, Phokas was not to be outdone by his predecessors.[36] Justinian had erected a column with his statue outside Hagia Sophia. Justin II had planned a column in some other location; according to John of Ephesus, it had an interior staircase. No less than three columns were projected to honor Phokas during his short reign, two in Constantinople and one in Rome. A massive marble capital bearing his monogram, and evidently made for some other such monument, was found at Synada in western Anatolia.[37] So it is clear that Phokas was motivated by a strong concern to impose, quite literally, his imperial image on the urban landscape of the empire, and to emulate his predecessors in his secular as in his religious patronage.

But churches were not just demonstrations of power. They were also expressions of piety, however insincere, and we have no reason to believe that Phokas was not

---

[32] Proc. *Aed.* 1,8,12–14.
[33] Proc. *Aed.* 1,8,15–16; *Patria*, ed. Preger, *Scriptores*, 260. The octagonal form of the church is basically confirmed by its physical remains, see Mathews 1971, 56–61; Niewöhner 2009, 1431–1452.
[34] Theophyl. Sim. *Hist.* 8,10, ed. C. de Boor (Leipzig, 1887), 303; *Chron. Pasch.* ed. L. Dindorf (Bonn, 1832), I, 693; Theoph. *Chron.*, ed. C. de Boor (Leipzig, 1883), 289.
[35] Cameron 1976, 251–253, 265–267. Phocas' reliance on the Blue faction has recently been brought out by Booth 2011, 555–601.
[36] C. Mango, *Studies on Constantinople*, supplement I.
[37] Asutay 2003, 417–423.

sincerely concerned for the salvation of his soul, however much his paranoid cruelty and vanity may have got in the way. In a society that was obsessed by the cult of saints, the dedication of an expensive sanctuary to one's patron saint was both an act of gratitude for past favor and a plea for continued intercession before the throne of God, in this life as in the next. In this sense, the church of St Phokas can be seen as a move to honor the great martyr from Sinope with due recognition of his proven and expected efficacy on behalf of his imperial namesake. Here too we may detect a sense of rivalry with previous emperors, notably Maurice. Maurice had not only completed a prominent public church in honor of the Forty Martyrs of Sebasteia;[38] he had also renovated a church dedicated to another Anatolian martyr, St Theodore, at a short distance from Hagia Sophia, and had added to this a church of St George, who was then in the process of becoming a local hero in Maurice's native Cappadocia.[39] Maurice's devotion to these and other saints had not saved him from a humiliating fall from power and a grisly death. In these circumstances, it was only appropriate that the patron saint of the man who had replaced Maurice with the aid of Divine Providence should be honored with a splendid house in close proximity to the Great Church of the Holy Wisdom of God.

But a public church built by an emperor was not just an act of private devotion. An emperor's piety was a public function that he performed on behalf of the state; he was himself an intercessor for the intercession for which he prayed, and a church that he dedicated to a saint was offered for the salvation of all orthodox Christians who worshipped in it. In this sense, it was an act of civic benefaction, and it was meant to complement, rather than compete with, earlier imperial foundations. However selfish Phokas' motives for building a new church, he presumably justified the project on the grounds that it made a significant addition to the spiritual capital accumulated by previous emperors, that it attracted a significant increase in the divine favor bestowed on Constantinople and the empire. What is not clear is how this accumulation of spiritual credits was believed to translate into spiritual benefits. In other words, we return to the question we posed at the outset: what was the point of building new churches in post-Justinianic Constantinople? Why add to the ecclesiastical stock of a city that was already well stocked, if not overstocked? One can never be entirely sure, but access to services, sacraments, and sermons does not seem to have been a problem. I think it is appropriate to focus attention, not on the visiting earthly congregations, but on the heavenly proprietors to whom the churches were dedicated: Christ, the Theotokos, the angels and saints. The point was to multiply and enhance the sacred *oikoi* in which they were at home, and thereby to guarantee their increased and continued presence and availability. Their presence became particularly urgent in the late sixth century, in order to refute contemporary doubts about the power of the saints to act after the separation of their souls

---

38 See above, n. 29.
39 *Patria*, ed. Preger, *Scriptores*, 225.

from their bodies.[40] In this, the accumulation of sacred space went hand in hand with the accumulation of relics, to which sixth-century emperors, like their predecessors, devoted much energy – here it is appropriate to recall the efforts by Maurice to obtain a body part of St Demetrius from Thessalonica,[41] and by his wife, Constantia, to obtain the head of St Paul from Rome.[42]

Heavenly beings needed to be present in order to hear prayers and work miracles. From the point of view of Constantinople as a whole, however, their most important function was to provide protection. The role of the Theotokos as supernatural defender of Constantinople against barbarian invasion was still to come at the time we are considering, but it had already been anticipated under Justinian, when Procopius described the extramural shrines of the Virgin at the Blachernae and Pege as outer defences that guarded access to the city gates.[43] Even without barbarians, there was much that Constantinople needed protecting against: it is sufficient to read Procopius on the plague of 542,[44] Agathias on the earthquakes and plague of 557–558,[45] and Malalas on the almost annual occurrences of natural disorders and civil violence in the second half of Justinian's reign.[46] The fact that a similar catalogue of woes is not recorded for the reigns of Justinian's successors reflects the changed priorities of the historians who took over the narration of events. It cannot be assumed to mean that disasters did not continue to happen. It certainly does not mean that they were not anticipated, and there is very eloquent evidence to the contrary in the *Life of St Theodore of Sykeon*. When Theodore visited Constantinople during the reign of Phokas, the patriarch urged the holy man to prolong his stay because of a popular scare that the city was about to sink beneath the sea.[47] It was not the first time the rumour had circulated; Malalas records a similar panic in 541.[48] Thus it was in a climate of recurrent anxiety about the future of the city that emperors from Justinian to Phokas adorned Constantinople with new churches. Since, presumably, they did not build those churches in order for them to perish in an imminent catastrophe, we may rather suppose that they built in the hope of preventing catastrophe, and the more catastrophe threatened, the more they continued to build. Thus

---

40 Dal Santo 2012.
41 *Miracula Sancti Demetrii* 1,5: ed. Lemerle, *Les plus anciens recuieils des Miracles de Saint Démétrius* (Paris 1979), I, 87–90.
42 Gregory the Great, *Letters*, IV 30: ed. D. Norberg, *S. Gregorii Magni Registrum Epistularum*, 2 vols., Corpus Christianorum Series Latina 140 (Turnhout 1982), I, 248–250
43 Proc. *Aed.*, 1,3,1–9.
44 Proc. *Bell.* 2,22.
45 Agath. *Hist.*, ed. R. Keydell (Berlin 1967), V 3–10; trans. J.D.C. Frendo, (Berlin-New York 1975), 137–146.
46 Ed. Dindorf, 483–496; trans. E. Jeffreys, M. Jeffreys, R. Scott, *The Chronicle of John Malalas* (Melbourne 1986), 288–307.
47 *Vie de Théodore de Sykéon*, ed. and trans. A.-J. Festugière, 2 vols Subsidia Hagiographica 48 (Brussels 1970), §135: vol. I, 107; vol. II, 111
48 Ed. Dindorf, 481; ed. Thurn, 228–229; trans. Jeffreys and Scott, 286.

I would conclude that the church foundations that ended with the church of St Phokas and St John had one common function among the various motives of the individual founders: they were all basically apotropaic. The accumulation of sacred space, of churches dedicated to heavenly patrons, was designed to make Constantinople too holy for God to destroy. It can be seen in the same apotropaic light as the renaming of Antioch, which Justinian in 528 officially designated as Theoupolis, the city of God, after the city had been repeatedly flattened by earthquakes with great loss of life.[49]

The case of Antioch reminds us that Constantinople was not unique, either in its natural disasters, or in its accumulation of churches that transformed the urban landscape during the fifth and sixth centuries.[50] However, I have the impression that the evidence for church construction after the mid sixth century is more plentiful in Constantinople than elsewhere, with the exception of the Holy Land. Moreover, natural disasters had symbolic implications for Constantinople that they did not have for any other city. Being the New Rome, which by the sixth century had definitively succeeded Old Rome as the sole imperial capital and as the greatest city in the *oikoumene*, Constantinople inherited the role that imperial pagan Rome had had in Jewish and Christian apocalyptic thought: the role of Babylon the Great, the rich and arrogant sink of worldly corruption, which oppresses and murders the saints of God, and which in the End Times will be completely destroyed. The idea that Constantinople had assumed the function and would suffer the fate of the biblical Babylon was basically endorsed by Andrew of Caesarea, in his commentary on the Apocalypse of St John, written at the beginning of the seventh century.[51] It was then taken up by the Byzantine apocalyptic tradition, along with two characteristic motifs. One was the epithet Heptalophos, which was derived from the Sibylline oracles, and which, as Wolfram Brandes has demonstrated, is the source of the entirely spurious modern notion that the site of Constantinople was planned in imitation of the seven hills of Rome.[52] The other important motif was the prediction that Constantinople would be swallowed up by the sea, just like Babylon the Great in the Apocalypse of St John.[53] In the light of this prediction, the recurrent fear of submersion recorded in Malalas and the *Life of St Theodore of Sykeon* takes on new meaning, and suggests that the assimilation of Constantinople to Babylon was already well established in popular belief in the early sixth century. It also suggests that the apotropaic agenda of church building in sixth century Constantinople went well beyond the prevention

---

49 Malalas, ed. Dindorf, 443; trans. Jeffreys and Scott, 258.
50 For Antioch, see now Mayer/Allen 2012.
51 See his commentary on Rev. 17, 1–3: ed. J. Schmid, *Studien zur Geschichte des griechischen Apokalypse-Textes*, I (Munich 1955–1956), part 2, 181. On the author and the date of composition, see the translation by E. Scarvelis Constantinou, Andrew of Caesarea, *Commentary on the Apocalypse*, The Fathers of the Church: A New Translation (Patristic Series) 123 (Washington D.C. 2011), and also Constantinou 2013.
52 Brandes 2003, 58–71.
53 Brandes 1999, 119–131.

of natural disasters: it aimed to refute the belief that Constantinople was Babylon the Great, by transforming the imperial capital into a holy city, where the saints were not persecuted but honored with magnificent dwellings, and sacred space predominated. In other words, the accumulation of churches was meant to change the apocalyptic identity of the New Rome from Babylon the Great to New Jerusalem.

That Constantinople aspired to be a New Jerusalem is almost a cliché, and that it claimed this status on the basis of its unrivalled concentration of churches and relics has become too self-evident to require demonstration. There is also a growing recognition that the time when the notion of Constantinople as a second Jerusalem first appears in literature, around the turn of the sixth century, was a time of widespread apprehension that the end of the world was imminent.[54] But no-one, to my knowledge, has hitherto made the connection between the two, and recognised that the desire to identify Constantinople with Jerusalem had a profoundly eschatological dimension, because it involved the denial of a deeply disagreeable but widely expected alternative: if Constantinople was not the New Jerusalem, then it was the ancient Babylon, with all that this implied. This alternative scenario was not only alarming to the inhabitants of Constantinople; it was also potentially subversive of imperial authority, which in the sixth century identified with the *urbs regia*/βασιλεύουσα πόλις as never before, and it affected the loyalty not only of Christians but of Jews, who continued to hope for the restoration of the kingdom of Israel.

The transformation of Constantinople into a New Jerusalem was a broad and largely unstated ideal rather than a fully articulated program. It had to be; anything more systematic would have been considered a presumptuous if not blasphemous interference in the workings of Divine Providence. In particular, official ideology carefully avoided any attempt to equate Constantinople with the heavenly Jerusalem, or to sanctify Constantinople at the expense of the terrestrial Jerusalem, which remained the official ἁγία πόλις of the Christian empire.[55] However, official ideology undoubtedly encouraged the interpretation of apocalyptic texts in a sense that was supportive of imperial pretensions. The sixth century saw two new developments in Biblical exegesis that sanctified the providential role of the Christian empire, and thus, by extension, of the imperial capital. One was the reinterpretation of the Four Kingdoms prophecies in the Book of Daniel to distinguish between the Roman Empire before and after Constantine: while the pre-Constantinian, pagan empire corresponded to the fourth in the series of transitory world powers, the Christian Empire was one with the kingdom of Christ, the kingdom without end. This interpretation first appears in the *Christian Topography* of Cosmas Indicopleustes, written in the

---

[54] First appearance: *Life of Daniel the Stylite*, ed. H. Delehaye, *Les saints stylites* (Brussels 1923), 12. Imminence of the end of the world at the end of the sixth cosmic millennium: Brandes 1997, 24–63; Magdalino 1993, 3–34, esp. 4–7; Magdalino 2008, 123–128.

[55] Cf. Congourdeau 2001, 125–136.

mid sixth century.⁵⁶ The other development was the rehabilitation of the Book of Revelation, or the Apocalypse of St John, which refined and elaborated the vision of Daniel. Since the third century, the Book of Revelation had been regarded with suspicion in the Christian East, largely because of its prophecy, in chapter 20, of a millennial reign of Christ and the saints on earth. But by the end of the sixth century, interest in the book had grown sufficiently to prompt the first Greek commentary, written by one Oikoumenios, who declared that it was the authentic work of St John the Apostle, and effectively defused its controversial prophecies, by explaining them as allegorical allusions to events that had already taken place.⁵⁷ However, this historicist approach clearly failed to satisfy, because only a few years later a leading churchman, possibly the patriarch of Constantinople, asked Andrew, the archbishop of Caesarea, to write a new commentary.⁵⁸ Andrew guaranteed a long shelf life for his work by explicating Revelation as a book of prophecy that was still in the process of being fulfilled. Most crucially, he provided an explanation of chapter 20 that was both safe and pertinent for the age in which he lived: the millennium is the present age, which has begun with the Incarnation and will end with the reign of Antichrist, the age in which the saints "exercise priesthood and reign with Christ," "being venerated by pious rulers and faithful kings, manifesting God-given power against every bodily ailment and demonic activity".⁵⁹ This was essentially the interpretation of the millennium that had been given by St Augustine two hundred years earlier, and it is not impossible that Andrew derived it from a Latin source. Like Augustine, Andrew saw the millennial kingdom mainly in terms of the ministry of the Church, but he opened the way for equating it with the Christian empire, which the successors of St Constantine governed in co-rulership (συμβασιλεία) with Christ and the saints, whom the "pious rulers and faithful kings" venerated in the churches of Constantinople.⁶⁰

Similarly, while Andrew, as noted previously, was inclined to endorse the identification of Constantinople with Babylon the Great, he opened the way for identifying it with the New Jerusalem, by admitting the possibility that the prophecy of Gog and Magog, the savage tribes who are mobilised by Satan at the end of the millennium and besiege the holy city of the saints (Rev. 20, 7–9), refers to the Scythian nation, i.e. the Avars, who threatened Constantinople in the early seventh century.⁶¹ The logical conclusion was drawn after the Avar siege of Constantinople in 626. Theodore, Synkellos of the Great Church, celebrating the enemy's defeat and withdrawal

---

56 II 73–75: Cosmas Indicopleustès, *Topographie chrétienne*, ed. W. Wolska-Conus, I, Sources chrétiennes 141 (Paris 1968), 187–191; Magdalino 1993, 10–11.
57 Ed. H.C. Hoskier, *The Complete Commentary of Oecumenius on the Apocalypse* (Ann Arbor 1928).
58 Ed. Schmid; for the context of the work relative to Oikoumenios, I follow Scarvelis Constantinou (above n. 51).
59 Ed. Schmid, 216, 218, 221.
60 Magdalino 2003b, 250–251.
61 Ed. Schmid, 223–225.

due to the miraculous intervention of the Virgin, declared that the prophecy of Gog and Magog was thereby fulfilled. And since the Avars were Gog, "rightly have I interpreted the land of Israel to be this city, in which God and the Virgin are piously glorified and all mysteries of pious devotion are performed ... What else ... is this city, which one would not be wrong to call in its entirety a sanctuary of God?"[62] Theodore was referring to the Old Testament version of the prophecy, as it occurs in the book of the prophet Ezekiel, and his message was aimed at the Jews, but he and his audience would surely have had the Apocalypse of St John, and Andrew's recent commentary, in mind.

Andrew of Caesarea was writing his commentary on Revelation close to the time when the new round church of the emperor Phokas was taking shape at the entrance to the Hippodrome. Let us now return to this building and to the question of motivation that remains unanswered: why, when Heraclius took Constantinople and overthrew Phokas in 610, did he complete the church of St Phokas with a new dedication to St John the Apostle? Clearly, he did not want to let a good building go to waste, and clearly he wanted to disassociate it from his hated predecessor, whom he subjected to a thorough *damnatio memoriae*. But why St John the Apostle? Unless Heraclius had a personal attachment to the Apostle that is not recorded, he is likely to have taken the advice of the recently elected patriarch Sergios, with whom he developed a close collaboration over the next twenty-eight years.[63] As patriarch, Sergios would have been well aware that the Apostle John lacked a major sanctuary in the center of Constantinople where his annual *synaxis* could be celebrated at a convenient processional distance from the Great Church. The omission was all the more glaring in view of the fact that Justinian and Justin II had provided other leading apostles with centrally located churches: St Peter's next to Hagia Sophia, St Paul's at the Acropolis point, and St James's at the Chalkoprateia.[64] The re-dedication to St John of another church close to Hagia Sophia thus filled a conspicuous liturgical gap. At the same time, it coincided with two other developments that brought the figure of St John into sharp and unprecedented focus in Constantinople during Heraclius' reign.

Heraclius came to power at a moment of unprecedented world crisis, when the Roman Empire was in the process of losing ground to Sassanian Persia in the "last world war of antiquity". In the decade after 610, the Persians conquered Syria, Palestine and Egypt, and their armies ravaged Asia Minor as far as the Bosphoros. Christian sanctuaries throughout these areas faced desecration by the invaders. This happened most famously at Jerusalem, where the Persians, on taking the city in 614,

---

62 Ed. L. Sternbach, "Analecta Avarica," *Rozprawy Akademii Umiejętności, Wydiał filolog.*, 2nd series, 14 (Cracow 1900), 298–320, esp. 316–317.
63 Kaegi 2003, 60.
64 St Peter's was located near the *skeuophylakion* of Hagia Sophia, that is near the north-east corner of the building: Preger, *Scriptores*, 78 apparatus; Janin 1969, III, 398–399. It must have been built together with or after the Great Church. For St James and St Paul, see above, nn. 2, 27.

sacked the churches and deported the relic of the True Cross to Ctesiphon. What happened in Jerusalem was to be anticipated elsewhere, as the emperor and patriarch clearly did anticipate it in the case of a recently deceased holy man, Theodore of Sykeon in Galatia: fearing that his relic would be despoiled by the Persians, but also desiring its protective presence for the capital city, they had it translated to Constantinople.[65] The same concerns were surely raised with regard to other sacred sites in Asia Minor, and especially the most sacred and splendid of all: the shrine of St John the Apostle at Ephesus. Ephesus was partially destroyed in 614, and whether the destruction was caused by the Persians or by an earthquake, the security of the church and of pilgrim access to the site was clearly disrupted.[66] It is therefore a reasonable hypothesis that at this point the authorities removed a part of the Apostle's tomb – his only available 'relic,' together with the sacred dust or 'manna' that it gave off[67] – to a newly completed church in Constantinople that was rededicated for the occasion. Anthony of Novgorod reported that the church in question contained "the stone that was placed under the head of St John the Theologian in his tomb".[68] The same rationale of removing relics to Constantinople in the face of the Persian invasion may explain why the church of St John Diippion housed the cults of other important saints of Asia Minor, notably St Antipas of Pergamon, St Tryphon of Nicaea, and St Orestes of Tyana.

By causing death, destruction and desecration throughout the East, the Persian invasions, coupled with the Avar and Slav invasions and the internal violence that accompanied the overthrow of Maurice and Phocas, undoubtedly intensified the mood of apocalyptic anxiety about the future of the world and the eschatological identity of Constantinople. The end of the empire and of the world was anticipated as never before. In these circumstances, the officially prompted confirmation, by Andrew of Caesarea, that the Book of Revelation was not only the divinely inspired work of an apostle and evangelist but also highly relevant to the current situation could only increase the reverence for St John the Theologian in Constantinople and encourage the idea of honouring him with the new church that Heraclius was completing. Here it is worth recalling, too, that Andrew of Caesarea's interpretation of the millennial prophecy in Revelation 20 repeated that of St Augustine. Heraclius came to Constantinople from North Africa, where Augustine had written and taught, and his legacy must have remained strong. Thus, we cannot rule out the possibility that the

---

65 Kirch 1901, 252–272.
66 Persians: Foss 1975, 739. Earthquake: Foss 1979.
67 Like Christ and the Virgin Mary, it was believed that St John had left no corporeal remains on earth. According to the hagiographical tradition that came to prevail in Constantinople, his body was miraculously removed (μετετέθη) after its burial, and the manna was produced annually on 8 May: *Synaxarium*, ed. Delehaye, cols. 82, 8 May. This tradition of a bodily *metastasis* was clearly related to the belief that St John would remain alive on earth until the reign of Antichrist, see below.
68 Ed. and trans. G. Majeska in Spingou 2022, 512–513.

emperor himself brought the Augustinian exegesis to Constantinople, although there were certainly other routes by which it could have arrived.

Finally, we should recall one detail from the travel account of Julien Bordier, who saw the church of St John just before its demolition at the beginning of the seventeenth century. He says that it was decorated with mosaics depicting scenes from the Apocalypse. It would be unwise to place too much weight on this short statement, which neither tells us exactly what iconography Bordier saw, or how he identified it. Nevertheless, it is perhaps significant that he mistakenly thought the church was dedicated to St John the Baptist: in other words, he did not interpret the iconography on the basis of the church's real dedication to St John the Apostle. The possibility therefore remains that this was a rare, if not unique, cycle of images from the Revelation of St John, commissioned by Heraclius on his completion of the church, although a substantial input by Romanos I, who restored the building in the tenth century, cannot be ruled out. Mosaics or no mosaics, however, Heraclius' completion and rededication of the church added St John the Apostle to the supernatural defenders of Constantinople, and gave him an interest in ensuring that he would recognize it as the city of the saints, the New Jerusalem, and not the other city he had seen in his vision.

The apotropaic function of church building was never explicitly articulated, which may occasion some doubt as to whether it actually existed. One later text, indeed, explicitly denied any hope that Constantinople would be saved because its churches and relics made it too holy for God to destroy. In the *Life of St Andrew the Fool* (10th c., set in the 5th c.), the saint delivers a long apocalyptic prophecy in response to a certain Epiphanios who asks him, "How will this our city, the New Jerusalem, pass away? What will become of the holy churches which are here, and the crosses and the precious icons and the books and the relics of the saints?" Andrew replies that the city will remain safe under the protection of the Theotokos until the end. Eventually, however, it will be desecrated and defiled by the rule of a wicked woman who will burn icons, crosses and sacred books, and will seek to destroy the relics of the saints, although God will spirit them away. After that, God will uproot the city and hurl it into the sea like a millstone.[69] But Epiphanios has a problem: "Some people say that the Great Church of God will not be submerged with the city but will be suspended in the air by an invisible power". To which Andrew replies, "When the whole city sinks into the sea, how can the Great Church remain? Who will need her? Do you think God dwells in temples made with hands?" Only the column of Constantine in the Forum would remain above water, because it contained the "precious nails" with which Christ had been fixed to the Cross.[70]

---

[69] Just like Babylon the Great in Revelation 18, 21.
[70] Ed. and trans. L. Rydén, 'The Andreas Salos Apocalypse. Greek Text, Translation, and Commentary,' *DOP* 28 (1974), 197–261, at 201–202, 208–209, 211 (text); 215, 220–221, 222 (translation); L. Rydén, *The Life of St Andrew the Fool*, 2 vols (Uppsala 1995), II, 274–279.

The apocalyptic section in the *Life of Andrew the Fool* thus offers, through the mouth of the fictitious saint, an orthodox view of the end of Constantinople, the Empire, and the world, which is ultimately pessimistic. It corresponds to the idea, which we find in other contemporary texts, that Constantinople was both Jerusalem and Babylon[71] – literally the city to end all cities. Along with these texts, it shows that the apotropaic battle to canonize an optimistic vision of the fate of Constantinople was lost as the millennium loomed. Yet insofar as Andrew is made to disappoint the wishful thinking of the inquirer, the *Life* reflects that such wishful thinking still lingered. A similar concern to refute a persistent alternative viewpoint can be seen in another passage, where the saint denounces what is clearly a messianic prophecy about the ultimate salvation of the Jews and their return to Jerusalem.[72] His narrative of the fate of Constantinople may similarly be read as a refutation of a more optimistic scenario that is implied in the questions posed by Epiphanios. In these questions, we can read the pious hopes of the generations of emperors and other Constantinopolitans who invested in the building of churches, the collection of relics, and the production of icons and precious liturgical books. And in Andrew's responses we can read the nightmare scenario that all this investment was meant to avoid, and which made all of it redundant: the mutation of the New Jerusalem into Babylon the Great. It was not a mutation that St John the Theologian had foreseen in Revelation. However, it was one that the biographer of Andrew the Fool expected him to live through, for elsewhere in the text, he has Andrew state that St John "is alive and in the world".[73] This controversial but widely accepted belief, that Christ's beloved Apostle would not see death until the reign of Antichrist,[74] had huge unstated implications for the churches dedicated to St John, in Constantinople, Ephesos and elsewhere. Those implications are interesting to contemplate but, unfortunately, impossible to document.

Bibliography

Asutay, N. (2003). 'Ein unbekanntes Ehrenmonument des Kaisers Phokas aus Synada bei Akronion (Afyon),' *ByzZ* 95, 417–423.

Asutay-Effenberger, N. & Effenberger, A. (2004). 'Zur Kirche auf einem Kupferstich von Ğugas Inciciyan und zum Standort der Chalke-Hirche,' *ByzZ* 97, 51–93.

Bayram, F. (ed.) (2009). *Araştırma Sonuçları Toplantısı 26, 26–30 Mayıs 2008, Ankara* (vol. 3), Ankara.

Beaton, R. & Roueché, C. (eds.) (1993). *The Making of Byzantine History. Studies dedicated to Donald M. Nicol*, Aldershot.

Berger, A. (1988). *Untersuchungen zu den Patria Konstantinupoleos*, Bonn.

---

71 Mahé 2018, 503; Flusin/Detoraki 2018, 520.
72 Rydén, 'Andreas Salos Apocalypse,' 210–211 (text), 221–222 (translation); cf. Magdalino 2014.
73 *The Life of St Andrew the Fool*, ed. and trans. Rydén, 218–219.
74 Magdalino 2016, 132–133; cf. Detoraki 2012, 53–55.

Booth, Ph. (2011). 'Shades of Blues and Greens in the Chronicle of John of Nikiu,' *ByzZ* 104, 555–601.

Brandes, W. (1997). 'Ἀναστάσιος ὁ δίκορος: Endzeiterwartung und Kaiserkritik in Byzanz um 500 n. Chr.,' *ByzZ* 90, 24–63.

Brandes, W. (1999). 'Das "Meer" als Motiv in der byzantinischen apokalyptischen Literatur,' in Chrysos et al. 1996, 119–131.

Brandes, W. (2003). 'Sieben Hügel: Die imaginäre Topographie Konstantinopels zwischen apokalyptischem Denken und moderner Wissenschaft,' *Rechtsgeschichte* 2, 58–71.

Brandes, W. & Schmieder, F. (eds.) (2008). *Endzeiten. Eschatologie in den monotheistischen Weltreligionen*, Berlin.

Cameron, Al. (1976). *Circus Factions: Blues and Greens at Rome and Byzantium*, Oxford.

Cameron, Av. (1980). 'The Artistic Patronage of Justin II,' *Byzantion* 50, 62–84.

Chrysos, E. et al. (eds.) (1999). *Griechenland und das Meer. Beiträge eines Symposions in Frankfurt im Dezember 1996*, Mannheim.

Congourdeau, M.-H. (2001). 'Jérusalem et Constantinople dans la littérature apocalyptique,' in Kaplan 2001, 125–136.

Dagron, G. (2000). 'L'organisation et le déroulement des courses d'après le Livre des cérémonies,' *T&MByz* 13, 1–200.

Constantinou, E.S. (2011). *Andrew of Caesarea: Commentary on the Apocalypse*, Washington D.C.

Constantinou, E.S. (2013). *Guiding to a Blessed End: Andrew of Caesarea and his Apocalypse Commentary in the Ancient Church*, Washington D.C.

Dal Santo, M. (2012). *Debating the Saints' Cult in the Age of Gregory the Great*, Oxford.

Detoraki, M. (2012). 'Livres censures: le cas de l'hagiographie byzantine,' *Bulgaria Medievalis* 3, 45–58.

Flusin, B. & M. Detoraki (2018). 'Les histoires édifiantes et Constantinople,' *T&MByz* 22/1, 509–565.

Foss, C. (1975). 'The Persians in Asia Minor and the end of Antiquity,' *EHR* 90, 721–747.

Foss, C. (1979). *Ephesus after Antiquity*, Cambridge.

Grélois, J.-P. (2007). 'Note sur la disparition de Saint-Jean au Dihippion,' *REByz* 64, 369–372.

Grélois, J.-P. (2010). 'Western Travelers' Perspectives on the Hippodrome/Atmeydanı: Realities and Legends (Fifteenth-Seventeenth Centuries),' in Pitarakis 2010, 213–239.

Janin, R. (1969). *La géographie ecclésiastique de l'empire Byzantin; Pt. 1: Le siège de Constantinople et le patriarcat OEcuménique* (vol. 3: *Les églises et les monastères*), Paris.

Kaegi, W. (2003). *Heraclius, Emperor of Byzantium*, Cambridge.

Kafesçioğlu, Ç. (2009). *Constantinopolis/Istanbul. Cultural Encounter, Imperial Vision and the Construction of the Ottoman Capital*, University Park, PA.

Kaplan, M. (1976). *Les propriétés de la couronne et de l'Église dans l'Empire byzantine (V^e–VIe siècles)*, Paris.

Kaplan, M. (ed.) (2001). *Le sacré et son inscription dans l'espace à Byzance et en Occident. Études comparées*, Paris.

Kirch, C. (1901). 'Nicephori sceuophylaci encomium in S. Theodorum Siceotam,' *AB* 20, 252–272.

de Lange, N. & Tolan, J. (eds.) (2014). *Jews in Early Christian Law. Byzantium and the Latin West, 6th–11th Centuries*, Turnhout.

Lopez Estrada, F. (ed.) (1943). *Ruy González de Clavijo: Embajada a Tamorlán*, Madrid.

Magdalino, P. (1993). 'The history of the future and its uses: prophecy, policy and propaganda,' in Beaton/Roueché 1993, 3–34.

Magdalino, P. (ed.) (2003a). *Byzantium in the Year 1000*, Leiden.

Magdalino, P. (2003b). 'The Year 1000 in Byzantium,' in Magdalino 2003a, 250–251.

Magdalino, P. (2008). 'The End of Time in Byzantium,' in Brandes/Schmieder 2008, 119–133.

Magdalino, P. (2014). '"All Israel will be saved"? The forced baptism of the Jews and imperial eschatology,' in de Lange/Tolan 2014, 231–242.
Magdalino, P. (2016) 'The Apostolic Tradition in Constantinople,' *Scandinavian Journal of Byzantine and Modern Greek Studies* 2, 115–141.
Mahé, J.-P. (2018). 'Joseph, traducteur arménien à Constantinople au Xe siècle,' *T&MByz* 22/1, 499–508.
Mango, C. (1950). 'Le Diippion. Étude historique et topographique,' *REByz* 8, 152–161.
Mango, C. & Scott, R. (1997). *The Chronographia of Theophanes Confessor*, Oxford.
Mathews, T.F. (1971). *The Early Churches of Constantinople: Architecture and Liturgy*, University Park, PA.
Mayer, W. & Allen, P. (2012). *The Churches of Syrian Antioch (300–638 CE)*, Leuven.
Niewöhner, P. (2009). 'Byzantinische Gebälke im archäologischen Museum Istanbul,' in Bayram 2009, 1431–1452.
Pitarakis, B. (ed.) (2010). *Hippodrome/Atmeydanı. A Stage for Istanbul's History* (2 vols.), Istanbul.
Spingou, F. (ed.), (2022). *Sources for Byzantine Art History*, (vol. 3: *The Visual Culture of Late Byzantium*), Cambridge.

James Howard-Johnston
Jerusalem in 630

Jerusalem was not one of the great cities of the Middle East in antiquity. Its position, set well back from the coast, a stiff climb from the rich plain of Sharon, on the edge of the dry Judaean upland, inhibited its development into a metropolis. It was no more than a bloated fortress, occupying a natural acropolis, the Temple Mount, and several nearby defensible hills. It had been able to develop into a respectable urban settlement, thanks to a relatively abundant water supply. In human terms, it did not stand out from the mass of cities which studded the Middle East in its late-antique heyday.[1] But its past history invested it with extraordinary status. For it was the meeting-place between the immaterial and material worlds. In the deep past God had directed his chosen people across the Jordan. He had aided Joshua as he led the army of Israel into their allotted land and conquered it, city by city. He had authorized David to bring the Ark of the Covenant into the city and to place it in the Holy of Holies in the Temple. Jerusalem was thus the central place in his providential scheme for mankind, in that early era when the Jews were the instruments for the realizing of his will on earth.[2]

With each new stage in the development of monotheism, the status of Jerusalem was enhanced. It provided the setting for the drama which inaugurated the second era of human history. It was there that God incarnate, the single person of Christ, perfect in his divinity and perfect in his humanity, submitted to a human court, was convicted and sentenced to a lingering, painful death by crucifixion. It was there that, by the climactic act of the Resurrection, the godhead enmeshed in the flesh had opened the way to salvation for all mankind. It was no wonder then, that the supernatural aura of Jerusalem grew ever stronger, that places associated with the Passion were increasingly venerated, as this new, complex, proselytizing form of monotheism infiltrated the Roman empire, east and west. So intense was the devotion of Christians to the holy places that a direct link was soon established between them and the imperial authority, once Constantine had adopted the new faith. The legend of the discovery of the True Cross by his mother Helena, and the dispatch of a fragment to the new imperial city which bore Constantine's name, provided the vital connection between the Gospel story and the role of the Christian Roman empire as the divinely authorized director of earthly affairs.[3]

Jerusalem thus acquired unrivalled status as a sacred place in late antiquity. In religious terms, it was the *omphalos* of the earth, that central point from which the divine debouched into the human world. As holy city, it easily outranked the great

---

[1] Liebeschuetz 2001, 54–63, 295–303; Avni 2014, 109–125, 138–145.
[2] Peters 1985, 1–130; Wilken 1993, 1–19, 46–64.
[3] Klein 2004, 31–59; Shalev-Hurvitz 2015, 43–73.

metropoleis of the Mediterranean, which, by virtue of their wealth and political dominance, had become the principal cities of the Christian world. If, breaking loose from the trammels of chronology, we look ahead for a moment into the third, Islamic era, in which a purer, more austere monotheism was disseminated throughout the world, we will see that Jerusalem's role was yet more elevated, raised up to a cosmic level. A strange rock which wells up from the surface of the Temple Mount was identified as the place where God's feet had rested when he created the whole visible universe. It was also scheduled to be the place where the Last Judgement would take place at the end of time.[4]

Despite its special providential role, despite the strength of its natural and manmade defences, Jerusalem was not impregnable. Its capture by Pompey in 63 BC, like its earlier sack by Nebuchadnezzar in 587–6, marked a key stage in its history and that of the Jews – the incorporation of the city and the people into the Roman empire, in preparation for the inauguration of a new era in the reign of Augustus with the Incarnation and the supersession of the Old by the New Testament.[5] Over the next thousand years or so, four armed assaults were successfully made – by Roman legions against rebel Jewish forces (twice), by Persians in the course of the last Persian-Roman war (603–630), and by the First Crusade.[6] Each caught the attention of a listening world and resonated down the years, none more so than its capture by the Persians in May 614. For it fell to the forces of a great rival power, devoted to an alien dualist and idolatrous faith. Damage was done to the holy places and there were atrocities in the course of the city's sack which could be and were magnified in the propaganda subsequently pumped out by the Roman authorities.[7] Worst of all – at least this became the central theme of Roman propaganda – the fragments of the True Cross were unearthed, torn away from their proper setting and deported to Ctesiphon-Veh Ardashir, capital of the Persian Sasanian empire.

The fall of Jerusalem came at a low point in the Roman empire's fortunes, when its innermost line of defence on the Euphrates had been breached and Persian forces had conquered Syria, from which they had pushed south into Palestine and occupied

---

4 Elad 1992, 33–58, and van Ess 1992, 89–103.
5 The most scholarly of Byzantine universal historians, George Syncellus, duly divided his history in two at 63 BC – Torgerson 2015, 93–117, at 97–111.
6 There was no Arab siege. The city submitted along with the rest of Palestine in 634 (Howard-Johnston 2010, 466).
7 A mass burial in a cave by the pool of Mamilla (or Maqella) outside the Jaffa Gate corroborates the massacre there reported by Strategius, c.11.2, ed. & trans. G. Garitte, *La prise de Jérusalem par les Perses en 614*, CSCO 202–3, Scriptores Iberici 11–2 (Louvain, 1960) and *Expugnationis Hierosolymae A.D. 614 recensiones Arabicae*, CSCO 340–1 & 347–8, Scriptores Arabici 26–9 (Louvain, 1973–4). Several hundred skeletons were found piled up in a cave which is fronted by a funerary chapel, with a mosaic inscription praying for the salvation and succour 'of those whose names the Lord knows'. The latest of the 130 coins found in the cave was a gold solidus of the Emperor Phocas (602–610). See Reich 1996, 26–33, 60; *Corpus inscriptionum Iudaeae/Palaestinae*, ed. H.M. Cotton et al., I.2 (Berlin, 2012), 245–246 (no. 869).

the provincial capital, Caesarea. While the commander-in-chief, Shahrbaraz, showed good sense and kept his forces away from the holy city, content merely to send in a small control commission, feelings began to run high inside the city as Easter approached, eventually breaking out into riots in the course of which the members of the control commission were killed and a pogrom began. The Jews appealed for help. Shahrbaraz had no choice but to intervene.[8]

He advanced swiftly. The Patriarch Zacharias was filled with foreboding and bewailed what he saw lying in store for his flock and the holy places. His policy of accommodation was in ruins. All he could do was to send off an emissary, Modestus, abbot of St Theodosius, to ask the Roman force at Jericho to launch a diversionary attack.[9] The siege began at the very end of April when the Persians surrounded the city and began to construct siege-towers and artillery pieces. Inevitably damage was caused to sites in the vicinity. The size of the Persian army deterred the Roman force summoned from Jericho, which promptly withdrew. Their departure allowed the Beduin to raid widely, prompting a general evacuation of the monasteries in the Judaean desert immediately to the east of Jerusalem. The mood plummeted inside Jerusalem. There were premonitions of disaster outside. A monk of St Sabas had a vision first of Christ on the Cross at Golgotha, turning away from the entreaties of the faithful, and then of the church of the Holy Sepulcher awash with mud. He was killed a few days later. Two prisoners, monks from Phoenicia, were watching the city, when they saw its protective angels leave under orders from above, sixteen or seventeen days into the siege. Three days later, probably on 17th May, the walls were breached by mining, by the Damascus Gate on the north-east side, and the Persians fought their way into the city.[10]

Shahrbaraz probably did what he could to restrain his men during the sacking of the city. When order was restored three days later, his chief concern was to identify and remove trouble-makers, the political and religious leadership headed by Zacharias, and those with useful skills. He also sought out the fragments of the Cross, probably so as to assuage the feelings of the large Christian communities of Mesopotamia who might otherwise become restive at the news from Palestine. He then withdrew, back to Caesarea, still reluctant to impose Persian rule directly on the holy city and most of Palestine. There was no question, though, of the Roman government's neglecting the opportunity to make capital out of the episode. The only way to strike back at the enemy and to sustain spirits (and the regime's standing) at home was by a propaganda campaign. Every stop was pulled out to blacken the Persians. Much

---

8 The best source is the history attributed to Sebeos – *Patmut'iwn Sebeosi*, ed. G.V. Abgaryan (Erevan, 1979), 114.29–115.23, trans. R.W. Thomson in R.W. Thomson & J. Howard-Johnston, *The Armenian History Attributed to Sebeos*, TTH 31, 2 vols. (Liverpool, 1999), I *Translation and Notes*, II *Historical Commentary* (n. 34 for the siege of Jerusalem). See also Strategius, cc.2.8–3.5.
9 Ps.-Sebeos 115,23–5; Strategius c.5,1–20.
10 Ps.-Sebeos 115,25–31; Strategius cc.5,21–8.6. *Cf.* Flusin 1992, II, 141–142, 147–159; Magness 2011, 85–98, at 88–94.

was made of the capture and removal of the Cross, presented as a latter-day analogue to the Babylonian Captivity. Such propaganda was, however, double-edged. It could and did, indeed, cause damage to east Roman prestige in Latin Christendom, undermining the empire's status as an *empire*, as a superordinate power.[11]

Two years after the fall of Jerusalem, the Persians resumed their advance. They occupied the whole of Palestine in 616 and restored order and security. Two large raiding expeditions across Asia Minor in 617 – intended probably to distract the Romans – were followed, after a year's preparations, by the invasion in massive force of Egypt in 619. Alexandria was captured and within little more than a year the whole of Egypt was brought under effective Persian control.[12] Then, in 622, came the final phase of the long war, the phase which would lead to the annihilation of the Roman empire. Notwithstanding the Emperor Heraclius' bold but forlorn counteroffensive targeted on Transcaucasia in 624–625, the Persians retained the initiative and organized an attack on Constantinople and the metropolitan area, from east and west, by two Persian armies and a 80,000-strong host led by their ally, the khagan of the nomadic Avars.[13] One of three contemporary sources for the ten-day siege which followed (29th July–7th August 626), a long sermon delivered probably within a month of the siege's end by the Patriarch Sergius' Syncellus, Theodore, latched on to an Old Testament episode which prefigured Constantinople's survival, when Jerusalem weathered a concerted attack from Samaria and Assyria in the time of Ahaz. The awkward fact that Heraclius, like Ahaz, had sinned, could be passed over, since Heraclius, unlike Ahaz, was not in the city. Theodore's sermon is a fine example of the art of giving historical depth and significance to contemporary events, and of avoiding the giving of offence. A certain superiority was imputed to Constantinople, since it had not fallen unlike Jerusalem later to Nebuchadnezzar.[14]

The turning point in the war came in August 626. Not only were the Avars thwarted by the entirely manmade fortifications of Constantinople, despite the array of advanced siege-engines which they brought to bear and waves of attack by land and, eventually, sea, but also one of the two Persian armies was defeated in northern Asia Minor and, even more ominous from the Persian point of view, the great power of the northern world, the Turkish khaganate, which controlled the steppes from the inner Asian frontiers of China to the Crimea, intervened on the Roman side, an army being dispatched across the Caucasus with an ultimatum instructing the Sasanian king. Khusro II, to withdraw from Roman territory and to return all prisoners of war, or

---

11 An important source for the dissemination of this propaganda was Strategius' account of the sack and its aftermath (cc.8–12). *Cf.* Flusin 1992, II, 159–172.
12 Flusin 1992, II, 177–181; Altheim-Stiehl 1992, 5–8.
13 Howard-Johnston 1999, 1–44, at 1–4, 14–19 (repr. in Howard-Johnston 2006, Ch. VIII); Howard-Johnston 1995, 131–142, at 131–138 (repr. in Howard-Johnston 2006, Ch. VII).
14 Theodorus Syncellus, ed. L. Sternbach, *Analecta Avarica*, Rozprawy Akademii Umiejętności, Wydział Filologiczny, ser. 2, 15 (Kraków, 1900), 298.1–320.29, at 298.29–300.20.

else face Turkish might.[15] It was assuredly the grim prospect of war in the north rather than a last foolhardy thrust by Heraclius and his small expeditionary force across the Zagros and south against the Sasanian metropolitan region which triggered the successful palace revolution which dethroned Khusro, ended the fighting and opened the way for peace negotiations in spring 628.[16]

Eventually, in a third round of negotiations with a third Sasanian regime, that of Khusro's daughter Boran, terms for peace were agreed. They included the symbolically all-important return of the True Cross to Christian Roman hands, those of Heraclius, and its restoration to its proper place in Jerusalem in a carefully choreographed ceremony on Wednesday 21st March 630.[17]

How on earth is the modern observer, living in an irreligious age, to retroject himself into a distant time where notions about the supernatural role of Jerusalem were deeply embedded in the collective consciousness of Christians, Jews and, later, Muslims? How is one to breathe something of the charged atmosphere at the end of the greatest war between the Roman and Persian empires, as Heraclius prepared to restore the True Cross to its proper place on Golgotha? No contemporary could deny that God had intervened in human affairs with the most spectacular results. None, however eminent their position in the hierarchies of state or church, could emancipate themselves from the ambient thought-world. But ideas, hopes and fears, attitudes surely varied considerably between milieux and individuals. And there is no single source which can be used as an authoritative guide. Thus, we cannot simply extrapolate from the views expressed by George of Pisidia, who wrote a short poem about the restoration of the Cross but did not witness it in person. He may well have been more representative of contemporary views than usual when, ten days after the ceremony, the news reached Constantinople and the poem began to take shape in his mind. He seems to have been in a state of high excitement, his attention shifting hither and thither (like the eye of a spectator flitting over the procession) as different thoughts came into his head. But even in this comparatively artless poem, written, one suspects, in some haste, he avoids the obvious Biblical comparisons of Heraclius with Joshua and David, and introduces one with Jason (retrieving the golden fleece) which is unlikely to have crossed anyone else's mind.[18]

---

15 Howard-Johnston 1995, 137–142; Howard-Johnston 1999, 19–20, 22–26, 40–42.
16 Howard-Johnston 1995, 137–142; Howard-Johnston 1999, 19–20, 22–26, 40–42; Howard-Johnston 2004, 93–113 (repr. in Howard-Johnston 2006, Ch. IX).
17 Mango 1985, 91–118, at 112–114; Howard-Johnston 1999, 26–29; Flusin 1992, II, 293–309. But see Zuckerman 2013b, 197–218, who shifts the ceremony to 21st March 629, has Heraclius to send the Cross to Constantinople for veneration in August 629 and places its *re-installation* in Jerusalem in 630 (before 30th March).
18 Georg. Pisid. *In rest. S. Cruc.*, ed. & trans. A. Pertusi, *Giorgio di Pisidia poemi: I Panegirici epici* (Ettal, 1959), 225–230.

Still the imaginative leap must be made. We must strive to view events from within as well as without, with the aid of other extant accounts of the solemn ceremony which celebrated the triumph of the Romans as Christians, as agents of God's will.

Heraclius waited at Hierapolis for the return of the delegation which he had sent to Ctesiphon.[19] This distant heir of Constantine the Great (something advertised by the name which he gave his eldest son) readied himself to receive back the Cross which God, in his anger, had allowed to fall into Persian hands.[20] He had outdone Constantine. He had not merely threatened war but with the boldness of an Alexander had penetrated deep into the interior of the Persian empire.[21] Both these images were in the air, but Heraclius preferred to portray himself more modestly as Pious Basileus in Christ, stripping off the other titles (Imperator, Augustus) and honorifics which exalted Roman imperial power. His authority was shown thus to be derived from God rather than (manipulated) human election.[22] Like an Old Testament king, he had been acting as God's agent in his campaigns. Just as God had encouraged the Israelites by sending down manna, he had given Heraclius' men a sign of his favor on their entry into Persian territory in 624 when they saw what should have been a desiccated landscape bathed in unseasonal dew.[23] Heraclius had campaigned with all the tactical acumen of Joshua, achieving surprise by ambush and night march, and with the same God-sanctioned ruthlessness in victory. Like Joshua, he had conquered the holy land, although, in his case, the fighting had taken place far away.[24] It was therefore as much as Old Testament king as Roman emperor that he was going to take the Cross back to Jerusalem.

The instrument of degrading punishment had long since been transformed into the symbol of Christian victory.[25] For contemporary observers the wooden fragments of the original Cross were imbued with awesome supernatural power. When they described it as instrument of Christian victory, they were not simply speaking figuratively. The Cross became the inanimate pendant to Heraclius in the working out of God's will on earth. It was guarantor of the safety of the whole civilized world for a contemporary Palestinian monk. Sophronius, future Patriarch of Jerusalem, at the time a refugee in north Africa, described it as destroyer of death and demons,

---

19 *Chron. M. Syr.*, ed. & trans. J.B. Chabot, 4 vols. (Paris, 1899–1910), II, 427 (trans.), IV, 418 (text); *Chron. 1234 pertinens*, ed. J.-B. Chabot, CSCO 81, scriptores syri 36 (Paris, 1916), 238.7–13, trans. A. Palmer, *The Seventh Century in the West-Syrian Chronicles*, TTH 15 (Liverpool, 1993), 142.

20 Heraclius the New Constantine, born 612 – *Chronicon Paschale*, ed. L. Dindorf, Corpus Scriptorum Historiae Byzantinae (Bonn, 1832), 702.16–18, trans. M. & M. Whitby, *Chronicon Paschale 284–628 AD*, TTH 7 (Liverpool, 1989). *Cf.* Drijvers 2002, 175–190, at 181–183.

21 Reinink in Reinink/Stolte 2002, 81–94, at 84–86, 90–91.

22 Shahid 1972, 293–320; Chrysos 1978, 29–75; Kresten 2000, 178–179; Zuckerman 2010, 865–890.

23 Exodus, 16:4–35; Theoph. *Chron.* ed. C. de Boor, 2 vols. (Leipzig, 1883–5), I, 307.21–3, trans. C. Mango & R. Scott, *The Chronicle of Theophanes Confessor: Byzantine and Near Eastern History AD 284–813* (Oxford, 1997).

24 Joshua, 8:1–29, 10:1–12:24.

25 Drijvers 2002, 179–180.

grantor of life to mortals, in the anacreontic poem which he wrote to celebrate its return. In his anger, God had allowed the Persians to capture it as they rampaged over Roman territory, but the Cross had killed Khusro, "the generator of war, the evil king of evil, the cruel persecutor of sweet peace," rolling that perpetrator of universal slaughter easily out of life.[26]

George of Pisidia touched on this obvious theme. For him too the Cross was laden with power, a Christian analogue to the Ark of the Covenant which likewise belonged properly to the holy city. He too saw its removal by Khusro, described as the plaything/sport of error, as a punishment for sin. But it had been retrieved from the Persian furnace. Its wood had quenched Persian fire. The spiritual missiles it shot had caused internecine conflict. The Cross was the most precious, the most powerful of Christian relics. Universally venerated, its return to Golgotha could be universally celebrated by Christians.[27]

Not by Jews, though. It is here that we touch on the grim underside of the celebrations. At each stage of its progress through Roman territory, the Cross was not only reminding Christians of what they had in common but of what the Saviour had suffered at the hands of the Jews. The Cross, as instrument of crucifixion, could not but rouse anti-Jewish feeling, could not but direct the collective Christian memory back to the ills inflicted on them by the Jews. There had been some active collaboration on the part of the Jews of Palestine at the time of the Persian invasion. But it was Persian intervention to stop the Jerusalem pogrom, the atrocities (much exaggerated but real) committed after the fall of the city, and the unusual license enjoyed by the Jews of the city over the following two years of indirect Persian rule, which had firmly cast the Jews as allies of the Persians. The return of the Cross, which had been torn with their help from the holy city, was bound to re-activate Christian rancor, to heighten tension wherever Jews and Christians lived side by side, to lead to violence on a greater or lesser scale.[28]

The True Cross was received reverently by Heraclius at Hierapolis, probably towards the end of February 630. He had a large body of troops with him, representing the army which had, by its endeavors, recovered it. He was also accompanied by dignitaries, who formed a peripatetic court. He set off on a solemn progress south. Besides the Cross, he was taking back precious vessels belonging to the churches of Jerusalem which had been spirited out the city and kept safe in Constantinople.[29] He travelled south through Galilee, where, according to a plausible story retailed by Eutychius, he received a warm welcome from the Jews and promised that there would be no reprisals. However, the conversion, under pressure, of a rich Jew in whose house he stayed at Tiberias, did not augur well for the future, and, on his arrival at Jerusalem, Heraclius is said to have rescinded his promise when he saw with

---

26 Sophron. *Anacr.* 18, ed. & trans. M. Gigante (Rome, 1957).
27 Georg. Pisid. *In rest. S. Cruc.* 9, 32–34, 58–68, 73–82.
28 *Cf.* Olster 1994, 82–84.
29 Ps.-Sebeos, 131.9–14.

his own eyes the mass grave of executed Christians at Maqella, just outside the western wall. That was probably the occasion for his declaration of a three-mile exclusion zone around the city, which is reported by Theophanes.[30] Unequivocal evidence of anti-Jewish sentiment in high places at this time is provided by two well-placed observers: Sophronius ended his short poem with the wish that Jewish diatribes against the Cross might rebound against their heads, while George of Pisidia slipped in an aside calling on them to abandon their misguided ancestral faith.[31]

Only the barest outlines can be recovered of the ceremony which took place at Jerusalem. The most informative source – an early medieval sermon known under the title of *Reversio Sanctae Crucis* – is, in essence, a miracle story. Whatever happened has been reworked, embellished and re-interpreted. It is hard to separate solid substance from elaboration and invention, save on *a priori* grounds. Still it is worth entertaining, at least as a possibility, the scenario which it suggests. As Heraclius, whose name is deformed into Gracchus, approaches, the people go out to meet him rejoicing, carrying palm leaves, candles and lights, singing hymns and psalms. He rides down the Mount of Olives and stops outside the Golden Gate on the east side of the Temple Mount, because, according to the *Reversio*, at that moment the gate was miraculously blocked and an angel instructed Heraclius to take off his imperial regalia. He obeys, and walks barefoot, clad in nothing save a loincloth, and, as the stones which have fallen miraculously rearrange themselves around the gate, enters the city, carrying the Cross.[32]

There are two key points to this miracle story: the vice-gerent of God enters the city by the same route as Christ took on his way to the Passion; he discards his imperial robes and shoes, then passes through the gate and enters the city as a humble mortal, carrying the Cross. Risky it may be, but I see no reason to reject this picture.[33] It may exaggerate the lengths to which the emperor went in his self-abasement but it does accord with an already documented downgrading of the emperor's earthly authority. It may also be conjectured that the Golden Gate, a large and ornate vestibule with two domed passageways through it, was built to commemorate the ceremony. If its construction (known to antedate the Arab conquest) can be placed in the early

---

30 Eutychius' notices about the Jews of Palestine (ed., M. Breydy, *Das Annalenwerk des Eutychios von Alexandrien: Ausgewählte Geschichten und Legenden kompiliert von Sa'id ibn Batriq um 935 A.D.*, CSCO 471, Scriptores Arabici 44 [Louvain, 1985], 127.10–129.14, trans. op.cit., CSCO 472, Script.Ar. 45 [Louvain, 1985], 107–109) are partially corroborated by Theoph. p. 328.15–23 de Boor. There was no question, it should be noted, of Heraclius' expelling Jews with established residence from the city. The widespread unrest which such an act would have caused, would have greatly complicated the already difficult task of reimposing Roman authority across the Middle East. Unequivocal evidence for the presence of a large and influential Jewish community in Jerusalem shortly after the Arab conquest is provided by Ps.-Sebeos 139.25–140.22.
31 Sophronius, *Anacreontica*, 18.85–88; GP, *In Restitutionem*, 25–26.
32 *Reversio sanctae atque gloriosissimae crucis Domini nostri Jesu Christi*, PL 110, cols. 131–134, at 133C-134C; see Borgehammar 2009.
33 But see Viermann 2021, 293–303.

seventh century, as is suggested by the style of its sculptural decoration, it must surely be dated after the end of the war, when defensive strength was no longer a vital necessity. A connection is also suggested by its alignment, more or less on the axis of the Holy Sepulcher, the destination of the procession led by Heraclius.[34]

The emotions roused on Wednesday 21st March 630 as the procession made its way into the city before a large crowd of spectators are caught best by Ps.-Sebeos. 'There was no little joy on that day as they entered Jerusalem. There was the sound of weeping and wailing; their tears flowed from the awesome fervor of the emotion of their hearts and from the rending of the entrails of the king, the princes, all the troops, and the inhabitants of the city. No one was able to sing the Lord's chants from the fearful and agonizing emotion of the king and the whole multitude'.[35] The two great poles of the empire had come together. The Cross was in the hands of an emperor, who was, for the first time, visiting the holy city. It was an extraordinary conjunction which impressed itself deeply on the collective consciousness. No wonder George of Pisidia, invited Constantine to return and to applaud Heraclius and viewed the Cross as the Ark of the new dispensation.[36]

Heraclius and the dignitaries with him led the way up onto the Temple Mount, then down into the city, along the Via Dolorosa to the complex of shrines enclosed in the church of the Holy Sepulchre.[37] It was there, at the small protuberant rock identified as Golgotha, that a small piece of public theatre was staged (if we can trust the report of it given by Nicephorus). Heraclius handed the reliquary containing the Cross over to Modestus, the senior churchman left in Jerusalem after the deportation of the Patriarch Zacharias in 614. Modestus inspected the seal and declared that it was intact. A hymn of thanksgiving was sung. The Cross was taken out of the reliquary, unlocked by the key which Modestus had kept, restored to its proper place on Golgotha and venerated by all who were there.[38]

---

[34] Mango in Raby/Johns 1992, I, 1–16, at 6–16; Burgoyne, 'The Gates of the Haram al-Sharif,' in op.cit., 105–124, at 106, 111–115. Arab conquest: Howard-Johnston 2010, 380–381, 465–467.

[35] Ps.-Sebeos, 131.15–20, with T'ovma Artsruni, Patmut'iwn Tann Artsruneats', ed. K. Patkanean (St Petersburg, 1887), 97.7–13, trans. R.W. Thomson, Thomas Artsruni: History of the House of the Artsrunik' (Detroit, 1985); Strategius, c.24.8–9.

[36] Translatio reliquiarum S. Anastasii, c.1, ed. & trans. Flusin, Saint Anastase, I, 98–9; GP, In Restitutionem, 49–63, 73–74. A visit by the last emperor to Jerusalem where he hands his crown back to God was to become a key element in the scenario of the last days presented in the late seventh century Apocalypse of Ps.-Methodius – ed. & trans. G.J. Reinink, Die syrische Apokalypse des Pseudo-Methodius, CSCO 540–1, Scriptores Syri 220–1 (Louvain, 1993) and B. Garstad, Apocalypse Pseudo-Methodius, An Alexandrian World Chronicle (Cambridge, Mass., 2012), 1–139.

[37] Shalev-Hurvitz 2015, 55–76.

[38] Strategius, c.24.9; Nicephorus, Breviarium, ed. & trans. C. Mango, Nikephoros Patriarch of Constantinople, Short History, CFHB 13 (Washington, D.C., 1990), c.18.8–16, who goes on to report (c.18.16–17), mistakenly, that Heraclius immediately sent the Cross off to Constantinople; Seert Chron., ed. & trans. A. Scher & R. Griveau, Histoire Nestorienne (Chronique de Séert), PO 13, 556.8–10. Cf. Booth 2014, 159–161.

The solemn, contrite mood which had gripped all participants and spectators at this awesome ceremony probably lightened somewhat when it was over. Heraclius resumed the demeanor of an emperor. Soon afterwards, possibly on the same day, he appointed Modestus Patriarch in succession to Zacharias who had died in exile.[39] He stayed on for a while, conducting the everyday business of government. He was still there when a bishop arrived from Persian Mesopotamia with a letter from the new Nestorian Catholicos, Ishoyahb. He had time to visit and take pleasure in the holy places, outside as well as inside Jerusalem. He bestowed largesse on the patriarchate, returned the church plate which had been kept safe in Constantinople, distributed alms to the poor and made grants to cover the cost of incense in the city's churches. He also made plain his regard and respect for the whole body of Palestinian monks, whose ascetic striving and prayers benefited all their fellow men.[40]

Steps were also taken to enhance the new confidence engendered in Christians. Modestus himself sponsored a new cult, that of St Anastasius the Persian martyr. The Life which he commissioned was completed during his short tenure of the patriarchate (between March and September 630).[41] It provided an additional illustration of the power of the Cross. For it was the news of the arrival of the Cross in Mesopotamia which had set Anastasius on the road to conversion. And it provided an uplifting example for the monks of Palestine and elsewhere. By the death for which he had striven, inspired by voracious reading of the acts of the early Christian martyrs, Anastasius had shown that martyrdom was still within man's reach in that late age. A Life, however, could not by itself create an enduring cult. A shrine was needed to act as a focal point, and that shrine should contain authentic relics for veneration by the faithful. So one of the two monks who had accompanied Anastasius on his journey towards death was sent back to Mesopotamia, on an officially sanctioned mission to recover the martyr's body. He travelled out in the party of the Nestorian bishop who had been negotiating with Heraclius and Modestus, and, with the backing of the Catholicos (and some apparently supernatural help), managed to spirit the body out of the monastery where it was already highly venerated, consoling the monks with a small piece of it, thanking the Catholicos with another.[42]

Rather more than a year after the restoration of the Cross, there was much rejoicing when the martyr's body was brought back to Palestine. Large crowds turned out to watch its arrival at the main cities, Tyre and Caesarea, on its circuitous route to Jerusalem. Popular enthusiasm generated a subsidiary cult at Caesarea (paralleling those which sprang up in Mesopotamia). The celebrations reached a climax on the 2nd of November 631 when the procession reached Jerusalem and the martyr's

---

[39] Strategius, c.24.10; *Translatio*, c.2.3–8.
[40] *Translatio*, cc.1.7–2.8; Ps.-Sebeos, 131.21–23.
[41] Flusin, *Saint Anastase*, II, 191–193.
[42] *Translatio*, cc.2.8–5.6.

body was installed in the monastery which had sheltered him during his seven years of ascetic striving and earnest study.[43]

Anti-Jewish sentiment was fanned by the religious fervor generated by these celebrations. There is no solid evidence of an official, empire-wide campaign of coerced baptism, but the imperial government made no move to protect its Jewish subjects. Programmed as it was to defend and propagate Christianity, it could not adopt an even-handed policy as the Persians had. For Jews, the ambient Christian world was becoming increasingly threatening. Pressure to accept Christianity grew stronger.[44] Rabble-rousers were all too likely to cause trouble in the streets, and the local authorities might, in a surge of religious enthusiasm, introduce a campaign of conversion (as they did in north Africa in 632). In Jewish eyes, Heraclius' image darkened and merged with that of the embodiment of evil, Armilus or Hermolaos (a combination of Romulus and Eremolaos, 'Waster of Peoples'), son of Satan and a stone statue, who would be a fierce, merciless adversary of the Jews on the eve of the last days.[45]

Christians, for their part, regarded Jews as misguided adherents of an outmoded faith. They tested their attachment by applying social pressure to convert. They also prised the Old Testament away from their possessive grasp, taking current events to have been prefigured, like the Gospel story itself, in the Biblical past. The final step in this assault on Judaism would have been for Christians to appropriate the Temple Mount, which had been left derelict throughout late antiquity. The construction of the Golden Gate, if it can be securely associated with Heraclius, and the contemporary, similarly decorated double gate on the south side, may perhaps be taken as a first move in a staged appropriation of the site. Then, if the *Reversio* is to be believed, the Cross itself was carried in procession over the Temple Mount, a ritual act of great importance in which the assembled dignitaries of the Christian empire implicitly asserted a claim to the site. It may be possible to discern a third planned move, namely permanent occupation, if we attend carefully to the clues left by an extraordinary artefact of a later age.

The Joshua Roll is an archaizing illuminated manuscript, securely dated to the middle of the tenth century. Fifteen sheets of parchment were glued together to form a roll, just over 10.5 m long and 30–31.5 cm high. It presents a continuous picture frieze, which illustrates Joshua's campaigns of conquest in the holy land (I Joshua 1–12, of which the first and last chapters are not covered in the roll which is in-

---

[43] *Translatio*, cc.5.6–6.18.
[44] Olster 1994, 84–92; Dagron/Déroche 1991, 17–273, at 30–38; Drijvers 2002, 188–190. Evidence: Devreesse 1937, 25–35; *Doctrina Jacobi nuper baptizati*, ed. & trans. V. Déroche, in Dagron & Déroche, 'Juifs et Chrétiens,' 47–229, at 70–73; Fredegar, iv.65, ed. & trans. J.M. Wallace-Hadrill, *The Fourth Book of the Chronicle of Fredegar with Its Continuations* (London, 1960); Mich.Syr, II, 414, IV, 413; *History of the Patriarchs of the Coptic Church of Alexandria (St Mark to Benjamin I)*, ed. & trans. B. Evetts, *PO* 1, 492.
[45] Levi 1914, 129–160; 1919, 108–121; 1920, 57–65; van Bekkum 2002, 81–112, at 103–110.

complete). Short excerpts from the Biblical text act as captions. The action is set in an illusionistic landscape, individual episodes being separated by trees, steep hillsides, and pieces of classical architecture. Personifications, familiar in late-antique secular art, materialize from time to time. The Joshua Roll looks out of place in the tenth century: its form, a roll, is classical (as against the medieval codex) and the lines of text run parallel to the main axis of the visual field (as in antiquity), rather than descending vertically (as in the middle ages); style and iconography are equally redolent of late antiquity. It seems virtually certain that it is a tenth century copy of an earlier illustrated roll, faithful save for a few lacunae in the captions (where the text in the original was illegible) and some parallel pictorial errors (betraying misunderstanding of minor iconographic details).[46]

The motivation behind so extensive an illustration of Joshua's campaigns was surely contemporary relevance. They were taken to prefigure parallel military feats in the Christian era which had a similar result, conquest of the holy land. Of the two historical episodes which spring to mind, John Tzmiskes' single, swift thrust towards Jerusalem in 975 can be ruled out, because the extant Joshua Roll is a mere facsimile of an earlier roll (and, insofar as it can be dated on stylistic grounds, appears to predate Tzimiskes' campaign). That leaves Heraclius' Persian campaigns as the likely latterday analogue to those of Joshua and the religious celebration of victory at Jerusalem as the occasion for its production.[47]

What, though, was the intended function of the original roll? To judge by the later copy, it was not a finished work – the rendering of figures and settings is spare, executed with a handful of colors. If anything, it looks like a cartoon for a larger, monumental work. There is indeed a sculptural quality about the frieze of figures, which recalls the traditional Roman triumphal column. It is but a small step, from these widely canvassed hypotheses of art historians, to conjecture that the original Joshua Roll was a cartoon, commissioned by Heraclius, for a triumphal column to be erected in Jerusalem to commemorate the victory of the Christian empire with the same combination of biblical iconography and classical styles as was used in the David Plates.[48] It is a rather larger step to conjecture that the chosen site lay on the Temple Mount, but that was where the statement of Christian victory would be most visible, that was where the beginning of new era of Christian solidarity and dominance could be publicly declared to greatest effect. A surge of Christian confidence at the end of the great war may, on these conjectures, have emboldened the authorities of state and church to embark on a final act in the long process of Christianization of the Near East – the full incorporation of the holiest of Jewish pla-

---

46 Wander 2012, 17–82.
47 Wander 2012, 93–97, 133–138.
48 Dalton 1906, 1–24, at 1–13, 23–24 (circumstances of discovery and other items concealed); Dodd 1961, no. 58–66 (stamps and date); Weitzmann 1979, 475–483 (the best short description, save for the identification of the covenant of David and Jonathan as the scene depicted on the most problematic of the small plates); Wander 1973, 89–104 (full analysis of iconography).

ces into the Christian city of Jerusalem. The Joshua Column would presumably have been followed by a larger building program. Discarding hindsight, and staring forward into a murky future from the year 630, we might pick out the dim outline of a massive domed structure or a great basilica or a complex of both standing on the Temple Mount, built as a focal point for the whole of Christendom in what was hoped would be a new era of unity ...

Bibliography

Altheim-Stiehl, R. (1992). 'Zur zeitlichen Bestimmung der sāsānidischen Eroberung Ägyptens,' in Brehm/Klie 1992, 5–8.

Avni, G. (2014). *The Byzantine-Islamic Transition in Palestine: An Archaeological Approach*, Oxford.

Bekkum, W.J. van (2002). 'Jewish Messianic Expectations in the Age of Heraclius,' in Reinink/Stolte 2002, 81–112.

Booth, P. (2014). *Crisis of Empire: Doctrine and Dissent at the End of Late Antiquity*, Berkeley.

Borgehammar, S. (2009). 'Heraclius Learns Humility: Two Early Latin Accounts Composed for the Celebration of Exaltatio Crucis,' *Millennium* 6, 145–201.

Brehm, O. & Klie, S. (eds.) (1992). *ΜΟΥΣΙΚΟΣ ΑΝΗΡ. Festschrift für Max Wegner zum 90. Geburtstag*, Bonn.

Chrysos, E.S. (1978). 'The Title Βασιλεὺς in Early Byzantine International Relations,' *DOP* 32, 29–75.

Dagron G. & Déroche, V. (1991). *Juifs et Chrétiens en Orient Byzantin*, Paris.

Dalton, O.M. (1906). 'A Second Silver Treasure from Cyprus,' *Archaeologia* 60, 1–24.

Devreesse, R. (1937). 'La fin inédite d'une lettre de Saint Maxime: Un baptême forcé de Juifs et de Samaritains à Carthage en 632,' *RSR* 17, 25–35.

Dodd, E.C. (1961). *Byzantine Silver Stamps*, Washington D.C.

Drijvers, J.W. (2002). 'Heraclius and the Restitutio Crucis: Notes on Symbolism and Ideology,' in Reinink/Stolte 2002, 175–190.

Durand, J. & Flusin, B. (eds.) (2004). *Byzance et les reliques du Christ*, Paris.

Elad, A. (1992). 'Why did 'Abd al-Malik Build the Dome of the Rock? A Re-Examination of the Muslim Sources,' in Raby/Johns 1992, 33–58.

Ess, J. van (1992). ''Abd al-Malik and the Dome of the Rock: An Analysis of Some Texts,' in Raby/Johns 1992, 89–103.

Flusin, B. (1992). *Saint Anastase le Perse et l'histoire de la Palestine au début du VIIe siècle* (2 vols.), Paris.

Gnoli, G. (ed.) (2004). *La Persia e Bisanzio*, Rome.

Holum, K.G. & Lapin, H. (eds.) (2011). *Shaping the Middle East: Jews, Christians, and Muslims in an Age of Transition 400–800 C.E.*, Bethesda Ma.

Howard-Johnston, J. (1995). 'The Siege of Constantinople in 626,' in Mango/Dagron 1995, 131–142 [repr. in Howard-Johnston 2006, Ch. VII].

Howard-Johnston, J. (1999). 'Heraclius' Persian Campaigns and the Revival of the East Roman Empire, 622–630,' *War in History* 6, 1–44 [repr. in Howard-Johnston 2006, Ch. 8].

Howard-Johnston, J. (2004). 'Pride and Fall: Khusro II and His Regime, 626–628,' in Gnoli 2004, 93–113 [repr. in Howard-Johnston 2006, Ch. IX].

Howard-Johnston, J. (ed.) (2006). *East Rome, Sasanian Persia and the End of Antiquity: Historiographical and Historical Essays*, Aldershot.

Howard-Johnston, J. (2010). *Witnesses to a World Crisis: Historians and Histories of the Middle East in the Seventh Century*, Oxford.

Jankowiak, M. & Montinaro, F. (eds.) (2015). *Studies in Theophanes. The Chronicle of Theophanes: Sources, Composition, Transmission*, Paris.

Klein, H.A. (2004). 'Constantine, Helena, and the Cult of the True Cross in Constantinople,' in Durand/Flusin 2004, 31–59.

Kresten, O. (2000). 'Herakleios und der Titel βασιλεὺς,' in Speck 2000, 178–179.

Levi, I. (1914–1920). 'L'Apocalypse de Zorobabel et le roi de Perse Siroès,' *REJ* 68 (1914), 129–160; 70 (1919), 108–121; 71 (1920), 57–65.

Liebeschuetz, J.H.W.G. (2001). *Decline and Fall of the Roman City*, Oxford.

Magness, J. (2011). 'Archaeological Evidence for the Sasanian Persian Invasion of Jerusalem,' in Holum/Lapin 2011, 85–98.

Mango, C. (1985). 'Deux études sur Byzance et la Perse sassanide,' *T&MByz* 9, 91–118.

Mango, C. (1992). 'The Temple Mount, AD 614–638,' in Raby/Johns 1992, 1–16.

Mango, C. & Dagron, G. (eds.) (1995). *Constantinople and Its Hinterland*, Aldershot.

Olster, D.M. (1994). *Roman Defeat, Christian Response, and the Literary Construction of the Jew*, Philadelphia.

Peters, F.E. (1985). *Jerusalem: The Holy City in the Eyes of Chroniclers, Visitors, Pilgrims, and Prophets from the Days of Abraham to the Beginnings of Modern Times*, Princeton.

Raby, J. & Johns, J. (eds.) (1992). *Bayt al-Maqdis, I 'Abd al-Malik's Jerusalem*, Oxford.

Reich, R. (1996). '"God Knows Their Names": Mass Christian Grave Revealed in Jerusalem,' *Biblical Archaeology Review* 22.2, 26–33.

Reinink, G.J. (2002). 'Heraclius, the New Alexander: Apocalyptic Prophecies during the Reign of Heraclius,' in Reinink/Stolte 2002, 81–94.

Reinink, G.J. & Stolte, B.H. (eds.) (2002). *The Reign of Heraclius (610–641): Crisis and Confrontation*, Leuven.

Shahid, I. (1972). 'The Iranian Factor in Byzantium during the Reign of Heraclius,' *DOP* 26, 293–320.

Shalev-Hurvitz, V. (2015). *Holy Sites Encircled: The Early Byzantine Concentric Churches of Jerusalem*, Oxford.

Speck, P. (ed.) (2000). *Varia, 7*, Bonn.

Torgerson, J.W. (2015). 'From the Many, One? The Shared Manuscripts of the Chronicle of Theophanes and the Chronographia of Synkellos,' in Jankowiak/Montinaro 2015, 93–117.

Viermann, N. (2021). *Herakleios, der schwitzende Kaiser. Die oströmische Monarchie in der ausgehende Spätantike*, Berlin.

Wander, S.H. (1973). 'The Cyprus Plates: The Story of David and Goliath,' *MMJ* 8, 89–104.

Wander, S.H. (2012). *The Joshua Roll*, Wiesbaden.

Weitzmann, K. (ed.) (1979). *Age of Spirituality*, New York.

Wilken, R.L. (1993). *The Land Called Holy: Palestine in Christian History and Thought*, New Haven.

Zuckerman, C. (2010). 'On the Titles and Office of the Byzantine Βασιλεὺς,' *T&MByz* 16, 865–890.

Zuckerman, C. (ed.) (2013a). *Constructing the Seventh Century*, Paris.

Zuckerman, C. (2013b). 'Heraclius and the Return of the Holy Cross,' in Zuckerman 2013a, 197–218.

Lutz Greisiger

From 'King Heraclius, Faithful in Christ' to 'Allenby of Armageddon': Christian Reconquistadores Enter the Holy City

On the pleasant, sunny afternoon of December 11th 2017, Jerusalem saw an unusual crowd gathering upon the ramp of the ancient citadel, the 'Tower of David,' on other days used as the entranceway to the city history museum inside. Men and women in suits positioned themselves at the guard rail, together with men wearing the vestments of Greek Orthodox, Armenian and Coptic clergymen, the dark suits and fezzes of Turkish officials and the thawbs and agals of Arab gentlemen. Dressed in a khaki field uniform, riding boots, belt and peaked cap, one of them planted himself behind the microphone stand in the center and, addressing "the Inhabitants of Jerusalem the Blessed and the People Dwelling in Its Vicinity," read a proclamation of martial law over the city and solemnly declared inviolable the holy sites and traditional rights of all resident religious communities.[1]

With this event the Jerusalem municipality marked the centenary of the official seizure of the city by the British Egyptian Expeditionary Force under the command of General Edmund Allenby, after four hundred years of Ottoman rule. To honor this occasion the Tower of David Museum also opened an exhibition entitled "A General and a Gentleman: Allenby at the Gates of Jerusalem." The reenactment took place in the presence of mayor Nir Barkat and the famous general's great-grandnephew Henry J.H. Allenby, among other dignitaries, who in their speeches praised the world-historical significance of the "liberation of Jerusalem." Five days prior to the celebration, the US president had, opportunely enough, announced his country's recognition of Jerusalem as the capital of the State of Israel.[2]

One hundred years before, the real general Allenby had dismounted his horse outside of Jaffa Gate, entered the city on foot, then climbed the ramp to the citadel's portal, and had addressed the local and global public in English, French, Italian, Hebrew, Arabic, Russian, and Greek.[3] In all its matter-of-factness and sobriety that ceremony could scarcely belie the fact that it made Allenby the latest in a long and formidable series of conquerors and pilgrimaging rulers[4] – of particular significance

---

[1] See www.timesofisrael.com/history-repeats-itself-as-lord-allenby-captures-jerusalems-old-city-again (last accessed August 8, 2022).
[2] Cf. www.nytimes.com/2017/12/06/world/middleeast/trump-israel-speech-transcript.html (last accessed August 8, 2022).
[3] English text in Horne 1923, 417.
[4] A tentative list of such entries into the Holy City/al-Quds includes the following figures (episodes commonly or frequently seen as 'mythical' marked with *): King David of Judah and Israel* (ca. 1010 BCE); King Alexander of Macedon* (ca. 332 BCE, mythologically constructed as a Christian king *avant*

ⓐ OpenAccess. © 2022 Lutz Greisiger, published by De Gruyter. [CC BY-NC-ND] This work is licensed under the Creative Commons Attribution-NonCommercial-NoDerivatives 4.0 International License.
https://doi.org/10.1515/9783110718447-013

obviously being the professed Christians among them – whose entries into the Holy City had each marked a more or less momentous historical change. This article aims to determine in how far such entries followed a performative tradition, or to which extent their representation in texts and other media conformed to a narrative tradition, by gathering, analyzing and comparing source materials on a number of significant cases. Of interest is the impression they were meant to make on the public. Whether, therefore, the sources document a performative practice or instantiate a representational paradigm is of secondary importance.

Prototypes

In an episode much pondered over since time immemorial, chapter 14 of the Book of Genesis narrates how Melchizedek, "the king of Salem" (i.e. Jerusalem[5]) and "priest of the most high god" once "brought out bread and wine" to host Abram and to "bless him of the most high God, possessor of heaven and earth." In return for the divine protection that the priest-king of Jerusalem had thus conveyed to him, Israel's progenitor henceforth was to pay tithes to him, i.e. to submit himself to his rule.[6] Shortly afterwards God had made a covenant with Abram, renaming him Araham and promising him offspring as countless as the stars of heaven and to them the possession of the "land from the river of Egypt unto the great river, the river Euphrates."[7]

---

la lettre); Judah Maccabee (25 Kislew 3925/27 November 164 BCE), first Ethnarch of the Hasmonean state (later Kingdom) of Judah; Jesus of Nazareth* (ca. 30 CE); St Helena, mother of Constantine the Great, Roman Empress (326); Aelia Eudocia, wife of Emperor Theodosius II (spring 438 or 439); Muḥammad* (621); Heraclius I, Roman-Byzantine Emperor (March 21, 630); ʿUmar ibn al-Khaṭṭāb, second Caliph (15/636, 16/637 or 17/638); Abū Jaʿfar al-Manṣūr, second Abbasid Caliph (136/754); Charlemagne,* Frankish King and Emperor of the Romans (shortly after 800); Godfrey of Bouillon, Duke of Lower Lorraine, first ruler of the Kingdom of Jerusalem (July 15, 1099); Saladin, first Ayyubid sultan of Egypt (Rajab 27, 583/October 2, 1187); Frederick II, Emperor of the Holy Roman Empire (March 17 1229); Hethum II, King of Armenia (October 1299); Selim I, first Ottoman Caliph (Ṣafar 25, 923/March 20 1517); Shabbatai Zevi, King Messiah (1663); Caroline of Brunswick, Queen Consort of King George IV (July 12, 1816); İbrahim Paşa, son and general of the Wāli of Egypt, Muhammad (Mehmet) Ali Paşa (1250/1834); Maximilian Joseph, Duke in Bavaria (1838); Leopold II, Duke of Brabant, later King of the Belgians (March 30, 1855); Grand Duke Konstantin Nikolayevich, brother of Tsar Alexander II of Russia (April 30$^{Jul.}$/May 12$^{Greg.}$ 1859); Edward, Prince of Wales, later King Edward VII (April 1, 1862); Friedrich Wilhelm, Crown Prince of Prussia, later Emperor Friedrich III (November 4, 1869); Franz Joseph I, Emperor of Austria (November 9, 1869); Wilhelm II, German Emperor (October 29, 1898); General Edmund Allenby (December 11, 1917); Moshe Dayan, IDF Commander-in-Chief (June 8, 1967/Iyyar 29, 5727). Two conquerors, Pompey (63 BCE) and Titus (70 CE), can be omitted since they did not regard Jerusalem as a holy city.

5 Cf. Psalm 76:3. But see the references to Jewish and Christian texts that do *not* identify 'Salem' with Jerusalem given by Bernhardt 1992, 415.
6 Gen. 14:18–20.
7 Gen. 15.

Of Melchizedek (Malkī-Ṣedeq, "King of [or: My King is] Righteousness," in Hebrew), furthermore, the Bible mentions neither his birth nor death (nor, for that matter, any other biographical detail),[8] a fact that came to be widely understood as indicating that he was not bound to the laws of becoming and passing in time and, by implication, his was an everlasting priest-kingship.[9] A complex interpretative process then led to the attribution of this twofold dignity to his 'servant' Abraham.[10]

The Second Book of Samuel narrates that David, after having been anointed king of both the southern kingdom of Judah and its northern counterpart Israel, invaded the ancient Jebusite city of Jerusalem with the fortress Zion, situated right on the border of the two states, to make the city his residence, the dwelling place of YHWH, and the capital of the united kingdom.[11]

When, according to another tradition, Jacob, the father of the Israelite people, on his deathbed bid farewell to his twelve sons and patriarchs-to-be of the twelve tribes, the fourth of them, Judah, David's ancestor, received a peculiar blessing. Judah, Jacob said, was irresistible like a lion; he would overcome his and his brothers' enemies and his brothers would "bow down before" him. And he prophesied that "the scepter shall not depart from Judah, nor a lawgiver from between his feet, until Shiloh come; and unto him shall the gathering of the people be." This verse came to be understood to mean that some day, Judah's, David's and their descendants' reign would be assumed by a messianic ruler named Shiloh, but until that remote moment, it would last uncontestedly, by divine warrant.[12]

Finally, in order not to leave room for any doubt about the full validity of the Davidian prerogatives, Psalm 110 added that "The lord hath sworn, and will not repent: Thou art a priest for ever after the order of Melchizedek."[13] Thus David had inherited three titles from the primeval ruler Melchizedek, that of the eternal kingship over God's people, the high priesthood, and the right to Jerusalem. By implication, the ruler who would one day rise to establish the true theocracy would be a priest-king like Melchizedek and David, and restorer of their sovereignty.

After his conquest of Jerusalem, the biblical narrative continues:

> David went and brought up the ark of God ... into the city of David with gladness. And it was so, that when they that bare the ark of the LORD had gone six paces, he sacrificed oxen and fatlings. And David danced before the LORD with all his might; and David was girded with a linen ephod.[14]

---

[8] In contrast, some apocryphal works offer more information on Melchizedek – see e.g. '(Slavonic Apocalypse of) Enoch,' transl. Anderson 1983 (repr. 2009), 91–221, there 207–211.
[9] Cf. e.g. Hebr. 7:1–3.
[10] Astour 1992, 684–686; Bernhardt/Willi/Balz 1992, 414–423.
[11] 2 Sam. 5; cf. 1 Chron. 11:1–9.
[12] Gen. 49:8–10; cf. de Hoop (1999), s.v. Gen. 49:8–10; שילה.
[13] Psalm 110:4.
[14] 2 Sam. 6:12–14; cf. 1 Chron. 15–16.

Afterwards, his wife Michal would deride him for his shameless self-exposure, even before "the eyes of the handmaids of his servants." The ephod, a type of long shirt, was part of the ceremonial vestment worn by the high priest in the tabernacle and later in the Jerusalem temple.[15] This episode about David leading a procession, wearing a cultic garment, and offering sacrifices is the closest to officiating as high priest as he is ever described in the biblical tradition. Yet the narration about him consecrating the new capital by installing the sacred ark there obviously implied presenting him as political ruler *and* as chief religious official.

According to the First Book of Chronicles, the Ark had been brought from a place called Kirjathjearim that, in the Book of Joshua, is also named Kirjathbaal.[16] Today Qiryat Yearim is a Jewish religious community just outside the ancient Arab village of Abu Ghosh, about 15 km west of Jerusalem. The remains of the biblical site are currently being excavated.[17]

Samuel 2 further narrates that King David bought a threshing floor on Mount Moriah from its Jebusite owner, Araunah, for the price of fifty silver shekels, in order to "erect an altar to the Lord"[18] – a place commonly identified with the Temple Mount. But it was not granted to David to build a house for God, a task that he had to leave to his son Solomon. And it was through Solomon, too, God promised David, that "thine house and thy kingdom shall be established for ever before thee: thy throne shall be established for ever."[19] To officiate as high priest, however, was not given to David but to Zadok the Levite, descendent of Aaron. The Temple, eventually, would be built by David's son, Solomon.

To summarize this complex of ideas as suggested by the scriptural tradition: David, conqueror of Jerusalem and unifier of all the twelve tribes of Israel is king and high priest like Melchizedek before him; his descendants nominally are kings and high priests forever, until a man by the enigmatic name of Shiloh – none other than the messiah – will appear, take over these offices and, by virtue of them, will rule over the peoples of the world. Spatially, the claim to power thus expressed, is most closely connected with the city of Jerusalem, while the claim to the priesthood is bound to the Temple Mount in that same city.

These notions were to be inherited, whether actually or implicitly and potentially, by later, Christian conceptions of legitimate imperial rule.[20]

When, a millennium later, the gospels tell us, Jesus of Nazareth arrived at Jerusalem it was no less revolutionary an event. A large crowd, present for the imminent feast of Passover, received him outside the gate, "took branches of palm trees, and

---

15 Cf. Exod. 28:4–8, 29:5, 39:2–5; Lev. 8:7.
16 1 Chron. 13:5; Joshua 15:60.
17 Cf. 'Strata: Temporary Home of the Ark of the Covenant,' *Biblical Archaeology Review* 43.4, 2017.
18 2 Sam. 24:18–25; 1 Chron. 21:18–30.
19 2 Sam. 7; 1 Chron. 22:1–16.
20 Cf. Dagron 2003, 49–52.

went forth to meet him, and cried, Hosanna: Blessed is the King of Israel that cometh in the name of the Lord." The Gospel of Matthew has the crowd further hail Jesus as the "son of David;" in the Gospel of Mark they praise the coming "kingdom of our father David."[21] All four gospels present the event as the fulfilment of Zechariah's prophecy about a messianic king, "righteous and redeeming," riding on "the foal of an ass."[22] The narrative is also reminiscent of Psalm 118 with its imagery of a solemn passage: "Open to me the gates of righteousness: I will go into them, and I will praise the lord ... Blessed be he that cometh in the name of the lord."[23] In addition, chapters 5 to 7 of the Letter to the Hebrews state that Christ had been appointed "high priest for ever after the order of Melchizedek."[24] A genealogy constructed to firmly establish the combined royal and sacerdotal charismata by ascribing to Jesus (and his mother Mary) a lineage going back to Judah and Levi would be added in the third century – "the 'divine economy' which assured the Messiah the double title of king and priest."[25]

Thus, there remains little uncertainty about the claim raised by the evangelists and Paul: Jesus of Nazareth is the foretold descendent of King David who has come to restore the kingship of his ancestor and to assume his eschatic priest-kingdom over Israel; hence, the ancient royal residence in Jerusalem belongs to him, too. And finally, the implication that he was also identical with Shiloh whose coming the patriarch Jacob had prophesied, that he, therefore, had come to rule over all the other nations as well, immediately suggested itself.

All four gospels relate that Jesus approached Jerusalem from the Mount of Olives to the east. There were two entryways to the city on its eastern side, the Lions' Gate, later also known as St Stephen's Gate and, leading straight onto the elevated plaza that formed the precinct of the Temple (considered to be identical with the Ḥaram al-Sharīf of Muslim lore), the Gate of Mercy (Shaʿar ha-Raḥamim in Hebrew, Bāb al-Raḥma in Arabic) or Golden Gate. It has widely been assumed that it was this latter gate through which Jesus the Christ had entered the Holy City, an inference suggested by the gospels themselves since their narrations all proceed directly to the episode of the Cleansing of the Temple.[26]

The entry of King David, and that of the "son of David," Jesus of Nazareth, into Jerusalem were both perceived as markers of epochal changes. The first instituted the

---

[21] John 12:12–15; cf. Matt. 21:1–9; Mark 11:1–10; Luke 19:28–38.
[22] (Deutero-)Zechariah 9:9 "Rejoice greatly, O daughter of Zion; shout, O daughter of Jerusalem: behold, thy King cometh unto thee: he is just, and having salvation; lowly, and riding upon an ass, and upon a colt the foal of an ass."
[23] Psalm 118:19.20.26.
[24] Hebr. 5:6.10.
[25] Dagron 2003, 315–317, cit. 316.
[26] Mark 11:11 even deals with the change of scene in one concise sentence: "And he went into Jerusalem, into the temple." However, the earliest extant source that explicitly mentions Jesus's entry through the *Porta Aurea* is a homily on Palm Sunday by Ps.-Bede, dated 8th/9th c.: *Patrologia Latina* vol. 94, col. 507.

divinely ordained eternal kingship in Israel and made Jerusalem a sacred city; the second signaled a revolutionary universalization of the salvation that had previously been reserved for Israel alone, making Jerusalem the center of this universal order of salvation, the capital of a symbolical world empire.

Heraclius

Almost exactly 600 years after Jesus's atoning sacrifice in Jerusalem and around 300 years after the beginning of the Christianization of the Roman monarchy, a Roman emperor for the first time bothered to come to the Holy City in person. Neither Constantine nor Justinian had deigned to do so, even while the former's mother Helena, by finding the True Cross and by overseeing the construction of the Church of the Holy Sepulcher, had made the rock of Golgotha and the tomb of Christ the physical center of the Christian world and bound the Christian emperors' throne to it, and even though the latter had one of the most formidable projects of his building program realized here, the great Nea Church. One may wonder, therefore, if the significance ascribed to the earthly, the real Jerusalem did not only fully catch up with that of the spiritual and symbolic one by the time of Heraclius.[27]

During the first three decades of the seventh century, the Byzantine Imperium Romanum went through a profound crisis. In 602 the *centurio* Phokas seized power, only to be overthrown by a counter-usurpation from Heraclius senior, exarch of Carthage, and his son, who was crowned emperor in 610. In addition to this domestic crisis, an even more severe one appeared in the realm of foreign policy. From 603 onwards, the Romans' centuries-long arch-enemy, the Persian Empire, reigned over by the Sasanian dynasty since 224, relentlessly conquered province after province of Byzantine territory, in 626 even threatening, together with its Avar allies, the capital Constantinople.[28]

Already in 614 Persian troops had conquered Jerusalem and not only deported its Christian population to Mesopotamia but also carried off to Ctesiphon (near today's Baghdad and not far from ancient Babylon) the relic of the True Cross that had been enshrined in the Church of the Holy Sepulcher since its construction in the time of St Helena. As attested by literary works such as the Syriac *Cave of Treasures* and the Ethiopic-Arabic *Book of Adam and Eve*, the inhabitants of the eastern provinces of the Empire regarded Golgotha as the actual center of the world. The Cross, in their view, was made from the very wood of the Tree of Life in Paradise which was the same wood as that of the tree in whose branches the ram had been caught that Abra-

---

[27] For a wider contextualization of these partly legendary events cf. Wilken 1992 and the contribution of Howard-Johnston to this volume.
[28] For a comprehensive overview of the period cf. Greatrex and Lieu (2002), 182–228; Dignas and Winter (2007), 44–49, 115–118, 148–151.

ham sacrificed instead of his son Isaac,[29] as well as the wood that had been used to build the Ark of the Covenant roughly a millennium later.[30] Viewed in this light Shah Ḳosrow II (590–628) had not merely heisted the most sacred relic of Christendom, he had uprooted the wooden axis around which the whole of salvation history revolved – a disaster of cosmic proportions.

The significance of this loss seems to have dawned only gradually on the Constantinopolitan government after the fall of Jerusalem, perhaps because one half of the Cross was kept (together with the Holy Nails, Lance and Sponge) in the Hagia Sophia. It was at this very time, however, that the celebration of the Feast of the Cross on September 14th appears to have been introduced in the Constantinopolitan Church, and soon the retrieval of the True Cross became an official war objective. From 622 onward, the Byzantine army conducted a large-scale counterattack under the personal command of Emperor Heraclius and, after six years, forced the enemy to surrender. The Persian troops withdrew and Byzantine ones moved back into their former fortresses and garrisons. The Cross was restituted to Heraclius who transferred it back to Jerusalem in triumphal procession. What transpired upon his arrival is related in the Latin translation of a lost contemporary Greek document. The *Reversio Sanctae Crucis*, a text frequently adapted throughout the Middle Ages (perhaps most influentially in Jacobus de Voragine's *Legenda Aurea*[31]), describes the memorable event as follows:

> Thus, taking charge of the wood of the most glorious Cross that the impious one (i.e. Ḳosrow) had carried off, he (i.e. Heraclius) hurries to Jerusalem. All the people are rejoicing, with palm fronds, candles and torches or other signs of glory, with hymns and canticles, some proceeding to meet him and others following in his train.
>
> But when the Emperor, coming down from the Mount of Olives, sitting on a royal horse decorated with imperial ornaments, wanted to enter by the same gate that the Lord had entered when coming to His passion, the stones of the gate suddenly descended and joined themselves to one another, making a solid wall.
>
> As they were wondering in astonishment, constricted by exceeding sorrow, they looked up on high and saw the sign of the Cross in the sky, shining brightly with flaming splendour. An angel of the Lord took it in his hands, stood above the gate and said: When the King of the heavens, the Lord of all the earth, entered through this gate on his way to fulfilling the mysteries of the passion, he did not appear in purple or a shining diadem, nor did he ask for a strong horse to carry him, but sitting on the back of a humble donkey he left his servants a paradigm of humility. This said, the angel quickly returned to heaven.
>
> Then the Emperor rejoiced in the Lord because of the angelic visit, and having removed the tokens of imperial rank he proceeded without shoes, girded only with a linen belt, took the Cross of the Lord in his hands and hastened forward, face covered in tears and eyes raised to the sky, making his way to the gate. As soon as he approached with humility the hard stones sensed the

---

[29] Gen. 22:1–13 Exod. 25,10–22.
[30] La Caverne des Trésors, ed., trans. Ri (1987), IV,2–3; XXIX,4–9; LIII,6.11.
[31] For a comprehensive reconstruction of the reception history in Medieval Europe, see Baert 2004, 133 et seqq.

celestial command, and raising itself at once the gate gave free access to those who were going in.³²

The palm branches, the route taken from the Mount of Olives through the Eastern Gate, the enthusiasm of the crowd, and the numerous miraculous healings, raisings from the dead, and castings out of demons that, we are told, subsequently came to pass, all unmistakably remind the reader/listener of Jesus's entry on Palm Sunday, so that the text's explicit linking of the two events almost appears as a redundancy.

Around 630, the time of his victory, Heraclius renounced the title of emperor (*imperator/autokrator*) – which, formidable though it might have been, was no more than the designation of an administrative office – and assumed that of a "king faithful in Christ" (πιστὸς ἐν Χριστῷ βασιλεύς), implying a right to rulership and entitlement to dynastic succession ordained by God.³³ Unlike his predecessors and immediate successors Heraclius furthermore was frequently presented as a New David.³⁴ As David had once brought the Ark of the Covenant to Jerusalem, now the New David brought the Ark of the New Covenant, the Cross, back to Jerusalem. Like David, he stripped down almost completely on the occasion, wearing not a linen ephod but a linen belt, and like David, he was said to have received the ordination to the priesthood.³⁵ And finally a rumor spread that Heraclius had not only defeated the Persians but had them converted to the Christian faith, had disabused the sole opponent of the Christian empire from unbelief and, therefore, had removed the main obstacle to the worldwide expansion of the gospel.³⁶

All this taken together, Heraclius seemed to be on the verge of founding nothing short of an everlasting dynasty of priest-kings with a God-given right to world power. That this pledge remained unfulfilled, therefore, might be ascribed to the advance of the Arabs. Only a decade after Heraclius's splendid victory the Roman troops had to withdraw from Palestine; shortly thereafter Egypt fell, and the Sasanian Empire collapsed. The "king faithful in Christ" sank into a deep depression and would never more leave his summer residence on the shore of the Bosporus opposite the capital.

But even though Heraclius's salvation-historical mission never advanced beyond its early stages, there remained one more task to be performed. Establishing a universal Christian empire could not restrict itself to an implementation of the Great Commission as it was given in Matthew 28: "Go ye therefore, and teach all nations, baptizing them in the name of the Father, and of the Son, and of the Holy Ghost." It was also necessary for the people of the Old Covenant to be regarded in a way adequate

---

32 *Reversio Sanctae Crucis* 14–17; cf. *Sermo de exaltatione Sanctae Crucis* 17–21, ed./trans. Borgehammar 2009, 145–201, there 186–189, cf. 198–201.
33 Shahîd 1981, 288–296; Dagron 2003, 29–32.
34 Alexander 1977, 217–237; Dagron 2003, 29; Zahnd 2008, 71–87.
35 As attested in the 'Khuzestan Chronicle' (also 'Guidi's Chronicle') ed. Guidi 1891 (repr. Nendeln 1974), 23; trans. Nöldeke 1893, 28.
36 Greisiger 2014, 117–121.

to its salvation-historical weight. Regardless of their rejection of Christ, God had, according to Romans 11, never abandoned His people to simply replace them with the New Israel, the Church, but had preserved them for their unification with the latter.

Jews, especially in the Galilee, their main area of settlement, had by all accounts supported – not least militarily – the Persian advance. After 614, the occupiers granted a messianic king and high priest, named Neḥemyā ben Ḥushīēl in the apocalyptic midrashim that mention him, the sovereignty over Jerusalem and permitted some kind of cultic and sacrificial routine to be put into practice on the Temple Mount. Christian sources accuse 'the Jews' of destroying numerous churches and even of trying to forcibly convert a multitude of civil detainees and of committing a mass execution among those who would not obey. In Edessa, Jewish combatants were resisting the Byzantine reinvasion as late as 628.[37]

Heraclius exercised clemency. When he arrived at Edessa, he granted a general amnesty to all members of the Jewish resistance. In Tiberias, he and his entourage were hosted by a wealthy member of the Jewish community named Benjamin, who had apparently been involved in the Galilean movement, the insurgents' collaboration with the Persians, and the persecution of Christians. Heraclius took him along on his further journey to Jerusalem and converted him at their stopover in Neapolis (Nablus/Shekhem) in Samaria.[38]

Upon his arrival in Jerusalem, the emperor granted a writ of protection to all the Jews of Palestine – but after his solemn entry he revoked the promise at the insistence of the Christian population and Patriarch Modestus (r. 614–634) and renewed the old prohibition of access to the city for Jews. A few years later he even decreed that all the Jewish subjects of the empire must be baptized.

Thus, all indications are that Heraclius and his advisors initially hoped that the Jews, realizing that in Neḥemyā ben Ḥushīēl they had backed the wrong horse, would now submit themselves to the victorious and benevolent "king faithful in Christ," and realize, just like Benjamin of Tiberias had, that Jesus of Nazareth was their Christ, too. Shortly afterwards this benevolence once more changed into repression, but the goal of the conversion of all the Jews remained. Orthodox circles would regard these efforts as tantamount to meddling in God's design, maintaining that He had provided for the salvation of Israel not until for the end of time.[39]

Heraclius's entry into Jerusalem was obviously meant to mark an epochal change, not without striking eschatological undertones: the "king faithful in Christ" assumed world rulership, complying with God's will (to which the Jews were also bound), bringing in a new age of unprecedented splendor, peace and prosperity for the Christian Imperium Romanum.

---

37 For an attempt at a reconstruction of the events, which, for want of straightforward historical accounts, largely depends on *vaticinia ex eventu* from apocalyptic texts, see Greisiger 2014, 46–63, 68–77.
38 Greisiger 2014, 94–97.
39 Greisiger 2014, 97–106.

Godfrey

On 15 July 1099, after an eight-day siege, thousands of armed Frankish pilgrims invaded Jerusalem and – according to the chronicle of William (ca. 1130–1186), archbishop of Tyre and chancellor of the Kingdom of Jerusalem – caused an appalling bloodbath among the Muslim and Jewish civilians. Regardless of these horrors the chronicler felt compelled to imbue his narrative with salvation-historical significance:

> It was a Friday at the ninth hour. Verily, it seemed divinely ordained that the faithful who were fighting for the glory of the Savior should have obtained the consummation of their desires at the same hour and on the very day on which the Lord had suffered in that city for the salvation of the world. It was on that day, as we read, that the first man was created and the second was delivered over to death for the salvation of the first. It was fitting, therefore, that, at that very hour, those who were members of His body and imitators of Him should triumph in His name over His enemies.[40]

The first crusaders to enter the Holy City, William informs us, were Godfrey, Lord of Bouillon and Duke of Lower Lorraine (ca. 1060–1100), and his brother Eustace.[41] William notes that Godfrey's men participated in the looting and bloodshed[42] but another historian, Albert of Aachen (fl. ca. 1100) (relying on the chronicle of an eyewitness, one of the duke's vassals), draws a different picture of Godfrey:

> [W]hile all the princes were gazing open-mouthed at the possessions and the turreted buildings, and all the common crowd was … inflicting a massacre with excessive cruelty on the Saracens, Duke Godfrey soon abstained from all slaughter, and … took off his hauberk and linen clothes, went out of the walls with bare feet and made a humble procession around the outside of the city; then, entering through that gate which looks out on the Mount of Olives, he presented himself at the Sepulcher of Lord Jesus Christ, son of the living God, keeping up steadfastly tears, prayers, and divine praises, and giving thanks to God because he had earnt the sight of that which had always been his greatest desire.[43]

The enactment – real or fictitious – of Godfrey's pious and humble entry into the Holy City was obviously meant to emulate that of Heraclius as the *Reversio Sanctae Crucis* had depicted it.[44] Just like Heraclius, barefoot and dressed only in his shirt, the coming ruler of the Christian Kingdom of Jerusalem (he would renounce the

---

[40] *Willelmi Tyrensis Chronicon*, ed. Huygens 1986, 8,18; *A History of Deeds Done Beyond the Sea*, trans. Babcock 1941–1943, vol. 1, 369–370.
[41] Wilhelm 8,18. In Albert's account, Godfrey and Eustace were preceded by Lithold and Engilbert, see n. 43. below, 6,19–428–429.
[42] Wilhelm 8,19.
[43] *Albert of Aachen*, ed. and trans. Edgington 2007, 12,7–440–441.
[44] Menzel 1992, 1–21.

royal crown) enters through the gate opposite the Mount of Olives and, drowned in tears, thanks God for the grace He has bestowed on him.

Throughout the Middle Ages, Heraclius's entry would remain an inherent part of the collective memory of Christians.[45] A thirteenth century Old French translation and continuation of William's chronicle even bears the title *Estoire d'Eracles*.[46] Moreover, liturgical customs attest to a belief held among Jerusalemites of the Crusader period, that it was through the Golden Gate that the Lord and Heraclius had entered the city. Kept closed throughout the year, the gate was opened twice, once on Palm Sundays and once on the feast of the Exaltation of the Cross on September 14th, to allow for processions which connected the gate with the Dome of the Rock (at that time a church dedicated to the Mother of God and named *Templum Domini*) and with the Holy Sepulcher.[47] Through Godfrey and his literary 'voice,' Albert, this tradition of commemorating Jesus's and Heraclius's entries via the Eastern Gate was further amplified.

The Nineteenth Century

In the course of the nineteenth century, especially following the 'Oriental Crisis' of 1839–1841, Palestine's geopolitical significance dramatically increased once again. Western powers, including the Russian Empire, were now able to assert their and their subjects' interests in the Middle East more forcefully. This was further facilitated by improved traveling conditions resulting from innovations in steam navigation and railway construction, while the 'Holy Land' witnessed a steadily increasing influx of Christian pilgrims and a growing presence of Christian, by now also Protestant, religious institutions.[48] One of the most significant of these new foundations was the establishment of the first Protestant bishopric in Jerusalem in 1841, a Prussian-Evangelical and Anglican cooperation that was to last until 1886.[49] In order not to fall short of their political and religious aspirations, various royal families also dispatched members, among them at least two crowned heads of state, to make their appearance in the Holy Land.

---

45 Baert 2004, 167 et seqq.
46 *Recueil des historiens des croisades* (1859); pt. I: *Historiens occidentaux*; vol. 2, Paris (repr. Farnborough 1969); *Guillaume de Tyr et ses continuateurs* ed. Paulin (1879–1880).
47 Johannes of Würzburg: 'Descriptio Terrae Sanctae,' in Huygens/Pryor 1994, 78–141, there 96; John of Würzburg, *Description of the Holy Land*, trans. Stewart 1890, 19; Morgenstern 1929, 1–37, there 1, 3–5; Kedar/Pringle 2009, 133–149, there 147–148.
48 See e.g. Vogel 1993; Bar/Cohen-Hattab 2003, 131–148; Murre-van den Berg 2006; Kark 2008, 14–29; Trimbur/Aaronsohn 2008; Tejirian/Simon 2012, 69–93; Merlo 2013, 48–67.
49 Perry 2001, 65–80.

The first example concerns Russia, the longstanding protecting power of the Orthodox Christian communities under Ottoman rule.[50] In the spring of 1859, Grand Duke Konstantin Nikolayevich, brother of Tsar Alexander II (r. 1855–1881) traveled to Palestine for an official visit, accompanied by his wife Alexandra Iosifovna and his son Nikolai. Subsequently one of the largest urban building projects in nineteenth century Jerusalem – and one of the first quarters outside of the city walls – was carried out: the Russian Ecclesiastical Mission. Known among the locals as *al-Muskubīya* in Arabic, *Migraš ha-Rūsīm* in Hebrew or "the Russian Compound", the building complex comprising pilgrims' hostels, residences for priests and clerics, cathedral, mission, marketplace, and the Russian consulate, left an unmistakable mark of the Russian claims to the Holy City and the Holy Land.

Konstantin von Tischendorf (1815–1874), the renowned discoverer and editor of the *Codex Sinaiticus*, who had already won the Grand Duke's and the Tsar's favor and accompanied the imperial pilgrims, portrayed their journey for *Die Gartenlaube*, the newly founded first German illustrated magazine. On his way, Konstantin Nikolayevich rode at the head of his large entourage and baggage train on a white Arabian horse that the governor of Jerusalem had sent him – a splendid sight, Tischendorf writes, "the like of which the great pilgrims' road scarcely may have seen since the time of the Crusades", a thought that "stirred a sublime emotion of Christian patriotism within my soul."[51]

Christian pilgrims or settlers in Palestine apparently never passed up an opportunity to see in their present reality a reverberation of the glorious days of the Crusades. Thus, when British and Austrian troops occupied the Ottoman sea fortress of Acre in 1840 – they had actually come to the aid of Sultan Abdülmecid I (r. 1839–1861) against the defecting governor of Egypt, Muhammad Ali Pasha – James Edward Hanauer (1850–1938), an Anglican priest and photographer born and raised in a German-American family in Palestine, perceived this as a repetition of Richard the Lionheart's conquest of the city during the Third Crusade in 1191.[52] In a similar vein, the Swiss Oriental scholar Titus Tobler (1806–1877) exclaimed in the report of his fourth exploratory journey to Palestine in 1865, in view of the heavily increased number of European Christian settlers in the Holy Land: "The peaceful crusade has begun. Jerusalem must become ours."[53]

The Russian travelers' party stayed the night at the residence of Mustafa Abu Ghosh where, according to historical tradition, the Crusaders had also lodged on their way from the coast to the Holy City. Sometime in the twelfth century, the Knights Hospitaller had taken over a fortified compound with a church there,

---

50 Hopwood 1969; Carmel 1985, 45–77; Kane 2006, 177–198.
51 Tischendorf 1862, 251.
52 Hanauer 1900, 124–142. For a connection with the Crusades made by contemporaries, cf. also von Bergmann 1857, 41, n. *. For the events of 1191, cf. Runciman 1955, 50–51.
53 Tobler 1868, 322. For an overview of the role crusader imagery played in 19th c. religious and political discourses cf. also Knobler 2006, 293–325.

which henceforth served pilgrims as sleeping quarters. At that time, the tradition that connected the place with the Ark of the Covenant had not entirely been forgotten, although in the Crusader period it seems to have been (partly) replaced by another tradition that identified it with the biblical Emmaus (Luke 24:13–35).[54]

On the following day, the Greek Patriarch of Jerusalem Cyril II (r. 1845–1872) and provincial governor Mustafa Süreyya Paşa (1825–1879) came to meet the caravan. On their arrival, Tischendorf relates, "the Patriarch and the Grand Duke both dismounted their horses. Then the former blessed the guest and exclaimed: 'Blessed be he that cometh in the name of the Lord.'" Few of those present may have been more keenly aware of the messianic implications of this utterance than the Greek-Orthodox ecclesiastical prince who made it and the Lutheran New Testament scholar who preserved it for posterity.

Konstantin Nikolayevich, however, would not go so far as to emulate the one who had first "come in the name of the Lord" by entering Jerusalem from the east. He took the Jaffa or Hebron Gate on the opposite side of the city, which was traditionally also known as the Pilgrims' Gate. Having arrived at the portal, we are further told, "the Grand Duke ... descended in order to enter, according to ancient custom, the city on foot." Inside the city the Russian bishop received the distinguished pilgrims "with the cross and holy water;" to the cheering of the crowd they proceeded from there without delay to the Church of the Holy Sepulcher.

Now, that "old pious custom" to dismount one's horse at the gate had most certainly been common practice among Christian Jerusalem pilgrims since time immemorial. In the account of his great Oriental journey in the 1750s, for example, Stephan Schultz (1714–1776), the director of the *Institutum Judaicum et Muhammedicum* in Halle, writes that Christians had been expressly forbidden to enter in any way other than by foot.[55] However, given the ubiquity of memories of the Crusader past in nineteenth-century Palestine, one is justified in seeing in this custom a reflection of Godfrey of Bouillon's entry as well, not just its historical antecedents.

To Tischendorf, however, the Grand Duke's journey seemed to point not only to the splendid past but also to an even more glorious future:

> That [the entry into the City of God] turned out more solemn than that of virtually every other European prince ... since the Crusades, carried the more weight the more it resulted from the interaction of so many and diverse forces ... The entry of the Tsar's intimate friend and brother turned into a beautiful manifestation of the most animated sympathies. I am convinced that it kindled in many a heart the desire that it may foretell another entry of enduring importance. And also this I know, that many others conceived this entry and everything it was tied up with as significant for the future of the Holy City.[56]

---

54 Pringle 1993–2009, vol. 1, No. 1, 7–8; Gadrat-Ouerfelli/Rouxpetel 2018.
55 Schultz 1771–1775, vol. 5, 67–68.
56 Tischendorf 1862, 251–253, there 253.

Few of the actors or those who recorded their acts had dared to be this explicit. Nonetheless, the German scholar's remarks demonstrate that contemporaries could see such processions of mingled triumph and humility as also alluding to the eschatic re-entry of Christ in Glory, whether as anticipating a future moment or as asserting that the redemptive events were unfolding before their very eyes.

A particularly significant figure to visit Jerusalem was Franz Joseph I, Emperor of Austria, King of Hungary (r. 1848–1916) who travelled to the Orient in order to attend the opening of the Suez Canal in 1869 and on his way made a detour to Palestine. Even though his precursor, Franz II (r. 1792–1806), had already renounced the crown of the Imperium Romanum sixty years earlier, and Franz Joseph himself could no longer lay claim to the leadership of Greater Germany following the Battle of Königgrätz in 1866, the Emperor's visit was still special because as a member of the house of Habsburg he also bore the title of King of Jerusalem.[57]

The Benedictine abbot Beda Dudík (1815–1890), who accompanied the royal traveler as his chaplain, and published a comprehensive account of the journey in the following year, relates that "as the Crusaders of old had done, so also the crowned pilgrim spent the night at the biblical site near Abu Ghosh, whence the Ark of the Covenant was carried to Jerusalem." And he continues: "Although the emperor did not bring the Ark of the Covenant with him, he carried a pious and faithful heart to the Holy City, and the determination to pray for his empire, for himself and for his house at the grave of the Savior, and to do deeds of charity and Christian love."

On November 9th, 1869 – only weeks before the twentieth anniversary of his coronation – Franz Joseph, too, dismounted his horse outside Jaffa Gate and entered the city on foot. The entire Catholic clergy stood ready for his reception and a bishop who deputized for the Patriarch presented him the cross for a kiss and, when the festive procession proceeded to the Holy Sepulcher, "bell-ringing and the thunder of cannons announced to the world that after 600 years once again a Christian Emperor made pilgrimage to the holy place."[58]

Only five days earlier, the Prussian Crown Prince Friedrich Wilhelm, the future German Emperor Friedrich III (r. 1888), and father of Wilhelm II, likewise on his way to attend the opening of the Suez Canal (November 17th), had visited Jerusalem. The prince's sojourn was less magnificent and ceremonious, and he did not exercise any caution at the gate but went in with his entourage on horseback, "in the face of the narrow streets and the awful pavement, only concerned that we might at any moment end up sprawled on the ground with our horse."[59]

---

[57] For the emperor's full "Great Title" cf. e. g. *Hof- und Staats-Handbuch des Kaiserthumes Österreich für das Jahr 1857*, Vienna 1857, pt. 1, p. 1.
[58] Dudík 1870, 180–182; cf. Fischer 2006, 199–209.
[59] *Tagebuch meiner Reise nach dem Morgenlande 1869: Bericht des preußischen Kronprinzen Friedrich Wilhelm über seine Reise zur Einweihung des Suez-Kanals*, ed. Rothfels 1971, 45–47.

Emperor Franz Joseph, in contrast, exercised humility. As soon as the city first came into view he knelt down and kissed the earth, and remained in silent meditation for several minutes, contemplating, as Dudík suggests, the images that crossed his mind, considering that he bore the title of King of Jerusalem.[60] The chaplain's reckoning that this was the first time in six hundred years that a Christian Emperor visited the Holy City was a reference to the *stupor mundi et immutator mirabilis*, Frederick II (r. 1220–1250), who had led the Sixth Crusade in 1228/29 and had occupied the city not by force of arms but by treaty concluded with the Ayyubid Sultan al-Kāmil (r. 1218–1238). We do not know any details about the manner in which he made his entry on 17 March 1229, but we do know that on the following day he assembled clerics and knights in the Church of the Holy Sepulcher and crowned himself King of Jerusalem.[61] Thus Franz Joseph I was indeed a remote heir to both of the crowns of that other Holy Roman Emperor and King of Jerusalem – leading, as it were, a crusade by peaceful, symbolic means. The Austrian Hospice, a landmark building opened in 1863 at the Third Station of the Via Dolorosa, was to commemorate the Emperor's sojourn on the occasion of its fortieth anniversary with a monumental mosaic on the chapel wall entitled "The Military and Peaceful Pilgrimages of Austria-Hungary to the Holy Land since Ancient Times," showing an ensemble of figures replete with references to the Crusades.[62] Thus, Franz Joseph, too, made performative references to King David, Jesus Christ, Heraclius, as well as Godfrey of Bouillon, and combined them with an allusion to Frederick II.

Much better remembered than the journeys of other nineteenth-century royal figures such as Konstantin Nikolayevich and Franz Joseph is that of the German Emperor (1888–1918) Wilhelm II in 1898. The visit was a genuine media event: newspaper reports, picture postcards and numerous promptly published illustrated luxury volumes covered the meticulously orchestrated sequence of public acts performed by Wilhelm and his wife Augusta Victoria: their glamorous sea voyage to Constantinople and onwards to Haifa, the trek of the enormous retinue for several days southwards, the visits to the various German communities, the consecration of the neo-Romanesque Church of the Redeemer in Jerusalem specially built for the occasion, the handing over of a plot of land on Mt. Zion, recently procured from the Sultan, to the German Catholics to build the Abbey of the Dormition, and the endowment of the malaria hospital (opened in 1910) with the soaring neo-Byzantine Church of the Ascension ('Augusta Victoria Church') on the Mount of Olives, overlooking all of Jerusalem and its surroundings.[63]

---

[60] Dudík 1870, 180 181.
[61] Runciman 1955, 188–189.
[62] Arad 2015, 251–280.
[63] For a detailed account and in-depth analysis of the events and their broader context, see Benner 2001.

The event displayed an equally weighty symbolism that, however, had its own peculiarities. Under the legal principle of the Territorial Sovereign's Church Government ("landesherrliches Kirchenregiment"), then in force in Protestant German states, Wilhelm, in his capacity of King of Prussia, also held the office of *Summus episcopus*, chief bishop and head of the Prussian Evangelical Church, by far the largest territorial Evangelical Church in the Empire. Indeed, he often conducted services, especially when no ordained minister was at hand, among the inner circle of courtiers and confidants. Of course, millions – more than a third – of his subjects were Catholics whose spiritual leader resided in Rome, not Berlin. Nevertheless, there was a recognizable, if ultimately not enforceable, tendency among civil servants and Evangelical clergy towards equating Germanness with Protestantism and, by implication, the Imperial Office with that of the highest religious authority. This near-conflation of secular and spiritual power at the head of the Empire, moreover, echoed medieval attempts at sacralizing the earthly monarchy, connections made to Old Testament models of kingship and even representations of the emperor as vicar of Christ.[64]

Despite having reason to stress these quasi-messianic claims in the performance of Wilhelm's visit to the Holy City, remarkably, they remained in the background. Not unlike with Grand Duke Konstantin Nikolayevich or Franz Joseph I, it was instead the Palestinian population who struck such undertones when receiving the Emperor. The Arab Muslim and the Jewish communities both had erected triumphal arches where the royal visitor and his entourage would stop and listen to welcome addresses from the respective dignitaries and receive ceremonial ovations. The Jewish arch was inscribed with Psalm 118:26: "Blessed be he that cometh in the name of the LORD: we have blessed you out of the house of the LORD," in Hebrew and German, and was crowned with a depiction of the breast-plate of the high priest.[65] A boy's choir intoned a song each of whose nine strophes ended with "Blessed be he that cometh in the name of the LORD," which even some of the Emperor's attendants found "more suitable for welcoming the messiah than for that of the German Emperor."[66]

The Palestinian German Protestants had a similar message to the distinguished visitor: when he came for the dedication of the Church of the Redeemer on October 31st – Reformation Day – the congregation sang the famous Advent song *Tochter Zion, freue dich* ("Zion's daughter, rejoice"), composed by George Frideric Handel, the words of which, written by Friedrich Heinrich Ranke in 1823, revolve around the themes of the Son of David coming to Jerusalem, riding on a donkey, to erect His eternal kingdom.[67] The messianic exaltation of the earthly ruler implied in *this* festive performance seems not to have met with any disapproval from the German public.

---

64 Benner 2001, 28–43, 45, 108–113, *passim*.
65 See www.loc.gov/pictures/item/mpc2004007274/PP (last accessed August 8, 2022).
66 Von Mirbach 1899, 193 (quotation); cf. Schneller 1899, 90.
67 Benner 2001, 285.

Not only does Wilhelm appear to have been little inclined to encourage such fulsome reverence by religious audiences, the dignity that the head of the World Zionist Organization, Theodor Herzl (1860–1904), envisioned for him ultimately did not appeal either. The Austrian Jewish journalist and political visionary met no fewer than three times with the imperial traveler, trying to engage him for his project of an autonomous Jewish settlement in Palestine under German protectorate – which he argued would also be advantageous for Germany's ally, the Ottoman Empire, given its current economic plight. After some initial signs that Wilhelm sympathized with the Zionists' proposal he eventually, not least in deference of Sultan Abdülhamid's aversion to it, declined the opportunity to go down in history as the emancipator of the Jewish people.[68]

In the afternoon of October 29th, the Emperor rode into the Holy City – not on a donkey but on his white stallion *Kurfürst* ('prince-elector'), and followed by the Empress in a dress coach-and-four. They did not enter through the Jaffa Gate, the "Pilgrims' Gate" of old, which would have been too narrow for the Empress's carriage, but took the newly opened access-road just beside the gate.[69] Only a hundred meters into the city, at the beginning of David Street, when forced by "the narrow streets and the awful pavement" Wilhelm's father had once complained about, did the couple descend and proceed on foot towards the Church of the Holy Sepulcher.[70]

It would appear, then, that Wilhelm himself, otherwise not exactly renowned for his sense of tact on the stage of international politics, did everything he could to divert the innuendoes that had long been customary with princes, monarchs, and conquerors when entering the Holy City. His careful avoidance of any religious, messianic, or Crusader reminiscences is a curious exception to the established rule that awaits further elucidation.

Edmund Allenby

As early as in the summer of 1917, at the beginning of the Palestine campaign under the command of General Edmund Allenby, the London War Office asked the newly-appointed field commander to make a Christmas present of Jerusalem to the increasingly war-weary British population. Allenby was to comply with this request, on December 9th, after the surrender of the Ottoman garrison.

---

[68] Benner 2001, 210–227, 245–254, 279–281, 306–313.
[69] A persisting rumor has it that it was at Wilhelm's request that Ottoman authorities tore down part of Suleiman the Magnificent's city wall between the Gate and the Tower of David, in order to make way for the Emperor's entry. In fact, when he got wind of the project he was horrified and tried to prevent it, but it turned out that the works had long been planned in order to broaden the access road there – Benner 2001, 285.
[70] Benner 2001, 282–289.

At the same time, his superiors did their best to dampen overly high religious expectations of the populace. When, after two weeks, the advance began to bear fruit, the War Office issued a "D-notice," (short for "Defence Advisory notice"):

> The attention of the Press is again drawn to the undesirability of publishing any article, paragraph or picture suggesting that military operations against Turkey are in any sense a Holy War, a modern Crusade, or have anything whatever to do with religious questions. The British Empire is said to contain a hundred million Mohammedan subjects of the King and it is obviously mischievous to suggest that our quarrel with Turkey is one between Christianity and Islam.[71]

Prohibitions are only needed against things that are frequently done. In fact, with the growing success of the campaign, suggestions that it was a "modern Crusade" and a "Holy War" grew rampant. Moreover, Foreign Secretary Arthur Balfour (1848–1930) had recently sent his famous Declaration to the Zionist Federation of Great Britain and Ireland, in which the King and the British Government declared "the establishment in Palestine of a national home for the Jewish people" to be an objective of British foreign policy. It was an obvious presumption, therefore, that the Empire was preparing for liberating Palestine from the rule of the infidels not least *on behalf of the Jews*. Signals of this kind went down well with British Christian circles that cherished a biblicistic 'philosemitism' – and with which senior state officials and politicians, such as Lord Balfour himself and, by his own account, Prime Minister David Lloyd George (1863–1945), were also associated. This philosemitism was closely connected, not unlike its present-day Evangelical counterpart (especially in the U.S.), with an eschatology in which the restoration of the People of Israel to their ancestral home, followed by their eventual acceptance of Jesus Christ as their savior, played a central role.[72]

On December 11th General Allenby formally took possession of Jerusalem on behalf of the British Crown. He had been instructed on how to proceed by the Chief of the Imperial General Staff, William Robertson (1860–1933):

> In the event of Jerusalem being occupied, it would be of considerable political importance if you, on officially entering the city, dismount at the city gate and enter on foot. German emperor rode in and the saying went round, 'A better man than he walked'. Advantage of contrast in conduct will be obvious.[73]

Allenby, ever the dutiful soldier, fulfilled these instructions to the letter. The photograph of his "humble entry" (Fig. 23) literally went around the world. In order to ef-

---

[71] *The National Archives of the UK*: PRO, FO 395/152/218223, Notice D.607, 15 Nov. 1917, quoted in Bar-Yosef 2005, 249; Mazza 2009 (repr. 2014), 124.
[72] Lewis 2010 (repr. 2013).
[73] *Allenby in Palestine: The Middle East Correspondence of Field Marshal Viscount Allenby, June 1917– October 1919*, ed. Hughes 2004, 92–93.

fect the requested "contrast in conduct" he did not take the gap in the city wall that had allegedly been made for Wilhelm II, but had the long-shuttered Jaffa Gate opened for himself.[74] As he wrote to his wife, he himself would have preferred to enter through the Golden Gate[75] – a messianic gesture that obviously would have gone against all political reason. In order to hint at his famous predecessors, Godfrey, Heraclius, Jesus, and King David, he had to content himself instead merely with ostentatious humility. Hence, the address he subsequently delivered to the population exuded a very British sense of sobriety, fairness, prudence and reliability.

The crusading enthusiasm so dreaded by the authorities, however, proved unavoidable. Most famously, the satirical magazine *Punch* published a full-page cartoon with the caption "The Last Crusade," showing the King of England, Richard the Lionheart, overlooking Jerusalem, the city he had been unable to conquer in 1191, exclaiming "My dream comes true!"[76] The Anglophone markets were flooded with books and booklets celebrating Allenby and his soldiers as victorious Crusaders.[77] Sales of such literary classics as Walter Scott's *Ivanhoe* and *Tales of the Crusaders*, and Torquato Tasso's *La Gerusalemme liberata*, soared. The London actor Vivian Gilbert (1882–1932), who in the 1920s went on a tour of the United States to promote his war memoirs, *The Romance of the Last Crusade*, concluded: "In all the ten crusades organized and equipped to free the Holy City, only two were really successful, – the first led by Godfrey de Bouillon, and the last under Edmund Allenby."[78]

Attempts to win the hearts of the Palestinian Muslims likewise resorted to religious themes. According to a story whose origin is hard to trace, going around in varying versions in the heroic literature of the time and even frequently re-emerging in present-day popular accounts of World War I and the Palestine campaign, the British victory resonated with an alleged ancient Muslim prophecy according to which "a prophet from the west" would one day arise and expel the Turks, and that the General's name was understood by the Arab population to mean "the prophet" – "*al-nabī*." Apparently, this odd story was devised by some British army officer and it certainly appealed more to the English than the Arabic-speaking audience.[79]

Already by the time the Ottoman troops had left the city to the British forces, an additional keynote resounded among the advancing soldiers – and soon after in the

---

[74] *A Brief Record of the Advance of the Egyptian Expeditionary Force under the Command of General Sir Edmund H. H. Allenby, G.C.B., G.C.M.G.: July 1917 to October 1918*, ed. Pirie-Gordon 1919, opposite plate 28; Finley 1919, 8.
[75] Goldhill 2008, 144: "This plan was 'unfortunately' scrapped, as Allenby ruefully wrote to his wife."
[76] *Punch*, December 19, 1917, p. 415 – https://archive.org/details/punchvol152a153lemouoft/page/n889 (last accessed April 8, 2022).
[77] Siberry 2000, 94–97; Bar-Yosef 2005, 247.
[78] Gilbert 1923, 171; cf. Bar-Yosef 2014, 51–71.
[79] E.g. *A Brief Record*, loc. cit.; Finley 1919, 16–17. In actual Arabic pronunciation it ought to be *an-nabī*, not '*al-nabī*.' Even worse, other versions cite the fake Arabic formula as "Allah nabī" and the like; further references in Cline 2004, 247; Bar-Yosef 2005, 261–262; Goldhill 2008, 144.

Fig. 23: Frank G. Carpenter: *The Holy Land and Syria. Frank G. Carpenter's World Travels*, vol. 1, Garden City, NY, 1922, Frontispiece.

press. The exclamation "The day of deliverance is come!" is said to have spread – and is again hard to trace to its origin. Its frequent appearance in print, however, is indicative of a widespread sense that the Empire had not just won a decisive victory but that it had brought mankind to the brink of redemption. Not only had the "war to end (all) war(s)" become "the last crusade," it was also seen as the final battle between good and evil.

It was, however, only in the following year, from September 19th to 25th 1918, that the British victory was completed, in a number of skirmishes fought in the vast area between the cities of Haifa, Damascus and Amman. These events collectively went down in military history as the "Battle of Megiddo." Indeed, the ancient site in the Valley of Yezreel lay within the contested area but no significant military action took place anywhere close to it. In recognition of his achievements, Edmund Allenby subsequently was not only promoted to the rank of Field Marshal but also raised to the peerage and henceforth bore the title 1st Viscount Allenby of Megiddo and of Felixstowe.

In the title of one of the many popular biographies of the great commander, playing on the common equation of the Old Testament city of Megiddo with the site of the great battle of the last days according to Revelation 16:16, he was forthrightly dubbed "Allenby of Armageddon."[80]

Onset or Suspension: Two Salvation-Historical Passage Ways

The ceremonial entries of Christian sovereigns and other supreme leaders into Jerusalem and their occupations of the city – whether factual or symbolic – were *rites de passage* from the profane space of the general surface of the earth into a sacred precinct with its own material-spiritual texture and corresponding rules of human conduct. By the same token, these passages marked a transition, as it were, from the current salvation-historical dispensation to another, more advanced one. Thus, the actor of such a rite performed it vicariously for God's people. Since in the Christian conception of history there remained only one more epochal threshold to be crossed, that of the Second Coming, any such entry inevitably suggested that it was meant to herald the expected eschatic events, and the entrant was the harbinger of Christ returning.

In the course of the eight centuries from the Crusaders' capture of Jerusalem to the seizure of the city by the British in World War One, those performing this rite appear on the whole to have grown increasingly cautious of invoking these grave impli-

---

80 Savage 1925.

cations,[81] in deference of the contemporaries' sensitivities – both religious and non-religious –, or to prevent wide-ranging political consequences of their action. However, to avoid the procedure and its inherited sacred significance altogether was not an option available.

The original locale of such (proto-)redemptive passages, the Golden Gate was mostly kept closed from the Crusader period onwards, until it was finally walled up altogether under Süleyman the Magnificent (1520–1566),[82] thus effectively blocking the way for the anticipated messianic breakthrough.

While the entry to the Holy City thus retained its symbolic quality as a gesture that heralded the dawning of a new age, the corresponding ceremony at the access to the *capital* city of the holy empire appears to have borne virtually an opposite significance. As a rule, the entry of a crowned head into Constantinople was a re-entry: the Roman emperor's own homecoming from a victorious military campaign to restore the appropriate imperial power relations, or similarly, the return of orderly, righteous rulership, embodied by the restored emperor – either way, reconfirming the world-political *status quo*. The many rites of passage at the emperors' entries to the city thus were less celebrations of epoch-altering revolutions than of restorations, in tune with the theme of a regularly recurring, even perpetual *restauratio* or *renovatio imperii*, of a salvific stability and persistence that ran through the representations of imperial rule.[83] Future comparative studies would shed light on the extent to which this concept is evident in the representations used at these events.[84]

The ceremonial entry in practice may be tentatively reconstructed as follows: typically (or, rather, ideally) the emperor would make his way into the city through the southernmost entrance of the Theodosian wall that was, strikingly enough, likewise called the 'Golden Gate' (*Chryseia Pyle*, *Porta Aurea*, *Altınkapı*). After acts of humility by the emperor, such as dismounting his horse and prostrating himself toward the east, the procession would follow a ca. 5.5 km long route that has been called the

---

81 The post-Crusader entrants' avoidance of the Golden Gate may not only have been prompted by the walls that blocked its two passageways, but partly motivated by the legend that the returning Christ would enter Jerusalem there, of which the Iraqi Karaite commentator Yefet b. 'Ali (fl. 10th c.) seems to have left the earliest extant testimony – cf. Bargès (ed. and trans.) (1846), on Psalm 122:2.
82 Pringle 1993–2009, vol. 3, 106–107.
83 Girardet 2000, esp. 104–107; Gutteridge 2006, 574–581. In the introduction to his *New Constantines* collected volume, Paul Magdalino referred to the fact "that the emperors who made the most noise about imperial renewal cast themselves, or were cast, in distinctly eschatological roles" as "hard to interpret" (1994, 8–9), a state of affairs that seems not to have changed much since. For the role attributed to Constantinople in the projections of the Byzantine apocalyptic tradition, see Kraft 2012. For an attempt to come to terms with this deep contradiction in the sources' representations of Heraclius (in association with whose reign it appears first to have occurred in full, inspiring the most influential Apocalypse of Ps.-Methodius) cf. Greisiger 2014.
84 Cases that would have to be covered in such a comprehensive comparative study include those of Theodosius I (386 and 391), Heraclius (629/630), Leo III (717), Theophilos (838), Basil I (871 and 882), Nikephoros II Phokas (963), John I Tzimiskes (971), Basil II (1019), Alexios Komnenos (1081), John II (1133), Manuel I (1159), Andronikos I (1182), and Michael VIII Palaiologos (1261).

Constantinopolitan *via triumphalis*, along the southern branch of the *Mese* through the Fora of Arcadius and of Constantine, and reaching the Milion in the actual center of the city, and thus of the Empire, between the Hippodrome and the Hagia Sophia. The emperor would then enter the imperial church for a thanksgiving service, solemnly deposit his crown on the altar, and have himself crowned anew, as it were, by the patriarch.[85]

The reassuring impression of these magnificent public performances naturally became unsettled after the Frankish invaders of the Fourth Crusade held their entry in 1204 and maintained their hegemony for almost six decades. Accordingly, in the late Byzantine period the Golden Gate was increasingly seen as a location of the vulnerability and frailty, rather than the constant rejuvenation, of the Empire. As early as 1190 the gate seems to have been walled up and, after these walls had been broken down by the fleeing Byzantine troops in 1204, they likely were restored. Following the accession of Michael VIII in 1261 – a veritable restoration of the Byzantine Empire – none of his successors seems to have taken this way into the city anymore, probably indicating that it remained closed or walled up.[86] After the conquest of the city by Mehmed II in 1453, the Ottomans inherited this wariness regarding the gate, considering that it might serve for a Christian re-conqueror to enter the city, claim the imperial throne, and to put an end to their rule. In 1457/58, the gate was integrated into a structure known as the Castle of the Seven Towers (*Yedikule Zindanları*) and thereby lost its function as an entryway for good.[87] Legends of a Byzantine emperor in some subterranean hideout, waiting for the divinely ordained day to reappear and restore the Christian empire, remained current among Constantinopolitans, Greeks and Turks alike, well into the modern age.[88]

If the above reconstruction is correct, we may conclude that, while the Golden Gate of Jerusalem served the mytho-ideological function of one day giving access to the redeemer, a new King David or Melchizedek, the Golden Gate of Constantinople embodied, as long as the Empire lasted, not a messianic but a *katechontic* promise. Ceremonial entries into both cities inevitably reflected the respective, opposed salvation-historical roles they were assigned for.

---

85 Treitinger 1938, 146–147, 149–150; Mango 2000.
86 Madden 2012, 320–322.
87 Müller-Wiener 1977, 293, 295, 297–300; Ousterhout 2019, 139–140; Mango 2000, 181; Madden 2012), 322–323; Asutay-Effenberger 2007, s.v. Konstantinopel, Theodosianische Landmauer, Goldenes Tor; and cf. the contribution by Asutay-Effenberger and Weksler-Bdolah to this volume.
88 Madden 2012, 323–326.

Bibliography

Alexander, S.S. (1977). 'Heraclius, Byzantine Imperial Ideology, and the David Plates,' *Speculum* 52, 217–237.
Arad, L. (2015). 'Realising a dream: Emperor Franz Joseph I and his peoples at the Austrian Hospice in Jerusalem,' in Bugnyar/Wohnout 2015, 251–280.
Astour, M.C. (1992). 'Melchizedek (Person),' *The Anchor Bible Dictionary* 4, 684–686.
Asutay-Effenberger, N. (2007). *Die Landmauer von Konstantinopel-İstanbul: Historisch-topographische und baugeschichtliche Untersuchungen*, Berlin.
Atwater Babcock, E. (trans.) (1941–1943). *A History of Deeds Done Beyond the Sea, by William, Archbishop of Tyre* (2 vols.), New York.
Baert, B. (2004). *A Heritage of Holy Wood: The Legend of the True Cross in Text and Image*, Leiden.
Bar, D. & Cohen-Hattab, K. (2003). 'A new kind of pilgrimage: The modern tourist pilgrim of nineteenth-century and early twentieth-century Palestine,' *Middle Eastern Studies* 39, 131–148.
Bargès, J.J.L. (ed., trans.) (1846). *Rabbi Yapheth ben Heli Bassorensis Karaitæ in Librum Psalmorum commentarii arabici...*, Lutetiæ Parisiorum.
Bar-Yosef, E. (2005). *The Holy Land in English Culture, 1799–1917: Palestine and the Question of Orientalism*, Oxford.
Bar-Yosef, E. (2014). 'Theatre, masculinity, and class in the First World War: Vivian Gilbert performs the last crusade,' *The Drama Review* 58, 51–71.
Benner, Th. (2001). *Die Strahlen der Krone: Die religiöse Dimension des Kaisertums unter Wilhelm II. vor dem Hintergrund der Orientreise 1898*, Marburg.
Bernhardt, K.-H. (1992). 'Melchisedek I. Altes Testament,' *Theologische Realenzyklopädie* 22, 414–417.
Bernhardt, K.-H., Willi, Th. & Balz, H. (1992). 'Melchisedek,' *Theologische Realenzyklopädie* 22, 414–423.
Borgehammar, S. (2009). 'Heraclius learns humility: Two early Latin accounts composed for the celebration of Exaltatio Crucis,' *Millennium* 6, 145–201.
Bugnyar, M. St. & Wohnout, H. (eds.) (2015). *At Home in the Orient: The Austrian Hospice in Jerusalem*, Vienna.
Carmel, A. (1985). 'Russian Activity in Palestine in the Nineteenth Century,' in Cohen 1985, 45–77.
Charlesworth, J.H. (1983). *The Old Testament Pseudepigrapha* (vol. 1: *Apocalyptic Literature and Testaments*), ed. James H. Charlesworth, New York (repr. 2009).
Cline, E.H. (2004). *Jerusalem Besieged: From Ancient Canaan to Modern Israel*, Ann Arbor.
Cohen, R. (ed.) (1985). *Vision and Conflict in the Holy Land*, Jerusalem.
Dagron, G. (2003). *Emperor and Priest: The Imperial Office in Byzantium*, Cambridge.
De Hoop, R. (1999). *Genesis 49 in its Literary and Historical Context*, Leiden.
Delzant, J.-B. (ed.) (2018). *L'église d'Abu Gosh: 850 ans de regards sur les fresques d'une église franque en Terre Sainte*, Paris.
Dignas, B., Winter, E. (2007). *Rome and Persia in Late Antiquity: Neighbours and Rivals*, Cambridge.
Di Nepi, S. & Marzano, M. (eds.) (2013). *Quest: Issues in Contemporary Jewish History* (Issue 6: *Travels to the 'Holy Land': Perceptions, Representations and Narratives*), Milan.
Dillmann, A. (trans.) (1853). *Das christliche Adambuch des Morgenlandes*, Göttingen.
Dudík, B. (1870). *Kaiser-Reise nach dem Oriente*, Vienna.
Edgington, S.B. (ed./trans.) (2007). *Albert of Aachen, Historia Ierosolimitana – History of the Journey to Jerusalem*, Oxford (repr. 2009).

Eisler, J. (ed.) (2008). *Deutsche in Palästina und ihr Anteil an der Modernisierung des Landes*, Wiesbaden.

Finley, J.H. (1919). *A Pilgrim in Palestine, Being an Account of Journeys on Foot by the First American Pilgrim after General Allenby's Recovery of the Holy Land*, New York.

Fischer, R.-T. (2006). *Österreich im Nahen Osten: Die Großmachtpolitik der Habsburgermonarchie im Arabischen Orient 1633–1918*, Vienna.

Gadrat-Ouerfelli, C., Rouxpetel, C. (2018). 'Emmaüs, un épisode biblique, deux sites. Concurrence et coexistence dans les sources latines, grecques et orientales (xiie–xve siècle),' in Delzant, J.-B. (ed.), *L'église d'Abu Gosh: 850 ans de regards sur les fresques d'une église franque en Terre Sainte*, Paris 2018, 41–62.

Girardet, K. (2000). 'Renovatio imperii aus dem Geist des Christentums: Zu Herkunft und Umfeld des Begriffs,' *ZAC* 4, 102–115.

Gilbert, V. (1923). *The Romance of the Last Crusade: With Allenby to Jerusalem*, New York.

Goldhill, S. (2008). *Jerusalem: City of Longing*, Cambridge, MA/London.

Grabar, O. & Kedar, B.Z. (eds.) (2009). *Where Heaven and Earth Meet: Jerusalem's Sacred Esplanade*, Jerusalem.

Greatrex, G., Lieu, S.N.C. (2002). *The Roman Eastern Frontier and the Persian Wars*, London.

Greisiger, L. (2014). *Messias · Endkaiser · Antichrist: Politische Apokalyptik unter Juden und Christen des Nahen Ostens am Vorabend der arabischen Eroberung*, Wiesbaden.

Guidi, I. (1891). 'Un nuovo testo siriaco sulla storia degli ultimi Sassanidi,' in *Actes du huitième congrès international des orientalistes*; vol. 2,1: *Section sémitique et de l'Islâm. B: Langues sémitiques, autres que l'arabe; textes et écritures cuneiforms, etc.*, in Congrès International des Orientalistes, Leiden 1891 (repr. Nendeln 1974), 1–36.

Gutteridge, A. (2006). 'Some Aspects of Social and Cultural Time in Late Antiquity,' in Bowden, W., Gutteridge, A., Machado C. (eds.), *Social and Political Life in Late Antiquity* (Late Antique Archaeology 3,1), Leiden, 569–598.

Hanauer, J.E. (1900). 'Notes on the Modern Colonization in Palestine,' *Palestine Exploration Fund Quarterly Statement* 32, 124–142 (= in *The Jewish Era: A Christian Quarterly in Behalf of Israel* 9,3 [July 15], 1900, 74–80; 10 [January 15], 1901, 15–20).

Hopwood, D. (1969). *The Russian Presence in Syria and Palestine 1843–1914: Church and Politics in the Near East*, Oxford.

Hughes, M. (ed.) (2004). *Allenby in Palestine: The Middle East Correspondence of Field Marshal Viscount Allenby, June 1917–October 1919*, Stroud.

Huygens, R.B.C. & Pryor, J.H. (eds.) (1994). *Peregrinationes tres: Saewulf, John of Würzburg, Theodericus*, Turnhout.

Huygens, R.B.C. (ed.) (1986). *Willelmi Tyrensis Archiepiscopi Chronicon*, Turnhout.

Huygens, R.B.C. (ed.) (1994). Johannes of Würzburg: 'Descriptio Terrae Sanctae,' in Huygens/Pryor 1994, 78–141.

Kane, E.M. (2006). 'Pilgrims, Piety, and Politics: The Founding of the First Russian Ecclesiastical Mission in Jerusalem,' in Tamcke/Marten 2006, 177–198.

Kark, R. (2008). 'Missionary Societies in the Holy Land in an International Context,' in Eisler 2008, 14–29.

Kedar, B.Z. & Denys Pringle, R. D. (2009). '1099–1187: The Lord's Temple (Templum Domini) and Solomon's Palace (Palatium Salomonis),' in Grabar/Kedar 2009, 133–149.

Knobler, A. (2006). 'Holy Wars, Empires, and the Portability of the Past: The Modern Uses of Medieval Crusades,' *CSSH* 48, 293–325.

Kraft, A. (2012). 'Constantinople in Byzantine Apocalyptic Thought,' in *Annual of Medieval Studies at CEU* 18, 25–36.

Lewis, D.M. (2010). *The Origins of Christian Zionism: Lord Shaftesbury and Evangelical Support for a Jewish Homeland*, Cambridge (repr. 2013).

Madden, T.F. (2012). 'Triumph Re-imagined: The Golden Gate and Popular Memory in Byzantine and Ottoman Constantinople' in Gertwagen, R., Jeffreys, E. (eds.), *Shipping, Trade and Crusade in the Medieval Mediterranean: Studies in honour of John Pryor*, Oxford, New York, 317–328.

Mango, C. (2000). 'The Triumphal Way of Constantinople and the Golden Gate,' *DOP* 54, 173–188.

Mazza, R. (2009). *Jerusalem from the Ottomans to the British*, London (repr. 2014).

Menzel, M. (1992). 'Gottfried von Bouillon und Kaiser Heraclius,' *AKG* 74, 1–21.

Merlo, S. (2013). 'Travels of Russians to the Holy Land in the 19th Century,' in Di Nepi/Marzano 2013, 48–67.

Morgenstern, J. (1929). 'The Gates of Righteousness,' *HebrUCA* 6, 1–37.

Müller-Wiener, W. (1977). *Bildlexikon zur Topographie Istanbuls: Byzantion – Konstantinupolis – Istanbul bis zum Beginn des 17. Jahrhunderts*, Tübingen.

Murre-van den Berg, H. (ed.) (2006). *New Faith in Ancient Lands: Western Missions in the Middle East in the Nineteenth and Early Twentieth Centuries*, Leiden.

Nöldeke, Th. (1893). *Die von Guidi herausgegebene syrische Chronik*, Vienna.

Ousterhout, R.G. (2019). *Eastern Medieval Architecture: The Building Traditions of Byzantium and Neighboring Lands*, New York.

Paulin, M. (ed.) (1879–1880). *Guillaume de Tyr et ses continuateurs, texte français du XIIIe siècle* (2 vols.), Paris.

Perry, Y. (2001). 'Anglo-German Cooperation in Nineteenth-Century Jerusalem: The London Jews' Society and the Protestant Bishopric,' *Jewish Culture and History* 4, 65–80.

Pirie-Gordon, D.H.C. (ed.) (^{2}1919). *A Brief Record of the Advance of the Egyptian Expeditionary Force under the Command of General Sir Edmund H. H. Allenby, G.C.B., G.C.M.G.: July 1917 to October 1918*, London.

Pringle, D. (1993–2009). *The Churches of the Crusader Kingdom of Jerusalem: A Corpus* (4 vols.), Cambridge.

Ri, S.-M. (1987, ed. trans.). *La Caverne des Trésors: les deux recensions syriaques*, (Corpus Scriptorum Christianorum Orientalium, vol. 486–487 = Scriptores Syri, vol. 207–208), Lovanii.

Rothfels, H. (ed.) (1971). *Tagebuch meiner Reise nach dem Morgenlande 1869: Bericht des preußischen Kronprinzen Friedrich Wilhelm über seine Reise zur Einweihung des Suez-Kanals*, Frankfurt a. M.

Runciman, S. (1955). *A History of the Crusades*; vol. 3: *The Kingdom of Acre and the Later Crusades*, Cambridge (repr. 1965, 1979, 1997).

Şahin, K. (2010). 'Constantinople and the End Time: The Ottoman Conquest as a Portent of the Last Hour,' *Journal of Early Modern History* 14, 317–354.

Savage, R. (1925). *Allenby of Armageddon: A Record of the Career and Campaigns of Field-Marshal Viscount Allenby*, London.

Schneller, L. (1899). *Die Kaiserfahrt durchs Heilige Land*, Leipzig.

Schultz, S. (1771–1775). *Der Leitungen des Höchsten nach seinem Rath auf den Reisen durch Europa, Asia und Africa* (5 vols.), Halle.

Shahîd, I. (1981). 'On the Titulature of the Emperor Heraclius,' *Byzantion* 51, 288–296.

Siberry, E. (2000). *The New Crusaders: Images of the Crusades in the Nineteenth and Early Twentieth Centuries*, Aldershot.

Stewart, A. (trans.) (1890). *John of Würzburg, Description of the Holy Land*, London.

Tamcke, M. & Marten, M. (eds.) (2006). *Christian Witness Between Continuity and New Beginnings: Modern Historical Missions in the Middle East*, Berlin.

Tejirian E.H. & Simon, R.S. (2012). *Conflict, Conquest, and Conversion: Two Thousand Years of Christian Missions in the Middle East*, New York.

Tischendorf, C. (1862). 'Großfürst Constantin und sein Einzug in Jerusalem,' *Die Gartenlaube* 16, 251–253.

Tobler, T. (1868). *Nazareth in Palästina. Nebst anhang der vierten wanderung*, Berlin.

Treitinger, O. (1938). *Die oströmische Kaiser- und Reichsidee nach ihrer Gestaltung im höfischen Zeremoniell*, Jena (repr. Darmstadt 1956, 1969).

Trimbur, D. & Aaronsohn, R. (eds.) (2008). *De Bonaparte à Balfour: La France, l'Europe occidentale et la Palestine, 1799–1917*, Paris.

Trumpp, E. (ed.) (1880). *Der Kampf Adams (gegen die Versuchungen des Satans), oder: Das christliche Adambuch des Morgenlandes*, Munich.

Vogel, L.I. (1993). *To see a Promised Land: Americans and the Holy Land in the Nineteenth Century*, University Park, PA.

von Bergmann, J. (1857). *Erzherzog Friedrich von Oesterreich und sein Antheil am Kriegszuge in Syrien im Jahre 1840*, Vienna.

von Mirbach, E. (1899). *Das deutsche Kaiserpaar im Heiligen Lande im Herbst 1898*, Berlin.

Wilken, R.L. (1992). *The Land Called Holy: Palestine in Christian History and Thought*, New Haven, CT.

Zahnd, U. (2008). 'Novus David – Νεος Δαυιδ. Zur Frage nach byzantinischen Vorläufern eines abendländischen Topos,' *Frühmittelalterliche Studien* 42, 71–87.

General Index

Acacian Schism 217, 256
Al-Aqsa Mosque 179
Antichrist 273, 275, 277
Antonia (fortress) 14
Apocalypse 56, 74, 265, 271, 273–274, 276–277, 289, 297, 316
apostles 7, 15, 27, 31, 51, 122, 133, 143, 147, 151–152, 154, 170, 200, 218, 263–265, 267, 269, 271, 273–277
apostolic succession 241
Arab conquest 2, 7, 288–289
Arianism 13, 19–20, 29, 32
Ark 227, 281, 287, 289, 297–298, 301–302, 307–308
Armageddon 7, 295, 315
Armenian lectionary 147, 191–192
ascetics 20–21, 28, 34, 46, 118, 290–291
Avars 47, 57, 75, 273–275, 284, 300

Babylonian Exile 222
baptism 17, 199, 220, 291, 303
Basilica Cistern 215, 235
Baths of Zeuxippos 266
battle of Adrianople 29, 41, 71
battle of Chrysopolis 194
battle of Königgrätz 308
battle of Megiddo 315
Belgradkapı 74, 81, 83, 87
Bible 11–12, 18, 189, 297
Binbirdirek Cistern 144
Blachernai 75, 103
Blachernai Wall 75, 87
Black Sea 1, 48, 72, 121
Book of Daniel 177, 272
Book of Kings 175
Book of Revelation 56, 273, 275
burials 57, 132, 156, 187–188, 275, 282

calendar 2, 5, 53, 173–174, 191, 264
Calvary. See Golgotha.
Canaanites 226
cardo 152, 161–163, 167–168, 171
Castle of the Seven Towers 317
celebrations. See festivities.
Christmas 225, 231, 311

Churches in Constantinople and its vicinity
– Church of SS Peter and Paul 145–146, 224
– Church of SS Peter and Paul (Chalcedon) 145
– Church of SS Sergius and Bacchus 146, 224, 263
– Church of St Acacius 144, 200
– Church of St Anastasia 143
– Church of St Anthony 74
– Church of St Demetrius 75–76
– Church of St Euphemia 217
– Church of St George 267, 269
– Church of St Ioannophokas 264. See also Church of St John the Apostle.
– Church of St James at the Chalkoprateia 267, 274
– Church of St John the Apostle 7, 263–267, 269, 271, 273, 275, 277
– Church of St John the Baptist at the Hebdomon 268
– Church of St Lawrence 144–145, 153–154
– Church of St Mary of Blachernai 75, 270
– Church of St Menas 143
– Church of St Mocius 144, 200
– Church of St Panteleemon 267
– Church of St Paul 143, 152, 263, 267, 274
– Church of St Phokas 264, 267, 269, 271, 274. See also Church of St John the Apostle.
– Church of St Polyeuctus 6, 145, 151, 153–154, 172, 177, 216–225, 263
– Church of St Theodore 145, 267, 269
Church of St Thomas 145
– Church of St Thyrsus 145
– Church of the Apostles 15, 51, 143, 151, 154, 170, 200, 218
– Church of the Archangel Michael 48, 54, 268
– Church of the Forty Martyrs 145–146, 267, 269
– Church of the Theotokos ta Areobindou 267
– Church of the Theotokos tes Diakonisses 267

- Church of the Theotokos tes peges   75, 270
- Hagia Irene   51, 53, 143–145, 147, 152, 200, 225, 227, 263–264, 267, 269, 273–274, 276
- Hagia Sophia   7, 52–53, 55, 57, 169–170, 172, 174, 177, 215–216, 221, 225, 227, 229–235, 263–264, 266–269, 274, 301, 317
- Nea Ekklesia   235
- Peribleptos church   235

Churches in Jerusalem and its vicinity
- Augusta Victoria Church   309
- Church of SS Cosmas and Damianus (Kidron Valley)   151
- Chapel of St George   149
- Chapel of St Menas   150, 156
- Church of Holy Sion   20, 96, 101, 147, 149, 152, 172
- Church of St Mary at the Pool of Bethesda   173
- Church of St Stephen   24, 54, 148, 150–152, 155
- Church of the Ascension (Augusta Victoria Church)   309
- Church of the Ascension (Eleona)   13, 16, 100, 147
- Church of the Redeemer   309–310
- Church of the Tomb of Mary   173
- Holy Sepulcher   1, 5, 12, 14–17, 25, 100, 141–142, 145, 147–149, 151, 163, 165, 167, 170–171, 173, 186–195, 202, 228, 283, 300, 304, 307, 309, 311
- Nea Maria   5, 32, 139, 152, 161–179, 217, 224, 235, 300
- Templum Domini   305

Churches elsewhere
- Church of Paulinus (Tyre)   216, 221
- Church of St John (Ephesus)   170, 275
- Church of the archangel Michael (Germia)   133
- Church of the Nativity (Bethlehem)   16, 162, 168
- Constantinian church at Mamre   13, 144
- Theotokos church (Mount Garizim)   162

circus factions   45, 230
cisterns   144, 162, 166, 169, 215, 235
citadel   90, 295
City of David   89–90, 93, 95, 102, 297
clergy   20, 45, 151, 178, 191, 247, 308, 310
clerics   21, 27, 45, 52, 189, 191, 199, 205, 306, 309
columns   14, 147, 167–169, 175–176, 201, 265–266, 268, 276, 292–293
conquests
of Jerusalem (by David)   297
of Jerusalem (70 AD)   176
of Jerusalem (614 AD)   7, 168, 178
of Jerusalem (c. 637 AD)   34, 58, 288–289
of Jerusalem (1099 AD)   7, 315
of Constantinople (1204 AD)   75
of Constantinople (1453 AD)   61, 85, 317
councils
- of Nicaea (325 AD)   13–14, 26, 131, 186, 190–191, 242
- of Tyre (335 AD)   17, 189, 200, 202
- of Jerusalem (335 AD)   190–191
- of Constantinople (381 AD)   41, 52, 114, 264
- of Ephesus (431 AD)   173, 246
- of Ephesus (449 AD)   244
- of Chalcedon (451 AD)   6, 26–28, 30–32, 52, 114, 142, 154, 217, 241–257
- of Jerusalem (518 AD)   250
- of Constantinople (536 AD)   33
- of Constantinople (553 AD)   33
- of Constantinople (681 AD)   264

Cross. See Holy Cross.
Crucifixion   22, 149, 187, 281, 287
crusades   7, 49, 60, 75, 282, 304–309, 31–313, 315–317
cult of saints   5, 12, 132–133, 143, 148, 151, 153, 155–156, 172, 269, 290
cursus publicus   113–114, 118, 120, 128, 130

Damascus Gate   90, 92, 94, 152, 283
David's Tower   90, 95
dedication. See inauguration.
desert   3, 28–33, 113, 115, 117, 140, 150, 154–156, 162, 164–165, 172, 281, 283
dies Solis   193, 196
Diippion   264, 266–268, 275
Dome of the Rock   179, 293, 305
dynasty   16, 32, 71, 75, 186, 191–192, 194–196, 205, 209, 300, 302

earthquake   54, 56, 74, 76, 79, 87, 97, 124, 130, 178, 225–227, 231, 233, 265, 270–271, 275
Easter   170, 283

Edirnekapı 76, 86–88
encaenia 15, 174, 187, 189, 191–195, 197, 202, 264. See also inauguration.
encomia. See panegyrics.
entries (adventus) 2, 7–8, 150, 153, 173–174, 286, 295–296, 299, 302–305, 307–309, 311–312, 315–317
epigrams 6, 219–225, 229, 234–235
Epiphany 151, 174
eschatology 2–3, 6–7, 11, 56, 59, 222–223, 272, 275, 303, 312, 316
eulogies. See panegyrics.
Euphrates 115, 124, 135, 282, 296

festivities 5, 17, 54, 57, 173–174, 186–194, 199–200, 219, 264, 266, 274, 286–287, 290–292, 295, 301 308, 310, 316
First Wall (Jerusalem) 88, 95, 101
fortifications 4, 48–49, 71–72, 78–79, 82, 88, 94–95, 99–101, 115, 163, 284, 306
Forty Martyrs 51, 142, 145–146, 267, 269
Forum of Arcadius 317
Forum of Constantine 72, 201, 276, 317
Forum of Theodosius 41, 151, 218

Gate of Charisios 86
Gate of Pempton 86
Gate of St John 86
Gate of St Romanos 83, 85–86
Gethsemane 20, 173
Golden Gate (Constantinople) 56, 74, 80, 82–83, 85, 87–88, 316–317
Golden Gate (Jerusalem) 288, 291, 299, 305, 316
Golden Horn 49, 72, 74–76, 87, 119, 121, 144
Golgotha 13, 15, 24, 34, 100, 115, 147, 188, 192–193, 283, 285, 287, 289, 300
Gospels 7, 11–12, 20, 27, 148, 170, 173, 192, 226, 228, 281, 291, 298–299, 302
governors 14, 19, 25, 31, 60, 123, 127, 199, 306–307

Hasmoneans 90, 95–96, 141, 296
Heavenly Jerusalem 11, 23, 222, 272
Hebdomon 40, 51, 268
Henotikon 28, 246–247, 252, 254–255, 257
heresy 29, 32, 208, 232
hermits 29
Hezekiah's Wall 95

hippodrome 3, 7, 16, 22–23, 41, 44–45, 55–56, 58–59, 144, 149, 176, 192, 201, 209, 227, 230, 264–266, 268, 274–275, 317
Holy Cross 3, 7, 16, 18, 22–24, 34, 56, 58–59, 77, 100, 114–115, 120, 140, 149, 156, 188, 192–193, 275–276, 281–291, 300–302, 305, 307–308, 317
Holy Lance 58, 301
Holy Land 1–3, 5, 11, 13, 15, 17–34, 50, 102, 114–115, 117, 125, 127–128, 132–133, 135, 140–141, 146, 151, 154–155, 161–163, 168, 176, 178–179, 188, 197, 199, 203, 209, 245, 253, 255–256, 271, 286, 291–292, 305–306, 309, 314
Holy men 4–5, 24, 28, 32–34, 46, 129, 132, 140, 145–146, 156, 270, 275
Holy Nails 301
Holy places 4, 12–13, 17–20, 22–27, 29, 31, 99, 111, 116, 126, 128, 132, 141–143, 146, 148–149, 162, 170, 190, 252–253, 256, 281–283, 290, 295, 308
Holy Sponge 58, 301
Holy War 7, 312
Holy women 118, 140
Homoeans 41, 51, 54
hospices 25, 149–150, 168–169, 309
house of Pilate 142, 147
Huns 46, 49
hymns 18, 55, 172–174, 216, 221, 225–226, 228–235, 288–289, 301

imperial cult 191, 193
imperial family 30, 52, 54, 102, 199
inauguration 5, 15, 17, 143, 164, 166, 172–174, 186–191, 193–195, 199, 202, 216, 221, 225, 231, 233, 235, 269, 282, 310. See also encaenia.
incarnation 13, 31, 195, 229, 231, 233, 273, 282
inscriptions 6, 49, 74, 78–80, 82–88, 98, 102–103, 118, 123, 125, 127–129, 143, 149, 166, 169, 171, 178, 216–219, 221, 224, 230, 282
İsa Kapısı Mescidi 74
Islam 7, 39, 49, 60–61, 179, 282, 293, 312
Israel 57, 60–61, 90–91, 103, 135, 228, 232, 272, 274, 281, 295–300, 303, 312
Israelites 142, 226–227, 286

Jachum and Baaz (columns) 175
Jaffa Gate 90, 93, 282, 295, 307–308, 311, 313
Jews 7, 11, 18–19, 56, 60, 141, 175–177, 232, 272, 274, 277, 281–283, 285, 287–288, 291, 293, 303, 312
Jordan 17, 125, 130, 199, 281
Joshua Column 293
Joshua Roll 291–292
Judah 295–297, 299
Judaism 4, 11, 15, 96–97, 103, 171, 178, 291

Kalagros Gate 83
khagan 284
King David's Tomb 96
Kıyâmet-i Suǧra 74
Land Walls (Constantinople) 72–77, 81, 139
Lycos 76

Madaba Map 89, 100, 164
martyrs 5, 12, 24, 51, 130, 132–133, 142–146, 149–155, 170–171, 200, 218, 220, 253, 264, 266–267, 269, 290
mausoleum 200
Mese 85, 144–145, 151, 201, 218, 317
Mesoteichion 85
Mevlevihanekapı 78, 80, 83, 87–88
Milion 264, 266, 268, 317
miracles 11, 18, 147–148, 151, 163, 170, 270, 288
monarchy 2, 4–5, 16, 33, 45, 185, 188, 191–193, 195–196, 198–200, 204–205, 208–209, 234, 243, 250, 300, 310
monasteries
– monastery of the Dormition 309
– monastery at Xanxaris 132
– monastery of Bassianus 139
– monastery of St Dalmatius 146
– monastery of St Dios 145
– monastery of Euthymius 150, 156
– monastery of Flavia 150, 156
– monastery of St John the Baptist 145
– monastery of Martyrius 166
– monastery of Matrona 139
– monastery of Melania the Elder 20
– monastery of SS Cosmas and Damianus 145
– monastery of St Andrew 144
– monastery of the Nea Maria 166, 168–169

– Theotokos/Diomedes monastery 56
monasticism 3, 28–29, 34, 257
monks 20, 27–33, 45, 115, 117, 141, 156, 162, 165, 178, 242, 244–245, 247–249, 251–253, 256, 283, 290
monophysitism 28, 235
mosaics 89, 96, 103, 141, 163, 171, 178, 265–266, 276, 282, 309
Mount Carmel 124–125
Mount Garizim 162
Mount Sinai 139, 162, 175
Mumhane 75–76
Muslims 285, 293, 299, 304, 310, 313
Myriandrion 83
mythology 198, 201

navel (omphalos) 50, 57–58, 61, 141, 281
Nestorians 32, 244, 290
New Jerusalem 4, 7, 14–15, 56, 61, 75, 171, 193, 234, 263, 265, 267, 269, 271–273, 275–277
New Rome 234, 271–272
New Testament 18, 130, 176, 192, 226, 250, 282, 307
Nicaeans 13, 41, 51, 54
Nika riot 172, 217, 225, 227, 230–231, 234
Nile 124
nomads 162, 284
novels 163, 263

Oak of Mamre 17
obelisk 41
Old Jerusalem 1, 15, 56–57, 146, 171, 193
Old Testament 6, 13, 55, 57, 141, 145–146, 175, 177, 215, 220, 222, 225–235, 274, 284, 286, 291, 310, 315
Ophel 89–90, 93–95, 102
orations 5, 17, 185–187, 195–196, 202, 204–207
Origenists 32–33, 162, 166
Orontes 124, 150
Ottomans 61, 74, 80, 83, 85–86, 88, 90, 93, 95, 167, 265, 295–296, 306, 311, 313

paganism 3, 11–12, 14–15, 17–18, 50, 60, 96–97, 118, 128, 130–132, 139, 144, 190–191, 193, 196, 198, 201, 221, 271–272
palace 5, 16, 24–25, 44, 47–48, 54, 61, 75, 103, 144–145, 155, 176–177, 186–187,

190, 194, 198–199, 201–202, 205–206, 224, 231, 235, 268, 285
Palestinian Union   244–246, 254
Palm Sunday   299, 302, 305
panegyrics   149–150, 153, 155, 165, 167, 169, 186–187, 189, 198, 203–208, 216, 219, 228, 233
Passion of Christ   4, 13, 149, 171, 281, 288, 301
Passover   298
patriarchate   6, 26, 28, 53, 114–115, 123, 142, 241–244, 250, 254–256, 290
patronage   4, 24, 39, 117–118, 127, 130, 147, 268
peace   1, 31, 74, 146, 190–191, 194, 197, 232, 247, 285, 287, 303
Pentecost   149, 170
persecution   51, 144, 189, 195, 198, 245, 303
Persians   7, 19, 41, 46–47, 57–59, 115, 124, 155, 165, 168, 178–179, 189, 219, 274–275, 282–287, 290–293, 300–303
Peutinger Map   123, 132
Phoenicians   128
pilgrims   2–4, 12, 16, 20–22, 24, 26, 31, 98–99, 101, 111–123, 127–135, 141–142, 147–148, 150, 152, 154, 162, 188, 304–309, 311
plague   53, 56, 124, 226–227, 270
polytheism   195, 199, 204, 208
Pool of Bethesda   173
Pool of Mamilla   282, 288
Pool of Siloam   99, 101
popes   27, 153, 217, 220, 224, 243, 245–246, 251–252, 254, 256
porphyry column   201
ports   80, 119, 124–125, 130, 135
prophecies   11, 18–19, 57, 189, 272–277, 299, 313
prophets   6, 57, 114, 141, 174–175, 190, 274, 313
quarries   167–169, 192
relics   2–3, 7, 22–25, 41, 51, 54–56, 58–59, 114, 123, 130, 142–145, 148–149, 151, 153–156, 170, 176, 192, 224, 234, 270, 272, 275–277, 287, 290, 300–301
resurrection   12–14, 100, 144, 171, 178, 187–188, 195, 228–229, 281
revelation   11–12, 56–57, 139, 149, 195, 203, 273–277, 315
Rhesion gate   83

Russian cathedral   168
Russian Compound   100, 306

sack of Rome   177
salvation   4–5, 11, 21, 57, 61, 146, 188, 190–193, 195, 197, 202, 207, 226–227, 230, 234, 269, 277, 281–282, 299–304, 315–317
Samaritans   32, 113, 162
Saracens   115, 304
Sasanians   3
Scamander   141
Scythians   273
Sea of Marmara   72, 75–76, 80, 119, 121
Second Wall (Jerusalem)   88, 95, 192
senate   40, 43–44, 113
Septuagint   141, 175
ships   119, 121, 198
siege of Constantinople (626 AD)   57, 273, 293
Sigma   76, 80, 87
Sion   20, 25, 57, 72, 88–90, 93, 95–96, 99–102, 147, 149, 152, 172, 228, 297, 299, 309–310
Slavs   275
soldiers   16, 25, 27, 43, 45, 47, 118, 196, 264, 313
spolia   87–88, 96–97, 102–103
Strata Diocletiana   115
Strata Nova   82
Suez Canal   308
Sultan Ahmed Mosque   265
Sulukulekapı   78, 86, 88
summus deus   188, 195–196
sun worship   196
synods. See councils.
Syriac   98, 100, 148–149, 151, 300
Syrian Gates   121

Taurus mountains   113, 120–121, 134
Tekfur Sarayı   75–76, 87
Temple Mount   14–15, 95–97, 100, 103, 146, 163, 170–171, 179, 193, 281–282, 288–289, 291–293, 298, 303
temples
Jewish Temple   5–6, 11, 14–15, 19, 34, 56, 88, 97, 148, 152, 161, 168–169, 171–179, 193, 215–216, 219, 222–225, 228–235, 298–299
of Ezekiel   6, 145, 222

of Jupiter 14–15, 192
of Venus 14, 192
Tenth Legion 15, 88, 95–96, 115
Tetrarchy 113
Third Wall (Jerusalem) 88, 95
throne 1, 32, 46, 202–204, 206, 223, 228–230, 269, 298, 300, 317
Tigris 123–124
tombs 12, 14–15, 57, 88, 96, 99, 142, 150, 156, 188, 190, 192–193, 202, 266, 275, 300
Topkapı gate 86
Topkapı Sarayı 72
towers 49, 74, 76, 78, 80–81, 83–84, 86–87, 89–90, 92–93, 95, 283, 295, 311, 317
trade 4, 111–112, 116, 124, 127, 133–135
translation of relics 2, 24, 51, 153–154, 156, 234, 275
tricennalia 17, 185–187, 190, 194, 196–197, 206–207
Trisagion Riot 217–218
triumphal arches 82, 310
triumphs 2, 7, 82–83, 176–178, 255, 286, 304, 308
Turks 61, 313, 317

Unkapanı 74
usurpations 18, 28, 40, 43, 45–46, 83, 245, 300

Valley of Yezreel 315
Vandals 26, 176–177
Via Dolorosa 289, 309
Via Egnatia 82–83, 121
Via Sebaste 123
Via Tauri 134
vicennalia 190, 198
victories 1, 4, 7, 14, 28, 48, 54–55, 82, 96, 103, 144, 171, 177, 190–191, 194, 207–208, 227, 286, 292, 302, 313, 315

wine 4, 116–117, 134–135, 296

Xylokerkos gate 83

Zagros 285
Zion. See Sion.

Names

Aaron   146, 298
Abba Romanus   150
Abdülhamid, sultan   311
Abdülmecid I, sultan   306
Abgar, king   146
Abraham   13, 146, 297
Abramius, monk   166
Abū Jaʿfar al-Manṣūr   296
Acacius of Caesarea, bishop   19, 185
Acacius of Constantinople, bishop   245–246, 251
Acacius of Nicomedia, martyr   143–144, 146, 152, 200
Acacius, comes   17, 144, 152
Agape, martyr   152
Agathias   270
Ahaz   284
al-Kāmil, sultan   309
Alaric   177
Albert of Aachen   304–305
Alcison of Nicopolis   244, 256
Alexander Acoemetus   146
Alexander II of Russia   296, 306
Alexander of Cappadocia   12
Alexander the Great   286, 295
Alexander, fictitious knight   139
Alexandra Iosifovna   306
Alexios II Komnenos   264, 316
Allenby, Edmund   7–8, 295–296, 311–313, 315
Allenby, Henry J. H., 295
Alypius   19
Amantius, imperial official   255
Ambrose of Milan, bishop   23
Ammianus Marcellinus   19
Ananias, servant of Abgar   146
Anastasius of Jerusalem, bishop   156, 245, 251, 253–254
Anastasius the Persian, martyr   290
Anastasius, dux   31
Anastasius, emperor   30–32, 48, 113, 155, 162, 170, 217–218, 223, 243–244, 247–256
Andrew of Caesarea, bishop   271, 273–275
Andrew the Fool, saint   276–277
Andrew, apostle   51, 144, 146
Andrew, monk   156

Andronikos I Komnenos   316
Anicia Juliana   6, 56, 145, 171–172, 177, 179, 216–224, 229–230, 234–235, 263
Anna Komnene   263
Anthemius of Tralles   169
Anthemius, praefectus   74, 102
Anthony of Novgorod   264, 275
Anthony, saint   74
Antiochus Strategos   115, 168
Antiochus, eunuch   144
Antiochus, fictitious knight   139
Antipas, saint   264, 275
Araunah   298
Arcadia, daughter of emperor Arcadius   144
Arcadius, emperor   24, 42, 51, 54, 71, 74, 101–102, 128, 140, 317
Areobindus   217–218
Armilus (or Hermolaos)   291
Artemidorus   102
Arthur Balfour   312
Athanasius of Alexandria, bishop   173, 187, 200, 202
Augusta Victoria   309
Augustine, bishop   273, 275
Aurelianus, praetorian prefect   145
Auxentios   264
Auxitius, comes   129
Avitus of Vienne   256

Balaam the Seer   146
Balak   146
Barachos   164
Baras   145
Barkat, Nir   295
Basil I, emperor   216, 235, 316
Basil II, emperor   316
Basiliscus, emperor   245, 251, 253
Bassa, noblewoman   150–151, 155–156
Bassianus, monk   139
Belisarius, general   174, 176–178
Belshazzar, king   177–178
Benjamin of Tiberias   303
Beor   146
Bethuel   146
Bezalel   232–233
Boran   285

Bordier, Julien   265, 276
Brown, Peter 29

Caesarius   120, 122, 145
Caracalla   123
Caroline of Brunswick   296
Cassiodorus   100–101
Castinus, magister militum   42
Charlemagne   296
Christ. See Jesus.
Clavijo   264–266
Constans   194
Constantia, wife of emperor Maurice   270
Constantine I, emperor   1, 3, 11–14, 16–20, 22–25, 39–40, 43–44, 49, 56, 72, 74, 83, 98, 127–128, 132, 139, 142–144, 146–147, 149, 163, 171–172, 185–186, 188–190, 192–201, 203–209, 219–220, 228–229, 234, 272–273, 276, 281, 286, 289, 296, 300, 317
Constantine II, emperor   194
Constantine, hegumen   166
Constantius I, emperor   194
Constantius II, emperor   18–19, 22, 40–41, 51, 123, 186
Cosmas Indicopleustes   272–273
Cosmas, saint   145, 151
Crispus, son of emperor Constantine   16, 128, 194
Cristoforo Buondelmonti   76, 265
Cyril of Alexandria   25, 148, 153, 173, 175
Cyril of Jerusalem   18–20, 22–23, 97, 142, 148
Cyril of Scythopolis   24–26, 28–33, 150–151, 161, 164–165, 169, 244
Cyril II of Jerusalem, bishop   307

Dalmatius   146, 193–195
Damianus, saint   145, 151
Daniel, prophet   177–178, 272–273
David, king   7, 57, 174, 227, 229–230, 281, 285, 292, 295, 297–299, 302, 309–310, 313, 317
Demetrius, saint   75–76, 270
Diocletian, emperor   15, 43, 88
Dionysius of Tarsus, bishop   255
Dios, monk   145
Dioscorus of Alexandria, bishop   244–245
Domitianus, husband of Matrona   139
Dudík, Beda   308

Edward VII, king   296
Egeria   20, 22–23, 98–99, 121–122, 132–133, 140–142, 146–147, 188, 191–192
Eleazar   146
Elias of Jerusalem, bishop   28, 30–32, 156, 164–165, 169–170, 247–254
Elijah, prophet   141, 146
Elpis, martyr   152
Engilbert   304
Epiphanius of Constantinople, patriarch   32
Epiphanius Monachus Hagiopolita   125
Epiphanius of Tyre (Flavian's brother)   255
Epiphanius, literary figure   276–277
Eremolaos. See Armilus (or Hermolaos)
Eucherius of Lyons, bishop   99–101
Eudocia, Theodosius II wife   5, 22, 24–25, 27–28, 31, 34, 88, 93, 100–102, 117–118, 145, 148–156, 163, 217–218, 220, 222, 296
Eudoxia, Arcadius's wife   101–102
Eudoxia, Theodosius II's daugther   21, 25, 42, 101–102, 130, 144, 153
Eudoxius, hegumen   166
Euphemia, saint   132, 144, 146, 217
Euphemius of Constantinople, bishop   247, 254
Eusebia, noblewoman   145
Eusebius of Caesarea, bishop   5, 12, 14–18, 22, 34, 117, 171, 173, 175, 185–209, 216, 221
Eusebius of Nicomedia, bishop   186
Eustace III, count of Boulogne   304
Eustochium   21
Eustratios   264
Euthymius, monk   28–29, 150, 154–156, 247
Eutropia, mother-in-law of emperor Constantine   17
Eutyches, monk   244, 246–247
Eutychius of Alexandria   178, 287–288
Evagrius   118, 252–253
Ezekiel   6, 57, 141, 145, 175, 222, 274

Fausta   16
Faustinus   99
Fidus, disciple of Euthymius   156
Flavia, noblewoman   150–151, 156
Flavian of Antioch, bishop   247–249, 251–255
Flavius Anicius Olybrius   217
Flavius Areobindus Dagalaifus   217

Franz II, emperor   308
Franz Joseph I, emperor   8, 296, 308–310
Frederick II, emperor   296, 308–309
Frederick III, emperor   296, 308
Fritigern   71

Gabrielius, monk   150–151, 156
Gad   146
Gaiseric   176–177
Galla Placidia   42
Gelasius of Caesarea, bishop   23
George, saint   149–150, 155
George IV   296
George of Pisidia   285, 287–289
George Syncellus   282
Gerlach, Stefan   266
Gilbert, Vivian   313
Godfrey of Bouillon   7–8, 296, 304–305, 307, 309, 313
Gog   57, 273–274
Goliath   227
Gorippus   216, 233
Gracchus   288
Gregory of Nazianzus   131–132, 144
Gregory of Nyssa   22
Gregory of Tours   117, 224
Gregory the Great   53, 270

Hadrian   11, 43, 152
Hanauer, James Edward   306
Handel, George Frideric   310
Helena, mother of emperor Constantine   16–17, 22–23, 25, 117, 132, 142, 149, 172, 192, 194, 199, 228, 281, 296, 300
Helena of Adiabene   99
  Helpidius   146
  Heraclius, emperor   2, 7, 33–34, 47, 50–51, 54, 58, 76, 124, 263–264, 266–267, 274–276, 284–293, 295–296, 300–305, 309, 313, 316–317
  Heraclius senior, exarch   300
  Herakles   88
  Hermolaos   291
  Herod   90, 94, 96–97, 103, 178
  Herzl, Theodor   311
  Hethum II, king   296
  Hiram of Tyre   175
  Honorius, emperor   23, 42, 71, 128
  Hormisdas, pope   224, 256
  Huneric   26

Hypatius of Ephesus, bishop   32
Hypatius, nephew of emperor Anastasius   31
İbrahim Paşa   296
Isaac, monk   51, 145–146
Isaac, son of Abraham   301
Isaiah   151, 174–175
Ishoyahb   290
Isidorus of Miletus, architect   169
Ismael   7

Jacob, son of Isaac   146, 151, 297, 299
Jacobus de Voragine   301
Jason   285
Jerome   21–22, 98–99, 114, 126, 128, 130, 142
Job   146
John, emperor   42, 55, 83
John II Komnenos, emperor   316
John Chrysostom   52, 54, 140, 143, 173, 175
John Moschus   151, 166, 178
John of Ephesus   268
John of Jerusalem, bishop   31, 170, 249, 251, 253, 255
John Rufus   22, 25, 98, 100–101, 148, 150, 154–155
John Stoudios   264
John Stratiotes   264
John the Apostle   263–264, 267, 273–276
John the Baptist   145–146, 149, 151, 268, 276
John the Eunuch, monk   166
John the Evangelist   148, 271, 273–274,
John the Theologian   275, 277
John Tzmiskes   292, 316
Jordanes   177
Joseph   146
Joshua   146, 281, 285–286, 291–293, 298
Judah   295–297, 299
Judah Maccabee   296
Julian, emperor   19–20, 40, 121, 124, 128, 150, 194
Julian of Bostra   255
Jupiter   15, 192
Justin I   162, 218, 223, 223–224, 250, 255
Justin II   117, 216, 233, 263, 267–268, 274
Justinian   5–6, 11, 32–33, 48, 51–53, 56, 113, 115, 121, 124, 129–130, 139, 145, 152, 161–179, 215–217, 223–235, 263, 268, 270–271, 274, 300

Juvenal of Jerusalem, bishop   25–28, 242, 244–245, 250–251, 253–254

Khusro II   284–285, 287, 293, 301
Knapheus   246, 251
Konstantin Nikolayevich   8, 296, 306–307, 309–310
Kosmas of Epiphania   255
Kyriakos, bishop   178, 267–268

Laban   146
Lawrence, saint   144–145, 153–154
Lazarus   147
Leo the Great, pope   27–28, 153, 242, 245, 251, 254
Leo III, emperor   316
Leopold II, king   296
Licinius, emperor   14, 190, 194
Lithold   304
Lloyd George, David, prime minister   312
Lot   146
Lubenau, Reinhold   265
Lucan   141
Luke, evangelist   19, 51, 144

Macarius of Jerusalem, bishop   14, 17, 142
Macedonius of Constantinople, bishop   144, 247–248, 251, 253
Magnentius, emperor   18
Magnus Maximus, emperor   82
Malalas   25, 100–101, 217, 230, 270–271
Malek   128
Manasseh   146
Manuel I Komnenos   316
Manuel II Komnenos   75
Marcellinus Comes   144, 153–154, 217
Marcellus, monk   146
Marcian, emperor   26–28, 46, 150, 242, 244–245, 250–251, 254
Marcianus, saint   144
Marcus Aurelius, emperor   43
Mardarios, saint   264
Maria Komnene   264
Marianus, imperial official   189
Marinus of Berytus   255
Martha, sister of Lazarus   147
Martyrius   28, 156, 166, 244–247, 254
Mary   23, 75, 140, 148, 152, 155, 166, 172–174, 269–270, 275–276, 299
Mary, sister of Martha   147

Matrona, noblewoman   139–140, 144, 146
Maurice, emperor   33, 46–47, 55, 124, 267–270, 275
Maximilian Joseph, duke   296
Mehmed II   317
Melania the Elder   20–21, 142
Melania the Younger   21–22, 25, 34, 118, 122, 130, 151, 155
Melchior Lorich   265
Melchizedek   7, 146, 296–299, 317
Melito of Sardis   11
Menas, martyr   143, 150, 156
Michael II, emperor   87
Michael VIII Palaiologos   316–317
Michael, archangel   48, 54, 133, 268
Michal, daughter of Saul   298
Mocius, martyr   144, 146, 200
Modestus of Jerusalem, bishop   283, 289–290, 303
Monaxius, praetorian prefect   71
Moses   57, 146, 174–175, 226–227, 229–230, 232
Moshe Dayan   296
Muhammad   296
Muhammad (Mehmet) Ali Paşa   296, 306
Mustafa   306–307
Mustafa Abu Ghosh   306
Mustafa Süreyya Paşa   307

Nabarnugios. See Peter the Iberian.
Nahor   146
Narses, imperial official   267
Nebuchadnezzar   282, 284
Neḥemyā ben Ḥushīēl   303
Nephalius, monk   248
Nestorius   30, 246–247
Nicephorus   289
Nikephoros Gregoras   263
Nikephoros II Phokas   316
Niketas Choniates   75, 264
Nikolai (Nicholas Konstantinovich)   306

Oikoumenios   273
Olympus, dux   31
Orestes, martyr   132, 264, 275
Origen   11, 33

Palladius of Helenopolis   149
Pamphilus, martyr   51
Pasicrates   149

Passarion 24
Paul the Apostle 122–123, 143, 145, 152, 270, 299
Paul of Ankara, bishop 129
Paul of Ephesus 245, 251,
Paul the Confessor 51, 144, 146, 152
Paul the Silentiary 221, 231
Paula, pilgrim 21, 98–99, 126, 128, 142
Paulinus of Nola 21–22
Paulinus, court advisor 145
Peter the Apostle 27, 145, 148
Peter of Jerusalem, bishop 164, 166, 170
Peter, brother of the emperor Maurice 267
Peter Knapheus of Antioch 246, 251
Peter Mongus 244, 246
Peter of Damascus 255
Peter the Iberian 22, 98, 100, 155
Philon of Byzantium 76
Philoxenus of Hierapolis 248, 253–254
Phocas, emperor 7, 124, 264, 266–270, 274–275, 282, 300, 326
Phocas, martyr 51, 264, 267–269, 271, 274
Piacenza Pilgrim 100–101, 124–125, 128, 130, 147, 149, 152, 168, 178
Pieter Coeck van Aelst 265
Pilate 142, 147–148
Pilgrim of Bordeaux 20, 22, 98–100, 120–122, 126, 132, 134, 142, 146–147
Pistis, martyr 152
Plato of Ancyra, martyr 132–133
Poemenia 20, 147
Polyeuctus, martyr 6, 145, 151, 153–155, 171–172, 177, 216–225, 229, 234, 263
Pompey 282, 296
Porphyry of Gaza 120
Priscus, magister militum 47
Proc[u]lus 128
Procopius of Caesarea 72, 75, 129, 161–162, 165–172, 174–178, 268, 270
Procopius, emperor 40
Ps.-Sebeos 283, 287–290
Psellos 235
Publilius Optatianus Porfyrius 198
Pulcheria 24, 142, 144–145, 150, 153–154, 156

Rabbi Shefatiya 216
Rachel 146
Ranke, Friedrich Heinrich 310
Rebecca 146

Richard the Lionheart 306, 313
Robertson, William 312
Romanos I Lekapenos, emperor 264, 276
Romanos III Argyros 235
Romanos the Melodist 172, 225–231, 234
Romulus 291
Rufinus, church historian 22–23, 149
Rufinus, praetorian prefect 26, 145

Sabas, monk 29–33, 113–115, 164–165, 172, 244, 247–249, 251–256, 283
Saladin 296
Sallustius, bishop 247, 254
Sanderson, John, 265
Samuel 114
Sarah 146
Sasima 131–132
Satan 273, 291
Saturninus, attendant of monk Isaac 145
Schedel, Hartmann 265
Schultz, Stephan 307
Scott, Walter 313
Sebeos 283, 287–290
Selim 296
Septimius Severus, emperor 72
Sergius of Constantinople, bishop 47, 284
Sergius, saint 146
Severianus of Arethusa 255
Severus of Antioch, bishop 30–31, 248–255
Severus, patron of Bassianus 139
Shabbatai Zevi 296
Shahrbaraz 283
Shiloh 297–299
Silvester, pope 220
Simeon 123, 150
Simeon the Elder, stylite 123
Socrates, church historian 55, 117, 143
Sol invictus 193, 196
Solomon 6, 146, 172, 175, 177, 215–216, 218–225, 228–235, 298
Sophia, wife of Justin II 267
Sophia, legendary figure 118, 140, 152, 155
Sophronius of Jerusalem, bishop 286, 288
Sozomen, church historian 117, 143–144, 153–154
Sphoracius 145
Stephen, martyr 5, 24, 56, 144–147, 149, 151–154

Studios, consul 145
Süleyman the Magnificent 316

Terah 146
Thecla 132
Theodora 174, 194, 227, 229, 231
Theodora, second wife of emperor Constantius 194
Theodora, wife of Justinian 174, 227, 229
Theodore 1, 51, 57, 59, 129, 145, 150, 267, 269–271, 273–275, 284
Theodore of Sykeon 51, 129, 270–271, 275
Theodore the Syncellus 1, 57, 59, 273–274, 284
Theodoret, bishop of Cyrrhus (Syria) 129
Theodosius, bishop of Jerusalem 149–150, 155, 242, 244–245, 251
Theodosius I, emperor 20, 23–24, 41–44, 51–52, 82, 87, 142, 219–220, 234, 316
Theodosius II, emperor 21, 24, 26–28, 42, 46, 51, 55–56, 71, 74, 82–83, 87–88, 101–102, 114, 118, 143–144, 148, 153, 217, 296
Theodosius, bishop of Jerusalem 149–150, 155, 242, 244–245, 251
Theodosius, archdeacon/author 127, 133, 147–148
Theodosius, monk 29–31, 244, 247–249, 251–253, 255–256
Theodota, martyr 149
Theodotus of Ancyra, martyr 150
Theophanes, chronicler 24, 114, 120, 288
Theophilos, son of emperor Michael II 87, 316
Theotokos. See Mary.
Tiberius II 48, 263, 267
Tiberius II, emperor 48, 263, 267

Tiberius, emperor 43
Timotheus Aelurus 245
Timothy 51, 144
Titus Tobler 306
Titus, emperor 163, 176, 296
Torquato Tasso 313
Tryphon, saint 264, 275
Tyche of Constantinople 201

Umar I, caliph 7
Umar II, caliph 296

Valens, emperor 29, 40–41, 51, 113, 123, 151
Valentinian I, emperor 40
Valentinian III, emperor 21, 42, 118
Vespasian, emperor 11, 15, 163
Victor Vitensis 177
Victor, attendant of monk Isaac 145
Vitalian, comes 48, 249–250, 255
Vitalian, magister militum 48, 249–250, 255
von Tischendorf, Konstantin 306
Wilhelm II, emperor 8, 296, 308–313
William of Tyre, bishop 304

Yefet b. 'Ali 316

Zacharias Rhetor 245
Zacharias, imperial official 31
Zacharias, patriarch 283, 289–290
Zadok 298
Zechariah 299
Zeno, emperor 28, 53, 145, 162, 245–247, 251–254
Zeus 128, 132
Zippor 146
Zosimus 26

Places

Abu Ghosh   298, 306, 308
Adana   121, 129
Adiabene   99
Adrianople   29, 41, 71
Aelia (Capitolina)   1, 11–15, 34, 88, 93, 95, 102, 296
Africa   32, 47, 49, 165, 275, 286, 291
Aila   15, 31, 71, 95, 98, 115, 117
Akko   124
Alexandria   6, 25, 50, 52–53, 61, 115, 119, 121–124, 127, 134, 139, 148, 153, 173, 175, 178, 242–247, 252–254, 284, 291
Alexandria ad Issum   121
Alexandria Troas   122
Amman   315
Anatolia   113, 121–123, 130–134, 268
Ancyra (Ankara)   113, 119–121, 128–129, 131–133, 150
Andabilis   131–132
Antioch   6, 25–26, 41, 50, 53, 59, 61, 101, 113, 115–116, 118–124, 127–129, 134, 139, 142, 150, 242–243, 252–253, 271
Antioch, Pisidia   122
Antipatris   126
Aqua Calidae   132
Arabia   28, 142
Armenia   29, 296
Ascalon   117, 125
Asia   28, 42, 47–48, 52, 114, 119–120, 123, 128, 131, 133–134, 145, 274–275, 284
Asia Minor   28, 42, 47–48, 52, 114, 119–120, 123, 128, 131, 133–134, 145, 274–275, 284
Assyria   284
Athens   22

Baalbek   124
Babylon   7, 271–273, 276–277, 300
Babylonia   19, 175, 177, 222, 284
Baghdad   300
Bakatha   164
Balkans   46–47, 121, 223, 249, 251, 256
Batos   132
Beirut   125, 139
Beit Nattif   116
Belen   121
Berlin   172, 185, 263–264, 270, 282, 310

Berytus   125, 255
Bethlehem   13, 16, 21, 25, 155, 162, 168
Bithynia   128, 190
Black Sea   1, 48, 121
Bordeaux   20, 22, 98–100, 112, 120–122, 126, 132, 134, 142, 146–147
Boreium   175
Bosphoros. See Bosporus
Bosporus   1, 3, 5, 15, 39–41, 43–44, 48, 56, 61, 119, 121, 187, 200, 268, 274, 302
Byblos   125
Byzantium, city of   1, 39–40, 48–51, 72, 145, 234
Caesarea (Maritima)   13, 26, 31, 60, 71, 98, 115–116, 119, 125–126, 142, 199 242, 249, 283, 290
Caesarea (Cappadocia)   47, 133
Cappadocia   12, 28, 121, 129, 131, 269
Capri   43
Carcassonne   177
Carthage   50, 176–178, 300
Catania   97
Caucasus   284
Chalcedon   6, 24, 26–28, 30–32, 52, 114, 119, 121, 132, 142, 145, 150, 154, 156, 162, 217, 241–249, 251, 254–255
China   284
Chrysopolis   194
Cilicia   121, 129
Crimea   284
Ctesiphon (Veh Ardashir)   275, 282, 286, 300
Cyprus   119

Dara   165
Delphi   201
Diospolis. See Lydda.
Dor   119, 130, 142

Edessa   221, 303
Egypt   28, 47, 114, 123, 142, 145, 150, 162, 243, 245–246, 254, 274, 284, 296, 302, 306
Emmaus (Nikopolis)   126, 130, 307
Ephesus   26, 32, 50, 122–123, 132–133, 170, 173, 244–246, 268, 275
Euchaita   133
Europe   39, 48, 115, 122, 301

Faustinopolis 131

Galatia 48, 129, 133, 275
Galilee 125, 142, 287, 303
Gangra 133
Gaul 44, 177, 224
Gaza 117, 120, 125, 130, 143
Georgia 98, 100, 174
Germia 48, 133
Great Britain 312
Greece 1, 48–49, 317

Haifa 125, 309, 315
Hammat Gader 118
Helicon 201
Heraclea 52
Hierapolis 248, 286–287

Iconium 122–123
Ireland 312
Isauria 129
Istanbul 39, 61, 73–74, 85, 111, 145, 217
Italy 42, 44, 49, 95, 165, 216, 243

Jericho 100, 115, 130, 178, 283
Joppa (Jaffa) 125
Judaea 11, 60, 140, 281, 283

Khirbet al Atrash 130
Kirjathjearim (Qiryat Yearim) 298

Laodicea 124
Latium 49
Lebanon 124, 175
Levant 59, 89, 113, 115, 119–120, 122, 124, 130–131
Libya 175
Lorraine 296, 304
Lydda 126–127

Madaba 89, 96, 100, 141, 163–164, 171
Mainz 288
Mamre 13, 17, 144
Megara 1
Melitene 29, 145
Mesopotamia 113, 283, 290, 300
Middle East 8, 39, 281, 288, 305, 312
Milan 23, 42, 113, 151
Mopsuestia 121, 129
Moscow 61

Nablus 303
Nahr al-Kalb 125, 128
Nazareth 12, 142, 296, 298–299, 303
Neapolis 151, 173, 303
Near East 123
Negev 115, 117
Nicaea 13–14, 26, 121, 131, 186, 190–191, 242, 246, 275
Nicomedia 113, 143, 186, 190
Nikopolis. See Emmaus.
Nitria 28
North Africa 275, 286, 291

Oriens 26, 123, 253

Palaestina 60, 98, 102, 113–114, 119, 126–127, 130
Pamphylia 139
Pergamon 275
Perge 139
Persia 24, 128, 135, 274, 293
Philadelphia 129
Pontus 128
Porta (Portella) 121
Propontis 48–49
Ptolemais 119, 124–125, 130

Qiryat Yearim. See Kirjathjearim.

Ravenna 42–43, 113
Red Sea 15, 98, 116–117, 123
Rhodes 119–120
Rome 3, 6, 14–15, 21, 32, 39–46, 48–50, 52–54, 61, 113, 116, 145, 151, 153–154, 176–177, 219, 234, 242–243, 246–247, 251–254, 256, 268, 270–272, 287, 310
Russia 61, 296, 306

Samaria 162, 284, 303
Scythopolis 24–26, 28–33, 71, 98, 102, 150–151, 161, 164, 244
Sebaste 123, 142
Sebastia 133
Seleucia Pieria 124, 129
Seleucia ad Calycadnum 132
Shekhem 303
Sidon 25, 128
Sinai 115, 139, 142, 162, 175, 242
Sinope 269
Sion. See general index.

Sirmium   113
Sosthenion   48
Sykeon   129, 270–271, 275
Synada   268
Syria   28–29, 47, 113, 122–124, 129, 145, 162, 243, 245–246, 248–249, 252, 255, 274, 282, 314

Tarsus   120–121, 129, 131–132, 255
Taurus   113, 120–123, 134
Theoupolis. See Antioch
Thessalonica   42, 270
Thrace   48–49, 52, 121

Tiberias   118, 287, 303
Transcaucasia   284
Trier   24, 56, 113
Tripoli   118
Troy   141
Turkey   61, 312
Tyana   121, 123, 132, 275
Tyre   17, 125, 175, 189, 200, 202, 216, 221, 255, 290, 304

Veh Ardashir. See Ctesiphon.

Xanxaris   132

Literary Sources

Acta Conciliorum Oecumenicorum
- I,1,3 77,79–80   153
- II,1,1 pp. 27–30   46
- II,1,2 p. 16   46
- II,1,2 p. 29   46
- II,1,2 p. 61,7–16   251, 254
- II,1,2 pp. 128–130   244
- II,1,2 pp. 160–161   53
- II,1,3 pp. 88–89   53
- II,1,3 pp. 119–124   251
- II,1,3 pp. 131–132   242
- II,1,3 pp. 494–495   150
- II,2,2 p. 652   264
- II,3,1 p. 21   46
- II,3,1 p. 23   46
- II,4 pp. 70,19–71,22   254
- II,4 pp. 81,31–82,13   245
- II,4 p. 92,7   27
- II,4 p. 138,12   27
- II,5 p. 9,1–29   245

Agathias, *Histories*
- 5,3–10   270

Ambrosius, *On the Death of Theodosius*
- 40–51   23
- 47–48   23

Ammianus Marcellinus
- 16,3,3   124
- 22,6,4   121
- 23,1,2   19
- 23,1,2–3   19
- 31,16,4–7   71

Anna Comnena, *Alexiad* (ed. Reinsch/Kambylis)
- 15,7,4   263

Anthologia Palatina
- 1,8   224
- 1,10   172, 217–222
- 1,12–17   217

Armenian Lectionary
- 2,225   192

Athanasius, *On the Incarnation*
- 8,3   173

Aurelius Victor, *The Lives of the Caesars*
- 41,15   194

Bible, Old Testament
Genesis
- 14:18–20   296
- 15   296
- 22:1–13   301
- 49:8–10   297

Exodus
- 25:10–22   301
- 28:4–8   298
- 29:5   298
- 39:2–5   298

Leviticus
- 8:7   298

Joshua
- 8:1–29   286
- 10:1–12:24   286
- 15:60   298

1 Samuel
- 4:1–5:12   227
- 17   227

2 Samuel
- 5   297
- 6:12–14   297
- 7   298
- 24:18–25   298

1 Kings
- 6–7   145
- 6:2   222
- 2:13–51   222
- 17:3–6   141

1 Chronicles
- 11:1–9   297
- 13:5   298
- 15–16   297

– 21:18–30   298
– 22:1–16   298

2 Chronicles
– 3–4   145, 222
– 3:3   222
– 6:18   231

Psalms
– 50:20–21   25
– 76:3   296
– 110:4   297
– 118:19   299
– 118:20   299
– 118:26   299
– 131   174
– 137:5–6   141

Proverbs
– 8:22–25   143

Isaiah
– 2:2   174–175

Ezekiel
– 9:37   141
– 39:10–11   58
– 40   175
– 40:5–42:20   222
– 40–43   145
– 41:13–15   222

Daniel
– 5:1   178
– 9:26   19

Zephaniah
– 3:16–17   58

Bible, New Testament
Matthew
– 15:21–28   226
– 21:1–9   299
– 24:2   19

Mark
– 11:1–10   299
– 11:11   299
– 13:2   19

Luke
– 19:28–38   299
– 19:44   19

John
– 9   147
– 12:12–15   299
– 18:36   250

Romans
– 13:1–7   250

Hebrews
– 3:1–6   174
– 5:6   299
– 5:10   299
– 7:1–3   297

Revelation
– 18   250

Apocrypha
(Deutero-)Zechariah
– 9:9   299

Canones Conciliorum Oecumenicorum (CCO)
– I. Const. 3   52
– Nic. 7   13, 242
– Chalc. 9   53
– Chalc. 17   53
– Chalc. 28   53

Cassiodorus, *Exposition of the Psalms*
– 50   100

Cassiodorus, *Variae*
– 3,49   97

Cristoforo Buondelmonti, *Liber insularum archipelagi*
– 50   76

Collectio Avellana
– 116,25   52
– 137,12   256
– 164   217
– 179   217
– 187   224
– 198   217

Collectio Sabbaitica
- 28   250
- 30   250

Cosmas Indicopleustes
- 2,73–75   272–273

Georgius Cedrenus (ed. Bekker)
- p. 523   51

Chronicon Paschale (ed. Dindorf)
- p. 534   40
- p. 542   51
- p. 585   25, 100
- p. 618,14–19 121
- p. 693   268
- p. 703   47
- p. 705   58
- p. 707,16–18 286
- pp. 713–714 47
- pp. 715–726 75

Chronicle of Seert (ed. Scher/Griveau)
- 556,8–10   289

Chronicle of the Year 1234 (ed. Chabot)
- 238,7–13   286

Codex Iustinianus
- 1,1,8,8   53
- 1,1,8,12   53
- 1,1,8,22   53
- 1,2,16,1   53
- 3,12,2   193
- 8,10,10   71

Codex Theodosianus
- 2,8,1   193
- 5,1,2   40
- 5,6,3   49
- 15,1,51   49, 74
- 15,3,1–6   128
- 15,3,4   128
- 16,2,26   20, 142
- 16,2,45   52

Consularia Constantinopolitana
- s.a. 356–357 51

Corripus, *In Praise of the Younger Justin*
- 4,6   117
- 4,283   172

Cyril of Jerusalem, *Catecheses*
- 4,10   22
- 10,19   22
- 13,4   22

Cyril of Jerusalem, *Letter to Constantius*
- 1   18
- 3   18, 22
- 6   18
- 7   19

(Ps-)Cyril of Jerusalem, *Letter About the Earthquake of AD 363*
- 6   148

Cyril of Scythopolis, *Life of Euthymius*
- 2   29
- 16   24
- 27   28
- 30   25, 28
- 32   28
- 35   25, 156
- 37   151
- 40   156
- 42   156
- 45   28
- 49   164

Cyril of Scythopolis, *Life of John the Hesychast*
- 4   25, 52, 149

Cyril of Scythopolis, *Life of Sabas*
- 30   24, 30, 247
- 50   30, 248
- 50–54   248, 254
- 50–55   113
- 51–55   30
- 52   30
- 53–54   26
- 56   31, 248, 249
- 57   32, 244, 249, 250, 252
- 60   250
- 70–73   164
- 70–74   32
- 71–74   113
- 72   115, 164–165

– 73	164
– 78	150
– 86	166

Cyril of Scythopolis, *Life of Theognius*
– 1	150

Digesta Iustiniani Augusti, Constitutio Deo Auctore
– praef.	33

Eucherius
– 6,25,2	99

Evagrius, *Ecclesiastical History*
– 1,20	25, 101
– 1,20–21	118
– 1,22	25, 148
– 2,4	253
– 2,5	242
– 2,18	241
– 3,8–9	251
– 3,14	246
– 3,30	247
– 3,31	244, 249, 256
– 3,32	248
– 3,33	244, 248, 256
– 3,4	245
– 3,7	245
– 3,34	255

Eusebius, *Ecclesiastical History*
– 4,25	19
– 4,26,14	11
– 6,11,2	12
– 10,4	216
– 10,4,3	216

Eusebius, *In Praise of Constantine*
– prol.	186
– prol. 4	199
– 1,1	186
– 2,5	186
– 3,1–2	186
– 3,4	186
– 5,3–4	208
– 6–7	207
– 6,1	186
– 6,10	186
– 6,18	186
– 9,9–10	196
– 9,11	186
– 9,17	13
– 9,18	186
– 10,7	186
– 11–18	17
– 14,3	173

Eusebius, *Life of Constantine*
– 1,1,1	186
– 2,24–42	17, 142
– 2,40	142
– 3,3,48–49	200
– 3,10–15	191
– 3,11	186
– 3,25	14, 192
– 3,25–28	192
– 3,25–41	13
– 3,26–28	14
– 3,28	12, 192
– 3,30–31	14
– 3,30–32	17
– 3,31–32	165
– 3,31,3	14
– 3,33	193
– 3,33,1	15, 171, 193
– 3,33,1–2	228
– 3,41–43	16
– 3,42,2–3	16
– 3,44	16, 118
– 3,48,1	200
– 3,48,2	200
– 3,52	144
– 3,52–53	17
– 3,54,2–3	201
– 4,18–20	196
– 4,18,3–20,2	196
– 4,33	17, 186, 202
– 4,33,1	206
– 4,40,1–2	194
– 4,40,2	17, 188–189
– 4,43	189
– 4,43–47	17
– 4,43–47	186
– 4,44	189
– 4,45	186, 189
– 4,45,1	189
– 4,45,2	191
– 4,45,3	189–190, 197
– 4,46	185–186, 207

– 4,47	190	– 5,39	53
– 4,58–60	200	– 5,41	53
– 4,62	199	– 5,44–45	53
– 4,62,2	17	– 7,24	53
		– 7,28	53

Eusebius, *Martyrs of Palestine*
- 11,10–12   13

Eusebius, *Proof of the Gospel*
- 3,140–141   97

Eusebius, *On the Sepulcher of Christ*
- 11,7   203–204
- 11,8   196
- 17,5   195, 204
- 17,11   195
- 17,12   197

Eutychius, *Annales* (ed. Breydy)
- 127,10–129,14   288

Expositio totius mundi et gentium
- 29   117

George of Pisidia, *In Bonum patricium*
   (ed. Pertusi)
- v. 5–9   47

George of Pisidia, *In restitutionem Crucis*
   (ed. Pertusi)
- v. 9   287
- v. 25–26   288
- v. 32–34   287
- v. 49–63   289
- v. 58–68   287
- v. 73–74   289
- v. 73–82   287

George of Pisidia, *Expeditio Persica*
   (ed. Pertusi)
- 1,108–157   47
- 2,8–3,340   47

Gerontius, *Life of Melania the Younger*
- 50–56   22, 118
- 58–59   25

Gregory the Great, *Letters*
- 4,30   270
- 5,37   53

– 7,30–31   53
– 8,29   53
– 13,41   53

Gregory of Nazianzus, *Carmina*
- 2,1   131

Gregory of Nazianzus, *Letters*
- 125   132
- 126   132

Gregory of Nyssa, *Letters*
- 2   22

Gregory of Tours, *Glory of the Martyrs*
- PL 71, 793–795   224

Gregory of Tours, *History of the Franks*
- 5,30   48
- 7,29   117

Hydatius, *Chronicle*
- s.a. 424   42

Itinerarium Burdigalense
- 570–591   120
- 571   121
- 592   99
- 594   13
- 595   13
- 598   13
- 599   13

Itinerarium Egeriae
- 2,1   146
- 4,2   146
- 4,4   146
- 5,4   146
- 7,7   146
- 7,9   146
- 10,4   146
- 10,7   121
- 12,2   146
- 12,10   146
- 13,1   146

– 13,4	146
– 14,2	146
– 15,1	146
– 16,3	141
– 17,1	146
– 20,4	146
– 20,5	146
– 20,9	146
– 20,10	146
– 20,11	146
– 21,1	146
– 21,4	146
– 22,1–23,6	133
– 23,8	121
– 25,11	147
– 29,3–6	147
– 36,1–2	147
– 36,3	99
– 37,1–3	23
– 43,7	99
– 48–49	191
– 48,1	192

Itinerarium Antonini Placentini
– 1c	100
– 1–2	124, 130
– 2	128
– 4–7	142
– 4–17	125
– 7	118
– 16	150
– 22	147, 149
– 23	147, 178
– 24	147
– 25	147
– 27	147, 150

Jerome, Against Vigilantius
– 5	114

Jerome, Letters
– 46,9	22
– 58,2	22
– 58,3	192
– 108,8	126, 128
– 108,8,2	142
– 108,9	99

Jerome, Lives of Famous Men
– 54	12

John Chrysostomus, *On Saint Phocas*
– 1 (PG 50,699–700)	51

John of Nikiu
– 89,69–70	248
– 89,87	48

John Malalas (ed. Dindorf / ed. Thurn)
– 14 (pp. 351–357 / pp. 277–278)	101
– 14,8 (pp. 356–357 / pp. 276–277)	25
– 14,8 (pp. 357–358 / pp. 277–278)	100
– 16,16 (pp. 401–407 / pp. 329–332)	48, 249
– 18,28 (p. 443 / pp. 370–371)	271
– 18,71 (p. 476 / pp. 398–400)	230
– 18,90 (p. 481 / pp. 406–407)	270
– 18,96–153 (pp. 483–496 / pp. 408–432)	270

John Moschus, *Spiritual Meadow*
– 6	166, 178
– 61	178
– 68	166, 178
– 187	166, 178

John Rufus, *Life of Peter the Iberian* (ed. Horn/Phenix)
– 26–28	155
– 31–35	155
– 38	100
– 40–44	22
– 49	148
– 64	98
– 71	25
– 166	154

John Rufus, *On the Death of Theodosius of Jerusalem* (ed. Horn/Phenix)
– 2–3	150

Josephus, *The Jewish War*
– 5,136	88
– 5,142–149	88
– 7,1–4	88

Leo the Great, *Letters*
– 109	27
– 114	254
– 126	245
– 139	27

Libanius, *Orations*
- 21,15   120

Liberatus of Carthage
- 17,113–117   246
- 18,128   248

Life of Alexander the Sleepless
- 43   146

Life of Andrew the Fool (ed. Rydén)
- pp. 218–219   277
- pp. 221–222   277
- pp. 274–279   276

Life of Barsawma
- 93,4   155

Life of Daniel the Stylite
- 10   57, 234
- 12   272

Life of Isaac
- 18   51

Life of Matrona
- 4   139
- 13–14   139
- 25   139
- 29   144
- 33   144
- 36   139
- 38   144

Life of Theodore of Sykeon
- 3   129
- 6   129
- 58   129
- 79   129
- 135   270
- 152–153   47
- 166   47

Lucan, *Pharsalia*
- 9,973   141

Marcellinus Comes, *Chronicon*
- s.a. 439   25, 56, 144, 153
- s.a. 453   144
- s.a. 453   154
- s.a. 514–515   249

Marcus Diaconus, *Life of Porphyry*
- 26–27   52, 120
- 34   120
- 37   120
- 37–40   52
- 42–43   52
- 45–46   52
- 50–54   52
- 53   130
- 56–57   120

Michael Glykas, *Annales*
- 4,268–269   215

Michael the Syrian, *Chronicle* (ed. Chabot)
- 4,418   286

Miracula Sancti Demetrii (ed. Lemerle)
- 1,5 (1,87–90) 270

Nicephorus, *Breviarium*
- 2   47
- 8   47
- 12   47
- 18   58

Nicephorus Gregoras, *History*
- 1,1   263

Nicephorus Sceuophylax, *Encomium on Theodosius*
- 44–48   51

Niketas Choniates, *History* (ed. van Dieten)
- 1,236   264

Novellae Iustiniani
- 40 praef.   163
- 103 praef.   163
- 123,9   52, 53
- 131,2   53

Notitia Urbis Constantinopolitanae
- 231   143
- 233   143
- 235   143
- 237   143
- 238   144

– 240	143	– 1,3,5–10	75
– 241	143	– 1,4,1–8	224
– 242	143	– 1,6	145
		– 1,7,3–5	51

Oikoumenios, *Commentary on the Apocalypse*
(ed. Schmid)

		– 1,8,12–14	268
– 216	273	– 1,8,15–16	268
– 218	273	– 2,11,2	175
– 221	273	– 5,4,4	129
– 223–225	273	– 5,5,1–3	129
		– 5,5,4–20	129
		– 5,5,6	129

Olympiodorus. *fragments* (ed. Blockley)

– 43,1	42	– 5,6	165
		– 5,6,2–7	167
		– 5,6,3	165

On the Hagia Sophia (ed. Preger)

– vol. 1 p. 105,4–5	172	– 5,6,4	170
		– 5,6,8	167
		– 5,6,9–13	167

Optatianus, *carmina*

		– 5,6,14–15	167
– 19	198	– 5,6,16	169
		– 5,6,17–18	167

Origiens, *Commentary on the Gospel of John*

		– 5,6,19–22	168
– 6,40–41	12	– 5,6,23–26	168
		– 5,6–9	162

Palladius, *Dialogue on the Life of St John Chrysostom* (ed. Malingrey)

		– 5,8,8	175
		– 5,8,9	115
– 14 (p. 278)	52	– 5,3,10	72
		– 6,2,22	175

Patria Constantinopoleōs (ed. Preger)

– pp. 168–170	264	**Procopius, *Secret History***	
– p. 180	47	– 7	230
– p. 225	269		
– p. 249	267	**Procopius, *Wars***	
– p. 250	267	– 2,13,26	165
– p. 260	268	– 2,22	270
		– 4,9,5	177

Paul of Elusa, *Life of Theognius*

		– 4,9,5–9	176
– 5	156	– 5,12,41–42	177

Paulinus of Nola, *Letters*

		Protoevangelium Iacobi	
– 29,10	21	– 7–8	173

Philostorgius, *Ecclesiastical History*

		Reversio Sanctae Crucis	
– 2a	51	– 14–17	302
– 3,2	51		
– 12,13	42	**Romanos the Melodist, *Hymns***	
		– 35,2,5	174

Procopius, *Buildings*

		– 54,4	227
– 1,1,25–26	169	– 54,8–9	226
– 1,3,1–9	270	– 54,11–12	226
– 1,3,2	173	– 54,12	226

– 54,13	226	– 7,10,4	51
– 54,13–25	226	– 7,21,1–16	51
– 54,15–16	227	– 7,22,15–18	55
– 54,17	227	– 7,23,1–10	42
– 54,18	227	– 7,23,11–12	55
– 54,19	227–228	– 7,28,2	52
– 54,20	228	– 7,47	25, 117
– 54,21	228	– 7,47,3	148
– 54,21–24	226		
– 54,21–22	172		
– 54,22	228		
– 54,23–24	229		
– 54,24–25	230		

Sophronius, *Anacreontica*
- 18   287
- 18,85–88   288

Rufinus, *Ecclesiastical History*
- 10,7–8   23

Sozomen, *Ecclesiastical History*
- 2,1   117
- 2,26,3   14
- 4,3   144
- 4,5   18
- 7,1,2   71
- 7,10   143
- 8,17,5   200
- 9,2   142
- 9,5   49

(Ps-)Šapuh (ed. Darbinjan-Melikjan)
- 70–71   58

Ps-Sebeos, *History* (ed. Abgaryan)
- pp. 112–113   47
- pp. 114–115   47, 283
- p. 115   283
- pp. 123–124   47
- p. 131   58, 287, 289, 290
- p. 136   58
- p. 433   58

Spelunca Thesaurorum (ed. Ri)
- 4,2–3   301
- 19,4   301
- 53,6   301
- 53,11   301

Sermo de exaltatione Sanctae Crucis
- 17–21   302

Strategius, *Expugnatio Hierosolymae*
- 5,1–20   283
- 5,21–8,6   283
- 8–12   284
- 11,2   282
- 24,9   289
- 24,10   290

Severus of Antioch, *Letters*
- CL 37, pp. 292–293   255
- CL 51, pp. 325–326   255
- SL 1,21   255

Simplicius, *Epistula ad Acacium*
- 121,25–30   245

Synaxarium ecclesiae Constantinopolitanae (ed. Delehaye)
- February 16   51
- March 11   266
- May 8   275
- September 26   264

Socrates, *Ecclesiastical History*
- 1,6   146
- 1,16   200
- 5,1,3   71
- 5,8,13   52
- 5,9   143
- 5,9,1–2   51
- 6,8,1–9   54
- 6,23   200
- 7,1,3   49

Theodoret of Cyrus, *Ecclesiastical History*
- 1,7,10   186
- 2,27   19

Theodoret of Cyrus, *Letters*
– 81   129

Theodore Lector, *Epitome*
– 360   46
– 483   54

Theodore of Petra, *Life of Theodosius*
(ed. Usener)
– 24 (pp. 60–61) 32

Theodore Syncellus, *Homilia de depositione vestis deiparae in Blachernis*
– 3   56

Theodore Syncellus, *Homilia de obsidione Avarica Constantinopolis* (ed. Sternbach/Makk)
– 2–3 (pp. 298–299) 57, 284
– 8 (p. 301)   57
– 11–12 (pp. 302–303) 47
– 12 (p. 302)   47
– 12 (p. 303)   47
– 17–18 (pp. 304–305) 57
– 20 (p. 306)   57
– 27–31 (pp. 309–310) 57
– 38 (p. 313)   57
– 40–47 (pp. 314–318) 57
– 50 (p. 319)   57
– 52 (p. 320)   57

Theodosius, *De situ terrae sanctae*
– 4   127
– 6   150
– 7b   147
– 8b   147
– 9   150
– 15   133

Theophanes, *Chronicle* (ed. de Boor)
– AM 5920 (pp. 86–87) 24, 56, 115
– AM 5945 (p. 107) 242
– AM 5964 (p. 118) 26
– AM 5991 (p. 142) 252
– AM 6003 (p. 153) 249
– AM 6004 (p. 156) 248
– AM 6005 (p. 157) 248
– AM 6006 (pp. 160–161) 249
– AM 6056 (p. 240) 48
– AM 6064 (p. 244) 267
– AM 6080 (p. 262) 55
– AM 6083 (pp. 268–269) 47, 267, 269
– AM 6091 (p. 277) 267
– AM 6094 (pp. 283–290) 33, 268
– AM 6113 (pp. 302–306) 47
– AM 6114 (p. 306) 47
– AM 6114 (p. 307) 286
– AM 6120 (p. 328) 58
– AM 6125 (p. 337) 58

Theophylact Simocatta, *History*
– 5,16,1–6,3,8   47
– 6,8,8   55
– 8,10   268

(Ps-)Zacharias Rhetor, *Ecclesiastical History*
– 3,3   242, 244
– 3,5   244
– 4,7–8   52
– 5,2   245
– 5,5   245
– 5,6   244, 246
– 5,8   246
– 5,12   244, 246
– 6,1   246
– 7,1   247
– 7,8   248
– 7,10   248, 249
– 7,12   255
– 7,13   249
– 8,1   255

(Ps-)Zacharias Rhetor, *Life of Severus*
– 102–103   248
– 114   255

Zosimus
– 5,8,2   26

Epigraphic Sources

CIIP
– 1,800   166
– 1,869   282

IGLS
– III.2 no. 1142   129

ILS
– 5339   49

RRMAM 3,2
– 115(4)   128
– 184–185   128

RRMAM 3,3
– 87(A)   128

– 139   128
– 166   123, 134

SEG
– 8,315   17

www.ingramcontent.com/pod-product-compliance
Lightning Source LLC
Chambersburg PA
CBHW080910170426
43201CB00017B/2280